DATE DUE

SE 23 '94			
AP 30 '98			
MR 19 '99			
NO 25 '02			
NV 19			

DEMCO 38-296

HUMAN RIGHTS WATCH WORLD REPORT 1994

Featured in World Report 1994

■ Featured in World Report 1994

HUMAN RIGHTS WATCH WORLD REPORT 1994

Events of 1993

HUMAN RIGHTS WATCH

New York · Washington
Los Angeles · London

ISBN 0-300-05993-0
ISSN 1054-948X

Proofreading, cover, and page design by Robert Kimzey.

Human Rights Watch
485 Fifth Avenue
New York, NY 10017-6104
Tel: (212) 972-8400
Fax: (212) 972-0905
email: hrwatchnyc@igc.apc.org

Human Rights Watch
1522 K Street, N.W., Suite 910
Washington, DC 20005-1202
Tel: (202) 371-6592
Fax: (202) 371-0124
email: hrwatchdc@igc.apc.org

Human Rights Watch
10951 West Pico Blvd., Suite 203
Los Angeles, CA 90064
Tel: (310) 475-3070
Fax: (310) 475-5613
email: hrwatchla@igc.apc.org

Human Rights Watch
90 Borough High Street
London, UK SE1 1LL
Tel: (071) 378-8008
Fax: (071) 378-8029
email: hrwatchuk@gn.org

HUMAN RIGHTS WATCH

Human Rights Watch conducts regular, systematic investigations of human rights abuses in some seventy countries around the world. It addresses the human rights practices of governments of all political stripes, of all geopolitical alignments, and of all ethnic and religious persuasions. In internal wars it documents violations by both governments and rebel groups. Human Rights Watch defends freedom of thought and expression, due process and equal protection of the law; it documents and denounces murders, disappearances, torture, arbitrary imprisonment, exile, censorship and other abuses of internationally recognized human rights.

Human Rights Watch began in 1978 with the founding of Helsinki Watch. Today, it includes Africa Watch, Americas Watch, Asia Watch, Helsinki Watch, Middle East Watch, and four collaborative projects, the Arms Project, Prison Project, Women's Rights Project, and the Fund for Free Expression. It now maintains offices in New York, Washington, Los Angeles, London, Moscow, Belgrade, Zagreb and Hong Kong. Human Rights Watch is an independent, non-governmental organization, supported by contributions from private individuals and foundations. It accepts no government funds, directly or indirectly.

The executive committee includes Robert L. Bernstein, chair; Adrian W. DeWind, vice chair; Roland Algrant, Lisa Anderson, Peter D. Bell, Alice L. Brown, William Carmichael, Dorothy Cullman, Irene Diamond, Jonathan Fanton, Alan Finberg, Jack Greenberg, Alice H. Henkin, Stephen L. Kass, Marina Pinto Kaufman, Alexander MacGregor, Peter Osnos, Kathleen Peratis, Bruce Rabb, Orville Schell, Gary G. Sick, and Malcolm Smith.

The staff includes Kenneth Roth, executive director; Holly J. Burkhalter, Washington director; Gara LaMarche, associate director; Susan Osnos, press director.

ACKNOWLEDGMENTS

A compilation of this magnitude requires contributions from a large number of people, including the entire Human Rights Watch research staff. The contributors were:

Aziz Abu-Hamad, Abdullahi An-Na'im, Kenneth Anderson, Cynthia Arnson, Sarvenaz Bahar, Deborah Blatt, Cynthia Brown, Mary Jane Camejo, Joel Campagna, Therese Caouette, Holly Cartner, Allyson Collins, Stephen Crandall, Erika Dailey, Rachel Denber, Chris Derry, Alison DesForges, Richard Dicker, Hamilton Fish, Janet Fleischman, Patrick Gilkes, Eric Goldstein, Stephen Goose, Patricia Gossman, Sasha Greenawalt, Jeannine Guthrie, David Holiday, Mike Jendrzejczyk, Sidney Jones, Farhad Karim, Robin Kirk, Jeri Laber, Sarah Lai, Gara LaMarche, Anthony Levintow, Ivan Lupis, Ellen Lutz, Bronwen Manby, Anne Manuel, Juan E. Méndez, Ivana Nizich, Christopher Panico, Alexander Petrov, Dinah PoKempner, Regan Ralph, Jemera Rone, Kenneth Roth, Awali Samara, Virginia N. Sherry, Karen Sorensen, Mickey Spiegel, Judith Sunderland, Dorothy Q. Thomas, Isabelle Tin-Aung, Lee Tucker, Alex Vines, Daniel Vogt, C.M.F., Joanna Weschler, Andrew Whitley, Lois Whitman.

Cynthia Brown edited the report. Holly Burkhalter reviewed the sections on U.S. policy.

CONTENTS

Human Rights Watch

INTRODUCTION

Nineteen ninety-three marked an evolution in the human rights movement. For many years, the preoccupation has been marshaling the collective will to uphold human rights. This year, with the expansion of multilateral operations in the name of human rights, an additional concern emerged: ensuring that the collective defense of human rights remained true to the principles that stirred it to action.

It has long been tempting to assume that the protection of human rights was simply a matter of collective will. So rarely had a common response been mustered to the horrific crimes of this century, it had been possible to hope that abuse might end and freedom might prevail if only the international community would rally to the human rights cause.

Several times in 1993 a common defense of human rights was mounted or continued, but the results were disappointing. A punishing embargo was imposed on Haiti, a massive humanitarian operation was pursued in Bosnia, a military intervention was continued in Somalia, yet the killing of civilians persisted. Blockades, airlifts and assaults were undertaken, yet the murderers' guns still pounded. Despairing at the failure to stop these atrocities, many began to question the utility of collective action.

Yet the tragedies of Bosnia, Haiti and Somalia reflect less the limits of collective action than a failure of collective vision. The fault lay not in the impetus to stop extreme cruelty, but in the tendency to abandon human rights principles, particularly concerns with justice, once joint action began. The lesson of Mogadishu, Sarajevo and Port-au-Prince is not the futility of collective action, but the importance of justice remaining central to the cause. Until the rule of law is understood as essential to peace, until the end to murder and torture is seen as lying in accountability rather than accommodation, the growing number of states willing to join a collective defense will remain insufficient to secure respect for human rights.

In this introduction, we also address other themes that emerged in our review of events from December 1992 to November 1993. We devote particular attention to a less visible but extremely dangerous challenge to the human rights cause, a conceptual attack launched by abusive governments against such basic principles as the indivisibility and universality of human rights, and the duty to ensure that international assistance does not underwrite repression. We address the governmental role in the spreading plague of communal violence. We note nine human rights monitors who were killed during the year and two who forcibly disappeared. Finally, we discuss the trends apparent in the Clinton administration's emerging human rights policy: its strong theoretical defense of human rights; the mixed message it has sent on the issue of accountability for gross abuses; its expansion of the terrain of human rights activism, sometimes qualified by wavering resolve in pressing human rights concerns; its neglect of human rights in several countries where the U.S. government could be particularly influential, especially in Mexico and the Middle East; and its troubling record toward the rights of migrants and refugees seeking to enter the United States.

The Absence of Justice in Multilateral Action

The quest for justice has long been central to the human rights cause. The goal is to ensure that those responsible for gross abuse face, at minimum, dismissal from their official positions and, whenever possible, criminal prosecution and punishment. The human rights movement seeks justice out of respect for the victims of abuse and their families, as a step toward redressing the wrongs they have suffered, and to deter future abuse, by sending a message that one cannot victimize others without suffering severe consequences oneself.

The new collective resolve on behalf of human rights in Bosnia, Somalia and Haiti has shown an unfortunate neglect for justice. The oversight is hardly coincidental. The extraordinary human cost of an embargo or military intervention naturally discourages the patience and commitment needed to subject abusive forces to the rule of law. Particularly when U.N. troops are at risk in hostile territory, the temptation is tremendous to opt for the quick fix, to settle for a superficial peace or political accord that neglects the problem of impunity.

But the absence of justice makes its mark in heightened passions for revenge and undeterred impulses to abuse. Peace without justice is a perpetual source of discontent for victims of abuse and their families. And once troops have literally gotten away with murder, they are tempted to try again when they perceive new threats to their interests. The continuing human rights disasters of 1993 are illustrative.

· After international intervention halted the devastating famine in Somalia, U.N. forces seemed to abandon concern with human rights as they moved to the difficult stage of building a stable political order. They went to extraordinary lengths for several months to arrest Gen. Muhammad Aideed for the alleged role of his forces in ambushing U.N. troops. Yet they made no effort to establish any form of accountability, whether current or prospective, for the devastation and mass starvation that Aideed and other warlords had visited upon Somalia. Nor did the U.N. publicly scrutinize its own forces' compliance with international standards, continuing a disturbing tradition prominently displayed during the Persian Gulf War. The U.N.'s preoccupation with justice on behalf of its own dead, and its apparent indifference to justice on behalf of Somali victims, reduced U.N. peacekeepers to the level of another fighting faction. A principled defense of human rights would have signaled the importance of the rule of law to any lasting political order. Instead, the im-

punity tolerated by the U.N. inspired those willing to use arbitrary violence for their own political ends.

· A disregard of justice also plagued U.N. action toward Haiti. The abbreviated deployment of international monitors reflected the recognition that human rights would be central to any lasting political accord. But when it came to trying to break the impasse in Port-au-Prince, the U.N., and primarily Washington, quietly backed an amnesty, not only for the army's crimes against the state, such as the act of rebellion, but also for crimes against individual Haitians, such as murder. Similarly, under the guise of crafting a broad consensus government, Washington endorsed the army's attempts to control the Defense and Interior Ministries, an obvious impediment to dismissal of the officers responsible for mass murder. Because of divisions within the army and a growing split with the country's traditional elite who financed the original coup, the army's leadership at the end of November was under considerable pressure to negotiate an orderly transition out of the current stalemate. But Washington's willingness to compromise the principle of accountability had emboldened the army to hold out for guarantees of impunity, and prolonged the suffering of the Haitian people.

· In the former Yugoslavia, the U.N. took painfully slow steps to establish a functioning war crimes tribunal. The torpid pace reflected British and French fears that the active pursuit of justice would delay the opportunity to withdraw their U.N. troops—an ironic twist on a deployment that was meant to serve the residents of that embattled territory. An institution of potentially monumental significance, the tribunal is supposed to indict, try and punish those responsible for such crimes as rape, torture, execution, indiscriminate shelling and forced starvation. But nine months after the Security Council vowed to create it—and, in this case, despite constructive pressure from Washington—the man chosen to serve as chief prosecutor, Ramón Escovar Salóm of Venezuela, had yet to assume his duties or to hire a staff, and the U.N. had yet to provide the necessary funding. The separate war crimes commission established in 1992, an investigative but not a prosecutorial body, tried to compensate for this lethargy, but had to beg for funds from private sources to make up for the U.N.'s lack of financial commitment. This visible indifference to the pursuit of justice was particularly troubling once the U.N. declared certain "safe havens" in Bosnia, since by doing so it effectively assumed the responsibilities of a state toward the local population, including the duty to seek justice for gross abuse. The devaluation of justice also squandered an unprecedented opportunity to draw the line on the growing scourge of communal violence.

These three prominent cases were not alone in reflecting a tendency to devalue justice in the course of multilateral operations. In Liberia, for example, the West African peacekeeping force known as ECOMOG met a serious rebel challenge by teaming up with forces tied to the highly abusive army of former President Samuel Doe, the same forces it should have been seeking to exclude from Liberia's political future. In Cambodia, despite success in sponsoring an election, repatriating refugees and building a rudimentary legal system, the U.N. neglected its explicitly delegated power to take "corrective action" to remedy abuses, leaving a troubling precedent of impunity for political and ethnic killings.

The case that best proves the importance of U.N. operations being guided by a concern with justice is El Salvador, where an effort to establish accountability for human rights abuse was central to the U.N.-sponsored peace plan. In March 1993, the Truth Commission issued its report on the atrocities of the prior twelve years—an important formal acknowledgment of responsibility for these abuses. The report also heightened the pressure to comply with the December 1992 recommendations of the Ad Hoc Commission for the purge of 103 senior officers of the Salvadoran army, including the Minister and Vice-Minister of Defense. The Truth Commission named Defense Minister René Emilio Ponce as having ordered the 1989 murders of six Jesuit priests, their housekeeper and her daughter. Ponce and several other senior officials who had resisted the Ad Hoc Commission's recommendations finally stepped down in July 1993. Because a broad amnesty for political and common crimes was enacted shortly after the release of the Truth Commission's report, justice remains incomplete, and there was a troubling increase in death squad activity in late 1993. Still, the important steps taken toward establishing accountability for the most serious human rights crimes have left El Salvador with a relatively solid foundation for a lasting peace.

The lesson, we believe, is that peace is likely to be elusive without justice, despite the extraordinary attention of the international community. The festering wounds of victims and their families, coupled with the message that there is no price to be paid for complicity in slaughter, makes a volatile combination. Until the international community recognizes that troops and blockades cannot substitute for structures of accountability, its massive rescue operations risk failure.

We believe the disregard for justice shown in 1993 highlights the urgent need for a U.N. High Commissioner for Human Rights—a senior official who, among other important duties, would ensure that human rights considerations are not neglected once the U.N. launches major operations. The U.N.'s inattention to matters of justice also reinforces the importance of the much-studied but long-neglected permanent international tribunal to try those responsible for gross abuses, as a mechanism to avoid the short-term political calculations that tend to thwart the quest for justice.

The Conceptual Challenge
to the Human Rights Cause

The challenges to the human rights movement in 1993 were not limited to the terrain of repression. Some of the toughest tests emerged not under the barrel of the gun but in the confines of the conference room, particularly during the World Conference for Human Rights, the assembly of governments that met in Vienna in June, for the first time in twenty-five years, to review global progress on human rights. As human rights gained acceptance as a central element of international relations, a number of governments, mainly from Asia, tried to strike back. They included highly abusive governments, such as China, Burma and Iran, as well as governments that champion closed political systems, such as Singapore, Malaysia and Indonesia. No longer credibly able to deny the significance of human rights concerns, they sought to dilute or redefine some of the most basic human rights principles.

The attack took three basic forms. These governments challenged the indivisibility of human rights, by arguing that economic development should precede respect for civil and political rights. They attacked the principle that human rights apply equally to all people, by arguing that human rights standards should vary according to a government's view of local culture. And they sought to undermine one of the most effective means of human rights enforcement—application of the duty of donor governments and institutions not to become complicit in abuse by underwriting those who engage in repression.

The Development-First Argument

The argument that economic development must precede respect for civil and political rights falls on many receptive ears. From the despots of underdeveloped countries who sought a convenient banner under which to cling to power, to the officials of developing countries who found it useful to attribute economic progress to their own authoritarian rule, to governments in the developed world that were eager to justify windfalls to be made by ignoring the misdeeds of potentially profitable trading partners, the argument that civil and political rights must await economic progress often finds ready appeal. Invariably, it masks a primary concern with preserving the political status quo, even at the cost of popular well-being.

Some countries have managed to develop despite their repressive governments. Their leaders often claim credit for economic progress, but the claims are at best unprovable, since it is impossible to know how much farther an economy might have advanced with a less abusive government. Moreover, governments that follow a repressive route to development risk the handicap of competing in an information age without the free flow of information. Some also face the loss of many of their most talented citizens, who shun the sterility of a controlled environment. And all face the prospect of political turmoil, as authoritarian leaders confront growing demands for popular participation in government and respect for civil and political rights that often accompany improved living standards.

More often, repressive governments simply preside over stagnation and decline, as in much of Africa, the former Soviet bloc, and significant parts of Asia. These examples of repressive impoverishment reflect the impediments that violations of civil and political rights often place on the path to realization of economic rights. An inability to criticize government policies or to report truthfully their consequences can turn food shortage into famine, or humanitarian hardship into calamity. Censorship of reporting on corruption can encourage official preying on the economy and stifle development. Restrictions on the right to organize prevent workers from earning a subsistence wage. Limitations on the ability to publicize and campaign against threats to the environment can lead to environmental degradation. A weak or corrupt judicial system will tolerate the use of violence to dispossess peasants of their land. Discrimination against women can leave them powerless and dependent.

In these very concrete terms—the values of health, land, income, and environment on which people build their lives—repression is the nemesis of economic rights, particularly for the least powerful members of society. Indeed, it is to disguise such individual deprivations that proponents of authoritarian models tend to speak in terms of "development," presumably measured in collective terms, rather than the economic rights of individuals. We believe that respect for civil and political rights is the best guarantor of the economic rights that abusive proponents of development-first theories purport to champion.

The Argument of Cultural Relativism

Many of the same governments argue that members of their cultures prefer consensus to political competition—an orderly, if controlled, society, to the diverse and vibrant civil society that emerges when freedom of expression and association are respected. The same asserted cultural preferences, often wrapped in a religious veneer, are cited to justify restrictions on the rights of women. To respond to these supposed sentiments, some governments press for international human rights standards that vary with local cultural desires.

This argument, usually made by those in positions of power, smacks of self-justification and convenience. Restrictions on free expression and association facilitate the suppression of dissenting views, and a lack of equal rights for women perpetuates male dominance. In the absence of an opportunity to hear freely from those forced to relinquish their freedom and equality, the assertions of cultural or religious preference usually go untested.

In 1993, however, opportunities did arise to hear from the supposedly willing victims of culturally and religiously based restrictions on their rights. Asian nongovernmental organizations met in Bangkok,

and women's rights activists from around the world met in Vienna; they offered anything but assent to this restricted view of rights. Indeed, even the world's governments assembled in Vienna offered strong affirmation of the universality of human rights. While noting that "the significance of national and regional particularities and various historical, cultural and religious backgrounds must be borne in mind," they reiterated "the duty of states, regardless of their political, economic and cultural systems, to promote and protect all human rights and fundamental freedoms." A similar affirmation of universality can be found in the broad ratification of the leading human rights instruments by governments from all regional, cultural and religious traditions.

Respect for human rights is important, in part, to permit different cultures and religions to flourish, through the free choices of individuals. The rights to equality and to free expression and association—indeed, the right to practice one's culture or religion freely—permit all citizens of the world to select their personal way of life. But suppressing freedom and equality in the name of culture or religion is a corruption of the concept of rights. Rights should serve as a check on collective action, even when that action is embraced by a majority. To view rights as varying with governmental interpretations of culture or religion is to eviscerate the power of rights.

The Argument Against Aid Conditioned on Respect for Human Rights

In addition to challenging the definition of important rights, these governments and others set out to undermine one of the principal means for enforcing fundamental rights: the often very effective strategy of denying certain forms of international assistance to abusive governments. Economic sanctions were used effectively in 1993, for example, to press for reversal of a coup attempt in Guatemala, to encourage a referendum on multiparty elections in Malawi, and to promote compliance with U.N. recommendations that abusive army officers be dismissed from their positions in El Salvador. Such sanctions ensure that repressive regimes pay a price for their abuse, through restrictions on their access to international assistance. Aid conditions also reflect a growing realization that if the purpose of international assistance is to promote economic rights, respect for civil and political rights must be a central concern.

Human Rights Watch has long supported withholding military aid, police aid, arms transfers and security assistance from governments that consistently commit gross abuses of human rights. These abuses include summary execution, torture, systematic invidious discrimination, and prolonged arbitrary detention. We also oppose certain infrastructure development projects that lend more prestige and legitimacy to an abusive government than direct benefits to the needy. To avoid harming those who suffer poverty and humanitarian disaster, we do not oppose development and relief assistance that meets basic human needs, but urge whenever possible that such aid be channeled through nongovernmental organizations.

Maintaining this linkage between aid and human rights reflects several concerns: the principle that all rights are indivisible, that economic rights cannot be ensured in an environment of disrespect for civil and political rights; the duty of donor nations to avoid becoming complicit in human rights abuse by funding the machinery of repression; and the importance of deterring abuse, by promising an interruption in the flow of material support to those tempted to commit serious human rights violations.

This strategy was attacked by many governments that have felt the sting of economic sanctions. They argue that the victims of abuse should not be deprived of economic assistance simply because of their government's misdeeds. But this logic conveniently confuses the abuser with the abused. Precisely because of concern with the victims of abuse, restrictions on economic assistance seek to deny abusive governments the tools of repression, while preserving as much as possible the flow of assistance to the needy through alternative channels.

In a variation on this argument, the opponents of sanctions attempt to place government-to-government aid in the context of global inequalities of wealth. Any denial of economic assistance, they argue, impedes efforts to establish a more equitable distribution of resources. Yet if a transfer of wealth from North to South, from developed to developing countries, is sought in the name of Southern people rather than Southern oppressors, that will hardly be accomplished by the provision of guns and bullets, or the funds to purchase them, to abusive regimes of the South. The repression underwritten by aid to such governments impedes development and perpetuates inequalities of wealth.

Others argue that linking economic assistance to the human rights record of the recipient amounts to imperialist bullying. But the imperialist label misrepresents the duty to guard against international support of repressive regimes. That duty extends to all governments, whether the support they lend is economic, moral or diplomatic. Nor is the duty extinguished by recasting in nationalist or anti-imperialist rhetoric the tired and discredited argument that human rights are an internal affair, and not the proper concern of the international community.

We recognize that the argument about economic sanctions is advanced not only by self-interested governments but also by others who are concerned that broad embargoes and similar trade sanctions may indiscriminately harm innocent individuals. Human Rights Watch shares these concerns and refrains from advocating general economic embargoes. We also believe that any blockade, or militarily enforced embargo, must comply with international standards against the starvation of civilians as a method of warfare. While we do advocate selected trade sanctions, we attempt to do so in a manner that targets the abuser, not the abused: by seeking, for example, to deny beneficial trade terms to governments that commit or tolerate violations of labor rights, to block export of goods made with forced labor, or to restrict trade benefits to state enterprises of governments that commit gross abuses. We believe that such targeted sanctions enhance the welfare of the victims of abuse, by ensuring that those who violate human rights do not profit from their crimes. We object to governments that deliberately equate the issue of trade sanctions with the goal of preventing international funding of governmental repression. Fine-tuning trade sanctions in the interest of avoiding harm to innocent victims is perfectly appropriate, but there should be no exception to the effort to avoid financing government abuse.

We also share the concern of many that economic sanctions are often used inconsistently. But the same inconsistency can be found, for example, in such widely accepted tools as U.N. resolutions on human rights. We believe the solution lies not in abandonment of such powerful tools for promoting human rights, but in a quest for more principled application.

The Epidemic
of Communal Violence

Among other disturbing trends in 1993, communal violence continued to pose the major threat to human rights in many regions. Once more, contrary to conventional wisdom, its usual cause was not age-old animosity among different groups, but governments and political groups that fomented strife for their own political gains.

- Over 700 were killed, mostly Muslims, when police and mobs went on a rampage in Bombay in January. The killings marked the second major outbreak of communal violence in India following the destruction of a sixteenth-century mosque in Ayodhya in December 1992, inspired by a Hindu nationalist political party.

- President Mobutu Sese Seko of Zaire instigated and manipulated communal conflict, particularly in Shaba, where 90,000 were displaced by mob vio-

lence, and in North Kivu, where at least 7,000 appear to have been killed, and over 200,000 displaced. His apparent goal was to destabilize his political opposition and to make the point that Zaire was ungovernable without him.

- In parallel fashion, Kenyan President Daniel arap Moi, determined to prove that multiparty democracy would spark ethnic tensions, continued to foment violence between his Kalenjin ethnic group and the majority Kikuyu community. As in Zaire, the violence began to take on a life of its own.

- Longtime persecution of Tutsi in Rwanda as part of the government's effort to maintain Hutu solidarity yielded, in 1990, a largely Tutsi-based guerrilla movement and, in the following years, including 1993, severe government repression against Tutsi.

- In neighboring Burundi, an attempted military coup in late October and the assassination of Burundi's elected president set off a wave of communal violence that within one month had claimed the lives of an estimated 10,000 to 20,000 and displaced as many as one million. As in the case of Rwanda, the violence was between the Hutu majority and Tutsi minority, with military and civilian authorities playing a large role in fomenting the violence.

- Three days after the German Bundestag voted in May to restrict the right of asylum, tacitly blaming the victims for the continuing escalation of right-wing violence against foreigners, five Turkish residents died when skinheads set fire to their house in the town of Solingen. In a speech the next month before the Bundestag, Chancellor Helmut Kohl blindly denied any "connection between the asylum law and the arson attacks in Solingen and elsewhere," underscoring a failure of moral leadership that only exacerbated the problem.

Other examples of government-inspired communal violence include the Kurdish insurgency in Turkey, which was fueled by years of official restrictions on the ability of Kurds to practice their culture; the decade-long war in southern Sudan, triggered by Khartoum's effort to impose its radical version of Islamic law, in which well over a million have died from abusive fighting and related starvation and disease; the ongoing political violence in South Africa, largely fomented by those who resisted the passing of the apartheid order; and the killing in the former Yugoslavia, sparked by deliberate campaigns of hatred in the officially controlled media.

Resistance to Elections

Efforts to block elections, or to deny the will of the electorate in choosing its government, continued to reap devastation in 1993. While elections alone cannot guarantee respect for human rights, the year showed repeatedly that disregard for free and fair elections can breed disaster.

- In Angola, some 500,000 have died from the renewed fighting, and related starvation and disease, caused by the rebel force UNITA's rejection of September 1992 elections found by foreign observers to be "generally free and fair."

- In Algeria, the government's 1992 cancellation of elections won by an Islamic party yielded a bloody conflict plagued by assassination and torture.

- The Nigerian military's refusal to recognize the results of presidential elections in June 1993 threw the country into political turmoil that resulted in a coup d'etat in November.

- Since the Haitian military's September 1991 coup against President Jean-Bertrand Aristide's freely elected gov-

ernment, the army has clung to power through ruthless repression. Its grievances against President Aristide pale in comparison with the killing, brutality and impoverishment that it has visited upon the Haitian people.

- In Burma, the military continues to reject the results of the May 1990 elections. In January 1993, it initiated a National Convention to draft a constitution guaranteeing itself a primary governing role.

The Death Penalty

In what seemed to be an accelerating trend, many countries imposed the death penalty in 1993 in circumstances of, at best, serious due process deficiencies.

- In Algeria, twenty-six death sentences were carried out, most of them after trials in special courts with severe due process restrictions, including the use of confessions secured through torture. Over 350 were sentenced to death, mostly in absentia, and thus with a theoretical right to contest the sentences if apprehended.

- In Egypt, thirty-nine civilians were sentenced to death and seventeen were hanged by military courts that lacked the independence of Egypt's civilian courts, and from which there was no right of appeal.

- In Saudi Arabia, executions imposed after summary trials proceeded at a rate of more than double that of 1992, with sixty-three executed, most by beheading, in the first seven months of 1993. Most defendants were not represented by lawyers at trial or assisted in preparing their defense.

- In Kuwait, seven Iraqis and ten Palestinians were sentenced to death in 1993, and another Iraqi was executed in May after having been sentenced to death in

1992. Their trials featured confessions obtained through torture, and legal counsel before trial was not permitted.

· In Nigeria, thirteen death sentences were imposed (though later commuted) by special tribunals with no right of appeal.

· Peru approved a new constitution that increases the number of crimes carrying the death penalty despite a bar to such expansion in the American Convention on Human Rights. The extensive use of "faceless courts" only compounds the seriousness of this step backward.

· In addition to continuing large-scale judicial executions in Iran, there were at least four assassinations of Iranians linked to exile opposition parties.

· In the United States, where thirty-six of fifty states permit the death penalty, the Supreme Court in 1993 continued to restrict appeals available to death-row defendants, including a ruling that new evidence of innocence is not enough to grant a hearing, let alone a new trial. Thirty-five people were executed in the first eleven months of 1993, the most in thirty years. Several of those killed had the mental capacity of children, a transgression of at least the spirit of the international prohibition on the execution of minors.

The Right to Monitor

While in some cases in 1993 the international community showed itself increasingly willing to adopt extraordinary measures to protect human rights, local human rights monitors often were the most important actors in the struggle to hold their governments accountable. The threat they posed was most evident in the lengths to which abusive forces went to silence their reports. At least nine human rights monitors were killed in the year under review, and two forcibly disap-

peared.

Some countries, such as Burma, Iraq, Iran, North Korea and Vietnam, remained too dangerous, or too closed, even to attempt human rights monitoring. Of the places where it was possible to attempt human rights monitoring in the past year, Kashmir and Turkey were the most dangerous. Three human rights monitors were killed in each, under circumstances suggesting retaliation for their public criticisms.

· In Kashmir, a prominent human rights activist, Hirdai Nath Wanchoo, was shot dead by unidentified gunmen in December 1992. The government's refusal to conduct an independent investigation raises questions about its complicity. Dr. Farooq Ahmed Ashai, a doctor and outspoken critic of the government's human rights record, was shot and killed by Indian paramilitary troops in February 1993. Dr. Abdul Ahad Guru, a surgeon and critic of Indian human rights practices (who was also a member of the Jammu and Kashmir Liberation Front) was assassinated by unidentified gunmen in March 1993, and his brother-in-law was killed by police during the funeral procession.

· In Turkey, two officials and one member of the Human Rights Association were assassinated, all in February. They included Metin Can, the president, and Dr. Hasan Kaya, a member, of the Elazig branch, and Kemal Kilic, a founding member of the Urfa branch. The government has failed to investigate the murders.

Other countries where human rights monitors were killed in 1993 include the following:

· In Guatemala, rights activist Tomás Lares Sipriano was murdered in April by an army-organized civil patrol, the day after he had organized a demonstration protesting military pressure to join the supposedly voluntary patrols. In October, Francisco Guarcas Ciphiano, a member of Guatemala's oldest human rights organization, the Mutual Support Group, was kidnapped by civil patrol members in the Guatemala City bus terminal and disappeared. Guatemalan human rights groups also continued to suffer threats, intimidation, and detention.

· In Algeria, Djilali Belkhenchir, a pediatrician who was vice-president of the Algerian Committee Against Torture, was felled in an attack attributed to Islamists in October.

· In El Salvador, José Eduardo Pineda, a lawyer who had been working for the newly created office of the human rights ombudsman, died in March of injuries sustained in a violent attack in July 1992. Other human rights monitors were threatened and attacked in 1993.

· In Colombia, Delio Vargas, president of the Colombian Association for Social Assistance, a refugee organization, disappeared in April after being forced into a car by five men in circumstances suggesting the involvement of security forces. Human rights activists also suffered threats and surveillance by state security agents.

Apart from murder, governments took other steps in their effort to silence the human rights movement:

· The Rwandan government threatened and attempted to assassinate human rights activists and witnesses in advance of a January visit by an international human rights commission that included one of our representatives. Beginning hours after the commission's departure, government-sponsored violence left 300 dead, including a student who had provided information to the commission, and thousands driven from their homes. The family of one young man who aided the commission was attacked by a mob incited by local officials, and the father of the family was forced to commit suicide. Attacks on human rights monitors continued throughout the year.

· Fifteen Syrian human rights monitors remain in prison, serving long prison terms or awaiting sentencing. The Committees for the Defense of Democratic Freedoms and Human Rights in Syria has been decimated in its home country, and now operates out of Paris.

· The Saudi government banned the Committee to Defend Legitimate Rights, established in May by six prominent Islamist jurists and university professors, for purportedly violating Islamic law. The committee was the first nongovernmental organization of its kind to be formed in Saudi Arabia in decades. Several members lost their government jobs or had their private offices closed, and fifteen were detained.

· Those who reported on Chinese human rights practices continued to risk lengthy prison terms. For example, Fu Shenqi, a Shanghai dissident, was sentenced in July to three years in a re-education camp for mounting a letter-writing campaign on behalf of a political prisoner. No international human rights organization was permitted to conduct a fact-finding mission in China in 1993, although the head of China's bid for the 2000 Olympics issued one invitation five days before a decision on the site was to be made.

· Human rights monitors in Haiti were subject to death threats and physical attacks. Haitians who cooperated with the international civilian mission were threatened and arrested.

· Cuba continued to imprison pro-democracy activists, and to restrict access by U.N. and nongovernmental human rights investigators.

· For the first time in ten years, the Peruvian government obstructed our own attempts to visit prisons. It asserted trumped-up charges of "terrorism" against human rights activists. To obstruct inquiries into its death-squad activity, it also intimidated Peruvian congressional investigators and impeded proper forensic inquiry.

· In a move aimed at the country's six human rights and humanitarian groups, the Kuwaiti government banned all unlicensed organizations, after having repeatedly refused their requests for licenses. Some of the groups continued to meet privately.

· Sudan persisted in its strategy of effectively replacing the nation's leading human rights organization and bar association with government-controlled entities.

· The Yugoslav government obstructed international monitoring efforts in Kosovo, Sandzak and Vojvodina. It forced the Conference on Security and Cooperation in Europe to close down its mission, and refused permission to the U.N. Special Rapporteur to open an office.

· The Iranian government also denied access to the U.N. Special Representative, as well as to nongovernmental organizations that sought to monitor Iranian practices.

The Clinton Administration's First Year

President Bill Clinton's inauguration has brought to U.S. policy a heightened emphasis on human rights, but a stress that still falls significantly short of principled support. He has appointed several officials who are vig-

orous advocates for human rights. But their latitude to set U.S. policy has been regularly constrained by the administration's competing concerns. Rather than articulating a vision of human rights as an essential element of world order, the Clinton administration has only cautiously embraced the cause, jettisoning human rights when the going gets rough. This lack of consistent leadership has sapped much authority from the administration's advocacy of human rights, and has left unfulfilled Washington's potential to advance respect for human rights.

Doctrinal Advances

The administration was at its strongest in advancing human rights at the level of theory. At the World Conference on Human Rights in Vienna, it abandoned the U.S. government's recent hostility to international human rights law, embracing the full scope of international standards and vowing to study or seek ratification of outstanding human rights treaties. At Vienna and elsewhere, the administration also affirmed the interdependence of human rights, democracy and development. It stressed that "democracy" involves more than competitive elections, but also such democratic institutions as an independent judiciary and law-abiding prosecutors and police.

These doctrinal advances positioned Washington in the mainstream of the human rights debate for the first time in many years. Instead of contesting first principles, the administration accepted the positive law on human rights and worked to defend it. The shift was timely, and effective, in combatting the fundamental challenges to the human rights cause launched by a collection of abusive governments in Vienna.

The administration also took important steps to remedy a traditional neglect of women's rights. Speaking at the World Conference, Secretary of State Warren Christopher called the promotion and protection of women's rights a "moral imperative." In congressional testimony, John Shattuck, the Assistant Secretary of State for Democracy, Human Rights and Labor, said that "the

Clinton administration regards promoting the cause of women's rights as a key element of our overall human rights policy." He pledged to "lead the effort in the United Nations Human Rights Commission toward appointing a Special Rapporteur on Violence Against Women," to improve U.S. reporting on women's rights in the State Department's annual human rights survey, and to seek ratification of the Convention on the Elimination of All Forms of Discrimination Against Women.

Mixed Messages on Accountability

While the administration's vision of democracy was more complete than that of its predecessors, its record in pressing for accountability for those who commit gross abuse—also a critical element of any meaningful democracy—was mixed. In a November speech, Madeleine Albright, the U.S. ambassador to the U.N., rejected amnesty for war criminals in the former Yugoslavia, and raised the specter of sanctions if governments refuse to extradite indicted defendants for trial before the international war crimes tribunal. The speech was tremendously important in rebuffing those governments (particularly Britain and France) that would risk the long-term dangers of impunity for gross abuse in favor of the short-term attractions of peace without justice and a quick exit for their U.N. troops. By setting forth a workable plan to try war criminals, the speech went a long way toward silencing skeptics who say that the pursuit of justice is available only to a battlefield victor.

The administration also sought accountability in Iraq by supporting the U.N.'s establishment of a separate U.N. war crimes tribunal to address atrocities committed by Baghdad's troops during the Persian Gulf War and its aftermath. However, little progress was made on this campaign in 1993.

Since no U.S. troops were in harm's way in Iraq or the former Yugoslavia in 1993, the administration's support for accountability would have been much more principled, and powerful, if it had extended to Somalia, where U.S. troops are deeply involved, or to Haiti, where U.S. interest in a political solution is high. Instead, while the Clinton administration was preoccupied with U.N. efforts to arrest General Aideed for the alleged role of his troops in attacking U.N. troops, it made no effort to hold accountable those responsible for the mass starvation of Somalis, let alone to ensure an independent investigation into the conduct of U.N. forces. In Haiti, it exerted quiet but strong pressure on President Aristide to close off the possibility of prosecution for human rights crimes and to abandon his quest to dismiss from the Haitian military those behind widespread atrocities.

An Expanded but Uncertain Terrain of Human Rights Activism

The Clinton administration significantly expanded the terrain of U.S. activism on human rights, including by challenging the practices of several important U.S. friends, although it sometimes wavered in the resolve it showed in addressing their abuses.

· After years of substantial U.S. neglect of serious abuse in Indonesia and East Timor, the Clinton administration supported a U.N. resolution criticizing human rights practices in East Timor, and undertook a systematic review of Indonesia's labor rights practices under threat of revoking trade benefits.

· In notable contrast to the Bush administration's refusal to meet with Salman Rushdie, President Clinton granted the writer a formal audience to illustrate Washington's firm support for freedom of expression in Iran, and its continuing objection to the death sentence imposed by Iran's leaders for a novel that they deemed blasphemous. Other elements of the Clinton administration's tough policy toward Iran included opposition to World Bank loans, and an effort to deny Iran "dual-use" technology with both military and civilian applications.

· During a visit to Turkey in June, Secretary Christopher broke Washington's traditional public silence on Ankara's abysmal human rights record (apart from the State Department's annual worldwide human rights report) by announcing the goal of improving freedom of expression and eliminating torture and arbitrary killing. He promised a carrot-and-stick approach, but without the slightest human rights concession from Turkey, the administration announced an intention to deliver $336 million in aircraft and other military equipment. In October, during a meeting with Turkish Prime Minister Tansu Ciller, President Clinton cited Turkey's "shining example of cultural diversity," while ignoring the severe abuses committed by the government against the Kurdish minority.

· Breaking with President George Bush's insistence on separating human rights from China's Most Favored Nation (MFN) trading status, President Clinton in June issued an executive order extending MFN unconditionally for a year but linking further extension to a series of human rights conditions. However, the conditions were troublingly elastic, and the administration refused to spell out the specific improvements that must precede renewal of MFN. This refusal left the impression that the White House might try to sell to Congress even minimal concessions from Beijing. The administration, primarily through Secretaries Christopher and Shattuck, did deliver the message that lack of "overall significant progress" by June 1994 would mean loss of MFN. But by November, when President Clinton met Jiang Zemin, the General Secretary of the Chinese Communist Party, in Seattle, the message was more mixed. At the same time as the President reinforced the need for human rights progress, he allowed the sale of a supercomputer to China, lifting one of the few remaining sanctions imposed by the Bush administration. The Clinton administration's clear desire for enhanced trade with China risked sending a signal that Washington's threat to withdraw MFN was not serious.

Inconsistent Support for Elected Government

Like its predecessor, the administration was often a strong proponent of elected government, but the absence of strong advocacy was notable in the case of several important countries. On the positive side:

· The administration's prompt and forceful response to Guatemalan President Jorge Serrano's "self-coup"—stopping foreign aid and threatening to suspend trade benefits and to oppose multilateral bank loans—contributed to reversing the coup attempt.

· The administration's reaction to the military's annulment of elections in Nigeria—including a rare suspension of licenses for commercial arms sales—was also tough, though, as of the end of November, less effective.

· In Malawi, Vice President Al Gore and other administration officials pressed for the release of political prisoners and the lifting of restrictions on civil society in advance of the June referendum on multiparty democracy, in which Malawians rejected the country's thirty-year dictatorship.

The administration's wavering support for elected government was most visible in its backing of Russian President Boris Yeltsin when he dissolved a parliament chosen in relatively free elections in 1990. President Clinton and Secretary Christopher justified this compromise of principle by reference to President Yeltsin's purported democratic commitment. It was difficult to dispute the enormity of the problems facing Yeltsin, and the importance to Washington of an orderly transition from Communist rule in Russia. But as President Yeltsin suspended the Constitutional Court, closed newspapers, banned political parties, vacillated on his pledge of early presidential elections, and allowed Moscow authorities to banish non-ethnic Russians from the city, the ends-justifies-the-means contentions that underlay U.S. policy looked increasingly dubious and dangerous. Indeed, they were disturbingly reminiscent of the Bush administration's unqualified backing of Mikhail Gorbachev. A similar tendency to back a leader, rather than human rights principles, could be seen in the Clinton administration's support for Eduard Shevardnadze in Georgia.

The administration also did not allow its quest for elected government to interfere with its relations with major oil producers. Saudi Arabia's authoritarian monarchy remained beyond public criticism, as did Kuwait's royal family, which continued to sponsor abuses despite the election of a parliament with limited powers.

Progress toward acceptance of the North American Free Trade Agreement (NAFTA) provided an important opportunity to promote political freedom in Mexico. But evidently out of fear of jeopardizing the Congressional vote on NAFTA, the administration lost its critical voice when it came to Mexican abuses, other than to speculate that NAFTA would improve Mexican human rights practices. We hope that with NAFTA approved by Congress, that voice will now be found.

A Troubling Silence on the Middle East

The Middle East and Northern Africa seemed to have disappeared altogether from the administration's human rights agenda, although it was not for want of problems. Egypt, Algeria and Israel confronted violence from Islamic militants, but their response included torture, the excessive use of lethal force, and restrictions on association and expression. These acts, themselves violations of human rights standards, fueled a climate of extremism by closing off legiti-mate avenues of dissent. Yet the administration greeted them with virtual silence and unconditional support for the governments in question.

The administration took U.S. policy a disturbing step backward when it came to Israel's deportation of 400 Palestinians to Lebanon. Following longstanding U.S. practice, the Bush administration had condemned the deportations as violations of the Fourth Geneva Convention. Ignoring the law, the Clinton administration treated the deportations as a mere political problem, accepting Israel's decision to return one-fourth of the deportees as sufficient compliance with a U.N. Security Council resolution demanding immediate repatriation of them all.

Regression was also apparent in the administration's reversal of an eight-year ban on lethal sales to Lebanon without linking the resumption to human rights progress. The administration exchanged high-level visits with Lebanese officials, but the meetings seemed designed to bolster the Lebanese government and to ensure active participation in the Middle East peace process, rather than to address the Lebanese government's campaign against the press, jailing of opponents, banning of demonstrations, and attacks on peaceful demonstrators. Indeed, less than a month after the Lebanese army killed eight peaceful demonstrators and injured dozens, Edward Djerejian, Assistant Secretary of State for Near Eastern and South Asian Affairs, in a major policy address, expressed only praise for the army and argued for increased aid.

The administration's disregard for human rights in the Middle East is particularly troubling in light of the peace accord between Israel and the Palestine Liberation Organization. A major obstacle to a successful peace effort is the threat of severe abuse by Israeli or Palestinian forces and their allies. Washington risks squandering this tremendous opportunity by diminishing its human rights advocacy in the region. The wrong message was sent when the regional press quoted President Clinton, in a telephone conversation with President Hafez al-

Asad, as effectively urging that critics of the peace accord be silenced. The White House never denied the accuracy of the quote. It is hoped that Secretary Shattuck's scheduled visit to Israel, the occupied territories and Egypt in late 1993 will provide an occasion to redress this neglect.

The Treatment of Migrants and Refugees

The administration set a far more productive tone than its predecessor in addressing abuse by the U.S. Border Patrol against undocumented migrants along the Mexican border. The Bush administration had dismissed out of hand our investigation in 1992 showing a pattern of unredressed physical abuse by Border Patrol agents. The Clinton administration responded to an updated probe in 1993 with a detailed list of reforms that it was studying or implementing.

Yet the administration's attention to human rights standards dropped precipitously when it came to Haitian asylum-seekers. Despite escalating violence of such severity that international monitors were forced to evacuate the country, the administration insisted on summarily returning Haitian boat people to the Haitian army, on the same dock where its own observer troops would not land, without any attempt to identify and exempt those who risked persecution. U.S. government centers set up in Haiti to interview would-be refugees offered small consolation, as those willing to risk travel to the centers faced indefinite waits.

The administration successfully defended a stingy reading of refugee law before the U.S. Supreme Court, by arguing that the prohibition against forcibly repatriating refugees applied only once refugees reached land. It then showed a similar lack of generosity when it stopped three boats laden with Chinese migrants of the coast of Mexico, undertook only superficial attempts to screen for refugees, and then pressured Mexican authorities to accept and repatriate their passengers.

The Work of Human Rights Watch

The increasing willingness of the United Nations to initiate peacekeeping and humanitarian operations in defense of human rights prompted a corresponding shift in emphasis in the work of Human Rights Watch. While encouraging U.N. involvement in appropriate cases, we felt a duty to scrutinize U.N. operations, to ensure they remained true to the human rights principles that in theory were guiding them. We examined the conduct of U.N. representatives in Angola, Cambodia, El Salvador, Iraq, Liberia, Somalia, Sudan and the former Yugoslavia. As outlined earlier, we found U.N. actions wanting in significant respects, particularly the tendency to devalue the importance of justice.

Our work on the United Nations was facilitated by our receipt of formal consultative status. The last time our application for U.N. consultative status was considered, in 1991, it was blocked under a voting system that gave a veto to any member of the pertinent committee. In light of this privilege, many of the most abusive governments flocked to the committee, and our application was rejected with vetoes by Cuba, Iraq, Libya and Sudan. In 1993, when similar vetoes seemed likely, the U.N. broke its usual procedure and, for the first time in memory, called for a vote. Our application was approved by an overwhelming majority.

Our monitoring of U.N. field operations was also facilitated by our broad mandate, which has long extended not only to traditional violations of civil and political rights, but also to violations of the laws of war, including such abuses as indiscriminate shelling, the targeting of civilians, the use of starvation as a weapon of war, forcible displacement, and the use of indiscriminate weapons such as chemical weapons and landmines. This mandate also permitted us to address conduct by both governmental and guerrilla forces. We devoted extraordinary attention to the conflict in the former Yugoslavia, and also investigated or reported on abuses in the course of conflicts in Angola, Burundi, Cambodia, Colombia, Georgia, Iraq, Kashmir, Lebanon, Liberia, Mozambique, Nagorno-Karabakh, Northern Ireland, Peru, Rwanda, Somalia, Sudan, Tajikistan, and Turkey.

As this introduction demonstrates, we attach special importance to seeking accountability for gross abuses of human rights. We collected large quantities of evidence of war crimes and crimes against humanity in the former Yugoslavia, which we shared with the U.N. War Crimes Commission and hope to share with the War Crimes Tribunal, once it is functional. For much of the year, we pressed for the establishment of the tribunal, the naming of an aggressive prosecutor with a record of action on behalf of human rights, and appropriate funding. While the tribunal has been established and a prosecutor has been named, we fear that continuing critical scrutiny will be needed in 1994.

Our emphasis on accountability was also reflected in our massive research project into the genocidal campaign, known as the *Anfal*, waged by Iraq against its northern Kurdish population in 1988. We have collected some 350 testimonies from victims and survivors of the Anfal, and are well along in our review of literally tons of documents of the Iraqi secret police that were seized by the Kurds during the 1991 uprising and airlifted to the United States. We are in the process of seeking a governmental plaintiff to bring a case against Iraq before the International Court of Justice, the World Court, for violating the Genocide Convention. The quest for accountability was also central to our work in such places as Cambodia, El Salvador, Guatemala, Haiti, Peru, and Somalia.

We devoted substantial resources to an effort to stop the growing epidemic of communal violence. As in 1992, we saw our function as highlighting the governmental role in such violence, to point the way toward ending the violence and avoiding new outbreaks. Our broad mandate allowed us to address problems of discrimination, which often spark communal strife. Illustrative of our work was our reporting in 1993 on India, Kenya, Latvia, South Africa, the former

Yugoslavia, and Zaire.

Despite the compelling nature of wartorn situations, we devoted considerable attention to addressing traditionally repressive governments. We sought to protect and enlarge the political space for the independent institutions that make up civil society. Foremost among our concerns was protecting nongovernmental human rights organizations. Again our broad mandate, which allows us to address not only issues of imprisonment but also noncustodial restraints on civil society, was central to the task. In addition, we kept up pressure on governments where the emergence of civil society is still limited, as in Burma, China, Cuba, Kuwait, Lebanon, and Saudi Arabia.

With an office in Moscow, we closely scrutinized the Russian government's human rights practices. Our monitoring addressed the government's conduct toward its own citizens and, through its military policies, toward the governments of the "near abroad" of the former Soviet Union.

We sent a substantial delegation to the World Conference on Human Rights, where we sought to highlight the conceptual threat to the human rights movement noted above, and to rally sympathetic governments to respond forcefully. We also published two reports to contribute to the discussion in Vienna, a worldwide survey of prison conditions, and a review of U.N. field operations.

Perhaps our most visible presence in Vienna was our Women's Rights Project, launched in 1990 to remedy traditional neglect of women's rights issues. In 1993, the Women's Rights Project addressed rape in the course of conflicts in Peru and Bosnia, forced trafficking of Burmese women and girls in Thailand, discriminatory forced virginity exams in Turkey, and mistreatment of Somali refugees in Kenya.

Our Arms Project, formed in late 1992, made its mark with a groundbreaking global report on the scourge of land mines. The report was timed to correspond with efforts at the United Nations to amend the Land Mines Protocol from a regulatory to an abolitionist legal regime. The Arms Project also investigated arms transfers and related abuse in Argentina-Brazil-Chile, Georgia, India-Pakistan, Lebanon, and Rwanda.

We continued to devote substantial time and effort toward shaping U.S. foreign policy. The advent of the Clinton administration, including several officials who are strong advocates for human rights, provided new opportunities. But the need for strong vigilance remained, since the administration often allowed countervailing interests to prevail over the consistent promotion of human rights.

In keeping with our belief that third-party governments and institutions can exert considerable influence on behalf of human rights, we took steps in 1993 to expand our advocacy work to the European Community. In early 1994, we plan to open an office in Brussels to address the E.C.'s human rights policy, and to scrutinize compliance with its stated commitment to link external assistance to the human rights record of the beneficiary. Several chapters of this report include discussion of the policy of the E.C. or its member states. We also continued to work with the Japanese government to encourage it to live up to its commitment to condition foreign aid on human rights grounds. The chapter on Japan in this report analyzes Japan's evolving human rights policy.

We have always prided ourselves on the flexibility of our advocacy efforts, and one particularly noteworthy undertaking was our campaign to deprive Beijing of the prestige of hosting the 2000 Olympic Games because of its deplorable human rights record. The hard-fought campaign, launched when it seemed only a pipedream, paid off in September when the International Olympic Committee rejected Beijing's bid by the narrowest of margins. In countries where international assistance was not substantial, particularly in China and Central Asia, we also increased our efforts to enlist the support of the business community in promoting human rights.

Our work on human rights in the United States in 1993 focused on the treatment of migrants and refugees seeking to enter U.S. territory. We investigated and reported on abuse by the Border Patrol along the U.S.-Mexican border, the U.S. government's summary repatriation of Haitian asylum-seekers, its inadequate attempts to compensate for this illegal policy by substituting an in-country processing center in Haiti, and its proposed restrictions on asylum procedures in the United States. In addition, in a joint project with the American Civil Liberties Union, we are scheduled to publish in late 1993 an assessment of U.S. compliance with the International Covenant on Civil and Political Rights, which the U.S. government formally ratified in September 1992.

What follows is a review of human rights in 68 countries. As noted, the report covers 1993, through the end of November, plus the last month of 1992. For each country, we describe some of the major human rights developments of the year, restrictions on human rights monitoring in that country, U.S. human rights policy toward the country (sometimes supplemented by a discussion of the role of other governments and international actors, such as the U.N.), and our own response to these developments. This is our eleventh annual review of U.S. human rights policy, and the fourth report that also describes human rights developments worldwide.

This volume does not include a chapter on every country on which we have worked. Nor does it discuss every issue of importance. Rather, the countries and issues treated reflect the focus of our work, which in turn is determined by a variety of factors: the seriousness of abuses, our access to information about them, our ability to influence abusive practices, and our desire to balance our work across various political and other divides.

HUMAN RIGHTS WATCH WORLD REPORT 1994

AFRICA
WATCH

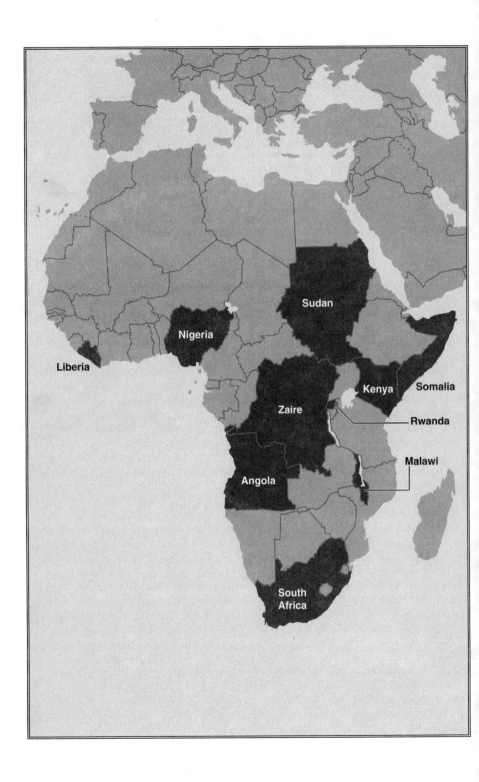

AFRICA WATCH OVERVIEW

Human Rights Developments

In 1993 the twin themes of peacemaking and democratization, on the one hand, and descent into chaos and humanitarian disaster, on the other, continued to dominate human rights developments in Africa, presenting a mixed picture of precarious improvement in some countries, stalemate or deadlock in others and unmitigated catastrophe in a few cases. The political manipulation of ethnic tensions and conflicts also had serious human rights consequences in Kenya, Burundi, Rwanda, Zaire and elsewhere.

In contrast to the tragic situations in Angola, Liberia, Somalia and Sudan, there was the somewhat positive and hopeful case of, for example, Mozambique. As both types of cases clearly indicated, however, some form of international intervention (multilateral peacekeeping and peace-enforcement operations) was becoming an increasingly common, though highly problematic and controversial, factor in the status of human rights in Africa. Africa Watch was particularly concerned that unless human rights standards and mechanisms were fully integrated into the concept and implementation of intervention, if and when it occurred, it was unlikely to achieve its objectives. We have therefore always insisted on such integration, and called for rigorous monitoring and accountability for human rights violations in all cases and situations.

Calls for international intervention are made in a wide variety of situations, and rationalized in different ways. They may be made during peacemaking negotiations to end a civil war and rationalized as necessary for regulating transitional processes, as in Namibia, Angola, Liberia and Mozambique. Intervention may also be called for at times of severe national crisis, as in Burundi after the failed military coup of October 21, 1993. However, the actual conception and implementation of an intervention initiative are conditioned by many factors, including the realities of international power relations, competing perceptions of national interest and the dynamics of domestic politics at any given point in time. This appears to be true whether the initiative purports to be global, as in the case of Somalia, or regional, as in the case of Liberia.

In this light, the precise outcome or consequences of intervention would be difficult to predict in advance with any degree of certainty. There will also probably be enduring disagreement about its appropriateness, timing and implementation in any given case. It is beyond doubt, however, that the integration and rigorous observance of human rights norms is essential for the success of any intervention, if and when it is justified.

Africa Watch was also particularly concerned about mounting evidence that some governments were either actively engaged in the manipulation of so-called ethnic violence among their citizens, or at least failing to take necessary action to prevent and control it. As clearly shown in country reports below, and other Africa Watch publications, the governments of Kenya, Rwanda, South Africa and Zaire, as well as Angola, Liberia and Nigeria, have been implicated in either encouraging or condoning ethnic-based violence within their respective countries. All governments must be held accountable for their responsibility in this regard.

The Right to Monitor

As can be seen from the various country sections of this report, opportunities for human rights monitoring generally improved with greater democratization in many parts of Africa. There was also a growing body of independent African monitoring organizations and groups which could act in partnership with international NGOs in this regard. It was also encouraging to observe the development of inter-African networks of human rights monitors, like the Union Inter-Africain des Droits de l'Homme et des Peuples (Inter-African Union for Human and People's Rights), based in Ouagadougou, Burkina Faso. The Union participated with Africa

Watch in an international commission, which conducted a very successful mission to Rwanda in the early part of 1993.

There was, however, an urgent need to strengthen the capabilities of African human rights organizations, and to promote a culture of independent, nonpartisan human rights monitoring and advocacy. African human rights groups also need to develop a stronger sense of consistency, continuity and accountability to their local constituencies. African human rights organizations must see consistency, continuity and local constituency building as essential elements of their right to monitor.

U.S. Policy

U.S. policy in Africa was dominated in 1993 by the issue of American military involvement in Somalia. What began as a humanitarian effort in early December 1992, when President Bush deployed some 25,000 U.S. troops to break the strangle-hold of Somali warlords over the country's food supply, by year's end had become a tangled military engagement costing American lives. Congressional outrage over some nineteen American casualties incurred as U.N./U.S. forces pursued factional leader Muhammad Farah Aideed forced President Clinton to promise to withdraw the American force by March 1994, and cast a shadow over the possibilities of U.S. humanitarian intervention elsewhere.

The disaster in Somalia may be traced to the lack of clear purpose by the U.S./U.N. in that country, and in late 1993 the Clinton administration's overall policy towards Somalia was no clearer than it was when the President took office in January. A lack of attention to human rights had characterized U.S. policy toward Somalia, which in turn ensured that the U.N. would not incorporate human rights guarantees into its operations there.

On a positive note, U.N. operations outside of Mogadishu appeared to be bearing fruit, with much of Somalia conflict-free and a large portion of the country's displaced people returning to their homes and villages.

Regrettably, however, little headway was made by the U.S./U.N. effort in establishing mechanisms to bring those responsible for gross abuses against Somalis to account, and to build institutions of civil society that might help avert a repetition of the human rights disaster that cost some 300,000 Somali lives before the international intervention.

Elsewhere in Africa the Clinton administration's human rights policies were influenced by its emphasis on democratization and conflict resolution. Speeches about Africa by key figures in the administration—including National Security Advisor Anthony Lake and Secretary of State Warren Christopher—were meant to signal a new commitment to Africa, especially in the areas of democracy and human rights. While this effort was most welcome, the effects were largely symbolic, and most of sub-Saharan Africa remained marginal for the Clinton administration.

In the area of conflict resolution, crises in Liberia, Angola, and Sudan continued despite the administration's diplomatic efforts. In Liberia, the administration recognized the need to provide financial support to the U.N. and African peace initiatives which resulted in some progress, however tentative, by year's end. In Angola, one of Africa's worst human rights disasters, the U.S. did not succeed in its mediation efforts. The upsurge in the civil war following the National Union for the Total Independence of Angola or UNITA's refusal to cede to the results of U.N.-sponsored elections in October 1992 resulted in tens of thousands of civilian deaths due to abuses by both UNITA and government forces. The Clinton administration, which recognized the MPLA government in May 1993, had the opportunity to use the occasion of recognition to press the government for human rights commitments. There was no evidence that the administration did so, nor did it make any public statements about abuses by either side throughout most of the year. The announcement of the appointment of a special U.S. envoy to Angola by late October did indicate, however, a significant improvement in the level of U.S. involvement in that country.

U.S. human rights policy in Africa was more successful in the area of promoting democracy in several countries where governments attempted to thwart the will of their electorate. In Malawi, for example, the Banda regime, under pressure from the U.S. and other international donors, held a referendum on multiparty democracy in June. But the country's single political party, dominated by Life President John Tembo and his henchman, did everything in its power to guarantee a result in its favor: detaining the country's best-known political dissident, Chakufwa Chihana, and denying the pro-democracy movement access to the media. The U.S. played an important role in the process by strongly pressing the Malawian government to release political prisoners, and beaming independent news reports in the Chewa language through the Voice of America. The referendum was held in time and the electorate voted for multiparty democracy.

Nigeria was another country where the U.S. was helpful to the development of democracy. When Nigerian President Babangida refused to announce the results of the country's presidential election and then annulled the elections themselves, the U.S. immediately imposed sanctions on the regime, cutting off bilateral assistance, suspending commercial arms sales, and threatening opposition to Nigerian loans in the multilateral financial institutions. The strong American response encouraged some moderation on Nigeria's part, leading to the formation of an interim government headed by Ernest Shonekan.

With regard to some African countries, the U.S. failed to exercise the leverage it possessed as effectively as it might have. In the case of Kenya, where the United States had the potential to exercise significant leverage, an important opportunity to pressure the Kenyan police was missed when the U.S. provided some $3.73 million in military assistance for border security. Certainly the Kenyan government faces a serious security

problem on its Somali border, where Somali and Kenyan bandits committed all sorts of atrocities against both local and refugee populations in the area. But to have provided the assistance without first receiving a commitment on the part of the government of Kenya to discipline its own police—which has been responsible for the rapes of Somali women in the area—was a lost opportunity to promote badly needed reforms.

In Sudan, one of worst human rights trouble spots on the continent, the U.S. government had little leverage to exercise with the Al-Bashir regime. Bilateral assistance from the U.S. was limited to humanitarian assistance, and real leverage to encourage human rights improvements was not available. The Clinton administration, like the Bush administration before it, spoke out frankly about abuses in Sudan, but the Sudanese government, increasingly isolated in 1993, appeared undeterred by pressure from the West.

One area where the U.S. ought to have been more effective was with the anti-government Sudan People's Liberation Army (SPLA) forces in southern Sudan. Both SPLA factions, the Garang (Main-stream) and Riak (United), engaged in gross abuses of human rights against civilians from each other's communities. Although the U.S. had criticized these abuses in a few public statements, it did not succeed in influencing the behavior of the SPLA factions in southern Sudan. Gross and systematic human rights abuses continued to be committed by both factions. Given the commonly assumed susceptibility of such groups to external pressure, it may be asked whether the SPLA factions were receiving mixed messages from the U.S. administration and Congress: condemnation of their human rights record in public and expressions of "understanding and support" in private.

The Work of Africa Watch

Throughout 1993, Africa Watch continued its work of monitoring and documenting human rights abuses in about a dozen countries in Africa. An effort was made to maintain a balance between the work on humanitarian disasters—Somalia, Sudan, Liberia, and Angola—and reporting on abuses in those countries claiming to be establishing democracy, including Nigeria, Zambia, Rwanda and Mauritania. It is only by illustrating the range of abuses, from violations of free expression to manipulation of ethnic conflict to massacres of innocent civilians, that a picture of Africa's diversity and complexity can emerge.

Not surprisingly, Africa Watch devoted considerable resources to work on the Horn of Africa, particularly the crises in Somalia and Sudan. Two separate missions were sent to both countries during 1993 in order to provide consistent information on the pattern of abuses and, in the case of Somalia, the role of the U.N.

A theme that was woven through much of Africa Watch's work involved the government's role in manipulating ethnic conflict. Publications examined the government's incitement of communal violence in Zaire and Rwanda, the ethnic clashes in Kenya, and the KwaZulu conflict in South Africa.

Africa Watch also conducted studies of the international peacekeeping operations in Africa, with particular emphasis on the U.N. operation in Somalia and the West African intervention in Liberia. In both cases, the lack of a human rights component was found to undermine the success of the missions.

During 1993, Africa Watch produced several joint projects with Human Rights Watch's Prison Project, Women's Rights Project and Arms Project. These focused projects enabled Africa Watch to conduct in-depth studies on prison conditions in Zaire and South Africa, the rape of Somali women refugees in Kenya, and the civilian toll from land mines in Angola and Mozambique.

As in the past, Africa Watch was called to testify before congressional hearings on Africa: before the Senate Foreign Relation's Subcommittee on Africa dealing with Liberia, and before the House Foreign Affairs Subcommittee on Africa dealing with Nigeria. In addition, Africa Watch continued to

be an important source of information for the U.S. and international press, and provided numerous interviews about human rights conditions in Africa.

ANGOLA

Human Rights Developments

In 1993 Angola returned to full civil war. The September 1992 elections had provided Angolans with their first opportunity to express their will in what the U.N. and other foreign observers concluded was a "generally free and fair" process. In the presidential election President dos Santos, as winner, received 49.56 percent of the vote compared with 40.7 percent for rival National Union for the Total Independence of Angola (UNITA) leader Jonas Savimbi. In the legislative election, the Popular Movement for the Liberation of Angola (MPLA), dos Santos's party, obtained 53.7 percent of the votes compared to UNITA's 34.09 percent. Under Angolan law, the failure of the winner in the presidential election to receive 50 percent of votes cast requires an election runoff. But a second round of the 1992 election did not occur because UNITA rejected the results and returned the country to civil war, such that 500,000 Angolans died in the renewed fighting or from a combination of starvation and disease. Toward year's end, some three million people, particularly children, women and the elderly, were suffering from the consequences of the conflict, including an estimated 1,000 people a day dying in a conflict that neither side could win outright.

Fighting first broke out in the central city of Huambo on October 17 and 18, 1992, and by the end of the month in Luanda also, culminating November 1 in street battles in the city center and in residential districts with at least 1,200 people killed, many of them innocent civilians. Savimbi's nephew and right-hand man, Elias Salupeta Pena, and UNITA vice-president Jeremias Chitunda, were shot dead by soldiers on

November 1 as they were trying to flee from Luanda. Top UNITA military commander Gen. Arlindo Pena Ben-Ben escaped with injuries, but his foreign affairs spokesperson, Abel Chivukuvuku, was injured and taken into government custody. The government also captured fifteen other senior UNITA officials. Fighting ended in Luanda on November 2 but continued in other provinces.

UNITA's strategy was one of brinkmanship, in clear violation of the May 1991 Bicesse peace accords. It pushed the government to the breaking point and prompted a vicious backlash: the seventy-two-hour attack by government forces and vigilantes on UNITA positions in Luanda and in towns across the country. Police and civilian supporters of the government razed UNITA offices, extrajudicially executed UNITA sympathizers and purged UNITA from the towns. Eyewitnesses interviewed by Africa Watch said that there were deliberate mass killings by pro-government forces. During those seventy-two hours the government made little effort to stop the killings. Militarily, the government destroyed a significant portion of UNITA's political leadership and support structure by destroying the guerrillas urban and armed militia. However, the government failed to confront UNITA's armed forces (FALA).

By mid-November 1992, the U.N. reported that fifty-seven of Angola's 164 municipalities were under UNITA control and that UNITA maintained an advantage in forty additional ones. UNITA also occupied several provincial capitals, including Uige (Uige province), Huambo (Huambo province), Benguela (Benguela province), Caxito (Bengo province) and Ndalatando (Cuanza Norte province). In spite of U.N. mediation attempts and a cease-fire agreement in November, UNITA continued to make territorial gains in the north. As these military gains continued, the position of those in the MPLA seeking a military response strengthened. President dos Santos installed a new government on December 2, 1992. Of its fifty-three members, eleven were affiliated with other parties that had won seats in the legislative elections. UNITA was offered five posts: Ministry of Culture and four vice-ministries. Among the other appointments was Gen. Joao Baptista de Matos as the new armed forces chief, replacing Gen. Antonio Franca ("N'dalu") who had been negotiating with UNITA in an attempt to avoid renewed civil war.

On December 27, 1992, the government launched its counter-offensive against UNITA. This marked a return to full-blown civil war. Fighting spread across the country with UNITA forced to retreat from many locations and government forces regaining control of Benguela city and Lobito (Benguela) after fierce fighting. Although the MPLA captured Huambo, the government's objective of dealing UNITA a final blow on the battlefield failed because its forces over-extended themselves and could not sustain their gains under renewed pressure from UNITA. At the end of January 1993, the U.N. estimated that UNITA controlled 105 of the 164 municipalities.

From January 3, UNITA battled to capture the second city, Huambo, shelling it despite a majority of its residents having voted for UNITA in the elections. The town fell to the rebels on March 8, at a cost, according to U.N. estimates, of 15,000 casualties. In January UNITA captured the oil town of Soyo (Zaire) but the government soon recaptured it only to lose it to UNITA once again in May. After June, the major focal point of the conflict for the rest of the year was Cuito, capital of Bie province. The city came under UNITA seige in January. In nine months of siege 35,000 people died, according to U.N. estimates. U.N. relief reached the city in late October following a local cease-fire. Two-thirds of Angola had fallen under UNITA control by November.

A number of attempts were made by the U.N. and its member states in 1993 to mediate in the conflict. In January, peace talks between UNITA and the MPLA in Addis Ababa failed on key issues. A projected second round of talks did not take place. Talks in Abidjan between May 12 and 21 came the closest to agreement of any negotiations so far; a thirty-eight-point protocol was drawn up. But the talks finally failed because of UNITA's inability to compromise. Agreement was reached between both sides on a power-sharing formula, but UNITA refused to agree to an article that demanded its fighters' withdrawal from areas they had occupied since fighting broke out in October 1992. Attempts to reach a compromise on this point were frustrated by the U.N. UNITA wanted the symbolic presence of U.N. peacekeeping forces in the areas from which it withdrew. This would, in UNITA's view, protect its supporters from MPLA retaliation. The U.N. indicated, however, that such a force could only be sent after a full ceasefire had been signed, and then only six to nine months after the event. The talks failed.

Violence also continued in Cabinda, an oil-rich Angolan enclave between Zaire and the Congo, where separatist factions fought for independence. There was a spate of killings and abductions in the region. In mid-1993 one faction, Front for the Liberation of the Cabindan Enclave-Armed Forces of Cabinda (FLEC-FAC), seemed to have suffered a serious internal struggle, accompanied by killings and disappearances. Both UNITA and the Angolan government held talks with the separatist factions in an attempt to form alliances, and those approaches may have contributed to the fighting among the various FLEC factions.

Renewed conflict was being fueled by new arms and foreign expertise actively procured by both the MPLA and UNITA. The government used its oil revenue remittances to fund the conflict; UNITA used its access to diamond-producing areas to fund purchases of weaponry to augment what it captured from government forces. On April 23 the government unilaterally declared that the Triple Zero clause in the Bicesse accords, which prohibited either side from purchasing arms, was obsolete. Both sides also sought recruits in the mercenary market in South Africa and Europe. Britain and several other European Community countries lifted their arms embargo against the government in August.

The numbers of people displaced by the conflict continued to grow, estimated at two million by June 1993. According to the government, Angola required 27,000 tons of food per month plus medical supplies. Commercial food imports into Luanda diminished due to the lack of foreign exchange, with the government forced to spend money on armaments and exporters reluctant to send ships into a war zone. A U.N. World Food Program report suggested that a significant proportion of Angola's harvest would rot due to disruption caused by the fighting, and estimated that 1.9 million conflict- and drought-affected persons would require 337,000 tons of food assistance.

Reports of human rights abuses by both sides increased as the conflict intensified and civilians became victims of calculated violence. Reports from the central and northern provinces indicated that both sides have engaged in killings and intimidation of civilians, especially if they were not from the home ethnic group. These tactics caused massive civilian displacement, especially out of UNITA, held areas, and have encouraged ethnic divisions.

Africa Watch also received frequent reports of violations of the laws of war by both sides, including executions of captured soldiers and cases of children forced to fight on the war front. UNITA was also responsible for gross human rights abuses, including executions of civilians and other deliberate and arbitrary killings. Near Quipungo (Huila), UNITA attacked a train on May 27 in which 225 people were killed and several hundred injured, most of them civilians.

Humanitarian efforts were also hampered by the war. Several relief flights were hit by UNITA fire. In April, a World Food Programme (WFP) aircraft was shot down by UNITA in eastern Angola. UNITA attempted to deny the delivery of food aid to isolated government towns in order to capture them. There were frequent suspensions of relief flights because of these attacks. The government also sought to deny food aid delivery to rebel-held areas. In July, an agreement reached between the government, UNITA and the U.N. allowed the resumption of some relief flights to agreed locations. Only in late October was the U.N. able to fly again to all towns across the country.

In August, the bombing of Huambo as part of a major government offensive against UNITA destroyed the International Committee of Red Cross (ICRC) headquarters in the city. In August, a WFP convoy of seventy-five trucks transporting relief aid to some 145,000 war-affected people in Caimbambo and Cubal was attacked by unidentified gunmen who destroyed one truck and damaged two more. Four members of the convoy were killed.

The Right to Monitor

As Angola descended into renewed civil war, human rights monitoring as well as international relief efforts faced extreme dangers. The threat of violence came not only from the warring sides but from freelance bandits and looters.

Both the government and UNITA limited journalistic access and coverage as part of their war effort. More than twenty Angolan journalists died while trying to cover the fighting.

U.S. and U.N. Policy

The Clinton administration initially delayed recognizing the MPLA in the hope that this would give it extra leverage over UNITA. But increasing frustration at UNITA's continued intransigence convinced the administration to recognize the Angolan government on May 19. Soon after recognition, the U.S. opened an embassy in Luanda and sent its first ambassador. An arms embargo on selling U.S. government nonlethal military equipment to the Angolan government was lifted in June.

Formal military assistance to the Angolan government did not appear to be on the immediate agenda of the U.S. administration, although the Defense Intelligence Agency (DIA) expanded its presence in Luanda. Except for recognition of the MPLA government, there was a strong sense of

continuity from previous administrations' policies. For more than half the year, U.S policy towards Angola was ad hoc; only in August did Robert Cabelly, special advisor to Assistant Secretary of State for African affairs George Moose, draft a policy document for the first time. Apparently as a result of this advice, emerging U.S. policy towards Angola appeared to concentrate on diplomacy rather than a military approach, encouraging both sides to return to peace talks. At the urging of key members of Congress, for example, the administration in late October appointed a special envoy to assist U.N. peace efforts and attend the talks that began that month in Lusaka. Testimony by administration officials in Congress concentrated on the peace process; apparently in order to foster progress in the negotiations, officials said virtually nothing about abuses by either side. Nor did Congress press for a stronger human rights stance; rather, Congress continued to be preoccupied by events elsewhere, such that Angola policy remained determined by the State Department and favored the MPLA. The Defense Department, however, believed that U.S. policy should be even-handed between both sides, inasmuch as eventually stability in Angola would require a major role in government for UNITA.

In the context of this inchoate policy, the administration and Congress approved the selling of nonlethal military equipment to Luanda beginning in June. The equipment included the sophisticated U.S.-made Global Positioning System (GPS), a guidance system for relief drops and/or bombing. Sales of military items of any kind to a government engaging in a pattern of gross abuses of human rights like the Angolan government, is prohibited under human rights provisions of the Foreign Assistance Act, and should not have occurred in this case.

The U.N. presence in Angola was greatly reduced by renewal of the conflict. Staff of the United Nations Angola Verification Mission (UNAVEM II) in September 1993 numbered forty-three international civilian staff; fifty military observers; eighteen police observers; eleven military paramedics, and seventy-five local staff. UNAVEM military and police staff continued to be deployed at five locations (Luanda, Lubango, Namibe, Benguela and Sumbe).

After the presidential and legislative elections of September 29 and 30, 1992, UNAVEM II sought to mediate actively in the conflict despite its increasingly irrelevant and limited mandate for monitoring and verification. Eight Security Council resolutions, beginning in October 1992, have gradually extended UNAVEM's mandate and condemned UNITA for violating the Bicesse accords. In January 1993, while extending UNAVEM's mandate, the Security Council also advocated greatly reducing UNAVEM staffing levels, to thirty military observers, eighteen police observers and forty-nine international staff. UNAVEM withdrew from the oil-rich Cabinda enclave in early March following an attack on its compound by unidentified gunmen. A March resolution of the Security Council appealed to both sides to "strictly abide by applicable rules of humanitarian law, including unimpeded access for humanitarian assistance" to the civilian population in need.

At the end of April, showing increasing exasperation with UNITA, the Security Council condemned attacks on humanitarian flights, particularly by UNITA. UNAVEM's staffing levels were reduced further after a June resolution that also held UNITA responsible for the breakdown of peace talks and for thereby jeopardizing the peace process. On July 15, the Security Council warned UNITA that international sanctions might be imposed unless it signed a cease-fire by mid-September. As UNITA continued military actions past that date, the Security Council warned that an oil and arms embargo would be imposed in the absence of a cease-fire by September 25. When the deadline passed, sanctions were imposed.

The U.N. Special Representative on Angola, Margaret Anstee, retired following the collapse of the peace talks in May. Her replacement was a former Malian foreign minister, Alioune Blondin Beye. U.N. Sec-

retary-General Boutros-Ghali had selected Sergio Viera de Mello, who represented the U.N. High Commissioner for Refugees (UNHCR) in Cambodia, but UNITA opposed his nomination on the grounds that his country of origin, Brazil, has been too friendly with the Angolan government.

UNAVEM's mandate was to be renegotiated whenever a cease-fire could be reached, and UNAVEM III created for the next stage.

The Work of Africa Watch

Africa Watch was active in monitoring human rights abuses in the conflict and held meetings with senior government, UNITA and U.N. officials. In January, Africa Watch released *Land Mines in Angola*, the result of extensive research carried out in the country in 1992. It contained a technical assessment of mine-laying in Angola and examined the makes and types of mines that have been used, and the methods of their use. The report also examined the human impact of land mines, finding that civilians were the most common victims. In examining mine clearance initiatives during the interim period up to the September 1992 elections Africa Watch discovered that some of these were seriously flawed. The report concluded that only a complete ban on the use of anti-personnel mines could remove the unreasonable danger they posed to civilians. Information obtained subsequent to publication of the report indicated that many land mines had been planted by both sides in the renewed conflict.

Africa Watch also worked closely with humanitarian organizations in drawing attention to Angola's plight and briefed and lobbied politicians and the media. Africa Watch staff gave a series of public talks and press interviews on Angola in the United States, southern Africa, Australia, France, Portugal and Great Britain.

KENYA

Human Rights Developments

On December 29, 1992, Kenya held its first genuinely multiparty elections since independence. Incumbent President Daniel arap Moi was reelected, and the Kenya African National Union (KANU), the ruling party since independence in 1963, returned as the largest party to the National Assembly. Although the political system was opened up to some extent by the elections, Kenya's government remained intolerant of criticism. Attacks on opposition politicians and on journalists, use of excessive force by police in the control of demonstrations, and the enforcement of repressive legislation remained serious concerns in Kenya in 1993. The politically motivated ethnic violence that had convulsed large areas of rural Kenya during 1992 returned intermittently during the first half of 1993, and erupted with renewed force towards the end of the year, amid continuing allegations of government involvement. As corruption scandals shook the government, Kenya's economy continued to decline.

Observers from Kenya and abroad concluded that, although there were significant irregularities in the conduct of the elections, the results substantially reflected the will of the Kenyan people. The reelection of President Moi and KANU, owed much to the division of the original main opposition party, the Forum for the Restoration of Democracy (FORD), into two parties, FORD-Kenya and FORD-Asili, joined by a breakaway group from KANU, the Democratic Party. Moi himself received only 36 percent of the vote. KANU nevertheless secured one hundred of the 188 seats being contested in the National Assembly. Seven parties altogether were represented in the new parliament. Divisions within the opposition increased throughout the year: in September, FORD-Kenya split once more, as well-known lawyer Gitobu Imanyara was fired as secretary-general of the party, in a conflict with Raila Odinga, the son of the party's leader Oginga Odinga; Vice-Chair Paul Muite and several others resigned from party offices in protest.

On January 27, 1993 the new parliament was suspended, legally, by President Moi one day after it was convened; it reopened only in March. Although debate on controversial government policies did occur, the opposition was frustrated by the bias of the speaker in favor of the government, and no significant reforms were introduced through parliament during the year. Despite plans announced in June by Attorney General Amos Wako to look into the need for law reform, repressive legislation such as the Preservation of Public Security Act, the Public Order Act, the Societies Act, the Nongovernmental Organization Coordination Act, the Chiefs' Authorities Act and the Local Authorities Act remained in force and in use. More positively, the much-vilified British expatriate chief justice, Alan Hancox, was replaced in March by Ghanaian judge Fred Apaloo, who indicated that he would be more supportive of an independent judiciary.

The most disturbing trend of 1993 was the continuation of political violence in rural Kenya. Although many predicted that the so-called tribal clashes that erupted at the end of 1991 and became fiercer as the 1992 election campaign progressed would cease once elections were held, this was not the case. In late 1993, Africa Watch estimated that 1,500 Kenyans had been killed and 300,000 internally displaced since the clashes began. During 1993, conflict was concentrated in Rift Valley Province, and pitted members of Moi's ethnic group, the Kalenjin, against Kenya's majority community, the Kikuyu. Allegations of government promotion of this violence, verified by the report of a parliamentary committee in 1992, continued to be made in 1993.

The Kenyan government failed to take adequate measures to stop the violence. Although arrests were made, those arrested were often released without charge, or charges were not vigorously pursued. Strong action was taken in response to inflammatory statements by opposition figures, but similar comments made by ministers were ignored. In September, the government declared several districts to be "security operation zones" where emergency-type laws would apply. Regulations promulgated under the Preservation of Public Security Act also restricted access to these zones. Government officials denied later reports that violence was still continuing despite these measures. A challenge to the constitutionality of the regulations was filed in court.

The bulk of relief to the victims of the violence was carried out by church groups, principally the National Council of Churches of Kenya (NCCK) and the Catholic church. Church members engaged in relief efforts were subject to official harassment for their efforts. Others attempting to draw attention to the political violence were also attacked. Wangari Maathai, the well-known environmental activist, attempted on three occasions in February and March to hold a meeting for clash victims in Nakuru, which were all prevented by police action. On February 25, John Makanga, a pharmacist associated with Professor Maathai was arrested, assaulted, detained for two weeks, and charged with sedition for distributing leaflets accusing the government of responsibility for the violence. In what was widely presumed to be officially-sponsored harassment, an exhibition of photographs depicting victims of the clashes—organized by Maathai at the U.N.'s Vienna conference on human rights—was stolen by a group of Maasai who had been taken to the conference by a minister as representatives of Kenya's "indigenous" peoples.

Political violence also erupted in Kenya's coastal cities, where the Islamic Party of Kenya (IPK), denied permission to register as a party for the elections, clashed both with police and with a rival party, the United Muslims of Africa. In May, the leader of the IPK, Sheikh Khalid Balala, was arrested and charged for threatening to kill KANU leaders. Released on bail, amid unprecedented security precautions, he was re-arrested five days later. In September, Mombasa saw renewed rioting as Muslims protested the visit of President Moi to the city.

Freedom of political expression and assembly was threatened by police action on numerous occasions in 1993. In January, members of the security police attempted to abduct Paul Muite of FORD-Kenya from his office. In April, police violently dispersed a peaceful demonstration in Nairobi called to protest high food prices and the deteriorating economy. FORD-Kenya leader Raila Odinga was arrested and charged with joining an illegal procession. One month later, Odinga was again arrested, with five other opposition parliamentarians, while campaigning for a by-election in the western town of Kisii. In May, the leader of the Central Organization of Trade Unions, Joseph Mugalla, was arrested and charged with inciting workers to break the law, by calling for a general strike. At the opening of parliament in March, a band of armed Maasai warriors, acknowledged to have been organized by government ministers, attacked opposition demonstrators outside parliament; some weeks later, police charged a crowd that was outside parliament heckling cabinet ministers. In June, riot police broke up a rally held by Martin Shikuku, deputy leader of FORD-Asili. Shikuku and a colleague were arrested and held overnight, then released without charge. In August, a peaceful demonstration in the coastal tourist town of Lamu turned into a riot when police tried to disperse it.

Although increased press freedom did allow greater scrutiny of government activity following the election—revealing, for example, official involvement in the "Goldenberg" corruption scandal—the independent press most critical of the government remained under threat in 1993. Numerous issues of *Finance* and *Society* magazines were confiscated throughout the year, either before distribution or from street vendors in Nairobi. The editor of *Finance*, Njehu Gatabaki, was detained for twenty-three days in February, briefly detained again in May, and held for three days in June after being arrested as he was about to leave Nairobi to attend the World Conference on Human

Rights in Vienna, where he was to speak on government attacks on the press. On April 30, armed uniformed police went to the premises of Fotoform Limited, the printers of both *Society* and *Finance*, and immobilized the printing machines by taking away essential components. Publication of both magazines was halted for several weeks.

Other publications were also objects of harassment. On February 13 and 14, police confiscated copies of *Watchman*, a church magazine, and of *People*, a new weekly newspaper financed by Kenneth Matiba, leader of FORD-Asili. On February 16, police arrested Rev. Jamlick Miano, the editor of *Watchman*, and another journalist with the magazine. They were charged with sedition and held for three weeks before being released on bail. These charges were dropped on June 28. In March the Kenya Television Network local news, which had established a standard of reporting far superior to the propaganda broadcast by the government-run Kenya Broadcasting Corporation, was taken off the air, after broadcasting statements by Wangari Maathai and Kenneth Matiba criticizing the government for its role in the clashes.

The situation in Kenya's North East province, along the border with Somalia, remained extremely insecure. Bandits known as *shiftas* operated throughout the region, preying on local residents, refugees and relief workers. Refugee camps housing Somalis fleeing civil war were especially unsafe, and women in particular were at risk of rape. In some cases these rapes involved Kenyan security forces. Efforts by the Kenyan police to control the situation led to armed clashes in which several scores of bandits were killed, in addition to numerous police.

The Right to Monitor

The government showed itself to be particularly sensitive to any attempt to report on or investigate the Rift Valley clashes. Journalists working in the areas and activists attempting to take action were repeatedly harassed. Although representatives of Africa Watch toured the clash areas without official obstruction in June and July, more high-profile visits provoked a strong reaction. The declaration of security zones in the Rift Valley, with no access for any outsiders, followed wide publicity of visits to the clash areas made in August by Kerry Kennedy Cuomo of the Robert F. Kennedy Memorial Center for Human Rights and by Lord David Ennals, on behalf of the British Refugee Council. The Kenyan government had, however, given visas to representatives of the RFK Center after many rejected requests in previous years.

In early September, after the declaration of security zones, a visiting group of Dutch members of parliament was barred from visiting the clash areas. Shortly thereafter, thirteen opposition MPs were arrested as they tried to travel to Molo, one of the worst areas. Bedan Mbugua, editor of *People*, was later arrested together with two ministers of the Presbyterian church, as they were traveling towards Molo. On September 13, they were charged with organizing an unlawful public procession and obstructing the police then released on bail.

The partial relaxation of political repression that accompanied the election campaign allowed the operation of a handful of new organizations examining human rights, including the Kenya Human Rights Commission and the Legal Education and Aid Program (LEAP). In June 1993, the creation of another new human rights organization was announced. The National Democratic and Human Rights Organization (NDEHURIO), led by former parliamentarian Kiogi wa Wamwere and lawyer Mirugi Kariuki (both ex-political prisoners), stated that its principal purpose was to stop torture and mistreatment of detainees in Kenya. Wamwere and Kariuki and five others were arrested in September as they were traveling in one of the clash areas, after it had been declared a security zone, and charged with entering into a prohibited area and being in possession of a firearm. Wamwere and Kariuki were held in custody for more than a month before finally being released on bail. In November, Wamwere was rearrested and charged with stealing guns that had been raided from a police station in the Rift Valley area.

U.S. Policy

Ambassador Smith Hempstone, regarded as a hero by many Kenyans for his leadership of the international pressure on President Moi to hold elections, resigned from his position, as is customary, at the end of the Bush administration. Aurelia Brazeal, a career diplomat previously ambassador to Micronesia, was finally confirmed as Hempstone's replacement in August, and took up her position in September. U.S. policy towards Kenya in 1993 was conducted in a somewhat more restrained style than Kenyans had become used to.

Following the elections, the Kenyan government lobbied intensively for the restoration of bilateral and multilateral aid, suspended in November 1991 in protest at human rights abuses and economic mismanagement. Since that date, all U.S. aid had been channeled through nongovernmental organizations. However, in September 1993, the State Department announced the release of $3.73 million of pipeline money in military assistance to assist the Kenyan government in providing security along the border with Somalia. The department issued a public statement that "[t]he decision to release these funds is based solely on the need to respond to an extraordinary security threat. The release does not constitute satisfaction with the human rights situation in Kenya, a matter which remains of deep and fundamental concern to the United States."

Several statements were also issued throughout the year, by the department or by the embassy in Nairobi, protesting actions taken by the government against freedom of expression. Nevertheless, in contrast to the critical stand previously taken by Ambassador Hempstone, the U.S. failed to take a strong position holding the Kenyan government responsible for the violence in the Rift Valley province. In September, the only statement issued on the violence publicly welcomed the government's decision to declare security zones, showing unwarranted faith in the good behavior of the security forces in these circumstances. The statement was conditioned only by the "hope that the increased security measures will be accompanied by measures to allow access to the affected areas by the press and political representatives of all concerned."

The Moi government had received extensive U.S. military aid in previous years. That aid largely ended during the Bush administration as a response to Kenyan human rights abuses and President Moi's suppression of democracy. The Clinton administration requested $600,000 in military training for fiscal year 1994. Military sales to Kenya continued, with an estimated $343,000 in commercial sales estimated in fiscal year 1993, and $172,000 expected in fiscal year 1994. The U.S. continued to provide approximately $18 million in development assistance to Kenya.

In March, the Kenyan government announced that it was abandoning the implementation of an International Monetary Fund (IMF) structural adjustment policy involving liberalization of prices and devaluation of the Kenyan shilling. The policies were reinstated the following month. In April, despite this suspension of cooperation with the IMF, the World Bank released $85 million, citing some economic progress. However, a second installment of that money was not released in July. Denmark cut its aid to Kenya in August, on the grounds of corruption and the inability to end the rural clashes, but Japan, Kenya's largest donor, announced in October that it was resuming balance of payments support. The consultative group of bilateral donors met at the end of November to decide whether the remainder of suspended aid would be restored.

The Work of Africa Watch

A joint Africa Watch/HRW Women's Rights Project newsletter on the rape of Somali refugees in Kenya was published in October in response to the critical situation along the border in north-eastern Kenya. In November, a report on the rural violence in Rift

Valley Province was published, to coincide with the meeting of the Paris Club group of donors to decide whether to resume aid to Kenya. A number of letters were sent to President Moi protesting the arrest and detention of journalists and human rights activists and urging respect for freedom of speech.

LIBERIA

Human Rights Developments

Although significant progress was made in the second half of 1993 toward ending Liberia's bloody civil war, combat involving the Liberian warring factions and the West African peacekeeping force took a heavy toll on the civilian population. The June massacre of almost 600 civilians in a displaced persons camp in Harbel served to heighten international attention to the war and pressure the parties to resume peace negotiations. Nevertheless, the lack of protection for civilians from abuses by all sides and the profound distrust among the warring factions remained obstacles to lasting peace. The peace agreement signed in July was believed to be Liberia's last, best hope.

Throughout 1993, Liberia remained divided: the Interim Government of National Unity (IGNU) governed the capital, Monrovia, backed by the West African peacekeeping force (ECOMOG); Charles Taylor's National Patriotic Front of Liberia (NPFL), the main rebel group, controlled some 60 percent of the country; and the United Liberation Movement for Democracy in Liberia (ULIMO), a rebel group made up primarily of soldiers from former President Samuel Doe's army, the Armed Forces of Liberia (AFL), controlled at least two western counties. The warring factions are based in part on ethnic affiliations: the AFL is composed mainly of Krahn, the ethnic group of former President Samuel Doe; ULIMO is supported largely by Mandingos and Krahns; and the NPFL was initially formed by Gios and Manos.

The event that set the stage for the developments of 1993 took place in October 1992, when the NPFL attacked Monrovia, ending two years of an uneasy peace and reigniting the civil war. Fighting raged in and around the city, with the suburban areas particularly hard hit. Approximately 200,000 people displaced from these areas flooded into the central city to escape the fighting, and hundreds of civilians were killed.

The offense caught ECOMOG unprepared, and thus compelled it to adopt a new strategy: in the interests of ending the war and defeating a seemingly intractable adversary in the NPFL, ECOMOG accepted the assistance of other Liberian factions in fighting the NPFL. The human rights record of these factions—ULIMO and the AFL—ranged from suspect to abysmal. The AFL was thoroughly discredited by its gross abuses during the 1980s and especially during the war in 1990, when it massacred civilians and devastated Monrovia. ULIMO is an offshoot of the AFL, and its conduct in the areas it captures have included attacks on civilians, looting, and executions of suspected NPFL sympathizers.

After first supporting the right of the AFL to defend itself from attack, ECOMOG soon permitted the AFL to operate alongside the multinational troops, although the AFL retained a separate command structure and controlled certain areas on its own. ECOMOG has claimed that ULIMO operated independently, but it was clear that some coordination existed. There was little indication that ECOMOG tried to curb excesses by these factions. The collaboration between ECOMOG and AFL/ULIMO changed the dynamics of the war, and raised questions about ECOMOG's commitment to human rights.

Meanwhile, refugees fleeing NPFL territory told of an ongoing pattern of NPFL abuses against the civilian population, especially harassment and looting, but also killings. For example, there were reports that in May the NPFL was responsible for a massacre at Fassama that left approximately one hundred civilians dead, although this was never fully verified. NPFL fighters continued to act with impunity in their territory. The human rights abuses and intransigent attitude of the NPFL constituted a serious obstacle to ECOMOG's efforts at peacekeeping.

There was increasing concern about ECOMOG air attacks on NPFL territory using Nigeria's Alpha jets. The NPFL had no air force, and ECOMOG planes could easily reach the whole country. Targets included the port of Buchanan and areas around Gbarnga, Kakata, Harbel and Greenville, as well as border areas in the Ivory Coast. There was also charges that ECOMOG violated medical neutrality by attacking hospitals— Phebe Hospital outside Gbarnga, F.J. Grante Hospital in Greenville, and the Firestone Hospital. Precise information about the targets and casualties were not available, because independent observers were prevented for security reasons from traveling to the sites. Relief convoys also were attacked, including a Médecins sans Frontières (MSF) convoy in April that was carrying medicines and vaccines.

There were consistent reports, by ECOMOG as well as other neutral sources, of the NPFL using the civilian population or civilian institutions as a shield for its military activities, which is a direct violation of the Geneva Conventions. Nevertheless, ECOMOG had an obligation under international humanitarian law to protect the civilian population, and was prohibited from conducting attacks that, while aiming at a military target, might be expected to inflict disproportionate harm on the civilian population.

The AFL maintained a fairly low profile from the November 1990 cease-fire until the NPFL offensive in October 1992. However, a pattern later emerged of AFL soldiers engaging in looting and armed robbery, with civilians fearing reprisals if they reported the incidents. One highly visible case illustrating the AFL behavior occurred on January 31, 1993; Brian Garnham, a British citizen working at the Liberian Institute for Biomedical Research, an affiliate of the New York Blood Center, was killed by the AFL.

Garnham and his American wife, Betsy Brotman, had lived in Liberia for many years. After the killing, AFL soldiers went on a looting spree, emptying the laboratory compound of whatever they could carry.

In late April, five AFL soldiers, including two officers, were charged in connection with Garnham's murder; however, none was charged with murder. The most severe charges were brought against the platoon commander, Capt. Gbazai Gaye, who was charged under Art. 131 of the Uniform Code of Military Justice for perjury, and under Art. 133, for conduct unbecoming an officer. As of November, the charges have either been dismissed or dropped against all the soldiers except one, who still faced charges of larceny.

For its part, ULIMO engaged in a pattern of abuses: it limited the free movement of people and goods in its territory; it denied Africa Watch a pass to travel to its areas without an ULIMO "escort"; and it established checkpoints along the roads, at which civilians and relief organizations often faced harassment. There were also reports of atrocities by ULIMO forces; Amnesty International received reports in March about the execution of fourteen young men suspected of supporting the NPFL in Zorzor, and the killing of thirteen civilians in Haindi. Liberian human rights monitors expressed concerns about summary executions, beatings and arbitrary arrests. Documenting human rights conditions in ULIMO territory proved to be difficult, largely because ULIMO denied access to independent observers.

One of the most vicious acts of the entire war was the June 5-6 massacre of approximately 547 civilians, mostly women and children, at a displaced persons camp outside Harbel. The victims were shot, beaten or hacked to death, and mutilated. Initial reports seemed to indicate that the NPFL was responsible, and the interim government issued a report confirming that assumption. However, a U.N. investigation later concluded unequivocally that the massacre was carried out by the AFL. (See below.)

The massacre heightened attention to

the Liberian war and set in motion a series of important international developments. On June 9, the U.N. Security Council condemned the massacre, requesting that the Secretary-General launch an immediate investigation and warning that those responsible would be held accountable for their actions. Secretary-General Boutros Boutros-Ghali dispatched his special representative to Liberia, Trevor Gordon-Somers, to investigate the massacre. Gordon-Somers's report to the Secretary-General was never published, nor were his conclusions made public.

On August 4, Boutros-Ghali ordered an independent inquiry into the Harbel massacre. A three-member panel, headed by Kenyan Attorney General Amos Wako, visited Liberia in August and concluded that the massacre was "planned and executed by units of the Armed Forces of Liberia (AFL)." The report went on to recommend that three soldiers be prosecuted in connection with the massacre. In September, the interim government detained the three soldiers named in the report, but openly questioned the U.N.'s findings.

Simultaneous with these initiatives, the peace process gained momentum. In a major breakthrough, on July 25 a peace agreement was signed in Cotonou, Benin, by the NPFL, ULIMO and IGNU. The accord followed U.N.-sponsored negotiations in Geneva involving representatives of all the factions. These negotiations were part of a series of peace talks led by Gordon-Somers. Representatives of the Economic Community of West African States (ECOWAS) and the Organization of African Unity (OAU) also served as sponsors of the Cotonou agreement. The accord called for a cease-fire on August 1, the formation of a transitional government, disarmament and encampment of combatant forces, followed by elections.

An important element of the plan involved the creation of a U.N. Observer Mission in Liberia (UNOMIL) to help supervise and monitor the agreement, in conjunction with ECOMOG. The plan also provided for an expanded ECOMOG force, under the auspices of the OAU, to be composed of

African troops outside the West African region. These new contingents would be responsible for disarmament and encampment, and would be monitored by UNOMIL.

The accord also provided for an amnesty for "all persons and parties involved in the Liberia civil conflict in the course of actual military engagements." Clearly, an amnesty for acts committed between combatants during a conflict is substantially different from one covering war crimes or crimes against humanity. The gross atrocities committed during Liberia's war should be excluded from any amnesty, as should attacks against civilians who took no part in the hostilities.

The peace accord stipulated that concomitant with disarmament, a five-person Council of State elected by all the factions would take power from the interim government until elections were held. A thirty-five-member transitional parliament would include thirteen members from the NPFL and the interim government, and nine from ULIMO. On August 16, the Liberian factions elected Bismark Kuyon, representing IGNU, as chair of the interim council, and Dorothy Musuleng Cooper of the NPFL as vice-chair. On October 20, the NPFL abruptly replaced Musuleng Cooper with Isaac Mussah, a notorious NPFL commander. On November 15, IGNU replaced Kuyon with Philip Banks, who had been serving as Justice Minister.

As of November, the process had reached a stalemate. The transfer of power hinged on the beginning of disarmament, which in turn depended on the arrival of the expanded ECOMOG troops. The countries that agreed to contribute those troops were Zimbabwe, Tanzania and Uganda, contingent on the provision of outside assistance. Finally, as part of the Benin meeting of November 3 through 6, the parties agreed that the transitional government would be installed upon the arrival of the first expanded ECOMOG troops.

In a disturbing development, a number of former officials of the Doe regime who were known for their involvement in human rights abuses were named to the transitional government and electoral commission. In addition to the nomination of Isaac Mussah, the most serious concerns focused on two ULIMO nominees—George Dweh, reputedly linked to killings at the height of the civil war; and Jenkins Scott, former Justice Minister and closely associated with Doe's repressive policies.

The situation of the displaced civilians and residents in many parts of central and northern Liberia became increasingly desperate by the summer of 1993. Relief assistance to these areas had been effectively cut off after the October 1992 offensive, although some food and medicine continued to flow through the Ivory Coast border. Relief groups found that up to 700,000 civilians in NPFL territory were in danger, with 200,000 already suffering starvation. Aid workers estimated that hundreds of children could die every week due to hunger and malnutrition.

Meanwhile, an estimated 652,600 Liberians remained as refugees in the neighboring countries: 380,000 in Guinea; 250,000 in the Ivory Coast; 12,000 in Ghana; 7,000 in Sierra Leone; and 3,000 in Nigeria. (The war also displaced some 200,000 Sierra Leoneans, 162,000 of whom went to Guinea and 105,000 to Liberia.) The issue of repatriation of the refugees remained subject to progress on the political front and the resolution of certain security concerns, and as of November no significant repatriation had occurred.

In a surprising development, on August 31, Ernest Shonekan, Nigeria's interim president, announced that Nigeria would withdraw its troops from Liberia within seven months. Nigerian troops formed the backbone of the ECOMOG force, and had become the principal enemy of Charles Taylor's NPFL. The Nigerians had also effectively financed the West African intervention, which was estimated to have cost well over $500 million.

The emergence in September of a new armed faction, the Liberian Peace Council (LPC), threatened to disrupt the peace accord by attacking the NPFL. Reports indicated that the LPC was largely Krahn and included many former AFL soldiers.

The Right to Monitor

A number of human rights organizations were established in Monrovia and were able to function without interference from the interim government or ECOMOG.

· The Catholic Peace and Justice Commission was the human rights and peace component of the Catholic church of Liberia. It sought to gather and disseminate information on human rights violations, and engaged in some humanitarian relief.

· The Center for Law and Human Rights Education aimed to create awareness among Liberians of their basic rights. It operated two education projects, a Legal Aid Clinic, and a Resource and Documentation Library.

· The Liberian Human Rights Chapter and the Association of Human Rights Promoters were formed to act as human rights advocacy groups, and the Human Rights Chapter published a bulletin on human rights.

However, these Liberian human rights monitors operated under the same constraints as their international colleagues in trying to document violations in territory controlled by the NPFL or ULIMO: access was often prohibited by the factions or became too dangerous due to the fighting.

There were no known human rights organizations operating in either NPFL territory or ULIMO territory.

The Role of the International Community

U.S. Policy

After years of supporting the brutal and corrupt regime of former President Doe in the 1980s, making it the largest recipient of U.S. aid in sub-Saharan Africa, the U.S.

withdrew from Liberia more or less completely once the war began in 1990. Toward the end of 1993, however, when it became clear that the latest peace plan required substantial U.S. assistance if it was to succeed, Liberia finally became a higher priority.

The main tenets of U.S. policy toward Liberia in 1993 were to support conflict resolution efforts by ECOWAS and the U.N., to withhold recognition of any government in Liberia—neither the interim government nor the National Patriotic Reconstruction Assembly, the civilian arm of the NPFL—and to promote ECOWAS and its peace plan. By year's end, the conflict resolution efforts had gained new momentum, leading to a significant commitment of American resources. On September 30, the U.S. obligated $19.83 million ($13 million in Economic Support Funds and the rest in Foreign Military Financing) to the U.N. Trust Fund for peacekeeping in Liberia. The money would be used by ECOMOG and the Organization of African Unity (OAU) to help finance the deployment of the expanded ECOMOG troops, but not for lethal assistance.

The U.S. was the leading donor to the victims of the war: since the beginning of the conflict, the U.S. had provided some $250 million in humanitarian assistance. According to the State Department's Office of Foreign Disaster Assistance, in fiscal year 1993 the U.S. provided approximately $62 million, including assistance to Liberian refugees in Sierra Leone, Guinea, Ghana and the Ivory Coast. An additional $28.7 million had been provided since April 1991 to assist the ECOWAS-led peace process. But, although the Clinton administration acted quickly to condemn the June massacre in Harbel and to welcome the July peace agreement, it did not stress adequately the human rights component of the crisis. The administration should have made clear to all the warring factions that human rights issues would directly impact U.S. foreign assistance to any future government, and that the U.S. would distance itself from any force that continued to violate human rights and international law.

The Clinton administration's human rights policy would have been enhanced by greater attention to abuses by the ECOMOG forces. The U.S. was clearly aware of the increasing human rights problems associated with the ECOMOG intervention, yet U.S. policy still revolved around full support for ECOMOG. There is an obvious discrepancy between what American officials say in private and their public positions. Given the Clinton administration's request for $12 million for ECOWAS's peacekeeping activities in fiscal year 1994, the U.S. was likely to have some leverage over ECOMOG's behavior. It was critical for the administration to make clear its concern about human rights violations by both ECOMOG and the forces with which ECOMOG was allied, and condition its aid on respect for human rights. The U.S. should also have supported enhanced training for the new ECOMOG forces, with an emphasis on internal disciplinary structures and procedures for addressing human rights complaints.

Liberia would have been an excellent test case for the approach enunciated by the U.S. at the United Nations Conference on Human Rights in Vienna, described in the U.S. Human Rights Action Plan. Under this plan, the administration called for human rights to be "an integrated element of all U.N. peacekeeping, humanitarian, conflict resolution, elections monitoring, development programs, and other activities."

On June 9, Assistant Secretary of State for African Affairs George Moose testified about U.S. policy toward Liberia before the Senate Foreign Relations Subcommittee on African Affairs. His statement reiterated the administration's objectives: a negotiated settlement, disarmament of the warring factions, return of the refugees and displaced persons, and free elections leading to the establishment of a unified government "based on respect for human rights, democratic principles and economic accountability."

The U.S. deserves credit for pushing the U.N. to include a human rights component to UNOMIL's mandate. Although the language was not as strong as might have been hoped—it did not establish a human rights office or provide for the deployment human rights monitors—at least the U.N. resolution acknowledged officially that reporting on human rights violations was part of UNOMIL's mandate in Liberia.

The U.N. Role

Although the United Nations has contributed significantly to the emergency relief and humanitarian aid that has gone to Liberia, it did not address the Liberian crisis in political terms until November 1992, almost three years after the crisis erupted. In 1993 all indications were that the U.N. considered Liberia a regional problem best dealt with by ECOWAS, the regional body. While strengthening and supporting the regional organization was a laudable effort, the U.N. should have ensured that human rights issues figured prominently in the regional organization's efforts.

After finally addressing the Liberian crisis in November 1992 and imposing an arms embargo (Security Council Resolution 788), the Secretary-General dispatched a special representative, Trevor Gordon-Somers, to investigate the situation. Human rights language was notably absent from his report released in March (not to be confused with his later report on the Harbel massacre), thus missing yet another opportunity to insert human rights protections into the peace process. The March report suggested that there might be a role for U.N. observers to monitor a new cease-fire agreement, but foresaw no human rights monitoring component in their mandate.

The U.N.'s humanitarian mandate in Liberia was challenged when ECOWAS stepped up its effort to block cross-border humanitarian assistance to NPFL territory from the Ivory Coast. In early May 1993, ECOWAS executive secretary Abass Bundu called on relief organizations to cease all cross-border relief operations. ECOMOG contended that Taylor uses the cross-border convoys to transport supplies for his forces, and told relief organizations that they must inform ECOMOG when they conduct cross-border operations. However, since humanitarian aid was exempt from the U.N. embargo of November 1992, ECOWAS's stand contradicted the U.N.'s mandate to deliver such assistance.

This tension between the U.N. and the international relief organizations intensified on July 30, when Gordon-Somers wrote a diplomatic note to the Ivorian Minister of Foreign Affairs urging that a Médecins Sans Frontières convoy not be permitted to cross from the Ivory Coast into Liberia "because it is in violation of the Cotonou peace agreement." The U.N. defended its decision on the grounds that all convoys had to be checked for arms by U.N. observers. Relief groups, including the International Committee of the Red Cross, strongly protested the U.N.'s actions.

After the Harbel massacre in June, Secretary-General Boutros-Ghali condemned the killings and instructed Gordon-Somers to conduct an investigation into the incident. While this quick response by the U.N. was welcome, it was ultimately undercut by the fact that Gordon-Somers's report to the secretary-general was not published, or his findings revealed. Questions were raised as to why the Secretary-General chose to send Gordon-Somers, when his role as a mediator of the conflict precluded him from making any findings that would antagonize any of the warring factions. As noted above, however, the Secretary-General did order a subsequent investigation whose findings were published.

On September 22, the Security Council adopted Resolution 866 establishing the United Nations Observer Mission in Liberia (UNOMIL) for seven months. UNOMIL was to comprise approximately 500 members, some 300 being military, and its primary purpose was military: to monitor the cease-fire, the arms embargo, and disarmament and demobilization of combatants. In addition, UNOMIL was to observe the electoral process, help coordinate humanitarian relief and report "any major violations of international humanitarian law to the Secretary-General." This last aspect was particularly welcome, but it would have been important to specify the need to report on violations of human rights and humanitarian law.

The Work of Africa Watch

Given the ongoing crisis in Liberia and the abuses committed by all sides to the conflict, Africa Watch decided to focus an investigation on the ECOMOG intervention in Liberia from a human rights perspective. The mission was conducted in March, and evaluated the West African peacekeeping force's three years in Liberia, with particular emphasis on the period of renewed warfare since October 1992. In June, Africa Watch published "Waging War to Keep the Peace: The ECOMOG Intervention and Human Rights in Liberia."

Africa Watch was actively engaged in advocacy about human rights in Liberia with the new Congress and administration, conducting briefings, drafting letters, suggesting language for legislation and highlighting issues that required action from the U.S. government. On June 9, Africa Watch testified on Liberia before the Africa Subcommittee of the Senate Foreign Relations Committee, and called on the United States and the United Nations to integrate human rights into the peace process. In addition, Africa Watch was called upon to conduct frequent radio and press interviews about human rights in Liberia with U.S., African and European journalists.

MALAWI

Human Rights Developments

In 1993, Malawi joined the pro-democracy trend in Africa by abandoning its twenty-seven-year-old system of one-party rule. In an unprecedented referendum held in June, 63.5 percent of voters opted for a multiparty system, thereby dealing a decisive blow to Malawi's nonagenarian ruler, then-Life President Hastings Kamuzu Banda, who has ruled the country with an iron fist since independence in 1964. ("Life" has since been removed from his title.) The opposition's margin of victory was particularly significant considering the number of obstacles that the government placed in its path during the campaign period, including violent attacks on and arrests of opposition members, arbitrary bans on rallies, lack of access to the state-controlled radio, and restrictions on the printed press.

The most severe human rights abuses characteristic of the Banda regime, including the assassination, torture, long-term detention and exile of opponents, eased in the post-election period. A number of problems remained, however, particularly abuses by the police, who held themselves above the law, and abysmal conditions of detention. In addition, the Malawi Young Pioneers, a paramilitary wing of the ruling Malawi Congress Party (MCP), defied orders to disarm and continued to pose a threat to opposition members and the transition process.

Popular demonstrations against the government began in March 1992, following the issuance of a letter by the country's Catholic bishops that candidly criticized human rights abuses. The government reacted harshly, and in May 1992 major bilateral donors agreed to an aid freeze based on the country's abysmal human rights record. Five months later, President Banda stated his agreement to hold a referendum on one-party rule, and he invited a technical mission from the United Nations to visit the country to offer advice on the referendum process.

The first U.N. mission arrived in November 1992 and recommended the repeal or suspension of all laws that placed restrictions on freedoms of expression and association. The group also advised a six-month campaign period, to allow opposition groups an adequate chance to prepare for the vote. In a New Year's Eve address to the nation, Banda promised to abide by the U.N. recommendations, while at the same time refusing to allow more than three months for the campaign. Another U.N. team visited Malawi in January 1993 and urged Banda to postpone the polling date and to respect the U.N. recommendations. In February, after receiving a letter from U.N. Secretary-General Boutros Boutros-Ghali, Banda finally agree to move the date to June 14.

In response to the U.N. recommendations regarding freedom of expression and association, the government adopted regulations in February to govern the campaign process. Although guaranteeing "complete and unhindered freedom of expression and information in the exercise of the right to campaign," the regulations included a prohibition on "language which is inflammatory, defamatory or insulting or which constitutes incitement to public disorder, insurrection, hate, violence or war." Only three "pressure groups" (the MCP was then the only legal party) were recognized: the Alliance for Democracy (AFORD), the United Democratic Front (UDF)—both of these later became parties—and the Public Affairs Committee (PAC), which was composed of members of pro-democracy religious and professional bodies and opposition groups.

The government's guarantees proved meaningless throughout the campaign period, as police regularly denied opposition groups permission for rallies and arrested, beat and otherwise mistreated opposition figures for possessing documents advocating multipartyism and even for wearing T-shirts bearing political slogans. At least 20,000 people attended the first officially sanctioned opposition rally in January, which was addressed by members of AFORD, the UDF and the PAC. Shortly thereafter, four churchmen belonging to AFORD—Revs. Aaron Longwe, who was charged with sedition in 1992 and released on bail, Peter Kaleso, John Mwambira and Willie Zingani—were prohibited from addressing public meetings, although a high court judge later ruled that the men had been unfairly banned. Members of the Young Pioneers physically assaulted opposition members; such incidents increased after Parliament in April granted the MCP legal immunity for any crimes committed during the pre-refer-

endum period.

Following the opposition's victory on June 14, Banda accepted defeat but refused to accept the opposition's claim that its victory required Banda and the MCP government to resign. Shortly thereafter, Parliament repealed the sections of the constitution that made Malawi a one-party state. Exiles were granted amnesty. The government agreed to the formation of a National Consultative Council (NCC), made up of seven representatives of each political party (of which seven existed as of November), to provide guidance to Parliament and to oversee the transition, the May elections and the drafting of a new constitution that would take effect following elections on May 17, 1994.

Banda fell ill in early October and was flown to South Africa for brain surgery. In accordance with constitutional provisions, a three-person presidential council was appointed in his place and given full powers to run the government. The council was headed by the controversial Secretary-General of the MCP, Gwanda Chakuamba, who had been appointed party head only a week earlier after a decade-long vacancy in the post. Chakuamba, the head of the Young Pioneers in its most violent heyday, was released from prison in June after serving thirteen years of a twenty-two year sentence for sedition after a falling-out with President Banda. After his release from prison in June, he had initially joined the UDF before rejoining the MCP. Another member of the presidential council was John Tembo, Minister of State in the President's Office, who, together with his niece, Banda's "official hostess" Cecilia Kadzamira, was believed to have assumed a large share of political power in the country. The third member of the council was Minister of Transport and Communications Robson Chirwa. The opposition protested the appointment of the presidential council, but the government refused its demand that an interim president acceptable to all parties be appointed instead.

In November, Parliament formalized reforms that the government had already agreed to in principle, including legalization of the NCC, the repeal of provisions for detention without trial, and passage of a bill of rights to take effect immediately following the election.

The conviction and sentencing in December 1992 of Chakufwa Chihana, Secretary-General of the Southern Africa Trade Union Coordination Council and leader of AFORD, was a devastating blow to the opposition. Chihana, a longtime critic of the government and an extremely popular leader, had been detained in 1992 on several occasions totaling approximately five months and charged with sedition. The charges related to papers he had delivered at a conference held in Zambia and an address he had planned for his return to Malawi on the prospects of multiparty democracy there, a topic that, following Banda's agreement to hold the referendum, was no longer off-limits. In December 1992, Chihana's conviction and sentence to two years in prison with hard labor sparked a demonstration at which some 260 protestors were arrested and held for five days; approximately 130 were charged with unlawful assembly. An appeal to the sentence was heard in March 1993, resulting in its reduction to nine months with hard labor. Some 6,000 demonstrators again protested, and police opened fire; at least five were wounded. While in prison, Chihana, who suffered from respiratory infections and headaches, was denied medical treatment, fed poorly and forced to engage in heavy labor throughout his illnesses. He was released on June 12, two days before the referendum.

One of Malawi's most celebrated long-term political prisoners, Vera Chirwa, was released from prison on humanitarian grounds in January after spending eleven years in prison on a treason charge. Her husband, Orton Chirwa, had died in prison the previous October. Both Orton and Vera Chirwa had been detained in harsh conditions, including confinement in leg irons at various times during their incarceration. Vera Chirwa had been allowed to see her husband only once during her imprisonment and was de-

nied permission to attend his funeral.

Opposition leaders who were arrested in the run-up to the referendum included Bakili Muluzi, chair of the UDF and a former cabinet member of the MCP, who was arrested and held for three days in February. He was charged with misappropriating MCP funds during the 1970s. Chakakala Chaziya, vice chair of the UDF, and three other UDF members were arrested in January and detained for two weeks. Rev. Peter Kaleso was arrested in January after addressing an AFORD rally; he was later acquitted of charges that he had insulted the Life President. Alice Longwe, the wife of Rev. Longwe, was arrested and charged with sedition. An assassination attempt was reportedly made on Rev. Chinkwita Phiri, who at the time was acting general secretary of the Christian Council of Malawi.

A number of exiles returning to Malawi were arrested, including members of the United Front for Multiparty Democracy, an alliance of veteran exile politicians, who were detained in February upon their return from Zambia. One of the group who was holding a Zambian passport was deported; another was held without charge until his release in April. Three officials of the Malawi Democratic Party returned from exile in South Africa in February and were charged with importing seditious literature.

Detainees endured inhumane conditions of detention, including severe overcrowding, inadequate food and torture. Amnesty International reported that one detainee, Flora Kapito, who was arrested for possession of multiparty literature, died in detention in February as a result of injuries sustained while in prison. All pro-democracy activists were eventually released following the referendum. Amnesty International reports that three political prisoners—Nelson Mtambo, Sidney Songo and Htwana Mlombwa, all imprisoned since the mid-1960s—remained in prison after twenty-nine years. They were reportedly arrested in the aftermath of an armed rebellion led by a former cabinet minister. The government has never publicly admitted their imprisonment.

Many political trials in 1992 did not meet international standards for fairness, but there were some surprising decisions, including one in May in which a Malawi high court judge ordered the government to pay Martin Machipisa Munthali, a political prisoner released in June 1992 after twenty-seven years of confinement, the equivalent of $1 million; the government has since complied. Many prisoners continued on death row after unfair trials conducted by the so-called traditional courts, which, among other restrictions, prohibited legal representation for defendants. In October, traditional courts were suspended pending the repeal by Parliament of the laws under which they were established.

Because of Malawi's low literacy rate, radio, which was controlled by the government, was perhaps the most significant political tool in the campaign period, and it remained, predictably, in the control of the government. President Banda was the only campaigner allowed to broadcast on Malawi radio, and opposition rallies were not permitted live coverage.

Despite the referendum regulations lifting restrictions on the press, freedom of the press was not tolerated in the early months of the year. Independent newspapers, which did not exist before 1992, were occasionally shut down. The editor of one such paper, *New Express*, Felix Mponda Phiri, was arrested on January 2 upon his return from Zambia with copies of the first issue of the paper. He was detained without charge for seventeen days. Two opposition newspapers—AFORD's *The Democrat* and *UDF News*—were temporarily banned in March.

Dozens of newspapers have now appeared in Malawi, and after the referendum they did not face any serious constraints. After the referendum, the government and opposition agreed on a code of conduct for radio broadcasts, which, however, was regularly flouted. Broadcasts continued to favor the government and ruling party, and government officials were able to censor news reports.

Serious human rights concerns that remained in Malawi included rampant abuses by the police force. Police continued to arrest and torture particularly outspoken critics of the government and regularly flout court orders. Conditions in the prisons, which were under police control, were deplorable due to abuses by guards, overcrowding and inadequate food and medical care. Another area of concern was Malawi's judicial system, which lacked the independence necessary to fulfill its role as a guardian of human rights. Rectifying these institutionalized forms of abuse will require the inclusion of rights guarantees in the new constitution, a redrafting of laws which contravene human rights guarantees, and the active support of government leaders for internationally accepted human rights norms.

The Right to Monitor

Because of the government's absolute intolerance of dissent, human rights monitoring by Malawians was impossible before 1993. Starting in the pre-referendum period, several groups expressed an interest in monitoring human rights and began to formalize their work. Three such groups are the Civil Liberties Committee, an independent group founded in February, and the Law Society of Malawi and Christian Council of Malawi, both well-established organizations. In addition, a lawyer affiliated with AFORD, who recently founded the Foundation for Justice and Human Rights, has successfully brought human rights cases to the courts, including the case of Martin Machipisa Munthali described above.

International human rights groups were permitted to visit Malawi in 1993 and were granted meetings with high-level government officials.

The U.S. Role

The U.S. government played an important role in maintaining pressure on Banda during the run-up to the referendum. An aid freeze, which excepted humanitarian assistance, was agreed to by Malawi's major donors in May 1992 and was maintained by the U.S. government throughout the first half of 1993. Citing significant progress in moving toward democracy, on August 11 the U.S. released $11 million of that aid to Malawi, which was specifically targeted for literacy and agricultural projects. Total aid for fiscal year 1993 was $15.5 million, earmarked for projects on family planning, agriculture, AIDS prevention, child mortality and election support. A total of $15 million was requested for fiscal year 1994, but the request was expected to increase by $10 million. Another meeting with western donors was expected to be held in December 1993. World Bank loans to Malawi continued during the aid freeze.

An unusual and welcome demonstration of support for human rights by the U.S. government occurred in April, when Vice President Al Gore summoned the Malawian ambassador, Robert Mbaya, to the White House to discuss the referendum. According to a press release issued after the meeting, the vice president made the following statement to the Ambassador:

The administration is deeply interested in the process of democratization in Malawi. The upcoming referendum on a multiparty system is an extremely important event, and both its conduct and results will be watched closely by the international community.

The press release also noted that Vice President Gore raised human rights issues with Ambassador Mbaya and called for Chihana's immediate release.

The Voice of America played a commendable role in the pre-referendum period by airing a six-part series in the local language on political developments not reported on state radio.

The American Federation of Labor and Congress of Industrialized Organizations (AFL-CIO) filed a petition on workers rights in Malawi in 1992, following which the review committee of the Generalized System of Preferences (GSP) agreed in 1993 to examine Malawi's labor practices. A State Department official told Africa Watch that improvements in labor practices since 1992 would likely result in a continuation of Malawi's GSP benefits.

Members of Congress were active on Malawi during the year. A letter signed by ten Senators was sent to President Banda on March 5 to protest Chihana's continued detention. Also in March, Senators Kennedy, Kassebaum, Simon and Spectre introduced a resolution condemning the incarceration and harassment of dissidents and the restrictions on freedoms of speech, press and assembly. The resolution, which was not passed because it was overtaken by the referendum itself, was nevertheless important in sending a strong message of support to the Malawian opposition.

The Work of Africa Watch

Africa Watch's work consisted of writing letters to the Malawi government regarding human rights issues relevant to the referendum. A January 11 letter protested the Chihana conviction. Later in January, in light of the government's pledge to respect the U.N. recommendations, Africa Watch wrote to request permission for an Africa Watch mission. Previous requests had been denied, and no reply was received to this letter. In February, Africa Watch protested the arrests of AFORD and UDF members. A letter in late March raised concerns regarding Chihana's health.

Africa Watch also wrote to the U.S. representative of the World Bank in March, urging opposition to loans for Malawi based on Section 701(A) of the International Financial Institutions Act of 1977, which obliges the U.S. to oppose multilateral loans to countries that engage in a consistent pattern of gross violations of international human rights.

NIGERIA

Human Rights Developments

Nigeria, which began the year with promise

of a presidential election, ended the year with the stark reality of the return of military dictatorship and the abolition of all democratic institutions. The November 17 coup was the direct result of a final attempt to cling to power by Nigerian leader Gen. Ibrahim Babangida, who annulled the results of a presidential election held in June. The furor that followed the election's annulment succeeded in sweeping General Babangida from power in late August but not in preventing the installation of an unelected civilian interim government hand-picked by the outgoing regime. In mid-November, Defense Minister Gen. Sani Abacha forced the head of the interim government to resign, effectively staging what is the seventh coup d'etat in Nigeria's thirty-three years of independence. On assuming power, Gen. Abacha banned all existing democratic institutions, including the legislature, the political parties, and state and local elected offices.

Although Babangida had manipulated the transition process and had seen to it that the presidential election would be contested by two of his friends, Moshood Abiola and Bashir Tofa, the June 12 election represented to the nation an important if imperfect opportunity to move toward democracy. One of the most unfortunate effects of the annulment was the impetus thereby provided to the divisive influences of ethnicity and regionalism, which have tainted Nigerian politics since independence. The three largest ethnic groups are the Hausa-Fulani, who dominate the northern half of the country; the Yoruba, who control the southwest; and the Ibo, who are the largest group in the southeast. Historically, political power has been dominated by the Hausa-Fulani, the majority of whom are Muslims. The Yoruba, who form the majority in the commercial centers of Lagos and Ibadan, and the Ibo are largely Christian. The strong showing throughout the country by Abiola, a Yoruba Muslim from the south, would have provided the nation's more than 250 ethnic groups an unprecedented opportunity for unity, which was lost in the post-cancellation crisis.

Although election observers gave their approval to the election, Babangida first suspended and later annulled the vote without announcing the final results, which were later published by the Campaign for Democracy (CD), a loose coalition of human rights and other grass-roots organizations. It remained unclear if the election would have been permitted to stand had Tofa, a northern Hausa-Fulani Muslim, won or whether Babangida would have been unwilling to leave office in any case.

Riots erupted in Lagos in early July after peaceful demonstrations organized by the CD were overtaken by local thugs. Over one hundred demonstrators and other innocent victims were reported killed by military and security forces. The Civil Liberties Organisation (CLO), a Lagos-based human rights group, reported that some 250 protestors were secretly detained for four weeks at a notorious, remote island detention camp. The British government, Nigeria's largest investor, the U.S., the European Community and Canada condemned the election annulment and cut off aid.

Additional strikes and demonstrations by the CD, the Nigerian Labor Congress, the oil workers unions and other organizations were held in August, September and October. Support for the strikes was generally strong in Lagos and Ibadan but less so in the northern and eastern areas of the country.

On August 26, due largely to opposition within the military to his continued stay in office, Babangida resigned as head of state and retired from the military. He named an "interim government," headed by industrialist Ernest Shonekan, to take over from the military. Shonekan had previously headed a group of civilians co-opted by General Babangida in an attempt to placate critics of his decision to postpone his departure from politics from January to August 1993, his third such postponement. Although Shonekan was named commander-in-chief of the armed forces, Defense Minister Gen. Sani Abacha, who was the only military holdover from the previous regime and who was widely believed to be responsible for pressuring General Babangida to leave office, actually held the reins of power.

Soon after assuming office, the interim government called elections for February 1994. However, a large segment of Abiola's party indicated it would not participate, and the CD called for a boycott of voter registration in November. The government postponed the convening of the National Assembly until November 4, citing financial constraints as the reason, but political dissention was believed to be the actual cause of the postponement.

The following week, two unannounced moves by the government followed immediately by a ruling in a Lagos High Court, increased popular disaffection with the government. On November 8, without warning, the government raised fuel prices by nearly 700 percent, prompting the NLC to call for a nationwide strike. The same day, Nigerian television announced that all elected local government council were to be immediately dissolved "in preparation for the local government elections scheduled for February 1994." Two days later, a Lagos High Court ruled that the interim government was illegal; the government immediately appealed the decision.

The next week, while the country was in the throes of strikes and demonstrations, came the announcement that had been feared since the political crisis began. Shonekan and his cabinet had been forced out of office by General Abacha, who banned the legislature, the political parties, the National Electoral Commission, and state and local governments, which were to be replaced by military commanders. All political meetings and associations were also banned. No timetable was set for the return to civilian rule.

Predictably, in this tumultuous year, human rights abuses were widespread, most notably ethnically-based attacks, killings of demonstrators, detentions of activists and journalists, and interference with freedom of expression and association.

The most devastating abuses were related to attacks against the Ogonis, a minority group inhabiting the oil-producing delta region of Rivers State, who have vocally protested the destruction of their land and culture by multinational oil companies and Nigerian military forces. From July onwards, approximately 1,000 Ogonis were killed in attacks believed to be sanctioned by governmental authorities. Villages were destroyed, and thousands of Ogonis were displaced. The government did not provide aid or investigate the attacks.

Ogoni spokesperson Ken Saro-Wiwa became the target of a government harassment campaign, and in June he was arrested and detained for over one month, during which time he was denied access to medical treatment despite a critical heart condition. On July 13, Saro-Wiwa was charged before a Port Harcourt magistrates court with six counts, including unlawful assembly and sedition, relating to a boycott by the Ogonis of the June election. Two other members of the Movement for the Survival of the Ogoni People, which Mr. Saro-Wiwa headed, were also charged. Later that month, all three were released on bail, and their trial was adjourned.

In another ethnically related incident, death sentences were handed down between December 1992 and March 1993 to thirteen alleged participants—all members of the Kataf, a largely Christian ethnic minority—in ethnic and religious riots that had taken place in May 1992, in the northern state of Kaduna. The riots began after Katafs attacked a community of Hausa-Fulanis, and then spread to the cities of Kaduna and Zaria, where they took on a religious dimension. Hundreds of Katafs were arrested after the riots, and at least thirty-seven languished in detention for over a year.

The trials were conducted before two Special Tribunals, where all constitutional guarantees were suspended and from which there was no right of appeal. One group of six defendants received widespread attention because of the extraordinary level of abuse at the trials and the prominence of one of the defendants, retired Maj. Gen. Zamani Lekwot. The six are believed to have been made scapegoats in reprisal for their criticism of abuses against the Katafs. The involvement of the government in ensuring the convictions of the Lekwot group was made most apparent by the promulgation of Decree 55, announced in December 1992 but made retroactive to the previous July, which barred inquiries into abuses of constitutionally guaranteed rights during the trial.

The death sentences were sent for review to the National Defense and Security Council (NDSC), which in January 1993 replaced the Armed Forces Ruling Council. A suit brought by the Constitutional Rights Project, a Lagos-based human rights organization, resulted in a stay of execution for the Lekwot group. In late August, the NDSC commuted all thirteen death sentences to five years in prison and ordered the immediate release of all detained Katafs held without trial.

The press, which became increasingly outspoken in 1993, suffered its worst government assault in the country's history, beginning in March, when the editor of the Kaduna-based *Reporter*, owned by a former presidential candidate banned by Babangida in 1992, was arrested. In late May, the paper was proscribed. Two new and outspoken publications, *The News* and *Tell*, endured an incessant campaign of government-sponsored harassment. In May, *The News* was shut down and its entire editorial staff declared wanted for arrest. The magazine was later banned for several months.

In May, the Nigerian government unveiled the Treason and Treasonable Offenses Decree, which, although never published, announced a prohibition on promoting "ideas that minimize the sovereignty of Nigeria." It was believed to have been directed at the Ogonis as well as at human rights activists and outspoken journalists. In announcing the decree, the Justice Minister said that it could be interpreted to convict "[a]nybody who acts alone or conspires with anybody... either by word or publication of any material capable of disrupting the general fabric of the country or any part of it." Conviction under the decree would result in death. Two weeks after the announcement, following

international protest, the decree was suspended, and it has not been revived.

After the election was aborted, the government assault on the press intensified. Five media were shut down in July—Concord Press, owned by Abiola; *Punch*; the *Sketch* group; *Abuja Newsday*; and *The Observer*. All except *Newsday* were proscribed by decree the following month. Four *Tell* journalists were arrested in August and detained for approximately two weeks.

On August 16, the Babangida government promulgated Decree 43, which contained a litany of restrictions on the press, including punishment by a ten-year prison term or stiff fine or both for publishing "false information"; the establishment of an office for each paper in Abuja within one year; and an order to submit all newspapers to the Information Secretary. If implemented, the decree's financial burdens alone would force the closure of most of the the country's independent press.

On taking power in November, General Abacha lifted the bans on the news media, but warned them to be careful about what they published.

Abuses by members of the police and security forces, a persistent human rights problem in Nigeria, remained severe, and virtually no members of these forces were held accountable for their actions. Cases of harassment and shooting of innocent travelers at illegal checkpoints, torture and extrajudicial killings of "suspects," and the widespread use of bribes to ensure release from detention continued throughout the year. There were no initiatives by the government to investigate the deaths in the July Lagos riots.

As in previous years, abysmal prison conditions, including overcrowding, insufficient and poor quality food, and the lack of sanitation, water and medical treatment contributed to an estimated prison death rate of more than 1,000.

Nigerian universities were closed down during most of 1993 largely due to strikes by various unions. In early May, the government lifted the seven-year ban on the National Association of Nigerian Students. After repeated unsuccessful attempts to negotiate with the government, the still proscribed academic staff union called a strike in May over issues including lack of autonomy and conditions of service. The government responded by announcing a decree that reclassified teaching as an essential service and called for the dismissal of striking teachers. After a public outcry the decree was "set aside." Following meetings with the interim government in September, the academic union agreed to call off its strike.

The Right to Monitor

Attacks on human rights monitors escalated shortly after Babangida's November 1992 decision to postpone the transition. A crackdown from late November through early January included the arrest and short-term detention of a number of individuals involved in pro-democracy activities; forcible police entry into the headquarters of the CD and CLO and the seizure of materials; the interruption of a number of gatherings sponsored by human rights and pro-democracy groups; and the confiscation of a magazine that carried an interview with Femi Falana, president of the National Association of Democratic Lawyers. Printers of human rights and pro-democracy materials were detained for several days and their print shops were temporarily closed by police.

Incidents of harassment continued through the winter and spring. In late February, security agents invaded the CLO offices, took away documents, and questioned CLO officers about their funding sources and other matters. Femi Falana and Dr. Beko Ransome-Kuti, CD chair and president of the Committee for the Defense of Human Rights, were briefly arrested in March. In April, Falana and Ransome-Kuti were again briefly arrested and CD leaflets were confiscated on several occasions. CD activists were also arrested elsewhere in the country.

Hundreds of human rights and pro-democracy activists, labor leaders, academics, students and workers were arrested after the elections were canceled. Many were held for weeks without access to their families or defense counsel. In addition to the detentions, security agents conducted raids on offices of human rights activists and pro-democracy groups. In one raid on CD headquarters on August 9, forty security agents arrested everyone in the office, including visitors, and removed files.

Ransome-Kuti, Falana and Chief Gani Fawehinmi, all leaders of the pro-democracy movement, were arrested in early July and detained at Kuje Prison near Abuja. The three were charged with sedition and conspiracy to incite violence and initially refused bail. They were informed that, in addition to their criminal charges, they were also subject to detention under Decree 2, Nigeria's administrative detention decree. The three were denied access to their lawyers, families and doctors, despite serious health concerns of both Dr. Ransome-Kuti and Chief Fawehinmi. The Abuja High Court granted them bail in late July, but they were not released then because of the Decree 2 detention orders. They were finally released in August as one of the first acts of the interim government.

Many other activists were arrested in early July as well, including three members of the CLO, Wale Shittu, Femi Adeluga and Emma Nweke, who were detained for twenty-five days for possession of CD leaflets. Hundreds of protestors were arrested throughout the country following various demonstrations held from August through October. Most were released, but it was feared that some unidentified activists might have remained in detention.

U.S. Policy

The U.S. had a strong human rights policy towards Nigeria throughout 1993, raising criticism of the government's abuses and its manipulation of the electoral process. In the period shortly before the election, the White House refused a request for a meeting with General Babangida, who was in the U.S. on other business. On June 10, Michael O'Brien of the U.S. Information Agency issued a statement that a threatened postponement of elections was "unacceptable" to the U.S. government. Following protests by the Nigerian government, the statement was amended to say that a postponement of the election would cause "grave concern" to the U.S. But even that was too much for Nigeria, which reacted by expelling Mr. O'Brien and by withdrawing the accreditation of eight nongovernmental observers from the U.S. to monitor the election.

Less than twenty-four hours after the election was canceled, the State Department released a statement "deploring" the move. The U.S. quickly cut off $450,000 in aid for military training and followed by canceling an $11 million grant to the Ministry of Health and other smaller grants totaling less than $1 million. The rest of the bilateral aid, which funded humanitarian programs through nongovernmental channels, was left intact. One of the State Department's most commendable actions on Nigeria was a suspension of arms sales, which has only rarely been used elsewhere and represents an important initiative by the Clinton administration. In addition to these steps, Nigeria's military attaché in Washington was ordered to leave and a U.S. security assistance officer was withdrawn from Nigeria. Military relations between the two countries were also reduced. In July, the U.S. announced that it would review commercial military sales on a case-by-case basis with the presumption of denial. U.S. citizens were urged to defer travel to the country.

At an August 4 hearing on Nigeria's political crisis before the Africa Subcommittee of the House of Representatives, Assistant Secretary of State for Africa George Moose promised "additional steps" if a civilian government was not in place on August 27. Following the installation of the interim government, some lower-level Nigerian government officials were permitted to meet with U.S. officials in Washington, but a meeting requested by Mr. Shonekan with high-ranking officials was refused.

An unfortunate aspect of U.S. policy towards Nigeria was the decision in the middle of the upheaval to replace Amb.

William Swing, who during his brief tenure strongly promoted observance for human rights in Nigeria. Ambassador Swing left Lagos in September to be replaced by Amb. Walter Carrington, who, among his previous academic and political posts, worked in the office of former Congr. Mervyn Dymally and also briefly served as ambassador to Senegal.

In a strong speech delivered at Ambassador Carrington's swearing-in ceremony on October 25 and released in Lagos, State Department Counselor Timothy Wirth criticized Nigeria's failure to further the transition process and promised that the U.S. would maintain the above-mentioned restrictions on aid and other forms of cooperation until there was "genuine progress toward fulfilling the aspirations of the Nigerian people for unhindered, democratically-elected civilian government."

In a statement on November 18, the State Department "condemn[ed]" General Abacha's coup, and said it was "assessing new measures...which may be necessary to reinforce those taken in the wake of the June 12 election."

The Nigeria chapter in the State Department's *Country Reports on Human Rights Practices in 1992*, released in January 1993, provided an accurate view of human rights abuses in Nigeria, devoting thorough discussions to such widespread problems as police abuses and prison conditions. One shortcoming of the report was the absence of discussion of the trials of the Kataf suspects and the promulgation of Decree 55.

The Work of Africa Watch

Africa Watch issued four newsletters on Nigeria. The first, released in December 1992, highlighted the renewed crackdown on human rights and pro-democracy groups. In March, "Military Injustice" discussed the death sentences of General Lekwot and the other convicted Katafs. A newsletter released in early June, "Threats to a New Democracy," was based in part on an Africa Watch mission to northern Nigeria to investigate the government's involvement in communal violence and discussed manipulation of the transition and interference with civil institutions. "Democracy Derailed," released in August, detailed human rights abuses surrounding the election annulment.

Africa Watch wrote protest letters to the government after the elections were suspended in June and again in July to protest the arrests of pro-democracy activists. A press release was distributed in June regarding the election's annulment. In August, Africa Watch testified before the Africa Subcommittee of the House of Representatives Foreign Affairs Committee.

Africa Watch wrote to Mr. Shonekan in September, raising issues including attacks on the Ogonis and restrictions on freedom of expression and asking him to respect the results of the June 12 elections. Also in September, Africa Watch called on the IMF/World Bank to take human rights into consideration in negotiating a new agreement with Nigeria. On October 6, to coincide with an address by Shonekan before the U.N. General Assembly, Africa Watch issued a press release raising various human rights concerns.

RWANDA

Human Rights Developments

The year 1992 ended and the new year began with another crisis for human rights in Rwanda. Local government officials, acting on orders from the general staff of the Rwandan army, organized attacks on Tutsi, a minority people, in several communes in the northwest. Three were killed, dozens injured and thousands forced to flee their homes for refuge in churches, schools or government centers. The operation was to "clear the brush" that might be used as "cover" by members of the Rwandan Patriotic Front (RPF) in their guerrilla war against the Rwandan government. Most members of the RPF are Tutsi, and, following their invasion of Rwanda in October 1990, the government had identified Tutsi within Rwanda as

RPF "accomplices" providing "cover" for the invaders. Using this excuse, the government killed approximately 2,000 Tutsi between 1990 and 1992, some singly or in small groups, others in massacres that took hundreds of lives at Kibilira, Bugesera and in northwest Rwanda. In addition, the government arrested or detained without charge about 10,000 Tutsi and members of the political opposition in 1990 and 1991, and dozens of others in 1992. Many of these were tortured or badly beaten; some were held incommunicado in military camps rather than in regular prisons.

The Tutsi, once a ruling aristocracy, had been driven from power by a revolution in 1959. Hundreds of thousands fled to surrounding countries, where many continued to live as refugees in 1993. The largely Tutsi RPF invaded Rwanda to back their demands that the refugees be allowed to return home and that the current government be changed.

President Juvenal Habyarimana, who first took power in a military coup twenty years ago, publicly deplored the attacks on the Tutsi. However, although he had widened his single-party government into a four-party coalition in April 1992, he had maintained his control over the party militia, police and local administration. This control allowed him to continue abuses against Tutsi and members of the opposition, and Tutsi were targeted in an effort to bolster crumbling solidarity among Hutu, who form about 85 percent of the population of Rwanda. President Habyarimana is himself Hutu as are virtually all officials. His role in the violence emerged clearly just prior to the December 1992 attacks when one of his spokesmen made a widely publicized speech calling on Hutu in the northwest to rid the region of Tutsi by all means necessary, including killing them and dumping them in the nearest river. President Habyarimana never denounced this inflammatory speech nor disassociated himself from this spokesman.

Several Rwandan human rights associations, united within the coalition known as the Liaison Committee of Associations in Defense of Human Rights in Rwanda (CLADHO), had been urging the creation of an international investigatory commission on human rights in Rwanda. During 1992, they asked Africa Watch, the International Federation of Human Rights (Paris), the Inter-African Union of Human Rights (Ouagadougou) and the International Center for Human Rights and Democratic Development (Montreal) to organize the inquiry. The commission, a ten-person panel representing eight nationalities, known as the International Commission of Investigation on Human Rights Violations in Rwanda since October 1, 1990, was co-chaired by representatives from Africa Watch and the International Federation of Human Rights. On their arrival in early January 1993, the commission's members were welcomed by President Habyarimana, a public posture belied by attempted assassinations and threats against potential witnesses that had taken place in the days immediately preceding. The commissioners collected testimony from hundreds of persons, ranging from ordinary cultivators out on the hills to the highest government officials. They engaged in formal interviews, but also collected information presented spontaneously, sometimes by persons who had learned of their presence in Rwanda from radio news broadcasts. They reviewed numerous official documents, including many judicial dossiers, and verified lists of victims presented by families, clergy and human rights associations. They excavated two mass graves where Tutsi victims had been buried, one in the backyard of a local government official.

While conducting its investigation, the commission had been told that the government was only awaiting its departure to launch new violence. Just hours after the commission left on January 21, 1993, supposedly spontaneous demonstrations against a recent political agreement between the RPF and the Rwandan government turned into attacks on the persons and property of Tutsi and opponents of the regime. Apparently wary of increased unfavorable atten-

tion to official participation in abuses, President Habyarimana this time had attacks led by militia of his political party, the National Republican Movement for Democracy and Development (MRND), and its ally, the Coalition for the Defense of the Republic (CDR), rather than by local officials. In the next five days, more than 300 people were killed, and thousands of others were driven from their homes.

On February 8, the RPF violated the cease-fire in effect since the previous July and drove Rwandan troops farther south. After this resumption of the conflict, Rwandan soldiers took vengeance on Tutsi civilians and opponents of the regime. They killed at least 147 persons and beat, tortured and raped many more, often after detaining them in military camps. They burned and looted hundreds of homes and businesses. In some cases, the soldiers acted alone; in others, they were joined by local mobs of civilians. In some communes where Tutsi had been repeatedly attacked in the past, the military distributed arms to groups of civilians known to support President Habyarimana.

These abuses came shortly after a group of Rwandan soldiers calling itself *amasasu* (meaning "bullets" in Kinyarwanda, the local language) threatened to "detect and destroy" opposition politicians and others who, in their view, were supporting the RPF. They declared themselves above the law and said they would deliver "an exemplary lesson to these traitors from inside." In early February, Prime Minister Dismas Nsengiyaremye, a member of the political opposition included in the government since April 1992, criticized the Minister of Defense for the official compilation of a list of "accomplices" of the RPF and asked that the names of those accused be turned over to the Ministry of Justice for prosecution by legal channels. As late as May, civilians were being detained without charge in military camps and were eventually delivered to the regular judicial system only after vigorous intervention by local human rights associations.

When the RPF launched its early February attack, it justified the offensive in part by the need to counter human rights abuses of the Rwandan government, such as the massacre two weeks earlier of hundreds of Tutsi. The Rwandan government in turn accused the RPF of massive killings of civilians, including thousands who had sought shelter in camps for displaced persons. While most of the government charges lacked credibility, investigations by local human rights associations established that the RPF had summarily executed sixteen civilians, eight government officials and eight others, mostly family members of the officials. One of those executed was the local official whose backyard contained a mass grave excavated by the international commission. According to information collected by local human rights groups and the clergy, the RPF killed more than one hundred civilians during its February attack. Open warfare was halted once more in March by a new cease-fire.

In a report published March 8, 1993, the international commission found the Rwandan government guilty of serious and systematic human rights abuses between October 1990 and January 1993, the period it investigated. The commission's report concluded that the majority of the approximately 2,000 victims of massacres and other abuses were Tutsi who had been targeted for the sole reason that they were Tutsi. It determined that authorities at the highest level, including the President of Rwanda, were responsible for these abuses, which were carried out by civilians, soldiers from the Rwandan army, and by the militias attached to the MRND and the CDR. Local administrative officials had coordinated the attacks in many cases. The report pointed out that the president and government of Rwanda tolerated the activities of armed militias attached to political parties, a clear violation of Rwandan law, and that these militia were playing an increasingly important role in violence against Tutsi and members of the political opposition. The commission also observed that the judicial system was paralyzed by political interference even more than by lack of resources and the poor training of judicial officials. Although hundreds of accused persons had been arrested following massacres, for example, all had been released shortly after and not one had actually been brought to trial.

The international commission also found that during the same twenty-seven month period, the RPF had attacked civilian targets and killed and injured civilians who were clearly protected by the Geneva conventions. It reported that the RPF had also kidnapped Rwandans and forced them to go to Uganda and has looted and destroyed the property of civilians.

The Rwandan government responded to the report of the international commission by "recognizing and regretting" the human rights abuses that had taken place in Rwanda. In a joint statement of acknowledgment and apology delivered in April, President Habyarimana and Prime Minister Nsengiyaremye promised a ten-point set of reforms that conformed closely to recommendations made by the international commission on March 8 and by Africa Watch in its February 1992 report. At the same time that they admitted and deplored the abuses, the Rwandan authorities promoted the formation of four supposedly autonomous human rights associations whose chief purpose was to denounce the international commission and its report. These associations, whose names sounded remarkably like those of the authentic human rights associations, published a pamphlet critical of the commission in Rwanda and held press conferences in Europe and the U.S. The leading propagandist for this effort was Ferdinand Nahimana, the official responsible for radio broadcasts that had provoked the massacre of hundreds of Tutsi in Bugesera in March 1992.

One of the reforms promised by the Rwandan government was administrative and judicial sanctions against authorities responsible for human rights abuses. Even before this date, several local officials (*burgomasters*) accused of abuses had been removed as part of a general administrative house-cleaning that had also removed officials guilty of corruption, negligence, or other shortcomings. The burgomasters were replaced in a restricted electoral process that represented a welcome, if limited, step toward democratization. The officials removed, however, were all low-level and none was brought to trial.

The Rwandan government instituted its own investigatory commission to look into the massacres of January 1993. Like several earlier internal commissions that inquired into abuses in 1992, this one produced a report that assigned responsibility to some local officials but obscured the role of higher authorities. As part of an agreement with the RPF, the Rwandan government replaced some of the officials implicated in the January killings, but as of November not one of them had been indicted or tried for participation in the violence.

The Rwandan government also undertook to prosecute individuals and organizations that promoted armed militias attached to political parties. For several months following the April 7 statement, the militia adopted a low profile, but in August and September, they became visible again, easily identifiable on the streets by their distinctive dress. No one has been prosecuted for supporting such militias. The post of Minister of Justice, vacant for six months following the December 1992 resignation of the incumbent to protest interference in the judicial process, was finally filled and the new minister began trying to reform the system.

Although the Rwandan government partially executed some of the reforms promised in April, by November 1993 it had not carried out its commitment to guarantee the security of all Rwandans. No large-scale killings took place since after April, but assassinations and a series of explosions took a number of lives. Among the victims of assassinations were Emmanuel Gapyisi, a leading opposition politician, killed in May, and Fidèle Rwambuka, a former burgomaster, shot down in his home in August. Attacks by bombs, grenades and land mines continued through fall 1993, with the worst, an explosion at Kirambo, killing sixteen and

injuring 127 in late May. Many of these killings were attributed to "death squads" reputedly operating under the direction of high authorities and hence protected from arrest and prosecution.

The insecurity and privations of war, coupled with open and easy trading of guns and grenades, fostered a rapid increase in crime of all kinds. In the face of the ineffectiveness of the police and judicial systems, private citizens organized neighborhood guards who were armed and who threatened and shot persons whom they suspected of wrongdoing. The government did nothing to halt the formation of such groups or to prosecute those who injured or killed alleged criminals.

Security within the prisons was also inadequate. In August, two prisoners who supposedly had provided information to the secret police were killed by fellow inmates at Kigali prison, while in the prison at Butate, thirteen prisoners were killed by their fellow inmates in the four hours that it took guards to intervene and reestablish order.

On August 4, the Rwandan government and the RPF signed, in Arusha, Tanzania, a peace treaty in which both sides reaffirmed their commitment to establishing human rights and a state of laws in Rwanda. The agreement transferred much of the Presidential power to a cabinet which would be staffed during a twenty-two-month transition period by representatives of the three political blocs: President Habyarimana's political party and its allies, the internal opposition parties, and the RPF. The accords named Faustin Twagiramungu of the MDR, the largest internal opposition party, as Prime Minister during the period of transition. The armies of the Rwandan government and of the RPF were to be combined into a single joint force of 13,000, considerably reduced from the 40,000 then under arms on the government side and the approximately 10,000 in the RPF army. The parties asked the United Nations to send a force to keep the peace during the twenty-two months leading to national elections. This force would replace troops provided by the Organization of African Unity (OAU) that had enforced the cease-fire in the year prior to the signing of the peace treaty. The transitional government was to take power after the arrival of the U.N. troops, on September 11. The U.N. force was delayed, however, and was expected to arrive in December 1993. In the meantime, the old government—a coalition of Habyarimana and internal opposition representatives—continues to function.

During the period of most intense warfare, nearly one million ·Rwandans—about one-seventh of the total population—were forced to flee their homes in the battle zone. Many took refuge in hastily improvised camps where shelter and sanitation were completely inadequate. They depended on food assistance delivered by the Red Cross, the World Food Program, and other agencies. In June, members of parliament and local human rights groups publicized thefts of food by local officials and aid workers, some of whom had been charging displaced persons for the supplies or confiscating them for resale on the open market. With the end of fighting, the displaced began returning to their homes, leaving about 300,000 in the camps.

The peace treaty guaranteed the right of all refugees living abroad to return to their homeland. Reintegrating the returnees and balancing their rights against those of other Rwandans was likely to prove a serious challenge to the new government.

Providing for the thousands of soldiers to be demobilized with the return of peace would pose significant problems as well.

Encouraged by the signing of the peace accords, Rwandans began to explore paths to national reconciliation. Human rights activists stressed the need to establish reconciliation on a foundation of honesty and justice and pressed for continued investigation and prosecution of those responsible for abuses in recent years. As of November, neither the Rwandan government nor the RPF had demonstrated a serious commitment to bringing the guilty to justice.

The Right to Monitor

While President Habyarimana made a show of welcoming international inquiry into the situation of human rights in Rwanda, his subordinates threatened or attacked those who could or did give testimony before the investigative commission. The family of one young man who aided the commission was attacked by a mob incited by local officials, and the father of the family was forced to commit suicide. A student who had provided information to the commission was among the victims killed in the massacres that began the day of the commissioners' departure. A human rights activist, Monique Mujawamariya, executive director of the Rwandan Association for Human Rights and Public Freedoms (ADL), who had been instrumental in organizing the visit of the commission, was injured in an automobile accident of suspicious origin shortly before the arrival of the commission. In addition, she was threatened with death by Capt. Pascal Simbikangwa, known to have tortured many persons detained by the secret police, in full view of members of the commission who were preparing to board the plane to leave Rwanda. In April, Gakwaya Rwaka, executive secretary of the human rights association, The Christian League for the Defense of Human Rights in Rwanda (LICHREDHOR), was threatened, as were members of his family. In May, Ignace Ruhatana, an activist with the human rights group Kanyarwanda, was attacked and wounded in his home and many of his papers were taken. Carpophore Gatera, another member of Kanyarwanda, was attacked five days later. In late 1992 and early 1993, the offices of Kanyarwanda were attacked three times. On November 14, 1993, Alphonse-Marie Nkubito, president of CLADHO, and one of the founders of the Rwandan Association for Human Rights (ARDHO), was attacked by several assailants who threw a grenade into his car, and he was hit in the back by a second grenade as he tried to flee. As of mid-November, he was in critical condition in a hospital in Kigali.

Despite official intimidation, five human rights associations actively monitored the situation and cooperated effectively in joint investigations, letters of protest, and press releases. They developed a network of contacts with international human rights organizations that enabled them to publicize abuses promptly to an audience outside of Rwanda.

The Role of the International Community

Belgium, the former colonial power in Rwanda, recalled its ambassador from Rwanda for consultations within hours of the publication of the report of the international commission. Subsequently the Belgian Senate unanimously passed a resolution acknowledging the report of the commission, condemning abuses by the Rwandan government and the RPF, and directing its own government to review aid policies towards Rwanda.

France has consistently supported President Habyarimana over the years and continued this policy during 1993 despite evidence of human rights abuses by his regime. Just after the beginning of the war in 1990, France sent a contingent of troops "to protect French citizens and other expatriates" in Rwanda. After the RPF violated the cease-fire in February, France sent an additional 300 soldiers, some of whom actively supported Rwandan troops in the combat zones. Some of the French troops were withdrawn after the March cease-fire, but others remained in Rwanda, in violation of accords which called for the departure of all foreign troops. France supplied Rwanda with arms and with political and propaganda support within the European Community.

The European Parliament reacted to abuses reported by the international commission with a March 11 resolution condemning the violations and asking increased financial and logistical support from its member nations for OAU observers in Rwanda to implement the cease-fire. The legislative body of the European Economic Community and its affiliated countries, the Assemblée Paritaire ACP-CEE, passed a stronger resolution condemning the abuses and asking the European Community to suspend price supports for agricultural products from Rwanda (STABEX) until reforms had been instituted.

The diplomatic community in Kigali, the capital of Rwanda, also intervened effectively on the spot to defend human rights. The ambassadors and other representatives of the United States, Belgium, Canada, Germany, Switzerland, the Vatican and the European Community protected individuals in danger and censured the Rwandan government at critical times. The ambassador of France joined in some of these protests even as his government continued to support President Habyarimana.

The Special Rapporteur on Extrajudicial, Summary or Arbitrary Executions appointed by the United Nations Commission on Human Rights investigated the situation in Rwanda in April. He issued a report that confirmed the findings of the international commission and called for a number of measures including a mechanism for protecting Rwandans against any further massacres, dismantling the armed militias, further investigations and bringing violators of human rights to account, an end to arbitrary detentions and arrests, and support for local human rights organizations.

The OAU played an important role in bringing the Rwandan government and the RPF to a final settlement of the war. In addition to facilitating the peace negotiations, the OAU provided a neutral peace-keeping force that effectively patrolled the cease-fire line from 1992 on.

U.S. Policy

During the first months of 1993, the United States showed increasing concern with human rights abuses in Rwanda. Following publication of the report of the international commission in March, the State Department announced it was "deeply disturbed" by the Rwandan violations. Soon after, the U.S. reduced to about $6 million its projected $19.6 million aid package for Rwanda. This decision resulted as much from dissatisfaction with the continuation of the war and with poor economic performance, however, as from concern with human rights abuses. The U.S. eliminated or froze funds for economic development, while amounts designated for humanitarian aid were increased. Rwanda had been a country targeted for special U.S. assistance but was now put on the "watch list," meaning that it could lose this status if it did not improve its performance in several areas, including protection of human rights.

The United States attributed human rights abuses largely to the tensions of wartime and expended great effort in obtaining a peace settlement for this as well as for other reasons. Once the peace treaty was signed in August 1993, the U.S. appeared ready to turn its attention to other issues. When President Habyarimana visited Washington for official conversations in October, Africa Watch urged Assistant Secretary of State George Moose to raise human rights questions with him, especially the important issue of accountability for past abuses. The U.S., however, appeared to place little if any stress on human rights during the talks so as not to spoil the "positive atmosphere" of the discussions.

The Work of Africa Watch

By immediate, direct and forceful communications to Rwandan authorities, the U.S. government and the press, Africa Watch intervened to call for a halt to abuses as they were happening, such as the massacres of January and February and the detention of civilians in military camps later in the spring. Through the same channels, it deplored violations brought to its attention after the fact, such as the executions by the RPF in February and the assassinations of Gapyisi and Rwanbuka, and pressed for those responsible for these crimes to be brought to justice.

Africa Watch continued to view certain reforms as essential for the establishment of the rule of law and the protection of human rights in the long term. It repeatedly brought such measures to the attention of the Rwandan government, the RPF and the U.S. govern-

ment through correspondence and through recommendations made in its reports. Those recommendations included:

- dissolving armed militias, the *amasasu* military association, and bands of armed neighborhood guards;

- strengthening the judicial system, including creating measures to protect the courts from political interference and improving training for magistrates and police;

- equal treatment for all Rwandan citizens, a measure which would mean ending classification according to ethnic group and removing such labels from all government documents;

- ending impunity for human rights abuses in order to end the cycles of violence that have killed thousands in Rwanda.

To assist in establishing accountability, Africa Watch helped organize the international commission that documented human rights abuses from October 1990 to January 1993. It also pressed the Rwandan government and the RPF to conduct serious and credible investigations of civilian and military authorities accused of such crimes and to prosecute all those implicated.

In both short-term crisis intervention and long-term initiatives, Africa Watch worked closely with Rwandan human rights associations. The international inquiry, initiated by the Rwandan associations and carried out by Africa Watch, the International Federation of Human Rights, the Inter-African Union of Human Rights, and the International Center for Human Rights and Democratic Development, was an important innovation in human rights intervention and a model of cooperation between locally-based and international associations. The continued strength and growth of the Rwandan associations is vital to improving the situation of human rights in the country.

In March 1993, Africa Watch together with the other sponsors of the international commission issued a one hundred-page report documenting the findings of the commission. Africa Watch issued an update, "Beyond the Rhetoric: Continuing Human Rights Abuses in Rwanda" in June 1993.

Africa Watch invited Monique Mujawamariya, executive director of the Rwandan Association for the Defense of Human Rights and Public Freedoms, to be honored by Human Rights Watch as part of its observance of Human Rights Day, December 10.

SOMALIA

Human Rights Developments

Despite a considerable improvement in the overall humanitarian situation in Somalia during 1993, after it became a major focus of international interest and the subject of United Nations intervention, the country remained in crisis. For several months in the middle of the year, U.N. forces, sent to Somalia to restore peace and reestablish a functioning civil society and state after a year of brutal clan warfare, found themselves caught up in a serious military confrontation in Mogadishu. Humanitarian and political issues took second place to military priorities. The whole process of U.N. intervention raised serious questions of accountability as well as various legal and ethical issues. The Somalia operation underlined the U.N.'s overall weaknesses in peacekeeping operations, and demonstrated problems inherent in the concept of peace enforcement.

The decision to send the predominantly U.S. forces of the United Nations International Task Force (UNITAF) to Somalia from December 9, 1992, was taken by outgoing U.S. President George Bush in response to reports that the majority of food arriving in Somalia for relief of the famine was being looted, and that relief agencies could not operate because of a general climate of insecurity. It was authorized by Security Council Resolution 794, under Chapter Seven of the U.N. Charter, "to establish a secure environment for humanitarian relief operations." The reports of food diversion may have been exaggerated, and earlier aid, together with a successful harvest following a drop in military activity, had already made a substantial difference in food supplies. Nevertheless, the famine was certainly not under control by December 1992, and mortality rates in the worst-hit areas remained high.

With the arrival of UNITAF forces (made up originally of some 24,000 U.S. troops and another 13,000 from other countries) the general climate of insecurity suffered for most of 1992 eased greatly. The port of Mogadishu, closed to the U.N. for weeks, was reopened; the airport was able to operate much more efficiently; international agencies and nongovernmental organizations were given military protection, and most of the protection rackets, food diversion and looting were brought to an end—at least in the areas in which UNITAF forces operated. Food distribution improved, and, in a matter of weeks, meals and supplemental food were being delivered to virtually all areas of southern and central Somalia without interference.

There were, however, unanticipated results to UNITAF activities. Hundreds of armed militiamen from Mogadishu together with their "technicals" (armed vehicles) dispersed to various other towns, including Baidoa and Kismayo. Between the arrival of the U.S. marines in Mogadishu and their presence in Baidoa ten days later, gunmen launched a wave of attacks. In Kismayo, dozens were assassinated before UNITAF forces reached the town. The presence of U.S. marines and subsequently Belgian troops did nothing to prevent control of Kismayo changing hands several times in severe factional fighting between Gen. Mohamed Siad Hersi "Morgan" (son-in-law of the former president of Somalia, Siad Barre) and Col. Ahmed Omar Jess.

The first effort at reconciliation came on December 11, 1992, when Gen. Muhammad Farah Aideed and "Interim President" Ali Mahdi, rivals for the control of Mogadishu and for the leadership of the Hawiye clan, shook hands in a public relations exercise, arranged by the U.S., which had no effect on the ground. With UNITAF firmly in place, the U.N. organized two peace conferences in Addis Ababa, Ethiopia, in January and March 1993. In January 1993, a large number of delegations from Somalia met in Addis Ababa under U.N. auspices. The meeting produced an agreement on disarmament, including a requirement to inform the U.N., by February 15, of the location and composition of clan militias and weapons held. The deadline was not met, and neither implementation nor verification made any significant progress before the second conference (or indeed subsequently). The March conference was essentially a meeting of the main clan-based factions. Agreement was reached on the establishment of a Transitional National Council (TNC), with four subcommittees covering disarmament and security, rehabilitation and reconstruction, restoration of property and settlement of disputes, and transitional mechanisms. Regional and district councils were to be set up, and an independent judiciary created.

One immediately controversial element was the application of these arrangements to the self-proclaimed Republic of Somaliland in the north of the country. The new leadership and elders of Somaliland categorically rejected the agreement's relevance to Somaliland. The elders had already made it clear that the planned deployment of U.N. troops in the north, announced in February, was unacceptable. Large public demonstrations in several towns underlined the point. The north made significant progress during 1992 and 1993, following its declaration of independence in 1991, in reestablishing functioning state structures and demobilizing clan militias.

Little progress had been made with other aspects of the March agreement by the time UNITAF, under U.S. command, was replaced, on May 1, by the United Nations Operation in Somalia (UNOSOM II).

UNOSOM II was authorized, by Security Council Resolution 814, to use force to bring peace, and to disarm and demobilize all troops. In addition, it was empowered to establish a police force and assist in the formation of government and legal structures. Many U.S. troops remained in Somalia, though the Pakistani detachment became the largest component of the U.N. force. Overlap between U.N. and U.S. command structures remained. The U.N. Special Envoy to Somalia, Jonathan Howe, was a retired U.S. navy admiral.

Some efforts were made by UNOSOM to establish regional and district councils, a judicial system and a police force. However, in some instances, premature efforts to establish district councils in contested areas caused problems. For example, twenty-three Somalis were killed in inter-clan fighting in Qorioley in early September after UNOSOM called for elections. Moreover, virtually all such political efforts were suspended after June 5, when twenty-four Pakistani soldiers died in a confrontation with General Aideed's forces. Exactly what happened was not investigated or established at the time, but UNOSOM immediately blamed General Aideed. On June 6, Security Council Resolution 837 authorized the arrest, detention and prosecution of those responsible for the attack. Admiral Howe also announced a $25,000 reward for information leading to the capture of Aideed. UNOSOM subsequently commissioned an internal investigation of the incident: the report produced in mid-August, a summary of which was later published, stated that there was *prima facie* evidence of General Aideed's responsibility.

All sides bear responsibility for the marked deterioration in security and the substantial increase in human rights violations over subsequent months. That included UNOSOM, which became drawn into open conflict with General Aideed, and in its military activities showed a disregard for the laws of war. The applicability of the Geneva Conventions and their Additional Protocols may not be clear with respect to U.N. military operations, but each component force is clearly bound to observe them at all times. Lawyers with the UNOSOM forces stated that the U.N. regarded the rules of international humanitarian law as binding on its forces.

On June 12, Pakistani troops fired on a small civilian demonstration close to the U.N. compound, killing at least two people. On June 13, Pakistani forces again opened fire on a crowd, this time killing at least ten, including women and children. UNOSOM claimed that the shooting was in self-defence, but the facts of the case were not clearly established. Journalists who were eyewitnesses to the incident stated that it was not clear that shots had been fired from the crowd before the Pakistani troops opened fire, and that in any event the response to any fire from the crowd was disproportionate to the threat faced and was not in conformity with the obligation to minimize the danger to noncombatants. No public investigation of this incident was carried out by UNOSOM.

In their search for General Aideed, UNOSOM forces attacked the clearly marked Digfer Hospital in Mogadishu on June 17, killing several patients and wounding others. Members of Aideed's militia had entered the hospital, and, in violation of the laws of war, used it as a vantage point to fire on UNOSOM forces that were pursuing them; the U.N. claimed that its troops were acting in self-defense. However, as in the June 13 incident, the UNOSOM forces were under an obligation to take action to minimize noncombatant casualties. Again, the facts of the case were not clearly established. The U.S. denied that its helicopters were used in the attack, though it admitted that eleven missiles were fired from helicopters on June 17, during the battle. Several otherwise unexplained missiles did hit the hospital, though it is not possible to say whether they were responsible for any deaths. At least five patients were killed during the battle. Damage to the hospital observed after the fighting was over indicated that the whole hospital had been targeted, and not just specific points where Somali militiamen might have been

seen. UNOSOM confirmed that no warning of the attack was given, stating that none was possible in the circumstances. On September 13, in a similar incident, U.N. forces fired on Benadir Hospital, near the U.N. compound.

On July 12, an attack was carried out on an alleged command center of General Aideed, using missiles fired from U.S. helicopters. UNOSOM originally claimed that only thirteen Somalis were killed in this attack, but the International Committee of the Red Cross later verified at least fifty-four deaths. No warning was given before the attack, and no fire had been aimed at UNOSOM from the building. The legality of the attack was questioned by UNOSOM's own justice division in a report that was not released to the public. The report concluded: "UNOSOM should anticipate that some organizations and member states will characterize a deliberate attack meant to kill the occupants without giving all the building occupants a chance to surrender as nothing less than murder committed in the name of the United Nations."

The use of air power supplied by the U.S., in particular Cobra helicopter gunships, resulted in the deaths of many Somali civilians from ill-directed rocket and cannon fire. Helicopters were used as a threat, hovering over buildings and houses, singly or in a mass, and homes were destroyed and civilians knocked over by the draught from their rotors. By the end of October, Africa Watch estimated that at least 500 to 600 Somalis, both civilians and combatants, had been killed by U.S. or UNOSOM forces, and more than 2,000 wounded. UNOSOM officials were quoted in mid-November stating that nearly one hundred UNOSOM or U.S. soldiers had died, including seventy-four killed and 325 wounded since June 5.

Several hundred Somalis were detained by UNOSOM forces, most of them following the June 5 attack on Pakistani forces. Although the great majority were released after short periods, many were detained without charge for several weeks. Some were held in secret locations and denied access to lawyers or family, only obtaining visits from the International Red Cross after long delays. There was no indication of what laws would apply to these cases, what rights the defendant would have, or indeed by what tribunal they would be tried. They were not allowed to consult with lawyers, nor to talk to reporters. In September, a rudimentary court system was set up, and many U.N. detainees were handed over to the newly established Somali police force for processing. Forty-three Somalis were still in U.N. custody in mid-November.

No procedures were established by UNITAF or UNOSOM for Somalis to lodge complaints in case of wrongdoing by U.N. forces, though some of the individual military detachments had their own procedures. This was the case for the U.S. forces, and for the Canadian and Australian forces serving with UNITAF. There were no such procedures for the other forces with UNOSOM. In April, a U.S. Marine was convicted for use of excessive force in an incident in which he killed two civilians. In mid-June, a U.S. soldier was arrested by military police, accused of subjecting a Somali to torture. The soldier was released, pending further investigation. Another soldier was convicted of aggravated assault of two civilians. Six Canadian soldiers were eventually charged with murder and torture in connection with the beating death of a Somali in their custody. A court martial proceeding was undertaken in Canada. Belgian forces operating in Kismayo instituted an inquiry in response to criticism of their behavior.

General Aideed's forces were also guilty of violations of the laws of war. The neutrality of hospitals was violated on at least the two occasions reported above. On several occasions, civilians seem to have been used to "shield" his troops, a serious violation of international humanitarian law that contributed to the high civilian casualties during exchange of fire with U.N. forces. Several Somalis working for the U.N. were killed, and there were reports that these were summary executions by Aideed's troops. Somalis working for locally produced newspapers critical of General Aideed, including a broadsheet published by the U.N., received death threats. Two U.N. soldiers, a Nigerian and an American, were captured by Aideed, but were not seriously mistreated, after initial manhandling by Somali civilians, and were ultimately released. The Red Cross visited them while they were in custody.

When the pursuit of General Aideed proved unsuccessful, elite U.S. Rangers were sent in August to reinforce the U.S.-commanded rapid deployment force left in Mogadishu after the handover from UNITAF to UNOSOM. On October 3, U.S. Rangers from this force were trapped by Aideed's forces in a densely populated area of narrow streets, while undertaking an armed sweep, ostensibly in search of weapons. Eighteen U.S. soldiers and one Malaysian were killed, seventy-five U.N. troops wounded, and one taken prisoner. According to eyewitness reports, several hundred Somalis may have been killed in this episode; Aideed himself claimed that 315 were killed and 812 wounded, figures accepted by the Red Cross as "plausible."

This attack resulted in a major review of U.S. and U.N. policy. In response to the domestic outcry at the American casualties, President Clinton sent in thousands more U.S. troops, but also announced a date, March 31, 1994, for the withdrawal of all U.S. forces from Somalia. He reappointed Robert Oakley as U.S. Special Envoy, a position he had held earlier in the year, with the task of organizing a fresh reconciliation conference, and announced that a commission of inquiry staffed by Africans would seek to establish responsibility for the June 5 deaths. It was also made clear that the U.S. would no longer look for General Aideed. In mid-November UNOSOM formally ended its search for Aideed; instead, the Security Council resolved that a special commission would determine who was responsible for attacks on U.N. forces. A conference on the economic reconstruction of Somalia, to which 150 Somali leaders were invited, was convened in Addis Ababa.

Nevertheless, towards the end of the year prospects for a settlement still remained poor. Almost as soon as it became clear that U.S. policy had changed, more arms began to appear on the streets of Mogadishu, and in rural areas there were signs of rearmament and some skirmishes. Several clashes between factions underlined the fact that nearly a year had been lost with no real progress towards any political solution. There were indications that some areas of the center and south of the country to which displaced people were returning might be on the verge of suffering food shortages again. Insecurity and banditry continued to be problematic throughout southern Somalia.

The Right to Monitor

Although the overall security situation in Somalia improved, human rights monitoring remained difficult. The most dangerous area was Mogadishu, affected as it was between June and October by the conflict between General Aideed's forces and those of UNOSOM. Both proved extremely reluctant to acknowledge violations and even more reluctant to assist in investigations. Local Somali organizations attempting to monitor human rights violations were ignored by the U.N. Elsewhere, the threat of violence was limited largely to free-lance bandits, and, at times, Somali factions.

U.S. and U.N. Policy

Suspicion over the intentions of UNITAF and then UNOSOM, and the role of the U.S. in both, crystallized quickly in Somalia. There was widespread concern that solutions were being imposed on the local population without regard for their views. Very few Somalis were consulted in advance of either operation, and even fewer involved as participants in subsequent processes. UNOSOM in particular, after the June 5 attack on Pakistani troops, took on the attitude and mentality of an occupying force, firing Somali staff, keeping its personnel in "safe houses," or in a guarded compound, and "offering" to protect journalists.

From the beginning, many Somalis were discouraged that the leaders responsible for gross violations of human rights under Presi-dent Siad Barre and after should be those that the U.S. and the U.N. turned to during 1993. It soon became apparent that the U.S. was prepared to deal with General Morgan, despite the declarations of the U.S. special envoy, Robert Oakley, that he would never deal with the "Butcher of Hargeisa," responsible for the destruction of 80 percent of that city in 1988 and the deaths of tens of thousands of its inhabitants. Within two months, the U.S. military's view of Morgan as a more reliable figure than General Aideed or his allies had been accepted, and Morgan's forces were in control of Kismayo, with his opponents disarmed by UNITAF. In Mogadishu, most of those disarmed belonged to General Aideed's forces. Other factions guilty of equally serious human rights violations during Somalia's civil war, including troops under "Interim President" Ali Mahdi, were not systematically disarmed.

Where UNOSOM attempted to fulfill its original humanitarian mission, it also failed to consult with Somalis. For example, little evaluation of local needs took place before attempts were made to set up the regional and district councils provided for under the March agreement in Addis Ababa. Considerable concern was also expressed that the rights of displaced people, or of refugees who might return, were being neglected. There is little indication that UNOSOM's political office consulted or worked through any of the local voluntary organizations that sprang up in many areas, and which often operated across clan lines. Their expertise, in some cases, was considerable. As the local councils were to have responsibility for law and order, these weaknesses were significant.

From May on, military priorities—the enforcement of law and order, and the subjugation of the so-called warlords—governed UNOSOM policy, rather than human rights or humanitarian concerns. This was supported by the U.S. However, at the end of the year, after the major reconsideration of policy caused by U.S. casualties, the U.S. was showing a much greater willingness to encourage the involvement of other African states in peacemaking efforts; UNOSOM was also trying to reestablish its own credibility by keeping control of the process, and giving its humanitarian functions priority. UNOSOM seemed reluctantly prepared to accept the role of regional powers, in particular that of President Meles Zenawi of Ethiopia, in reconvening the Addis Ababa conference.

The Work of Africa Watch

Africa Watch sent missions to Somalia in January and October, and, in association with the HRW Women's Rights Project, to Somali refugee camps in Kenya in July.

From the outset, Africa Watch raised general and specific questions of accountability of U.N. troops, whether under UNITAF or UNOSOM II, and emphasized the need for the U.N. to document past and present human rights abuses by all sides. Accountability for human rights abuses, including by U.S. or U.N. forces, should be insisted upon whatever future agreements are reached for the settlement of the conflict. In March, a newsletter detailed the need for the creation of a legitimate government and the fostering of a civil society. It drew attention to the need for a safe environment, and noted the problem of disarmament, arguing that, if undertaken, it should be even-handed and verifiable. The creation of a police force, the need for Somali participation, and for realistic clan and sub-clan involvement at all levels, were also emphasized.

Africa Watch wrote to the U.N. Secretary-General on June 15 and again on July 15. The letters protested attacks on Somali civilians, by both U.N. forces, principally from the U.S. contingents, and armed Somali factions. Africa Watch called for a special session of the Security Council to be held on Somalia to investigate human rights abuses; for an independent commission of inquiry to be set up to investigate all violations since June 5, including U.S. air attacks; for the U.N. to ensure that any future military operations should be conducted with "scrupulous regard" for the laws of war, and for the U.N. to start a vigorous policy of dialogue and negotiation. Other suggestions included relocating Pakistani troops out of Mogadishu. Finally, Africa Watch suggested a contingent of unarmed human rights monitors to be deployed throughout Somalia to collect information on abuses by all parties. Africa Watch also expressed concern over the failure of the resolution authorizing the arrest of those responsible for the attack of June 5 to detail the applicable legal procedures.

Africa Watch argued against any premature withdrawal of U.S. troops, for fear it might lead others to pull out and precipitate a sudden departure of all foreign troops. A probable consequence, in the absence of realistic peace agreements, would be renewed fighting and an upsurge in human rights abuses.

SOUTH AFRICA

Human Rights Developments

In 1993 a date was finally fixed for the end of white minority rule in South Africa. Multiparty negotiations that had been suspended in June 1992 were resumed, and April 27, 1994 was set as the date for the first multiracial general election in South Africa's history. In October the Nobel Peace Prize was awarded jointly to Nelson Mandela, President of the African National Congress (ANC) and to State President F.W. de Klerk, for their leadership of the negotiations since 1990. However, the transition period was threatened by the withdrawal from the negotiations of conservative groups, including Chief Gatsha Mangosuthu Buthelezi's Inkatha Freedom Party (IFP) and several right-wing white parties, and by the sudden escalation of political violence following the announcement of the election date. During 1993, some steps were taken to increase accountability in the law enforcement system, but abuses of human rights continued to be committed by the security forces, including detention without trial and torture and ill-treatment of detainees. South Africa signed several human rights treaties during 1993, including the Convention Against Torture and the Convention on the Elimination of All Forms of Discrimination against Women (CEDAW).

In February 1993, bilateral negotiations between the ANC and the National Party government, based on a September 1992 Memorandum of Understanding between the two parties, set the stage for the resumption of multiparty talks. A controversial agreement provided that an interim government of national unity, effectively a form of power sharing between the two parties, should rule South Africa for a period of five years after an election. A Multiparty Negotiating Forum (MPNF) began to sit in April, taking over the work of the Convention for a Democratic South Africa (Codesa) abandoned in June 1992. Two months later, April 27, 1994 was agreed, by twenty of the twenty-six parties to the negotiations, as the date for the election of a 400-member constituent assembly. In September, legislation was passed in the existing parliament for the establishment of a Transitional Executive Council (TEC), with extensive powers to promote free political activity during the election campaign. In November, the MPNF agreed to a new interim constitution to take effect after the elections, pending agreement on a final version. It included a bill of rights guaranteeing basic freedoms and abolished the ten nominally independent homelands.

Right-wing resistance to the negotiations process grew during the year. In May, a new coalition of twenty-one right-wing parties, known as the Afrikaner National Front (Afrikaner Volksfront, or AVF), was founded by several former leaders in the South African Defence Force (SADF). On the day the election date was supposed to be confirmed, approximately 3,000 members of the white supremacist Afrikaner Resistance Movement (Afrikaner Weerstandsbeweging, or AWB), crashed an armored vehicle through the glass-fronted entrance of the World Trade Centre in Johannesburg, location of the talks, and occupied the building. Several right-wing delegations—including the IFP and the governments of the homelands of KwaZulu, Ciskei and Bophuthatswana—refused to endorse the election date and walked out of the negotiations. In October, these and other members of the right-wing Concerned South Africans Group (Cosag), joined to form a new party, known as the Freedom Alliance. The Freedom Alliance did not endorse the new constitution, nor the abolition of the homelands.

However, political violence remained the most serious threat to the transition process. Violence had been on a downward trend in late 1992 and early 1993, but exploded with renewed force in July 1993, following the announcement of the date for multiracial elections. The July-August toll of 1,159 deaths, as monitored by the independent Human Rights Commission (HRC), was the highest ever two-month total. By the end of October, the organization calculated that 3,521 people had died in political attacks in 1993, the overwhelming majority in conflict between ANC and IFP supporters. However, as in previous years, allegations were made that a "third force," formed of security force and/or right-wing elements, was instigating much of the violence. In July, it was revealed after his death in custody that Victor Kheswa, a notorious criminal involved in many violent incidents, was a member both of the extreme right-wing World Preservatist Movement and of the IFP.

Earlier in the year, negotiations had been threatened by the highest-level political assassination in South Africa since President de Klerk unbanned the ANC in 1990. On April 10, 1993, Chris Hani, president of the South African Communist Party (SACP) and member of the National Executive Committee of the ANC, was shot dead outside his home by Janusz Waluz, a Polish immigrant and member of the AWB. In October, Waluz was found guilty of the murder of Hani, together with Clive Derby-Lewis, a Conservative Party member of parliament, who had supplied the gun. Both were sentenced to the death penalty.

Attacks on white South Africans also increased during 1993, although the vast majority of victims were black. In May, an attack on a hotel bar in East London carried out by the Azanian Peoples Liberation Army (APLA), the armed wing of the Pan Africanist Congress (PAC), killed five white men. In July, ten people were killed and fifty injured in an attack on a church in a white suburb of Capetown. Other whites died in attacks on farmers and travelers, many attributed to APLA. In the first six months of 1993, 109 policemen, black and white, were killed.

The government's response to political violence remained inadequate, despite several high-profile initiatives, and continued to rely on suppression of protest rather than attempt to address underlying problems of policing. The declaration of "unrest areas" under the Public Safety Act, where emergency-type legislation gives police the right to detain without trial and other powers, remained routine. At the end of October, twenty-seven districts were unrest areas; 609 people had been detained without trial during the year to that date. Although the MPNF voted in November to abolish detention without trial under the Internal Security Act, detention under unrest regulations was not affected. In March 1993, the government announced a "ten point plan" to combat violence, focusing on increased police presence and manpower. Stronger penalties for possession of illegal weapons and ammunition were brought into effect by an amendment to the Arms and Ammunition Act, passed in May. Following the upsurge of violence in July, the government flooded the townships with troops, in a manner reminiscent of the days of emergency rule in the mid-1980s.

Government action taken to address fears raised by attacks on white South Africans remained more forceful than the response to violence in the black townships. In April, the homeland of Transkei was surrounded by troops, as a response to a Goldstone Commission report indicating that the homeland was used as a base for APLA cadres. On May 25, partly in response to the attack on an East London hotel attributed to APLA, police arrested eighty-one members

of the PAC, in a nationwide sweep. Most were eventually released without charge. In the wake of the Capetown killings, the government announced that about 2,000 ex-policemen were to be re-employed, and 4,000 civilians to replace trained police in administrative posts. In October, SADF troops illegally entered Transkei, and raided a house in Umtata, the capital, killing five teenagers alleged to be APLA cadres. By contrast, the police failed to take prompt action to prevent the occupation of the World Trade Centre by the AWB. Sixty-nine of those involved were eventually arrested and charged with various offenses, but most were only fined for their behavior. At the same time, the government began distributing large numbers of sophisticated assault rifles to white farmers, following attacks on rural homesteads, under the "kommando" or reservist system for the SADF.

The structures of the September 1991 National Peace Accord (NPA), including the Goldstone Commission of Inquiry into the causes of the violence, continued to function during 1993. Measures taken under the NPA, especially the establishment of local dispute resolution committees, were widely credited with the decline in political violence in late 1992 and early 1993; however, they were unable to cope with increased tensions later in the year. The Goldstone Commission released reports or conducted investigations of numerous violent incidents during 1993. Some of these reports, especially those investigating the security forces, were strongly criticized for failing to allocate blame for the causes of the violence. To supplement these efforts, it was agreed at the MPNF that a multiparty national peacekeeping force should be established to counter political violence during the run-up to the elections. This was provided for by the act establishing the TEC.

In December 1992, following a raid by the Goldstone Commission on a secret military intelligence headquarters, President de Klerk fired twenty-three top army officers alleged to be involved in covert action aimed at undermining black opposition groups and provoking violence. However, some of the most notorious officers, including Gen. "Kat" Liebenberg and Lt.-Gen. George Meiring, were not removed. During 1993, the reopened inquest into the 1985 deaths of four anti-apartheid activists, including Matthew Goniwe, implicated General Liebenberg in his assassination and in attempts to destabilize the homelands of Ciskei and Transkei. In March, the notorious 31 and 32 Battalions, made up of Angolan soldiers under white command, were finally disbanded, more than a year after the government had promised it would do so; though the individual members of the battalions remained in the army. In August, Liebenberg retired as head of the army; but he was replaced by Meiring, rather than an officer with a relatively untainted image. Also in August, the Minister of Defense announced the end of military conscription for whites only and the forthcoming establishment of an all-volunteer army.

Police misconduct, including the indiscriminate use of lethal force in crowd control, and the torture and ill-treatment of individuals in police detention, remained routine during 1993. According to the HRC, 115 people were killed in actions by the security forces, and thirty-five people died in police custody in South Africa in 1993 up to the end of October. One of the most noteworthy incidents of bad crowd policing occurred in April, when police fired on a demonstration in Soweto protesting the death of Chris Hani, killing four people.

Some important measures were taken by the government to address these concerns. In January, ten regional police reporting officers were appointed under the NPA by the Minister of Law and Order to investigate allegations of police misconduct. The government announced additional measures in May, including the appointment of ten regional "ombudsmen" to whom members of the public could complain, a review of police training, and the introduction of "community supported" policing. In September, the government said that it would cease to employ about 13,000 rudimentarily-trained *kitskonstabels* ("instant constables"), respon-

sible for many abuses. In July, the Security Forces Board of Inquiry Act provided for a board, chaired by a judge, to investigate serious offenses by the police. The same month saw an agreement, under the NPA, to allow civilian inspection of police cells in the Vaal area. Despite these measures, the vast majority of security force abuses remained unpunished and uninvestigated, especially abuses committed by the homeland security forces, not affected by reforms introduced by the government in Pretoria.

The South African government retained extensive powers under the Internal Security Act to ban or restrict public gatherings. Although a new cooperation between government and political parties began to be evident in the planning of mass action, many demonstrations continued to be banned. Hundreds of arrests were made during the year for participation in illegal gatherings. In April, the Goldstone Commission published draft legislation for the regulation of gatherings in the future. The draft was widely criticized as giving too many powers to the police.

Government censorship of the media in South Africa continued to ease in 1993. As part of the negotiation process, the appointment of a new board for the government-operated South African Broadcasting Corporation (SABC) was agreed, to ensure balanced coverage of the election campaign. However, the airwaves remained restricted: the transmitter of Bush Radio, a community station in Capetown, was confiscated on April 30, and its operators charged with broadcasting illegally.

At the end of October, 316 prisoners were on death row in South Africa (excluding the nominally independent homelands). Although the South African parliament voted in June by a two-thirds majority to resume implementation of the death penalty, after a moratorium on executions of two years, the Minister of Justice stated that the government would not resume hangings without consulting with parties outside parliament, and no further executions did in fact take place before mid-November. The government of the homeland of Bophuthatswana announced a moratorium on executions in March. In the homeland of Venda two executions were threatened in May, but were postponed after national and international protest.

Abuses committed in the past by the ANC continued to receive attention in 1993. In August, a report was issued by the second internal commission of inquiry appointed by the ANC to examine allegations of torture and ill-treatment in detention camps in Angola and other southern African countries during the 1980s. The three-person commission confirmed the conclusions of previous investigations and named individuals responsible for torture and other abuse. The ANC, while accepting "collective moral responsibility" for the abuses and offering an apology to the victims, declined to take any further action. It called for the establishment after elections of a "truth commission" to examine and determine punishment for abuses by all sides during the apartheid era.

The ten homelands maintained their separate identity from South Africa during 1993, and their separate representation at the multiparty talks. Three of the homelands— Bophuthatswana, KwaZulu and Ciskei— continued to demand that an extreme form of federalism, effectively perpetuating the homeland system, should be entrenched in rules binding a constituent assembly. The governments of all three homelands joined the right-wing Freedom Alliance. However, the new interim constitution agreed by the MPNF in November provided for the reincorporation of the homelands after elections in 1994.

In Bophuthatswana, political organizations opposed to the regime, in particular the ANC, remained unable to organize within the homeland boundaries, as meetings were dispersed and activists detained under the homeland's extremely repressive Internal Security Act and other legislation. The University of Bophuthatswana and other educational institutions were particularly targeted for attack as a result of efforts by students and faculty to promote free political

activity. The university was closed down for several months during the year.

In Ciskei, 1993 saw continuing repression by the homeland government of opposition groups, and promotion of the African Democratic Movement, or its replacement, the Christian People's Movement, set up by homeland leader Brig. Oupa Gqozo. In May, an unconditional indemnity was announced for seventy soldiers and police involved in the shooting of twenty-eight demonstrators in the "Bisho massacre" of September 1992. However, in August, after being compelled by court order to give evidence, Gqozo was found by an inquest to be responsible for the 1990 death of former Ciskei Defence Force Commander Maj.-Gen. Charles Sebe, during an alleged attempted coup. In December 1992, in an interesting development for the future adjudication of a bill of rights in South Africa, the Appellate Division of the Ciskei Supreme Court overturned Section 26 of Ciskei's National Security Act, which allowed indefinite detention without trial. However, the homeland reintroduced detention powers in a September 1993 decree replacing the invalidated section.

Natal Province, the location of the KwaZulu homeland, remained the focus of some of the worst violence between supporters of the ANC and the IFP. Much of this violence was rooted in the lack of free political activity in the homeland, and in the arbitrary and illegal behavior of KwaZulu officials. The biased, incompetent and criminal behavior of the KwaZulu Police (KZP) led to repeated calls for the force to be disbanded. A limited investigation of the KZP was carried out by the Goldstone Commission during the second half of the year.

The Right to Monitor

The South African government continued to allow greater freedom than in the past to organizations monitoring human rights based both inside and outside the country. In January and February, Africa Watch was given permission to visit five prisons, as a follow-up to visits made by the Prison Project of Human Rights Watch in August 1992.

Several international and local networks monitored violence in South Africa, including teams from the United Nations, the European Community and the Commonwealth, with government consent. Both monitors and journalists reporting on the violence were targets of harassment and sometimes attack, but mostly by township youths rather than government forces.

In the homeland of Bophuthatswana, two South African human rights groups, the Black Sash and the Transvaal Rural Action Group, remain banned. U.N. and E.C. monitors were refused entry to the homeland in March, and two monitors from the Ecumenical Monitoring Programme in South Africa were arrested; in May the leader of the U.N. team in South Africa and four other U.N. monitors were also briefly detained. In December 1992, three lecturers at the university involved in human rights monitoring or political activity were "deported" to South Africa. The coordinator for the Mafikeng Anti-Repression Forum, a local human rights group, was detained in August, together with five members of the executive of the local ANC branch. Student leaders on the campus of the university protesting lack of political freedoms were repeatedly harassed and detained.

U.S. Policy

The election of Bill Clinton as President of the United States was widely expected in South Africa to lead to greater U.S. support for the ANC, as opposed to the government, in the negotiations process. Nelson Mandela was amongst the first world leaders that President-elect Clinton called after his election, and the only African leader invited to his inauguration. In 1993, the Clinton administration supported the negotiations process and showed itself more willing than the Bush administration to criticize those who obstructed it; in particular, Chief Buthelezi was strongly urged to resume participation in the talks when he refused to endorse the decision to fix April 27, 1994 as the date for elections and led the IFP out of the negotiating forum.

In April, after the assassination of Chris Hani, Secretary of State Warren Christopher sent letters of condolence to Nelson Mandela and to Hani's widow Limpho, in May, a high-level U.S. delegation, headed by Health and Human Services Secretary Donna Shalala, attended the funeral of Oliver Tambo, former leader of the ANC in exile, who died of natural causes. In August, officials confirmed reports that the State Department was providing security training for the protection of Mandela and other ANC leaders.

On July 4, Nelson Mandela and President de Klerk were joint recipients of the Philadelphia Liberty Medal, sponsored by We the People 2000, a business and civic organization. Both leaders visited the White House during their trip to the U.S., and had high-level meetings with administration officials and others, but Mandela received much more attention. After the presentation of the medal, he toured the U.S. fundraising for the ANC's election campaign and calling for renewed contacts with South Africa after the elections. In October, President Clinton welcomed the award of the Nobel Peace Prize to Mandela and de Klerk.

All U.S. aid to South Africa has, since 1985, been paid through nongovernmental channels. In 1993, the U.S. Agency for International Development (USAID) program in South Africa amounted to $80 million, making it South Africa's largest donor after the European Community. In addition, $10 million was allocated by the U.S. government in 1993 for support of the election process.

In September 1993, following the passage of the legislation to establish a Transitional Executive Council to regulate the period until elections in 1994, Nelson Mandela called on the U.N. General Assembly to lift all sanctions against South Africa except the oil and arms embargoes. Within hours, the United States, which had already removed most restrictions on trade with South Africa in 1991, announced that it would comply. Legislation lifting the ban on U.S. support for International Monetary Fund (IMF) and World Bank loans to South Africa, and removing all conditions on Export-Import Bank guarantees, was passed immediately in the Senate, and one week later in the House. President Clinton announced a trade and investment mission to South Africa to explore business opportunities. Other countries, together with the Commonwealth and the European Community, also lifted sanctions. The IMF announced that it would lend $850 million to South Africa for balance of payments assistance.

The Work of Africa Watch

Africa Watch's work in South Africa in 1993 followed themes established in previous years, focusing on abuses in the homelands and accountability. A representative of Africa Watch traveled to South Africa in January and February. In May, a report examined the official response to political violence, in light of recommendations made by Africa Watch in January 1991. In September, a newsletter examining human rights in KwaZulu continued a series of reports focusing on the homelands. A chapter on South Africa was included in the *Human Rights Watch Global Report on Prisons*, published in June 1993. A report focusing on South African prisons, undertaken with the HRW Prison Project, was scheduled for release in January 1994.

Several detailed letters were sent to the governments of South Africa and the homelands, protesting threats of execution in the homelands and interference with free political activity. A letter was also sent to the ANC urging the organization to accept the recommendations of the Motsuenyane Commission and take action against those found to be responsible for human rights violations in ANC detention camps.

SUDAN

Human Rights Developments

The human rights tragedy of Sudan, geographically the largest country in Africa, continued in 1993.

The repressive government headed by Gen. Omer al Bashir and controlled by the National Islamic Front (NIF) continued to consolidate the power they seized through a military coup that in 1989 overthrew the elected government. Its radical agenda was to impose its version of Shari'a (Islamic) law and convert Sudan into a totalitarian Islamic state. Sudan's thirty million citizens would be ranked according to religion, sect, political affiliation and sex and granted or deprived of rights accordingly.

This discriminatory agenda completely failed to respect the diversity of Sudan's more than 600 ethnic groups. None is in the majority although those who call themselves Sudanese Arabs are over 40 percent, Dinka 11 percent, and Nuba 8 percent. Only 73 percent of the population is Sunni Muslim (most of them followers of Sufi sects), followed by traditional African religions (16 percent) and Christians (9 percent).

All institutions, from the army to the courts to the schools, have been steadily purged of independent civil servants and staffed by NIF party loyalists, and all forms of civil liberties have been suppressed. Political parties are banned, religious intolerance is the order of the day, and arbitrary arrests and torture prevail.

More than twenty people were detained in April 1993 in connection with an alleged coup attempt. Some of these detainees were paraded on public television, chained and bearing signs of ill-treatment. Reports indicated that the accused were severely tortured. The government announced that they would have a fair and open trial, but no trial had yet taken place as of November.

A campaign against Islamic groups other than the NIF was carried out in mid-1993. The two largest political parties in pre-coup Sudan had roots in the traditional Islamic sects of Al-Khatmiya and Al-Ansar. The government confiscated an important mosque in Khartoum North belonging to Al-Khatmiya in late May 1993. On May 22, 1993, police troops took control of the Omdurman religious complex of the tomb of Muhammad Ahmed Al-mahdi, the most important shrine of the Al-Ansar sect, evacuating the buildings and confiscating the furniture. Many members of the Al-Ansar sect were arrested. Sheikh Al-Hadiya, the leader of Ansar Al-Suna Al-Muhammadiya, was arrested in June 1993.

The armed opposition, represented by two factions of the Sudan People's Liberation Army (SPLA), had a poor human rights record in the areas of south Sudan it controlled. The two factions were the SPLA-Torit faction headed by John Garang and the 1991 breakaway SPLA-Nasir/United faction led by Riak Machar.

The ten-year-old conflict in the south continued to bring famine, pestilence and death to the 3.5 million people who lived in that region. The violations of the rules of war committed by the government and the SPLA factions were a direct and important cause of food shortages and deaths.

South Sudan had, at best, only a subsistence economy intermittently disrupted by floods, droughts and disease. The precarious balance with the environment in which its people lived has been upset by war. Civilians have had difficulty planting and harvesting because they have been, more than once, displaced by the conflict. Fighting also impeded their search for work or food, and seasonal migration with their cattle. Armies engaged in burning villages and widespread looting of cattle, thus depriving civilians of another means of coping with grain shortages and rendering them vulnerable to disease and death.

Pockets of famine continued to exist in south Sudan, as they had throughout the decade of war. They shifted according to battle lines. In three southern areas of food shortages surveyed by the U.S. Centers for Disease Control and Prevention, in March 1993 (Ame, a displaced persons camp, Ayod and Kongor), half the deaths in the preceding twelve months were attributed to starvation, with diarrhoeal disease the second most frequent cause of death. The team found that the rates of severe under-nutrition were "among the highest ever documented," including in Somalia.

The U.N. estimated that approximately 800,000 people were in need of international food relief while another 700,000 need such non-food assistance as seeds, farming tools, fishing implements, and mosquito nets. Such implements, lost or destroyed in the war, are needed to restore self-sufficiency and reduce dependency on expensive imported food.

Not only personal tools but most infrastructure, electricity and communications had been destroyed during the war. The few roads were impassable during the rainy season, sprinkled with land mines and targets for ambush at all times. Commerce was reduced to barter in most areas. The rebel-controlled countryside and the government-controlled towns did not trade with each other; the government towns were besieged garrisons surviving on relief food, captive markets for army profiteering.

Included in the civilians dependent on relief food were some 250,000 residents of Juba, under SPLA-Torit siege for years. SPLA-Torit had indiscriminately shelled the government-held town, which continued to be ringed by land mines laid by both sides. The government prohibited movement out of the town, while engaging in iron-fisted repression of civil society and non-Muslims.

Indiscriminate government aerial bombardment produced hundreds of thousands of displaced persons and refugees during the year. Early in 1993, the government bombed the towns of Kayo Keiji, Mundri, Lotukei and Chikudum, causing numerous civilian victims. But the most damage was done in August by indiscriminate government bombing preceding a major military offensive in Western Equatoria, generating over 100,000 new Equatorian refugees who fled into Uganda; tens of thousands of already displaced Dinkas fled further north into Sudan.

The devastating impact of the prolonged war was illustrated by the decline in population for the three southern provinces from 5.2 million in the 1983 census to a U.N. estimate of 3.5 million in 1993. The U.S. Committee for Refugees estimated that in ten years of war 1.3 million people, southerners, had died because of the conflict.

Despite the shocking need for all kinds of assistance to the southern population, the government continued callously to obstruct relief efforts, as part of its strategy of punishing civilians living in rebel areas and strangling rebel forces. It permitted the U.N.'s relief effort, Operation Lifeline Sudan (OLS), to reach only six locations in south Sudan in 1992. In December 1992, however, the government was temporarily shocked into facilitating delivery of humanitarian relief by an avalanche of international pressure and the sudden appearance of nearly 30,000 U.S. troops under the U.N. flag to protect delivery of humanitarian assistance in nearby Somalia that month. OLS then was permitted to expand its deliveries to forty locations in south Sudan in 1993, but constant struggle is required to maintain the assistance. In mid-1993 the government refused entry to the Special Envoy for Humanitarian Affairs for the Sudan appointed by the U.N. Secretary-General, and only relented under pressure.

In May 1993, the government finally permitted the International Committee of the Red Cross (ICRC) to resume its operations in south Sudan. The ICRC's expulsion in March 1992 had put a halt to its work in the protection of war victims, particularly minors, and in visiting persons detained on account of the conflict.

The ferocity of the attacks on civilians had been heightened since 1991 by tribal revenge-taking between the Dinka aligned with SPLA-Torit and their traditional Nilotic cousins and rivals, the Nuer, aligned with SPLA-Nasir/United. In 1993, Equatorian tribes were increasingly affected.

Three Didinga villages near Chikudum in Eastern Equatoria were burned by SPLA-Torit troops in early 1993 for allegedly siding with the other faction. Several Didinga men were summarily executed after capture by SPLA-Torit. SPLA-Torit looted and burned the seven Pari villages of Lafon in Eastern Equatoria to the ground after occupying it in early 1993, causing many civilian deaths and displacing thousands. In both locations, civilians complained of SPLA-Torit's confiscation of their food.

A pocket of famine dubbed the "hunger triangle" was created by factional fighting in 1993 along the Nuer-Dinka territorial divide in Upper Nile, including the towns of Ayod, Waat, and Kongor.

The SPLA-Nasir faction occupied Kongor, where Dinka civilians complained of mistreatment, including killings, beatings and theft of food, by those forces. The SPLA-Nasir faction convened a meeting there to unite all SPLA dissidents, but the meeting was attacked by SPLA-Torit on March 27. The most prominent victim was an elder Equatorian statesman, Joseph Oduho, who had been released from long-term detention by SPLA-Torit in 1992. An expatriate U.N. World Food Program monitor was brutalized in the March 27 attack, forced to strip naked and walk through thorns, shot at eight times and left for dead. (In 1992, two U.N. relief workers were killed while in SPLA-Torit custody.)

Following the attack on Kongor, the SPLA-Torit forces swept north into Ayod and Yuai in Upper Nile in April, burning those two Nuer population centers to the ground, destroying the U.N. compounds, looting cattle, and causing heavy civilian casualties. They continued to justify these actions as retaliation for the Nasir faction's massacre of several thousand Bor Dinka in late 1991.

On May 28 the U.S. brokered a cease-fire and agreement to military withdrawal between the SPLA factions in the "hunger triangle." The cease-fire was broken in June. Although it is not clear which side struck first, both parties advanced on the territory of the other, killing civilians and burning villages. SPLA-Nasir/United manipulated relief food for military purposes. Recognizing that relief agencies would attempt to deliver food to the starving, and that the hungry would walk for days to reach a food source, the faction summoned desperate civilians to Yuai in the "hunger triangle" in early 1993, creating a town of thousands where fewer than one hundred had lived. Relief food followed, from which the new Yuai base, close to the Dinka/Nuer front line, could be illegally provisioned. Yuai was attacked in April and June and burned down by the SPLA-Torit faction, which killed scores of civilians.

In late July, the Nasir faction attacked Kongor, making it the sixth attack on the town in the last two years.

In late July, the government started an offensive from the garrison town of Yei into Kaya in Western Equatoria. The government's heavy indiscriminate bombardment of SPLA-held towns and villages resulted in a flow of 106,000 Equatorian refugees into nearby Uganda in less than four weeks, according to the U.N. High Commissioner for Refugees (UNHCR). The economy was severely disrupted, and the towns of Kaya and Yondu deserted and looted. Relief officials predicted that several hundred thousand more were at risk of starvation.

Finally, in the Nuba Mountains in South Kordofan, the "transition zone" north of the three southern provinces, the government army continued its counterinsurgency campaign: forced relocation of villagers and burning of their villages, forcible conscription, and killing of resistors. Nubans are non-Arab tribesmen of Muslim, Christian and animist faiths. The government armed and used tribal Arab militias (*murahaleen*) to raid the Nuba population with impunity. The murahaleen were then transformed into the Popular Defense Force (PDF).

The relocated were sent outside of the Nuba Mountains, although some were returned to work on "peace villages" serving as labor pools for large agricultural estates. Much of the Nuba civic urban leadership was eliminated through arrest and disappearance.

Despite reports of severe rural deprivation caused by the counterinsurgency campaign, the government adamantly refused permission for the U.N. or foreign agencies to bring assistance to nongovernment-controlled areas of the Nuba Mountains. The cruelty of this policy was reinforced by food shortages due to drought and locusts.

The government continued to subject southern and other displaced persons who fled north to Khartoum and other cities to discrimination and harassment. As of November, about 150,000 displaced persons remained outside Khartoum proper in unsuitable sites called "peace camps," far from any job possibilities; some 700,000 squatters and displaced had been forcibly relocated to these sites starting in early 1992, their possessions were destroyed in transit. Relief and development assistance by international nongovernmental organizations was severely restricted by government obstructionism, while access was wide open to Islamic agencies which used relief to proselytize.

The Right to Monitor

The Sudan Human Rights Organization (SHRO) was still banned in Sudan in 1993. The government's human rights organization, of the same name, served solely to defend the government from criticism of its human rights record. The original SHRO was re-launched in the United Kingdom in January 1992, and during 1993 was active in the U.K., Egypt, the Netherlands, former Czechoslovakia, Hungary, Canada, Sweden and the U.S.

Typical of the government campaign to close down civil society and block human rights monitoring was the destruction of the independence of the legal profession; attorneys had used the courts to fight human rights abuses. The Sudan Bar Association was banned on June 30, 1989 and replaced in September 1989 by a government-appointed "steering committee" for the Bar Association. This committee defended the government's abuses. A presidential decree of January 1993, amending the Advocate's Act of 1983, in effect put the bar association under the jurisdiction of the general law of trade unions (1992 Trade Unions Act). The legal profession thus fell under the supervision, for the first time in Sudan's history, of a nonjudicial government official, the Registrar of Trade Unions.

Government supporters then created the General Union of Sudanese Lawyers (GUSL) to serve as a new Bar Association.

They approached the Registrar of Trade Unions to call an election of officers for their organization. Obliging them and guaranteeing their electoral victory, the registrar called an election among attorneys on one day's notice in March 1993.

An Africa Watch researcher was extended a visa by the Sudan government to conduct a human rights fact-finding mission in mid-June. At the last minute, the government asked for a postponement of the visit until mid-July. In July, also at the last minute, the government reneged on that invitation. It has since abstained from contact with Africa Watch while maintaining a public posture of "openness" to foreign human rights visitors and others.

U.S. Policy

The U.S. condemned human rights violations by both the government and the SPLA factions. In its February 1993 annual *Country Reports on Human Rights Practices* (covering 1992), the U.S. State Department harshly and extensively criticized the human rights record of the Sudan government for total lack of political freedom, due process and civil liberties. It also criticized the government for extrajudicial executions and disappearances, and noted that "torture and other forms of physical mistreatment by official and unofficial security forces were widespread in 1992." The State Department also concluded that "the SPLA ultimately ruled by summary methods that included beatings, torture, and arbitrary execution." It also noted that SPLA shelling of Juba killed over 200 civilians.

Then on March 10, Assistant Secretary of State Herman J. Cohen condemned government bombing of rebel-held towns and rebel looting of relief deliveries. He reiterated U.S. shock and outrage over the government's execution of two employees of the U.S. Agency for International Development (USAID) in Juba in August 1992. Secretary Cohen listed as principal human rights concerns the forced removal of Khartoum's squatter populations, forced relocations and abuses against Nubans, infringement of women's rights, arbitrary detention, torture, repression of the press, restrictions on labor unions, and coercive Islamization.

On May 4, newly-appointed Assistant Secretary of State George E. Moose reiterated these concerns and added concern about massacres, kidnapping, forced labor, child conscription, forced displacement and Arabization in the transition zone between north and south.

In public testimony, in contrast with the *Country Reports*, little mention was made of human rights abuses by the SPLA factions. This criticism was couched in terms of "intra-SPLA fighting" that shut down relief operations and demonstrated the rebel leaders' lack of regard for their own people's welfare.

To further publicize abuses in the government-controlled areas, in May 1993 the State Department (at the request of Cong. Frank Wolf [R-VA]) declassified a cable from the U.S. Embassy in Khartoum describing widespread human rights abuses in Bahr El Ghazal and the Nuba Mountains. Since access to those areas was so limited, publication of this information played an important human rights role.

U.S. Ambassador to Sudan Donald Petterson visited both government- and SPLA-controlled areas of Sudan and brokered a cease-fire agreement whereby the two SPLA factions agreed as of May 28 to withdraw their troops from a famine-afflicted zone in south Sudan, in order to facilitate delivery of much-needed relief. But the cease-fire held only a few weeks.

In August 1993, the State Department designated Sudan a state sponsor of international terrorism under the Export Administration Act, as a result of the department's conclusion that Sudan allowed the use of its territory (including safe houses and training) by terrorists such as members of the Abu Nidal Organization, Hizballah and Palestine Islamic Jihad. The bombing at the World Trade Center in New York in early 1993 contributed to the downward spiral in U.S.-Sudan relations when it was discovered that some of the accused had Sudanese passports.

As a result of that terrorist listing, Sudan became ineligible for nonemergency assistance, certain benefits under the Trade Act, U.S. foreign tax credits, commercial sales of U.S. munitions, and other items. The U.S. also was required to vote against loans in international financial institutions and other uses of funds for Sudan.

Before being placed on the terrorist list, however, Sudan was already barred from economic or military aid by the Brooke Amendment, which prohibits countries in arrears on loan payments to the U.S. from receiving economic assistance, and Section 513 of the Foreign Assistance Act, which imposes the same prohibition on military rulers who have overthrown an elected government. The U.S. already routinely opposed development assistance to Sudan through the World Bank, and the State Department was hostile to Sudan's readmission to full membership in the International Monetary Fund.

Although development aid was prohibited by the terrorist listing, humanitarian assistance through voluntary agencies was not barred, and the U.S. was an important contributor to Operation Lifeline Sudan, the U.N. operation responsible for overseeing the delivery of assistance to 1.5 million Sudanese in need. In fiscal year 1993, the total U.S. government assistance to Sudan was over $85 million, most of it for emergency relief. From 1988 to mid-1993, the U.S. provided over $300 million in relief assistance to Sudan.

Sudan received increased attention in Congress concerning human rights and conflict resolution. Cong. Frank R. Wolf made his third visit to Sudan in February 1993, and denounced a government bombing of Kajo Keji, the aftermath of which he witnessed. He urged U.N. and U.S. pressure to stop government bombing and stem the flow of sophisticated military equipment.

The Senate Foreign Relations Committee held a hearing in May on Sudan, focusing on human rights issues and the nature of the conflict. The House Committee on Foreign Affairs, Subcommittee on Africa, held hearings on Sudan in March and its chair, Harry Johnston (D-FL), headed a congressional delegation to Sudan in July to raise human rights issues with all parties. The subcommittee co-sponsored a panel discussion by the parties in Washington on October 20 and 21, 1993.

That conference was followed by a breakthrough peace agreement dated October 22, 1993 between the two SPLA factions, facilitated by Representative Johnston and the State Department. Nowhere in the eight points of agreement, however, did the parties mention human rights or agree to cease their abusive treatment of the civilian population.

The Role of the United Nations

The U.N. increased its response to the human rights and humanitarian disaster in Sudan during 1993, but without including a human rights component in its relief operations. On December 18, 1992, the U.N. General Assembly had expressed "its deep concern at the serious human rights violations in the Sudan, including summary executions, detentions without due process, forced displacement of persons and torture." The General Assembly had called upon the government to ensure that all religious and ethnic minorities enjoy the rights recognized in the Convention on Elimination of All Forms of Racial Discrimination and called upon all parties to the hostilities to fully respect international humanitarian law.

On March 10, 1993, the U.N. Commission on Human Rights appointed a Special Rapporteur for Human Rights in Sudan, Gaspar Biro, who visited the country in September in preparation for a report to be delivered to the General Assembly in November 1993. The extensive U.N. relief effort for the displaced in the south, however, has no full-time human rights or protection function, despite the massive abuses of humanitarian law that were the root cause of civilian suffering, famine and death. The needs of Sudan for constant human rights protection were so great that a Special Rapporteur in twice-yearly visits could never meet them. The crisis required a large team of U.N. human rights monitors stationed throughout Sudan, especially in the south and the Nuba Mountains, to promptly document and denounce violations of human rights and humanitarian law.

The Work of Africa Watch

Africa Watch issued a report on the persecution of the Coptic minority in Sudan in February 1993. It conducted two fact-finding missions to south Sudan and Nairobi, in March and for five weeks in June-July 1993; after each mission, a summary of concerns was issued on the war in south Sudan. A more comprehensive report was planned for early 1994.

ZAIRE

Human Rights Developments

Human rights in Zaire deteriorated substantially during 1993, with pervasive lawlessness and government manipulation of ethnic conflicts leading to widespread abuses against civilians. This situation was intensified by the political deadlock between two rival governments: one loyal to President Mobutu Sese Seko, who had been in power for twenty-eight years; the other to Prime Minister Etienne Tshisekedi and the transitional parliament, the High Council of the Republic (HCR). The potential for even greater disintegration and human rights abuses loomed large, summarized in a confidential U.S. State Department cable in February warning that Zaire could turn into "Somalia and Liberia rolled into one, with vast potential for immense refugee flows, regional destabilization and humanitarian disaster."

President Mobutu repeatedly undermined the prospects for multiparty elections, which he had promised in April 1990, and made clear his disdain for the transition process. (His term of office actually expired in December 1991.) This attitude was demonstrated in his crackdown on members of the opposition and his willingness to use

force against civilians. As long as Mobutu controlled the elite army troops and the treasury, he was able to maintain power.

The economic crisis, characterized by soaring four-digit inflation and massive unemployment, produced serious starvation and malnutrition. Food shortages also resulted from the army rioting and massive looting that had taken place since 1991. Feeding centers were established around the capital by international relief organizations, and children were especially at risk.

Zaire was plagued by months of fighting between President Mobutu, Prime Minister Tshisekedi, and the HCR. On January 15, the HCR, a transitional legislative body elected by the National Conference and chaired by Archbishop Laurent Monsengwo Pasinya, claimed Mobutu was blocking "the functioning of the country's institutions at every level," and declared him guilty of high treason, for which he could face trial before the Supreme Court. Mobutu dismissed the threat on the grounds that he was not answerable to the HCR.

On January 28, government soldiers rioted when they discovered that they had been paid in new bank notes that could not be spent. Mobutu had ordered the five-million-*zaire* notes to be printed to keep up with inflation; Tshisekedi considered the move inflationary and called on shopkeepers to refuse to accept the banknotes. This developed into the worst unrest since unpaid soldiers rioted in September 1991, disturbances that had left at least 200 people dead and had prompted Belgium and France to send soldiers to evacuate some 20,000 foreigners.

In contrast to the 1991 riots in which the population joined the soldiers on a looting spree, the soldiers' rampage in 1993 terrorized the population. Hundreds of civilians were killed, including the French ambassador, Philippe Bernard, who was shot in an attack on the embassy, and the twenty-eight-year-old son of opposition leader Frederic Kibassa Maliba, who was killed during an attack on his father's home. Many more civilians lost their belongings in looting raids conducted by soldiers. There were numerous reports of rape by soldiers, and the Belgian government claimed that soldiers raped Belgian nuns in the Limete district of Kinshasa. Hundreds of foreigners were evacuated from Kinshasa by French troops; the Belgian troops worked to evacuate foreigners from Brazzaville in neighboring Congo to Europe, because Mobutu refused to allow them into Zaire.

Mobutu's elite troops took advantage of the chaos to attack newspapers, churches, and politicians opposed to the regime. Estimates of numbers killed range from 300 to more than 1,000, including many regular army soldiers who were killed by the presidential guard, the Special Presidential Division (DSP). Several hundred soldiers were arrested by the DSP, and there were fears that many were tortured.

Mobutu blamed Tshisekedi for the riots, and tried to dismiss him—for the second time in sixteen months, the first time being a week after he was appointed in October 1991. Tshisekedi claimed that since Mobutu did not hire him, he could not fire him.

Another showdown occurred in late February, when government troops held some 400 legislators hostage in the parliament for three days; the International Committee of the Red Cross was not allowed access to the hostages to feed them. Hundreds of other soldiers soon joined in, often with their wives and families. The soldiers demanded that the parliament approve the new banknotes as legal tender and require local merchants to accept them. They also rejected the interim constitution, approved by the National Conference. After finally releasing the legislators, on February 26 soldiers attacked the residence of Archbishop Monsengwo, who fled unharmed.

On March 29, Mobutu named Faustin Birindwa as prime minister to replace Tshisekedi, and revived the one-party National Assembly as a rival to the HCR. Birindwa was a former ally of Tshisekedi who was expelled from the Union for Democracy and Social Progress (UDPS). Neither Tshisekedi nor the HCR accepted Mobutu's move, reaffirming that since the HCR elected him, only it could remove him. Western countries and the HCR continued to recognize the Tshisekedi government.

In April, authorities launched a new crackdown on members of the opposition, including politicians, unionists, independent newspapers, and human rights activists—the first wave of political detentions by the security forces since 1990. During April, some twenty members of the Sacred Union, the coalition of opposition parties, were arrested. On April 6, gendarmes blocked off the parliament building, preventing the transitional parliament from meeting. On April 13, troops were sent to search the houses of Tshisekedi and his ministers, looking for government property; they claimed to have found proof of "sedition." Meanwhile, attacks on independent journalists continued: on April 23, Mukengeshayi Kenge, of *Le Phare* newspaper, was arrested and later charged with "spreading false rumors;" Mulumba Kandolo, from *Le Potentiel*, was arrested on April 28; and Kalala Mbenga Kalao, from *La Tempete des Tropiques* was arrested on August 25. Several trade union leaders were arrested in May, and were still in detention in late July.

The most visible illustration of the government's manipulation of the ethnic and regional conflict took place in Shaba, Zaire's mineral-rich province. A government-inspired campaign of terror had caused more than 100,000 residents with origins in the neighboring region of Kasai to be displaced from their homes since November 1991, and most since August 1992. Under the guise of promoting the interest of Shaban natives, or "Katangese," Mobutu's regional representatives attacked the substantial Kasaien community, which had been in place since well before independence, and raised a youth militia to reclaim the wealth of the region for its "original" inhabitants. As many as 90,000 were displaced by mob violence in March 1993.

Although there were historical roots to the animosity between the two communities, the explosion of violence in 1993 was largely explained by Mobutu's struggle to retain power: the violence erupted at the moment when Mobutu was forced to accept the appointment of Tshisekedi, who is himself Kasaien, as prime minister.

The attacks on Kasaiens and the promotion of Katangan interests took the form of a campaign, led by Gov. Gabriel Kyungu wa Kumwanza and Deputy Prime Minister Nguza Karl-I-Bond, for "regional purity" throughout Shaba. The governor turned the youth wing of Nguza's UFERI party into a security and intelligence apparatus, which was implicated in the attacks.

The pattern of attacks had begun in Likasi in August 1992; by year's end, an estimated 68,000 Kasaiens had been forced out of their homes. There was no effort to investigate or prosecute those responsible for the violence. The same tensions exploded in the mining city of Kolwezi in March 1993. But while it had taken six weeks to convince the Kasaiens of Likasi to leave their homes, the same process took only two weeks in Kolwezi. The facts surrounding the initial violence in Kolwezi are vague, but by March 22, Katangese youths carrying knives and machetes attacked Kasaiens—looting, burning homes and conducting house-to-house expulsions of Kasaiens. Again, the attacks were carried out with total impunity.

In an even more deadly explosion of regional violence linked to the political standoff, ethnic fighting broke out in North Kivu in March 1993. The conflict in North Kivu, which borders Rwanda, pitted the Nyanga and Hunde ethnic groups against Hutu and Tutsi of Rwandan origin (Banyarwanda). Reports from international relief organizations indicated that at least 7,000 people, mainly Banyarwanda, might have been killed, and over 200,000 more displaced. Some Banyarwanda reportedly staged counter-attacks, killing and wounding members of other ethnic groups. As in the case of Shaba, the fighting appeared to be instigated by the local authorities, and the central government did nothing to protect civilians.

In April, Tshisekedi asked the U.N. to send peacekeeping troops to Zaire to help stop the ethnic and political violence.

U.N. Secretary-General Boutros Boutros-Ghali appointed a special envoy to Zaire in July—Lakhdar Brahimi, a former Algerian foreign minister. Brahimi visited Zaire in August to investigate the political crisis. In early October, U.N.-brokered negotiations were reporting some progress. However, there was nothing to indicate that President Mobutu was willing to make any real concessions. By November, Mobutu's intransigence seemed to be paying off. His international image was enhanced after participating in the Francophone summit held from October 16 to 18 in Mauritius, where he was granted an audience with French President François Mitterrand. Although the two sides were nearing agreement on moving the country toward elections, they remained deadlocked on issues such as the role of the President and the selection of the interim Prime Minister.

The Right to Monitor

Several independent human rights organizations began functioning in Zaire. These monitors operated under difficult conditions, and were frequent targets of harassment by the Mobutu regime. Nevertheless, they became an important source of information about human rights abuses in Zaire, and collaborated with various international organizations including Africa Watch.

In 1992, a coalition of human rights organizations joined together to form Human Rights Now (Droits de l'Homme, Maintenant). The participating groups included: The League for Human Rights (Zaire); the Voice of the Voiceless for Human Rights (VSV); the Zairian Association of Human Rights (AZADHO); the Committee for Democracy and Human Rights in Zaire; the Group Amos; the Black Robes. Human Rights Now served as a forum to coordinate their activities and to resolve disagreements. Another human rights group was the Committee for Democracy and Human Rights. The groups in Human Rights Now differed slightly in focuses; for example:

- VSV, the oldest of the human rights groups, worked on educating Zairians about their rights, providing assistance to victims, conducting investigations, and producing reports.

- The League for Human Rights, founded in 1990, published periodic reports on human rights and waged campaigns in the press. It tried to work on a national and international level, and has branches in Shaba, Kasai, North Kivu, Maniema and Equateur, as well as a representative in Belgium.

- AZADHO, created in 1991, published reports on various human rights topics as well as a bi-monthly journal on human rights.

- The group Amos was not a regular nongovernmental organization but, rather, an independent group within the Catholic church. Amos was engaged in a range of activities involving education and sensitization on human rights, and played a major role in organizing within local churches, especially in Kinshasa.

- The Black Robes was an association of young lawyers and magistrates active in human rights. Individual members played a significant role in several human rights-related cases in the courts and prisons.

There were also specialized groups, including an association of prison professionals involving civilian prison employees in reporting on human rights and prison conditions.

The U.S. Role

As of early 1992, the Western governments that formerly supported Mobutu—the U.S., France and Belgium—collaborated to support the transition process headed by the National Conference and then the Tshisekedi government. All U.S. military aid was ended by Congress in November 1990, and most economic aid ended the following year, long after such measures had been urged by the U.S. Congress and human rights groups in Zaire and the United States.

On February 11, 1993, the State Department revealed possible steps that the U.S. and its allies might take regarding Zaire, including: freezing Mobutu's bank accounts in the U.S. and Europe; seizing his personal assets; denying visas to Zairians closely associated with Mobutu; suspending Zaire from the International Monetary Fund; and seeking an arms embargo and a ban on exports from Zaire. However, the U.S., France and Belgium were slow to take any further measures, except for restrictions on visas to President Mobutu and his close advisors.

The Clinton administration decided not to appoint a new ambassador to Zaire to replace Amb. Melissa Wells, who left in March 1993. The intention was to send a clear signal to Mobutu that the U.S. would not conduct normal relations with Zaire until the transition process was back on track. Nevertheless, many Zairians saw this as a sign that the U.S. was pulling away from the forceful position represented by Ambassador Wells.

The Clinton administration took a more forceful public line toward Zaire than its predecessor. In several public statements, senior U.S. officials distanced themselves from Mobutu and criticized the human rights abuses. In February 5 testimony before the Senate Foreign Relations Committee, then-Assistant Secretary of State for African Affairs Herman Cohen said, "Mobutu must effectively give up power so that a transition to a fair election can take place." In testimony before the Senate Foreign Relations Committee on June 9, Assistant Secretary of State for African Affairs George Moose put it more firmly: "There is no doubt about the cause of the problem. It is President Mobutu's stubborn refusal to honor his promise to permit a democratic transition process to proceed." He went on to note a "a pernicious pattern of government-provoked or -tolerated violence against minority ethnic groups," and a "sharp escalation of human rights abuse."

Assistant Secretary Moose described how the U.S. was working with the French and Belgian governments to increase political and economic pressure, using measures such as visa restrictions and prohibition of arms exports. In April, the U.S. did impose a ban on arms sales to Zaire.

On June 21, the State Department's spokesperson announced that President Clinton had banned entry to the U.S. to Zairians "who formulate or implement policies impeding a transition to democracy in Zaire or who benefit from such policies and the immediate families of such persons." This policy was to remain in effect for so long as Secretary of State Warren Christopher considered it necessary. The State Department explained the move as "a sign that the administration will not conduct normal business with President Mobutu so long as he thwarts a transition to democracy."

On July 19 and 21, Assistant Secretary Moose held meetings in Washington with Mobutu's envoy and notorious security official, Ngbanda Nzambo-ko-Atumba. The purpose of the meeting was for Mr. Ngbanda to deliver Mobutu's response to a letter from Secretary of State Christopher; not surprisingly, Mobutu blamed the opposition for Zaire's problems. According to the State Department, Moose informed Ngbanda that this response was "totally inadequate."

After the meetings, the State Department's spokesperson gave a strongly worded statement, holding Mobutu responsible for a situation that "puts at risk the lives and welfare of millions of his countrymen and the stability of an entire region."

On October 26, Assistant Secretary Moose testified again on Zaire, denouncing Mobutu's intransigence and stating that the U.S. was exerting "mounting pressure" on the regime. It was unclear, however, what concrete steps the U.S. was taking to pressure Mobutu, other than threatening economic sanctions.

As of July, the U.S. had obligated $1.5 million in fiscal year 1993 to assist displaced persons in several parts of Zaire, including the victims of civil strife in Kinshasa and the displaced in Shaba and North Kivu.

The Work of Africa Watch

In March and April, Africa Watch sent a mission to Zaire to investigate both prison conditions and the ethnic conflict in Shaba province.

The results of the study of prisons and police detention in Zaire first appeared in June as part of a larger report by Human Rights Watch's Prison Project, *The Human Rights Watch Global Report on Prisons*, and were to be issued in December as a separate report titled *Prison Conditions in Zaire*. Among our findings: that prisons in Zaire had become private enterprises and prisoners were slave laborers, with extremely high rates of death and disease. The prisons themselves were in an advanced state of decay, most of them dating from the period prior to independence in 1960. In addition to extreme overcrowding, inmates suffer from very limited drinking water and sanitary facilities that are, at best, semi-functional.

Also in June, Africa Watch published "Inciting Hatred: Violence Against Kasaiens in Shaba." The report documented the government-inspired campaign of terror threatening the lives and livelihoods of tens of thousands of Zairians who have their roots in Kasai. The violence was found to be the result of a cynical and politically expedient effort to shift popular grievances away from the failed Mobutu regime and onto one group of Zairians closely identified with the opposition. The events in Shaba were highlighted as an example of the suspicious re-emergence of regional violence linked to the political stand-off.

Africa Watch engaged in various forms of advocacy regarding Zaire, focused on informing members of Congress and the administration about the deteriorating human rights situation and the Mobutu regime's role in the violence. Africa Watch also conducted numerous press interviews about human rights in Zaire.

AMERICAS
WATCH

Human Rights Developments

On October 6, 1993, troops from the Palacé Battalion, under the command of Lt. Col. Luis Felipe Becerra Bohórquez, murdered thirteen peasants in the *vereda* El Bosque, in Riofrío, in the Colombian department of Valle. Lieutenant Colonel Becerra Bohórquez issued the official report, in which he claimed that his troops had sustained combat with guerrillas of the Ejército de Liberación Nacional (ELN), killing six women and seven men, including the chief of the guerrilla unit. Riofrío peasants filed complaints stating that the victims were not guerrillas but unarmed peasants who were killed in cold blood. The Procuraduría General de la Nación, an independent investigatory body that prosecutes disciplinary offenses committed by Colombian state agents, started an inquiry.

This episode would be sad but routine news in Latin America, except for the fact that this was not the first time Lt. Col. Becerra had been investigated for his role in a major massacre. On March 4, 1988, a group of gunmen arrived at the living quarters of banana workers in the *fincas* called Honduras and La Negra, in the Urabá region of northwestern Colombia. After identifying workers they had dragged away from their beds, the gunmen murdered twenty-three of them, many in front of their families. A Procuraduría investigation produced rare initial results: a startling one was that then-Major Becerra Bohórquez, at the time intelligence chief at the 10th Army Brigade, had used his own credit card to pay for the hotel stay in the region of some of the gunmen brought from other parts of Colombia to commit the murders.

The disciplinary and criminal inquiries dragged on for years, while Becerra remained on active duty. In the meantime, he attended courses in the United States required for aspiring chiefs (*oficiales superiores*). While a warrant for his arrest was pending in the public order courts for his role in Urabá, he was promoted to Lieutenant Colonel and posted as head of the public relations command at army headquarters in Bogotá. Based on the evidence in the Urabá record, the Procuraduría ordered his removal from the force, the most severe disciplinary measure at its disposal. Becerra exhausted his administrative appeals, and the order was confirmed in February 1993. Later, however, the Procuraduría reversed itself: it revoked the dismissal order, found that its own investigation was deficient, and ordered a new inquiry. On April 20, 1993, the Procuraduría's delegate office for the armed forces found that the five-year statute of limitations had expired and closed the Urabá file. Becerra recently told the press that he was willing to "subject himself" to the Procuraduría's investigation into the Riofrío massacre.

Impunity for major violations, as exemplified by the inability of Colombian institutions to discipline the likes of Becerra, remains the principal obstacle to improvement in human rights observance in the Americas. Its counterpart, the struggle for truth and justice as the means to achieve accountability, has become the dominant theme of the nongovernmental human rights movement in the hemisphere. As part of that movement, Americas Watch in 1993 made accountability its focus. Some signal progress was achieved in the course of the year in breaking the cycle of impunity. In March, a Truth Commission set up by the United Nations, as part of the peace agreements in El Salvador, produced a landmark report on the most tragic violations in the twelve-year conflict. The report was important not only because it validated the claims made for years by Salvadoran and international human rights monitors, but also because it was a successful first experiment by the United Nations in establishing the truth about abuses by all sides as part of a peace process. Although the Salvadoran government immediately issued a morally indefensible amnesty for abusers of fundamental rights, the achievement of the Truth Commission was not completely canceled, since its findings remain as the collective memory of the Salvadoran nation and nurture its decision not to let the carnage happen again.

Elsewhere, there were other encouraging steps in the direction of accountability. In Chile, the case against Pinochet's top henchmen for the 1976 murder in Washington of exiled former diplomat and cabinet minister Orlando Letelier and Ronni Moffitt, an American colleague, progressed towards a final decision. There were also a few other cases from those dark years that had a good chance of establishing responsibility for human rights crimes. In Guatemala, a land where impunity had been rampant for decades, some perpetrators of well-known abuses were convicted and others were being prosecuted. Bolivia's Supreme Court finally convicted former dictator Luis García Meza for the egregious violations against opponents of his "cocaine coup" government of the early 1980s.

Even where governments remained an obstacle to accountability, civil society organizations made some successful efforts at breaking the silence. In Honduras, the disappearances that took place between 1981 and 1984 remained unpunished, but the controversy about them was renewed in 1993 as an important issue in the presidential campaign. Leo Valladares, the human rights ombudsman, announced that he would produce a report on the fate of the disappeared at the end of the year; with funding from the international community, he has launched what appeared to be an important effort. Americas Watch made our files available to Valladares, including the documents we used in cases against Honduras before the Inter-American Court of Human Rights and that produced landmark decisions in the *Velásquez* and *Godínez* cases in 1989 and 1990, respectively. In Colombia, despite the many ways in which accountability was officially thwarted, independent human rights organizations produced carefully documented reports that named violators, cribbed from the paper trail left by official inquiries. By these and other examples, Latin American societies made it clear that the victims of gross

abuses were not forgotten; the collective will to preserve the memory of these crimes for future generations was an important aspect of accountability.

And yet the task remained daunting, and was made even more arduous by the so-called pragmatism with which the international community regards impunity. In Haiti, encouraging efforts to secure restoration of democracy, spearheaded by skilled United Nations mediators and supported decisively by the Clinton administration, were marred by a willingness to accommodate the blackmail of the military and their insistence on a blanket amnesty, not only for the offense of deposing Jean-Bertrand Aristide in 1991, but for the numerous ghastly crimes committed against democratic Haitians in the ensuing two years of dictatorship. In October 1993, as the *de facto* rulers reneged on their pledge to allow Aristide's return and held out for further, unacceptable concessions, the folly of a process that rewards political violence and countenances impunity for crimes against humanity became self-evident.

In Peru, deliberate official interference with investigations ensured impunity for the best-documented human rights crime of recent years: the disappearance and murder of nine students and one professor of "La Cantuta" University in July 1992, by a death squad called Colina, under the direction of military intelligence. A strong body of evidence, including the discovery of clandestine graves and the revelations of well-placed military sources, has yet to break the will of the Fujimori government to guarantee impunity to those who ordered and executed the grisly massacre. In 1993, impunity for Peruvian military also received a boost at an international level: the case for the 1988 massacre of villagers in Cayara, in retaliation for an attack by Sendero Luminoso guerrillas, was dismissed by the Inter-American Court of Human Rights because of serious procedural flaws in the preliminary handling of the case by the Inter-American Commission of Human Rights. The case was then taken to the General Assembly of the Organization of American States, but the region's most powerful political organ declined to take any action.

Impunity is not limited to abuses committed with clear political motivation. The inability of institutions to deal with crimes by police against prison inmates, shantytown dwellers, common crime suspects and spontaneous demonstrators, is the main cause for the repetition of these patterns of abuse and for their increase in many Latin American and Caribbean countries. In Venezuela, the hundreds of murders committed by the military and police during the February 1989 riots known as *el Caracazo* remain almost completely unsolved; only three of the more than sixty corpses of Caracazo victims, found in 1990, have been identified. No progress was made in all of 1993 in the investigation of the murder of several dozen inmates at Retén de Catia prison in November 1992. In Brazil, several years later, there has been scant progress in punishing military policemen for the murder of eighteen inmates in the São Lucas police precinct in São Paulo, in February 1987. The slow pace and the indifference of authorities made it possible for an even worse massacre to take place in October 1992 in the São Paulo Casa de Detenção in Carandiru, where military policemen killed 111 inmates. More than a year later, this case also languished in the intricate, ineffectual proceedings of Brazilian civilian and military courts.

Americas Watch and its parent organization, Human Rights Watch, have made accountability the centerpiece of our efforts to defend and promote human rights. We have insisted, first and foremost, on the right of the victims of egregious abuse to see justice done, a right that the State should have no power to take away, not even through the decision of a democratic majority. When it comes to crimes against humanity, governments have an effective obligation to investigate, prosecute and punish them, to disclose to the victims and to society all that can be known about them, and to grant the victims moral and material reparations. If effective punishment is not possible, govern-ments nonetheless are bound to promote an official account; to allow and encourage efforts by civil society to document and publicize the violations; and to purge the armed and security forces of those elements who have participated in or tolerated such abuses. We also believe that the United Nations, the Organization of American States and all inter-governmental bodies called upon to promote peaceful solutions and to restore democracy should incorporate accountability as a goal and as a tool of those efforts.

The Right to Monitor

As in recent years, 1993 witnessed the steady growth and diversification of the expanding Latin American human rights movement. Women's organizations particularly succeeded in establishing women's rights as human rights. Community groups, indigenous rights organizations, groups that defend the rights of street children, and many others made their presence known and found new ways of bringing specific human rights problems to the attention of the authorities.

Human rights advocacy continued to be hazardous, however. In Colombia and in Peru, highly respected human rights monitors were threatened with prosecution for their legitimate exercise of free expression. In October 1993 we published a briefing paper on the ways in which six different categories of civil society activists (including human rights monitors) have been objects of intimidation in Mexico, even as that country opened up to international trade and, reluctantly, to domestic and international scrutiny of government practices. Although the high visibility of Latin American human rights workers probably helped improve the conditions under which they worked, attacks still occurred. In Lima, a well-known community leader was almost murdered by Sendero Luminoso in an attack that left several school children wounded. In Guatemala, well-known monitors were harassed indirectly through violence and intimidation against their relatives and associates. In Colombia, a prominent human rights activist and refugee worker was disappeared in April.

His whereabouts were still unknown as of November. In other countries, even when monitors were left alone to conduct their work, they incurred the wrath of powerful sectors of society and became the objects of insidious attacks on their reputations through the media.

An organization that contributed in large measure to the prestige and credibility of the Latin American human rights movement officially closed down its operations in December 1992. The Vicaría de la Solidaridad of the Catholic archdiocese of Santiago, Chile, founded in the early years of the Pinochet regime, declared its job done with the advent of democracy. Many of its services were taken over by other organizations of civil society. In 1993, the legacy of the Vicaría, its insistence on the sacredness of human life, its attention to honest reporting and unfailing commitment to the defense of the most vulnerable in society lived on in the work of hundreds of organizations that strive to follow that sterling example. We include ourselves among the Vicaría's admirers and followers, and we know that its work will continue to inspire human rights monitors in Latin America for many years.

An encouraging development in human rights protection—which can be traced to the Vicaría's legacy—is the success achieved in Medellín by the Catholic archdiocese and by other nongovernmental organizations in sponsoring dialogue and thus reducing the extraordinary levels of violence. In the first half of 1993, as a result of dialogues between the various parties to the violence, homicides in Medellín fell by 36 percent compared to the same period in 1992. It is particularly inspiring to record that success in a city that for years has been besieged by drug trafficking, *sicarios* (hired guns), urban militias, private armies and paramilitary groups, and policemen both on and off duty. It is all the more remarkable that the nongovernmental human rights movement in Medellín has obtained this initial success, because in the 1980s its monitors were singled out for persecution, including our colleague Dr. Héctor Abad Gómez,

whose fond memory still inspires our work.

The strength of civil society in our hemisphere spawned another welcome development: the continued improvement of the role of the press as watchdog against government abuse. In many countries—and unlike earlier times when it contributed to official silence—the press has become a trustworthy source of information about human rights violations. Many newspapers and magazines devote increasing efforts to investigative reporting of human rights matters. In Peru, the discovery of the clandestine burials of the "La Cantuta" students and the revelations about the Colina death squad were made possible in large part by the courageous efforts of Peruvian journalists. Their status, nonetheless, continued to be precarious: *Sí* and *Caretas*, the leading Lima weeklies, continued to labor under the twin threats of prosecution and advertisement cuts.

Freedom of the press had its ups and downs in the continent. In Argentina, a long public debate resulted in July in the repeal of the Penal Code clause of *desacato* (contempt) that had been used to prosecute journalists who criticized high public figures. As a result of a case brought by prominent Argentine investigative journalist Horacio Verbitsky, with the assistance of Americas Watch, the Inter-American Commission on Human Rights was asked jointly by Verbitsky and the Argentine government to produce a report on the compatibility of *desacato* statutes with the freedom of expression provisions of the American Convention on Human Rights. Despite this example of the Argentine government's disposition to progress in this area, later in the year Argentine journalists were subjected to a series of threats and acts of intimidation, in some cases including beatings, by thugs linked to the ruling party. The wave of attacks subsided after parliamentary elections in early October, but the events have not been properly investigated.

The increased role of civil society and the press in most countries resulted during 1993 in a healthy debate about human rights issues. Americas Watch improved its access to larger segments of the population in most countries due to the increased attention that our reports, press releases, letters to officials and other initiatives received in the major media in most countries. Fortunately, our own increased visibility was only part of the larger attention given to the work of our domestic colleagues.

In 1993 Cuba remained a notable exception to this favorable trend toward the strength of civil society and freedom of the press. Though some monitors and other dissidents were released before the expiration of their unjust sentences, others continued to serve time for offenses such as "clandestine printings," "defamation of the head of state," and "enemy propaganda," in violation of Cuba's international obligations. Human rights monitoring remained a dangerous activity in Cuba in 1993, even though the orchestrated acts of "repudiation" dwindled in number and severity compared to previous years. Again, in 1993, Americas Watch was not allowed to visit the island to conduct our research and advocacy work, as we do freely elsewhere in the hemisphere.

Accountability and Civil Society

Accountability and civil society are the marks that we look for in assessing the status of democracy in the continent. Although most countries in the region are governed by regimes arising from elections, Latin Americans have a right to expect more from their fledgling democracies: more participation in decision-making, more transparency in government action, and more responsiveness in state institutions, particularly from those designed to protect citizens' rights. For us, a government cannot credibly call itself democratic unless its agents are accountable for their actions; its courts and prosecutors protect the rights of citizens and redress injustices; it allows and encourages the development of independent organizations of civil society; and social and political conflict is generally resolved through peaceful means.

In 1993 there were new threats against the stability of democracy in Latin America, but the defeats suffered in Haiti in 1991 and in Peru in 1992 were not repeated elsewhere. Venezuela endured both a second 1992 attempted coup (on November 27) by disgruntled members of its military, as well as a serious constitutional crisis resulting from the removal from office of President Carlos Andrés Pérez on corruption charges in May 1993. With its democratic institutions shaken, Venezuela faced new presidential elections in late 1993. President Jorge Serrano of Guatemala attempted his own version of a Fujimori-style, self-inflicted *coup d'etat*, but the firm reaction of Guatemalan society and international opinion forced a reversal. Democracy and human rights both were strengthened when Guatemala resolved the ensuing constitutional crisis by appointing Ramiro de León Carpio, the country's respected human rights ombudsman, to complete Serrano's term. On the negative side, the effort to restore democracy in Haiti seemed stalled and even floundering in early November, as this report was being drafted; also on the negative side, the authoritarian regime of Alberto Fujimori consolidated itself in 1993. The Fujimori-dominated Congress drafted a new constitution; on October 31, it received about 52 percent of the vote in a plebiscite. The principal features of the new constitution are the possibility of re-electing Fujimori and the expansion of the death penalty, in violation of Peru's international obligations. It is a sad comment on the state of democracy in Peru that popular sentiment in favor of the death penalty was the vehicle by which Fujimori sought a mandate for his own reelection.

The independence and impartiality of the judiciary suffered setbacks in 1993. Americas Watch placed increased attention on the independence and impartiality of the courts and of other institutions designed to protect rights, and believes the international community has not insisted enough on this aspect of democracy. Colombia's "faceless" judges, whose jurisdiction covers important criminal areas of drug trafficking and insurgency, not only failed to afford fair trials to those accused of those crimes, but increasingly seemed to direct their efforts against community and social activists whose non-violent actions bore no relationship whatsoever to drug trafficking or insurgency. The same was true, to an even larger extent, of the faceless judges and prosecutors created in Peru in the aftermath of Fujimori's self-coup. In Colombia, serious attacks against the lives of judges and court officials may have prompted a solution that nevertheless went too far in violation of due process and is now being misapplied. In Peru, threats to judges were real but the "remedy" is disproportionate and not reasonably designed to address the dangers. Moreover, the system of administration of justice of the Fujimori era makes no pretense of adherence to a democratic division of powers. In response to international criticism, the Fujimori-controlled Congress created a panel of jurists to review the performance of judges. Their non-binding opinions were then routinely ignored.

Peru also brought back military court jurisdiction to try civilians, which the Constitution of 1979 expressly forbade. Military courts are intrinsically non-independent; Latin American dictatorships have frequently resorted to them to prosecute and punish political opponents without even a semblance of due process. Faceless military courts in Peru have had a record 97 percent conviction rate in the Fujimori era. On the other hand, when their jurisdiction is limited to military defendants accused of human rights violations, military courts in Peru and everywhere else in Latin America enjoy a nearly perfect record of cover-up and impunity. In other countries, even though no special courts or similar schemes were created during 1993, the independence of the courts continued to erode through neglect, shrinking budgets, politicized appointments and steady decline in professional standards. This problem was particularly acute in Argentina. President Carlos Menem appointed fierce loyalists to the highest court as well as to newly created benches, and unduly protected some of them from impeachment procedures.

Independence and impartiality of the judiciary are fundamental traits of democracy, essential to the structural observance of human rights. An independent adjudicator is the ultimate guarantee for the exercise of rights. Procedural safeguards in criminal proceedings, important as they are in their own right, are meaningless if the judge is biased against the defendant. Access to justice by victims of abuse by state agents is equally illusory if courts are perceived to participate in the effort to cover up abuses. Fundamentally, when independent judges and prosecutors fulfill their duties, they convey a sense of trust and faith in institutions that is generally referred to as the rule of law; without it, majority decisions may be authentically representative of the will of the people, but they are not necessarily democratic.

If courts were more independent in Latin America they could be a powerful instrument in the effort to overcome the gaping inadequacy of many regimes to deal with non-politically-motivated patterns of violations of human rights. In July 1993, the world's conscience was shaken by the slaughter of street children by members of the Rio de Janeiro police. Unfortunately, violence against street children is almost endemic in many Brazilian cities, and it is also a problem in Guatemala City, Bogotá and other major urban areas. Police agents who take justice into their own hands and kill those they suspect to be criminals continue to plague Latin American law enforcement bodies. In the new democratic context in Latin America, Americas Watch documented some progress on this issue when the facts of police killings were publicized, as in Jamaica and Argentina. But in greater Buenos Aires, the effort to curb police killings suffered a new setback in 1993: a young student called Miguel Bru disappeared in August after he filed a complaint against some police officials of the province of Buenos Aires. His fate and whereabouts had not been clarified as of November. There were also instances when the police, accustomed to the impunity of dictatorial years, reacted with tragic excess against violent crime. On October 21, in a Santiago suburb, Chilean *carabineros* trying to thwart the escape of bank robbers alleged to be Lautaro guerrillas, shot indiscriminately against a bus that had been hijacked by the thieves; there were seven dead—three guerrillas, one bank guard and three innocent bystanders—and sixteen wounded.

In most countries, police forces continued to use torture as a routine interrogation technique against detainees. Closer societal scrutiny and court supervision have not made a dent in this practice. With some honorable exceptions, courts continue to foster this practice by admitting evidence obtained through torture and other illegal means. If police are a menace to those suspected of common crime (and almost by definition suspects tend to be young, male and poor), police forces fail miserably in protecting victims of certain abuses, such as women survivors of domestic violence. As in many other regions of the world, women in Latin America can expect little protection from police if they complain of beatings and threats by their husbands or lovers. A woman who failed to get the protection she requested was murdered by her ex-husband in Uruguay in 1993; a potentially precedent-setting case has been filed before the Inter-American Commission on Human Rights.

Prison conditions continued to deteriorate in the region during the year. For common crime offenders, overcrowding and brutal conditions are a function of neglect; when inevitable riots and escape attempts take place, the response can be unspeakable massacres like the ones in Brazil and Venezuela mentioned above. In Peru, inhumane conditions are deliberately, systematically inflicted upon certain categories of insurgency defendants, held in maximum-security facilities to which Americas Watch was denied access repeatedly in 1993.

Disputes about land tenure continued to generate a heavy toll in violence. Landless peasants and Indian communities are victimized by the power exercised by old and new rural landlords who manipulate local courts and security forces, or use their own "private armies." In Brazil in 1993, Americas Watch

once again documented the pervasive practice of some forms of forced labor, as well as the inability of the country's institutions to deal with it.

The increase and spread of these violations that were not directed against a particular political enemy were compounded by the relative lack of interest in the population at large in any effort to correct them, despite the courageous efforts of many Latin Americans. For large segments of the population—the poor, the disenfranchised and the marginalized—democratic regimes that pay no attention to these patterns of violations are failed democracies. The challenge for democracy at the end of the century in Latin America is to extend its benefits to these large categories of victims of human rights violations.

Armed Conflict and Human Rights Violations

Armed conflict continued to wane in the hemisphere in 1993, and that accounted not only for a reduction in general terms in abuses by guerrillas, but more specifically, murders, disappearances and other crimes associated with counterinsurgency. Despite their governments' proclamations of success against their guerrilla enemies, Peru and Colombia experienced continued armed violence, though in both countries some reduction in intensity could be verified. Efforts to generate processes leading to political settlements in either country were unsuccessful during the year. In Guatemala, the defeat of the Serrano self-coup brought hopes of renewed talks, but as of early November there had been no significant progress. The U.N.-brokered peace process in El Salvador took hold in 1993 despite dangers to guerrilla activists who had reentered the political process. In Nicaragua there were some serious acts of violence between government troops and reconstituted former *contra* and former Sandinista forces. The bloody confrontations signaled the weakness of the Nicaraguan democratic process, and resulted from the failure to reach a lasting and comprehensive settlement at the end of the contra war.

The remaining insurgency wars revealed an increasing tendency by guerrilla forces to disregard basic standards of the laws of war, together with their growing disinterest in their image in international and domestic public opinion. As a result, insurgency tactics in Colombia and Peru became more and more vicious and less respectful of the neutrality of unarmed civilians. In Colombia, some guerrilla units resorted not only to more kidnappings for ransom, but even to banditry, drug trafficking and lawlessness. In Peru, Sendero Luminoso has never shown any inclination to respect the Geneva Conventions standards, except in demanding prisoner-of-war treatment for their arrested militants. In spite of triumphant announcements by the Peruvian government of the willingness to negotiate by Sendero's jailed leader, Abimael Guzmán, towards the end of the year it appeared that Sendero's ability to wreak deadly havoc was still considerable.

On the side of government forces, "dirty war" tactics in Colombia and Peru were still used in 1993, albeit—in the case of Peru—with a notable reduction in the number of reported cases. As the examples cited earlier show, there was still pervasive impunity for past and new cases of disappearances and massacres, even if the security forces seemed to be more selective in applying those tactics. At the same time, the continuing counterinsurgency wars were the pretext for the governments' resort to emergency measures, and for the unfortunate tolerance of them in some sectors of society. Insurgency and counterinsurgency have generated great dislocation and turmoil in rural communities. It is virtually impossible to estimate the numbers of the displaced, but the phenomenon is widespread and no official effort has been made to provide much needed services. The domestic human rights movement in several Latin American countries is increasingly dedicating efforts to the plight of the internally displaced and of refugees. In 1993, with the support of the U.S. Jesuit Refugee Service, Americas Watch established a program of systematic monitoring of refugee policy, displacement, and repatriation as they affect Haitians and Guatemalans.

Though violations of the laws of war by both sides to the conflict continued in the Andean region, it was heartening to see that organizations of civil society have made a concerted effort to raise awareness in public opinion about the need to demand respect for the fundamental principles of international humanitarian law. Monitoring violations by guerrillas has become standard practice in many domestic human rights organizations, and major progress has been achieved in focusing attention on the need to protect civilians and noncombatants during counterinsurgency operations. The leadership of guerrilla groups, unfortunately, has remained largely immune to moral and political pressure from human rights groups.

The Response
of the International Community

The international community's response to human rights and democracy in Latin America continued in 1993 to lag behind the needs and exigencies of the times. In compliance with its charter, the United Nations leaves the initial response to crises to the regional body, the Organization of American States (OAS). At the OAS, governments pay lip service to a shared concern for human rights and democracy, but in practical terms misunderstood notions of sovereignty and non-intervention become an obstacle to collective action. Nonetheless, in 1993 the OAS response to attacks on democracy, embodied in the Declaration of Santiago of 1991, fared better than in previous years. Though actions by Guatemalan civil society and by the Clinton administration had more to do with the final outcome, the OAS did take an early and strong stance demanding the reversal of Serrano's dismissal of Congress and the courts.

In December 1992, the OAS requested the assistance of the U.N. in negotiations to bring Jean-Bertrand Aristide back to the presidency in Haiti. The U.N. and the OAS jointly appointed Dante Caputo, former Argentine foreign minister, as mediator. In the first half of the year, the process yielded some encouraging results. Borrowing a page from other successful ventures, the U.N. and OAS secured agreement to deploy a civilian mission with hundreds of human rights monitors. The U.N., especially, approached the planning and staffing of the mission very professionally, and the international monitors provided some important measure of protection for human rights throughout the year. The civilian mission also issued frank and credible reports, despite reported efforts by U.N. diplomats to tone them down in the name of protecting delicate negotiations.

In July, Haiti's *de facto* rulers agreed to the Governors Island Accord, by which Aristide would return on October 30; the leader of the *coup*, Gen. Raoul Cédras, agreed to step down by October 15, so that Aristide's government could appoint a new high command. By September it became clear that the usurpers of power in Haiti would not comply. When thugs prevented the deployment of international military and police advisors, the civilian mission monitors were evacuated. On October 30, Aristide was unable to return and the thugs supporting the military regime celebrated their successful defiance of the international community. The U.N.'s sole answer was to reinstate a targeted economic embargo and to threaten to strengthen it.

In contrast, U.N. involvement in the peace process in El Salvador continued to be perhaps the most successful of its recent ventures in conflict resolution. ONUSAL, the U.N.'s operation there, continued to monitor human rights violations, which were on the increase in anticipation of El Salvador's March 1994 elections. Salvadoran human rights organizations criticized ONUSAL's early periodic reports as too mild, but by the end of the year, ONUSAL was issuing more forceful denunciations of individual human rights cases. As stated earlier, another success of the U.N. effort was the publication in March of the report of the Truth Commission, documenting twelve years of abuses by official forces as well as the guerrillas.

International Mechanisms

The international protection mechanisms within the OAS to provide relief to victims of violations continued a precarious existence in 1993. The procedure before the Inter-American Commission on Human Rights (IACHR) was mired in uncertainty and frequently hampered by bureaucratic mishandling. An important defeat for the cause of human rights took place in early 1993 when the court declined jurisdiction in the case against Peru for the massacre of Cayara, citing the IACHR's violation of its own procedural regulations. Neither the complainants nor the families of the victims of Cayara were responsible for the error, which was at least in part caused by demands of the Peruvian representatives; yet the Cayara families were the most prejudiced by the result.

The court also issued an advisory opinion, acting on a request by Argentina and Uruguay—supported by Mexico—that, if successful, would have seriously curtailed the ability of the IACHR to rule on violations committed by democratic governments through legislation or court decisions. Americas Watch and other nongovernmental organizations (NGOs) were allowed a major role as *amici curiae* in the debate. The opinion vindicated the position adopted by the IACHR and the NGOs. Efforts to bring the IACHR under the control of the political organs of the OAS continued, however, under the pretense of "strengthening" the protection scheme. An effort to amend the American Convention on Human Rights to enlarge the commission (thereby allowing more political control of its members) was tabled at the 1993 OAS General Assembly.

Government representatives continued to dilute a draft convention on disappearances originally prepared by the IACHR. Some governments, including the United States, attempted to eliminate a clause that establishes that the practice of disappearances is a crime against humanity. This would signify an important retreat from positions already adopted by the general assemblies of the OAS and the U.N. The representatives of Chile, Costa Rica and

Argentina have stood fast in defense of the "crime against humanity" clause; Americas Watch and other nongovernmental organizations supported its retention.

Despite the difficulties of a system so obviously dominated by diplomatic and political considerations, Americas Watch and other nongovernmental organizations continued to dedicate serious efforts to strengthening it by using it on behalf of victims. In association with the Center for Justice and International Law (CEJIL), we continued to bring cases before the IACHR and the Inter-American Court. In July we presented evidence on the merits of a case against Peru for the massacre of prisoners on the island of El Frontón in 1986; a decision was expected in early 1994. CEJIL, Americas Watch, and the Andean Commission of Jurists–Colombia Section represented the widow of a disappeared teacher in the first Inter-American Court case against Colombia.

U.S. Policy

Early Clinton administration appointments at the State Department and other offices responsible for human rights and for policy towards the hemisphere were encouraging. In almost every case, experienced foreign policy professionals or persons with a solid record of concern for human rights and democracy were entrusted with positions of responsibility. Nonetheless, there were also hesitations and errors in judgment with detrimental effects for human rights. The first one took place even before the inauguration, when President-elect Clinton reneged on his campaign promises and decided to continue the policy of returning Haitian refugees found in the high seas, established by President Bush through the infamous "Kennebunkport order" of 1992. Later in 1993, the Supreme Court affirmed this policy, even though it flew in the face of fundamental principles of international law with regard to refugees and violated the spirit, if not the letter, of clear treaty obligations of the United States.

After that disturbing start, the policy towards Haiti took a positive turn when the Clinton administration lent considerable assistance and dynamic support to the efforts of the U.N. and OAS to obtain the return of President Aristide. One fatal flaw of that policy, however, attributable to mediator Dante Caputo but also to President Clinton's special envoy, Amb. Lawrence Pezzullo, was to put pressure on Aristide to give in to demands for a blanket amnesty for all crimes committed by the *de facto* regime since Aristide's ouster. Such a demand was immoral and illegal. Significantly, favoring such an amnesty proved in the end to have been bad political judgment: as the final implementation of the Governors Island Accord drew near, Gen. Raoul Cédras and his accomplices insisted once more on a blanket amnesty. They were emboldened to ignore the Governors Island pledges by the hesitation of the international community on this point. The international community's role was further weakened by President Clinton's unilateral decision to pull back the ship carrying American military observers and trainers, after a small number of thugs took over the Port-au-Prince harbor and prevented their landing. The deployment of military and police trainers had been agreed to by Haiti's *de facto* rulers at Governors Island in July; for that reason, it was meant from the start to be a consensual armed presence. But shooting their way into Port-au-Prince was not the only alternative to a unilateral withdrawal; the *U.S.S. Harlan County* should have remained at harbor to signal the fact that Cédras was reneging on his solemn undertaking, and to put pressure on him and his cohorts to comply. As it happened, President Clinton's decision handed a gratuitous victory to the thugs, forced the retreat of other officers already there, caused the evacuation of the civilian mission, and threw the U.N. plan into disarray.

As of November, Haiti remained under Cédras's control, human rights violations were rampant, and U.S. Coast Guard vessels still returned fleeing Haitians to a country the international community designated as a "failed state," and where massive, systematic human rights violations prevailed. The forcible return of fleeing Haitians, without affording them any opportunity to state a claim for asylum, was not only politically damaging to the effort to restore democracy in Haiti; it was also heartless, cruel and inhumane.

With respect to Peru, the administration had an early opportunity to show its concern for human rights, and used it to great benefit. In February, Peru needed the U.S. to convene the Support Group of countries to help Peru clear its arrears with international financial institutions. The Clinton administration told the Peruvian government that it should make some immediate human rights concessions or the support group would not be convened. The Fujimori government promptly agreed to five demands, although some of them were implemented only in words, not in deed. Later, the administration sent Peru mixed signals with respect to renewing direct economic assistance. With respect to a program to aid in the administration of justice, the State Department conditioned its approval on the report of a mission by four prestigious jurists from the United States, Italy and Argentina. The mission, chaired by Prof. Robert K. Goldman, of American University, visited Peru in September; its report was awaited in November, but was already having positive results as Peru announced (but did not immediately implement) some positive changes in criminal procedures.

A major objective of the administration during the year was to secure approval in Congress of the North American Free Trade Agreement (NAFTA), a tripartite comprehensive trade pact with Canada and Mexico, originally negotiated by the Bush administration. During his campaign, Clinton had announced that he would seek side agreements to secure protections for labor rights and the environment. The side agreements were signed in August 1993. Neither NAFTA nor the side agreements, however, included any mention of mechanisms to protect human rights. The environmental protections were stricter than those contemplated for complaints about labor rights. Americas

Watch deplored that the discussions surrounding NAFTA and the side agreements were not used by the United States government to put human rights on the table in Mexico and to encourage the Salinas government to take a more serious approach to long-term solutions to human rights violations.

In 1993, Americas Watch conducted research in several communities along the Southwest border of the United States, and published a second report on continuing violations of human rights by the U.S. Border Patrol and customs agents against persons suspected of illegal immigration. The acting commissioner of the Immigration and Naturalization Service (INS) wrote back a detailed letter and otherwise had an encouraging reaction: the acting commissioner sent a memorandum to all district offices of the INS with the recommendation that the abuses contained in our report be avoided. We then entered into a dialogue with the INS in hopes of producing structural changes in the way the agency behaves on the border. Since many of the victims of these crimes are Mexican nationals, we expressed our hope that the NAFTA negotiations could be the occasion for high-level discussions about human rights in the United States as well.

Policy towards Latin America, as exemplified by the steps taken so far, seemed to be still under formulation in the Clinton administration as of November. It was encouraging to notice shifts in the approach toward drug interdiction. The "war on drugs" under previous administrations was the occasion to overlook abuses by police and military partners and to introduce military and police assistance without human rights conditions or with only lip-service to those conditions. The Clinton administration has announced that human rights and the promotion of democracy will be central to its overall foreign policy in the post-Cold War world. The details of such an ambitious program had not been spelled out as of this writing. Americas Watch supports the idea that human rights and democracy, properly conceived, should be the guiding light for policies of cooperation with foreign governments. We hope, however, that the simplistic mistake of the Reagan and Bush administrations—of seeing progress in human rights where there were only elections and good words with no deeds—will be avoided. United States foreign policy must promote the content and not simply the form of democracy and human rights.

BRAZIL

Human Rights Developments

Three notorious massacres in Brazil in 1993 exemplified the serious human rights problems that continued to plague the nation. On July 23, a group of men shot and killed eight teenagers who were sleeping on the streets of downtown Rio de Janeiro, near the well-known Candelária church. Several weeks later, in early August, sixteen Yanomami Indians were murdered near Brazil's remote and forested border with Venezuela. Then, on August 29, a group of hooded gunmen killed twenty-one people in the Rio de Janeiro *favela* (shantytown) of Vigário Geral.

The three incidents were not aberrations but the most dramatic examples of violence against street children, violence against Brazil's indigenous population, and killings by off-duty police. Subsequent investigations revealed that off-duty police were involved in the Candelária and Vigário Geral killings; the Yanomami Indians were killed by Brazilian *garimpeiros* (gold miners). But these examples did not exhaust the forms of abuse against Brazil's civilian population, including rural violence often targeting the leaders of rural unions, the use of forced labor in agriculture, miserable prison conditions, inadequate investigations and prosecutions of violence against women, and torture and killings of suspected criminals by the police. Despite attempts by federal and state authorities to remedy Brazil's poor human rights record, many cases were characterized by official impunity.

Behind the phenomenon of violence against street children lay the extreme poverty of the majority of Brazil's population, domestic violence, and substance abuse. Although precise figures did not exist, estimates were that between seven and ten million children and adolescents were living and working on the streets of Brazilian cities. These children did what they could to supplement their families' incomes or ensure their own survival: sell candy and food, wash and "guard" cars, shine shoes, beg, steal, deal drugs, and engage in prostitution.

Because they were sometimes involved in crime—usually assaults and robbery—shopkeepers, the police, and at times the general public viewed these children as a threat to public safety. The perception overlapped with a general feeling that the justice system was corrupt and inefficient and that juvenile offenders, who could not be tried as adults, were never punished for their crimes. As a result, small businessmen sometimes hired private "security firms" to deal with children who stole from them or inconvenienced their clients. These groups, which engaged in death-squad activities, were frequently composed of off-duty policemen, who often became involved in organized crime themselves.

The majority of victims of the killing of street children were male teenagers, and a disproportionate share were black. According to statistics from the federal Procurador Geral (Attorney General), 5,644 children between the ages of five and seventeen were victims of violent deaths in the period between 1988 and 1991. Though more recent statistics were incomplete, it appeared that in 1992 and 1993, at least in the state of Rio de Janeiro, the killing of minors was increasing. In 1992, 424 children under the age of eighteen were victims of homicide in the state. In the first six months of 1993, 298 children were killed, a significant increase from the same period the previous year.

Investigations into the killing of children and adolescents were frequently inadequate, most often because of the involvement of off-duty policemen and because of witnesses' fear. Those fears were warranted; witnesses were frequently intimidated and sometimes killed.

Prosecutions of those engaged in the killing of street children were extremely rare, as the victims usually did not have family members who could maintain pressure on the authorities. The witnesses to these homicides were often other street children, who were easily intimidated or who, because of their unstable living situation, were not able to follow the case for the length of time necessary. As a result, it was rare for the killers of minors to be arrested, and even more uncommon for them to be convicted.

The Brazilian authorities took initial steps during 1993 to put an end to impunity, though the success of their efforts could not immediately be evaluated. In the Candelária killing of eight teenagers, four men, including three military policemen, were arrested and indicted for homicide in early August. The commander of the military police battalion in which the men served was dismissed. Prior to the shooting, the Rio de Janeiro state government had already established a special hotline for anonymous denunciations of death squad activity, which it claimed had resulted in the arrest of 250 people, including many policemen.

Shortly after the Candelária killings, twenty-one residents of a Rio de Janeiro slum were killed during an organized invasion of the favela by a group of hooded men carrying heavy-caliber weapons. The massacre occurred the day after four military policemen were murdered in the same neighborhood by drug traffickers. The governor of the state quickly stated that the killing "presented characteristics of an inadmissible operation of revenge" and dismissed the commander of the Ninth Battalion of the military police, responsible for patrolling the area. A subsequent investigation into the killing revealed a network of organized crime within the police force and resulted in the arrest and indictment of thirty-three men— twenty-eight of them military policemen— accused of being part of a death squad. As of October, it appeared that several top figures in the civil police would be indicted on charges of corruption and organized crime.

At the national level, the federal government instituted several important reforms, including establishing commissions to follow the most important cases and calling upon the federal police to set up a special unit to investigate police involvement in death squads. In one extreme case, the army assumed control over the military police in the state of Alagoas, after it was widely reported that the force was involved in political assassinations and organized crime.

The involvement of police in off-duty death squads was intimately related to another major human rights problem in Brazil, violence committed by on-duty policemen. Executions of civilians by the military police (responsible for patrolling and responding to crimes in progress) and torture by the civil police (responsible for investigating crimes) were the worst manifestations of police violence. In 1992, for example, the São Paulo military police killed 1,470 civilians, including 111 inmates at the Casa de Detenção prison. While the authorities claimed that many of the killings occurred in shoot-outs, the high number of civilians killed compared to the relatively low number wounded, and the low number of police deaths, undermined that assertion.

In the aftermath of the 1992 Casa de Detenção killings it appeared that killings by on-duty military police in São Paulo had decreased. In the first eight months of 1993, the São Paulo authorities stated that the military police killed 257 civilians, a significant decrease from 1992 though still an exceedingly high figure. The decrease in the number of killings showed that the military police could, however, curb their abusive practices when sufficiently pressured.

Despite the notable decrease in the number of killings by on-duty military police in São Paulo, the underlying situation that allowed this practice to continue remained unchanged: military policemen who committed crimes against civilians were judged in special military courts, which rarely convicted policemen for violent crimes. In numerous cases reviewed by Americas Watch, the military justice system either failed to convict abusive policemen, accepting their argument that violent acts occurred as a result of legitimate self-defense, or was so lethargic that it did not serve as an adequate curb on abusive behavior.

In February 1993, for example, state prosecutors with the military justice system recommended the indictment of 120 policemen for the Casa de Detenção killings, including ninety-eight for homicide. Those indicted included the commander of the operation, Col. Ubiratan Guimarães, and several other high-ranking officers. No one has been arrested or fired from the force, however. And in June 1993, three police officers who had participated in the attack on the prison were actually promoted, two of them for "merit." In a ground-breaking decision, on the other hand, a civil policeman was found guilty of participating in a notorious prison massacre in February 1989 in which eighteen inmates were killed in a jail in São Paulo. This was the first time that a policeman had been found guilty in a prison killing.

A positive step in 1993 to redress the problem of impunity for violent military policemen was the introduction of legislation to extend civil court jurisdiction in cases involving crimes against civilians committed by the military police. The legislation was passed by the lower house, the Câmara dos Deputados, in diluted form and as of November was now pending before the Senate.

Though there were no prison killings in 1993 comparable to those the previous year, prison conditions continued to be substandard and overcrowded, and beatings and mistreatment of inmates were common. In one notorious episode, as many as seventy-five boys at a São Paulo juvenile detention facility were beaten with sticks, truncheons and metal bars by prison officials and military police in the aftermath of a March 30 riot. Medical treatment was withheld and delayed. As a result of the poor conditions at the juvenile detention unit, the juvenile sec-

tion of the state prosecutor's office filed a suit against the state government, asking for an investigation into the beatings, mistreatment, and overcrowding at the facilities.

Violence against Brazil's indigenous population also grabbed international headlines in 1993, following the killing of sixteen Yanomami Indians by Brazilian garimpeiros near the community of Hwaximëŭ (Haximu), some fifteen kilometers across the border into Venezuelan territory. In one of several attacks in late July, it is thought that the garimpeiros shot, hacked, and beat to death four women, a man, three adolescents, and six children. Because of the difficulties of traveling in the area and due to the Yanomami practice of cremating their dead, it was unlikely that the total number of victims and the exact circumstances of the events would ever be known.

The authorities could have prevented the attacks had they heeded the warnings of indigenous rights organizations that Brazilian garimpeiros were invading the Yanomami reservation and crossing into Yanomami territory in Venezuela. Following the killings, the federal police arrested two men, and twenty-three garimpeiros were indicted on charges of genocide. President Itamar Franco appointed a new minister for the Amazon and announced that a federal police station would be opened in Surucucu, inside the Yanomami reservation. The office of the Procurador Geral was also particularly energetic in pressing for additional protection for the Yanomami. Some political and military authorities, however, minimized Brazil's responsibility for the killings and called for a reduction in the size of the Yanomami reservation.

Violence against Brazil's indigenous community, most frequently committed by garimpeiros, loggers or large landowners, has long been met with impunity. In 1992, it was estimated that twenty-four Indians were murdered, with none of those cases resulting in the punishment of the aggressors. Despite a constitutional deadline of October 5, 1993, the federal government failed to demarcate Indian reservations, a step urgently needed to protect indigenous communities from violence and disease. By the deadline, only 266 of 510 areas traditionally occupied by indigenous people had been officially demarcated.

Rural violence also appeared to escalate in 1993. In order to resolve conflicts over land tenure with small farmers and settlers, large landowners frequently hired gunmen to target leaders of rural unions, peasant organizers, squatters, and others who campaigned for agrarian reform. As of November 1993, at least forty-three peasants and agrarian reform activist had been killed. Very rarely were arrests made in those cases or the persons responsible brought to trial. Violence against peasants and small farmers also occurred when they were evicted from their farms, either by hired gunmen or by police sometimes acting without the necessary court orders.

The year saw a marked increase in targeted assassinations of rural activists, with at least eleven being killed by November. On March 16, the body of Mozarniel Patrício Pessoa was found on the banks of a stream in the state of Tocantins, with his skull shattered. He was the vice-president of the state Sindicato de Trabalhadores Rurais (Union or Rural Workers, or STR) in the town of Araguaina and the president of the local chapter of the Partido Comunista do Brasil (Brazilian Communist Party, or PC do B). Shortly after this murder, another rural union activist was killed in the neighboring state of Pará. Arnaldo Delcidio Ferreira, the president of the STR in Eldorado do Carajás, in southern Pará, was shot and killed on May 2. Ferreira had been repeatedly threatened with death, but local authorities had taken few steps to protect him. Then on June 29, unionist Raimundo Reis was shot and killed in the municipality of Turiaru, Maranhão. Reis had long been a leader in the struggle for agrarian reform in the area and had been living under threat for many years. The local rural union stated that after the killing neither the police chief nor the prosecutor was found in the area, and several weeks after the killing no investigation had been opened.

Killings of rural activists occurred in 1993 even in cases where the individuals had fairly high profiles. For example, on April 29, Paulo Vinha, a biologist and environmental activist, was shot and killed in the state of Espírito Santo. Vinha had been investigating environmental problems in the state and was also assisting local indigenous communities in their struggle to recover land that they claimed was taken from them by the Aracruz paper pulp company. As of November 1993, no one had been arrested for Vinha's murder, despite the fact that two suspects were quickly identified.

Impunity also prevailed in those cases which received prolonged international attention. In a major setback, the long-awaited trial of the killers of Expedito Ribeiro da Souza was indefinitely postponed in June 1993, only days before it was due to begin. Expedito, the president of the local STR and a vice- president of the PC do B, had been assassinated on February 2, 1991. At the time, he was the fifth person associated with the STR union who had been killed in the Rio Maria area of Pará in a period of ten months.

In an equally troubling case involving the murder of internationally recognized environmental activist Chico Mendes, two men found guilty of the 1988 murder escaped from prison. It was suspected that the police and prison authorities in the state of Acre were paid to allow the killers to escape. Environmental and human rights activists had long warned about the precarious security in the Rio Branco prison, where the two men were held. In the wake of the escapes, the federal police said that President Franco ordered them to make a man-hunt for the fugitives their "number one priority." However, the fruitless search was suspended after thirty days and not renewed.

Brazilian authorities also failed to take steps to curb the use of forced labor in rural areas. This practice was carried out by labor contractors who recruited workers from impoverished towns with false promises of high wages and good work conditions. Once the workers arrived at the job—often hundreds of miles away from their homes—they were told that the wages were lower than promised and that they owed money for transportation, food, shelter and tools. The workers were not allowed to leave until they paid their "debts," and were sometimes guarded by armed men. Noncompliant workers were often beaten and in some cases killed. In 1992, the Comissão Pastoral da Terra (CPT), a Catholic church-based group that monitors human rights, registered eighteen cases of forced labor involving 16,442 workers, a substantial increase in the number of victims from the previous year. As of November 1993, the organization had registered fifteen cases involving at least 5,540 workers. Despite the prevalence of this abuse, there was not a single conviction of labor recruiters, gunmen or landowners for involvement in forced labor.

Americas Watch also remained concerned about inadequate investigations and prosecutions of those responsible for violence against women. In June 1993, human rights organizations and local politicians reported that girls were being recruited and auctioned to brothels near gold mining areas in the Amazonian states of Acre and Rondônia. Many of these girls were recruited with false promises of well-paying jobs. Once they arrived at the gold mining areas, however, they were told that they must work as prostitutes. Some girls were beaten and killed if they refused to have sex. In prior cases local police authorities had refused to intervene and had even collaborated with brothel owners, and the federal police had to intervene to free the girls.

In a positive development, the federal Congress created a special investigation commission to look into child prostitution throughout the country. An initial report stated that there were approximately 500,000 girl prostitutes in Brazil.

The Right to Monitor

The Brazilian government imposed no formal obstacles to human rights monitoring, and there were many local organizations that actively promoted the rights of the rural and urban poor, street children, women, indigenous communities, prison inmates and other victims of human rights abuse. Many international organizations, including Americas Watch, conducted investigatory missions to Brazil without interference or obstruction by the government.

However, local organizations and individual human rights activists were sometimes threatened and harassed. Most frequently these threats could not be directly linked to the government. However, activists who worked with children on the streets of Brazil's cities reported to Americas Watch that they were frequently harassed and sometimes physically assaulted by the police. In one of the more prominent cases, on April 13, Pedro Horácio Caballero, a Catholic priest working with street children in downtown São Paulo, was beaten and harassed by military policemen after he tried to get the police to stop beating two twelve-year-old boys. Others who criticized the police or investigated crimes involving police were threatened. Federal congressman Hélio Bicudo, who proposed legislation seeking to change the military justice system, was also threatened with death.

In some cases the courts also were used in an attempt to silence human rights activists. São Paulo authorities filed a suit for slander against Frei Betto, a Dominican priest, theologian and writer, after he published an article in the *Estado de São Paulo* newspaper referring to police violence and the impunity that the São Paulo military police enjoyed. The charges against Frei Betto were later dropped. In a similar case, Darci Frigo, an activist with the CPT in the state of Paraná, had been convicted in 1992 on charges of slander resulting from statements that the CPT made linking a local politician to the practice of forced labor; in an important decision in April 1993, the state appeals court voted to reverse Frigo's conviction.

Lawyers who work with the human rights organization Gabinete de Apoio Juridico às Organizações Populares (Legal Suppport Group for Popular Organizations, or GAJOP) were threatened with death several times. On July 23, unknown men shot at

Jayme Benvenuto de Lima Júnior as he was driving home; he escaped injury. GAJOP was threatened because the organization had made public denunciations concerning corruption in the Pernambuco state judiciary. After the son of a local judge publicly stated that if he encountered any human rights lawyers he would shoot them, two GAJOP lawyers, Valdênia Brito and Kátia Costa Pereira, requested protection.

Activists who worked with indigenous people were also threatened in 1993. Sister Elsa Rosa Zotti, a Franciscan nun working with indigenous people in the state of Mato Grosso do Sul was threatened with death. According to the Conselho Indigenista Missionario (CIMI), Sister Zotti and several other nuns were threatened because they worked with the Rikbaktsa Indians, who were trying to secure the demarcation of their territory. The Catholic bishop of the state of Roraima, Dom Aldo Mongiano, also received a public death threat in February. On a live radio show, a man who identified himself as a "professional" offered to kill the bishop and leave his head in the town's main square. Dom Aldo had attracted the hostility of some of the state's population after farmers were expelled from land that was part of a Wapixana Indian reservation. Some accused Dom Aldo of helping the Wapixana to secure assistance from the federal police.

U.S. Policy

Despite close economic ties, the United States failed to use its considerable leverage to press for improvements in Brazil's human rights record during 1993. With the exception of the generally accurate chapter on Brazil in the State Department's Country Reports on Human Rights Practices for 1992, the U.S. government issued few public statement on human rights violations in Brazil. The State Department assured Americas Watch that human rights issues were frequently brought up in private conversations with Brazilian officials. However, in light of the high-profile massacres in 1993, the absence of public U.S. comment was particularly glaring.

Direct U.S. assistance to Brazil was low, compared with other countries in the region. In 1993 Brazil received approximately $1.3 million in anti-narcotics assistance, $250,000 for the International Military Education and Training Program (IMET) and some $13.8 million in development assistance. In its request for 1994 anti-narcotics and IMET assistance, the Defense Department emphasized Brazil's commitment to nuclear non-proliferation.

According to the State Department, anti-narcotics funding went to assist the federal police with law enforcement programs, and was used for training and non-lethal technical equipment.

Despite the lack of public statements, officials at the U.S. Embassy in Brasília actively followed human rights issues. Shortly after the news broke concerning the killing of the Yanomami, the embassy's political officer attempted to visit the Yanomami reservation but, along with several other diplomats, was turned back by military officials who claimed that she did not have the proper authorization to visit the area.

The private and cautious nature of U.S. policy stands in contrast to the public activism shown by the European Community. On September 16, the European Parliament approved a resolution condemning human rights violations by the Brazilian military police and the impunity that they enjoy. The resolution called for the punishment of those responsible.

Echoing world-wide concern about the Yanomami, the U.S. Congress also held hearings on indigenous rights in Brazil, on July 7, 1993. The hearing before the Western Hemisphere subcommittee of the House Foreign Affairs Committee included representatives of the Brazilian Congress and of the Kayapó Indian nation, and discussed the demarcation of reservations as well as steps to protect Brazil's indigenous population from violence.

Another new development in 1993 was the granting of political asylum to Marcelo Tenório, a gay Brazilian, by U.S. immigration authorities. Tenório claimed, and in a precedent-setting decision judge Philip Leadbetter agreed, that as a gay person he was a member of a persecuted social group in Brazil. Tenório stated that in 1989 he was beaten in front of a gay disco in Rio de Janeiro, and that in a different incident he was taunted and attacked by the police.

The Work of Americas Watch

In a press conference in São Paulo on May 31, Americas Watch released "Urban Police Violence in Brazil: Torture and Police Killings in São Paulo and Rio de Janeiro After Five Years," a newsletter issued jointly with the Núcleo de Estudos da Violência (NEV) of the University of São Paulo. After the release, Americas Watch participated in a roundtable discussion with representatives of the São Paulo section of the Ordem dos Advogados do Brasil (Brazilian Bar Association) and local human rights groups. On June 2, Americas Watch and the NEV also held a press conference and roundtable discussion on this newsletter at the federal Congress in Brasília, hosted by deputy Hélio Bicudo. These press conferences yielded widespread television, newspaper and radio coverage.

In June and July, Americas Watch conducted two missions to Brazil, investigating homicides of minors in the states of Rio de Janeiro, São Paulo, Pernambuco, and Espírito Santo, and forced labor in the states of Pará and Paraná. An Americas Watch representative was present during a raid on a forced labor site in the state of Mato Grosso. Along with the CPT, Americas Watch participated in a press conference in Pará, to protest the postponement of the trial of those accused of murdering Expedito Ribeiro de Souza, resulting in front-page news in the state capital's major newspaper. A newsletter about the forced labor investigations and a report about homicides of minors were scheduled for publication near the end of the year.

In September, after the killing of twenty-one people in the Rio de Janeiro slum of Vigário Geral, the vice-chair of Americas Watch met with state and federal authorities in Brazil and voiced Americas Watch's con-

cerns about police violence. A newsletter about this mission, titled "The Killings at Candelária and Vigário Geral: The Urgent Need to Police the Brazilian Police," was issued in October. The newsletter called for urgent reforms at the state and federal level, including joint federal and state investigations into police violence, improved administrative discipline, greater attention to the protection of witnesses, and expansion of the civilian courts to try crimes committed by the military police. The newsletter also proposed that the Brazilian government create a federal crime to punish police abuses, thereby allowing for federal prosecution should state efforts prove ineffective.

COLOMBIA

Human Rights Developments

A "macabre democratization" of violence is how Colombia's presidential human rights counselor Carlos Vicente de Roux described the predominant trend of 1993, referring to the appalling contempt for human life demonstrated by state forces, guerrilla groups, and drug mafias. In the first six months of 1993, an average of eleven people a day were killed or disappeared for political reasons: three in armed conflict, six in acts of outright repression, and one in "social cleansing." An average of one disappearance occurred every day, putting Colombia third in the world for disappearances.

Victims were a cross-section of Colombian society: peasants living in combat zones, leftists, trade unionists, human rights activists, ex-guerrillas who had laid down their weapons, prostitutes and other "social undesirables," soldiers, police, and combatants themselves. Human rights groups estimated that since the mid-1980s at least 300,000 Colombians had become internal refugees, forced to flee because of political violence. The refusal of both sides to respect the neutrality of the civilian population exacerbated suffering.

Yet the role of state agents and the

paramilitary groups allied with them stood out. According to the Andean Commission of Jurists–Colombian Section (CAJ–SC), of the political murders in which a perpetrator could be identified in 1993, approximately 56 percent were committed by state agents, 12 percent by paramilitary groups allied with them, 25 percent by guerrillas, and 7 percent by private individuals and groups linked to drug-trafficking. Monitors noted an upswing in "social cleansing killings," particularly threats against street children. For instance, between May and September, twelve youths participating in a gang rehabilitation project sponsored by the Cali mayor's office were killed in circumstances that suggested the participation of the police.

This grim picture was challenged by a report issued in June by the Procuraduría, the oversight branch of government, which minimized abuses committed by the state in 1992. Although containing important information and a critical analysis of violations and impunity, the report tended to absolve the military high command, arguing that abuses were committed by middle-level officers acting independently. This claim was difficult to defend given the military's structure and mode of operation. Fifty-eight percent of the approximately 2,600 complaints involved the police. Of those, 60 percent resulted in punitive action. Of the 191 cases involving members of the military, however, only twenty-four resulted in disciplinary action. The Procuraduría attributed this to the "deep-rooted sense of [protecting] the institution. . .which results in a notable lack of solidarity with the investigator, unable to gather information quickly and in confidence because of cover-ups, complicity, or simply the silence of fellow officers."

Specialized army counterinsurgency units continued to commit massive human rights violations, including indiscriminate attacks, bombings, murder, torture, the destruction of property, and arbitrary detention and incarceration. For example, soldiers from Mobile Brigade II detained peasants Armando Pérez Arévalo and José Rodrigo Caro in Los Canelos, Bolívar, on July 2,

accusing them of buying supplies for guerrillas. The next day, townspeople saw the pair in military custody, hooded, and dressed in fatigues. Two days later, a military helicopter brought their bodies to a nearby base; the military claimed they were "guerrillas killed in action."

Mobile brigades were also deployed against civilians engaged in peaceful protest. On September 14, Mobile Brigade II detained approximately 240 Segovia, Antioquia, residents participating in a civic strike, ostensibly to "prevent a disturbance." Held overnight with no shelter from rain, 238 were later released. Community leaders Héctor Múnera López and Joaquín Guillermo Vidales remained in incommunicado detention for several days.

Ties between the army and paramilitary groups remained strong. In November 1992, the Procuraduría issued formal charges against seven senior military officers for their illicit involvement with paramilitary groups in the Santander department. The highest-ranking officer indicted was Brig. Gen. Carlos Gil Colorado, former head of the Fifth Brigade and currently head of intelligence for the army general command.

Public complaints about police abuses reached a peak after a nine-year-old girl was raped and killed inside a Bogotá police station in February. (She was visiting her father, himself a police agent.) That month, the Procuraduría issued indictments against 150 members of the elite Anti-Kidnapping and Extortion Unit (UNASE), including eight police and four army officers, for kidnapping, torture, and disappearance. The Colombian press reported that kidnappers apprehended by UNASE were tortured to reveal the whereabouts of their victims. The kidnappers were then "disappeared" while the UNASE unit collected the ransom. In 1993 a governmental commission was formed to look into charges that members of UNASE, investigating the kidnapping of journalist Jaime Ardila, released in May, were involved with the army in the murder of Gregorio Nieves, an Arsario Indian, and the disappearance of eight others in April.

Three groups that looked into police abuses concluded that major reform was necessary. Perhaps most critical was the report submitted jointly by the Attorney General, Human Rights Ombudsman, Procuraduría and General Comptroller's office (Controlaría General), which called for "demilitarization," an end to the concept of "due obedience" which allows subordinates to claim innocence on the grounds that they were acting on superior orders, and a review of the constitutional provision that police be judged by military courts. Although the police were reorganized in 1993, change fell far short of the kind that would stem the worst abuses.

For their part, guerrillas continued to commit egregious violations of the laws of war, including murder, kidnapping, and attacks on civilian targets like media outlets and public transportation. In July a dissident faction of the Popular Liberation Army (EPL) murdered seventy-year-old priest Javier Cirujano ostensibly in retribution for his role in negotiating an EPL demobilization in 1991. The dissident faction of the EPL continued to target former associates who accepted a government amnesty, particularly in the banana-growing region of Urabá. Guerrillas also killed police captives after disarming and torturing them, as in the case of five Department of Administrative Security officers captured near Tuluá, Cauca, in April. Among the most prominent victims of the guerrilla offensive known as "Black September" was former Conservative senator Faisal Mustafá, shot by the National Liberation Army (ELN) at a political rally in Sucre, Santander, on September 12. Through imprisoned spokesman Francisco Galán, held in a Bogotá jail, the ELN vowed to continue threatening and attacking politicians opposed to renewed peace talks.

Although guerrilla bombings of oil pipelines reportedly dropped significantly compared to 1992—from twenty-four in the first six months of that year to three in the same period in 1993—ecological damage was severe in areas where crude oil spilled into wetlands and rivers.

Impunity remained the principal obstacle to long-term improvement in human rights protection. Despite sometimes vigorous investigative and disciplinary activity by governmental authorities, those who committed abuses were rarely apprehended and punished. Americas Watch knew of few cases in which military courts had sentenced officers or soldiers for human rights abuses, and even fewer for which the punishment was commensurate with the crime. To the contrary, 1993 saw several setbacks for accountability. In April, three Procuraduría delegates, reviewing a case connecting three members of the Army's 10th Airborne Brigade to the 1988 massacre of twenty banana workers on the Honduras and La Negra plantations in Antioquia department, ordered a new inquiry, claiming that the initial investigation—which had resulted in dismissal orders—was poorly conducted and lacked rigorous evidence. Later, the Procuraduría declared the case closed on statute of limitations grounds. One of the officers, Lt. Col. Luis Felipe Becerra Bóhorquez, was implicated during 1993 in the October massacre of thirteen people in Riofrío, Valle, by soldiers under his command. According to an eyewitness, hooded soldiers burst into the Ladino family home, beat family members, raped young women, and then executed them.

In the Urabá case, as in others, Americas Watch noted many instances where the "lack of evidence" rationale was used by the military to clear its members. "Lack of evidence" was also cited in the 1993 acquittal of police and army officers implicated in the disappearance, torture, and murder of twenty-six people from the town of Trujillo, Valle, during 1990, in circumstances that suggested cooperation with local landowners and paramilitaries.

Although the Procuraduría issued charges against two police officers for the 1991 massacre of twenty Páez Indians at El Nilo, Cauca, in July 1993 the two policemen were acquitted, prompting a protest from Colombia's human rights ombudsman. Meanwhile, a parallel investigation by civilian authorities was marred by delays and laxity, including the release of a principal civilian suspect and allegations by court officials that denunciations of the massacre were a guerrilla "show" to defame police.

The record of the Procuraduría's Delegate office for the armed forces was particularly poor in 1993. Repeatedly, cases were shelved or resulted in the acquittal of the soldiers involved. Often decisions were based on cursory investigations, which failed to take into account the testimony of victims or eyewitnesses. When such testimony was included, it was frequently disregarded. Procuraduría delegate César Uribe Botero defended military court jurisdiction to European Community representatives by claiming that without it, "the decisions of ordinary judges could become a tool that destroys the bulwark of democracy, which is the military forces. . .The enemies of the Colombian democratic system will say that there have to be daily dismissals, in order to weaken the army and our pluralistic democracy."

Meanwhile, thousands of other Colombians were charged with terrorism and drug trafficking and brought before "public order" courts in circumstances that violated basic due process rights. These courts, created to protect members of the judiciary from murderous attacks by drug traffickers and insurgents, involved "faceless" judges whose identities had been concealed, as well as secret witnesses and evidence. There was mounting evidence, however, that the public order jurisdiction was being used to suppress nonviolent social protest and to imprison peasants living in areas where the guerrillas were active. Among the most serious misapplications of the public order jurisdiction in 1993 involved thirteen members of the state telecommunications union (Telecom), imprisoned for participating in a 1992 strike. Although the workers were originally charged with sabotage amounting to "terrorism," the case was transferred to the ordinary justice system later in the year and the workers provisionally released in early November. The Telecom case had been the subject of broad national and international protest.

A study by the CAJ–SC found that many other cases referred to the public order courts were based on unsubstantiated and unsigned "intelligence reports" provided by the security forces, or evidence that had been falsified; because evidence was kept secret, the defense could not object to its use in court. Often the very poor were being tried without legal representation. Americas Watch received numerous reports indicating that defendants often underwent brutal treatment at the hands of their captors, including prolonged incommunicado detention, torture, and death threats. Despite obvious injustices, the Constitutional Court upheld the public order jurisdiction in March.

In a ruling criticized by the Gaviria administration, the Constitutional Court declared on August 3 that detainees held for "public order" crimes could not be deprived of conditional liberty for more than six months. Rather than permit a release of the 1,600 to 2,000 prisoners affected, however, President César Gaviria issued an emergency decree giving judges an additional period of time to rule on the charges. A law subsequently passed by Congress limited the period of investigation to six months.

The "state of internal commotion" invoked by President Gaviria in November 1992, ostensibly to combat Colombia's approximately 7,000 guerrillas, was renewed three times at ninety-day intervals during 1993 and remained in effect through November. While a number of the approximately forty emergency measures imposed by the executive were overturned by the Constitutional Court, others, including the executive's power to suspend local officials who hold unauthorized talks with the guerrillas and a prohibition on live broadcasts of guerrilla actions or interviews with the insurgents, were upheld.

In 1993, the Gaviria government resubmitted to the Congress a bill to regulate states of exception, criticized strongly by human rights groups and the human rights ombudsman, who termed it a "veiled prolongation of the situation of juridical abnormality." Although the congress removed some objectionable provisions, others were allowed, among them the security forces' right to carry out searches, detentions, and interceptions of communications without judicial warrant. Limitations on individual freedom and enhanced powers to a military establishment already renowned for brutality posed dangerous threats to Colombian democracy.

In addition, Congress upheld restrictions on the media and granted the President the power to modify definitions of crimes and penalties, used in April to double the maximum sentence for terrorism from thirty to sixty years. Concentrating extraordinary powers in the executive, this provision could allow the President to redefine crimes such as "rebellion" to cover not only armed revolt but also a broad range of activities considered "subversive" by the government.

The climate of war made it difficult to renew peace negotiations with guerrillas, strongly opposed by leading military commanders. Tirso Vélez, a poet and mayor of Tibú, Norte de Santander, was investigated for possible ties with guerrillas at the behest of the army after publishing a poem calling for peace and understanding between insurgents and soldiers. A fitful dialogue between the government and the Socialist Renovation Current (CRS), a dissident faction of the ELN, was abruptly suspended in late September following the murder of two CRS spokespersons in circumstances that suggested official complicity.

Drug kingpin Pablo Escobar remained a fugitive despite repeated claims by the government that his capture was imminent. In an effort to intimidate his pursuers, Escobar apparently ordered the killings of scores of policemen and random bombings in urban areas, one of which took fifteen lives in Bogotá in April. In response, a group known as "People Persecuted by Pablo Escobar" (Pepes) claimed credit for the murder of several Escobar henchmen and five former Escobar lawyers. Police in Medellín were also accused of carrying out random vengeance killings of young men in the city's poor slums, where the drug mafias recruited their irregular troops.

The Right to Monitor

Verbal and physical attacks on human rights monitors continued in 1993, born of the military's conviction that human rights advocacy equals subversion and the complete impunity for previous attacks on human rights activists. This attitude was encapsulated by a statement by Gen. Ramón Emilio Gil Bermúdez, Commander of the Military Forces, who described the activities of one Colombian human rights monitor in exile as part of an international campaign waged by guerrillas. General Harold Bedoya, commander of the army's Second Division, brought a charge of slander against the Permanent Committee for Human Rights and fifty other prominent human rights figures after the publication of an August communiqué calling for the release of trade unionists.

Four days before an April peace seminar he helped organize was scheduled to begin in Villavicencio, Meta, Delio Vargas, a human rights activist and coordinator of an association of internal refugees, was disappeared in circumstances that suggested the involvement of the security forces. The Regional Committee for the Defense of Human Rights (Credhos) in Barrancabermeja, Santander, continued to be the object of threats and harassment by the army's Nueva Granada Battalion.

Lawyers who prosecuted high-profile human rights cases or represented clients before the public order courts were also threatened. Rafael Barrios Mendivil, president of the "José Alvear Restrepo" Lawyers' Collective, was harassed and followed by members of the police, army, and state security agents and received numerous telephone death threats; he was counsel in the 1991 Los Uvos case involving the massacre of seventeen civilians, and in the El Nilo case involving the murder of twenty Páez Indians in December 1991. Dr. Eduardo Umaña Mendoza also received numerous telephone death threats after assuming the defense of the thirteen Telecom workers.

Guerrillas staged several attacks against journalists in 1993 for articles critical of guerrilla actions. In March, the ELN took responsibility for the murder of journalist and newspaper editor Eustorgio Colmenares, who had written about the guerrillas in the Cúcuta-based *La Opinión* newspaper. According to the newsweekly *Semana*, Colmenares was the hundredth journalist killed in four years of political violence and the first murdered by guerrillas. Journalist Jaime Ardila of *El Espacio* was kidnapped by guerrillas in April and remained in captivity for over a month.

U.S. Policy

Apart from the State Department's annual *Country Reports on Human Rights Practices*, no public statements were made during 1993 by U.S. Embassy officials concerning human rights. Although the Colombia chapter of the *Country Reports* issued in January did affirm that the security forces were responsible, in 1992, "for significant numbers of abuses," the main culprits were said to be guerrillas and drug traffickers. In addition, the Colombia chapter claimed that drug traffickers disseminated "false information about official human rights abuses," a claim that, while possibly true, did nothing to acknowledge or explain the high number of abuses by official forces documented by respected human rights groups.

The drug war continued to be the prime focus of U.S. policy, although the Clinton administration's strategy for narcotics control remained murky throughout the year. In what may mark a significant shift, the Defense Department's *Congressional Presentation for Security Assistance Programs* for fiscal year 1994 listed support for "counter-insurgency/counter-narcotics efforts" as the principal U.S. military assistance objective. Previously, the U.S. government had redirected resources away from the Colombian army to the police because the army was seen as uninterested in narcotics control efforts. Pentagon officials explained to Americas Watch that U.S. assistance programs were still dedicated to counter-narcotics purposes and not counterinsurgency. But the distinction may not be relevant given the Pentagon's

assessment that Colombia's two largest guerrilla groups have "evolved into criminal organizations, heavily involved in narcotics trafficking."

Although it represented a decrease compared to 1992, Colombia received an estimated $28.2 million in grants and loans under the Foreign Military Financing (FMF) and International Military Education and Training (IMET) programs in fiscal year 1993, more than any other Latin American country. Colombia also continued to head the list of numbers of students trained under IMET, a distinction it had held since fiscal year 1984. In fiscal year 1994, Colombia was again slated to receive more military aid than any other Latin nation, $32 million in FMF and IMET, or about half of proposed U.S. military aid to all of Latin America. An additional $25 million was requested for narcotics control programs run by the State Department. According to the department, approximately three-fourths of the fiscal year 1993 and 1994 aid was destined for the police.

Human rights controls over the disbursement of aid continued to be lax or nonexistent. According to a U.S. Government Accounting Office (GAO) report in August, U.S. officials had not developed procedures to determine whether U.S. aid went to Colombian units involved in human rights abuses, and end-use monitoring of equipment was inadequate. Moreover, GAO investigators found two instances in which Colombian security force officers who had allegedly committed human rights abuses came from units that received U.S. aid.

The Agency for International Development, funding a six-year, $36-million program for judicial reform, pointed repeatedly to the high conviction rate of the public order courts as a sign of improvement in civilian control of drug trafficking and terrorism, downplaying or ignoring the serious violations of due process inherent in their operation as well as the misuse of the public order jurisdiction. In interviews with Americas Watch early in the year, U.S. Embassy officials insisted that public order courts performed better on due process issues than ordinary courts, and defended the extension of their jurisdiction to cases such as that of the Telecom workers.

Out of growing concern for the human rights situation in Colombia, the U.S. Congress for the first time placed Colombia on the list of countries subject to special conditions for the disbursement of aid. Upon adopting conditionality, the Senate referred to a record "tarnished by continuing human rights abuses on a large scale" and expressed concern for the lack of access of the International Committee of the Red Cross to military and police detention facilities.

The Work of Americas Watch

Americas Watch expanded its focus on violations of the laws of war in Colombia, in view of the breakdown of the peace talks between the government and the insurgents and the sharp escalation of the war effort. A report on human rights violations committed by the Mobile Brigades, specialized counterinsurgency units, was due to be published in December, focusing on abuses by both the army and guerrillas. Research for this report led to a discovery of new cases of abuse in Colombia's public order court jurisdiction, which continued to be a central focus of investigation and advocacy. A Spanish translation of our 1992 report was released in March 1993, and rose to a place on Colombia's best-seller list.

Americas Watch registered frequent protests with Colombian government officials about the flood of human rights violations throughout the year. Together with the CAJ–SC and the Center for Justice and International Law (CEJIL), Americas Watch continued to represent past victims of abuses by pressing cases before the Inter-American Commission on Human Rights. One such case, the 1989 disappearance of rural teacher Isidro Caballero, came before the Inter-American Court of Human Rights during 1993, the first adversarial case against Colombia to be heard by that Court. Americas Watch representatives made two visits to Colombia during the year, meeting with Colombian and U.S. officials, human rights groups, and political and community leaders. In Washington, Americas Watch representatives focused on bringing Colombia's serious human rights situation to the attention of the U.S. Congress and pressed for human rights conditionally on U.S. aid. Americas Watch also participated in an ongoing dialogue with the Clinton administration and other human rights groups about U.S. funding for the public order courts.

Americas Watch invited Sister Nohemy Palencia, of the Civic Committee for Human Rights, in Meta, to be honored by Human Rights Watch at its observance of Human Rights Day, December 10.

CUBA

Human Rights Developments

In 1993, the Cuban government made a few important human rights gestures. It released a number of political prisoners before the end of their terms, in advance of the World Human Rights Conference in Vienna in June. It also slightly relaxed the travel restrictions on some former political prisoners and other dissidents. At least two were allowed to travel to the U.S. and return to Cuba, and others were permitted to leave permanently. Travel limits for the population as a whole also were reduced. There were fewer reports of mobs beating dissidents and vandalizing their homes in state-directed attacks; and while individual government critics continued to be fired from their jobs, there were fewer reports of mass expulsions.

Still, the thirty-five-year-old government of Fidel Castro only modified some of its behavior, without altering the laws that legalized and provided impunity for rights abuses.

The authorities continued to take legal and extra-legal reprisals against their opponents and critics, especially lesser-known human rights monitors and peaceful pro-democracy activists. Many peaceful dissenters continue to languish in prison serving some of the stiffest prison sentences for thought crimes in the last ten years. Cubans still must request permission from their government to leave their own country temporarily or permanently. Cuba continued to lack the laws and institutions that would protect civil and political rights on a permanent basis. There was no free press. The state continued to own all media. Speech was curbed by laws banning "enemy propaganda" and "clandestine printing." Dissidents were imprisoned on charges as serious as "rebellion." For offending the President, Cubans could be jailed for three years.

There were no legally recognized civic or political organizations independent of the government or Communist Party. Human rights and pro-democracy groups were denied official recognition. Free association and assembly were punished under laws prohibiting "illegal association" and "public disorder." There were no free and fair elections.

Cuban courts remained subordinate to the executive, and Cuban law dictated that judges must demonstrate their "active revolutionary integration." Due process was flouted, and defendants, especially in political cases, were almost always convicted.

Prison inmates—both political and common prisoners—reported that nonviolent protests such as hunger strikes spawned retaliation in the form of beatings, confinement in harsh punishment cells, denial of medical attention and relocation to prisons far from their families. Prisoners complained of inadequate food, unsanitary conditions, overcrowding, and insufficient or lack of time outdoors.

Violation of the right to privacy was systematic. Tight political control was maintained through extensive monitoring of Cubans' daily lives, conducted by state-security police who often coerced or blackmailed people into becoming informants, as well as by state-sponsored "mass organizations" such as the Committees for the Defense of the Revolution (CDRs), which operated in neighborhoods and workplaces.

Mass organizations, together with state-

security police, staged protests against "counter-revolutionaries" in ostensibly spontaneous "acts of repudiation." Mobs typically chanted slogans and often assaulted dissidents, defacing or destroying their homes. "Rapid-action brigades"—state-organized gangs of vigilantes—were deployed to crush forcibly any signs of popular discontent.

The loss of trade and subsidies from the former Soviet Bloc combined with the long-term U.S. blockade, had plunged Cuba into its most severe economic crisis since the 1959 revolution. Food rationing was tightened during 1993; transportation was drastically curtailed by a severe fuel shortage; electricity blackouts occurred regularly.

Extreme shortages and blackouts gave rise to unrest, including stone- or bottle-throwing anti-government protests, and increased crime. In response, in 1993 the government called on the population, including the brutal rapid-action brigades, to participate in its anti-crime campaign. According to the Communist Party daily, *Granma*, "delinquents and anti-social elements who try to create disorder and an atmosphere of mistrust and impunity in our society will receive a crushing reply from the people," as reported by Reuters on September 8.

Rights monitors reported the increased invocation of the "dangerousness" provision of the penal code in the context of the anti-crime campaign. Cuban law provided for the application of preventive measures, including imprisonment, against those who conducted themselves in a manner that contradicted "socialist morality," even without having committed a crime. Some fourteen anti-government activists were said to have been arrested in mid- to late-1993; some of them were held under the "dangerousness" provision, while others were charged with offenses that on their face violated internationally recognized standards of freedom of expression and association.

While the Cuban government considerably reduced travel limitations for the population in general, significant restrictions that ran contrary to international norms on freedom of movement remained. The extralegal harassment that once accompanied procedural requirements to leave the country by those who were stigmatized as "disaffected," reportedly diminished significantly. The growing number of *lancheros*, or boat people, who fled to the U.S.—more than 1,100 by mid-year—was caused less by Cuban restrictions than by the difficulty of obtaining U.S. visas. Still, Cubans were required to seek permission from their government to leave and return to their country—an inherent limitation—and those who wished to travel had to be age twenty-years-old and over. Those caught attempting to leave the country in makeshift vessels could expect to be detained for a period of time by state security police. Repeat offenders were likely to serve one year in prison.

In addition, the Cuban government continued to deny permission to travel to those with whom it might have a political quarrel. For example, Yara Silva Urquiza Bustamante, the thirteen-year-old daughter of Lissette Bustamante, a prominent journalist who defected to Spain in 1992, was refused permission to leave Cuba. In October 1993, prize-winning writer Norberto Fuentes was arrested for trying to leave the country illegally by boat after repeatedly being denied permission to travel.

Several shooting incidents were reported in mid-1993 involving people fleeing the country. On July 1, Cuban Coast Guards shot and killed three Cubans at the coastal town of Cojimar after they boarded a speedboat that had come from Florida to collect them. This was one of at least three incidents in which Cuban exiles in the U.S. attempted to bring back family members in boats and were captured by Cuban authorities for entering Cuban waters illegally. Around the same time, the U.S. State Department reported shooting and grenade-throwing by Cuban border guards against Cubans swimming to the U.S naval base at Guantánamo to seek asylum. According to the U.S. government, four Cubans were killed in two incidents at the end of June.

In a welcome development, in 1993 the Cuban government released several well-known political prisoners, including María Elena Cruz Varela, a prominent poet arrested in 1991 and sentenced to two years in prison for "illegal association" and "defamation of state institutions"; José Luis Pujol, a dissident arrested in 1992 and sentenced to a three-year prison term on charges of offending the government; and Marco Antonio Abad and Jorge Crespo, who were arrested in 1991 and sentenced to two-year prison terms for offending the president and spreading "enemy propaganda" in a film they made.

Despite having released some political prisoners, Cuban authorities continue to harass, arrest and imprison its critics and opponents. Rafael Gutiérrez Santos, an independent labor activist, was detained for six months in the first half of the year by state security police for alleged crimes against the security of the state. His arrest followed an announcement of the formation of the National Commission of Independent Unions. Other members of this group reportedly received official warnings from the police not to pursue their activities.

Guillermo Fernández Donate, of the Socialist Democratic Current, reportedly was arrested by state security police in mid-year for possessing "enemy propaganda." Over the last year, Fernández, also a member of the Cuban Committee for Human Rights, and his wife, Eurídice Sotolongo Losada, lost their jobs in a state architecture firm because of his opposition activities.

Domiciano Torres of the Democratic Civic Party, a pro-democracy group, was detained in August by state security police who beat him severely at the time of his arrest. Torres, a professor of architecture who lost his job in 1992 because of his dissident activities, reportedly faced charges of spreading "enemy propaganda." After being held for forty-two days by State Security, he was reportedly transferred to the Havana Psychiatric Hospital, a form of harassment commonly inflicted on jailed dissidents.

Rolando Roque Malherbe of the Cuban Civic Current, a pro-democracy group, was summoned for questioning by the police and the local CDR on September 23, the day before a party at his home in Havana, to which he had invited dissidents and diplomats. On September 24, plainclothes police surrounded Roque's home and prevented his guests from entering. Roque remained in detention until September 27. A prominent physicist, Roque lost his job in 1992 after signing an open letter to the participants in that year's Iberoamerican Summit in Spain calling on them to press the Cuban government to respect human rights.

Félix Bonne Carcasés of the Cuban Civic Current was held for three weeks in October by the Department of Technical Investigations in Havana. His arrest followed a search by state-security police, who confiscated some documents. Bonne, an electrical engineer, had also lost his job after signing the letter to the Iberoamerican Summit.

Pro-democracy advocates who continued to languish in prison included Yndamiro Restano of the Harmony Movement (MAR), who was arrested in Havana in 1991 and convicted with María Elena Aparicio, another MAR member, on charges of rebellion. They were serving terms of ten and seven years, respectively. Omar del Pozo, of the nongovernmental group National Civic Union, was tried in a military court in Havana in August 1992 along with three others including one state security agent. He was convicted of spreading "enemy propaganda" reportedly because he received information from the state security officer, and was sentenced to fifteen years in jail.

The Right to Monitor

Human rights monitoring continued to be illegal in Cuba. Despite numerous petitions for official recognition submitted to the Ministry of Justice by the various groups currently attempting to function in Cuba, none gained legal status. Laws restricting free expression and association, combined with near-constant surveillance by the state-security police, ensured that human rights monitoring was frequently punished.

Cuban rights activists were routinely harassed, questioned, and threatened by the security police, and often arrested. Since 1989, Cuban authorities have made hundreds of arrests of human rights monitors and pro-human rights political activists. During 1993 dozens were believed to be serving prison terms of up to fifteen years for their peaceful advocacy. Scores of others had been subjected to government-sponsored acts of repudiation and beatings by plainclothes state agents.

Security police frequently searched the homes of human rights monitors, confiscating typewriters, tape recorders and documents. Many activists had been fired from their jobs. They had been prevented from or pressured into leaving the country.

Rodolfo González González, a leading member of the Cuban Committee for Human Rights, was arrested at home by security police during the December 10 Human Rights Day crackdown on activists in 1992. He was being held in Guanajay prison in Havana and, after ten months, continued to await trial.

Amador Blanco Hernández of the José Martí National Commission on Human Rights was arrested at his home in Caibarién, Villa Clara province, also on December 10, 1992. Another member of the group, Joel Mesa Morales, was arrested in January 1993. Blanco and Mesa were tried in September 1993 on charges of spreading "enemy propaganda" and were sentenced to prison terms of eight and seven years, respectively.

On May 1, 1993, May Day, after attending mass at a Havana church, some fifty activists were attacked by scores of plainclothes police and "rapid response brigades" as they marched silently down the street carrying a Cuban flag. The marchers were beaten with pipes and clubs. César Guerra Pérez, Armando Sánchez and at least six others were reported to have been bloodied in the attack. The night before the attack, police arrested two organizers of the march, Paula Valiente and Juan Guarino. On May 17, they were each sentenced to a two-year suspended sentence on charges of inciting crime. Valiente was reportedly briefly detained on July 8 for planning another peaceful procession. Guarino was reportedly rearrested in September.

Others remained in prison, such as Sebastián Arcos, a leading member of the Cuban Committee for Human Rights who was arrested by state security police in January 1992 and sentenced (for spreading "enemy propaganda") to a prison term of four years and eight months. Luis Alberto Pita Santos, head of the Association of Defenders of Political Rights, who had been imprisoned since October 1991, was convicted on charges of offending the head of state, "clandestine printing," and "illegal association." He was sentenced to a five-year term. After reportedly spending seven months in an isolation cell in Boniato prison in Santiago de Cuba, Pita was moved to Kilo-8 prison in Camagüey, where he was said to have been beaten and, during the day, chained at the ankles for protesting his continued incarceration.

Pablo Reyes Martínez of the National Civic Union was arrested in 1992 and convicted of spreading "enemy propaganda." He was sentenced to eight years in prison for reporting on human rights abuses by phone for an exile radio station in the U.S.

The Right to Monitor

International human rights monitoring was severely curtailed after a brief opening in 1988 when Cuba was under international pressure to allow prison inspections by international organizations. Despite repeated requests, Americas Watch still did not receive permission from the Cuban government to conduct the kind of open investigation it undertakes routinely elsewhere in the region. Over the years, members of the Americas Watch board and staff have been allowed access to Cuba only under the auspices of other U.S. organizations.

For the second consecutive year, the Cuban government refused to cooperate with the resolutions adopted by the U.N. Commission on Human Rights, which provided for a special rapporteur to investigate human rights conditions in Cuba and report his findings to the commission. The Cuban government's 1988 agreement with the International Committee of the Red Cross granting access to Cuban prisons and political prisoners remained suspended, having been broken by the Cuban government in 1990.

U.S. Policy

The United States imposed a trade embargo against the government of Fidel Castro at the height of the Cold War, more than three decades ago. In 1992, three years after the demise of the Soviet Bloc, President Bush signed into law the Cuban Democracy Act, which expanded the embargo with the intent to speed the collapse of the Castro government and foster democracy.

While some saw the hostile U.S. posture towards Cuba as a way to pressure the Cuban government to initiate democratic reform, others considered it an excuse for the Cuban government to crack down on internal democracy advocates and deny civil and political rights. Americas Watch objected to aspects of U.S. policy that impeded human contacts by maintaining restrictions on travel by U.S. citizens and on telephone communications.

Under the 1975 Helsinki Final Act and successive accords reached by the Conference on Security and Cooperation in Europe (CSCE), the U.S. vowed to lift limits on "human contacts," including bans on travel and telephone communications. The principles set forth in the instruments clearly favored the removal of any barrier on such contacts raised by a CSCE government in its relations with other nations.

During 1993, the embargo allowed U.S. citizens to travel to Cuba, but prohibited them from spending money without permission from the U.S. Treasury Department. For defying the embargo, a U.S. citizen could be prosecuted for trading with the enemy, jailed for up to twelve years and fined up to $500,000 for corporations, and $250,000 for individuals. The Treasury Department was authorized to impose a civil penalty of up to $50,000 on violators of the Cuban Democracy Act.

Fines could not be levied against four categories of visitors to Cuba: U.S. government officials; family members with relatives in Cuba; academics, researchers with Cuba-specific expertise, and religious groups; and journalists. All other Americans traveling to Cuba were required to be guests of the Cuban government.

The Clinton administration embraced the Cuban Democracy Act but began to interpret its provisions in a way that, despite the restrictions enshrined in the law, would allow it slightly to increase human contacts. Since 1988, Americans who have been permitted to import books, films, records and art from Cuba, have been barred from traveling there to conduct business. In 1993, the administration allowed an American poster-art importer to spend money on travel to Cuba after years of repeated Treasury Department denials. However, the administration refused permission to a group of U.S. mathematicians to participate in an internationally sponsored conference in Havana in September 1993.

The embargo impeded telephone communications between Cubans and Americans by blocking payment of monies owed to Cuba that had been held in escrow for three decades. In 1993, the Cuban government announced that it was reducing the number of phone calls it would complete to and from the U.S. to a tiny fraction of normal demand. This may have been an effort to force U.S. callers to connect with Cuba via Canada, where phone companies paid Cuba its share of revenues. In response, while the U.S. banned the re-selling of calls through Canada in July, it issued new guidelines that could increase direct links to Cuba.

The administration lifted the limits on circuits between the U.S. and Cuba, and permitted U.S. long-distance companies to offer Cuba 50 percent of revenues for completing calls—most of which were billed in the U.S. However, it refused to allow Cuba access to the approximately $80 million that remained in a blocked account. The Cuban government rejected the U.S. offer.

The U.S. continued to fund TV-Martí,

the U.S. Information Agency's (USIA) television broadcast to Cuba, even though its transmissions had been successfully blocked by Havana and could not be seen in Cuba. The Cuban government retaliated by blocking the USIA's medium-wave radio broadcasts to Cuba, the widely-heard Radio Martí, which thereafter could be heard mainly on short-wave only. In 1993, the U.S. House of Representatives voted to stop funding both TV- and Radio Martí; the Senate voted to renew funding for both. As of early November, the matter was still undecided.

To its credit, the Bush administration's State Department once again produced a solid human rights report on Cuba. Its *Country Reports on Human Rights Practices for 1992* provided a largely accurate account of violations in Cuba, and was notable for the abundance of cases and issues it addresses in detail.

The U.S. delegation again led the campaign to censure Cuba at the United Nations Human Rights Commission (UNHRC) meetings in Geneva during the spring of 1993. Headed by Richard Schifter, the U.S. delegation balanced its initiative on Cuba with forceful efforts against other violator countries and avoided the ideologically-charged confrontations of past sessions. The 1993 UNHRC resolution on Cuba extended the mandate of the special rapporteur for another year. Again, the Cuban government quickly announced that Cuba would not cooperate with the rapporteur.

Mr. Carl Johan Groth of Sweden, named rapporteur by U.N. Secretary-General Boutros Boutros-Ghali in 1992, accepted the post for another year. Despite the fact that Mr. Groth had been denied permission to visit Cuba in 1992, he presented a report to the commission in February 1993 that reflected the broad range of concerns of Cuban human rights monitors while being thorough and balanced.

The Work of Americas Watch

Americas Watch published a lengthy newsletter on Cuba in February, "Perfecting the System of Control, Human Rights Violations in Castro's 34th Year," which covered the period January 1992 to February 1993. The release of the newsletter was timed to coincide with the meeting of the U.N. Commission on Human Rights in Geneva. In September 1993, Americas Watch met with the U.N. special rapporteur on Cuba.

EL SALVADOR

Human Rights Developments

The human rights situation deteriorated markedly in the second year since the signing of the January 1992 peace accord. By the end of 1993, politically motivated extralegal executions and death threats were on the rise and what the United Nations Observer Mission for El Salvador (ONUSAL) called "irregular groups" resembling death squads were once again responsible for violent murders.

The month of October alone witnessed the murder of four former combatants of the Farabundo Martí National Liberation Front (FMLN), two of them high-ranking. On October 25, FMLN leader Francisco Velis Castellanos was shot in San Salvador as he left his young daughter at a day-care center. Velis, an alternate candidate for the Legislative Assembly, was the highest-ranking FMLN leader killed since the advent of formal peace. Eight days later, former senior guerrilla leader Eleno Hernán Castro, a member of the FMLN's land commission, was murdered in San Vicente province. According to the Catholic church, two other ex-combatants, a married couple, were murdered in late October. In early November, local FMLN leader Gabriel Quintanilla was shot at close range in San Miguel and critically wounded, and the body of another ex-combatant was found stuffed in a garbage can in San Salvador.

The quickened pace of political murder posed a threat to the legitimacy of March 1994 presidential, legislative, and municipal elections, the first in which the FMLN was due to participate as a political force. In addition, the refusal of the government to undertake structural reforms to improve the administration of justice, so that crimes would be investigated and punished, became all the more critical in light of ONUSAL's plan to depart from El Salvador following the 1994 elections.

Continuing abuses, some of them serious and systematic, reflected the historical failure of El Salvador's judicial system to prosecute those responsible for human rights crimes. In 1993, however, there were dramatic attempts to challenge impunity. The United Nations-brokered peace accord established two commissions, one (the Truth Commission) to investigate past acts of violence and make recommendations for the future and another (the Ad Hoc Commission) to review the records of military officers in order to purge those involved in corruption and wanton violence. The findings of both commissions made human rights in El Salvador the subject of broad national and international debate. They also underscored the resistance of key Salvadoran military officers and civilian elites to making structural changes that would help institutionalize improvements in the respect for human rights.

In mid-March, the Truth Commission issued *From Madness to Hope: The Twelve-Year War in El Salvador*. The report examined assassinations, disappearances, and massacres attributed to official forces and death squads, and murders and kidnappings attributed to the FMLN. Renowned cases such as the 1980 murder of Archbishop Oscar Romero, the 1981 army massacre at El Mozote, and the rebel kidnapping and murder of municipal officials in the mid-1980s were examined in great detail alongside several other major cases that had never been publicized. A full 85 percent of the cases denounced to the Truth Commission were ascribed to state agents, paramilitary groups, or death squads allied with official forces. Five percent of the cases were attributed to the FMLN.

The commission's report also identified by name over forty military officers and eleven members of the FMLN responsible for ordering, carrying out, or covering up abuses and suggested that those named be banned from holding public office for ten years. (In mid-October, U.N. Secretary-General Boutros Boutros-Ghali reported that eight military officers, two judges, and one forensic doctor named by the commission still retained their posts.) The commission also made detailed recommendations for judicial reform, and cited the "tremendous responsibility" of the judicial branch for impunity in calling for the resignation of the entire Supreme Court. In perhaps its most spectacular finding, the Truth Commission named Minister of Defense René Emilio Ponce as having ordered the 1989 murders of six Jesuit priests, their housekeeper and her daughter. Previous investigations had involved Ponce and other officers in the planning of the Jesuit murders, but had not traced the direct order to the defense minister himself.

Military officers, conservative politicians, and government officials vehemently repudiated the report, a reaction stemming principally from its thoroughness in documenting official abuses. In an attempt to limit the impact of the report and prevent a full reckoning with its findings, President Alfredo Cristiani asked for an "immediate, general, and total amnesty" on the eve of the report's release. Within days, the Salvadoran Legislative Assembly, over the objections of the FMLN and opposition parties, passed a "broad, absolute, and unconditional amnesty" for political as well as most common crimes. As a result, those jailed in even the most notorious cases, including the Jesuit murders and the 1991 FMLN murders of two wounded U.S. servicemen, went free. The amnesty and its guarantee of impunity emboldened would-be killers to continue their murderous campaigns.

The Truth Commission was instrumental, however, in furthering the government's compliance with the recommendations of the Ad Hoc Commission for a purge of 103 officers, including the minister and vice-minister of Defense. President Cristiani failed to carry out the purge in late December 1992, transferring rather than dismissing seven senior officers and allowing another eight, including Ponce, to retain their posts. U.N. Secretary-General Boutros-Ghali stated in early January 1993 that the government's actions were "not in compliance" with the peace accord.

Once the findings of the Truth Commission regarding Ponce's involvement in the Jesuit murders were known, however, pressures mounted for his removal. Ponce publicly offered his resignation several days before the Truth Commission report's release. Not until July 1993 did he and several others step down from their posts.

Other aspects of the peace accord touching on human rights issues presented a similarly mixed picture in 1993. New units of the National Civilian Police (PNC) had replaced the National Police in five of El Salvador's fourteen departments by early November. But the U.N. noted on several occasions that the ranks of the existing National Police "increased significantly" rather than being reduced. Particularly troubling was the incorporation into the National Police of former personnel from the National Guard and Treasury Police, two security forces that were abolished because of their notorious involvement in human rights abuses. Members of the army's dissolved rapid reaction battalions, whose human rights record was similarly tarnished, were also incorporated into the National Police. These transfers represented a flagrant violation of the peace accord. The new PNC, meanwhile, continued to suffer from inadequate domestic and international funding, even while the Salvadoran government continued to direct new resources to the existing National Police. The appointment of a former military officer to the second-ranking post at the PNC also had the potential to undercut the peace accord's intention that it function as an entirely new security body.

In addition, President Cristiani announced in July his decision to deploy 3,000 army soldiers along the highways for an indefinite period of time, supposedly to fight common crime. Opinion polls showed that the Salvadoran public perceived there to be an increase in crime, and that fears for personal security ranked at the top of citizens' concerns. ONUSAL reported in May that a review of crime statistics "[does] not indicate a dramatic increase in common crime" even though figures for later in the year did show a rise.

Regardless of common crime, the deployment of the army for internal security functions contradicted provisions of the peace accord separating the military from the police and limiting the army's role strictly to matters of external defense. Americas Watch was also concerned that the government's dwelling on the issue of delinquency was intended to play on public fears, thereby generating support for a continued military role in strictly police matters. Moreover, we shared the fear expressed by ONUSAL as well as opposition forces that generalized violence could "become a front behind which serious violations of human rights, such as political murders, masquerade as ordinary crimes."

While government compliance with human rights provisions of the peace accord left numerous gaps, the FMLN also undercut the accord in ways that potentially jeopardized its full political participation. In May 1993 an arms cache in Managua, Nicaragua accidentally exploded. A subsequent investigation revealed that it belonged to the Fuerzas Populares de Liberación (FPL), one of the five groups composing the FMLN. Over the next several months, all five of the FMLN's constituent groups admitted to having over 114 other arms caches in and outside El Salvador. The existence of the weapons depots demonstrated that the FMLN had lied to the United Nations when it claimed to have fully disarmed late last year and to have turned over its arsenals for destruction.

The U.N. Security Council called the existence of the arms caches "the most serious violation to date" of the peace accord, and inside El Salvador there were calls for the FMLN's cancellation or suspension as a political party. A second process of verification and destruction of weapons belonging to the FMLN was completed in mid-August, but not after a serious breach of trust in the FMLN's commitment to peaceful political participation.

The climate for the 1994 elections was further marred by the government's failure to expedite the issuing of voter registration cards for 27 percent of El Salvador's potential voters, approximately 786,000 people. (The Supreme Electoral Tribunal was dominated by the right-wing ruling party.) Following an August freeze of $70 million in U.S. Economic Support Funds by the chairman of a congressional subcommittee, the pace of registration picked up. In October, members of ONUSAL's elections division expressed optimism that 90 percent of potential voters could be registered by the deadline of November 20. It remained to be seen whether that goal would be met, or whether the 1994 elections would fall short of their intended role as the culmination of the peace process.

The consolidation of democracy and the expansion of political participation were also undermined by the quickening pace of human rights violations as the year drew to a close. ONUSAL's eighth report issued in November, as well as reports by the newly-created office of the human rights ombudsman (Procuraduría para la Defensa de los Derechos Humanos), noted an increase in violations of the right to life, including outright assassinations and death threats. ONUSAL said in November that admissible denunciations of "deaths as a result of the violation of judicial guarantees and arbitrary or extralegal executions" had increased by 30 percent over the previous three-month reporting period. It noted as a positive development that there had been no forced disappearances during a thirteen-month period beginning in mid-1992 but also indicated an increase in arbitrary executions, not all of them political, as well as a handful of cases of torture. The ombudsman's office likewise signaled in October that "organized violence in the political arena" was worsening the situation of public security.

In July, ONUSAL engaged in a public dispute with Salvadoran human rights groups over the number of killings that could be attributed to death squads. ONUSAL's human rights division stated that several cases denounced by the archdiocese of San Salvador's human rights office, Tutela Legal, as having been committed by death squads were, in fact, common crimes without political motivation. At the same time, ONUSAL verified that certain homicides "involv[ed] methods and procedures similar to those which, in the past, were used by the death squads."

ONUSAL underscored that drawing the line between criminal and political acts was difficult when the government failed to investigate violent deaths. In fact, throughout 1993 the government failed to launch an investigation of death squad violence as recommended by the Truth Commission. By its October report, ONUSAL became less circumspect regarding death squad responsibility for murders, saying that it could not "rule out that former members of irregular groups like those who operated in the 1980s" were involved in violent deaths of unidentified individuals. ONUSAL also issued more frequent and prompt denunciations of individual cases, a positive development that helped generate pressure to resolve them.

The reports of ONUSAL's human rights division, issued at more frequent intervals than in the past, highlighted the persistence of:

· acts of "organized violence" carried out by ex-members of the armed forces and National Police;

· military personnel involvement in ordinary crime, in which some of the victims were members of the FMLN;

· abductions carried out by "irregular groups organized for that purpose" possibly involving security forces personnel;

· severe beatings and mistreatment of prisoners at the hands of the security forces, even though torture was not practiced on a systematic or massive scale;

· former FMLN compatants' participation in organized criminal bands;

· the murder of several former members of military intelligence, including those who had begun to share information with human rights groups.

It was difficult to see how these problems might be contained or eliminated as long as impunity remained the norm, and as long as the judicial system continued to fail at every level in the investigation and prosecution of crimes.

Given the history of political killings in El Salvador, and in light of the upcoming elections, Americas Watch was especially alarmed by several targeted attacks during the year. On May 20, 1993, the National Police opened fire on a peaceful demonstration by disabled veterans from both the armed forces and the FMLN, killing José Santos Martínez Pérez, a nineteen-year-old amputee. An investigating judge ordered the detention of police agent Alberto Ponce Zúñiga, but as of November, the leadership of the National Police had not turned him over to judicial authorities.

Moreover, in May, Gregorio Mejía Espinoza, secretary of the social-democratic Popular Social Christian Movement (MPSC), was abducted, tortured, and interrogated about the activities of the opposition Democratic Convergence, of which the MPSC is a member. (The Democratic Convergence was running a joint presidential ticket with the FMLN.) Mejía saved himself from execution when he jumped out of a vehicle into a ravine, thereby eluding his captors. He had previously received death threats. In June, Héctor Silva, another leading member of the Democratic Convergence, was attacked by a gunman who fired at him and his daughter as they were jogging in a Santa Tecla neighborhood. In early September, First Criminal

Court Judge Francisco Pléitez Lemus, who was responsible for investigating a prior attack on Silva's daughter, was murdered in front of his home. According to a family member, the judge had also previously received death threats.

Moreover, Oscar Grimaldi, a member of the FMLN, was murdered in the early morning hours of August 19 in San Salvador. His death was the subject of a rare immediate public statement by ONUSAL decrying a disturbing pattern of attacks with apparent political motivation; the main suspect in the case was killed in late October before he could be arrested. During the year, ONUSAL verified several other arbitrary executions of FMLN members, including Juan García Panameño who worked for the Committee of Mothers of the Disappeared (COMADRES).

Although the office of the human rights ombudsman increasingly made public pronouncements on human rights cases, it was faced with the need to improve dramatically its capacity to investigate and respond to cases if it was fully to assume its responsibilities by the time of ONUSAL's scheduled departure in early 1994.

The Right to Monitor

A number of nongovernmental organizations as well as ONUSAL actively monitored human rights in El Salvador during 1993; but attacks and threats against them were never investigated, let alone prosecuted. In March, lawyer José Eduardo Pineda Valenzuela died of injuries sustained in a violent attack in July 1992. At the time of the attack, Pineda Valenzuela was working for the newly-created office of the human rights ombudsman. Previously, he had been the leading government prosecutor in the Jesuit case, securing the 1991 conviction of two military officers. No one had been arrested in connection with the attack on Pineda Valenzuela as of November.

In December 1992, following publication of a series of ads denouncing human rights abuses by the military, Defense Minister René Emilio Ponce and Vice-minister Juan Orlando Zepeda filed a complaint against three members of the nongovernmental Human Rights Commission (CDHES) and six members of the National Union of Salvadoran Workers (UNTS) for defamation. The attorney general's office filed charges on December 9, 1992 and a San Salvador judge opened an investigation which proceeded slowly in early 1993. The army's attempt to prosecute members of the CDHES was only the latest manifestation of hostility. A number of CDHES workers were killed during the 1980s, most of them presumably by official forces.

While ONUSAL's human rights division continued to operate largely without restriction, it was the subject of renewed anonymous threats following the release of the Truth Commission report. In the wake of that report, the government also summarily canceled a scheduled visit of the Inter-American Commission on Human Rights (IACHR) of the Organization of American States. The IACHR denounced the government's cancelation as a "failure to comply with a previously-made commitment." In October, the IACHR said that the Salvadoran government had expressed renewed interest in a visit.

Americas Watch was also concerned about violent attacks and threats against other human rights monitors which, even if they might prove not to involve official responsibility, were not investigated by the authorities. In January, attorney Mirna Perla de Anaya, widow of murdered CDHES activist Herbert Anaya, was attacked along with her children on the road between San Salvador and Suchitoto as they returned from visiting a community of resettled refugees. In September, a law professor and member of the National Council on the Judiciary, René Madecadel Perla Jiménez, received several telephone death threats, including one from individuals identifying themselves as the Maximiliano Hernández Martínez Brigade, a notorious death squad. Dr. Perla Jiménez is Mirna Perla de Anaya's brother.

U.S. Policy

Given the billions of dollars in U.S. military and economic aid to El Salvador during the war, the report of the U.N. Truth Commission became a U.S. as well as a Salvadoran affair. The Truth Commission's acknowledgment and confirmation that U.S.-supported forces had engaged in massive and systematic human rights abuses led to congressional demands for an examination of past policy. In March, seventeen members of Congress asked President Clinton to declassify documents pertaining to cases examined by the Truth Commission. The President responded positively in June, promising that an initial review by the State and Defense Departments would be concluded by September. Over 12,000 documents were released in early November, identifying several current ARENA leaders as linked to death squad activities, and confirming that the U.S. government knew much more about the death squads than it had admitted to Congress or the public.

Secretary of State Warren Christopher, saying that he was "deeply shocked" by the Truth Commission report, also appointed a panel of retired foreign service officers and academic experts to review actions and statements by State Department officials regarding human rights. The report, issued on July 15, was a searing disappointment that some in Congress labeled a "whitewash". Despite years of U.S. official denial that Salvadoran government forces were responsible for systematic abuses, and despite prolonged efforts by past administrations to discredit human rights and humanitarian organizations working in El Salvador, the State Department panel found overall that foreign service personnel had "performed creditably" in advancing human rights.

It faulted officials of the Reagan administration for issuing false statements regarding the 1980 murder of four U.S. churchwomen and the December 1981 El Mozote massacre by the Salvadoran army. But the panel found such episodes to be the exception. Overall, according to the report, the State Department provided Congress with "factual and straightforward" information and officials acted, at times courageously, to advance human rights. These judgments were grossly distorted, as U.S. officials had routinely falsified the Salvadoran government's human rights record in order to maintain a steady stream of military aid to fight the insurgency.

After the publication of the reports of the Truth Commission and the State Department's El Salvador panel, congressional interest in El Salvador faded, although the House Foreign Operations Subcommittee did protest the Salvadoran government's failure to register eligible voters by holding up release of Economic Support Funds for El Salvador in August.

Earlier in 1993, the Clinton administration exerted helpful pressure on the Salvadoran military to comply with the recommendations of the Ad Hoc Commission. The State Department quietly suspended $11 million in U.S. military aid in February, after the army high command refused to implement the purge mandated by the peace accord. The funds were released later in September. The department and U.S. Embassy also issued strongly-worded condemnations of the October murder of FMLN party leader Francisco Velis Castellanos and agreed to provide investigative support, along with Spain and Great Britain, to bring the killers to justice.

The Department of Defense requested $2.7 million in new military aid for El Salvador for fiscal year 1994 and an additional $1.1 million for training, although the actual amounts were likely to be smaller. Apparently to offset the effect of this massive reduction in aid and to show continuing support for the Salvadoran armed forces, U.S. Southern Command chief Gen. George Joulwan traveled to El Salvador in early September to inaugurate the Fuertes Caminos (Strong Paths) joint military exercises. While the purpose of the exercises was to build infrastructure such as schools and wells, we were concerned that the maneuvers involved the armed forces in pursuits more appropriately undertaken by the civilian administration. This further weakened civilian control of the military—and thereby accountability—precisely when both needed to be enhanced.

The Work of Americas Watch

Through its representatives based in Washington and San Salvador, Americas Watch continued to play a widely-recognized central role in shaping the debate over accountability for human rights violations in El Salvador. Americas Watch staff continued to provide information and support to the Truth Commission during its final months in existence. Americas Watch representatives also figured prominently in the U.S. media before and after the release of the Truth Commission report, and worked closely with congressional offices and the Clinton administration in exploring possible U.S. policy responses. A representative of Americas Watch testified before the El Salvador panel established by Secretary of State Warren Christopher and provided the panel with additional background documentation.

In August, Americas Watch released "Accountability and Human Rights: The Report of the United Nations Commission on the Truth for El Salvador," evaluating the work of the Truth Commission and issuing specific recommendations for the Cristiani government and the Clinton administration. The report explored the origins of the Truth Commission in order to suggest ways that accountability might become part of future peace processes in other countries.

GUATEMALA

Human Rights Developments

This past year was one of breathtaking political changes in Guatemala, with important implications for the human rights situation. Dramatic events of May and June 1993 propelled a human rights advocate into the presidency and produced some positive steps, although in other areas, the new government failed to take strong action in defense of rights, apparently for fear of confronting the army.

The most important reform effort affected the abusive police force, whose corruption and subservience to the army had long crippled its ability to investigate crimes, especially those committed by the military or its agents. Areas where there was no evidence of change included the militarization of the countryside and the power of the civil defense patrols, which continued to commit grave abuses, including murder, death threats, forced displacement, and illegal detentions. Moreover, a kind of psychological war continues against popular organizations, human rights monitors, labor unionists, and independent journalists. The sources of the assaults, kidnappings, and death threats these individuals suffered were in many cases unknown, but the techniques of intimidation were consistent with clandestine methods used by the security forces. The government's response to new evidence of clandestine detention and death squad activity by the army were disappointing as well. And while there were some important prosecutions of members of the civil patrols and police for human rights violations after the new government came into office, impunity remained the norm.

Violations of international humanitarian law by guerrillas in 1993 included the use of child soldiers; in two incidents during the year, children fighting with the guerrillas were captured in combat—one was ten years old and the other thirteen.

On May 25, 1993, Guatemala's elected civilian president, Jorge Serrano Elías, set off a constitutional crisis when he closed down the congress, supreme court, and attorney general's office and suspended a broad range of constitutional rights. Remarkably, his efforts to establish a dictatorship were reversed, thanks to pressures from Guatemala's emerging civil society, the Clinton administration, some elements of the military, and the previously obscure constitutional court. One week after Serrano seized power, he was forced to resign. Less than one week after that, the nation's respected human rights ombudsman, Ramiro de León Carpio, was elected by the congress to finish out Serrano's term.

Resolution of this crisis through peaceful and legal means marked an important victory for the constitution, the rule of law, and Guatemala's civil society. Moreover, de León Carpio's ascension to the presidency raised hopes for an improvement in the human rights situation and for a civilian president who would finally be willing to challenge the overwhelming power of the armed forces. During his term as human rights ombudsman, de León Carpio had energetically investigated and publicly denounced human rights violations, something no government official had done before in Guatemala.

In the weeks after his sudden assumption of power, de León Carpio sent two successive defense ministers into early retirement because of their behind-the-scenes support for Serrano's coup. A third officer allegedly involved in the coup, Gen. Francisco Ortega Menaldo, was sent into diplomatic exile at the Inter-American Defense Board in Washington, D.C.

The president named individuals known and trusted by the human rights community to the posts of interior minister and head of the National Police. The new police director, Mario René Cifuentes, launched an ambitious program to eliminate military control over the police by removing military "advisors" to police department heads and by disbanding a joint military/police task force known as "Hunapú." Cifuentes announced plans, as part of a broad restructuring of the police, to create a special unit to investigate human rights violations, including extrajudicial executions, disappearances, and torture.

Some positive results of these efforts to reform the police have been the decisive intervention of police agents to save the life of Joaquín Jiménez Bautista, a refugee who returned to his village of Todos Santos, Huehuetenango, only to be captured and beaten by civil patrol members who accused him of committing atrocities as a guerrilla

commander in the early 1980s. Jiménez would undoubtedly have been lynched were it not for the intervention of an official of the governmental refugee authority, CEAR, and the police, who ultimately turned him over to the local human rights ombudsman. The police also took decisive action on September 23, when a prison riot resulted in the escape of Noel de Jesús Beteta, the convicted murderer of internationally known anthropologist Myrna Mack. Police captured Beteta and fourteen other convicts out of the thirty-seven who had escaped prison the same day.

Nonetheless, the police have failed to take effective action in other areas such as executing arrest warrants for members of the police and civil patrols accused of human rights violations. According to Casa Alianza, which operates a refuge and legal clinic for street children in Guatemala City, there were more than a dozen outstanding arrest warrants for police agents accused of violence against street children. Nor did the police detain several civil patrol chiefs whose arrest was ordered in July for the murder of human rights activist Tomás Lares Sipriano (described below).

On August 5, President de León Carpio announced the dissolution of the Presidential Security Directorate, a notorious intelligence unit commonly known as the "Archivos." The Archivos forms part of a large security apparatus operating from the presidency, and has for decades been pinpointed as a source of political repression. The trial and conviction of Beteta, an Archivos specialist, for the murder of Myrna Mack, opened a window into the secretive world of the Archivos and made the unit synonymous with repression in public opinion. This impression was reinforced in March 1993, when a secret office of the Archivos, used to intercept mail, was discovered in the General Post Office in Guatemala City.

Although the Archivos's dissolution was undoubtedly related to its criminal activities, the president never made such a link explicit. When the Myrna Mack Foundation, a human rights group formed by the sister of the slain anthropologist, called for an investigation into the Archivos's repressive activities, its demand went unheeded. Nor was it clear that Archivos activities would stop. They might simply be launched from a different location.

According to the Guatemalan newsweekly *Crónica*, the extensive files the Archivos kept on citizens and used as the basis for composing death lists were transferred to military intelligence (known as G-2 or D-2), despite widespread demand they be made public. Like the Archivos, G-2 had a long history of involvement in political repression. President de León Carpio reportedly sought to allay popular concerns by saying that if there ever were such files, it was "logical to believe" that they had been destroyed; but doubts persisted.

The president failed to take any action to curb the power and abuses of the civil patrols, which appeared responsible for the majority of human rights violations in Guatemala during 1993. Although as human rights ombudsman, de León Carpio had been a strong critic of the patrols' abuses, as president he rejected suggestions that they be dismantled, saying such a move should come only as part of peace negotiations with the guerrillas. Yet in many rural areas, the patrols usurped the functions of government and were a law unto themselves, as in the cases described below.

On April 30, patrols shot dead Tomás Lares Sipriano, a human rights activist from the village of Chorraxá, Quiché. The day before he was killed, Lares had organized a demonstration in the town of Joyabaj protesting military pressure on the area's inhabitants to join the civil patrols, which according to the constitution are strictly voluntary. Patrol leaders in Chorraxá had repeatedly threatened Lares in the past, and although the Quiché branch of the human rights ombudsman's office had ordered police protection for him, it had never been extended.

On May 1, patrollers killed ten alleged thieves outside the patrol-dominated town of San Pedro Jocopilas. Although the army and police claimed the victims died in a shoot-out, evidence collected by human rights monitors indicated that the eight men and two women were slain execution-style, some while tied to trees. Moreover, although the police reportedly arrived at the abandoned house where the patrollers had captured the ten alive, they left when the patrollers insisted on handling the matter themselves.

On August 3, patrollers fired on peaceful demonstrators in the village of Los Naranjales in Huehuetenango department, killing sixty-four-year-old peasant Juan Chamay Pablo and wounding several others. Although arrest warrants were issued on September 9 for fourteen patrollers, only one had been detained as of mid-November. Responsibility for this failure fell not only on the National Police, whose members were easily intimidated by the army-backed patrols, but also on the Mobile Military Police—the army's own police unit—which failed to respond to orders to detain the patrollers. A Colotenango patrol chief, Efraín Domingo Morales, was murdered on September 15, possibly in retaliation for the August 3 shootings and other patrol abuses, although it is unclear who was responsible. And on September 26, Andrés Godínez Díaz and María Pérez Sanches, his wife, who had participated in the August 3 demonstration, were tortured and killed after receiving numerous death threats from the civil patrols in Colotenango, Huehuetenango.

Some inroads were made into the impunity with which human rights violators had traditionally operated in Guatemala, while other cases suffered setbacks or went nowhere. In July, an appeals court overturned the acquittal of two civil patrol chiefs for the murder of two human rights activists from the village of Chunimá, Quiché, and sentenced them to thirty years imprisonment. Also in July, a court sentenced the third-in-command of the National Police and four other officers to prison terms for violently breaking up a peaceful demonstration which took place in July 1992 in front of the National Palace. An appeals court toughened to thirty years the sentences imposed on other police officers who murdered a student in April 1992 as well.

On the other hand, although an army captain was convicted in the 1990 murder of U.S. citizen Michael Devine, he promptly escaped from the barracks where he was detained and remains at large. Instead of being punished, the colonel in charge of the barracks, Luis Felipe Miranda, was promoted to general by de León Carpio on October 1. Nor did the government take steps to prosecute cases the president investigated when he was human rights ombudsman, such as the murder of peasant Lucas Pérez Tadeo, whose tortured body was found on September 3, 1992, in Nentón, Huehuetenango. When he was still human rights ombudsman, Ramiro de León Carpio issued a resolution blaming the local Las Palmas military base for the disappearance, torture, and murder of Pérez Tadeo.

The Right to Monitor

Those who sought to defend human rights in Guatemala continued to suffer harassment, intimidation, and physical violence for their work. The change of government in June brought a welcome end to the climate of intense official hostility towards human rights monitors prevalent under the Serrano administration—during which the president himself and his defense minister frequently issued baseless accusations against human rights monitors for purported links to the guerrillas.

The director, staff, and clients of Casa Alianza, a center for street children in Guatemala City, suffered a steady stream of threats during the year. Collective written death threats were issued to journalists, human rights monitors, development workers, and other activists in March and October.

The staff of the Association for the Advancement of Social Sciences in Guatemala (AVANCSO) were the objects of intimidation and threats culminating in the ransacking of their Guatemala City office on August 31. The harassment appeared to be a response to AVANCSO's calls for prosecution and punishment of the perpetrators of the murder of Myrna Mack, one of AVANCSO's founders. Witnesses and judges involved in the Mack case also received threats during 1993, as did Mack's sister, Helen.

As in past years, the indigenous human rights group known as the Counsel of Ethnic Communities "We Are All Equal" (CERJ), suffered serious persecution. Tomás Lares Sipriano, whose murder by civil patrollers is described above, was an active CERJ member. On May 8, three CERJ members— Pablo Itzep Hernández, Cruz Luz Hernández, and Manuel Batén Hernández—were detained and tortured at the military post in Chiul, Quiché. The officer in charge of the base, Capt. Aníbal Roberto Landaveri Martínez, was convicted of battery by a military court and sentenced to two-and-a-half years in prison. Also on May 8, the Guatemala City office of CERJ was raided by armed assailants and its staff threatened. Finally, CERJ members Juan Ren González and Alberto Calvo were imprisoned on trumped-up charges from October 1992 until their acquittal in June 1993.

Even governmental authorities who attempted to protect human rights faced persecution. On May 21, the local human rights ombudsman for the department of Huehuetenango, attorney Tibaldo Ricardo Gámez López, was detained and threatened by civil patrolmen when he traveled to the village of Llano del Coyote to investigate a case.

The executive secretary of the Guatemala Association of Jurists (AGJ), Fernando René de León Solano, was harassed several times during the month of July, and a trade unionist who had recently visited de León was abducted and questioned about him and others before being released. On September 10, the Guatemala City office of the AGJ was damaged by an explosive placed outside it.

In March in collaboration with the Archbishop's Office of Human Rights, the San Pedro parish in El Estor, Izabal began a program of training human rights monitors in the villages inhabited by Qeqchi Indians. Due to harassment and warnings by local patrol leaders, one-third of the monitors were forced to withdraw from the program.

The Mutual Support Group—which represents relatives of the disappeared and is Guatemala's oldest human rights group—suffered several incidents of harassment. In two office break-ins during October and November, documents regarding human rights violations and office equipment were stolen. A member of the group, Francisco Guarcas Ciphiano, was reportedly kidnapped by civil patrol members in the Guatemala City bus terminal on October 19.

U.S. Policy

The Clinton administration played an extremely important role in frustrating Serrano's coup by suspending all government-to-government aid and threatening to suspend trade privileges under the Generalized System of Preferences. The State Department also warned that it might oppose loans to Guatemala in international financial institutions if the coup were not reversed. The administration's unequivocal rejection of the coup consolidated opposition in Guatemala and motivated the business community and some sectors of the military to throw their weight against the coup. Washington's diplomacy also contributed to the building of a constitutional outcome to the crisis, instead of what at first appeared destined to be a military solution.

Since her arrival after the coup, the U.S. ambassador to Guatemala, Marilyn McAfee, has used her position creatively to further human rights in Guatemala, speaking out publicly about human rights abuses, visiting victims of human rights violations on several occasions and helping them get access to senior government officials. She told Americas Watch that she maintained a regular dialogue with Defense Minister Mario Enríquez and other senior officials in which she pressed for investigation of human rights violations.

The administration was eager to support de León Carpio's government and discussed expanding its police criminal investigations program and providing support to the police academy. Military training and joint exercises were renewed, after a brief hiatus during the coup, and the administration promised at a donor's meeting sponsored by the World Bank in September to provide $10 million in economic support funds to help with balance of payments strains. Approximately $11 million in military aid which had been suspended because of human rights violations since December 1990 remained on hold pending measurable improvements in the human rights situation and reforms in the military.

In August, two senior U.S. military officials visited Guatemala to express support for President de León and for the role of the military during the constitutional crisis. The generals, Army Chief of Staff Gordon Sullivan and George Joulwan, chief of the U.S. Southern Command, announced the resumption of joint civic action projects to be undertaken by the U.S. and Guatemalan militaries. Americas Watch objected to the U.S. promotion of the Guatemalan military's role in development and what it termed "nation building," as areas which should be the clear domain of the civilian government. We urged the Clinton Administration to end its support for military involvement in what should be civilian affairs such as vaccination campaigns and the building of schools. Regrettably, Generals Joulwan and Sullivan did not use the occasion of their visit to express publicly U.S. concern over the August incident in which civil patrollers shot peaceful demonstrators in Huehuetenango, killing an elderly peasant man and wounding several others. As the number of patrol abuses rose under the new government and the authorities' failure to prosecute and punish those responsible became more apparent, the need for public pressure from the United States became greater. We urge the Clinton administration to press for a dissolution of the patrols which, in addition to being involuntary in many parts of the country, remain the major source of human rights violations in Guatemala.

The Work of Americas Watch

An Americas Watch representative traveled to Guatemala the day of Serrano's coup to emphasize the organization's interest in a peaceful and legal restoration of constitutional government and our concern over the possibility that the coup would give rise to human rights violations and the persecution of monitors. In June, Americas Watch representatives met with government officials and human rights groups, and traveled in the countryside to investigate human rights violations. A report on the new government's human rights record and challenges was scheduled for publication in December.

Before the coup, Americas Watch sought to draw attention to clandestine detentions by the military, publishing a short report in March. Clandestine detention had been practiced for decades, but had been consistently denied by the authorities. Follow-up to the report was pursued through correspondence with the government on individual cases. An Americas Watch consultant specializing in issues of displacement and the repatriation of refugees traveled twice to Guatemala and Mexico to conduct research for a forthcoming report. Together with the Jesuit Refugee Service and other Washington-based groups, Americas Watch organized a series of roundtable discussions among nongovernmental organizations to heighten awareness of human rights and humanitarian issues in Guatemala.

HAITI

Human Rights Developments

In the second full year since a military junta overthrew freely elected President Jean-Bertrand Aristide on September 30, 1991, Haiti descended further into the depths of terror and lawlessness. Held hostage to the personal whims of army commander Gen. Raoul Cédras, police chief Lt. Col. Michel François, and the paramilitary death squads under their command, Haiti was brutalized into submission.

Well over 1,500 people were estimated by Haitian and international human rights monitors to have been killed by soldiers and paramilitary thugs from the 1991 coup through most of 1993. All forms of popular organization, crucial to the survival of those for whom there was no infrastructure in a country that is three-quarters rural, were ruthlessly suppressed by a regime that had no inclination, much less authority, to govern. Students, peasant leaders, the clergy, human rights monitors, journalists, politicians and anyone else associated with Aristide were subject to arbitrary arrest, torture or extrajudicial execution.

The army attempted systematically to eviscerate all civic, popular and professional organizations opposed to its authoritarian rule. The military junta banned meetings throughout Haiti's nine departments. All signs of public protest were swiftly and violently repressed. Wide-scale, short-term detention served successfully to intimidate and subdue. During detention, vicious beatings were the rule rather than the exception. Almost all arrests were warrantless and illegal. In 1993, among the most fiercely repressed popular organizations were the Papaye Peasants Movement and the Perodin Peasants Association.

Section chiefs, the rural military overlords, were reinstated. Soldiers and section chiefs preyed on their victims, demanding payment in exchange for freedom or to avoid torture. Those in hiding were told that they might return to their homes if they paid a fee. At military checkpoints, soldiers extorted from any who dared to travel the roads. For this, the army enjoyed absolute impunity.

With the July 3 signing of the Governors Island Accord between President Aristide and the Haitian armed forces—an accord that was to set in motion the return of Aristide's elected civilian government—generalized violence began to escalate. What is known in Haiti as *insecurité*—ostensibly random violence like shootings and robbery—by heavily-armed thugs increased as the military saw its prerogatives threatened. Labeled variously as *tontons macoutes, zenglendos,* and *attachés,* these paramilitary death squads had functioned over the years alternately as agents of political control or destabilization, responsible for a now-familiar pattern of egregious human rights crimes, that have rarely been punished.

As the various parties to the accord negotiated at Governors Island, New York at the end of June, the incidence and ferocity of army repression grew noticeably, with attacks rising exponentially in the months before President Aristide's scheduled October 30 return. This surge in violence was consistently reported by the Organization of American States/United Nations International Civilian Mission of human rights observers deployed since February 1993 to monitor and deter violence throughout the country.

In its press releases, the OAS/U.N. mission documented random and targeted shootings by police and armed civilians in Port-au-Prince on June 24, the day of a national strike called by various labor unions; beatings and arrests by Haitian troops and armed civilians of participants in a religious commemoration at the church of Notre Dame du Perpétuel Secours, in Port-au-Prince on June 27; and an increase in arrests and torture of nonviolent pro-Aristide demonstrators, grassroots organizers, and journalists in the towns of Gonaïves, Zabricot, Léogâne and Les Cayes.

By mid-August, the OAS/U.N. mission reported that thirty-six arbitrary executions and suspicious deaths had occurred since July 1—the time of the Governors Island negotiations—in Port-au-Prince alone. At the end of August, the civilian mission noted an increasing number of kidnappings and forced disappearances of grassroots activists by armed civilians, reporting ten cases in August alone. At the same time, the number of killings had risen to fifty. The OAS/U.N. mission reported the shooting deaths of at least twelve people in Port-au-Prince in just a two-day period, September 11 and 12.

On September 8, gunmen and machete-wielding thugs attacked well-wishers at the reinvestiture of democratically-elected Port-au-Prince mayor Evans Paul, a close ally of President Aristide. Three people were killed and some thirty wounded. Police agents were present but did nothing to stop the violence.

On September 11, a paramilitary death squad executed in broad daylight Haitian businessman Antoine Izméry as police agents looked on. Izméry, one of the most outspoken and best-known supporters of President Aristide, was murdered at a commemoration service at a Port-au-Prince church for the victims of the 1988 massacre at Father Aristide's St. Jean Bosco church.

On October 5, some thirty gunmen searching for Mayor Evans Paul opened fire on a political meeting being held at a Port-au-Prince hotel. Paul had fled the scene only moments before the attack. Later that day, gunmen fired on the home of Information Minister Hervé Denis.

On October 7, one day after the first foreign troops began to arrive in Haiti under a U.N. mandate (as contemplated in the Governors Island Accord), a newly created Duvalierist organization, the Front for Advancement and Progress of Haiti (FRAPH), announced a general strike. In Port-au-Prince, armed civilians and uniformed Haitian police successfully closed down the city by shooting automatic weapons at street merchants, seriously wounding at least two, according to press reports.

Minister of Justice Guy Malary, a leading attorney, was assassinated along with his driver and a bodyguard on October 14 as they were leaving the minister's office. Justice Minister Malary, a highly respected member of the interim civilian government, was responsible for introducing legislation to separate the police from the army and had worked closely with the OAS/U.N. Civilian Mission.

Throughout the year, Haiti's journalists, in their attempts to document such abuses, were among the most consistently targeted groups. In February, Radio Tropic-FM reporter Colson Dormé was knocked unconscious and abducted by thugs who accused him of belonging to President Aristide's political movement. When found on the street outside the radio station's offices six days later with his hands and legs tied and his head shaved, Dormé had been badly beaten. In June, the military cracked down on vendors of Libeté, a Creole weekly critical of the *de facto* regime. Only five of the nine radio stations that were attacked and forced to shut down during the 1991 coup resumed broadcasting.

The Right to Monitor
Human rights activists were among the first targets of the military in the early days of the coup. As the year drew to an end, they operated under increasingly menacing conditions.

On February 25, police and paramilitary thugs beat and arrested mourners at a memorial service for the victims of the Neptune ferry disaster, in which about 1,000 people died. The service had turned into an anti-government protest, with people shouting "Aristide or death." Among those who were attacked outside the national cathedral were Bishop Willy Romelus, president of the Catholic church's Justice and Peace Commission, a prominent human rights monitoring group, and human rights advocate Paul Dejean of the Karl Leveque Center and the Platform of Haitian Human Rights Organizations.

Three armed assailants looking for Jean-Claude Bajeux, head of the Ecumenical Center for Human Rights and longtime critic of the Haitian military's human rights record, descended on his home on October 4. Unable to find Mr. Bajeux, the attackers tied up and beat two housekeepers, and shot in the stomach and gravely wounded a neighbor who heard noises and came to check what was happening.

In mid-October, the Haiti office of the U.S.-based National Coalition for Haitian Refugees received a phone threat from a caller who identified himself as being under orders from the commander of the army garrison at St. Marc, a town north of Port-au-Prince. The caller also said he belonged to FRAPH, the newly formed Duvalierist organization.

Individual members of the leading monitoring group, the Platform of Haitian Human Rights Organizations, also received death threats.

The OAS/U.N. Civilian Mission was harassed by the military. Paramilitary attachés and informers for the army often sat in or loitered around the offices of the civilian mission in towns around the country. Haitians who cooperated with the Mission were arrested or threatened, especially in the Plateau Central and the Artibonite. In October, the offices of the civilian mission in Hinche in the Plateau Central were attacked by attachés, and a Haitian cleaning woman working at the offices was beaten.

U.S. Policy and Other International Response
In one of the first major human rights setbacks of the new administration, President Clinton reneged on his campaign promise not to summarily return Haitian boat people to Haiti. In January, the incoming and outgoing administrations agreed to blockade the island with U.S. Coast Guard cutters, Navy ships and helicopters in order to prevent refugee flight. In June, the U.S. Supreme Court upheld the Bush and Clinton administrations' interdiction policy. In a decision deservedly criticized by human rights and refugee policy groups, the court found that forcibly returning boat people without allowing them to state their case for asylum was not a violation of U.S. or international law. The Clinton administration then stepped up efforts to press for a negotiated solution to the crisis that had spurred some 40,000 Haitians to flee their country. Nonetheless, even with the support of the Clinton administration, international efforts to mediate a negotiated reversal of the coup—an effort led by the U.N./OAS special envoy to Haiti, former Argentine foreign minister Dante Caputo—were repeatedly frustrated by the Haitian military leaders.

In 1993, as previously, the issue of army accountability was a recurring stumbling block in negotiations to restore President Aristide and democracy in Haiti. While the Clinton administration and the U.N. promised large amounts of economic and military assistance to entice the military, and to a lesser extent President Aristide, to pursue negotiations, the carrot-and-stick approach foundered on the issue of accountability. Aristide was under consistent pressure from U.N. Special Envoy Caputo and from Amb. Lawrence Pezzullo, special envoy for President Clinton, to make concessions on the Haitian army's accountability for its crimes.

Before coming to a settlement, General Cédras required guarantees that President Aristide's opponents would be immune from prosecution and protected from acts of vengeance for participating in the military coup, and that U.N. observers would play a protective role. Cédras demanded amnesty and protection for himself, his family and other members of the high command. The U.S. and U.N. supported these conditions and put Aristide in the position of making or breaking the settlement.

In June, as the *de facto* leaders in Haiti were faced with increasingly harsh sanctions, Cédras agreed to negotiate with Aristide, and Aristide agreed on condition that they negotiate a date that the army and police chiefs would step down and be replaced; a date of his own return; and the nomination of a new prime minister. The U.N.-mediated talks began on June 27 at Governors Island in New York Harbor.

The ill-fated Governors Island Accord was signed on July 3. It called for the resignation of General Cédras shortly before the return of President Aristide to Haiti on October 30. U.N. and OAS economic sanctions would be lifted and more than $1 billion in international assistance was promised to begin with President Aristide's appointment of a new prime minister. Haiti was to receive technical and military assistance to promote development and administrative, judicial and military reform, namely the separation of the police from the army. The agreement also called for President Aristide to issue an amnesty in accordance with the Haitian Constitution, which allows amnesty for political crimes but not for common crimes. Aristide interpreted this constitutional norm as allowing an amnesty for the crime of overturn-ing the constitutional order, but not for the murders, disappearances and torture that had taken place since the coup.

On July 25, President Aristide named Robert Malval, a politically moderate publisher, as prime minister. After the Haitian parliament confirmed him one month later, the U.N. Security Council lifted its oil and trade embargo against Haiti with the proviso that it would be reimposed if the Haitian military did not comply with the Governors Island Accord.

The Clinton administration also proposed a military assistance package, pending the outcome of negotiations, which included $1.25 million under the International Military Education and Training Program (IMET) and close to $1.2 million in Foreign Military Financing (FMF) for military professionalization; $10 million in Economic Support Funds (ESF) for the U.N./OAS observer mission; $4 million in ESF for International Criminal Investigations Training Assistance Programs (ICITAP) police professionalization; $3 million in ESF for the administration of justice program of the U.S. Agency for International Development (USAID); plus developmental assistance and economic stabilization support, for a total of $37.5 million for fiscal year 1993. For fiscal year 1994, the administration requested $40 million in developmental assistance; $15 million in ESF; and $400,000 in IMET for a total of $80.8 million. Congress conditioned U.S. aid by prohibiting military assistance or training in which there would be participation by any member of the Haitian military involved in drug trafficking or human rights abuses.

In September, the U.N. Security Council also approved a U.S.-sponsored resolution to send 567 U.N. police monitors and 700 military personnel, including some sixty military trainers. These forces were to include about 500 U.S. troops. After concerns were raised about the lack of adequate screening procedures for trainees, the new U.S. ambassador to Haiti, William Lacy Swing, announced that the U.S. would no longer be training an interim police force. Instead,

U.N. police monitors and trainers (not including U.S. participants) would conduct the training and, with the Malval government, would be responsible for screening out human rights abusers. Swing added that the U.S. Embassy, working with the U.N./OAS mission, would screen trainees involved in the IMET program, and vowed to make vetting of human rights abusers from U.S. training and human rights monitoring a priority of his embassy.

Implementation of the Governors Island Accord began to unravel on October 11 when a gang of armed paramilitary "attachés" protesting the arrival of the *U.S.S. Harlan County* prevented the ship from docking in Port-au-Prince. According to the *New York Times*, "the demonstrators, who were allowed into the port area by police officers rerouting traffic to clear the way, beat on the cars of diplomats and kicked reporters waiting at the gates of the port, screaming, 'We are going to turn this into another Somalia!'" With no mandate to force its way on shore and failing to gain Haitian army guarantees of cooperation, President Clinton ordered the *Harlan County* to retreat. A contingent of Canadian police trainers already in Haiti as part of the accord departed the following day. On October 14, the U.N. Security Council reimposed an oil and arms embargo on Haiti, as well as an international freeze on the financial assets of the *de facto* authorities.

After the *Harlan County* withdrawal, General Cédras set new conditions for his resignation by demanding that the Haitian parliament pass legislation on an amnesty for crimes committed in connection with the coup. (President Aristide had already issued a decree in early October in accordance with the Governors Island process providing amnesty only for crimes against the state, not for crimes against human rights.) Although Cédras claimed he merely wanted Aristide's decree reinforced by amnesty legislation, it was understood that he sought a broader amnesty that would cover human rights crimes, or common crimes such as murder and torture; such an amnesty would violate the Haitian Constitution. In response to this new demand, the Clinton administration failed to state clearly that it supported the scope of Aristide's decreed amnesty or to oppose Cédras's demand for total impunity.

In an apparent effort to guarantee their safety in an increasingly hostile situation, the U.N./OAS mission of human rights observers was evacuated to neighboring Dominican Republic on October 15. President Clinton ordered six U.S. warships to patrol the waters off Haiti to step up enforcement of the embargo, with U.N. Security Council authorization forthcoming a day later.

Even though political violence in Haiti had escalated enough to prevent U.S. and Canadian military trainers from landing at the Port-au-Prince dock and to force the withdrawal of U.N./OAS human rights monitors, the U.S. declared its intention to continue to repatriate forcibly any refugees who attempt to flee Haiti. The Clinton administration announced that it would continue to rely upon its in-country processing (ICP) program in Haiti to consider Haitians' applications for political asylum in the U.S. Americas Watch, which denounced the continuation of the forcible repatriation policy, has investigated the ICP program and found that it offers no protection to applicants during the asylum application process; adjudication of cases is inconsistent; standards for asylum and credibility determinations are unfairly applied; and potential asylum seekers who do not feel that they can safely avail themselves of the program are left with no option.

As the U.S. Congress debated U.S. policy in Haiti, a controversy was ignited by a CIA report describing President Aristide as mentally unstable and by reports of human rights violations allegedly committed by Aristide during his presidency. During a briefing organized by Sen. Jesse Helms (R-NC), an intelligence officer who had reportedly earlier assessed General Cédras as a member of one of "the most promising group of Haitian leaders to emerge since the Duvalier family dictatorship," testified on Aristide's mental health.

As this report was written, the October 30 deadline for President Aristide's return to

Haiti had passed, with the Haitian military resisting a resumption of negotiations. Meanwhile, the U.S. government continued to debate what role it should play in restoring democracy to Haiti.

The Work of Americas Watch

Throughout the year, Americas Watch supported the restoration of Aristide to the presidency of Haiti, as the only proper way to respect the exercise of political rights by 67 percent of all Haitians. We urged that all the negotiations include precise human rights conditions so that re-democratization of Haiti results in deep, structural improvements in the protection of citizens' rights. We tried to prevent an outcome in which, in exchange for Aristide's return, the military could get away with total impunity for their crimes.

In our view, a minimal measure of accountability should demand that the armed and security forces of a reconstituted Haiti be purged of abusers of human rights. We also tried, unsuccessfully, to ensure that U.S. policy with respect to fleeing Haitians remained consistent with the U.S.'s obligations under international law.

Americas Watch continued to cooperate closely with the National Coalition for Haitian Refugees (NCHR). In February, we published our fifteenth joint report on Haiti, *Silencing a People, The Destruction of Civil Society in Haiti*. The 152-page report documents the military's systematic decimation of all sectors of civil society in the first year since the coup.

In September 1993, Americas Watch, together with NCHR and the Jesuit Refugee Service/USA, co-published a thirty-seven-page report, "No Port in a Storm: The Misguided Use of In-Country Refugee Processing in Haiti," a critique of a policy which had historically been conceived as an additional avenue of protection for refugees in selected countries, but had become in Haiti the only option for victims of Haiti's repressive military regime.

In an ongoing effort to call attention to the cycle of impunity that has fueled Haitian army violence—an issue that had been deliberately disregarded by international negotiators in the Haiti crisis—Americas Watch and NCHR issued a series of press releases and letters to the U.N./OAS Special Envoy to Haiti, Dante Caputo, and to Clinton administration officials involved in Haitian policy formulation.

Human Rights Watch also worked to inform Congress about the issue of accountability and other human rights issues as in July 17 testimony before the House Subcommittee on Western Hemisphere Affairs. Americas Watch followed up on that effort with letters to members of Congress urging them to convey to the administration their interest in ensuring accountability, by insisting that any Haitian army and police officers who were scheduled to receive U.S. military training be held responsible for any crimes they may have committed in the past.

HONDURAS

Human Rights Developments

This was a year of contradictions for human rights in Honduras. Although the government devoted unprecedented attention to fundamental human rights problems and took important steps towards their correction, members of the security forces continued to commit violent human rights violations. Abuse of authority, excessive use of force, and torture in custody were still common practices by the armed forces and the military-controlled police (FUSEP).

While structural problems in the administration of justice and the vast economic and political power of the armed forces continued to shield most military violators of human rights from prosecution, several cracks appeared in the armor during 1993. In July, history was made when civilian Judge María Mendoza de Castro sentenced retired Col. Angel Castillo Madariaga to sixteen years and six months in prison for the 1991 rape and murder of student Riccy Mabel Martínez Sevilla. He received ten years and six months for second-degree murder and six years (three less than the maximum penalty) for rape. Retired Sgt. Santos Eusebio Llovares Fúnez was sentenced to ten years and six months for second-degree murder. The third defendant in the case, Capt. Ovidio Andino Coello, was acquitted. To the best of our knowledge, this was the first time a high-ranking Honduran military officer had been convicted for a human rights violation.

The brutality of the case mobilized public opinion against the military. Students, women's groups, human rights organizations, and unaffiliated citizens joined forces to pressure the government for justice. Seventeen-year-old Martínez's mutilated body was found on July 15, 1991. She had last been seen two days earlier at the Las Tapias military base, seeking the release of her boyfriend who had been forcibly recruited.

U.S. Amb. Cresencio Arcos played a crucial role in the case by publicly demanding that justice be served and providing FBI services for forensic analysis that proved pivotal in the case.

On behalf of the Martínez family, lawyer Linda Rivera appealed the case, charging that Castillo and Llovares should have been convicted for first-degree murder, which carries a longer prison term and no chance of pardon.

Accusations of systematic violations of human rights were bolstered in February when former investigative-police agent Josué Eli Zúñiga Martínez publicly implicated the army and the police in at least seven assassinations, including the January 29, 1993, murder of businessman Eduardo Piña Van Tuyl. Zúñiga alleged that the army's infamous Battalion 3-16 was still in operation in San Pedro Sula, although the military had testified before the Inter-American Court of Human Rights of the Organization of American States that it was dissolved in 1987. Battalion 3-16's role in the disappearance of approximately 150 individuals between 1981 and 1984 was proven in a trial before the Inter-American Court of Human Rights, which concluded in 1989. And although the military stated that the battalion had been dismantled, Americas Watch received testimony from a military defector in 1989 alleging that Battalion 3-16 continued to operate out of the 105th Infantry Brigade in San Pedro Sula long after its purported dissolution.

Public outrage provoked by the Piña case and Zúñiga's declarations, combined with significant pressure from the U.S. government, created a momentum against the armed forces difficult for the Rafael Callejas administration to ignore. In March, President Callejas created a high-level "Ad Hoc Commission" composed of representatives from the executive, legislative, and judicial branches of government, the armed forces, the Catholic church, political parties, and the media. The commission's most important recommendation was the creation of a new Public Ministry as an "independent, autonomous, professional and apolitical" government office to defend citizens' collective rights, headed by a civilian prosecutor elected by Congress. A new investigative police force called the Department of Criminal Investigations (DIC) was to form part of the new Public Ministry.

The DIC was to replace the National Investigations Directorate (DNI), a police investigations unit notorious for egregious human rights violations. A three-member supervisory board, composed of two civilians and one military officer, was created to evaluate DNI personnel and prepare the transition. Americas Watch was concerned, however, that the new DIC would simply recycle the same agents who have been responsible for violent abuses at the DNI. We urged the government to screen the new personnel thoroughly to ensure that those with a history of abuse were not employed in the new police force.

Another concern was the evident reluctance of the armed forces to allow an effective transfer. Americas Watch learned from reliable sources that the military was stripping the DNI of its computers, telephones, and other equipment. This would leave the new DIC with little or no basic infrastructure and would contribute to the fulfillment of the military's prophecy that a civilian body could not function as well as one controlled by the armed forces.

The law to establish the Public Ministry was still on the agenda for debate in Congress as of November. Discussion of the law had been postponed until after the November 28 presidential elections, and there was little hope that Congress would debate the law in December when it was due to reconvene to discuss the 1994 budget. Even though Callejas originally said the office would be in operation by January 1994, it seemed more likely that the next administration, to assume power on January 27, would oversee its implementation.

The Ad Hoc Commission failed to deal directly with the issue of military control over the police force (FUSEP), the fourth branch of the armed forces since 1965. Instead of recommending a transfer into civilian hands, as many hoped the commission would, it created a National Study and Advisory Group to consider the matter. The group was intended to evaluate the police force and design a professionalization program. There were no indications that the group—created in April but unable to produce any findings as of mid-November—had been diligent in fulfilling its mandate.

The commission acknowledged the institutional weakness, inefficiency, and corruption of the criminal justice system as fundamental obstacles to the rule of law in Honduras. An inventory of all pending court cases was recommended to ensure that cases were processed expeditiously, as was the immediate creation of a judicial honor committee to investigate corruption. A new judicial code of ethics, to be binding on all judges, was written and approved by the Supreme Court.

One of the structural reasons why military human rights violators had almost never been punished was the practice by military courts of claiming jurisdiction over all such cases, although the Honduran Constitution seemed to establish that human rights violations, or crimes in which the victim was a civilian, should be the domain of the regular court system. Military courts gave benevo-

lent treatment to members of their own ranks accused of violating citizens' rights. The commission's recommendations on the matter supported the notion that human rights violations should be tried in civilian courts. The commission suggested that the Supreme Court settle all cases of jurisdictional conflict within sixty days. In response to this recommendation, the Supreme Court ruled in favor of civilian jurisdiction after two years of inaction in a case known as the El Astillero massacre. With the transfer of jurisdiction, a colonel was arrested and as of November was awaiting trial.

On March 25, Congress reinterpreted Article 90 of the constitution to limit military jurisdiction to prosecutions of "strictly military" crimes committed by armed forces personnel on active duty. It further held that cases where jurisdiction was unclear be automatically turned over to a civilian court. Although many hailed the interpretation as a definitive settlement of the conflict, it provided convenient loopholes for the military to claim jurisdiction in human rights cases by arguing that a soldier or officer was on active duty at the time of the crime and that the crime committed fell under the military code.

One positive development was the activity of the National Human Rights Commission, created by presidential decree in June 1992. While lacking adequate funds and unequivocal government support, the commission played an important role in its first year in providing Hondurans with a place to denounce violations. The commission was established to "work towards the respect for human rights by the State and individuals; give immediate attention and follow-up on any denunciation of human rights violations; elaborate and propose preventive and development programs on human rights, on judicial, education, cultural, and other aspects; and ensure compliance with international conventions and accords ratified by Honduras and promote the adoption of other similar instruments [to protect human rights]."

Human rights issues played an important, albeit polemical, role in the election campaign leading up to the November 28 general elections. Both major parties indulged in mutual accusations of responsibility for the disappearances in the early 1980s in a manner which human rights organizations felt trivialized the issue. In August, the candidates agreed to eliminate the issue from their campaigns in an accord negotiated by Archbishop Oscar Andrés Rodríguez. Although proposals by human rights groups for a Truth Commission to conduct a thorough study of the disappearances were rejected by the President, National Human Rights Commissioner Leo Valladares offered to produce a report on the disappeared by December 31, 1993.

The national security doctrine, which governed Honduras throughout the 1980s, continued to come under reevaluation. Over 150 leftist exiles had returned to their homes since Callejas decreed an amnesty in 1990. Among the exiles returned over the past three years were former members of clandestine armed groups as well as members of the peaceful opposition who fled the repression of the 1980s. Clandestine political organizations and parties, subject to repression throughout the past decade, were seeking to enter mainstream politics.

Contrary to statements in August by U.S. Army Gen. Hugh F. Scruggs—in Honduras for joint U.S.-Honduran army exercises—that there remained a "latent" threat of subversion in Honduras, armed leftist groups had little presence in the country. There were two minuscule groups considered to be still active: the Morazanista Patriotic Front and a radical splinter group of the Cinchoneros. Analysts concurred that these groups had scarce material and human resources and posed virtually no threat to the established regime.

Despite the government's increased rhetorical attention to human rights and the conviction in the Martínez case, security forces continued to commit gross human rights violations with impunity, especially in rural areas. While political violence significantly diminished, the military, including FUSEP, were accustomed to settling economic and personal differences with violence. Abusers were rarely held accountable, "punished" most often with a transfer to another area where they continued to violate citizens' rights.

In one particularly egregious case, José Reina Aguilar was shot to death in the middle of Las Lajas, Comayagua, on January 27 by a patrol composed of fifteen to twenty members of the FUSEP, who later claimed they had orders to disarm him. His son-in-law, Roberto Girón, witnessed the crime. The extrajudicial execution may have been a reprisal; Reina Aguilar was apparently a suspect in the murder of a FUSEP sergeant in 1992. Although the execution was witnessed by many, few were willing to testify for fear of retaliation from the four permanent FUSEP police who, Girón claimed "do whatever they want" in town.

Reports of torture and mistreatment while in police custody continued. José Efraín Orellano García told Americas Watch that he was arrested by two police officers in San Juan Pueblo, Atlántida, for no apparent reason on February 28. He was held in a cell for twenty-four hours, during which time he was beaten, kicked while lying on the ground, doused with water, and released only after paying a 300-lempira ($50) "fine." Complaints filed with the FUSEP's office of professional responsibility and in the courts led nowhere.

Forced recruitment by the army was often a brutal, discriminatory practice that disproportionaly affected the poor in rural areas. Bystanders got caught in violent episodes in which army soldiers used fatal force to recruit young men. On March 6 in La Cumbre de La Masica, José Roberto Romero was having a drink at a street stand when three FUSEP agents apparently attempted to recruit him. When Romero tried to escape, the police shot him in the lower right abdomen. He was in the hospital for six days and was rendered unable to work.

In a case which achieved widespread notoriety, eighteen-year-old Glenda Patricia Solórzano was shot to death on May 21 as she traveled in a bus near La Balsa, Olancho. Soldiers from the 15th Infantry Battalion were attempting to forcibly recruit a young man who had managed to get off the bus. He was running behind the moving bus when the soldiers fired two shots, which missed him, shattered the two back windows, and killed Solórzano. Three others were injured. This last incident occurred only days after the armed forces chief, Gen. Luis Alonso Discua Elvir, temporarily suspended recruitment until after the elections, as mandated by law.

The Right to Monitor

Monitors in Honduras were accustomed to phone tapping and occasional vigilance, which were common. In addition, there were sporadic efforts to discredit or threaten human rights groups. In January, a so-called Group of Four, claiming to be the "armed wing" of the human rights organization Codeh, took responsibility for a bomb which destroyed the car belonging to two sons of the former armed forces chief, retired Gen. Humberto Regalado Hernández. At the time of the explosion, the car was parked near Codeh's San Pedro Sula office while the two sons apparently shopped in a nearby store. Codeh president Dr. Ramón Custodio publicly denied any relationship to the incident or the group.

In February, Human Rights Commissioner Valladares received strong verbal pressures from armed forces chief Discua to discontinue his work, which Discua found damaging to the army's prestige.

U.S. Policy

For ten years, successive U.S. administrations provided Honduras with massive military aid designed to mold it into a bulwark against the perceived communist threat in Nicaragua, El Salvador, and Guatemala. Part of that policy was the systematic whitewashing of the Honduran military's human rights record. With the end of the Cold War, the U.S. began to exert more pressure on the Honduran armed forces to end human rights abuses and reduce their quota of power.

Ambassador Arcos left in mid-1993 with an impressive record of human rights advocacy from the U.S. Embassy, pressure that was particularly important in the Martínez case.

Military aid to Honduras declined after 1990, although foreign military sales by the U.S. government remained relatively high. The U.S. provided an estimated $1.5 million in military aid to Honduras in fiscal year 1993 and spent $1.1 million training the army. In addition, the administration provided approximately $9.7 million in Economic Support Funds (ESF), cash payments to the Callejas government. The Clinton administration requested similar levels of military aid for fiscal year 1994, but only $7.5 million in ESF. Foreign military sales agreements worth $10 million were reached in fiscal year 1993 and a similar level was expected to be approved in fiscal year 1994. Americas Watch urged the administration to use its remaining security assistance program, and other sources of influence, as a lever for human rights improvements, including the total separation of the police from the military, and prosecution of those responsible for human rights violations.

The 1992 State Department *Country Report on Human Rights Practices*, for Honduras, although far from exhaustive, directly implicated the armed forces in human rights abuses. The report cited "the tendency of [armed forces] personnel to protect officers accused of abuses; the inability of civilians to levy formal accusations before military courts; ill-trained and poorly equipped judiciary and police forces; and an endemically corrupt and inefficient criminal justice system" as obstacles to overcoming military impunity. The State Department asserted that a fundamental problem was "the failure of the Supreme Court to render decisions about the jurisdiction of the civilian courts over [armed forces] personnel accused of offenses involving civilians."

In July 1993, William Pryce, a Latin America specialist on the National Security Council during the Bush administration, became the new U.S. ambassador in Honduras. Pryce told Americas Watch that human rights were a pivotal aspect of U.S. policy of promoting democracy in Honduras. It was unclear, however, whether the new ambassador would use his position of considerable weight to pressure the Honduran government as his predecessor did.

The Work of Americas Watch

The unprecedented reform efforts underway in Honduras during 1992 and 1993 warranted new research by Americas Watch to evaluate the evolving human rights situation. Two Americas Watch researchers conducted a fact-finding mission in October 1993, taking testimony from victims and witnesses of human rights violations and holding meetings with the national human rights commissioner, a member of the Ad Hoc Commission, the U.S. ambassador, and human rights organizations.

During the meeting of the General Assembly of the Organization of American States in Managua in June, Americas Watch and the Center for Justice and International Law (CEJIL) publicized Honduras's failure to comply fully with the decision of the Inter-American Court of Human Rights holding the government responsible for the disappearance of Manfredo Angel Velásquez in 1981 and Saúl Godínez Cruz in 1982. Although the court in August 1990 adjusted the amount of damages that Honduras owed to the victims' families to compensate for Honduras's delinquent payment, the Callejas government still failed to compensate the families in accordance with the court's ruling. Americas Watch and CEJIL continued in 1993 to press members of the U.S. Congress to make full compliance with the court's verdict a condition to receive U.S. security assistance.

MEXICO

Human Rights Developments

Despite the Mexican government's efforts, in connection with the North American Free Trade Agreement (NAFTA) debate, to portray its human rights problems in the best possible light, Americas Watch's concerns in 1993 were virtually unchanged from prior years. Torture and police abuse; election-related abuses; and interference with freedom of expression and association of human rights monitors, independent trade unionists, peasant and indigenous rights activists, election observers, and journalists, were still pervasive problems. Moreover, notwithstanding legal reforms and personnel changes, impunity for those responsible continued.

In January 1993, President Salinas heightened expectations that he would restrain abuses when he named Dr. Jorge Carpizo as his third attorney general. Carpizo, a distinguished jurist and scholar, had solidified his reputation for integrity and commitment to human rights during his tenure as the first president of the National Human Rights Commission (CNDH). In his new role, one of his principal tasks was to clean up the Federal Judicial Police (FJP), an agency contaminated by ties to drug traffickers, whose agents had tortured and even murdered with impunity.

Attorney General Carpizo announced several rounds of dismissals of FJP agents identified as having connections with drug traffickers. He also filed criminal charges against Guillermo González Calderoni, a senior FJP Commander under his predecessor, Ignacio Morales Lechuga. González Calderoni had been implicated in human rights abuses, including the 1991 torture and murder of the Quijano brothers, and corruption. Unfortunately, the charges against him did not include torture or homicide.

In spite of Carpizo's efforts, the FJP remained plagued by corruption and human rights abuses. On March 1, 1993, former FJP agent Jesús Rioja Vázquez was arrested after he went on a rampage in Hermosillo, Sonora, during which he machine-gunned to death four people and ran over a fifth with his truck. At the time he was working for the FJP commander in Hermosillo as a *madrina*, or free-lance police agent. Rioja Vázquez had previously been implicated in the January 1990 FJP murders of the Quijano brothers, and a warrant for his arrest had been issued. Although his whereabouts were known, no steps were taken to bring him to justice and thus prevent the massacre. In addition, the investigation into the May 24, 1993 murder of Cardinal Juan Jesús Posadas Ocampo and six other persons in the Guadalajara airport revealed that several FJP agents were involved.

Attorney General Carpizo compromised his reputation as a human rights champion by supporting certain measures that violated fundamental rights. Those measures included a new law that doubled the amount of time prosecutors were permitted to detain criminal suspects involved in organized crime before presenting them to a court (most torture occurs in the period before criminal suspects are brought before a judge). Carpizo also implemented a new federal highway roadblock program to thwart arms and drug trafficking and prevent kidnappings (the move reversed President Salinas' July 1990 decision to eliminate checkpoints on the nation's highways, as these had long been used by police for extortion); he refused to meet face to face with the press and to disclose the names and criminal charges, if any, brought against fired FJP officers. Contrary to his record at the CNDH, as attorney general Carpizo did not prosecute to the fullest extent of the law those officers who engaged in human rights abuses. In September, Carpizo's hand-picked human rights liaison officer, children's rights activist María Guadalupe Andrea Bárcena, resigned complaining that deceit, corruption, and the lack of will to uphold justice in the attorney general's office made her job impossible.

Salinas's most significant human rights reform was the creation, in 1990, of the CNDH, an ombudsman agency authorized to investigate human rights complaints. By 1993, the CNDH had become an enormous, constitutionally mandated government bureaucracy with more than 600 staff members and its own building. It was hampered by mandate limitations that barred it from investigating violations of political and labor rights and from looking into matters that were under consideration by a court. The CNDH's inability to enforce its recommendations—which all too often were ignored by responsible government agencies—further hindered its effectiveness. Hundreds of recommendations from the CNDH about murder, torture, arbitrary detention, and other abuses were an important step in the direction of ending impunity; nevertheless, they also proved that serious human rights problems persisted.

The CNDH's independence—in fact as well as in law—from all authorities and its support for Mexican nongovernmental human rights organizations needed to be strengthened. For example, in Chiapas, senior military officials accused the Catholic church-affiliated Fray Bartolomé de las Casas Human Rights Center of spreading "odious lies" about the military, "defending criminals," and "obstructing justice." In March 1993, soldiers searching for two fellow officers who had vanished while on patrol, illegally raided homes, confiscated or destroyed property, tortured suspects, and arbitrarily arrested at least seventeen persons. The center denounced the abuses, after which the military charged that the center had coached witnesses into fabricating testimony. The CNDH investigated the incident and in its recommendation backed the military's assertion. Independent human rights groups, including the Minnesota Advocates for Human Rights, looked into the military's and the CNDH's accusations and found them to be unfounded.

The CNDH also needed to be more responsive to individual victims of human rights violations. During 1993 the CNDH only condemned torture in cases in which there was physical evidence of torture; it failed to consider evidence of psychological torture. Moreover, the CNDH did not recommend compensation for victims. Nor did it complain when persons accused of torture were charged with lesser crimes, such as abuse of authority or administrative infractions, even though, under Mexican law, this could prevent a victim from obtaining redress.

In response to internal pressure and mounting international publicity about electoral fraud during the NAFTA debate, the Salinas administration pushed through the legislature a series of bills to overhaul election procedures. While the new laws addressed campaign financing, the voter registration process, the number and apportionment of seats for members of Congress, electoral observation, and oversight of the ballot count, they carefully avoided any genuine threat to the monopoly on political power enjoyed by the ruling Partido Revolucionario Institucional (PRI). Steps to ensure free and fair elections would include: granting all political parties equal access to campaign financing, the media, and the use of the national colors; permitting professional, independent and impartial election observers to monitor elections and have full access to all election machinery, including computers; barring the military from putting on displays of force on election day that could deter voters from going to the polls; and establishing an independent, impartial electoral commission in which no political party or alliance of parties would dominate and the Minister of Government would play no role.

One measure that appeared progressive was in fact carefully crafted to remove an opposition candidate from contention in the 1994 presidential election. Article 82 of the Mexican Constitution was amended to allow persons born in Mexico whose parents were born outside the country to run for President. But that provision was not due to go into effect until the year 2000, thereby blocking the candidacy of Vicente Fox Quesada, a popular and charismatic Partido de Acción Nacional (PAN) leader whom the government considers a worrisome challenger.

The Right to Monitor

Individuals who publicly challenged the government or the PRI during 1993 faced an array of tactics to bring them into line or immobilize them. Independent human rights activist Víctor Clark Alfaro, director of the Binational Center for Human Rights (CBDH)

in Tijuana, was subjected to repeated efforts to silence him. In April 1993, the CBDH published a report on torture and corruption in the Baja California state judicial police that included eighty-four cases of torture, and alleged that drug traffickers were buying police credentials from corrupt officials. Many of the report's findings were independently supported by the state's own human rights commission. Nonetheless, the chief of security for the state attorney general alleged that he had been defamed and slandered, and the public prosecutor filed criminal charges against Clark. An appellate court later dismissed those charges on grounds of insufficient evidence. Meanwhile, Clark's offices were broken into, staff members received telephone death threats, and *madrinas* watched the office. While he continued his work, Clark was preoccupied with the security of his staff and the police informants who provided him with the data for his report.

Arturo Solís Gómez, president of the Centro de Estudios Fronterizos y Promoción de los Derechos Humanos, A.C. (CEFPRODHAC) in Tamaulipas, was the focus of similar intimidation by state authorities. Many of those abuses were linked to drug trafficking and the associated corruption of police and prison guards. While in the past many of the cases documented by CEFPRODHAC involved federal judicial police, in 1993 the dominant pattern changed and the most serious cases of torture and abuse reported to CEFPRODHAC involved state police in the border cities of Matamoros, Reynosa, and Río Bravo. At the same time, reported cases of abuse in the state prison persisted at previous levels.

According to CEFPRODHAC, this increase in state cases coincided with the inauguration of Gov. Manuel Cavazos Lerma in February 1993. Instead of receiving the cooperation of the new state leadership in combatting these abuses, CEFPRODHAC found itself the object of a public campaign to discredit it. CEFPRODHAC reported that it had been accused by State Attorney General Raúl Morales Cadena and State Director of Prisons Francisco Castellanos de la Garza of protecting criminals. It further claimed that it had been accused by the PRI and two smaller political parties in Matamoros of spying for foreign interests because it had received funding from the Ford Foundation and other U.S.-based nongovernmental philanthropic institutions. Finally, a CEFPRODHAC bulletin charged that the director of prisons "asked several journalists whose salaries are paid by the state government to accuse the CEFPRODHAC of being financed by drug traffickers and to state that the group charges money to detainees who have brought legal action to win their release from prison."

Independent union leaders and their lawyers were vulnerable to pressure tactics, including misuse of the criminal justice system, designed to convince them to curtail their activities. Agapito González Cavazos, head of the Day Laborers' and Industrial Workers Union in Matamoros, led the fight to win higher wages for workers than allowed by a longstanding pact between the government and the official union. At a critical moment in the negotiations, the seventy-six-year-old González was arrested by the FJP on four-year-old tax evasion charges. Although he was released several months later, the settlement reached with the workers while he was in prison was substantially less than he had been seeking.

According to press reports, Carlos Enrique López Barrios, a lawyer defending Tzotzil Indians in Chiapas, was beaten on April 27, 1993 by three unidentified men who seized the lawyer's appointment book and identification cards. The beating occurred while the group he worked with, Abogados y Asesores Asociados, was defending Tzotzil Indians from San Isidro el Ocotal who had been accused of a recent killing of two soldiers.

Despite steps taken by the Salinas administration in 1992 to modernize relations between the federal government and the media, in 1993 journalists still were subject to pressures to conform. Miguel Angel Granados Chapa, one of Mexico's most re-

spected political columnists, was required by the private radio station for which he worked to submit for prior approval the names of guests he intended to feature on his program. The demand occurred just after Granados Chapa hosted opposition presidential candidate Cuauhtémoc Cárdenas. The radio station's license was under review by government authorities at the time. Granados Chapa resigned rather than comply with the censorship demand. After he went public with his accusations, President Salinas called him to say that the government had nothing to do with his departure and to offer him a program on a government-owned radio station. Manuel Villa, the government official in charge of radio and television licensing, was removed from his post and named to head the newly formed National Institute of Migration.

U.S. Policy

Mexico was a U.S. policy priority in 1993 as a result of the intense debate concerning the North American Free Trade Agreement (NAFTA). Shamefully lacking during both the negotiations and the ratification debate was any genuine concern about Mexico's failure to protect fundamental human rights and to ensure political accountability. Even the supplemental agreements that were negotiated by the Clinton administration to repair deficiencies in the text it inherited from the Bush administration ignored these issues. While the environmental side agreement established a trilateral commission with the authority to investigate complaints about noncompliance with environmental standards, no similar mechanism was created in the labor side agreement, nor did that agreement affirm the rights of workers to organize and strike. By downplaying rights abuses and serious restrictions on democracy in Mexico, while engaging in the most profound restructuring of economic relations ever between the two countries, the Clinton administration missed an unprecedented opportunity to help Mexico's people achieve badly needed human rights reforms.

The Clinton administration passed up

another important opportunity to press Mexico on labor rights concerns when it announced in October that it was refusing to accept for review a petition on worker rights filed by the International Labor Rights Education and Research Fund 1993, pursuant to the mandatory labor rights conditions on the Generalized System of Preferences, a U.S. trade benefits program.

The administration's approach to Mexican human rights was characterized by the testimony of John Shattuck, the assistant secretary of state for human rights, democracy and labor, at an October 19 hearing before the House Foreign Affairs Committee. Secretary Shattuck described abuses frankly, but used the occasion as an opportunity to defend vigorously the NAFTA agreement, and made the claim, debatable at best, that adoption of the trade agreement would enhance human rights in Mexico.

Americas Watch was heartened by Ambassador-Designate to Mexico James R. Jones's testimony during his Senate confirmation hearings in September, in which he promised to promote human rights in Mexico at the Organization of American States (OAS) and U.N. and to "work with the Mexican government to carry out democratic reforms." We also were pleased to see that in the Congressional Presentation for Security Assistance Programs for fiscal year 1994, the department of defense identified as a central program objective the encouragement of "greater support among Mexico's military for democratization and respect for human rights." Unfortunately, the Pentagon did not explain how it planned to encourage support for democracy and respect for human rights in a military force that is absolutely loyal to the President, shielded from the press, and as much a part of the monolithic political system as any other institution in Mexico.

The Work of Americas Watch

In October, Americas Watch released a briefing paper on intimidation of activists in Mexico that examined government interference with core political rights of six catego-

ries of governmental critics or opponents: human rights monitors, labor organizers, *campesino* (peasant) and indigenous rights activists, environmentalists, journalists, and election observers.

In November, Americas Watch participated in a conference in Mexico City sponsored by Mexican nongovernmental organizations and focusing on police abuse in that city. At the conference, Americas Watch released a report on police abuse in Mexico City. In addition, a chapter on prison conditions in Mexico was included in the *Human Rights Watch Global Report on Prisons*. Work continued on the forthcoming Human Rights Watch-Yale University Press book on human rights in Mexico and on a report with the Natural Resource Defense Council on intimidation of environmental activists in Mexico.

NICARAGUA

Human Rights Developments

The human rights situation in Nicaragua during 1993, as in recent years, continued to be shaped by a highly polarized political environment, a weak central government (including a feeble judicial system), and violent actions by rearmed groups of ex-*contras* and former Sandinista army soldiers, including two major hostage-taking episodes in mid-year.

The Popular Sandinista Army (EPS) and police engaged in an excessive and disproportionate use of force in several instances when responding to rearmed groups, striking workers, and peaceful protesters. The general reign of impunity and the inability of the Nicaraguan state to administer justice continued to be the greatest obstacles to an improved human rights situation.

The crisis of governability experienced by the administration of President Violeta Chamorro, which spent most of the year veering from one political crisis to another, was rooted in the government's loss of support by political sectors that had previously constituted its base. The United Nicaraguan Opposition (UNO) that supported the Chamorro candidacy in the 1990 elections formally declared itself in opposition in early 1993. The government consequently relied largely on the bloc of deputies from the Sandinista National Liberation Front (FSLN) in the National Assembly to pass legislation. The FSLN, however, experienced its own divisions over this alliance, and by mid-year had made its support for the Chamorro government conditional. Several half-hearted attempts at national dialogue failed. In addition, a crippling economic recession—government figures placed the unemployment and underemployment rates at 50 percent—exacerbated social instability.

Because of the polarized political atmosphere and the lack of any effective state mechanism for the investigation and prosecution of violent crimes, the vast majority of deaths and other injuries with apparent political overtones remained the subject of a heated polemic between opposing forces. Both the Sandinista leaders, on the one hand, and the former contras and anti-Sandinista forces on the other, claimed that hundreds of their supporters have been systematically killed by the other side. State responsibility for this violence added to political polarization, since Sandinista officers still headed the military apparatus and were largely in charge of the police, although there had been substantial turnover among the rank-and-file.

The judiciary continued to be ineffective. The public perception that judges were partial to the Sandinistas lingered despite the fact that some 70 percent of judges had been replaced during Chamorro's term in office. Judicial actions in high-profile murder cases, such as that of former *contra* leader Enrique Bermúdez (in which Scotland Yard detectives gave some assistance during 1993) and teenager Jean-Paul Genie, also did not progress.

In the Genie case, the government refused a request by the OAS Inter-American Commission on Human Rights to accept the jurisdiction of the Inter-American Court of Justice in Costa Rica. By mid-November the Nicaraguan Supreme Court had yet to rule on whether the military or civilian courts should have jurisdiction, given that the alleged suspects were bodyguards of Gen. Humberto Ortega. Some analysts believed that progress might occur in this case in 1994, when the terms of four of the five Sandinista appointees on the Supreme Court expired and the Chamorro government replaced them.

The government was also unable to capture and prosecute former EPS lieutenant colonel Frank Ibarra, head of the so-called Fuerzas Punitivas de Izquierda (Leftist Punitive Forces, or FPI), which took credit for the November 23, 1992, murder of property-rights activist Arges Sequeira. With assistance from the Spanish police, the government carried out a credible investigation into Sequeira's murder, identifying Ibarra and several others as the culprits.

The one development that could have contributed to de-politicizing the human rights debate in Nicaragua was the creation of the Tripartite Commission, an investigative body composed of government representatives from the Interior and the Foreign Affairs Ministries, the Verification Commission headed by Cardinal Miguel Obando y Bravo, and the OAS's International Commission of Support and Verification (CIAV), which had monitored the fate of the demobilized contra forces since 1990. The Tripartite Commission was formed in September 1992 to review some 600 cases of abuses against and by former contras. The commission decided to focus on some one hundred cases of political violence—half involving deaths of former contras, and half in which the victims are presumed to be Sandinistas—in order to arrive at a consensus position as to who was responsible and to evaluate the role of the judiciary, police, and military in investigating and punishing those responsible.

The initial findings of the commission, which dealt only with homicides of former contras, provided a more complex picture of the security situation of ex-rebels than was normally portrayed by either their supporters or opponents. The first report, presented to President Chamorro in February, dealt with nine cases of killings of former contras and one case of the killing of a family member of a former contra.

In only three of these cases did the commission find the state directly responsible for the killings: in two cases, the army (EPS) was responsible, and in the third the police were responsible. In all the other cases, civilians were held responsible, while in one case the perpetrator could not be determined. In three of these civilian cases, members of Sandinista cooperatives were cited as responsible in various land disputes. In the one case involving the *recompas*, or re-armed former Sandinista military, there was testimony given to the commission that indicated the direct collaboration of the EPS.

The outstanding common denominator of these cases was the fact that all but one of them were inadequately investigated and punished by police and judicial authorities. The creation of the Tripartite Commission did stimulate the government to carry out investigations for the first time or to reopen cases that it had previously closed. However, in only one of the first ten cases presented had anyone been detained (a policeman), and that only came about, apparently, after the Tripartite Commission began its investigation.

A second report detailing eighteen cases (including forty-two violent deaths of former contras, their family members, and other civilians) was presented to the government in June 1993. Of these eighteen cases, the EPS was found to be responsible in four, although two of these were deemed common crimes. A more serious case was one in which members of the EPS were found to have placed mines on a road that resulted in the deaths of fourteen civilians and former contras in Pita del Carmen, Jinotega, on August 21, 1991. No police investigation was ever carried out.

In four of the eighteen cases, the authors were identified as recompas. The commission received evidence of police complicity in one recompa action; at the same time, the only case among the eighteen in which someone was detained involved recompa responsibility. Civilians were responsible in nine cases (three of these accounted for the only "normal" police investigations), the police in one case, and in one case the author was unidentified. While the state was not predominantly responsible for these killings by civilians, the police and judicial investigations were, as noted in the first report, largely "irregular," "insufficient," "incomplete," or "nonexistent."

A third report, due out in late 1993, was to be the first to deal with cases of Sandinista victims. A comparison of the efficacy of police and judicial investigations in such cases with those already studied would allow for a judgment as to whether cases involving Sandinista victims had been taken more seriously by the state. Previous experience by Americas Watch would lead to the conclusion that they have not been. The commission is also expected to make recommendations for the reform of the law governing the Auditoría Militar, the military body which investigates and sanctions abuses committed by the army and police.

The Tripartite Commission has faced innumerable problems and obstacles in its work. First, the government has pledged to respect the recommendations of the commission (reopen cases, prosecute those responsible, etc.), yet only one of the handful of reopened cases of homicide committed by police or military officers and sent to the Auditoría Militar resulted in a conviction during 1993.

While there generally appeared to have been a good-faith effort by police authorities to carry out administrative sanctions, in one case cited by the Nicaraguan Association Pro-Human Rights (ANPDH), a police officer from Waslala who had supposedly been discharged in accord with the commission's recommendations later killed again while on active duty. The Auditoría Militar found this officer guilty *in absentia*, but he has not been detained. In many cases, the police have been unable to arrest suspects identified by the Tripartite Commission; military officers who have been held responsible by the Commission have also fled before they could be arrested.

In addition, the commission's work progressed more slowly than anticipated, due both to the difficulty of arriving at a consensus position on highly charged cases and to the inability of government representatives (who are also responsible for handling many of the political crises affecting Nicaragua) to attend meetings. The commission's discussion of deaths of Sandinista victims was likely to slow the process even further, since these cases had not been investigated by the CIAV and only rarely by human rights organizations.

Finally, there was no publicity given to the findings of the commission inside Nicaragua, an important oversight on the commission's part. The release of information could both generate public pressure for justice in the cases investigated, and at the same time lower the level of polemic around the deaths of former contras.

The most serious obstacle to the work of the Tripartite Commission, however, was the government's promulgation of an amnesty law on August 10 for all "political and related common crimes committed up to August 15" (later extended to August 28). The amnesty exempts crimes against humanity and violations of international humanitarian law, although it remained unclear how the government or individual judges would interpret these provisions. The law would also "not affect the functions and purposes" of the Tripartite Commission with respect to "clarification of the facts" and the "determination of the consequent responsibilities." The law was thus not meant to hinder the commission's investigative work, but did not specifically exempt from the amnesty the cases studied by the commission.

In practice, the issue of who should be covered by the August amnesty will depend on each individual judge. In the Arges Sequeira case, for example, a judge (with support from the attorney general's office) determined this to be a common crime that occurred outside of a conflictive zone. The judge thus brought Frank Ibarra and others from the FPI to trial *in absentia*, a move that raised serious questions of due process. A grave example of the kinds of pressures that can be exerted on judges making decisions on whether or not the amnesty should apply was evident on September 28, when gunmen forced a judge in Estelí to sign release papers for some seventy-two prisoners, some of whom had been sentenced for purely common crimes.

The amnesty was the third one promulgated since Chamorro's election in February 1990. The first was passed by the Sandinista-dominated National Assembly, with opposition support, in March 1990, shortly before the Sandinistas left office; another was decreed by Chamorro's government in December 1991. The National Assembly passed the August 1993 amnesty law by a vote of 45 to 4, with one abstention. The Sandinista bloc voted unanimously in favor of the law, while the UNO deputies walked out before the vote was taken. The Chamorro government had promoted the idea of an amnesty since May as part of an inducement to some 1,400 recontra and recompa forces that eventually disarmed and congregated in security zones. In our view, however, it is one thing to declare an amnesty for the purpose of allowing former combatants to lay down their arms and re-enter civilian life, and something quite different to extend that amnesty to those who have committed serious abuses during or outside a combat situation.

The ineffectiveness of the amnesty as both a deterrent and inducement to groups of *rearmados* to lay down their weapons was vividly demonstrated by a twin hostage-taking crisis in mid-August. A week after the amnesty law was first passed, recontras of the Frente Norte 3-80, headed by José Angel Talavera (alias "El Chacal") kidnapped a delegation of more than three dozen legislators, government officials, and soldiers who had ventured into the northern town of Quilalí to convince them to accept a government amnesty. The following day, a group of former Sandinista military officers calling themselves the National Dignity Command took over the UNO headquarters in Managua and took hostage dozens of opposition politicians, including Vice-President Virgilio Godoy.

After the crisis ended a week later, the recompa kidnappers, along with most other recompa groups, availed themselves of the amnesty. Meanwhile the recontras under the leadership of "El Chacal" entered into further negotiations with the government. These broke off in mid-October, after which the EPS launched a military campaign against them.

Criminal and political violence continued to plague the Nicaraguan countryside throughout 1993, as groups of former contras and Sandinistas rearmed themselves to press for economic demands (land and credit), political demands (such as recontra demands for the removal of army chief Gen. Humberto Ortega), or simply to commit robberies. The actions of such groups throughout the year left scores of persons dead and wounded. On May 18 President Chamorro decreed a thirty-day suspension of constitutional guarantees under Article 150 of the Constitution in several northern departments of Nicaragua as part of a program to concentrate and demobilize members of rearmed groups. The decree suspended rights regarding arbitrary detention and searches without warrants. No complaints of abuses emerged about its implementation, and the President restored full civil liberties on June 16. The government also continued its collection of arms through special disarmament brigades; by mid-year, they had retrieved over 120,000 arms.

Military tactics brought about a rare consensus among Nicaraguan human rights groups in 1993, which uniformly condemned army practices. The EPS launched an aggressive military campaign at the end of 1992 and the beginning of 1993 against the rearmed groups. But conservative critics of the army denounced not only the military's failure to act forcefully against rearmed Sandinistas; they also accused the EPS of aiding and abetting them.

Perhaps because of this criticism, the EPS responded with no holds barred to the takeover of Estelí on July 21 by recompas of the Workers and Peasants Revolutionary Front (FROC) under the command of a former Sandinista major, Victor Manuel Gallego (alias "Pedrito el Hondureño"). The army reported some forty-five dead and wounded in the fighting, although the Nicaraguan Center for Human Rights (CENIDH), the Permanent Commission for Human Rights (CPDH), and ANPDH said those numbers were inflated. All these groups criticized the armed assault by the recompas, including the incident in which some fifteen armed FROC took up positions in a local hospital, a serious and reckless violation of international humanitarian law. But human rights groups also criticized the ferocity of the army's counterattack. The ANPDH and CENIDH both singled out the army's counterattack on the hospital as unnecessarily endangering civilian lives.

Both the CENIDH and the ANPDH also criticized the military's response to the early September takeover of San Ramón, Matagalpa, by rearmed groups. In that instance, two recompas were killed after being taken prisoner, while three civilians were killed and four others wounded.

The National Police reacted more aggressively against striking unionists and ex-army officers (sometimes armed) during 1993, something that occurred in tandem with changes in the police, including replacing older Sandinista figures with younger ones. The replacement of Police Chief René Vivas with Fernando Caldera was seen by some as a positive step, although both the ANPDH and CPDH criticized Caldera's human rights record during the time of the contra war.

CENIDH, for example, reported in 1993 that the police had used excessive force in evicting striking workers from the central customs installations in Managua on June 9, had beaten several workers in jail, and had lodged trumped-up charges against them to justify its behavior. In an earlier episode in September 1992, students and ex-EPS officers demonstrating peacefully during independence day celebrations (at which President Chamorro was present) were beaten by the police without provocation.

Under international pressure, 1993 also saw renewed (albeit symbolic) efforts by the civilian government of Violeta Chamorro to bring under control the large security apparatus it inherited from eleven years of Sandinista rule. A September 2 announcement by the President that General Ortega would leave his post as head of the EPS in 1994 brought an angry response from the army and the FSLN. However, in early October, the UNO and the FSLN reached an agreement that Ortega would leave once a new military organization law was passed by the National Assembly. Ortega had come under increasing criticism since the May explosion of an arms cache in Managua belonging to the Salvadoran guerrillas and the subsequent suspicion that high-level military authorities must have known about its existence.

In October, President Chamorro created by executive decree a new civilian intelligence agency, called the Office of Intelligence Affairs, to replace the EPS's Defense Information Directorate. (The DID had been headed until then by Col. Lenín Cerna, previously director of State Security in the Ministry of Interior and singled out for numerous human rights violations). Chamorro appointed agronomist Sergio Narváez Sampson, a personal friend with no political party affiliation and no previous experience in intelligence matters. Cerna, meanwhile, was promoted to the post of Inspector General, the third-highest ranking position in the EPS, a move that demonstrated Chamorro's still-tenuous control over military matters.

The Right to Monitor

Human rights groups were largely able to operate within Nicaragua without restrictions. The Permanent Commission on Human Rights (CPDH) worked closely with the Ministry of Government in visiting prisons in 1992 and 1993. The CPDH, the ANPDH,

and CENIDH all assisted in the negotiations during the August hostage crisis.

CENIDH reported that Leonel González, a human rights promoter and justice of the peace in Muelle de los Bueyes, Chontales, was killed by unidentified members of a rearmed group on March 26. On August 13, a foreign journalist and two members of the ANPDH were shot at by unidentified gunmen as they were returning from a visit to Jalapa, Nueva Segovia, although there were no injuries.

The International Commission of Support and Verification (CIAV) of the OAS continued to operate in formerly conflictive zones, monitoring rights of the demobilized contras and their families. The CIAV also participated in the Tripartite Commission. In late October, during the military's campaign against the recontras under the command of "El Chacal," the CIAV denounced that several of its vehicles had been denied access to areas in the north, preventing monitors from investigating several denunciations of abuses.

In June, the CIAV's mandate was expanded to include all persons affected by the war, not just those of the demobilized Nicaraguan Resistance. This widened mandate, a welcome step, had yet to be implemented by late 1993.

U.S. Policy

The Clinton administration continued a policy of support for the fragile Chamorro government, simultaneously seeking to foster political reconciliation among all parties and to prod the government to reform the security apparatus and improve human rights.

On April 2, the State Department announced that it was releasing $50 million in economic aid held up by the Bush administration. The aid was released as a tentative sign of support for steps that Chamorro had taken in reducing the size of the army and reforming the economy. The State Department took note of the ongoing work of the Tripartite Commission, the suspension of several police officers named in its first report, and the government's request for a broadened and extended mandate for the CIAV.

After media accounts reported in mid-1993 that recontra groups were receiving aid from Cuban-American groups in Miami, the State Department issued a stern warning that such activities were possibly illegal and "particularly repugnant in that they could support violence directed against a friendly government." Assistant Secretary of State for Inter-American Affairs Alexander Watson reiterated in early October that the U.S. stood ready to prosecute those who violated U.S. neutrality or related laws.

The discovery in Managua of several arms caches left by the Salvadoran guerrillas and containing weapons, fake passports and identity cards, and references to an international kidnapping ring, aroused strong suspicions that senior members of the Sandinista security or intelligence apparatus had approved or known of the caches' existence. In late July, the U.S. Senate approved, by a vote of 77 to 23, an amendment offered by Sen. Jesse Helms (R-NC) to ban aid to Nicaragua due to alleged links to international terrorism.

This amendment was subsequently dropped in a House-Senate conference, but the foreign aid appropriations bill for fiscal year 1994 required the State Department to block economic aid until it reported to Congress that the Nicaraguan government had investigated and prosecuted those found to be responsible for the arms caches, and had made "significant and tangible" progress in reforming the security forces and judicial system and in implementing the recommendations of the Tripartite Commission.

Shortly after the passage of the bill, Assistant Secretary Watson told Congress that the U.S. was reasonably assured that the "current Government of Nicaragua is not involved" in international terrorism activities. In public and private, Watson continued to press senior Nicaraguan officials on key human rights cases as well as the need to exert civilian control over the security forces.

The Work of Americas Watch

Americas Watch visited Nicaragua four times from December 1992 through October 1993 as part of an effort to monitor human rights violations in the context of accelerating political violence. Through contacts with Clinton administration officials, local and international human rights groups, Nicaraguan government representatives, and the U.S. Congress, Americas Watch attempted to ensure that human rights issues were included on the broad agenda of political reconciliation. Our public opposition to the government's proposed amnesty in mid-1993 received wide attention in the Nicaraguan press, and, along with the efforts of Nicaraguan human rights and civic groups, may have resulted in several exemptions from the amnesty law.

Americas Watch continued to press the Nicaraguan government on individual human rights cases and due process issues, as part of a broader effort to end impunity. A report on the findings of the Tripartite Commission and efforts to reform the military and police was scheduled for early 1994.

PERU

Human Rights Developments

This was a year of consolidation for Alberto Fujimori, an elected president who seized dictatorial power on April 5, 1992. Although international pressure later forced changes favorable to human rights, President Fujimori marshaled unprecedented power over formerly autonomous institutions like the judiciary, Public Ministry, a newly-elected congress, and the security forces. A new legal apparatus suppressed individual rights while the institutions designed to protect them were weakened or eliminated.

For human rights, this meant isolated gains in the context of continuing, serious violations. According to the government's Public Ministry and the nongovernmental National Coordinating Committee for Human Rights (Coordinadora), the number of disappearances reported in the first nine months of 1993 dropped compared with the same period in 1992, from 168 to sixty-one. The number of extrajudicial executions attributed to the security forces also decreased. Violations of the laws of war by Peru's two guerrilla groups—the Communist Party of Peru-Shining Path or Sendero Luminoso and the Túpac Amaru Revolutionary Movement (MRTA)—also decreased in number, if not severity.

Yet these figures should not be taken out of context: reporting on human rights violations was complicated by the lack of independence of once-autonomous branches of government, threats against human rights monitors, and the criminalization of such vague offenses as creating "a state of anxiety" or "affecting international relations" (Decree Law 25475). Many officials feared losing their jobs, and ordinary citizens feared imprisonment, if they supplied information. In the central and southern jungle, where violence was intense, the coup had exacerbated the difficult task of documenting reports of human rights abuse.

And some individuals who in earlier years might have been disappeared or killed by the security forces were arrested in 1993 under special laws promulgated after the coup. Tried secretly inside prison by hooded or "faceless" judges and prosecutors, defendants were prevented from mounting a meaningful defense. Those charged with "treason"—a charge that incorporated such disproportionate offenses as distributing Shining Path propaganda in the classroom and detonating a car bomb—were tried by hooded military judges, who handed down convictions in 97 percent of the cases brought to them in 1992 and most of 1993. Lawyers were not permitted to represent more than one such client at a time; the rights to *habeas corpus*, and provisional liberty were suspended; and defendants could be held in incommunicado police detention for up to thirty days.

Except in rare instances, suspects were unable to present witnesses in their defense or confront the prosecution. Torture, including rape, in police detention remained frequent, and confessions were routinely coerced. Many prominent Peruvians chose exile rather than face judicial procedures stacked against them. Along with admitted guerrillas, the accused included human rights monitors, journalists, environmental activists, doctors who had treated guerrillas under threat of death, and common citizens caught in the wrong place at the wrong time.

In repeated instances, judges based convictions not on evidence but unproved allegations. For instance, Darnilda Pardavé Trujillo was imprisoned from October 1992 through October 1993 because her sister, Yovanka, was a Shining Path leader. In his indictment, the judge concluded that it was "impossible to discard the possibility" that Darnilda knew of her sister's crimes despite the lack of any evidence. On October 29, 1993, she was finally acquitted and released. María de la Cruz Pari, who went voluntarily to the anti-terrorism police to testify on behalf of a family member on January 6, 1993, was herself arrested and raped. Antero Peña Peña, a peasant leader from the department of Piura, was detained on May 27, 1993, by soldiers who claimed to have found a subversive leaflet in his home. Police tortured Peña over the course of four days. Although the public prosecutor found no merit to the case, Peña remained imprisoned as of November.

Peruvian human rights groups believed several hundred individuals being prosecuted for terrorism or treason were innocent. For many, their only hope of freedom lay in a personal appeal to President Fujimori. Thus, justice hinged on the whims of the chief executive, who boasted publicly that he followed certain cases and telephoned the attorney general or justice minister to register his opinion. In March, for instance, President Fujimori visited jailed journalist Danilo Quijano and declared him unjustly accused, even as Quijano's case was before a faceless court. Quijano was eventually acquitted.

Thirty-three army officers court-martialed for allegedly plotting a coup in November 1992 were also denied fair trial.

Among other things, the officers were held incommunicado for ten to twenty days (the Military Code of Justice allows for only five days). Four claimed they were tortured, an allegation that did not receive sufficient investigation. A request by Americas Watch to observe their secret trials was ignored by the government. Fujimori eventually pardoned eleven men.

In response to widespread criticism, President Fujimori announced in June that the attorney general would review cases to prevent the innocent from being unjustly sentenced. The new congress, Congreso Constituyente Democrático (CCD) formed an honor board to review claims from dozens of judges dismissed arbitrarily after the coup and to evaluate the performance of Fujimori appointees, both judges and prosecutors. However, once issued, the honor board's recommendations appeared to be ignored.

In October, the government submitted a bill to modify aspects of anti-terrorist legislation that violate fundamental rights. The bill would restore *habeas corpus* and *amparo*; lift the restriction barring attorneys from representing more than one defendant at a time; prohibit *in absentia* trials; and allow for a final appeal in terrorism and treason cases before the Supreme Council of Military Justice. This appeal, or "revision," would be used to correct "a flagrant judicial error," according to the Prime Minister. If incorporated, these revisions would represent an improvement. Nonetheless, the system would remain inherently abusive since secret trials, prolonged incommunicado detention, the inability to cross-examine prosecution witnesses, and overly broad definitions of terrorism and treason would survive intact.

On October 31, Peruvians narrowly approved a new constitution that expanded the death penalty, previously applied only in cases of treason in an external war, to include the crimes of treason in internal war and terrorism. This violated Peru's obligations under the American Convention on Human Rights, which both prohibits the expansion of the death penalty and bars its use for political or related common crimes. Human Rights Watch opposes the infliction of capital punishment in all circumstances because of its inherent cruelty and because its irreversible nature prevents miscarriages of justice from being corrected. We view this decision with alarm, especially since the judiciary is no longer independent and special courts violate fundamental rights to due process.

Lack of accountability for human rights abuses remained the rule in Peru, contributing to the perpetuation of abuse. As of November, there were 4,200 unresolved disappearances, and the government was making no attempt to review them. New disappearances fared no better. Among the most disturbing were those of at least thirty university students from the University of the Center, in Huancayo, Junín, most of which occurred in the second half of 1992. Subsequently, in Huancayo, ten heavily armed and hooded men, some wearing police uniforms, burst into the home of Camilo Núñez on June 17, 1993. The detention was witnessed by Núñez's wife and brother, Teófilo, who told authorities that Núñez was taken away in a police vehicle. Two months later, Teófilo was detained in the presence of his wife and father. Soon afterward, his wife discovered his corpse, blindfolded and showing signs of torture, according to the Peruvian human rights group Fundación Ecumenica Para el Desarollo y la Paz (PEDEPAZ). Police denied detaining him. Camilo Núñez remained disappeared.

As evidence emerged throughout 1993 implicating a government death squad in the disappearance of nine students and a professor from Lima's "Enrique Guzmán y Valle" (La Cantuta) University on July 18, 1992, the Fujimori government engaged in a blatant cover-up, which even included the deployment of tanks in the capital, in April, to intimidate legislators seeking to investigate the crime. The government's evasive tactics also included efforts by the pro-government majority in the CCD, military leaders, and a military tribunal to derail a congressional investigation of the La Cantura case; the public prosecutor's abdication of responsibility to investigate the crime; the attorney general's failure for six days to seal a site where remains of some of the La Cantuta victims were found; the refusal by the attorney general to accept badly needed international assistance in the exhumation and forensic analysis of the remains; and a propaganda campaign by the police aimed at discrediting the discovery of the remains. Peruvians who investigated the crime—including family members, journalists, members of the congress, and a lawyer representing family members—faced death threats and legal harassment. Finally in late October, President Fujimori announced that four army officers—who were not immediately identified—had been detained in connection with the case, the first official acknowledgment that the military was responsible for the crime. On November 9, a criminal court in Lima convicted several police agents of aggravated homicide for the June 1991 murder of three young men. Three of the policemen were sentenced to eighteen years each; two accomplices were sentenced to five and six years respectively. A major implicated as the intellectual author of the crime was not tried.

After the 1992 coup, the government had attempted to regain control of prison cellblocks taken over by the Shining Path and the MRTA. While recognizing the need to maintain authority in prisons, Americas Watch objected to several measures that violated the U.N. Standard Minimum Rules for the Treatment of Prisoners. Our objections were based on several prison visits in 1992 and an analysis of decrees affecting prisons. However, our ability to monitor prisons was complicated in 1993 when the government denied entry to Americas Watch, for the first time in ten years of work in the country. The denial flew in the face of a promise delivered by the prime minister to the United Nations Human Rights Commission in Geneva, in February, to provide "free access" to prisons for international humanitarian organizations. In March, the government reached an agreement allowing the International Committee of the Red Cross

(ICRC) access to prisons after suspending visits for eight months. Although an important deterrent to abuse, ICRC access does not take the place of visits by organizations that publicly report their findings. As we reported in the *Human Rights Watch Global Report on Prisons*, Peru's prisons remained plagued by multiple problems, including life-threatening shortages of food, medicine, water, and basic supplies; a high incidence of communicable disease; extreme violence between guards and prisoners; rampant corruption; a complete lack of legal assistance for poor and indigent prisoners; frequent reports of torture and abuse by police and guards; and severely restricted access to exercise, family visits, and medical care.

Although the capture of leaders and hundreds of militants severely weakened the Shining Path in 1993, it continued to launch brutal attacks on noncombatants and civilian targets like television stations, schools, and public transportation. On August 18, guerrillas seized twelve Asháninka villages and killed at least sixty-two people, including Amerindians and mestizo settlers, in the central jungle province of Satipo, Junín. Many were first mutilated by machetes and axes. Such attacks became a leading cause of forced displacement.

Guerrillas also continued to terrorize candidates for municipal office and other local officials. In the weeks leading up to January municipal elections, Shining Path guerrillas were implicated in twenty-eight murders. Among those killed was candidate Ramón Galindo, a member of the United Left party who had served as vice-mayor in Villa El Salvador, an immense Lima slum neighborhood, after former vice-mayor María Elena Moyano was slain by the Shining Path in February 1992. In June, former Villa El Salvador mayor Michel Azcueta narrowly escaped death when two Shining Path execution squads fired at him as he entered the Fe y Alegría High School, where he taught geography. A bodyguard and four children were seriously wounded. A peace proposal made by imprisoned Shining Path leader Abimael Guzmán to the government from his prison cell in September had little immediate effect. Less than a month later, guerrillas detonated a car bomb outside a Lima hotel, killing three people.

The Right To Monitor

Although the government proved more sophisticated in its human rights rhetoric internationally, at home the attitude remained one of denial, hostility, and thinly-veiled threats against monitors. As a result, it became almost impossible to discuss human rights without being accused of distributing false information, damaging the country's image, or sympathizing with terrorists.

On September 24, human rights activist Lily Maribel Olano Elera was arrested by police outside Picsi prison in Chiclayo, Lambayeque department. Police told human rights groups that she was being investigated for "terrorism-related" crimes, a charge those groups described as preposterous. Olano was later released. The interim ministry charged Father José Manuel Miranda, of the Ica Human Rights Commission, with collaboration with guerrillas because of his work in local prisons, an accusation dropped only after international protests.

Journalists critical of the regime or engaged in investigating human rights abuses or corruption by the state were targets as well. According to the Center for Study and Action on Peace (CEAPAZ), fourteen journalists were detained and charged with "apology for terrorism" in 1993. On June 2, police arrested Piura radio journalist Juan Guerra, whose news program ran reports on police brutality. Guerra had declared publicly that police threatened to kill him for his reports. He was later released. Francisco Reyes, a reporter for the national daily, *La República*, was detained and severely beaten by air force soldiers at the airport in Yurimaguas on September 19; he had reported on corruption among the police and air force in the area. Reyes was subsequently turned over to the police and released.

After graves containing the remains of some La Cantuta victims were discovered by Ricardo Uceda, director of the newsweekly *Sí*, the Public Ministry reportedly threatened to charge Uceda with obstructing justice, one of many acts of intimidation against those who have pressed for resolution of that case. Earlier in the year, *Sí* was also the target of a case launched by the Defense Ministry to punish the magazine for suggesting that the military's National Intelligence Service was implicated in the 1991 Barrios Altos massacre. *Caretas* journalist Cecilia Valenzuela was threatened numerous times during 1993, once receiving a package containing a clipping with her photograph smeared with blood and the head of a chicken.

U.S. and O.A.S. Policy

The Clinton administration was creative in pressing for human rights improvements, obtaining some positive results. Nonetheless, those results were matched by the intransigence of the Fujimori government on other, equally important fronts or reversed once pressure subsided. Meanwhile, the Fujimori government's one-step-forward, two-steps-back approach to human rights drew some unwarranted praise from Washington.

After the army tank parade to intimidate parliamentarians investigating the La Cantuta disappearance case, in April, then-Assistant Secretary of State for Inter-American Affairs Bernard Aronson called President Fujimori to protest what the State Department called "an unacceptable attempt to intimidate the legislative branch." That same day, Fujimori publicly defended the legislature's theoretical right to exercise oversight. Yet once U.S. attention was elsewhere, Fujimori supporters in the CCD and army found other ways to cripple the La Cantuta investigation.

Similarly, when the Clinton administration in February set conditions for its participation in the so-called Support Group of donor countries, Lima was quick to comply with the letter (but not the spirit) of most conditions. While the government renewed ICRC access to prisons, it barred Americas Watch and local human rights groups such access. The government began a dialogue with the Peruvian human rights organization's forming the Coordinadora, but stated that it did so only because Washington insisted.

The Clinton administration later appeared eager to normalize relations with Peru. In a statement at a meeting of bilateral donor countries on June 22, the U.S. lauded Peru's "progress in strengthening democratic institutions and the protection of human rights"—a statement difficult to defend in the wake of Fujimori's blatant manipulation of the judiciary and the military's brash threats against the legislature in the La Cantuta affair. Yet, in a July interview with a Lima daily, U.S. chargé d' affaires Charles Brayshaw expressed satisfaction that a military court was investigating the La Cantuta case, ignoring the question of civilian jurisdiction and the military's near-perfect record of protecting its members implicated in serious crimes.

Military assistance and Economic Support Funds (ESF: cash payments classified as security assistance and totaling $110 million by the end of the 1993 fiscal year) were suspended to Peru after the 1992 coup and remained so during 1993, while development assistance and anti-narcotics aid to the police, the latter worth $19 million annually, continued without interruption. During the year, the Clinton administration began to discuss with human rights groups and the U.S. Congress a gradual resumption of the ESF with conditions relating to human rights attached. One of the proposed conditions was the formation of a commission of four distinguished attorneys from Argentina, Italy and the United States to study judicial independence and due process. That commission traveled to Lima in September and was expected to make recommendations to bring Peru into compliance with international standards in a public report by the end of 1993.

Americas Watch opposed the resumption of ESF to Peru for so long as it takes the government to restore an independent judiciary and congress; end gross violations of human rights and punish those responsible; repeal or reform the anti-terrorism decrees

that created the faceless courts; and review the cases handled by those courts.

The involvement in the La Cantuta case of a death squad run out of the National Intelligence Service (SIN) by Fujimori confidante Vladimiro Montesinos again raised questions about relations between the SIN and the Central Intelligence Agency, publicly acknowledged by Fujimori in November 1992. Americas Watch recommended that any U.S. assistance to the SIN or Vladimiro Montesinos be terminated immediately, and that if any agency of the U.S. government had information on death squads operating under Peruvian intelligence services, the Clinton Administration should disclose such information to the public.

Other governments appeared to be following the U.S. lead in warming up to the Fujimori government. For example, Sweden, once a refuge for persecuted Peruvians, partially closed its doors during 1993, on the grounds that it did not want to give safe haven to Shining Path supporters. As a result of this shift in policy, Mónica Castillo Páez, whose brother Ernesto was disappeared by police in October 1990, was deported from Sweden to Holland in August 1993. Castillo had fled Peru after police several times visited her family's home looking for her. In March 1991 the lawyer representing her family, Augusto Zúñiga, received a letter bomb that blew off his arm. Zúñiga remained in exile in Sweden.

The Organization of American States continued to maintain a low profile on Peru, facilitating Peru's partial rehabilitation in the eyes of the world community. A trip by the Inter-American Commission on Human Rights (IACHR) in May resulted in a bland press release that the Peruvian government heralded as an important endorsement.

The cause of human rights in Peru received a blow in February when the Inter-American Court of Human Rights threw out the Cayara case, in which the government was to be held responsible for the massacre of at least thirty peasants and the disappearance and murder of witnesses in 1988. The court's decision was based on procedural errors by the IACHR, which acts as a prosecutor before the Inter-American Court. Subsequently, the IACHR completed a report on the Cayara case, which held the government responsible for serious violations of the American Convention, and submitted the report to the OAS General Assembly in June.

The Work of Americas Watch

Through reports, press releases, opinion articles and frequent correspondence with the government and its representatives in Washington, Americas Watch continued to condemn human rights violations and violations of the laws of war by both the government and armed insurgents. Several Americas Watch missions visited Peru to gather information, meet with government officials and speak with the press. As a result of missions, Americas Watch published two reports and a lengthy newsletter in 1993: *Untold Terror: Violence against Women in Peru's Armed Conflict* (with the Women's Rights Project of Human Rights Watch), *Human Rights in Peru One Year after Fujimori's Coup*, and "Anatomy of a Cover-Up: The Disappearances at La Cantuta." In addition, a section on Peru was contributed to the *Human Rights Watch Global Report on Prisons*.

In cooperation with Peruvian human rights organizations and the Center for Justice and International Law (CEJIL), Americas Watch acted as counsel for the relatives of the victims in two cases: the 1988 Cayara massacre and the disappearance of prisoners following the 1986 prison riot at El Frontón. In the Cayara case, Americas Watch executive director Juan Méndez argued preliminary objections at the Inter-American Court of Human Rights in San José, Costa Rica. He also represented relatives of the El Frontón victims in a trial at the court, which was expected to make a decision in January 1994. In October, Americas Watch and CEJIL presented a petition regarding the expansion of the death penalty, requesting that the IACHR declare it a violation of the American Convention on Human Rights.

VENEZUELA

Human Rights Developments

In the middle of 1993, President Carlos Andrés Pérez was suspended from office and ordered to stand trial on charges of misappropriating $17 million in public funds. Ramón J. Velásquez was selected by Congress to assume the presidency and finish out the remainder of Pérez's term until February 1994. The peaceful transfer of presidential power and the country's ability to withstand two military uprisings in 1992, testified to the strength of civilian constitutional traditions. At the same time, the political turmoil during 1993 underscored the challenges to Venezuela's democracy arising from widespread resentment and frustration over corruption, increasing poverty and crime, inadequate public services, and discredited political institutions.

Serious human rights violations also continued to undermine the country's commitment to the rule of law. The past year witnessed arbitrary detentions; torture; extrajudicial executions; the unlawful use of excessive force resulting in physical injury and death; and abhorrent prison conditions. At least fifty-seven inmates were killed during a prison outbreak in November 1992, and numerous abuses were committed during the government's response to a failed military coup attempt that month and the one preceding it in February 1992. The number and nature of these abuses continued to be cause for concern. The government persisted in its traditional failure to curb and redress human rights violations. In addition to the absence of political will, problematic laws and the longstanding critical condition of the courts also contributed to the paucity of cases in which state agents were held accountable for human rights abuses.

Repercussions from the two attempted coups in 1992 continued in 1993. Although the government was able to put down the rebels within a day each time, the attempted coup of November 27 was much more violent than the earlier one in February. Official sources estimated about 230 dead. Among these were at least twenty-six noncombatants killed by security agents, according to Venezuelan human rights monitors. Coup participants charged National Guard and Metropolitan Police forces with executing six rebels—three military men and three civilians—after they had surrendered at a Caracas television station that they had occupied. The rebels were themselves accused of executing a private security guard at the station who had pleaded for his life. Likewise, rebels were accused of killing three surrendered members of an honor guard defending the Miraflores presidential palace. As of November 1993, no judicial proceedings had been initiated in any of these cases.

Eighteen persons detained by the military after the November coup attempt charged that they were tortured by their captors during unlawful incommunicado detention. The Public Ministry, which is charged by law with defending human and constitutional rights and monitoring the conduct of state agents, failed to visit the victims during their detention.

Exercising his constitutional authority, President Pérez suspended a number of constitutional guarantees on November 27, 1992, including the prohibition of arrest without warrant, the inviolability of the home and freedoms of movement, expression and assembly. Most of these liberties were restored by mid-December, and all were again in place on January 18, 1993. During the unnecessarily prolonged suspension of guarantees, however, government forces detained hundreds of dissidents and others perceived as unsympathetic to the government; not one was charged with participating in the coup attempt. Unnecessary violence characterized some raids. For example, while raiding her house on November 28, police threw acid on the leg of Sonia Díaz, a relative of one of the February coup plotters. Americas Watch is aware of only one judicial proceeding initiated into any of the human rights violations associated with the November 27 coup attempt.

Judicial investigations were underway, although dangerously stalled, in the case of the killing of at least fifty-seven inmates of Caracas's Retén de Catia prison during a prison outbreak the day of the November 1992 coup attempt. Under circumstances that remained murky, most of the victims were fatally shot, most at close range and in or about the head. One guard was shot and killed by a prisoner, and another guard was injured. At least forty-five prisoners were injured, either during the retaking of the prison or during their transfer to other prisons. Although lawyers for the Public Ministry earnestly pursued their investigations, the cases languished due to a combination of governmental reluctance and the court's unwillingness or inability to proceed. In that sense, the case neatly fit the pattern of most human rights investigations.

At the time of the prison riot, between 3,400 and 4,200 prisoners were jammed into a facility meant to hold 700 to 900. While conditions at the Retén de Catia in November 1992 were particularly horrible, they were not significantly worse than those in the nation's thirty other facilities. The riot led to increased public attention in 1993 to the national scandal of overcrowded, filthy, and violent prisons and their poorly-paid, abusive and corrupt staff.

Two March 1993 court decisions had a direct bearing on human rights. On March 2, a military court of appeals found fifteen members of a since-disbanded police/military unit (the CEJAP) guilty of intentional homicide in the October 1988 killing of fourteen fishermen in El Amparo and handed down prison sentences of seven and a half years to each defendant. The court accepted the defendants' claim of having killed the victims in self-defense during an armed confrontation; it nonetheless refused to exonerate them completely because of their excessive use of force. The court's tortured and patently biased handling of the evidence and its weak reasoning supported a decision that was best understood as a political compromise: any decision completely absolving the accused would have caused a furor among those demanding justice, yet the military court evidently heeded the military's insistence for many years that an armed confrontation, not a massacre, had taken place.

The case was presented to the Inter-American Commission on Human Rights (IACHR). In their 1992 petition before the IACHR, the Caracas-based Programa Venezolano de Educación Acción en Derechos Humans (PROVEA), Americas Watch and the Center for Justice and International Law (CEJIL) challenged the legitimacy of Venezuela's military courts to hear cases of this nature. Venezuela's 1938 military justice code, a vestige of dictatorship, grants extraordinary powers to the President to interfere in military court proceedings at his sole discretion. Because of this interference, the military justice system in Venezuela violates the requirement of the American Convention on Human Rights that judicial review be impartial and independent.

On March 11, the Venezuelan Supreme Court declared unconstitutional the special ad hoc military courts established by President Pérez to try those involved in the November 27 attempted *coup d'etat*. Some 150 civilians and members of the military were tried by these courts and approximately fifty had been convicted at the time of the Supreme Court's ruling. Human rights groups and lawyers for the accused challenged the tribunals' constitutionality, objecting to expedited procedures that rendered impossible an adequate defense; the curtailed right of appeal; and military court jurisdiction over civilians. The Supreme Court ruled that the *ad hoc* courts violated the constitutional guarantees of the right to defense and the right to be tried by one's natural judge, guarantees which had not been among those suspended after the attempted coup. Venezuelan jurists and human rights advocates were troubled by the possibility, raised by the court's language, that the President could have legally suspended such guarantees and by the court's failure to address Venezuela's obligation under international law to grant due process.

The use of violence by police resulting in death and serious physical harm continued in 1993. Police committed human rights violations not only in criminal investigations, but also during control of public demonstrations and street protests. According to PROVEA, police agents were responsible for 128 unjustified killings between October 1992 and June 1993 (not including at least fifty-seven civilian deaths resulting from the suppression of the uprising at the Retén de Catia prison). The number represented an increase over previous years. Security forces—including the Metropolitan Police, the National Guard, the intelligence force DISIP and the Judicial Technical Police (PTJ), an auxiliary body to the courts operating under the Ministry of Justice—employed such abusive methods as force disproportionate to the circumstances, extrajudicial executions and physical abuse and torture. Police abuse took place at every stage of police contact with citizens, both during and after arrest and detention and in the suppression of civic protest.

For example, on the night of December 16, 1992, Metropolitan Police were dispatched to quell a motorcyclists' party in the Blandín area of Caracas. Police were reported to have arrived shooting. One police officer was shot in the arm. Angered over his injury, he ordered other officers to open fire on a group of detained persons lying prone on the ground. Three individuals were killed. Two more were killed by gunfire as they separately fled the scene on motorcycle. No one was detained for these killings. On April 29, 1993, DISIP agents were seen by witnesses as they arrested a twelve-year-old male street child in the Sabana Grande section of Caracas, took him to a remote area, poured gas on his genitals and abused him physically and verbally. Investigations into this case produced no results. Sergio Rodríguez Yance, a university employee, was fatally shot on September 23, 1993, when government forces fired on a student protest in Caracas.

Security-force agents were rarely indicted or convicted for abuses against civilians. State agents also continued to benefit from the *averiguación de nudo hecho*, a pre-trial procedure designed to protect state agents from frivolous criminal charges. In practice, this investigative procedure delayed criminal proceedings unnecessarily, creating a temporary immunity from prosecution. While state agents responsible for the massacre at El Amparo were convicted—although with shockingly light sentences—not one state agent had been detained or incarcerated, as of November 1993, for the unlawful violence during the mass *Caracazo* riots of February and March 1989. Thousands were injured and at least 398 persons were killed, most of them shot by the military and police. During 1993 there was no perceptible advance in some 260 judicial investigations into these cases in both civilian courts and the 2nd Military Court of Caracas.

Investigations into the mass burial of more than sixty Caracazo victims in the "La Peste" section of Caracas's General Southern Cemetery continued to be stalled. There was no progress in identifying the victims (only three had been identified, in 1991), although as of June 1993, five additional sets of remains were being examined by government forensic experts. No criminal responsibility was yet assigned for the unlawful manner of burial or the killings themselves.

The Right to Monitor

A number of human rights monitoring and advocacy organizations operated freely in Venezuela without government restriction or interference. Relations between the human rights community and the government, particularly the Public Ministry and courts, varied from cooperative (as in efforts addressing the prison outbreak at Retén de Catia) to unproductive and even hostile (as in the ongoing efforts to identify those buried in 1989 in mass graves during the Caracazo). Reports by the human rights groups were generally well-received by the Venezuelan press, which provided decent, although inconsistent, coverage of human rights issues.

Americas Watch and other international human rights organizations freely conducted investigative missions. The government did not, however, respond to all requests for information on human rights issues.

Human rights monitors typically did not face physical danger in their work. Sergio Rodríguez, killed when police fired on a student demonstration in September 1993, was a participant in PROVEA's human rights monitor training program. There did not appear to be any connection, however, between his involvement with human rights activities and his death. Some lawyers representing participants in the 1992 coup attempts were threatened by anonymous callers.

U.S. Policy

Venezuela is an important U.S. ally in the hemisphere, given its longstanding civilian government and its role as the second-largest supplier of oil to the United States. The U.S., in turn, is the largest importer of Venezuelan oil, and Venezuela's largest trading partner. With the attempted coups and the country's increased importance as a transshipment point in the flow of drugs from Latin America, the United States in recent years made the preservation and promotion of democracy a chief goal in its relations with Venezuela. The Bush administration condemned the February and November 1992 coup attempts, and stated on the morning of the November attempt that "The United States cannot have normal relations with a country that has abandoned democracy. . . ."

During a September 2, 1993 press conference, conducted while Venezuela's Foreign Minister, Gen. Fernando Ochoa Antich, was in Washington, Secretary of State Warren Christopher noted that the United States "strongly support[s] the democratic process" in Venezuela. He failed, however, to address human rights problems affecting the country. On September 15, 1993, President Clinton, perhaps responding to renewed rumors of military unrest, sent an encouraging note to his Venezuelan counterpart, stressing that "My administration wants to continue working with Venezuela to reinforce your democracy, affirm respect in all sectors for civilian government and constitutional rule and promote honest responsible governance throughout the hemisphere."

In February 1993, the Department of State issued its *Country Reports on Human Rights Practices*, in which Venezuela was strongly criticized for its human rights practices. The report stated that:

> . . . serious human rights abuses continued in 1992. They included arbitrary and excessively lengthy detentions, abuse of detainees, extrajudicial killings by the police and military, the failure to punish police and security officers accused of abuses, corruption and gross inefficiency in the judicial and law enforcement systems, deplorable prison conditions, and violence and discrimination against women. Police sweeps of poor, crime-ridden neighborhoods resulted in increased incidents of extrajudicial killings and arbitrary arrests.

Notwithstanding human rights violations committed by Venezuelan security forces, Venezuela received U.S. security assistance through the International Narcotics Matters (INM) and International Military Education and Training (IMET) programs, both designed primarily to professionalize security forces and train them to combat drug trafficking.

Venezuela received an estimated $1 million in INM assistance for fiscal year 1993, which did not include a human rights component. In addition, $500,000 was requested for fiscal year 1994. Venezuela received $175,000 in IMET assistance in fiscal year 1993, with a significantly increased $475,000 requested for fiscal year 1994. According to the Clinton administration, the expanded IMET program for fiscal year 1994 was to emphasize democratic values, human rights and civilian oversight of the military.

The effectiveness of U.S. assistance to professionalize police and military person-

nel and to combat drug trafficking was questionable. The three security forces principally responsible for interdicting drugs— the PTJ, National Guard and DISIP—frequently violated fundamental human rights. Moreover, there were persistent charges that members of the armed forces and police were themselves involved in the drug trade. Indeed the *Miami Herald* reported in August 1993 that an arrest warrant was issued against one of Venezuela's former top drug fighters, National Guard Gen. (Ret.) Ramón Guillén Dávila, and four other officers suspected of drug trafficking and related crimes.

After the attempted coup of February 1992, the Bush administration dedicated some $800,000 to an eighteen-month program (to end in December 1993) arranged by the State Department's Agency for International Development (AID) to train Venezuelan law enforcement officials, including police, prosecutors and judges, to work together more effectively against corruption. In April 1993 interviews with Americas Watch, U.S. government officials criticized the program as little more than a U.S. flag-waving exercise to support the ailing Pérez administration.

On July 20, 1993, Jeffrey Davidow testified before the Senate Foreign Relations Committee as President Clinton's nominee for ambassador to Venezuela. Although Davidow did not raise human rights in his prepared statement, he acknowledged under questioning that human rights abuse took place in the country and that the State Department's most recent human rights report was "accurate." Davidow stated in a July 27 meeting with Americas Watch that human rights would be a central concern of the U.S. Embassy in Caracas.

The Work of Americas Watch

Americas Watch increased its focus on Venezuela throughout late 1992 and 1993. Not having published reports on Venezuela, we made an effort to conduct research on all the features of human rights violations against a backdrop of social and political tension, which included serious challenges to the stability of democratic institutions. In December 1992 and in May and June 1993, we conducted fact-finding missions to Caracas and met with government officials, victims of abuse, members of the human rights community, journalists, lawyers and the U.S. Embassy.

In October 1993, Americas Watch released its first report on Venezuela, an attempt to draw a comprehensive picture of the human rights situation under a threatened democracy. *Human Rights in Venezuela* documented some of the most serious abuses that have occurred over the past five years and the government's failure to curb and redress them. The report was published during the last months of the presidential election campaign in the hope of contributing to the national dialogue concerning the country's commitment to fundamental human rights and the rule of law.

Americas Watch invited Father Matías Comuñas Marchante, a Spanish priest serving the parish of Petare outside Caracas and long an activist for human rights, to be honored by Human Rights Watch at its observance of Human Rights Day, December 10.

ASIA WATCH

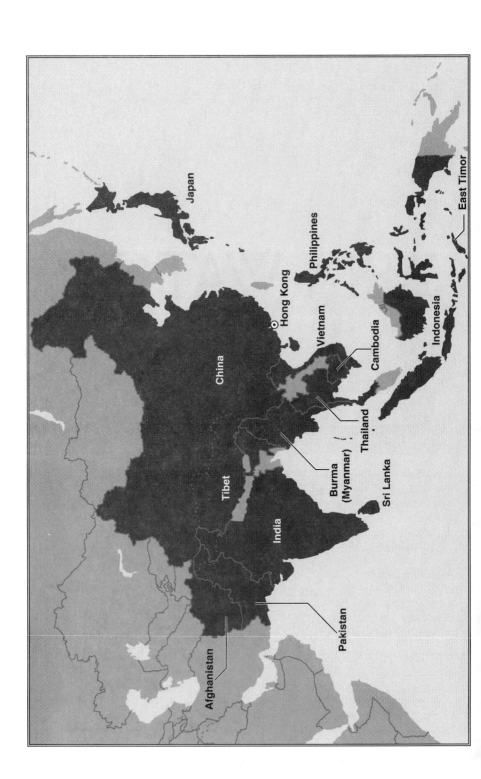

ASIA WATCH OVERVIEW

Human Rights Developments

While China, Burma and Kashmir exemplified the continuing human rights problems in Asia, the major development in the region was not so much the nature of the abuses but the debate over how to address them. Two factors had a major impact on this debate: the increased visibility of Asian nongovernmental organizations or NGOs and the growing economic power of East Asia.

Asian NGOs were able to articulate a vision of human rights that differed radically from that of their own governments and thus called into question the ability of the latter to define what is "Asian." They were more successful than their governments in blurring the traditional subregional distinctions of South Asia, Southeast Asia and Northeast Asia. And they helped redefine priorities for the human rights movement in a way that rendered obsolete the old division of labor among human rights, development, women's rights and environmental organizations.

These efforts culminated in the "Bangkok NGO Declaration on Human Rights" of March 27. Over one hundred NGOs from across Asia and the Pacific gathered in Bangkok on March 23 to coordinate their position for the Vienna World Conference on Human Rights, just as Asian governments convened a few days later, also in Bangkok, for the regional preparatory meeting of the same conference. It was clear from a series of statements they made during 1992 that China, Indonesia, Singapore and Malaysia, at the very least, were determined to promote an "Asian concept of human rights," which downplayed political and civil rights, highlighted the importance of economic development, stressed the need to take cultural, historical and religious factors into account when assessing human rights, and rejected aid conditionality and other forms of "interference in domestic affairs."

It was this concept that the Asian NGOs set out to rebut in Bangkok. The declaration they produced stated that because human rights were universal, "The advocacy of human rights cannot be considered to be an encroachment on national sovereignty." While noting the importance in the region of cultural pluralism, the NGOs declared, "Those cultural practices which derogate from universally accepted human rights, including women's rights, must not be tolerated." In reaffirming the indivisibility of political and economic rights, they stated, "Violations of civil, political and economic rights frequently result from the emphasis on economic development at the expense of human rights. Violations of social and cultural rights are often the result of political systems which treat human rights as being of secondary importance."

The Asian governments, at the official meeting from March 29 to April 2, produced a document that reflected much of the Chinese, Indonesian, Malaysian and Singaporean position (although since the U.N.'s definition of Asia includes Southwest Asia, it included the viewpoints of governments such as Syria and Iran as well). Some of the Asian democracies, including Japan, managed to moderate the tone of some provisions, such as that on aid conditionality, changing the word "reject" to "discourage." They also managed to include important clauses such as that emphasizing the need to encourage all states of the region to ratify the international covenants on human rights.

Ironically, however, it was the Asian governments' castigation of the West for failing to heed the importance of social and economic rights that led the American delegation to the Vienna conference to reverse the stance of earlier administrations and announce its intent to ratify the relevant conventions.

The NGOs succeeded in blunting the efforts of some governments to accentuate North-South and East-West fissures. But it was clear, not only from their stance in Bangkok but from NGO work more generally, that the Asian NGO agenda differed in some respects from that of counterpart organizations in the West, particularly in putting more stress on the need to address the linkage between human rights and development than on civil and political rights *per se*.

The focus on human rights and development did not mean that NGOs ignored abuses of basic political and civil rights. For many Asian NGOs, detained Burmese opposition leader and Nobel laureate Aung San Suu Kyi was a potent symbol of the Asian struggle for human rights and democracy. The communal riots that erupted in India following the destruction of the Ayodhya mosque led to abuses that horrified Indians of all religious and political backgrounds. Indian activists continued to fight against laws such as the Terrorist and Disruptive Activities Act (TADA), which severely restricted the rights of detainees. Treatment in detention centers was a major issue for Burmese refugees in Thailand. NGOs in Hong Kong were increasingly concerned about preservation of basic civil liberties, particularly freedom of the press, and as return to Chinese control in 1997 approached. Korean NGOs focused attention on the continued use of the National Security Law, and their concerns were reinforced when Cho Guk, an activist from the Korean organization KONUCH, who attended the U.N. human rights meetings in Bangkok and Vienna, was arrested shortly after his return from the latter and charged under that law with pro-North Korean and "anti-state" activities. Indonesian NGOs continued to defend political detainees, from suspected insurgents to students accused of criticizing the electoral process, and to call for greater freedom of association for workers.

Moreover, violations of political and civil rights, for the most part, were most severe in the countries where domestic NGOs were not allowed to operate: China, Vietnam, Burma, Bhutan, Brunei and North Korea. Elsewhere, there were areas that were also effectively closed to domestic and international human rights investigators, including East Timor and parts of Irian Jaya, Tibet, Khmer Rouge-held zones of Cambodia, and the Jaffna Peninsula. The Asia-wide coalition of NGOs thus spoke primarily to concerns in countries which already had a modicum of political openness; in countries without such domestic voices, there was no real alternative to international pressure as a way of drawing attention to human rights abuses and trying to curb them.

As noted above, however, Asian NGOs succeeded better than their respective governments in working together across sub-regional boundaries. The Bangkok conference highlighted regional solidarity and common interests, but there were many examples during the year of transnational cooperation. Sri Lankan and Thai human rights NGOs were particularly helpful to their newly-formed counterparts in Cambodia. In Korea, Indonesia, the Philippines and elsewhere, NGOs worked to document the use of "comfort women" during the Japanese military occupation of their respective countries during the Second World War; they then joined forces with NGOs in Japan to call for the Japanese government to acknowledge the abuses and compensate the victims. (By the end of the year, they had the acknowledgment but not the compensation.)

The breakdown of geographical barriers was somewhat offset by the need of NGOs to respond to developments within regional governmental associations like the Association of Southeast Asian Nations (ASEAN) and the South Asia Association for Regional Cooperation (SAARC). The ASEAN countries—Indonesia, Malaysia, Singapore, Brunei, Thailand and the Philippines—seemed well on their way by year's end to developing a regional mechanism to address human rights concerns. NGOs in the region were watching warily, doubtful that any mechanism that included among its founders Indonesia's President Suharto and Malaysia's Prime Minister Mahathir could advance the protection of human rights.

If the growing strength of NGOs in the region affected the human rights debate, so did the growing economic clout of East Asia, home of the "four dragons" (South Korea, Taiwan, Hong Kong and Singapore) and the future dragons (China, Indonesia, Thailand and Malaysia). For one thing, it meant that for much of the international community, "Asia" was East Asia; South Asia, comprising the countries of the Indian subcontinent, was largely ignored.

The "Asian concept of human rights" was the creation of East Asian governments, and authoritarian East Asian governments at that, which felt they deserved praise, not censure, for their efforts to alleviate poverty, even if some civil rights were curtailed in the process. Former Prime Minister Lee Kuan Yew of Singapore went to an extreme when he argued that Asians did not care about democratic government; they preferred efficient government. Other governments argued that it was simply a matter of time: Taiwan and South Korea were now well along in the democratization process, but their period of greatest growth came under authoritarian regimes. One problem with this argument, as the NGOs clearly saw, was that it left it up to non-democratic governments themselves to determine when the requisite level of development had been reached that would permit more political openness. More fundamentally, it has been shown that repression can impede development; inability to speak out against bad policies can stymie economic progress. Prior to the Vienna conference, fifty-six Indonesian NGOs said that time had now come in their country: "Now that development has been carried out for two decades," they said in a joint statement, "it is time for priority to be given to the realization of political and civil rights and democracy."

The experience of Taiwan and South Korea, however, also led many in the West who were uncomfortable with human rights advocacy to posit a direct relationship between economic liberalization and positive political change. Let the Chinese, Vietnamese and Indonesian economies continue to expand, the argument went, and an improvement in human rights will inevitably result, if only to satisfy the demands of a growing middle class. That argument, however, was of small comfort to the thousands detained in the region on political grounds. It belied the experience of China, where continued commitment to economic reform was accompanied by increased political repression, as China's leaders expressed a determination not to let the reforms affect Party control, and any signs of dissent were quickly crushed.

Economic growth in East Asia, however, also confronted the industrialized governments with some new problems for their human rights policies. Many Asian countries had the economic strength to resist economic sanctions or aid conditionalities imposed by donor countries. In 1992, the U.S. Congress cut off aid for advanced training for Indonesian military officers under the International Military and Educational Training Program; in 1993, the Indonesian government was planning to send officers to the U.S. for what was essentially the same program, but this time at its own expense. As trade and investment in the East Asian region became increasingly vital to the strength of industrialized economies, how far were the Western countries and Japan willing to press on human rights? One year into a new administration in the U.S. and six months into a new government in Japan, this question remained unanswered.

The Right to Monitor

As noted above, several Asian governments banned human rights organizations from operating in their countries altogether. No human rights monitoring was possible in China, Vietnam, Burma, Bhutan, Brunei or North Korea. In China, dissidents in Shanghai who tried to write letters on behalf of detained colleagues were briefly detained in June and one, Fu Shenqi, was sentenced to three years of re-education. The letter-writing campaign was one of the charges against him. In North Korea and Brunei, no one even attempted to form a human rights organization within the country.

In many other areas, human rights monitors faced harassment, intimidation and even murder by government agents or armed opposition groups. India and the Philippines, both functioning democracies, were the only countries during the year where monitors were killed, apparently for their human rights activities. Kashmir was a particularly hazardous place for human rights activists to work. In Indonesia, human rights activists working to defend peasants in a West Java land dispute case were detained for interrogation by police in October.

But thanks in part to the Bangkok and Vienna conferences on human rights in March and June, Asian human rights organizations had a higher profile than ever before. Their importance was perhaps demonstrated by the fact that the Chinese government felt it necessary to create a "nongovernmental" human rights organization, the China Society for Human Rights Studies, just so it would have access to discussions by NGOs in both meetings.

Several new regional human rights organizations came into being, such as Forum Asia and the Asian Regional Resource Center for Human Rights Education; other, long-standing organizations, such as the Asia and Pacific Women in Law and Development (APWLD) and the Asian Cultural Forum on Development based in Bangkok, took on a new prominence in organizing NGO activities in the region.

The issue for many human rights organizations in the region was no longer sheer survival but how to get a stronger voice within the U.N. and within international institutions such as the World Bank. Still, protection of human rights monitors remained a central concern. The Bangkok NGO Declaration of March 27 identified the "increasing restrictions" imposed on human rights defenders as one of the critical challenges facing the region. It stated, "As these groups voice the interests of the people and work for their advancement, it is imperative that they be permitted to work freely."

U.S. Policy

Fears in the region that Asia would be ignored by the Clinton administration, with its focus on domestic policy, were assuaged by over a dozen visits of senior administration officials during the year, including President Clinton's trip to Tokyo for the summit of the Group of Seven (G-7) industrialized countries in July where he extolled the virtues of what he called the New Pacific Community. The question, as it turned out, was not whether Asia would be neglected; it was whether the attention would be welcome.

The Asia-Pacific region was seen both as a critical area for American jobs and exports, and as a test case in the new administration's determination to promote democracy, open markets and human rights. As Winston Lord, the Assistant Secretary of State for East Asia and the Pacific said in a briefing on August 31, "We believe you can't have open economics and closed politics."

The Clinton administration made significant efforts to press individual countries in the region on particular human rights issues, such as access by the International Committee of the Red Cross to China, and labor rights in Indonesia. But these initiatives on behalf of human rights were overshadowed by the administration's tending to portray human rights and democracy as core American values, not as values underpinned by an international system of treaties that have been ratified by countries around the world. In a region where non-democratic governments had already made such political capital out of perceived North-South and East-West divisions, the failure to anchor the promotion of human rights securely in United Nations mechanisms was unwise.

Portraying human rights and democracy as quintessentially American, rather than universal, values might also have created problems for the administration's stated desire to see other countries join forces in their protection and promotion. On the other hand, it was not clear that the administration had aggressively sought allies on this issue, particularly in the region. Japan had the potential to be much more active on human rights, given its stated position that allocation of overseas aid should be determined, in part, by a recipient country's democratization and respect for human rights. The new cabinet, formed after the July elections, also included at least two men, including the new foreign minister, known to be interested in human rights. Yet when Secretary Christopher met Foreign Minister Hata in mid-September, the issue of a multilateral stance on human rights toward the major violators of the region apparently did not come up. The new Korean government also indicated its desire to play a greater regional role in fostering human rights and democracy; it was not clear whether the administration in Washington took the cue.

It was unclear how the administration would resolve the dilemma of promoting human rights and promoting jobs and exports in East Asia. But as the debates on trade benefits for China (MFN) and Indonesia (Generalized System of Preferences or GSP) made clear, a major player in addressing that dilemma would be the American business community. As the year opened, the business community was well aware of the increased readiness of the new administration to impose sanctions and of the ability of East Asian countries to withstand them. It feared that countries like China and Indonesia would retaliate against American companies if human rights pressure from Washington became too intense by giving future contracts to Japanese and European competitors. Some companies thus expressed an interest in working with Asia Watch and other human rights groups to head off a crisis before it arose or to work out a solution that might advance human rights at the same time that it eased the threat of sanctions.

By and large, however, the Clinton administration demonstrated a stronger rhetorical commitment to human rights than its predecessor, backed up, in a few cases such as China and Indonesia, by the threatened use of selective sanctions. It continued the policy of harsh words toward Burma and strongly criticized rights abuses by Indian security forces in Kashmir. But by the end of the year, the administration seemed to be having second thoughts about a tough human rights approach, particularly with respect to China, as anxiety rose about the political and economic implications.

The Work of Asia Watch

Asia Watch expanded its work during the year in terms of countries covered, issues addressed and advocacy techniques employed. It sought stronger coordination with local human rights organizations in setting priorities and increasingly looked beyond the United States to Europe and Japan for sources of pressure on human rights offenders in the region. It increased efforts to get donor nations to raise human rights concerns with recipients, and it increasingly saw the business community as a potential ally for the protection and promotion of human rights.

While Asia Watch continued to focus on a few key countries—China, India, Indonesia, Cambodia and Burma—it also sent a mission for the first time to Vietnam and intensified work on Pakistan, Thailand and Sri Lanka. Routine monitoring of Korea, Taiwan, Hong Kong, Singapore, the Philippines and Malaysia continued.

Each of the five key countries had a particular claim on Asia Watch resources. China, the largest country in the world, had an appalling record of arbitrary detentions and torture. Some of the worst carnage in Asia during the year took place in Kashmir, where Indian security forces tried to crush internal strife and armed insurgency, with methods that ranged from summary executions and disappearances to destruction of whole neighborhoods. Indonesia, the fourth-largest country in the world, was notable both for the scope of its abuses, ranging from arbitrary arrest in East Timor to worker rights violations in Java and Sumatra, and for its role in trying to define an "Asian" view of human rights. Cambodia was a test case of how the United Nations would balance peacekeeping and human rights monitoring, and Burma, a human rights disaster area, prompted a split between western proponents of sanctions and Asian proponents of "constructive engagement."

The range of human rights issues addressed became increasingly complex. Communal violence was a major issue in South Asia and in Cambodia, between ethnic Khmer and Vietnamese. Abuses related to the trafficking of women was the focus of Asia Watch work on the Thai-Burmese border. Trafficking of women was also an issue through much of the rest of the region, including India, Pakistan, China and Japan, and with it came a new set of human rights concerns linked to AIDS. Commercial logging throughout Southeast Asia led to violence against individuals who protested the logging itself or who resisted being evicted from their land; but the borderline between state and private sector involvement was sometimes hard to distinguish.

On the advocacy side, Asia Watch continued to build contacts in Japan and to engage Japanese officials in a discussion of the use of foreign aid (Official Development Assistance or ODA) as a tool for the protection of human rights. We tried to coordinate advocacy efforts with the work of NGOs and governments in Europe, particularly with respect to Indonesia, Sri Lanka and Burma. And in taking advantage of the debate on "good governance" within the World Bank, Asia Watch expanded contacts there. It also tried to ensure that human rights issues were raised at the annual donor meetings on Indonesia, India and Sri Lanka.

AFGHANISTAN

Human Rights Developments

The fall of the Najibullah government in April 1992 precipitated a bloody battle for control of Kabul that continued through 1993, with devastating loss of life. But despite the intensity of the fighting, Afghanistan remained largely ignored by the outside world, and there was little evidence of United Nations or diplomatic efforts to end the bloodshed. Most of the casualties resulted from indiscriminate rocketing and shelling by forces loyal to the Prime Minister, Gulbuddin Hekmatyar, a bitter enemy of the former Defense Minister, Ahmad Shah Massoud. Civilians were also targeted during sporadic battles between two communally-based political organizations, the Hezb-e Wahdat (Shi'ite) and the Ittehad-e Islami (Sunni Pashtun). Elsewhere in the country, regional councils or commanders consolidated power with little regard for events in Kabul. Hundreds of thousands of refugees returned from Pakistan, and thousands more were forcibly repatriated from Iran. Some 50,000 Tajik refugees who fled the civil war in Tajikistan remained in camps near the northern Afghan border. In July, Tajik and Russian forces shelled Afghan villages, killing an estimated 300.

On January 3, Burhanuddin Rabbani, the leader of the Jamiat-e Islami party, was sworn in as President. Rabbani's authority remained limited to only part of Kabul; the rest of the city remained divided among rival *mujahidin* factions.

On January 19, a short-lived cease-fire broke down when Hezb-e Islami forces renewed rocket attacks on Kabul from their base south of the city. Civilians were the principal victims in the fighting which killed some 1,000 before a peace accord was signed on March 8. Refugees continued to flee the city for Pakistan; others became part of the growing population of internally displaced, fleeing to Mazar-e Sharif and other areas north of Kabul.

Under the March accord, brokered by Pakistan and Saudi Arabia, Rabbani and Hekmatyar agreed to share power until elections could be held in late 1994. Hekmatyar was named Prime Minister, but by November he had not entered Kabul because of continuing opposition from forces loyal to Massoud and sometimes those allied to the Uzbek commander, General Dostum. The cease-fire broke down again on May 11, leaving more than 700 dead in bombing raids, street battles and rocket attacks in and around Kabul. The parties agreed to a new peace accord in Jalalabad on May 20 under which Massoud agreed to relinquish the post of defense minister. A council of commanders was to assume that office, as well as the office of Interior Minister, but by mid-November the power struggle remained unresolved.

Throughout the year, sporadic fighting

also continued between the Hezb-e Wahdat (which was aligned with Massoud and Dostum until January and after that with Hezb-e Islami) and Sunni Pashtun Ittehad-e Islami (which had aligned with Hezb-e Islami until January but then shifted allegiance to Massoud). Various commanders controlling sections of Kabul launched attacks on civilian areas in other quarters of the city. Rape, particularly of Shi-ite women, was reportedly one weapon in these attacks. While the rest of the country did not experience the intensity of fighting that took place in Kabul, conditions remained insecure for aid workers and returning refugees. On February 1 three United Nations workers and a Dutch engineer were murdered while driving from the Pakistani city of Peshawar to Jalalabad, in eastern Afghanistan. The incident prompted the United Nations to withdraw its staff from Jalalabad and Qandahar. U.N. staff who were evacuated from Kabul in August 1992 had not returned by November 1993. The U.N. continued to operate out of Mazar-e Sharif and Herat. Médecins Sans Frontières also closed down operations in the northern town of Kunduz after its workers there received threats.

Fierce fighting between rival leaders in Jalalabad in mid-October temporarily blocked one of the two main roads into Kabul, resulting in shortages of food and other supplies in the capital. Afghan refugees continued to return to areas in the east and north of the country, even though little mine clearance had been done in many of these areas. In July, the International Committee of the Red Cross (ICRC) reported a tripling of mine injuries since April 1992.

The Right to Monitor

No known domestic human rights organizations were functioning in Afghanistan during 1993, and the continuing chaos throughout the country made it unlikely that any such group would emerge in the near future.

U.S. Policy

The Clinton administration paid little attention to the crisis in Afghanistan in 1993.

In July, the Central Intelligence Agency stepped up efforts to buy back Stinger anti-aircraft missiles, which had been provided to the mujahidin in the last years of the war. The efforts were largely unsuccessful.

For fiscal year 1993, the U.S. requested $62 for humanitarian assistance and development aid for programs inside Afghanistan and for refugees in Pakistan.

Throughout 1993, the U.N. convened meetings of the "Friends of Afghanistan," including the U.S., Russia, Pakistan, Saudi Arabia and Iran, to discuss the continuing conflict. In a background briefing for the South Asia press on October 28, a senior administration official stated that the U.S. was urging the U.N. to convene another meeting of the group to send a fact-finding mission to Afghanistan to help focus world attention on the continuing crisis.

The Work of Asia Watch

In March an Asia Watch researcher traveled to Peshawar and Islamabad, Pakistan, to meet with officials of the U.N. High Commissioner for Refugees (UNHCR) and the U.N. Office for the Coordination of Humanitarian Assistance for Afghanistan (UNOCHA) officials to discuss attacks on civilians, obstruction of the delivery of relief supplies, and de-mining programs. A similar visit took place in October.

BURMA (MYANMAR)

Human Rights Developments

The ruling State Law and Order Restoration Council or SLORC continued to be a human rights pariah, despite its cosmetic gestures to respond to international criticism. Aung San Suu Kyi, winner of the 1991 Nobel Peace Prize, was permitted visits from her family but remained under house arrest for the fifth year. SLORC announced the release of nearly 2,000 political prisoners, but it was not clear that the majority had been detained on political charges, nor could most of the releases be verified. At least one hundred critics of SLORC were detained during the year, and hundreds of people tried by military tribunals between 1989 and 1992 remained in prison. Torture in Burmese prisons continued to be widespread. Foreign correspondents were able to obtain visas for Burma more easily, but access by human rights and humanitarian organizations remained tightly restricted. A constitutional convention met throughout the year, but over 80 percent of the delegates were hand-picked by SLORC.

Professor Yozo Yokota, the Special Rapporteur to Myanmar appointed by the U.N. Commission on Human Rights, issued a report in February on his December 1992 visit to the country. The report documented systematic violations of basic personal freedoms and physical intergrity and concluded that "serious repression and an atmosphere of pervasive fear exist in Myanmar." It also noted the lack of cooperation from SLORC and the intimidation and harassment of individuals wishing to provide testimony.

The human rights commission passed a resolution on March 10 which called on SLORC, among other things, to end torture, forced labor, abuse of women, enforced disappearances and summary executions; allow investigations of violations; improve prison conditions; cooperate with the U.N. High Commissioner for Refugees (UNHCR) for the safe return of refugees; and release Aung San Suu Kyi unconditionally. It also extended the mandate of the Special Rapporteur for one year.

To respond to international condemnation of its refusal to allow the National Assembly elected in May 1990 to meet, SLORC convened a national constitutional convention in Rangoon on January 9. Of some 700 delegates who attended, only 120 were elected parliamentarians. It was chaired by a fifteen-member commission, all of whom were active military officers, and delegates were divided into eight groups by occupation and background, such as peasants, workers and "national races." Each group was chaired by a military officer.

The convention met on and off throughout the year, and in September, six out of the eight groups agreed to a constitution that gave the military continued control of the government. The two groups that opposed it were the elected parliamentarians and representatives of political parties.

Many SLORC opponents were arrested in connection with the convention meetings. On August 4, Dr. Aung Khin Sint, a convention delegate and elected representative of the opposition National League for Democracy (NLD), and Than Min, alias Tin Tun Aung, an NLD executive committee member for Mingla Taungnyunt township, were arrested for distributing leaflets. They were accused of political agitation and intent to undermine the national convention. On October 15, they and nine others were sentenced to twenty years in prison. All were detained in Insein Prison in Rangoon.

Fighting between the Burmese military and various ethnic insurgencies along the Thai-Burmese and other borders was minimal during the year, in part because of a concerted effort by SLORC to negotiate cease-fires with different minority groups. In April, for example, a cease-fire was negotiated between SLORC and the Kachin Independence Army (KIA), and on October 1, SLORC signed a cease-fire agreement with the Kachin Independence Council (KIC). Thailand and China pressed insurgents based along their borders to negotiate or else lose their ability to shelter and mobilize on their respective territories.

Despite the low level of conflict, however, refugees continued to stream into Thailand. In June, NGOs estimated that 1,000 Burmese were crossing the border every day. The Thai government and international agencies were quick to refer to the newcomers as illegal immigrants, but many reported fleeing forced relocations, forced labor and forced conscription.

The state of Arakan in northwest Burma, home to the Rohingya Muslim minority, remained off-limits to outside observers, raising concerns about the possible repatriation of almost 300,000 Rohingyas who had fled to neighboring Bangladesh in 1991 and 1992. More than 13,000 refugees were repatriated in late 1992 and early 1993 without adequate screening procedures to determine if they were returning voluntarily or adequate monitoring mechanisms on the Burmese side. On January 31, UNHCR staff were allowed to interview refugees scheduled for repatriation in one transit camp in Bangladesh and found that nearly all were there against their will. In May, a memorandum of understanding was signed between UNHCR and the Bangladesh government ensuring UNHCR full access to all camps, and in July, Sadako Ogata, the head of UNHCR, reached an agreement in principle that her agency would be allowed a monitoring presence in Arakan. Details of the agreement were still being negotiated as of November.

SLORC took no steps to address the large-scale trafficking of Burmese women into forced prostitution in Thailand. Instead, it appeared to be arresting many women deported from Thailand on charges of illegally leaving the country and engaging in prostitution. It also routinely tested returning women for AIDS without their consent and without regard for confidentiality.

The Right To Monitor

No indigenous human rights groups were allowed in Burma, and passing information to outside groups was considered subversive.

The International Committee of the Red Cross had access neither to Burma's prisons nor to displaced populations along the border with China, Thailand and Bangladesh, although it did have a delegate based in Rangoon to run its prosthetics program for amputees.

SLORC tried to divert criticism of its refusal to allow access to prisoners by permitting individual foreign delegations highly controlled meetings with a few detainees.

U.S. Policy

The Clinton administration continued to be harshly critical of SLORC, and all economic assistance remained frozen, but the adminis-

tration made no effort to discourage investment by U.S. companies. On May 19 and July 20, President Clinton publicly called on SLORC to release Aung San Suu Kyi and other political prisoners, respect the 1990 elections and undertake genuine democratic reform.

Following a meeting with a group of Nobel laureates in July, President Clinton ordered a high-level interagency review to determine how the U.S. could increase pressure on Burma to address human rights abuses. As of November, the review was ongoing. No decision had been taken about such outstanding issues as whether to send an ambassador to Rangoon or to advocate corporate disinvestment in Burma.

At the Association of Southeast Asian Nations (ASEAN) Post-Ministerial Conference in Singapore on July 26, Secretary of State Warren Christopher repeated Clinton's statements of May and July, but took no action to encourage new initiatives by ASEAN towards Burma. Privately, U.S. officials acquiesced in ASEAN's "constructive engagement" policy.

Congress remained active on Burma. On June 22, more than forty members of the House of Representatives wrote to Prime Minister Chuan to urge Thailand to actively promote specific steps to improve human rights conditions in Burma. The Senate passed a resolution on April 19 calling for the immediate release of Aung San Suu Kyi, the transfer of power to those elected in May 1990 and an arms embargo to be effected through a resolution of the U.N. Security Council.

The Senate passed a resolution on April 19 calling for the immediate release of Aung San Suu Kyi, the transfer of power to those elected in May 1990 and an arms embargo to be effected through a resolution of the U.N. Security Council.

Administration policy was reflected in international agencies as well. The U.S. representative to the fortieth session of the governing council of the United Nations Development Program (UNDP) on June 9 announced that the U.S. would not support infrastructure development projects that could enhance SLORC's legitimacy in the eyes of the Burmese people. The U.S. contribution to UNDP for Burma was $7 million, to be used only for projects that promoted human rights and did not benefit SLORC.

The foreign operations bill adopted on June 10 by the House Appropriations Committee pledged $1 million for Burmese students displaced by civil conflict. The committee also called on the U.S. Agency for International Development (USAID) to support assistance to Burmese refugees and displaced people.

The Drug Enforcement Administration (DEA) continued a low-level liaison with SLORC, although direct assistance to counter narcotics production remained suspended. An April report by the State Department on narcotics strategy concluded that while Burma accounts for over 50 percent of illicit opium production, there were few signs that SLORC would commit itself to serious law enforcement in this area.

The Work of Asia Watch

Asia Watch sent missions during the year to Thailand and Bangladesh to interview Burmese refugees and victims of human rights abuses, including women trafficked over the Thai border. The missions to Thailand were jointly undertaken with the Jesuit Refugee Service.

A major report on the trafficking of Burmese women into Thailand was scheduled for release at the end of the year. A short report examining abuses of Rohingya refugees in Bangladesh was published in September, and Asia Watch issued several press releases during 1993 calling for the release of detainees in Burma and better protection for Burmese refugees.

Burma was a key issue in meetings Asia Watch held with Japanese officials in April. Asia Watch helped coordinate and circulate a letter issued jointly on June 22 by the U.S. Congress and the Japanese Diet. The letter was addressed to the prime minister of Thailand and requested his assistance in implementing the recommendations of the March

resolution on Burma of the U.N. Commission on Human Rights.

Asia Watch, in cooperation with the Lawyers Committee on Human Rights and the Jesuit Refugee Service, also held regular roundtable meetings on Burma in New York and Washington.

CAMBODIA

Human Rights Developments

With peaceful elections carried out in May, the promulgation of a new constitution in October and the restoration of Norodom Sihanouk to the throne as a constitutional monarch, Cambodia became the crown jewel of United Nations' peacekeeping efforts. But the success of the elections obscured the very real human rights problems that remained, including the failure to hold officials accountable for abuses, the treatment and status of ethnic Vietnamese, the continued presence of the Khmer Rouge, and the weakness of the legal system. The achievements of the United Nations Transitional Authority in Cambodia (UNTAC) on the political front pushed to the background but did not resolve the tensions inherent in the eighteen-month UNTAC mission between peace-keeping and human rights protection.

UNTAC struggled unsuccessfully to contain an explosion of political violence from January through May that threatened to undermine the elections. The Phnom Penh government (State of Cambodia or SOC) engaged in a series of attacks against political opponents, particularly those belonging to FUNCINPEC, the party headed by Norodom Ranariddh, Sihanouk's son. The Buddhist Liberal Democratic Party (BLDP) also came under attack. For example, on January 3, armed men attacked the FUNCINPEC headquarters in Sisophon, Banteay Meachay province, killing Roeun Sopheap, aged twenty-one, a security guard. The next day, two grenades were thrown at a house in Moung Russei district, Battambang province, owned by a BLDP official. One woman was injured. On the night of January 31, soldiers from the Fifth Division of the Cambodian People's Armed Forces (CPAF), the army of the State of Cambodia, detained six people in Sangke district, Battambang. Two were released, but four, who were all FUNCINPEC members, were taken to the Takok military camp and never seen again.

In the same period, the Khmer Rouge carried out numerous attacks on ethnic Vietnamese residents of Cambodia, including four in the month of March alone. By September, over one hundred ethnic Vietnamese had been murdered since the beginning of the UNTAC mission.

In January, UNTAC head Yasushi Akashi authorized the creation of a "special prosecutor" to bring criminal charges against human rights violators and empowered UNTAC police to arrest them. The effort came to little after the Phnom Penh government in February refused to allow its courts to try the case of Em Chan, a policeman accused of murdering a FUNCINPEC party officer. By the time UNTAC departed in September, it had arrested a total of four men, one of whom had died of natural causes. The other three were turned over to the new government for further proceedings.

In February and March 1993, UNTAC conducted a series of raids on police and military officers that yielded evidence showing the Phnom Penh government had set up undercover units to infiltrate and attack political opposition groups. Those raids were not made public until after the election when the *Washington Post* disclosed the existence of a secret UNTAC report, which Asia Watch subsequently published.

The extent of political violence by April was such that many people believed that the "neutral political environment," a prerequisite for the holding of elections according to the 1991 Paris peace accords, was lacking. But confounding all skeptics, almost 90 percent of registered voters went to the polls from May 23 to May 28. FUNCINPEC won 45.46 percent of the vote, taking fifty-eight out of 120 seats in the constituent assembly, with the Phnom Penh government's Cambo-

dian People's Party (CPP) winning 38.22 percent and taking fifty-one seats.

After the election, Vice-Prime Minister Prince Norodom Chakrapong, National Security Minister Sin Song and Gen. Bou Thang led a short-lived secessionist movement centered in the eastern provinces of Kompong Cham, Prey Veng and Svay Rieng. It lasted only a few days and collapsed by June 15.

Sihanouk brokered an interim power-sharing arrangement between FUNCINPEC and the Hun Sen government, which was carried over into the new government, with two Prime Ministers and two ministers of national security. Non-communist military units were incorporated into the Phnom Penh army, and towards year's end, there was speculation that the new government would launch a dry season offensive against the Khmer Rouge, which still controlled zones around Pailin. Although Prince Sihanouk in early July suggested that the Khmer Rouge might be allowed to play an unspecified role in the new government as "counselors," he cancelled scheduled talks with the party on July 20, citing interference from the United States. The U.S. had expressed hesitation at providing aid to the new government if the Khmer Rouge were included.

The Khmer Rouge continued to engage in attacks against the ethnic Vietnamese as some of the Vietnamese who had fled earlier assaults attempted, just after the elections, to return to their homes on Cambodia's great lake, the Tonle Sap. Ethnic animosity of Cambodians against Vietnamese remained a potent force, and it was unclear whether any ethnic Vietnamese would be granted citizenship under the new constitution. The new government moved cautiously to establish a technical committee with Vietnam on issues of citizenship and borders.

The continuing war with the Khmer Rouge also meant continued laying of land mines in a country that already had the highest proportion of amputees in the world. UNTAC trained and deployed forty teams of Cambodian de-miners, but progress was slow. Land that had been de-mined was mined again by opposing armies, and it was widely believed that as many new mines were laid as were cleared during the peacekeeping period.

In October, the Cambodian Mine Action Center, a joint U.N./government body that was to coordinate de-mining efforts after UNTAC's departure, was almost bankrupt and planned to close in mid-November. The U.S., which had offered $2 million to purchase UNTAC's de-mining equipment for Cambodia, had still not reached agreement with the U.N., which had valued the equipment at over $3 million. On October 8, the U.N. General Assembly passed a resolution stressing the urgency of de-mining worldwide and requesting the Secretary-General to advise on the establishment of a trust fund for mine clearance.

The situation of some repatriated refugees remained cause for concern. Over 360,000 Cambodians returned from Thailand in 1992 and 1993 under the auspices of UNTAC and the U.N. High Commissioner for Refugees. They had been promised land, but a shortage of mine-free land led to most receiving small cash grants instead. Although the repatriation in general went smoothly, it was too early to assess how the returnees would fare when U.N. rice subsidies ended. The one UNHCR experiment in supervising repatriation to a Khmer Rouge-administered area ended disastrously when the settlement became a war zone after the elections, forcing hundreds of refugees to flee to neighboring areas.

UNTAC made important progress in its efforts to rebuild a civil society in Cambodia. By the end of the year, more than a dozen independent newspapers were publishing regularly and nongovernmental organizations, including five human rights organizations and several professional associations, were operating more freely than at any time in Cambodia's history. UNTAC supervised Cambodia's accession to seven international human rights treaties, trained officials and ordinary citizens in basic principles of human rights, and drafted a new criminal law for the transition period that contained basic guarantees of procedural fairness. The law,

however, was rarely enforced, given the weakness of the judicial system and the deep politicization of the police and military.

The Right to Monitor

Four Cambodian human rights organizations emerged during UNTAC's tenure in addition to the Association de Droits de l'Homme au Cambodge (ADHOC), which was formed in January 1992. The new organizations were LICADHO (Cambodian League for Human Rights); Outreach; Human Rights Vigilance of Cambodia; and LCDHC (Cambodian League for Human and Citizens' Rights). With support from UNTAC, they began to teach human rights, monitor the elections, report abuses and publish magazines. In the period leading up to the elections, some local human rights activists became targets of violence and intimidation, and the Phnom Penh government discouraged Buddhist temples from allowing human rights offices on their premises. SOC authorities viewed the human rights organizations as political opponents in another guise, and monitors often reported being followed by government agents.

In general, however, the ability to carry out human rights monitoring was better than at any other period in Cambodian history. After the election, eight Cambodian human rights and development organizations made a bold statement on granting citizenship to long-term ethnic Vietnamese residents. They also urged that citizenship and residency rights be resolved according to humanitarian principles. The local organizations also played a critical role during the drafting of the constitution, pressing to open the process to public comment. They lobbied for specific human rights provisions, including independence of the judiciary and judicial review of executive acts as well as strong protections for the rights of women and children.

The Buddhist church, previously under complete state control, also showed signs of becoming more independent, and monks led several peace walks and public demonstrations.

During UNTAC's presence, international human rights organizations enjoyed free access to all areas of Cambodia except those controlled by the Khmer Rouge, and two international conferences were convened by UNTAC's Human Rights Component.

U.S. Policy

The Clinton administration firmly backed the U.N. peacekeeping mission in Cambodia and expressed support for a limited U.N. presence once UNTAC was withdrawn.

The U.S. contributed $517 million to UNTAC's total budget (approximately 30 percent). Additional funding for fiscal year 1994 was devoted primarily to economic development and de-mining, including $1 million pledged to HALO Trust, a de-mining group, plus another $700,000 to the Cambodia Mine Action Center; $2 million was also committed to help keep UNTAC's de-mining equipment in Cambodia. Another $2 million was contributed towards the expenses of the transitional administration.

At the 1992 donors conference in Tokyo, the U.S. joined with other donors in pledging $880 million in development assistance; at the Paris International Conference on Reconstruction of Cambodia in September 1993, it reported that over $135 million had been provided in fiscal year 1992 and 1993.

The administration put considerable emphasis, particularly in the lead-up to the elections, on supporting human rights and democratization projects, including training political parties and election observers.

State Departments officials described progress on human rights under UNTAC as "impressive," citing the release of political prisoners, accession to international human rights conventions, and formation of indigenous human rights groups. While studiously avoiding any public criticism of UNTAC's human rights activities, administration officials acknowledged in testimony before Congress on June 16 and October 27 that serious human rights problems remained. The U.S. backed the decision by the U.N. Human Rights Commission to appoint a Special Representative on Human Rights for Cambodia and to establish a field office to continue monitoring abuses.

While acknowledging the ongoing threat posed by the Khmer Rouge, the State Department maintained that encouraging economic development and rebuilding the country's communications and transportation infrastructure offered the most effective long-range strategy for denying the Khmer Rouge a base of political support.

The foreign aid appropriations bill for fiscal year 1994 contained explicit prohibitions on direct or indirect aid to the Khmer Rouge and "Cambodian organizations" cooperating militarily with them. The administration estimated commercial military sales to Cambodia of $22,000 in fiscal year 1994.

The administration gave mixed signals on the issue of whether U.S. aid to the new Cambodian government would be withheld if the Khmer Rouge were given a role. The State Department expressed the view that the new constitution effectively prohibited appointment of Khmer Rouge officials to ministerial or sub-cabinet level positions. The U.S. declined to call for Pol Pot or other high-ranking Khmer Rouge leaders to be put on trial by an international tribunal for atrocities committed during their rule, leaving this question for the new Cambodian government to decide.

The Senate's fiscal year 1994 State Department authorization bill (yet to be enacted by mid-November), contained a provision originally introduced by Sen. Charles Robb (D-VA) requiring the State Department to set up an office in Cambodia to investigate and gather documentation on "crimes against humanity" committed by Khmer Rouge leaders from 1975 through 1979, and to develop a proposal for an international tribunal.

The administration confirmed that cross-border smuggling and leakage of goods across the Thai border to the Khmer Rouge persisted as of mid-June, despite U.N. sanctions. But the State Department publicly praised Thai civilian authorities for trying to enforce the sanctions and defended Bangkok against Congressional criticism.

The chief U.S. representative in Phnom Penh, Charles Twinning, received wide praise for his public denunications of killings of ethnic Vietnamese and other human rights abuses.

The Work of Asia Watch

Asia Watch closely monitored human rights in Cambodia. A month-long fact-finding mission to Cambodia in February and March 1993 provided material for three published reports: "Cambodia: Human Rights Before and After the Elections;" the Cambodia chapter of *The Lost Agenda: Human Rights and U.N. Field Operations*; and "An Exchange on Human Rights and Peace-Keeping in Cambodia." Asia Watch also met with UNTAC officials in Washington to discuss its concerns and findings.

Asia Watch testified before Congress twice during the year on safeguarding human rights in Cambodia, the first time before the Senate Foreign Relations Committee on June 16, and the second before the House Foreign Affairs Committee on October 27. Among its recommendations were immediate funding for continued de-mining in Cambodia, the conditioning of any international aid to Cambodia's police or military on measures for strict accountability for human rights abuses, continued support for building a justice system in Cambodia, and the establishment of a human rights commission or ombudsman to investigate and expose human rights abuses.

Asia Watch invited Srey Chanphallara, a unique leading woman in the Cambodian human rights field, to be honored by Human Rights Watch at its observance of Human Rights Day, December 10.

CHINA
AND TIBET

Human Rights Developments

The Chinese government continued to ar-
rest, detain and torture peaceful critics and to interfere with freedom of expression, association, assembly and religion. International concern over these abuses led to the failure of China's bid for the 2000 Olympic games. Releases of dissidents were carefully timed to manipulate world opinion, as exemplified by the release days before the Olympic decision in September of writer and editor Wei Jingsheng after over fourteen years of solitary confinement. Foreign Minister Qian Qichen's statement on November 9, just before the Asia-Pacific Economic Cooperation (APEC) meeting, that China would be "willing to consider" access by the International Committee of the Red Cross (ICRC) to Chinese prisons was encouraging; it remained to be seen whether negotiations with ICRC would begin in earnest.

China's efforts to restrict freedom of expression reached beyond its borders. In May, it successfully prevented dissident-in-exile Shen Tong from holding a press conference at the United Nations, and in June, at the Vienna Conference on Human Rights, it tried to ban the Dalai Lama from speaking.

Within China, dissidents were sentenced for peaceful expression of political views. Plans to distribute handbills in Shanghai calling for the gradual introduction of democracy and political freedom to accompany economic reform led to the arrest of three Guangdong men, Li Guoheng, Liang Weiman and Wu Songfa, on April 6. Wang Miaogen, a former leader of the Shanghai Workers Autonomous Federation, was sent to a police-run psychiatric facility on April 27 to ensure no disruption of the East Asian Games in May. Members of the banned Shanghai Workers Autonomous Federation were arrested in May on charges of forming a "counterrevolutionary organization." Fu Shenqi, detained on June 26 to prevent him from speaking to journalists during the visit of Australian Prime Minister Paul Keating, was administratively sentenced on July 4 to three years in a "re-education through labor" camp for "inciting trouble" among Shanghai's dissidents and for speaking to foreign reporters. Two workers, Yao Kaiwen and Gao Xiaoliang, arrested in May, were secretly tried on September 24, the day following the Olympic decision, on charges of "forming a counter-revolutionary clique." Their activities allegedly included attempting to mark the fourth anniversary of the June 4 crackdown in Beijing. In October, in Hubei Province, Yu Zhuo, a graduate student in Wuhan Polytechnic's department of economic management, was sentenced to a two-year prison term for putting up more than thirty posters commemorating the events of June 4, 1989; he had been held incommunicado ever since September 3, 1992.

Nineteen dissidents, arrested in 1992 for their alleged involvement in underground dissident groups, were indicted in September 1993 in a move that indicated trials were imminent.

The State Security Law passed on February 22 had a particularly deleterious effect on journalists. Wu Shishen, an editor in the domestic news department of the official news agency *Xinhua*, was sentenced to life in prison for selling a Hong Kong reporter an advance copy of a speech by Party Secretary Jiang Zemin. An alleged accomplice, Ma Tao, an editor at the magazine *China Health Education News*, received a six-year sentence. In May, Bai Weiji and his wife, Zhao Lei, accused of "illegally providing national secrets to a foreigner," received ten- and six-year terms. Two friends, one a former journalist, were sentenced with them. Gao Yu, former deputy chief editor-in-chief of the now banned *Economics Weekly*, was charged on October 13, eleven days after her detention, with "leaking state secrets abroad." She was detained on October 2 as she was scheduled to leave China to take up a visiting scholarship at the Columbia School of Journalism in New York. On September 27, a Hong Kong reporter, Xi Yang, and a "co-conspirator" were arrested in Beijing for "stealing and spying on financial secrets of the state."

Press freedom was further curtailed by reprisals for "illegal publishing." Li Minqi, a former student who served a two-year sentence for pro-democracy activities, was detained briefly in June for printing an underground magazine. For selling pornography and trading in publishing quotas, Wang Shuxiang was sentenced to death with a two-year reprieve and his assets were confiscated. Li Dasheng received a twelve-year term for a similar offense, and in March, Wan Jianguo received a four-year prison term for reprinting some 60,000 copies of *Golden Lotus*, a 400-year-old Chinese erotic classic. The book, banned from public sale, is available to the Communist Party leadership under a system of restricted circulation.

Free expression restrictions extended to film, to "illegal" fax machines and private satellite dishes. "Farewell, My Concubine," co-winner of the Cannes Film Festival's Palme d'Or, could not be cleared for general release until substantial cuts were made. At the first Shanghai International Film Festival, works by China's independent filmmakers were banned without exception.

Wang Juntao, Bao Tong and Ren Wanding, all prominent dissidents, were denied release on medical parole despite serious problems. Ren was in danger of losing his eyesight from untreated retinal and cataract problems. Bao showed symptoms of colon cancer; a request by his family to allow him to see his own doctor was denied.

Those released from prison, either on parole or at the completion of their terms, continued to be harassed; many were without jobs, housing and medical benefits. Others were denied access to educational opportunities. Li Guiren, an editor and publisher from Xi'an, was critically ill when he left prison. Fired from his job and denied welfare benefits, he could not afford desperately needed hospitalization. Wang Xizhe, a prominent Democracy Wall activist who served almost twelve years, was prohibited from talking to the press or starting a private business.

Torture continued despite an upsurge in prosecutions of police and prison officials. Liu Gang, a student leader in Tiananmen Square, smuggled out accounts of his torture in a labor camp in Liaoning Province.

Li Guoheng, from Guangdong, reportedly was so badly beaten in detention that he asked his family for painkillers. And in Lianjiang county, Guangdong province, an accused chicken thief died after he was strung up in a police station window for three hours.

Freedom to leave and enter one's own country remained restricted. While some dissidents were granted passports, most notably Hou Xiaotian, wife of political prisoner Wang Juntao, others, such as Yu Haocheng, a sixty-five-year-old legal scholar, were not. Yu was considered a security risk because of his work as director of the Public Security Department's Masses (Qunzhong) publishing house.

On August 13, a day after he returned to China on a valid Chinese passport, Han Dongfang, a founder of the Beijing Workers Autonomous Federation, was seized in Guangzhou by the Public Security Bureau, roughed up and forced back across the border to Hong Kong. On August 21, Chinese officials invalidated his passport on orders from "concerned government departments." He effectively was rendered stateless.

Prison-made products continued to be exported in 1993. Xu Yiruo, a student detained three times between June 1989 and February 1993, reported that just before he left the Shandong No.1 Labor Re-education Center, he was mining flint clay for export to the U.S. and other markets.

Religious repression in China intensified throughout 1993 with the Protestant house-church movement coming under particularly severe attack. In one case, Lai Manping died from injuries sustained when public security officers broke into a religious gathering on March 27 in Shaanxi Province. In July, six Catholics were detained in Fujian Province after a raid on a house in which 250 youths were attending a class on religion and human quality. During interrogation, Public Security Bureau officials used guns and electric prods to beat some of the participants.

Catholic bishop Julius Jia Zhiguo was detained in April to prevent him from saying an anniversary mass for the late Bishop Fan Xueyan. Eight others were detained with him.

Heightened concern with so-called splittism resulted in an upsurge in arrests in Tibet, Xinjiang and Inner Mongolia. Between January and mid-August alone, there were some 119 political arrests in Tibet, almost half from rural areas and most involving peaceful protest. Two Tibetans, Gendun Rinchen and Lobsang Yonten, arrested in mid-May by state security officials, were still being held incommunicado at the end of the year for planning to inform a visiting European Community delegation of human rights violations. Farmers outside Lhasa, arrested for peacefully demonstrating in 1992, were sentenced in 1993 to terms ranging up to eighteen years. A mass demonstration in Lhasa on May 24 and 25 resulted in the arrests of at least thirty-five people by July; some were tortured. A Tibetan businesswoman, Damchoe Pema, twenty weeks pregnant when she was arrested in May, miscarried after police forced her to remain standing for over twelve hours and beat her with electric batons.

In Inner Mongolia, a Mongolian literature professor named Delger and a relative were detained for protesting the suppression of Mongol culture and formally charged with "counterrevolutionary propaganda" in January 1993.

In September, army troops were sent to the ethnically Uighur area of Kashgar, Xinjiang province, after a series of bombings and reported attacks on Chinese attributed to the East Turkestan Party, a separatist organization. On October 7, the official Chinese news agency reported that armed police "crushed" a protest by more than 10,000 Muslims in Xining, Qinghai over a children's book titled *Braintwisters*, which showed a pig next to a praying Muslim.

The Right to Monitor

No independent human rights organizations were allowed in China. Individual activists risked lengthy prison terms for disseminating information about prisoners, ex-prisoners, prison conditions and other human rights violations. One of the charges against Fu

Shenqi, the Shanghai dissident sentenced in July to three years in a re-education camp, was that he mounted a letter-writing campaign on behalf of Wang Miaogen, a former leader of the Shanghai Workers Autonomous Federation who was sent to a police-run psychiatric facility on April 27 to ensure he not disrupt the East Asian Games.

In Shanghai, members of the Study Group on Human Rights in China were harassed and in some cases briefly detained. In June, at least one member was forbidden to leave his apartment; another was threatened with incarceration in a mental facility if he persisted in a hunger strike. Other members were under surveillance. Another Shanghai group, with an overlapping membership, the Human Rights Association, applied in March to local authorities to register as an organization. Its petition was ignored.

No international human rights organizations were permitted to conduct fact-finding missions in China, but on September 18, five days before the site for the 2000 Olympics was named, the International Federation for Human Rights, based in France, was invited to send a delegation to China by the head of the Chinese Olympic Committee and former mayor of Beijing, Chen Xitong.

U.S. Policy

For the first half of the year, administration policy seemed focused less on improving human rights in China than on reaching an accommodation with Congress to prevent a bruising battle over China's Most Favored Nation (MFN) trade status, which is reviewed annually every June. The latter part of the year saw the initiation of a high-level review of China policy in response to growing concern within the administration and outside it over the poor state of U.S.-China relations.

The annual debate on MFN in Congress started early. Through March, Secretary of State Warren Christopher made only vague references to the need to use MFN to improve China's human rights performance. No one in the administration specified even in general terms what improvements would be sought before MFN was extended for another year nor what other governments such as Japan might do to help bring those improvements about.

Congress then took the initiative. On April 22, legislation was introduced in both the House and Senate detailing specific human rights conditions, as well as provisions dealing with trade and proliferation, for renewal of MFN in June 1994. Failure to meet the conditions would mean revocation of MFN for all goods produced or marketed by Chinese state-owned enterprises. (Similar legislation had been passed by large majorities in both houses in 1992 but had been vetoed by President Bush.) Rep. Nancy Pelosi (D-CA) and Sen. George Mitchell (D-ME), the lead sponsors, emphasized that the bill was intended to give Clinton leverage in dealing with China, and voiced their hope that the president would attach conditions himself when renewing MFN. China's trade surplus of $18.2 billion in 1992 helped fuel congressional concern.

On May 12, the American business community weighed in with an unprecedented letter to Clinton, signed by over 200 leaders of major U.S. corporations and business associations, arguing against conditions on MFN that might "lead the Chinese to engage in retaliatory actions."

By the time Assistant Secretary of State Winston Lord traveled to Beijing on May 12, it was clear that a compromise was being developed. The president would take the MFN issue out of Congress's hands and grant MFN for another year unconditionally, but the administration would craft its own conditions that would be broad enough to avoid provoking a strong counter-reaction from either the Chinese or from U.S. business. Some corporate representatives, aware of this compromise in progress, quietly urged moderation in Beijing. (Lord's visit was later credited for bringing about the release of a few prominent political prisoners, such as Xu Wenli, a Democracy Wall activist imprisoned for nearly twelve years. In addition, China issued passports and exit permits for others seeking to come to the U.S., such as Hou Xiaotian.)

On May 28, the president extended MFN for one year without conditions, noting the progress of economic reform in China and expressing hope that it would lead to "greater political freedom." At the same time, Clinton expressed "clear disapproval of [China's] repressive policies" and issued an executive order stipulating that to receive MFN in June 1994, China would need to make certain human rights improvements. Only two conditions were binding and absolute—promoting freedom of emigration under the Jackson-Vanik provision and abiding by the August 1992 bilateral agreement on prison labor exports—and these pertained to commitments China had already made. Otherwise, the secretary of state was to advise the president whether "overall, significant progress" had been made with respect to humane treatment of prisoners; protection of Tibet's cultural and religious heritage; release and full accounting of political prisoners; and unhindered television and radio broadcasts into China. Official reaction in China was muted, and Chinese leaders were said to be relieved that the executive order was not stronger.

Democratic congressional leaders closed ranks behind the president and gave the administration a grace period of one year to try to bring about substantive progress. (A resolution revoking MFN in 1993 was soundly rejected by the House on July 21 by a vote of 318 to 105.) In August, nearly a dozen congressional delegations visited China, echoing the administration's message that without real progress, MFN would be withdrawn next year.

To add teeth to the executive order, Asia Watch recommended that the administration give Congress a progress report after six months on China's compliance with the Order. Representative Sam Gibbons (D-FL), chair of the House Ways and Means Trade Subcommittee, at a hearing on June 8, endorsed this recommendation and announced that he would hold hearings early in 1994 at which the administration and human rights groups would be asked to testify. The

State Department, to its credit, used this Congressional requirement in its bilateral contacts to increase the pressure on China.

The U.S. also reacted vigorously to defend the right of the dissident, Han Dongfang, to return to China. On August 16 the State Department said it "deplored" the expulsion of Han and complained publicly when his passport was revoked.

A decision, as required by law, on August 25 to ban exports of satellites and related equipment to China in response to its sale of M-11 ballistic missile technology to Pakistan, complicated the administration's human rights policy. The impact of these sanctions on U.S.-China relations was increased when an inspection of a Chinese merchant ship, the Yinhe, suspected by the U.S. of carrying chemical weapons to Iran, came up empty. The Chinese accused the administration of bullying and retaliated by holding up a visit to Beijing by John Shattuck, Assistant Secretary of State for Human Rights and Humanitarian Affairs. The purpose of the visit, orginally planned for August, was to resume an official dialogue on human rights cut off by China in October 1992, and to spell out, more precisely, what was meant in the executive order by "overall progress." The administration seemed ill-prepared for the inevitable testing period in relations between the new president and Beijing.

China also resented a bipartisan congressional campaign to prevent Beijing from being chosen to host the summmer Olympics in the year 2000. On August 9, sixty members of the Senate, led by Sen. Bill Bradley (D-NJ), wrote to the members of the International Olympic Committee (IOC) declaring that awarding the games would "confer upon China's leaders a stamp of approval. . .they clearly do not deserve." On July 26, the House passed a resolution with a similar message by a huge margin (287-99), echoed on September 15 by a resolution in the European Parliament. The administration distanced itself from this campaign, while supporting, in a letter to Congress, the general principle that "a country's human rights performance should be an important factor" in the Olympic site selection. On September 23 the IOC voted to award the games to Sydney, Australia, despite a massive pro-Beijing lobbying effort. The release of China's most prominent dissident, Wei Jingsheng, just prior to the decision, was welcomed by the U.S. at the same time it called upon China "to release all persons like Wei imprisoned solely for the peaceful expression of their poltiical views."

On the prison labor issue, the administration frankly told Congress on September 9 that it was "regrettably at an impasse with the Chinese." The new comissioner of customs, George Weise, analyzing China's compliance with the August 1992 Memorandum of Understanding on prison labor, at a hearing on September 9, said China had responded to only sixteen of thirty-one requests for investigations of suspected prison labor sites, and had granted only one of five requests to allow U.S. customs officials to inspect facilities.

Congress took the lead in urging the administration to use the leverage of World Bank loans to China on behalf of human rights. The fiscal year 1994 foreign aid appropriations bill report called on the U.S. to "actively seek support among our allies for a policy of restricting loans to China until and unless there are fundamental human rights improvements" and requested a report back to Congress. From January to June, the U.S. voted to approve most loans to China but abstained on eight and voted against three major infrastructure projects. In fiscal year 1993, the World Bank's loans to China reached an all-time high of nearly $3.2 billion. Once again, China received more funds than any other country.

At the U.N. Human Rights Commission in Geneva, the U.S. co-sponsored and actively organized support for a relatively mild resolution condemning human rights abuses in China. It was defeated.

A high-level policy review initiated in September led the administration to use carrots as well as sticks to encourage the Chinese to be more cooperative on human rights. Resumption of high-level exchanges was

one tactic. Assistant Secretary of State for Human Rights John Shattuck visited China and Tibet from October 10 to 17, but only after the administration agreed to a meeting between President and Party Secretary Jiang Zemin and President Clinton at the summit meeting of the Asia Pacific Economic Community (APEC) on November 19 and 20 in Seattle and planned visits to Beijing by Treasury Secretary Bensten, Agricultural Secretary Mike Espey and others. Resumption of military exchanges, suspended after the crackdown in Beijing, began with a trip to China by Assistant Secretary of Defense Charles Freeman in November.

On September 29, President Clinton announced his national export strategy, including significant liberalization of controls on the export of supercomputers, which opened the door to the possible transfer of highly sensitive dual-use technology to China.

The Work of Asia Watch

China remained a key focus for Asia Watch, with work divided among Hong Kong, Washington and New York. The aim was to try to hold the new U.S. administration to its campaign position on China and to ensure that the international community did not lose sight of human rights abuses in China as it became awed by the country's growing economic might.

The Hong Kong office uncovered important new evidence on a range of human rights abuses, including confidential Chinese government documents sanctioning the use of executed prisoners' organs for medical transplants; fresh evidence of continued exports by Chinese authorities of prison-made goods; and evidence of forcible detention of political dissidents in asylums for the criminally insane.

The director of Asia Watch's Hong Kong office met frequently with government officials visiting Hong Kong to brief them on the human rights situation in China. He also maintained regular contact with the Beijing- and Hong Kong-based press corps. The Hong Kong office also continued to act as a liaison center for information on Chinese prisoners.

Recognizing the high stakes involved in Beijing's bid to host the 2000 Olympics, Human Rights Watch and Asia Watch launched an eight-month campaign to make human rights a factor in the International Olympic Committee's site selection process, focus attention on China's ongoing violations and oppose Beijing's bid.

Human Rights Watch initiated a correspondence with the IOC president and raised its concerns with the sports press. It also wrote the chief executive officers of sixteen major Olympic corporate sponsors—many of whom were believed to be supporting Beijing's bid—pointing out that their corporate image could suffer by an Olympiad tarnished by human rights abuses and urging them to use their influence on behalf of human rights.

Working with members of the European Parliament, Human Rights Watch helped generate an appeal to the IOC to reject Beijing's bid in a resolution condemning abuses in Tibet. This was followed by a separate letter from the European Parliament to the IOC President. In Monte Carlo, where the IOC voted, the Human Rights Watch representative distributed information to the press and helped ensure that human rights dominated the IOC decision-making process.

Asia Watch testified in Congress four times during the year: on May 20, before the House Foreign Affairs Committee, on human rights and U.S. policy toward China; on June 8, before the House Committee on Ways and Means, on human rights and MFN for China; on July 15, before the Senate Committee on Commerce, Science and Aviation, on human rights, China and the 2000 Olympiad; and on September 9, before the House Foreign Affairs Committee, on prison labor and U.S. policy toward China.

Asia Watch published two shorter reports on prisoners, "Economic Reform, Political Repression: Arrests of Dissidents in China since Mid-1992" and "Democracy Wall Prisoners." In June, Asia Watch published *Continuing Religious Repression in China*, updating its January 1992 report. For the *Human Rights Watch Global Report on Prisons*, Asia Watch researched and analyzed conditions in Chinese prisons, labor camps, detention centers and police lockups in several cities and provinces. Asia Watch also maintained a data base of all Chinese and Tibetan prisoners and ex-prisoners known to Asia Watch, and issued a comprehensive, detailed list of prisoners in November 1993.

Asia Watch continued to work closely with the Tibet Information Network to raise individual cases of Tibetan prisoners in various fora.

Asia Watch named Liu Gang, one of the leaders of the emerging student democracy movement in the mid-1980s, and imprisoned since 1989, as one of the international human rights monitors to be honored in 1993 by Human Rights Watch in observance of Human Rights Day, December 10.

HONG KONG

Human Rights Developments

China played hardball in its continuing dispute with Hong Kong Gov. Chris Patten over his modest proposals for legislative reform. Beijing's determination to win the greatest degree of control over Hong Kong, even prior to its legal resumption of sovereignty in 1997, underscored both the urgency of legal reform to more firmly secure the future observance of human rights, and the colonial government's lack of progress in this area.

At the end of 1992, Chinese officials hurled bitter personal invective against Governor Patten and threatened to set up "a new kitchen" or a parallel government for Hong Kong if his proposals were acted upon. Not until the governor published his proposals before the Legislative Council in April did Beijing agree to resume talks on the reforms, but little progress resulted. The governor in his annual policy speech in October suggested that the time left for reaching a mutual agreement was near an end, raising the prospect of further confrontation in 1994.

The government's pro-reform stance was tarnished somewhat in July, when Governor Patten argued that there was no need for an independent human rights commission, as called for by the Legislative Council. Proponents had argued that it was necessary to investigate official practices that might be in violation of the Bill of Rights, particularly as the cost of litigation in Hong Kong (where losers are liable for all fees and costs) greatly inhibits challenges through the courts.

Even so, many laws have been challenged under the Bill of Rights since it came into effect in 1991, in particular criminal laws that placed the burden of proof on the defendant. In October 1993, two activists who were arrested in June 1992 for breaking through a police cordon during a picket of the New China News Agency (*Xinhua*) office—China's *de facto* governmental presence—challenged their conviction by questioning the legality of police restrictions on peaceful assemblies.

China, which had opposed the Bill of Rights from the start, continued to hint that it would alter the legal landscape when it resumed control. In 1993 it unilaterally created the Preliminary Working Committee, a group that was to lay the groundwork for the eventual transfer of power, and one which was widely perceived as China's alternative to cooperating with the British. Simon Li Fook-sean, a co-convener of the committee's legal sub-group, suggested in September that the committee consider drafting laws to prohibit subversion against China. He also went on record in September as criticizing the Bill of Rights's supremacy over other Hong Kong laws, stating, "If we did scrap the Bill of Rights, the Basic Law, common law and all the ordinary ordinances would sufficiently protect human rights in Hong Kong. If people don't believe that, it's because they lack faith."

Precisely because they lacked faith in China's commitment to human rights, many Hong Kong legislators and nongovernmental organizations focused attention in 1993 on the government's failure to amend or repeal existing laws that were in conflict with the guarantees of the Bill of Rights. Some of the laws identified included provisions on censorship, police powers to license public demonstrations or compel evidence from journalists, and the Official Secrets Act. The government did, however, propose an amendment to the Television Ordinance that would remove the powers of executive authorities to revoke a television license on security grounds and to regulate the political content of programs. Legislators also decried the government's failure to introduce laws on sexual discrimination or freedom of information, and prepared to draft their own.

A new urgency infused concern over the future protection of press freedom when another Hong Kong journalist was arrested in China in September. Yang Xi of *Ming Pao* was accused of "espionage regarding state secrets on banking" because of an article about possible changes in interest rates. On October 2, a Chinese woman named Gao Yu was detained and accused of leaking state secrets for providing information to Hong Kong journalists. These arrests followed the 1992 arrest of Hong Kong writer Leung Wai-man, who had published a speech by China's Communist Party leader Jiang Zemin a week before it was given. Wu Shishen, a journalist with the New China News Agency who gave her the speech, was sentenced to life imprisonment.

The treatment of Vietnamese asylum-seekers detained in Hong Kong continued to pose grave human rights problems, even as Hong Kong authorities scrambled to comply with China's wish that the detention centers be emptied before 1997.

Screening for refugee status remained flawed, and Asia Watch was again obliged to intercede on behalf of rejected individuals at serious risk of persecution. In June, a Hong Kong court delivered a stinging indictment of the screening system, ordering reconsideration of the case of two Vietnamese, due to the government's failure to read back to them their immigration interview for completeness and accuracy, or to consider evidence of persecution they had proffered. Toward year's end, fewer than 3,000 of the approximately 35,000 Vietnamese asylum-seekers detained in Hong Kong remained to be screened, and the vast majority of the rest, who had been screened, had been rejected under flawed procedures. The government had appealed the court's decision.

The policy of incarcerating asylum-seekers also came under challenge in 1993. In mid-year, the U.N. Working Group on Arbitrary Detention began consideration of a complaint filed by the Lawyers Committee for Human Rights and the Women's Commission for Refugee Women and Children on behalf of all detained Vietnamese. In July, damages of over $25,000 were awarded to the first seven of 111 plaintiffs in the Boat 101 case, in which a court had previously ruled that the government illegally detained persons intercepted in 1989 en route to Japan.

The severely overcrowded detention centers for Vietnamese, often dominated by criminal gangs, were the site of yet more assaults and rapes. The overall atmosphere of intimidation and violence worsened as the Hong Kong government and the U.N. High Commissioner for Refugees (UNHCR) cut back services such as education and psychological counseling, and began systematically transferring asylum-seekers between camps, both to consolidate detention centers and to destabilize established communities in order to encourage people to volunteer to return to Vietnam. In May, tensions were so high in the Whitehead Detention Centre over a plan to transfer 4,000 detainees to a different section that the then-UNHCR chief of mission, Robert Van Leeuwen, made a personal visit. During the visit, asylum-seekers explained that every transfer put them at the mercy of criminal gangs, who would use violence to assert control and extort the transferred people. At the conclusion of Van Leeuwen's speech, in which he declined to address these concerns and instead focused on voluntary repatriation, three men slashed their stomachs in protest and had to be hospitalized.

The preoccupation with boosting the flagging numbers of volunteers for repatriation led the Hong Kong government, with the agreement of the UNHCR, to close off alternative sources of information to the incarcerated Vietnamese. In June, the government rejected a proposal from nongovernmental organizations for a forum on current conditions in Vietnam to be held in the detention centers; both Asia Watch and Amnesty International had been invited as participants. The government said the forum "could be counter-productive" given Asia Watch's past criticism of the government's policies. Early in 1993, *Freedom*, the premier news and commentary journal edited by detained Vietnamese was closed. UNHCR refused to reauthorize the magazine, citing lack of resources despite offers of financing and technical assistance from Hong Kong corporations and professionals; the journal's independence in publishing refugee views, however, was widely believed to be the real reason for its closure.

The Right To Monitor

Hong Kong generally respected human rights monitoring and advocacy, but the prognosis as 1997 drew near was uncertain. One possible harbinger of problems to come was the refusal of eighteen of Hong Kong's top law firms to accept as clients Martin Lee and Szeto Wah, two legislators and pro-democracy activists who were regularly reviled by China. Lee and Szeto sought to sue Simon Li Fook-sean of China's Preparatory Working Committee for defamation when he said in mid-July that the pair were unfit to remain in the legislature because they had urged runs on Chinese banks in 1989, after the Tiananmen Square massacre.

A similar problem that received growing attention was the frequent self-censorship the Hong Kong media practiced on topics sensitive to China. Although the colonial government used its broad powers of censorship infrequently, China systematically monitored Hong Kong journalists, punishing those it found irritating with denial of access to the mainland, or as described above, with arrest and imprisonment.

One of the notable areas where the Hong Kong government restricted media access during 1993 was the detention centers for Vietnamese. In April, the government opened files more than thirty years old to public inspection, and permitted residents to check personal files it held on them, but only with regard to information that was provided by the individual.

U.S. Policy

The Clinton administration supported the reform plans of Governor Patten, saying on March 30 in a report to Congress required under the U.S. Hong Kong Policy Act that the reforms were consistent with the Basic Law. Secretary of State Warren Christopher and Assistant Secretary of State for Asia and the Pacific Winston Lord also gave support for the plans, although Lord told the Senate on March 31 that the U.S. should stay out of negotiations between Britain and China over greater democracy.

Patten visited Washington from May 2 to May 8. The official purpose of his visit was to urge the U.S. to extend Most Favored Nation status to China without conditions, as Hong Kong would be hurt by withdrawal of MFN.

The Work of Asia Watch

Asia Watch was particularly concerned by the treatment of Hong Kong journalists as a harbinger of increased restrictions on freedom of the press when Hong Kong reverts to Chinese control in 1997. It continued to monitor the situation of Vietnamese refugees in Hong Kong.

INDIA

Human Rights Developments

The destruction of a sixteenth-century mosque in Ayodhya, in north India, on December 6, 1992, continued to have violent repercussions throughout the country as political leaders tried to exploit rising tension

between Hindus and Muslims. In January 1992, unprecedented communal violence in Bombay left at least 700 dead. Massacres of civilians by Indian security forces in Kashmir continued during the year; armed Kashmiri militants were also responsible for some summary executions of non-combatants. The conflicts in Punjab and Assam abated considerably, but security forces continued to commit abuses with impunity. Although the government of India found itself increasingly under pressure to respond to international and domestic criticism about human rights violations, it took few concrete steps to end them.

The razing of the Babri Masjid in Ayodhya was the culmination of a campaign by the Hindu nationalist political party, the Bharatiya Janata Party (BJP), together with other Hindu militant organizations, to challenge the Narasimha Rao government and assert the dominance of Hindu culture in India. Despite promises by BJP state government officials that the mosque would be protected, police at the site reportedly refused to intervene to prevent either the demolition or subsequent attacks on journalists and others. More than 1,000 died in the violence that followed in cities across north India. A disproportionate number of those killed were Muslims shot by police. In some cases, those shot dead were pulled from their homes and summarily executed. In Surat, in the state of Gujarat, attacks on Muslims included the gang-rapes of women.

In January, Muslims in Bombay were again the principal target during nine days of violence in which more than 700 people were killed. The Bombay police, many of whom reportedly support the Hindu militant Shiv Sena organization, deliberately targeted Muslims or stood back while mobs burned Muslims' homes. An official investigation into the violence and the police's role began in April; as of November, no findings had been made public. In August, the report of an independent commission, headed by two retired High Court judges, was published by the Indian People's Human Rights Commission, an independent group. It named eighty policemen and politicians from the BJP and the Congress (I) political party who were identified by eyewitnesses as participating in the violence.

On March 12, Bombay was rocked by a series on bomb blasts that tore through tourist hotels, markets and the stock exchange, killing at least 250 people. A police investigation blamed a prominent Muslim family involved in organized crime for the bombings. The motive for the attack remained unclear.

In Kashmir, the year began with the massacre of civilians by Border Security Force (BSF) troops in the western city of Sopore on January 6, in retaliation for a militant attack in which two soldiers had died. Eyewitnesses confirmed that the troops went on a rampage and killed at least forty-three persons, some of whom died of gunshot wounds, others of whom were burned alive when the troops set fire to their shops and homes. Although security officials first claimed that the victims died in cross fire, the government was forced to order a judicial inquiry and to suspend several officers in response to widespread publicity about the incident. By November, no details of the proceedings or findings had been made public. Human rights groups complained that the investigation was being hampered by the fact that it had been held in Srinagar, some twenty-five miles away, making it impossible for many witnesses to testify.

In February, the Indian government launched a new initiative, spearheaded by Union Minister of State for Internal Security Rajesh Pilot, to open negotiations toward a political settlement. Ironically, these efforts met with an upsurge in violence in March and April, provoked by hard-line elements in both the government and intelligence agencies and by extremist militant factions. As the government appeared increasingly divided over its Kashmir policy, human rights conditions in the state worsened dramatically. By November, human rights groups and journalists in Kashmir reported several hundred executions of detainees since mid-1992. The death of a police constable in army custody, on April 21, sparked a revolt by the local police force, which was widely believed to sympathize with the militants. Although several key political figures returned to the civilian administration in Srinagar in May, and the controversial head of the abusive BSF was transferred out of the state, abuses continued.

Tensions again escalated during a month-long standoff between the army and Muslim militants barricaded inside the Hazratbal mosque in Srinagar beginning on October 15. On October 22, BSF troops in the town of Bijbehara opened fire on protesters who were demonstrating against the army siege, reportedly after first blocking the street in which the marchers had assembled. The standoff at the mosque was brought to an end when the government agreed to permit the militants to surrender to local Kashmiri police rather than to the army.

Militant groups in Kashmir continued to murder suspected informers and other civilians, to launch attacks on civilian targets, and to commit rape and other abuses. On May 11, the Hezb-ul Mujahidin launched rocket-propelled grenades at the offices of the civilian administration in Srinagar, killing one employee and injuring three others. Militant groups also issued death threats against the press, including employees of the state-run television corporation, which was forced to withdraw a series on the Bible. The program resumed on April 11 after state officials provided extra security for the television station in Srinagar.

The brutal police crackdown in Punjab appeared to have brought an end to the ten-year-old conflict there but at the cost of massive police abuses. Director General of Police K.P.S. Gill's counterinsurgency efforts included torture, disappearances and a bounty system of cash rewards for the summary execution of suspected Sikh militants. The campaign succeeded in eliminating most of the major militant groups, and by early 1993, the government claimed that normalcy had returned to the state. Police abuses continued, however, and there was no effort to account for hundreds of disappearances and summary killings. Although Gill promised to take action against abusive policemen, he promoted them instead, meanwhile, similar operations were launched in neighboring states to kill suspected militants who had migrated out of Punjab. Government officials considered these brutal methods as a model to be applied elsewhere; the upsurge in summary executions in Kashmir was cited as an example of the "Punjab solution."

Sikh militants were believed responsible for a car bomb that exploded in New Delhi on September 11, killing eight people. The apparent target was a senior Sikh leader of the Congress Party, Maninder Singh Bitta, who was injured by the blast.

The repatriation of Sri Lankan refugees from Tamil Nadu resumed in August, under circumstances tantamount to *refoulement*. No international agency was permitted access to the refugee camps in Tamil Nadu to monitor whether the registration of refugees was voluntary; the United Nations High Commissioner for Refugees (UNHCR) was permitted to interview refugees only after they had been registered and moved to transit camps to await repatriation. Asia Watch representatives who visited the camps in April discovered that refugees had been subjected to direct and indirect coercion, including arbitrary arrest, withdrawal of stipends and food rations, and pressure to sign forms indicating their willingness to return. The refugees had no reliable means of getting information about conditions upon which to base their decision to return and were frequently unaware of bombing and fighting in their home villages.

Government efforts to check sectarian violence focused initially on attempts to impose sweeping bans on religiously-based political parties rather than to prosecute and punish political leaders and police responsible for inciting and participating in the violence. On December 10, 1992, the central government banned five organizations under the Unlawful Activities Prevention Act on the grounds that they had incited religious hatred and communal violence, but the bans were later overturned by the Supreme Court.

In late February 1993, thousands of BJP supporters who defied a government ban on a rally in central New Delhi were arrested, but they were released within a few days. Moves in August and September by the government to ban religiously-based political parties were obstructed by opposition parties. On October 5, forty politicians, including senior BJP and Shiv Sena leaders, were formally charged with criminal conspiracy and the destruction and defiling of a place of worship for their role in the violence at Ayodhya.

The militant Hindu organization Shiv Sena was responsible for a number of attacks on journalists in 1993, including the May 22 murder of Dinesh Pathak, the editor of *Sandesh*, who was stabbed six months after the former head of the Shiv Sena in Gujarat publicly threatened to eliminate him.

On March 30, Indian authorities canceled a $450-million World Bank loan for the controversial Sardar Sarovar dam on the Narmada River in western India because they were unable to meet environmental and resettlement standards established following a 1992 Bank-sponsored review of the project. Officials insisted, however, that the project would be completed without World Bank funding. Anti-dam demonstrations in April and May resulted in the arrests of hundreds of demonstrators and police raids of villages scheduled for inundation. As of November 1993, the project remained under government review.

A bill to establish a national commission to investigate reports of human rights violations was submitted to the parliament in May 1993. In September, Prime Minister Narasimha Rao established the commission by executive order and named former High Court justice Raganath Misra to head it. Although the commission's powers remained to be finalized, it appeared likely to have only a limited role in recommending action with regard to abuses by the military.

The Right to Monitor
Human rights monitoring continued to be extremely dangerous in areas of conflict in

India, especially Kashmir. On December 5, 1992, Hirdai Nath Wanchoo, one of the most prominent human rights activists in Kashmir, was shot dead by unidentified gunmen. Almost a year later, no one had been brought to justice for the murder. The government's refusal to conduct an independent investigation of the murder raised serious questions about the possibility of government complicity in the killing.

On February 18, 1993, Dr. Farooq Ahmed Ashai, fifty-four, chief orthopedic surgeon at the Bone and Joint Hospital in Srinagar, was shot and killed by Indian paramilitary troops at a security force post located near the Rambagh bridge in Srinagar. Dr. Ashai was an outspoken critic of the government's human rights record in Kashmir, and had documented cases of indiscriminate shooting and torture. The killing was apparently in retaliation for a militant grenade attack on the security forces about one-half hour earlier. An inquiry into the incident reportedly confirmed that the central reserve police force troops shot Dr. Ashai, but as of December 1993, the inquiry report had not been made public. Dr. Abdul Ahad Guru, a renowned Kashmiri surgeon, was assassinated by unidentified gunmen in Srinagar on March 31, 1993. Dr. Guru was a member of the governing council of the Jammu and Kashmir Liberation Front (JKLF), and his political position made him a target for rival militant groups as well as elements within his own organization. He was also an outspoken critic of human rights abuses by Indian security forces in Kashmir and met frequently with the international press and international human rights groups. He and his family had been harassed and assaulted by the security forces on several occasions. During the funeral procession, police opened fire on the mourners, shooting Dr. Guru's brother-in-law in the head and killing him instantly.

Jaspal Singh, president of the Ropar branch of the Punjab Human Rights Organisation, was detained by the Punjab police on the evening of August 16, 1993. The case attracted considerable attention from domestic and international human rights groups, and on September 8, Jaspal Singh was returned to his home by the Punjab police.

The government's policy on international human rights investigations was erratic. India does not officially permit international human rights organizations to conduct investigations, although it has permitted Asia Watch representatives to carry out research on tourist visas. In August, however, Minister of State for External Affairs Salman Khurshid stated that the government would not consider a request from Asia Watch for a research mission. In November 1992 the government had invited a delegation from Amnesty International for meetings in Delhi, but as of November 1993, the organization had not yet been permitted to carry out any investigations. The International Committee of the Red Cross (ICRC) has never been permitted to perform its protection activities in India, including prison visits. However, in September, the Indian government made it known that the home secretary had agreed to permit the ICRC to conduct human rights seminars for border security forces in Kashmir.

U.S. Policy

The first visit by a senior State Department official to New Delhi under the Clinton administration was marked by public criticism of India's human rights record. In May, then-Interim Deputy Assistant Secretary for South Asia John Malott stated that India "had to take steps to bring the behavior of its security forces into line with its constitutional commitment to human rights, especially in Kashmir." In his September 27 address to the United Nations, President Clinton mentioned Kashmir as one conflict that posed a threat to world peace.

During a briefing for the South Asia press on October 28, Assistant Secretary of State for South Asia Robin Raphel appropriately criticized paramilitary forces responsible for the October 22 massacre of thirty-eight demonstrators in Kashmir and stated that the administration was pushing India "very hard to clean up their act in terms of human rights violations" and "make the security forces accountable for their own behavior." She also stated that the "insurgency is not an excuse" for disappearances, extrajudicial executions and deaths in custody. The briefing, which was meant to be on background, became the subject of a diplomatic row between India and the U.S. following Secretary Raphel's observation that the U.S. did not recognize that Kashmir's accession to India was necessarily final.

Human rights issues also continued to be the subject of private discussions between India and the U.S. In fact, by early 1993, human rights was frequently cited as one of the three most contentious issues between the two countries, along with nuclear proliferation and trade issues. In private discussions with the Indian government, the U.S. raised human rights issues at the July 1 donors meeting in Paris, an initiative urged by several leading members of Congress.

On June 16, the House of Representatives voted to condition future International Military Education and Training (IMET) assistance on presidential certification of improvement in India's human rights record. The move was opposed by the administration and was not included in the Senate authorization bill, which however noted the need for swift investigation of human rights abuses and punishment of those responsible as well as access by international human rights groups to areas of conflict in India.

In a report accompanying the 1993 appropriations bill, the Senate Appropriations Committee expressed its disappointment that the ICRC had not been permitted access to Kashmir and called on the Indian government to act forcefully to end abuses. It also urged the U.S. executive directors to the World Bank, Asian Development Bank and IMF to "use their voice and vote, in accordance with United States human rights law, to promote improvements in human rights by the Indian government."

U.S. military assistance and military sales to India in fiscal year 1993 included the IMET program, estimated at $345,000, com-

mercial military sales licensed under the Arms Export Control Act, estimated at $54.6 million and military sales under the Foreign Military Sales Program, estimated at $40 million. World Bank loans planned for 1993 totaled $3.7 billion.

The Work of Asia Watch

India remained a high priority for Asia Watch in 1993. Asia Watch's statements calling for investigations into the role of the police during the communal violence that followed the destruction of the mosque at Ayodhya received wide coverage.

In order to focus international attention on the crisis in Kashmir, Asia Watch, together with Physicians for Human Rights (PHR), published a series of reports throughout the year on torture, rape, extrajudicial executions and violations of medical neutrality. The reports received extensive press coverage in India and were widely circulated in Kashmir. Asia Watch also publicly called on the U.S. to suspend all military assistance and military sales to India until the government took steps to end abuses.

In March 1993, Asia Watch held discussions with government officials and representatives of human rights organizations in Delhi. On April 28, Asia Watch testified about human rights in India at a hearing before the House Subcommittee on Asian and Pacific Affairs. Asia Watch also released a newsletter on abuses in Assam on April 18.

INDONESIA AND EAST TIMOR

Human Rights Developments

Despite some signs of increasing receptivity to human rights concerns, Indonesia continued to detain critics arbitrarily, restrict freedom of expression, and obstruct the emergence of independent associations. Abuse of detainees immediately after arrest remained routine. Indonesian military abuses continued, but in two major cases, the killing of a young labor activist and the shooting of demonstrators at a dam site in Madura, army personnel were arrested or disciplined.

The appointment of President Suharto to a sixth term by the People's Consultative Assembly in March; the successful campaign by the armed forces to have its commander-in-chief, Try Sutrisno, appointed vice-president; and major cabinet changes announced at the end of March heralded little change in the government's approach to human rights.

Shortly before the Vienna World Conference on Human Rights in June, Indonesia announced the establishment of a national commission on human rights, headed by a former military judge and head of the Supreme Court, Ali Said. The twenty-five-member commission was set up by presidential decree and appeared to have neither independence nor investigatory powers.

Access to Indonesia by international human rights organizations remained limited, although Asia Watch and the International Commission of Jurists were permitted in March to send observers to the highly-charged political trial of Xanana Gusnao, leader of the East Timorese independence organization and guerrilla army.

Asia Watch received no reports of disappearances during the year, although outstanding cases of disappearances in Aceh and East Timor from 1990 and 1991 remained unresolved. The government appeared to be making no effort to find the missing or punish those responsible, and in both areas, the disappeared were presumed dead.

Several killings were attributed to the armed forces and police. On March 25, two men from the transmigrant community of Sei Lapan in North Sumatra were reported to have died in custody after having been beaten following their arrest in connection with a longstanding land dispute. On May 9, a young labor activist named Marsinah was found raped and murdered after a strike at her factory in Sidoarjo, East Java, in which the military had intervened. A special police

investigation had uncovered no suspects by October. In late July, the body of Hans Soaf, believed to be a political activist in Irian Jaya, was found buried shortly after his arrest in Waskee, West Sarmi. Suspected leaders of Aceh Merdeka, the armed nationalist organization, continued to be shot dead by soldiers, rather than captured; two were killed in August. On September 25, soldiers opened fire on a group of peaceful demonstrators in Madura, off the coast of East Java. Three people, including a fourteen-year-old boy, were killed instantly; another died later of his injuries. The demonstrators were protesting the construction of a dam. The army announced that the killings would be investigated, and later transferred four officers from the area.

Freedom of expression continued to be tightly controlled, with dozens arrested for a wide variety of offenses. In early January, two young men, Djoni Purwoto and Sugiri Cahyono, were sentenced to four and three and a half years in prison respectively on blasphemy charges for insulting Islam during a comic theatre performance in Salatiga, Central Java.

Two students from Semarang, Central Java, were tried in October for criticizing the electoral process during the parliamentary election campaign in May 1992. Both were accused of "spreading hatred of the government." Another student, David Ramone, was sentenced to six months in prison on slander charges for his role in a demonstration in which students carried posters asking a university administrator to account for his use of student fees. In late June, the trial of a young activist, Buntomi, opened in absentia in Salatiga; he was accused of distributing a calendar in 1991 that bore unflattering caricatures of President Suharto and his wife.

Freedom of association was a major issue, particularly with respect to labor and religion. The government continued to harass people associated with the independent labor union, Indonesia Prosperous Workers Union (SBSI). In June, soldiers arrested two SBSI leaders in Medan, North Sumatra, for their role in a strike at a local shrimp farm.

Both men were severely beaten; they were released after a week. On July 29, the government prevented SBSI from holding its first national congress. The Indonesian military continued as a matter of routine to intervene in labor disputes and sit in on negotiations between labor and management.

The military also intervened heavily in a leadership dispute within the Huria Kristen Batak Protestan or HKBP, the largest Protestant congregation in the country, based in North Sumatra. Beginning in January and continuing throughout the year, protests against the government-installed *ephorus* or archbishop led to over one hundred arrests, many of them involving physical abuse. On July 25, a photographer hired by one faction to document the clashes was arrested by the district military command in Bongbongan and beaten. He suffered several broken ribs. Many of those detained tried to bring *habeas corpus* petitions against the army officers who arrested them, but the courts refused to hear them on the grounds that according to the Criminal Procedure Code, they only had authority to rule on irregular arrest and detention procedures involving police.

East Timor continued to receive international attention for the human rights violations committed there. The trial of Xanana Gusmao in Dili District Court from February to May 1993 was, until the end, more open than any East Timorese trial in memory, with foreign journalists, diplomats and human rights organizations all in attendance—until the defendant abandoned his hitherto passive stance and began his defense. The government first refused to let him read his defense plea in Portuguese; it then tried to prevent diplomats from attending the final sessions; and finally it barred Gusmao from reading the plea at all, declaring it to be irrelevant to the charges against him. Gusmao was sentenced to life in prison, later reduced through a disputed plea for clemency to twenty years. He began serving the sentence in Cipinang Prison in Jakarta.

Between May and July, the military commander responsible for East Timor, General Theo Syafei, tried to prevent the International Committee of the Red Cross from visiting East Timorese detainees on the ICRC's terms. Visits were resumed on July 29.

In early September, prior to the visit of a delegation of congressional staff members, over fifty East Timorese were detained for what were euphemistically referred to as "courses." They were released after the delegation returned to Jakarta.

The Right to Monitor

Human rights organizations continued to be subject to harassment and threats from the government, even as their visibility and influence increased. In September, Vice-President Try Sutrisno warned darkly of traitors who gave information to foreign organizations. He made the remarks in connection with an announcement from the office of the U.S. Trade Representative that tariff benefits could be revoked unless labor rights practices improved.

Several activists from LBH-Ampera, a legal aid organization, were detained after a peasant demonstration on October 6 in Bogor, West Java. The police chief of Bogor accused the group who organized the demonstration of being linked to the banned Communist Party. Jauhari Ahmed, who works for the organization, received death threats from unidentified men who vandalized his home at 2 A.M.

U.S. Policy

The Clinton administration was particularly active and outspoken on the issues of East Timor and workers' rights in Indonesia, raising these concerns at the highest levels with Indonesian officials.

At the U.N. Human Rights Commission in Geneva in March, the U.S. played a pivotal role in generating support for a resolution expressing concern about human rights abuses in East Timor, clearly signaling to Indonesia that it intended to take a tougher line on human rights than the Bush administration. The resolution was adopted by a vote of 22 to 12 (with 15 abstaining).

At the World Bank-convened donors

meeting of eighteen nations in Paris on June 30, the U.S. raised East Timor and worker rights during the general discussion and in its bilateral talks. The Consultative Group pledged $5.1 billion in development assistance, with no specific human rights conditions attached. Several governments including the U.S., Canada, Austria and Switzerland, referred to human rights and the issue of "good governance."

On July 3, forty-three senators wrote to President Clinton urging him to bring up East Timor with President Suharto at the G-7 summit meeting in Tokyo. The president did so.

In response to petitions filed in June 1992 with the U.S. Trade Representative or USTR's office by Asia Watch and the International Labor Rights Education and Research Fund, Mickey Kantor announced on June 25 that Indonesia's GSP (Generalized System of Preferences) export benefits would be in "serious jeopardy" if "substantial concrete progress" was not made to protect workers' rights. The USTR announced it would develop an "action plan" with Jakarta and would decide by mid-February 1994 whether to continue the GSP program in Indonesia. The GSP report, issued in July, was especially critical of the lack of freedom of association for workers and the role of the military in labor relations. The Indonesian government's moves to ban the national congress of the independent union SBSI, in the midst of the GSP review, sparked a strong denunciation by the U.S. Embassy in Jakarta and a stern statement from Timothy Wirth, State Department Counsellor.

On September 20, an interagency team, led by the USTR, visited Indonesia for five days of talks with Indonesian officials, nongovernmental organizations, independent union organizers, and others. Such a visit had never taken place before during the annual GSP review.

Throughout 1993, congressional concern on human rights in Indonesia was focused almost exclusively on East Timor. A Congressional staff delegation visited Indonesia, and briefly went to East Timor, from August 21 to September 5.

The fiscal year 1994 foreign aid bill continued the ban on International Military Education and Training (IMET) to Indonesia enacted by Congress in 1992.

Indonesia was due to receive $46 million in development assistance, plus an increase in foreign military sales estimated at $15 million in fiscal year 1994, and an additional $15.8 million in commercial military sales. An amendment to the Senate authorization bill, sponsored by Sen. Russell Feingold, was approved by the Foreign Relations Committee on September 8, linking future military sales to Indonesia to human rights progress in East Timor. The administration opposed the Feingold amendment, however, on grounds that it would hamper other efforts to address Indonesia's human rights behavior.

In August, following consultations with Congress, the administration had rejected a request by Jordan to sell U.S. F-5 jet fighters to Indonesia, partly on human rights grounds. At that time, the State Department emphasized that the decision was "not a precedent for other arms transfer decisions."

The U.S. Embassy in Jakarta in 1993 continued energetically to raise concerns about human rights abuses.

The Work of Asia Watch

Asia Watch worked with Indonesian human rights organizations to define priorities and tried to mobilize pressure from governments including the U.S. and Japan to address those concerns. Six short reports and several press releases were issued, and consultants and interns visited the country three times. Although Executive Director Sidney Jones remained banned from the country, the government permitted an Asia Watch consultant to observe one session of the trial of East Timorese leader Xanana Gusmao and gave her full access to military and civilian officials. She was offered an opportunity to meet with Gusmao, as well, but turned it down after certain safeguards requested to ensure continued access by outsiders to Gusmao after the interview were not forthcoming.

Asia Watch continued to meet with Indonesian officials from the ministries of Foreign Affairs and Manpower during their visits to New York and Washington, and was in regular contact with a wide range of non-governmental organizations based in Indonesia.

Asia Watch gave particular attention to restrictions on freedom of expression and labor rights, especially the right to organize trade unions. Much of the work on the latter involved ensuring that demands raised by worker organizations inside Indonesia were reinforced by publicity and pressure from outside.

Concern in the business community about Indonesian government retaliation for threatened U.S. sanctions over labor practices led to fruitful explorations into how U.S. businesses and the human rights community might work together for the protection of human rights. One result was that Asia Watch was able to open new channels for raising concerns in situations where American companies themselves were involved with the Indonesian government in possible rights violations.

JAPAN

Human Rights Developments

Japanese politics were thrown into a state of flux and uncertainty in 1993 as the Liberal Democratic Party, which had ruled for almost four decades, ceded power to a coalition government after elections on July 18. The new cabinet contained two men who had been active in human rights committees in the Diet, including Foreign Minister Tsutomu Hata, and the initial statements on human rights of Prime Minister Morihiro Hosokawa were promising. By the end of the year, it was too early to tell whether Japanese policy on human rights would substantially change, particularly with regard to foreign aid (Official Development Assistance, or ODA).

At the U.N. human rights conferences in Bangkok and Vienna, Japan underscored the role of development assistance in promoting human rights. In October, the Foreign Ministry published a "white paper" on ODA, reiterating the guidelines first adopted in April 1991, that allocation of aid would take into consideration respect for human rights and democratization shown by recipient countries. "Democratization" appeared to be understood as synonomous with free market reforms. The report, however, specified for the first time that a long-term objective of the ODA program was to encourage "good governance" (a term borrowed from the World Bank) as essential to sustainable development.

ODA for fiscal year 1992 totalled $11.3 billion, again making Japan the largest foreign aid donor worldwide, with Asian countries receiving 65 percent of that total. Japan announced in June 1993 that it would increase its ODA spending over the next five years by 50 percent, to a total of $70 to $75 billion.

The ODA guidelines were loosely applied in 1993, as the government relied on "policy dialogues" with recipient governments as the primary method for addressing human rights concerns, rarely engaging in public criticism of abuses or linking ODA decisions directly to human rights.

For example, when Vo Van Kiet, Vietnam's prime minister, met with then-Prime Minister Kiichi Miyazawa in Tokyo on March 25, seeking further ODA assistance, Miyazawa raised human rights concerns only in a general way and set no specific conditions for Vietnam to meet. Human rights issues did not appear to affect the resumption of ODA to Vietnam in November 1992 ($370 million) or the willingness of Japan to provide grants and loans to help repay Vietnam's debt to the International Monetary Fund. To assist with Vietnam's market reforms, Tokyo announced in October 1993 that it would send a team of legal experts to help in drafting commercial and investment laws; no similar interest was evinced in criminal or national security laws.

On China, Japan, anxious to prevent a

deterioration in U.S.-Sino relations, was willing to play an intermediary role between Washington and Beijing but refrained from exerting any direct economic pressure on Beijing. Foreign Minister Michio Watanabe was the first high-ranking official to meet with the Clinton administration. In talks with Secretary of State Christopher and President Clinton from February 11 to 14, he urged the administration to take a "moderate approach" and to renew Most Favored Nation status (MFN) for China unconditionally. Both governments agreed to do what they could to "help political reforms catch up with economic reforms" in China. The same message was delivered directly to the White House when then-Prime Minister Miyazawa met with President Clinton in Washington on April 15.

Various Japanese government officials visited Beijing in 1993, and while it was not clear that they had made specific appeals for human rights improvements, Japan quietly lobbied for the release of individual political prisoners as well as access to prisoners by international humanitarian organizations. In early April, an official Japanese delegation visiting Tibet to discuss cultural exchanges also raised prisoner cases and asked to visit a jail.

The Hosokawa government was likely to continue Japan's policy of building strong political and economic relations with China, despite its human rights record, and Hosokawa was expected to make an official visit to Beijing as early as March 1994.

On Burma, there was a split in the Japanese government early in 1993 over the posssible resumption of new ODA to the military government in Rangoon if the SLORC-sponsored constitutional convention showed any positive result. (See section on Burma.) By November 1, there was no change in the existing ODA policy, although Foreign Minister Hata, during a visit to Bangkok in September, said that Japan wanted to help bring Burma's government out of isolation. The government was considering inviting some SLORC officials to Tokyo "for technical training." Behind the scenes, Tokyo played an important role paving the way for Sadako Ogata's visit to Burma in July 1993 to discuss the role of the U.N. High Commissioner for Refugees (UNHCR) in monitoring repatriation of refugees from Bangladesh.

In the Diet, more than 400 members from all parties signed an appeal for restoration of human rights and civilian rule in Burma, delivered to the U.N. Secretary-General in New York in March by Satsuki Eda (then a member of the House of Representatives, later a cabinet minister.)

At the U.N. Human Rights Commission in Geneva, Japan played an ambiguous role: co-sponsoring a resolution on human rights in China which failed, but abstaining on a crucial resolution on human rights in East Timor, which passed. The Japanese embassy in Indonesia, however, did send representatives to attend the trial of a major East Timorese political prisoner, Xanana Gusmao, between February and May.

The Right to Monitor
Human rights groups in Japan faced no legal restrictions.

U.S. Policy
The Clinton administration was slow to recognize the enormous potential of Japan in promoting human rights as part of its "global partnership" with the U.S. and its commitment to Clinton's "New Pacific Community." The State Department, for example, was reluctant to act on the suggestion that Japan might assist with specific human rights issues in Vietnam.

Members of Congress expressed concern about the "comfort women" issue. A group of twenty Representatives sent a letter to Prime Minister Hosokawa in October, urging Japan to cooperate fully with the U.N. investigation into sexual slavery and to take other steps to clarify accountability for abuses during World War II, such as paying compensation to the victims.

The Work of Asia Watch
Asia Watch sent a mission to Tokyo in April

1993 to continue its dialogue with government officials, NGOs, academics and others. Asia Watch representatives gave several seminars and made a presentation at the Institute for International Cooperation of the Japan International Cooperation Agency; the Institute had been assigned by the Foreign Ministry to examine methods for assessing human rights progress in countries receiving ODA.

Other Human Rights Watch visits to Japan took place in connection with international conferences. The chair of Africa Watch attended, as an unofficial observer, a conference in Tokyo on African development issues co-sponsored by Japan and the U.N. on October 5 and 6.

In December, an Asia Watch board member was scheduled to speak on the role of business and human rights at a meeting hosted by the Council for Better Corporate Citizenship of Keidanren, the powerful Japanese business association.

The Asia Watch office in Washington maintained regular contact with the Japanese embassy, and Asia Watch representatives met the new U.S. ambassador, Walter Mondale, prior to his posting to Tokyo.

PAKISTAN

Human Rights Developments

The continuing power struggle between the prime minister and the president dominated political developments for much of the year. With the exception of Pakistan's support for Muslim militants in Kashmir and elsewhere, human rights issues attracted little international or domestic concern; nor did they feature significantly as an issue in the October parliamentary elections that returned Benazir Bhutto to power as Prime Minister.

The riots that followed the destruction of a sixteenth-century mosque in Ayodhya, India, in December 1992 were replicated in Pakistan. Hundreds of Hindus were assaulted throughout the country and at least six, a woman and her five children, burned to death. Hundreds of homes and some 120 temples were burned or damaged. In many of the incidents, local police and government officials passively watched and did not intervene to stop the violence.

The sudden death of the army chief of staff, Gen. Asif Nawaz, in January, upset the traditional balance of power between Pakistan's ruling troika: the President, Prime Minister, and army commander. Irregularities surrounding Nawaz's death prompted calls for an inquiry that was still underway as of November. On April 18, the power struggle between Prime Minister Nawaz Sharif and President Ghulam Ishaq Khan culminated in the President's dismissal of Sharif's government. In a landmark decision on May 26, the Supreme Court declared the President's actions unconstitutional and restored Nawaz Sharif as prime minister. But under pressure from the army, both Ghulam Ishaq Khan and Nawaz Sharif resigned, and an interim Prime Minister, Moeen Qureshi, and President, Wassim Sajjad, were appointed.

Qureshi implemented a number of reforms that attempted to address political corruption, curb the activities of drug traffickers, and tax agricultural lands. In addition, his reforms curtailed the ability of a number of groups to illegally influence election results.

In October elections were held for the national and provincial assemblies. Popular disgust with the political leadership was apparent in the low voter turnout of 40 percent, and 15 percent in Karachi where a local party enforced a boycott. Although no single party won an absolute national majority, the Pakistan People's Party (PPP) led by Benazir Bhutto took the most seats and formed a government. The principal Islamic parties received a record low number of seats.

The political turmoil had little effect on the country's pervasive human rights problems. Legal discrimination against minorities was particularly apparent during the October election. Members of Pakistan's Hindu, Christian, Ahmadi, Parsi, Sikh, Buddhist, Bahai, and Kalash minority communities had been banned from contesting general seats in elections since 1985 and were restricted to voting in a system of separate electorates for minority candidates. Electoral discrimination affected not only minorities but also residents of the federally administered tribal areas whose representatives are elected not by the general population but by a limited number of local notables.

The Ahmadi community officially boycotted the October election to protest their designation as a religious minority. Ahmadis had suffered widespread discrimination by the state as a result of being declared non-Muslim in 1974. Moreover, in the past several years hundreds of Ahmadis were arrested on charges of "insulting Islam" and "posing as Muslims" under the Anti-Islamic Activities Ordinance of 1984. The broad and vague provisions of a series of laws known collectively as the "blasphemy" laws, also dating from 1984, which strengthened criminal penalties for offenses against Islam, were used to bring politically-motivated charges against members of the Ahmadi and Christian communities as well as against some Muslims. Several hundred people were arrested under these laws over the years, including Salamat Masih, an eleven-year-old boy arrested in May 1993 on charges of writing blasphemous statements. As of November, two men, a Christian and a Muslim, had been sentenced to death for blasphemy and the cases remained on appeal.

Women in Pakistan also continued to suffer severe discrimination under the law. Over 60 percent of women in Pakistani jails were sentenced under Islamic penal laws called the *Hudood* ordinances. Because of the bias against women in the courts and unreasonably high standards of proof for rape allegations, rape victims were prosecuted under these laws for adultery or fornication. Before the October election, Benazir Bhutto repeated her earlier promise to repeal the *Hudood* ordinances, although it remained unclear whether she would be able to muster the political support to do so.

Abuse of women in custody continued to be reported. On February 27, policemen from the Tando Jam police station near Hyderabad severely beat a fourteen-year-old low-caste Hindu girl, Shakina, after arresting her on charges of theft. Pakistani women were not the only victims. Hundreds of Bangladeshi women were jailed in Pakistan and subjected to similar treatment after having been smuggled into the country—at a rate of over one hundred a month—and forcibly sold into prostitution or domestic servitude. No prosecutions for trafficking in women, however, took place during the year.

Torture and deaths in custody occurred throughout the country, particularly in Sindh province where some forty cases of deaths in custody and "encounter" killings of suspected criminals or political detainees were reported in the first six months of the year. Torture was used both to extract information and to intimidate or humiliate the victim. Police also routinely tortured detainees in order to extract bribes. In May 1993, Nazir Masih, a Christian, was beaten to death in police custody in Faisalabad, reportedly because he refused to provide alcohol for the police. Beatings, electric shock and crushing the muscles with a heavy roller were common forms of torture.

Proscriptions against child labor were ignored, and children often worked as bonded laborers. Over 6,000 children a year were being kidnapped and smuggled to the Gulf States where their small size and light weight made them ideal camel jockeys. The state did little to combat the trade, and Pakistani human rights organizations claimed local officials were involved.

A law providing for automatic bail for children under age fourteen was rarely applied, and thousands of children were held in jails throughout the country.

The Right to Monitor

Human rights groups generally functioned freely in Pakistan during 1993. However, on April 1, three staff members of the Human Rights Commission of Pakistan, including the organization's director, I.A. Rehman, were detained by police and documents from the commission's office confiscated. The three men were released later that day. The police questioned them about a poster published by the commission which depicted Pakistan's president beating the country with the eighth amendment to the constitution— an amendment which gives the president overriding powers over the prime minister and national assembly. The police confiscated all the posters and several other papers from the office. In response to protests by civil rights organizations and the press, the deputy commissioner of police reportedly issued a statement accusing the Human Rights Commission of publishing an "objectionable poster."

U.S. Policy
Throughout the Cold War, Pakistan enjoyed a close relationship with the U.S. because it was seen as an important ally against Soviet influence in the region. To that end, U.S. policy was concerned with supporting Pakistan as a military power. Human rights concerns never figured prominently in the relationship. Following the Soviet withdrawal from Afghanistan in 1989, Pakistan's relationship with the U.S. deteriorated precipitously. Growing concern in the U.S. about Pakistan's nuclear weapons capability and the threat of an arms race in the subcontinent culminated in the suspension of all U.S. economic and military aid to Pakistan on October 1, 1990. However, commercial arms sales have continued.

In late 1992 and early 1993, the U.S. increased pressure on Pakistan to end its support for militant groups in Kashmir. After the U.S. threatened to include Pakistan on its list of countries sponsoring terrorism, Pakistani officials launched a public relations campaign to counter the charges and by mid-year claimed that the flow of arms into Kashmir had been stopped. A police crackdown on suspected militants from Tunisia, Saudi Arabia and Egypt living in Peshawar resulted in scores of arrests and deportations. On July 14 Pakistan was removed from the U.S. State Department's terrorist watch list.

Public statements have tended to focus on the holding of elections. At an October 28 background briefing for the South Asia press corps, a senior administration official commended Pakistan for conducting "as free and fair an election as you can get in that part of the world." During a visit to Pakistan in November, Assistant Secretary of State for South Asia Robin Raphel raised the case of eleven-year-old Salamat Masih, detained in May on blasphemy charges. Within hours the boy was released on bail, but charges were not immediately dropped.

The Work of Asia Watch
In a report issued in June on the conflict in Kashmir, Asia Watch condemned Pakistan's role in supporting abusive militant groups. Following the killing of twenty Somali civilians by Pakistani troops on June 13, Africa Watch urged Secretary-General Boutros Boutros-Ghali to ensure that the soldiers responsible were returned to Pakistan with the recommendation that the government of Pakistan carry out court martial proceedings.

In September, Asia Watch issued a report on Pakistan's blasphemy laws, which concluded that these laws impose dangerous restrictions on internationally recognized rights of freedom and expression and freedom of religion, and have led to serious abuses particularly against the country's minorities.

An Asia Watch mission to investigate bonded labor took place in October. The report was planned for 1994.

PHILIPPINES

Human Rights Developments
Disappearances and summary executions continued to be reported, although at a lower level than in previous years. Members of the paramilitary force, CAFGU (Citizens' Armed Forces–Geographical Unit), continued to be among the perpetrators. The death penalty was reimposed in August after being abol-

ished by the 1986 constitution. The government of President Fidel V. Ramos continued to review cases of detained and convicted political prisoners, and many were amnestied. The remaining number of political prisoners, most held under criminal charges, was a source of dispute between the government and human rights groups. Little progress was made in peace talks between the National Democratic Front (the front organization of the Communist Party of the Philippines and its armed wing, the New People's Army) and the government; talks began in October in Jakarta between the government and the Moro National Liberation Front (MNLF). The MNLF was blamed for several kidnappings and bombings during the year, including the bombing of Manila's Light Rail Transit line on May 11 which injured twenty-six people.

The National Unification Commission (NUC), the government's peace negotiating body, ended its term on July 31 after eleven months of talks between the National Democratic Front and the government. President Ramos named Justice Secretary Franklin Drilon as acting presidential adviser on the peace process in preparation for the creation of a National Amnesty Commission. In its final report, the NUC recommended an absolute and unconditional amnesty for all rebels. The Clinton administration urged Ramos not to include in any future amnesty the men convicted of killing a U.S. army officer, Col. James Rowe, in Manila in 1989.

CAFGU members continued to be responsible for grave human rights abuses, including extrajudicial executions. On February 23, human rights worker and tribal activist Chris Batan, twenty-six-years-old, was shot and killed in *barangay* (district) Betwagan, Sadanga, Mountain Province. A member of the Igorot tribe, Batan had worked with Task Force Detainees and the Cordillera People's Alliance. His killing was witnessed by two colleagues who said they were approached by five or six armed men. A CAFGU member named Agustin Afawan was arrested and pleaded not guilty in May. On July 17, another tribal activist, William

Rom, head of Research and Documentation for SILDAP-Sidlakan, a tribal group based in Butuan City, Mindanao, was killed by CAFGU after returning from a visit to the Mamanwa tribal community. Rom and a companion, Carolina Salas, were followed and then attacked with machetes by four men identified as CAFGU recruits. Salas, who sustained a facial cut, said the attackers accused them of belonging to the New People's Army (NPA). One of the attackers, Mario Muyon, turned himself in to the police of Gigaquit, Surigao del Norte.

Many other instances of CAFGU harassment of suspected NPA supporters were reported during the year. On September 3, for example, a doctor named Hendry Plaza, the first doctor to join the Department of Health's "Doctors to the Barrios" program, was harassed by CAFGU members as he was immunizing children in San Luis, Agusan del Sur. In October, the military acknowledged that Plaza was on the military's wanted list or "order of battle," suspected of links to the NPA when he was a medical student in 1988. Later that month, President Ramos's Secretary of Health ordered Plaza transferred out of the province, saying, "We don't need dead heroes."

CAFGU members were also suspected in the killing of Exquito Lasquite, thirty-three, the local coordinator of the National Federation of Sugar Workers in Hacienda Culminares, barangay Minnoyan, Marcia, Negros Occidental. He died of multiple gunshot wounds to the head on April 17. According to local human rights workers, CAFGU members had frequently come to Lasquite's house to question him about his activities and his relation to the NPA.

The Human Rights Committee of the Philippines House of Representatives said in April that there had been an increase in reported incidents of forced recruitment by CAFGU.

Journalists also came under attack during the year. In January, a journalist named Romeo Legaspi was abducted by men believed to be members of the Philippines National Police after he published an article in the newspaper *Voice of Zambales* criticizing the police. His family also received death threats. As of December, he was still missing. On June 14, Clovis Nazareno, thirty-three, a newspaper columnist, was attacked by a local businessman in barangay Loon, Bohol province, in the presence of the municipal police chief. He suffered serious injuries, including a broken shoulder blade, but the police chief arrested Nazareno instead of his attacker. Charges were later dropped. Nazareno had written articles critical of illegal logging and had been accused in 1991 of supporting the NPA. On June 22, he filed charges against the businessman and police chief, but the case was dismissed when witnesses refused to testify, fearing reprisals.

July 31 was the deadline for filing claims with a U.S. federal court in Honolulu against the estate of Ferdinand Marcos for human rights abuses suffered during Marcos's years in power. As of July 12, only 2,000 people had filed, out of an estimated 10,000 victims. Spurred by the damage claims, a Manila newspaper, the *Philippines Daily Inquirer*, released a list of the top twenty military officers implicated in cases of torture under Marcos. Some of those named were still on active duty.

On August 6, a well-known political prisoner, Jaime Tadeo, chairman of the left-wing peasants' organization, Kilusang Magbubukid ng Pilipinas or KMP, was released from Bilibid Prison in Manila. He had been jailed in May 1990 on a charge of embezzlement, but he accused the government at the time of imprisoning him to stop his efforts on behalf of peasant rights. In October, the KMP split into two factions, after efforts to remove Tadeo from office failed.

On August 12, the Philippines Senate passed a bill reimposing the death penalty for six "heinous" crimes: murder, rape, arson resulting in death, kidnapping or serious illegal detention, graft and corruption, and drug trafficking.

Asia Watch documented numerous instances of threats, beatings and occasional murder of people trying to document illegal logging or who lived in areas where such logging was taking place.

The Right to Monitor

Human rights monitoring was still a hazardous profession in the Philippines as indicated by the deaths of Chris Batan and William Rom, noted above. On October 11, two other human rights activists, Neil Ballesteros and his wife, Maria Socorro, were abducted from a supermarket in the Manila suburb of Quezon City by six men who identified themselves as police, forces into a van and taken to a barracks where they were interrogated for about three hours. Ballesteros's interrogators demanded that he become an informer for the military in exchange for his wife's life. He was asked specifically to inform on the leader of a faction of the Communist Party, Filemon Lagman. Ballesteros agreed in order to secure the release of himself and his wife; they later appealed to President Ramos for protection. Ballesteros was an organizer for an urban poor organization, Kongreso ng Pagkakios ng Maralitang Lungsod or KPML; his wife worked on human rights education for Amnesty International.

U.S. Policy

Although the Clinton administration was generally supportive of President Ramos, U.S. aid to the Philippines fell sharply in 1993 and promised to continue to decline in 1994. The U.S. requested $2 million in funding for officer training (IMET) for fiscal year 1994, a decrease of $300,000 from the previous year; $10 million in Economic Support funds, down from $25 million in 1993. The request for Foreign Military Funding (FMF) dropped by $7.3 million to a total of $7.7 million for fiscal year 1994. In its funding request for Security Assistance for fiscal year 1994, the Clinton administration stated that U.S. assistance was "essential to the ability of the Ramos government to counter the communist insurgency, improve respect for human rights, consolidate democratic processes and institutions, and to sustain economic reforms."

According to the House Foreign Affairs Subcommittee Funding Recommendation for 1994, during fiscal year 1993 the U.S. contributed $157 million in total aid to the Philippines. It noted that although this was the largest amount of U.S. aid provided to any Asian country, the amount was less than half that provided to the Philippines in 1991. The dramatic decline of U.S. aid to the Philippines followed the Philippines Senate's rejection of a new base treaty in September 1991—a policy the U.S. Senate's appropriations bill for 1993 characterized as "punitive rather than productively serving any clear long term purpose."

That bill recommended $40 million for the Multilateral Assistance Initiative for the Philippines for fiscal year 1993 (half the requested amount) and required that the President channel at least $25 million of those funds through private voluntary organizations and cooperatives.

The Work of Asia Watch

In January, Asia Watch held talks with human rights organizations in Manila.

In September, Asia Watch sent a mission to the Philippines to investigate the relationship between human rights and illegal logging activities.

Asia Watch invited Cecilia Jimenez, Secretary-General of PAHRA (Philippine Alliance of Human Rights Advocates), to be honored by Human Rights Watch at its observance of Human Rights Day, December 10.

SRI LANKA

Human Rights Developments

The human rights situation in Sri Lanka was marked by the ongoing civil war in the northeast, the problems of repatriated refugees and a spate of political killings. Political violence in Sri Lanka reached a climax in 1993 with the assassination of President Ranasinghe Premadasa on May 1, and of his chief political rival, Lalith Athulathmudali, one week earlier. The deaths were seen by many Sri Lankans as evidence of a profound erosion of Sri Lanka's political process by years of repression and violence.

A decade of civil war between government forces and Tamil separatists, two violent insurgencies, and counterinsurgency efforts in which police and soldiers have engaged in arbitrary arrests, torture, murders and disappearances have claimed tens of thousands of lives. In this atmosphere of lawlessness, during 1993 death threats and physical assaults were aimed at politicians from many parties, at journalists covering political rallies, human rights lawyers and trade unionists.

Athulathmudali, head of the Democratic United National Front (DUNF), was shot while addressing an April 23 campaign rally for the upcoming provincial council elections. Although the government accused the guerrilla group, the Liberation Tigers of Tamil Eelam (LTTE) of the murder, many Colombo residents blamed the ruling party. At least twelve other violent attacks against opposition politicians were reported during the campaign, as well as more than eighty arrests.

Athulathmudali's funeral on April 28 became a massive anti-Premadasa demonstration at which two people were killed and more than forty injured when police opened fire on some of the marchers.

Two days later, President Premadasa himself was assassinated in a bomb blast at a May Day rally for the United National Party (UNP). Twenty others were also killed. Police superintendent Ronnie Gunasinghe, who had been implicated in the 1990 death-squad murder of journalist Richard De Zoysa, was among the casualties. The bombing was again attributed to the LTTE.

Former Prime Minister Dingiri Banda Wijetunga was immediately sworn in as Acting President and was unanimously elected by the parliament on May 7.

Although several human rights agencies designed to investigate disappearances and protect the rights of detainees had operated since 1991, and abusive provisions of emergency regulations were revised in 1993, prosecution of state forces for abuses remained rare.

As of November 1993, a verdict had still not been reached in the case of twenty-three Sri Lankan soldiers tried in civilian court on charges of massacring thirty-five Tamil civilians in the village of Mahilanthani in eastern Batticaloa District in August 1992. The soldiers pleaded innocent when the hearings opened on March 2.

In response to internal and external criticism, Wijetunga announced in mid-May that he would consider constitutional amendments to limit the powers of the presidency, and that he had dissolved a secret police force established under Premadasa which kept dossiers on political opponents and influential businessmen. Wijetunga also promised to end government interference with the press. On May 26, *The Island*, an independent Colombo newspaper, reported that the government had issued instructions to the police and other authorities not to interfere with media freedom because such interference could "have deleterious international repercussions."

Even so, in October, Iqbal Athas, a senior journalist who covers military affairs for the *Sunday Times*, and had been critical of army operations, received phone calls threatening his life and the kidnapping of his daughter. Army commander Lieutenant General Cecil Waidyaratne has been accused of issuing the threats.

Leaders of the Lanka Samasamaja Party (LSSP), journalist Saman Wagaarachchi, Secretary of the Free Media Movement, an organization that monitors press freedom, and *Yukthiya*, the newspaper Wagaarachchi works for, also received death threats after releasing statements criticizing the threats against Athas.

In July, doubts resurfaced about Wijetunge's commitment to human rights accountability when the government pardoned the former deputy inspector general of police, Premadasa Udugampola, and appointed him vice chairman of the Sri Lankan Ports Authority, after he rescinded his accusations of government complicity in the operation of death squads. Udugampola is thought to be the architect of some of the most brutal counter-terrorist tactics against the Sinhalese Marxist Nationalist Janatha Vimukthi Peramuna (JVP), a militant insurgency that was reponsible for several thousand deaths in the late 1980s.

The civil war in Sri Lanka entered its tenth year in 1993 with the LTTE and the Sri Lankan government continuing to battle for control of the northern and eastern parts of the country. Both LTTE militants and paramilitary groups affiliated with the army engaged in killings, abductions and torture of suspected informers and enemy sympathizers.

Massive repatriation of Sri Lankan refugees from India continued (see section on India), adding to the more than 600,000 persons already displaced by the war. Returnees and the internally displaced in Sri Lanka complained of harassment; arbitrary arrests and mistreatment by police and pro-government Tamil paramilitary groups; and the threat of violence from the LTTE against suspected government sympathizers.

Although the number of reported disappearances committed by government forces continued to drop in 1993, the Human Rights Task Force (HRTF), a government agency, reported that it had received over 2,000 complaints of missing persons since August 1992, some of them dating back to 1991. Of those reported missing, 114 persons were traced to police stations and army detention centers. The missing included sixteen Tamils who disappeared around Batticaloa after their arrest by the army in February 1993.

The army and police, often with the help of PLOTE (People's Liberation Organization of Tamil Eelam), a former Tamil separatist group that now aids the government in counterinsurgency, and two other armed groups, the Tamil Eelam Liberation Oganization (TELO) and the Eelam People's Democratic Party (EPDP), continued to engage in massive and arbitrary search and arrest operations, which targeted Tamils throughout the island. Arrests escalated following the assassinations of Premadasa and Lalith Athulathmudali.

Despite a government agreement in June to implement safeguards to prevent mistreatment of detainees and discourage arrests based solely on ethnicity, large-scale arrests of Tamils in and around Colombo continued. More than 2,000 Tamil civilians were picked up for questioning during the second week of October; most were released shortly thereafter.

In October 1993, President Wijetunga announced to a delegation of European parliamentarians that the government had established a special agency to investigate disappearances reported during the eight-year period from 1983 to 1991.

The Right to Monitor

Although nongovernmental human rights organizations enjoyed more freedom to operate than in previous years, and intimidation of human rights lawyers eased in 1993, threats continued to be reported. A lawyer involved in a much-publicized disappearance case against army officers in the south left the country in July after having received anonymous threats warning him to withdraw the case.

Labor unionists involved in peaceful protests and journalists covering labor rights issues also faced harassment and assaults by police officers.

U.S. Policy

The U.S. government continued to raise human rights issues with the Sri Lankan government. From October 13 to 19, Prime Minister Wickremasinghe visited Washington and was told by Secretary of State Warren Christopher, among others, that the human rights situation left room for improvement.

On June 18, the thirteen-member Sri Lanka Aid Group of donor nations, including the U.S., pledged $840 million for 1994, a $15-million increase over 1993. The U.S., while noting "continuing improvement in the human rights picture," urged the Sri Lankan government to "redouble" its efforts to implement commitments made to the U.N. Human Rights Commission, specifically to "prosecute those responsible for abuses"; to "further revise the Emergency Regulations to reduce the opportunities for abuse and to remove non-emergency related provisions"; and to "investigate the conditions under which detainees and prisoners are interrogated." The U.S. also condemned LTTE abuses.

The administration planned to continue IMET (International Military Education and Training) assistance to Sri Lanka, estimated at approximately $225,000, including training in military justice systems and human rights norms; the fiscal year 1994 security request proposed expanded IMET training. No Foreign Military Sales aid was expected; commercial military sales were expected to drop from an estimated $2.6 million in fiscal year 1993 to $1.3 in fiscal year 1994.

The Work of Asia Watch

Asia Watch's work in Sri Lanka focused on refugee protection and the repatriation of Tamil refugees from India because of reports of violations of humanitarian law in areas to which refugees were being returned as well as reports of abuse by paramilitary forces guarding resettlement centers. In April, Asia Watch sent a delegation to Sri Lanka and southern India to investigate reports of involuntary repatriation and human rights violations against returnees.

In June Asia Watch addressed a memorandum to countries providing assistance to Sri Lanka, raising the above concerns.

In August, Asia Watch released a report, calling on the governments of both India and Sri Lanka to halt a planned repatriation until there were firm guarantees that the refugees were going back voluntarily and would not be subjected to any form of persecution on their return.

In October, Asia Watch met with Prime Minister Wickremasinghe in Washington, D.C. to discuss human rights concerns and government initiatives to address abuses.

THAILAND

Human Rights Developments

Thailand continued to recover from political upheaval in 1993, but its chronic human rights problems remained: treatment of non-Thai nationals and trafficking in women in particular. A full accounting of events of May 1992, when the army opened fire on mass demonstrations in Bangkok, had yet to be made, and some senior officers involved in the May events were promoted in the annual military reshuffle in September. Violations of labor rights continued, as exemplified by a fire that swept through the Kader toy factory in mid-May, killing more than 200 women workers who had been locked in. As of August, 217 prisoners were under death sentence in Bang Kwang prison, mostly for murder and drug trafficking, but no prisoners had been executed since 1989.

On the positive side, the civilian government of Chuan Leekpai resisted military pressure and allowed a group of Nobel Peace Prize laureates to visit Thailand to campaign for the release of imprisoned Burmese opposition leader Aung San Suu Kyi. At the regional Asian preparatory meeting leading up to the Vienna World Conference on Human Rights, held in Bangkok from March 29 to April 2, Thailand also reaffirmed its intention to ratify the International Covenant on Civil and Political Rights and other important human rights instruments; by mid-November, however, it had not done so.

The treatment of Burmese and Cambodian refugees was a major cause for concern. Members of Burma's ethnic minority groups continued to flee into camps along the Thai-Burma border. The camps were set up at the discretion of local authorities with little control from Bangkok; by the end of the year, they housed 72,000 refugees, who found themselves increasingly vulnerable to *refoulement*. On April 7, two camps were burned to the ground by the Thai army's 9th Division, and 545 residents were forced back into Burma. In August, Camp No. 2 in Mae Hong Son Province, housing members of the Karenni ethnic group, was ordered vacated and its occupants forced back to Burma. On September 17, after extensive negotiations and a written agreement between Thai officials and leaders of the Mon ethnic minority that Mon refugee camps would be permitted to remain on Thai soil, the Mon were pressured to begin relocating refugees back to Burma. The Thai military escorted some 140 Mon refugees from the Loh Loe camp back to Burma to begin clearing land around Halockhane village, only an hour's walk from a Burmese military base camp. The entire Loh Loe refugee population of nearly 7,000 was expected to be moved back to Burma by early 1994.

The Thai government was quick to label the majority of Burmese coming across the border as "illegal immigrants," despite the fact that many were reportedly fleeing forced relocations, forced labor and forced conscription. The influx of refugees peaked in June, when nongovernmental organizations estimated that over 1,000 Burmese were crossing the border each day.

The Thai government treated Burmese students and intellectuals differently from the ethnic refugees. On January 14, the Thai Standing House Committee on Justice and Human Rights called on the government to grant Burmese students political refugee status. The call followed the announcement of the United Nations High Commissioner for Refugees (UNHCR) in late 1992 that it would cut off assistance to 516 Burmese "students" recognized by the Thai Ministry of Interior (MOI) unless they agreed to go to a camp in Ban Maneeloy commonly called the "safe area." Questions about how the Thai government determined who was a student and which students were valid refugees were not resolved; it was clear, however, that the camp was designed to keep the politically active refugee population out of Bangkok. By February, only a handful of Burmese students had gone voluntarily to the camp, but as third-country resettlement was made conditional on passing through the camp, the number of students going there slowly increased. The number of camp inhabitants also rose after some Burmese detained in the immigration detention center in Bangkok were given the option of going to the camp or being deported.

In April, the UNHCR cut off assistance to another 222 Burmese "intellectuals" selected by the Interior Ministry for the Maneeloy camp. If they refused to go, they faced destitution and possible arrest and deportation as illegal immigrants. Despite these risks, only a little over one hundred Burmese were living in the camp by the end of the year. Many Burmese were afraid to go because the camp was seen as little more than a prison, albeit a relatively open one, and there were only imperfect safeguards against abuse by Thai military guards and infiltration by the military intelligence of the State Law and Order Restoration Council (SLORC), the ruling junta in Burma.

Thailand's treatment of Burmese reflected its relatively close relationship to SLORC. On September 15, Thailand's foreign minister announced his government's intention to invite Burma to apply for observer status to the Association of Southeast Asian Nations (ASEAN).

The orderly repatriation of nearly 300,000 refugees back to Cambodia was marred by the incident that marked its conclusion. On May 7, hundreds of Thai military arrived at the Site 2 refugee camp in buses with UNHCR markings. The military then forced 400 to 500 Khmer refugees, who had been unwilling to return, onto eight of the buses and returned them to Cambodia. At the same time, as repatriation concluded and fighting inside Cambodia escalated in the run-up to the elections, the Thai Interior Ministry on May 4, 1993 ordered all provinces bordering Cambodia to take tough action against Cambodians who illegally entered Thailand.

The Thai government on October 26 reportedly removed over 300 Hmong refugees from the Phanat Nikhom Center and held them in detention until they could be repatriated in November. It was clear that they were forcibly removed from the camps; it was not clear if any had been adequately

screened to determine whether they had valid claims to refugee status. The move appeared to be linked to a July agreement between UNHCR and the governments of Thailand and Laos that all refugee camps in Thailand housing Hmong people would be closed by the end of 1994.

Thai officials made little effort to stop the trafficking of foreign girls and women, particularly Burmese and Chinese, into Thai brothels where the women faced debt-bondage, physical abuse and conditions akin to slavery. Involvement of local police was extensive. The raid of three brothels in Ranong, in southern Thailand, on July 14 highlighted the pattern of abuse. In the raid, 148 Burmese women were "rescued" by Thai police from brothels surrounded by electrified barbed-wire. All were sent the same night to the immigration detention center in Ranong and charged with illegally residing in Thailand. Two weeks later, witnesses saw fifty-eight of those rescued deported to Kawthaung, Burma, where they were subsequently arrested on charges of illegally leaving Burma and prostitution. The whereabouts of the other ninety remained unknown. Several nongovernmental organizations tried to negotiate on behalf of the women to provide alternative shelter and an orderly repatriation, but without success. None of the brothel owners was arrested, but eleven pimps and guards (mostly Burmese) at the brothel were taken to the police station. The charges against them were not known.

Two leading dissidents, Pra Prachak and Sulak Sivaraksa, went on trial during the year. Pra Prachak, a monk arrested in connection with his efforts to protest logging operations, was sentenced in January to eighteen months in prison and six months suspended sentence for charges which included trespassing on national forest land.

Freedom of expression was the key issue in the trial of Sulak, a Buddhist leader and social critic, who was charged with *lese majesté* for insulting the King during a 1991 speech at Thammasat University. The trial was ongoing as of November, but Sulak continued to travel freely and speak publicly. Freedom of expression also came into question when a dictionary was banned in July for defining Bangkok as a city of prostitutes.

The Right To Monitor

Thai organizations were allowed to operate without obstruction in Thailand. Many regional human rights organizations had their headquarters in Bangkok, as it was one of the few capitals in Asia where they could operate without harassment. (Hong Kong, the other center, was becoming increasingly less attractive as the prospect of China resuming control in 1997 approached.) Nevertheless, many Thai organizations felt subtle pressure not to criticize the government too harshly or raise particularly sensitive issues publicly.

U.S. Policy

The administration concentrated on strengthening relations with the new Thai government, seeking continued cooperation on regional security matters and copyright laws. When the new Thai army commander-in-chief, Wimol Wongwanich, visited Washington in September, the U.S. pressed for greater assistance in implementing U.N. sanctions against Khmer Rouge cross-border trade, but Thai actions on the Burma border were not discussed.

While no Foreign Military Financing (FMF) was requested in fiscal year 1994, the administration resumed International Military and Educational Training (IMET) following the September 1992 elections and budgeted $1.8 million for IMET. Commercial military sales continued to be brisk, projected at $140 million for fiscal year 1994.

U.S. officials did not raise concerns with Thai officials about the trafficking of Burmese women, but the Senate report accompanying the 1994 Foreign Appropriations Bill, urged the Thai government to prosecute those responsible for trafficking, forced labor, and physical and sexual abuse of these women.

On refugee issues, the administration tended to support, with little or no qualification, Thai government policy, backing the Ministry of Interior on the so-called safe area for Burmese students and providing funds for programs in the camp.

As part of its annual Generalized System of Preferences (GSP) review, the office of the U.S. Trade Representative extended its review of Thailand through 1993, monitoring child labor concerns and government efforts to reform the State Enterprise Labor Relations Act. This law restricts freedom of association and the right to organize for employees of state enterprises. The review period was extended for six months in June 1993 following the Thai government's stated commitment to take steps to end these abuses.

The Work of Asia Watch

Much of Asia Watch's work during the year focused on human rights violations associated with the trafficking of Burmese women into Thailand. A report scheduled for publication in December analyzed the abuses inherent in trafficking, the level of state involvement and how the Thai government's efforts to crack down on brothel operations sometimes further victimized the women involved.

Asia Watch continued to be concerned about the protection of Burmese refugees in the "safe area" and communicated its concerns both to the Thai government and UNHCR officials. In August, together with the Jesuit Refugee Service, Asia Watch sent a mission to the Thailand to interview Burmese coming into Thailand about human rights violations taking place across the border in Burma. Asia Watch also monitored the abuses of Burmese in Thailand by Thai authorities.

Asia Watch maintained close ties to Thai organizations and in March sent an observer to the Asian NGO Forum that preceded the official Asia regional preparatory meeting for the World Human Rights Conference.

VIETNAM

Human Rights Developments

Vietnam's efforts to pursue market reforms and improve relations with the U.S. and the international community while keeping the lid on political and religious dissent produced a mixed human rights performance. The government released or reduced prison sentences for a number of well-known dissidents at the same time that it imprisoned others for peaceful expression of their views. Dialogue on human rights with foreign governments and nongovernmental organizations, including Asia Watch, increased, but human rights investigations were not possible and political trials remained closed to foreign observers—and often to the general public. Penal and legal reforms continued, but few tangible improvements were discernible. Both the media and religious institutions remained under state supervision.

Several bomb plots by overseas anticommunist groups heightened Vietnam's concern with internal security. Continuing protests by the Unified Buddhist Church also resulted in clashes between government forces and demonstrators. The government, however, often failed to distinguish between opponents who used violence and peaceful critics, punishing both on national security charges.

Dr. Doan Viet Hoat, a professor of English literature and a former university administrator, was sentenced to twenty years in prison on March 29 for "attempting to overthrow the government." His offense was producing four issues of a typed newsletter called "Freedom Forum," in which he advocated democratic reform, and recording his ideas on democratic change on a cassette tape. Nowhere did he advocate violence against the government. Two other defendants, Pham Duc Kham and Nguyen Van Thuan, were convicted of producing "Freedom Forum," and five more were found guilty just for possessing copies of it. On July 9, the Ho Chi Minh City Court of Appeals reduced Dr. Hoat's term to fifteen years and five years of probation. Three other defendants were given similarly token reductions.

The government released some political prisoners, but many others remained in jail. U.S. citizens Nguyen Si Binh and Aloysius Hoang Duy Hung were released in June and July respectively, both men having been accused of trying to start alternative political organizations in Vietnam. Do Ngoc Long, a business consultant who was held under a three-year order of administrative detention because of his association with American businessman Michael Morrow, was released on April 6, but Doan Thanh Liem, a law professor also linked to Morrow, continued to serve a twelve-year sentence for "counterrevolutionary propaganda."

Although in recent years Vietnam had allowed citizens greater freedom of worship and has permitted religious communities to resume a limited role in social work, the government kept a tight rein on most other aspects of religion, approving candidates for the priesthood and religious orders, controlling the clergy's movements, and punishing those whose statements offended the Party or who conducted unauthorized meetings.

The greatest conflict has centered on the demands for autonomy of the Unified Buddhist Church (UBC), known for its protests against the Diem regime in the 1960s. Venerable Thich Huyen Quang, who assumed leadership of the UBC in 1992, has been living in government-imposed exile in Quang Nai province since 1982. He made numerous public appeals for the return of church property, the release of imprisoned Buddhist monks, respect for human rights, and freedom from state control. The government responded by searching pagodas and monasteries for his writings and detaining monks and lay Buddhists believed to support him.

Tensions came to a head on May 24 in Hue, when a man immolated himself at the pagoda where the former UBC Supreme Patriarch is buried. Local police immediately removed the man's body and detained the head of the pagoda, Thich Tri Tuu, for questioning. Monks who feared that Venerable Tuu had been arrested organized a sit-down protest in Hue, drawing a large crowd and blocking traffic. Persons in the crowd surrounded a security vehicle transporting Venerable Tuu, removed him and other passengers, and set the vehicle ablaze. At least six monks were arrested in conjunction with the May 24 demonstration, among them Venerable Tuu. On November 15, Venerable Tuu and three others monks were convicted of "public disorder" in a one-day, closed trial and sentenced to four and three year prison terms; five laypersons were also sentenced that day to terms between six months and four years on the same charges.

Another violent confrontation occurred in July, when police forces surrounded the Son Linh pagoda in Ba Ria-Vung Tau province, arresting a number of monks. Among those arrested was Thich Hanh Duc, the head of the pagoda and an open supporter of the UBC leader, who had been ordered evicted by the local government. The conflict began when Thich Hanh Duc challenged the validity of the eviction order in a public letter.

Sources within Vietnam claimed that police and other armed forces used tanks and tear gas to break through a ring of some 2,000 Buddhists surrounding the pagoda. The government charged that monks in the pagoda had collected arms, held an official hostage, and attacked police with rocks and sticks, and it denied that military tanks or units were involved in dispersing the crowd. No independent investigation of the incident had taken place by mid-November.

Asia Watch was concerned that in both confrontations, some monks and supporters of Thich Huyen Quang may have been arrested solely for their religious and political beliefs, rather than for acts of violence. This concern was heightened in August, when the People's Committee of Quang Nai province forbade Venerable Quang to continue any activities in the name of the UBC and ordered him to cease "sowing disunity among the religious" through his demands for church autonomy and religious freedom.

Tensions also remained between the Vatican and Hanoi, despite continued high-level contacts. The government permitted more frequent ordinations but maintained control over the number of candidates for seminary and their selection, and continued to restrict the transfer or movement of clergy within the country.

One well-known Catholic prisoner, Father Dominic Tran Dinh Thu, was released during the year, but at least fifteen other members of the Congregation of the Mother Co-Redemptrix remain imprisoned on charges of "counterrevolution." Also still imprisoned were Father Nguyen Van De and ten other members of the Sacerdotal Maria Movement and the Association of Humble Souls. Protestant pastors Dinh Thien Tu, Tran Dinh Ai and Tran Mai were released from labor camps on April 6, but many other pastors and lay Christians, especially from the highland regions, remained imprisoned for conducting unauthorized religious activities such as home prayer meetings and Bible classes.

Conditions for prisoners of all types remained poor, with continuing reports of abusive treatment, especially during the period of pre-trial investigation. Food and medicine appeared to be grossly inadequate, and prisoners generally relied on supplies brought by their families for sustenance. In at least one labor camp, however, political prisoners were segregated during the year from common criminals, a move that may improve their physical security.

Government officials acknowledged that improvement in prison conditions was needed, and in March, a Law on Imprisonment was passed, prohibiting torture or humiliation of convicts and ordering the separate accommodation of women and minors from other prisoners. The law also gave prisoners the right to complain about official abuses and required investigation of deaths in custody. It was too early to tell how well the law was being implemented.

Vietnam continued to oversee the state-controlled media, which was nevertheless quite lively, especially on officially-condoned subjects such as exposés of government corruption. The press, however, also continued to publish condemnatory articles about political detainees before their trial.

In July, the National Assembly approved a new law on publishing that gave citizens the right to demand corrections or charge libel. But the law also affirmed the government's right to pre-publication censorship "in necessary circumstances decided by the Prime Minister" and maintained state control of all publishing houses. It also set forth many substantive restrictions on the content of published materials, and stipulated as one policy goal "fighting against all ideas and actions which are detrimental to the national interest."

Examples of state censorship abound. At the end of 1992, authorities closed *Co Viet*, a Quang Tri literary journal, for publishing writings implicitly critical of the government. In September 1993, the *Far Eastern Economic Review* reported that a leading social scientist, Hoang Chi Bao, was ordered to make self-criticism for failing to emphasize in his monograph on social policy the achievements of the international communist movement and the role of the "imperialist forces" in the fall of Eastern Europe and the former Soviet Union. Some of contemporary Vietnam's best-known authors, such as Duong Thu Huong, continued to find it impossible to get their works published in Vietnam, and publication of many South Vietnamese writers from the pre-1975 era remained banned.

The Right To Monitor

Vietnam continued to punish open criticism of its human rights record by its own citizens through vaguely-written laws against "counter-revolutionary propaganda" and other political offenses. After UBC leader Thich Huyen Quang publicly demanded that state authorities account for Buddhists who were arrested or who died in custody, the government finally gave a public response, in which it formally denied abuses against some of the individuals whose cases had been raised by Venerable Quang. But it also accused him of raising trumped-up charges

of human rights violations in order to turn believers against the state and to encourage foreign trade and investment embargos against Vietnam. He was not arrested, however.

Vietnam allowed restricted access to the country by some international human rights and humanitarian agencies. In March, Asia Watch sent its first mission to Vietnam to initiate a dialogue on human rights with the government. The United Nations High Commissioner for Refugees (UNHCR) maintained a small staff in Vietnam to monitor the treatment of returning boat people. Several foreign delegations were also permitted to visit prisons, but on at least one such occasion, political prisoners were relocated for the duration of the visit.

For the thirteenth year in a row, however, no agreement was reached with the International Committee of the Red Cross or any other nongovernmental group on the regular monitoring of prison conditions.

U.S. Policy

Human rights took a back seat to POW/MIA issues in the Clinton administration's agenda on Vietnam. New opportunities to raise human rights issues were missed. By the end of the year, the U.S. had cleared the way for the resumption of international financial lending to Vietnam, permitted U.S. companies to bid on projects financed by those loans, and sent three diplomats to Hanoi on an unofficial basis to supplement the U.S. personnel investigating POW/MIA cases.

U.S. officials did consistently include human rights as a policy goal in relations with Vietnam and mentioned both general concerns and specific cases at meetings with Vietnamese counterparts during the year. In July, Assistant Secretary of State Winston Lord returned from a trip to Hanoi and announced at a Senate Foreign Relations Committee hearing that Vietnam had agreed to open a high-level dialogue on human rights issues; such a dialogue had yet to begin as of early November. At the same hearing, Senator Robert Kerrey (D-NE), proposed the establishment of a high-level delegation to conduct regular talks with Vietnamese counterparts on human rights issues, similar to the regular high-level meetings on POW/MIA matters. This proposal drew no response from the administration.

As in the Bush years, Congress was considerably more voluble in defending the rights of Vietnamese political and religious prisoners than the administration, with members addressing numerous public and private appeals on their behalf to the government of Vietnam. A concurrent resolution adopted by Congress and added as an amendment to foreign aid legislation on September 23 called on the U.S. to support human rights, the rule of law and democratization in Vietnam.

In August, Sen. Charles Robb (D-VA), was rebuffed in an attempt to visit one of Vietnam's best-known political prisoners, Dr. Nguyen Dan Que, an endocrinologist who was serving twenty years of hard labor for his public call for political reforms and respect for human rights. Although Vietnamese officials had approved the visit as part of Senator Robb's itinerary in Vietnam, on arrival Robb was told the visit was indefinitely postponed. Senator Robb criticized the decision, saying it was a missed opportunity for Vietnam to demonstrate sensitivity to human rights concerns. The State Department also expressed disappointment that the visit had been canceled. According to sources in Vietnam, after Senator Robb's visit, Dr. Que was removed to another section of his labor camp, placed in solitary confinement, and assigned hard labor.

On September 13, the White House renewed the embargo against Vietnam, but in an announcement that was conspicuously silent on the issue of human rights, allowed U.S. businesses to participate in projects funded by international financial institutions. This action followed the administration's decision in July to drop its objections to international lending to Vietnam. In October 1993, the World Bank announced approval of two loans to Vietnam worth $228 million, with another loan of $121 million pending for agricultural development.

Section 701 of the International Finan-

cial Institutions Act requires the U.S. to cast its vote against loans, other than those for basic human needs, to countries that engage in a consistent pattern of gross human rights abuses. In keeping with this obligation, the U.S. voted for the loan for primary education but abstained on the loan for road improvements. The Asian Development Bank also became a significant lender to Vietnam in 1993, and projected lending as much as $1 billion to Vietnam by the year 1996. It remained unclear to what extent the U.S. was prepared to urge major donors countries, such as Japan, to use their influence to press for human rights improvements.

Limited U.S. aid for humanitarian projects in Vietnam continued in 1993. The Agency for International Development allocated $3.5 million in assistance to private voluntary agencies operating in Vietnam for programs benefiting civilian victims of war and displaced children and orphans. The State Department's Bureau of Refugee Affairs in 1992 had allocated $2 million for projects to benefit returning boat people and their communities, most of which was disbursed in 1993. For 1994 it planned to continue such programs at similar levels of funding. In October, the U.S. Department of Defense flew approximately 2,000 pounds of textbooks to Vietnam under a program that allows nongovernmental organizations to use government transport for free when space is available.

The Work of Asia Watch

Asia Watch strategy on Vietnam had two elements: initiation of a dialogue on human rights with the Vietnamese government and efforts to convince other countries, including the United States, to bring more pressure to bear on Vietnam to improve its human rights record.

In March, an Asia Watch mission visited Vietnam for two weeks, meeting with senior officials in various agencies and ministries, including the ministries of interior, justice, and foreign affairs. The delegation also met with journalists, lawyers, scholars, clerics and returned asylum-seekers. Discussions were lively and wide-ranging, although Vietnamese officials were reluctant to discuss specific cases of political or religious prisoners. Subsequent meetings with government officials took place in New York.

On July 21, Asia Watch submitted testimony on human rights conditions in Vietnam to the Senate Committee on Foreign Relations, Subcommittee on Asia and the Pacific. Asia Watch did not take a position on normalization of diplomatic relations with Vietnam, which the U.S. had conditioned on factors other than human rights. Asia Watch did, however, recommend that the administration vigorously raise human rights concerns and press for the release of political and religious prisoners, through public statements if necessary. It also urged the U.S. government to support increased contact and exchange between Vietnam and the international community and recommended that American businesses urge Vietnam to reinforce the rule of law and respect internationally recognized human rights.

Asia Watch continued to publish detailed reports on the cases of particular individuals imprisoned for peaceful expression of their views, urging members of Congress, the administration, and representatives of other governments to advocate their immediate release. In January, Asia Watch published "The Case of Doan Viet Hoat and *Freedom Forum*: Detention for Dissent in Vietnam," which was placed into the Congressional Record in April by Sen. Paul Wellstone (D-MN). In March, Asia Watch asked to send an observer to Dr. Hoat's trial, a request the Vietnamese government denied. Asia Watch also raised in publications and private meetings with Vietnamese government officials the plight of prisoners suffering from poor health or poor conditions of detention. It maintained regular contact with representatives of the business community and international lending institutions.

Although Vietnam appeared to be making strong efforts to treat repatriated asylum-seekers fairly and reintegrate them into their communities, Asia Watch remained concerned about the international community's ability to monitor closely the increasingly large and dispersed returnee population.

HELSINKI WATCH

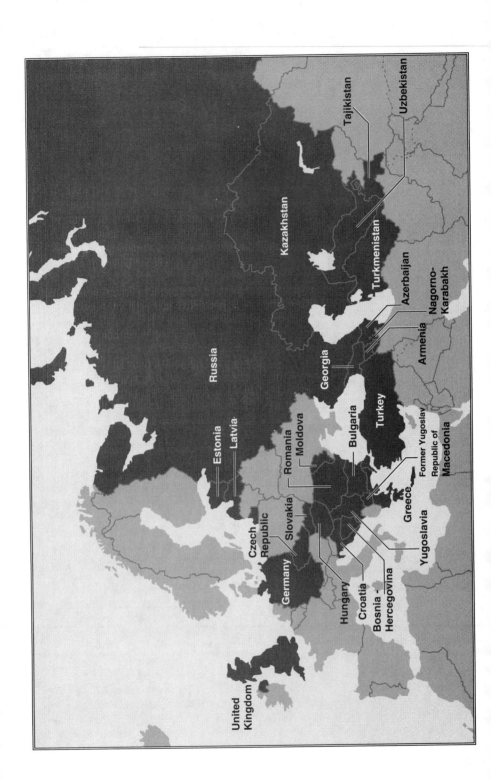

HELSINKI WATCH OVERVIEW

Human Rights Developments

The demise of communism in Europe has led to significant expansion in the work of Helsinki Watch. With countries fragmenting into their constituent parts, the number of signatories to the 1975 Helsinki accords grew from thirty-five to fifty-three countries, all within the same geographic area that we have traditionally covered. Whereas in 1992 the Helsinki Watch section of the *Human Rights Watch World Report* dealt with eight countries, this year we cover twenty-four, and the situations that we monitor are increasingly complex.

The nature of the human rights abuses that we are monitoring has changed radically. The rigidly uniform system of repression that existed under the communists in Eastern Europe and the Soviet Union has given way to a range of human rights abuses that covers the gamut from violations of the laws of war and unchecked violence against minorities and foreigners, to suppression of free speech and association and the imposition of unjust citizenship and residency laws. A few of the countries monitored by Helsinki Watch have maintained systems of repression reminiscent of the totalitarian rule of the communists, while others have seen the eruption of fierce armed conflicts, sometimes ethnic in origin, sometimes reflecting an internal struggle for power, and sometimes a combination of both. Many of the new countries were unstable in 1993, their governments barely able to maintain power and seemingly unable to enforce their own laws. Some, impoverished, looked to the west for aid and trade. Most seemed eager to privatize quickly and viewed the market system as their salvation. Following the collapse of central authority in both the former Yugoslavia and the former Soviet Union, struggles for power and manipulation of nationalism led to bloodshed and/or repression on an astounding scale, with no solution to the conflicts on the horizon.

Warfare in Bosnia-Hercegovina continued to rage as of early November, the time

of this writing. Largely as a result of Western inaction to halt past abuses, the war escalated during 1993, with all of the three factions fighting each other in various parts of the region. Gross abuses continued against civilians, hundreds of thousands of whom had been forcibly displaced as part of "ethnic cleansing." Several eruptions of warfare on Croatian soil, demonstrating the ineffectiveness of the United Nations peacekeeping forces sent there to maintain an uneasy cease-fire, indicated that more trouble might be brewing between Serbs and Croats in Croatia, as well as in Bosnia. In Kosovo, an ethnic Albanian province in Serbia, unwarranted arrests, abuse in detention, and police beatings of civilians escalated in the latter half of 1993, after Serbia expelled the Conference on Security and Cooperation in Europe (CSCE) human rights monitors stationed there.

Fierce conflicts were also being waged on the territory of the former Soviet Union, especially in Nagorno Karabakh and surrounding areas where the warfare between Armenians and Azerbaijanis entered its fifth year, in Georgia where the government was fighting a two-sided struggle against Abkhazian separatists and against the forces of ousted President Zviad Gamsakhurdia, and in Tajikistan where fierce clan battles resulted in incredible brutality. Civilians were subjected to egregious violations of humanitarian law, including indiscriminate attacks, summary executions, forced removal from their homes and abuse in detention. In each of these conflicts, as in the now quiescent conflict in Moldova, the direct or indirect role of Russian armed forces remained a deeply troubling factor.

In Tajikistan, the Rakhmonov government that took power after a fierce civil war was engaged during 1993 in a ruthless campaign of revenge against those who sympathized with or supported the opposition. In Azerbaijan, the Aliev government that essentially took power by force at first used violence, then censorship to suppress the opposition.

In Russia, hopes for a steady movement toward democracy were dashed by the events of early October, when President Boris Yeltsin illegally dissolved the Russian parliament, and the parliament staged a violent rebellion against the President's authority. Yeltsin's suppression of the reactionary forces that had taken over the parliament building was excessively harsh, resulting in many deaths and injuries. Nor were his actions after the uprising comforting: the Constitutional Court was suspended, leaving only executive power in place in Russia until the elections on December 12. Yeltsin issued decrees banning some newspapers and television programs as well as a number of political parties. The Moscow police behaved with excessive brutality, and the local government, with Yeltsin's tacit approval, sent thousands of people who did not have residency permits out of Moscow, focusing almost exclusively on people from the Caucasus and Central Asia, most of whom had nothing to do with the insurrection at the parliament building and many of whom were refugees from violence elsewhere in the former Soviet Union.

In two of the former Soviet republics—Uzbekistan and Turkmenistan—former communist leaders maintained control in a fashion not dissimilar to that of the past. Both governments maintained complete censorship of the media, prohibited free expression and association and kept dissenters under control either by arresting and trying them or by holding them under constant surveillance and *de facto* house arrest. The presidents of both of these Central Asian states maintained a cult of personality, which was used to bolster their centralized control.

The wave of xenophobia and violence against foreigners that swept over most parts of Western and Central Europe resulted in many disturbing incidents in Romania, Hungary, Bulgaria, the Czech Republic, Slovakia, and Germany. Skinheads and other neo-Nazi groups especially targeted Romas (Gypsies), often the first scapegoats of fascism and neo-nationalism. Romas were beaten in the streets and discriminated against without legal recourse; in Romania their homes were burned and they were imprisoned in connection with riots, while their attackers were not investigated or prosecuted. Other minorities were also targeted, either by violent means or more subtle forms of discrimination: Turks in Germany; Hungarians in Romania and Slovakia; Vietnamese in the Czech Republic; Turks and Macedonians in Greece; Macedonians in Bulgaria; Greeks in Albania; Serbs and Muslims in Croatia; Muslims, Albanians, Croats, Slovaks and Hungarians in Yugoslavia; and Kurds and Greeks in Turkey.

The state of the press and media in Croatia, Serbia and Montenegro, Slovakia, Poland, Hungary, Romania, Turkey and other countries was also very worrisome. The state employed a variety of tactics to keep the media under control, often very subtle ones: purging editors and radio and television directors who disagreed with the authorities, ostensibly for reasons unrelated to their politics; denying applications for joint ventures on various pretexts; blocking access to radio and television frequencies due to an array of technicalities; limiting access to newsprint and other facilities to squeeze independent journalists out of the market.

Many countries in the region passed, or maintain, laws that prohibit insulting the President or the state. In Poland and Kazakhstan, these laws were used to stifle dissent.

The granting of citizenship in some of the new states was also a problem with human rights dimensions. Particularly in Latvia, Estonia, Croatia, Yugoslavia and the Czech Republic new legislation limited the citizen body and created non-citizen minorities.

Elsewhere in the region, human rights abuses remained unchanged, despite widespread international protests. In Turkey, a longtime violator of basic human rights protections, the situation, if anything, worsened. In addition to the continuing practice of torture in police detention, the escalating war against the rebel Workers' Party of

Kurdistan (PKK) forces in eastern Turkey resulted in violence and abuse by both sides. Hundreds of civilians suspected of sympathy for the PKK were either assassinated, death-squad style, or "disappeared," including a large number of journalists. Deadly force was used against demonstrators and suspected "terrorists," and free expression was sharply limited. In Northern Ireland violations of due process, the use of lethal force and abuses in detention continued. Serious curbs on free expression continued in the United Kingdom and Greece.

The Right to Monitor

Opportunities to monitor human rights in Eastern Europe and the former Soviet Union were considerably greater in 1993 than they were under the communists, when people who attempted to monitor their governments were arrested and imprisoned and people abroad who were known to be human rights activists were denied permission to enter most Warsaw Pact countries. Nevertheless, Helsinki Watch recorded a number of violations of the right to monitor in the regions that we cover. In armed conflict areas, such as Bosnia, Tajikistan, and, to a lesser extent, Croatia, internal monitors and outside observers were impeded by the armed forces and by the government and were prevented from conducting investigatory missions. In Turkmenistan and Uzbekistan, local monitors were persecuted, and outside observers were prevented from conducting fact-finding missions. In Azerbaijan and Turkey, local monitors were harassed and, in Turkey they were also murdered, but outside observers were allowed to conduct fact-finding missions with relative freedom. In Greece, local monitors were harassed, but outside monitors were allowed to conduct fact-finding missions. In Serbia, local monitors were given a certain amount of freedom, but people from abroad who were known to be human rights observers were frequently prevented from entering or were forced out of the country.

President Milosevic of Yugoslavia and President Karimov of Uzbekistan flatly re-fused to meet with Helsinki Watch representatives in 1993. The Uzbek government also refused to issue visas to Helsinki Watch representatives, becoming the first country to employ this tactic toward Helsinki Watch in the post-communist era.

U.S. Policy

The Clinton administration's policy toward the newly independent states of the former Soviet Union and the post-communist countries of Eastern and Central Europe was focused, during 1993, on bringing about a speedy transition to a market economy. This focus was based on two assumptions: that free enterprise and democracy go hand-in-hand and that democracy guarantees respect for human rights. Neither assumption is necessarily true. It was especially worrisome that these assumptions, on many occasions, served as the justification for a lack of forthright criticism of countries that were violating the human rights of their citizens. The administration not only failed to articulate basic human rights principles as part of its foreign policy, but also in effect, failed to establish any guiding principles with which to deal with other countries. The result was a weak, inconsistent and often contradictory set of actions and leaders who appear to be repeatedly buffeted by competing forces.

The Clinton administration cited Russia as one of its major foreign policy successes, but its response to the October events in Moscow would indicate that Washington had scant interest in the human rights ramifications of all that happened there. The Clinton administration appeared to be following the Reagan and Bush administrations by adopting a policy designed to support one man, in this case President Yeltsin. In doing so, it was implicitly condoning the very real human rights abuses that had taken place under the Yeltsin government since October. Yeltsin was not the only President in the former Soviet Union to rule without constitutional legality: Shevardnadze in Georgia, Rakhmonov in Tajikistan, and Aliev in Azerbaijan were each in power as the result of violence or a violent overthrow of a former

regime. Yeltsin's apparent impunity in taking power himself might send a sign to other
leaders who had done the same, or who
might take the same route in the future—that
power is there to be taken by those who have
the forces to do so.

With regard to other parts of the former
Soviet Union, the U.S. administration's
policy was inconsistent and reactive, rather
than principled and forward-looking. Old
ties from the past played a role, which may
explain, for example, Secretary Christopher's
praise on October 21 of Georgian President
Shevardnadze "for his commitment to democratic values," despite the fact that
Shevardnadze's beleaguered government in
Georgia had taken no steps to improve the
rough justice meted out by police and paramilitary groups as well as in its prisons, and
other human rights abuses that were within
its power to correct. The administration appeared to be trying to please a variety of
constituencies in the United States, such as a
business community interested in joint ventures with the Newly Independent States.
Presumably in response to a well-organized
Armenian lobby, the administration did not
speak out about Armenia's support of the
Karabakh Armenians, even though sanctions were placed on Azerbaijan for its involvement in the Karabakh war.

But the main factor leading to inconsistency derived from the U.S. administration's
uncritical commitment to President Yeltsin's
Russia, which had a vested interest in sus-
taining the repressive governments of
Tajikistan, Uzbekistan, and Turkmenistan,
for example, because they were "stable," did
not overtly persecute their Russian minorities, and continued to acknowledge Russia's
military and economic hegemony. Although
U.S. embassies in the region weighed in
forcefully on human rights issues, Washington was virtually silent about the campaign
of revenge against political opponents that
was pursued by the Rakhmonov government
in Tajikistan. It weighed in more strongly in
the cases of Uzbekistan and Turkmenistan,
especially when U.S. diplomats came face to
face with actions by those governments to

prevent U.S. officials from meeting with
outspoken local critics. But the
administration's public statements about the
human rights failings of Uzbekistan and
Turkmenistan lacked force because the government failed to use economic development aid as leverage in a campaign to improve human rights behavior. State Department officials, in meetings with Helsinki
Watch, made it explicit that they were disin-
clined to link the provision of aid to human
rights behavior.

The U.S. remained silent about Russia's
military involvement in the former republics. Despite evidence available to Helsinki
Watch that Russian armed forces were implicated in the conflicts in Tajikistan, Georgia
and Moldova, all areas in which the laws of
war were being grossly abused, the U.S.
remained silent about Russia's role in these
conflicts, while Russia sought to portray
itself as both protector and peacekeeper in
the region. In August, a controversial article
in *The Washington Post* and a subsequent
briefing by an administration official indicated that the U.S. not only had no plans to
become involved in conflicts in the former
Soviet Union, but had "no plans to condition
our assistance to Russia on our judgement of
Russian policy and behavior towards the
other newly independent states. . . .We have
a dialogue with Russia, a partnership with
Russia."

In Bosnia, a disaster that has become a
symbol of the failure of the international
community, U.S. policy was characterized
by astounding inconsistency and indecision.
Instead of marshalling U.S. public opinion
in response to the unrelenting bloodshed in
Bosnia, the Clinton administration claimed
to be responding to an electorate that did not
want American lives to be lost in a foreign
country. At times in 1993 the U.S. tried to
assume its traditional role as world leader
with regard to Bosnia, only to back off again
and again, lacking the will to follow through
on its own threats.

The U.S. virtually ignored human rights
problems in Eastern and Central Europe and
made no public statements of any signifi-

cance. An exception was Germany where the U.S. ambassador spoke out against racist violence. The U.S. ambassador in Hungary also spoke out against violence toward minorities.

The U.S. government sent mixed signals with regard to human rights abuses in Turkey. In June, Secretary of State Christopher spoke openly in Turkey about widespread human rights abuses. But in October President Clinton hailed Turkey as a "shining example of cultural diversity," ignoring its longstanding repression of the Kurdish minority, a source of many of the human rights problems in Turkey today. In a welcome development, the State Department Bureau of Human Rights developed a written strategy for improving human rights practices in Turkey, concentrating on torture, extrajudicial killings and the stifling of free expression. Unfortunately, the paper itself did not address other forms of human rights abuse that were common in Turkey; moreover, there was no indication as of early November that the strategy has been put into action.

The Work of Helsinki Watch

In 1993 Helsinki Watch conducted more than twenty missions, many of them to new states where we had not been before or to places that have been so totally transformed that it was if we had never been there before. In the course of the year, Helsinki Watch published some thirty newsletters and reports, as well as numerous articles, press releases and lengthy letters of protest to the leaders of offending states.

Helsinki Watch also continued its traditional efforts to influence the U.S. government to use its leverage to promote human rights. We urged the U.S. government to end its one-sided approach to the participants in the Nagorno Karabakh struggle and employ sanctions against Armenia as well as Azerbaijan. We were successful in urging the U.S. government to take up the call for a war crimes tribunal for the former Yugoslavia and to speak out forcefully against any amnesties for war criminals. We urged the

U.S. government to speak out forcefully against human rights abuses in Russia after the October rebellion, rather than blindly supporting President Yeltsin in whatever he might do. We urged the U.S. government to use aid as a form of leverage in a number of the newly independent states of the former Soviet Union.

New problems in the region required new and diverse strategies on the part of Helsinki Watch. Throughout the year we defined new approaches and tailored them to meet the needs of particular situations and particular problems.

Because U.S. aid to the newly independent states of the former Soviet Union was relatively insignificant and in many cases primarily of a humanitarian nature, we urged that the U.S. government utilize the leverage of OPIC, the Overseas Private Investment Corporation. OPIC is a U.S.-government-funded corporation which provides risk insurance for American investments in the developing world. It is one of the most important sources of long-term risk insurance for overseas investment. If a decision is made to deny OPIC coverage to American companies, it can be an extremely important form of leverage. OPIC incorporates section 116 of the Foreign Assistance Act, which provides that no assistance should be given to countries engaged in a consistent pattern of gross human rights abuses.

Helsinki Watch also began a campaign aimed at foreign businessmen involved in private ventures in Uzbekistan and Turkmenistan, which are both rich in natural resources. We brought human rights violations to the attention of such companies and urged them to raise human rights issues in their dealings with repressive governments. It is our belief that "stability" based on repression is as bad for business as it is for human rights.

Helsinki Watch continued to engage foreign government leaders in a dialogue about human rights abuses in their countries. In 1993 we met with top officials in Azerbaijan, Georgia, Tajikistan, Armenia, Estonia, Latvia, and Russia, and kept up contact with many others, some of whom we had met with in past years when visiting their countries. Although these leaders often took issue with our criticisms, most of them were open to maintaining a dialogue with us, a significant change compared to the atmosphere that existed under the communists.

Another new strategy that Helsinki Watch employed for the first time in 1993 involve monitoring the flow of arms in various armed conflicts. Together with the Human Rights Watch Arms Project, we traveled to both sides in the Georgian conflict and gathered considerable evidence pointing to Russian involvement in arming and aiding the Abkhazians in their separatist struggle. In late 1993 Helsinki Watch sent a letter to President Yeltsin giving details we have assembled about the involvement of Russian armed forces in the armed conflicts in Abkhazia, Moldova and Tajikistan and asking for an explanation and for those responsible to be disciplined.

Helsinki Watch continued to be the primary source of detailed information on human rights abuses in the former Yugoslavia, scrupulously documenting and publicizing abuses by all sides in the conflict. Throughout 1993 we maintained a staff in the field at all times, documenting cases that might become part of the evidence for a U.N. war crimes tribunal. We made this evidence available to the U.N. Commission of Experts appointed to investigate such abuses. Simultaneously we kept up pressure for the establishment of a war crimes tribunal, calling for faster action by the U.N. when such efforts appeared to be lagging, demanding that amnesties not be granted to accused war criminals, and urging that witnesses and victims be granted adequate protection in line with the rights of the accused. Human Rights Watch and Helsinki Watch met with U.N. Secretary-General Boutros Boutros-Ghali in an effort to speed along the naming of a prosecutor.

In addition to monitoring violations of the laws of war in Bosnia-Hercegovina, Helsinki Watch also investigated and reported on violations of civil and political rights in Croatia and in Serbia and Montenegro.

In Eastern and Central Europe, Helsinki Watch took up a few over-arching issues that were problems in most of the region: the persecution of Romas, violence against foreigners, discrimination against minorities, and the restriction of press and media freedom. We accumulated a significant body of documentation on each of these issues, which we brought to the attention of various international bodies. We also criticized citizenship laws in Latvia, Estonia, Croatia and the Czech Republic and raised these issues with the appropriate officials in these countries. We sent trial observers to Kosovo, Uzbekistan, and Kazakhstan, and monitored trials in Moldova from afar.

Helsinki Watch continued its program of training human rights monitors, especially in the former Soviet Union. Our Moscow office set up a half-dozen training seminars in 1993, bringing people to them from other states of the former Soviet Union. We also worked with groups in other Western democracies to accomplish our common ends. In 1993 we organized a day of action by international groups focused on Turkey and participated in a number of joint actions with regard to the former Yugoslavia, including the filing of an *amicus* brief in opposition to Bosnian Serb leader Radovan Karadzic's motion to dismiss charges of human rights abuses brought against him in a U.S. court. Helsinki Watch continued its association with the International Helsinki Federation for Human Rights and recently rejoined its executive committee.

ARMENIA

Human Rights Developments

Most human rights developments in Armenia in 1993 were closely connected to the war in Nagorno Karabakh. Azerbaijan's blockade of Nagorno Karabakh and Armenia left Armenia's civilian population in devastating isolation and privation. At the same time, Armenia's assistance to its ethnic brethren in Nagorno Karabakh allowed the latter to capture at least six Azerbaijani towns outside Nagorno Karabakh proper, with severe casualties on all sides.

Electricity, gas, oil and grain—necessary for the basic human needs of civilians in Armenia—were in extremely short supply, the consequence of Azerbaijan's blockade, Turkey's close ties to Azerbaijan, and civil unrest in Georgia. The daily per person bread ration was raised from 250 to 350 grams only in September. Civilians could look forward to electricity for at most two hours per day, which affected the water supply. Armenia's main source of natural gas, a pipeline that runs through Georgia, was blown up regularly, most likely by Azerbaijanis living in the region. The lack of gas and electricity deprived Armenians of heat in the freezing winter.

The human toll of the blockade was reflected in a 1993 survey revealing that 70 percent of Armenia's population wanted to emigrate before the onset of winter, expected to be worse than the winter of 1992-93, when a rise in deaths among the newborn and the elderly was accompanied by a higher suicide rate and growing incidence of mental illness. The blockade had ruined Armenia's industry, and had reduced its mass media operations to 60 percent capacity.

While its own civilians have suffered from these privations, Armenian government officials have provided much-needed support to Nagorno Karabakh. High-level government officials stated to Helsinki Watch in June that Armenia provided everything necessary for Nagorno Karabakh's economy and security. While Armenia's former minister of defense said that the only military hardware Armenia provided to Nagorno Karabakh was anti-aircraft equipment, U.S. military analysts reportedly believed its military assistance was much more substantial. The former defense minister also maintained that Armenian army regulars did not serve in Nagorno Karabakh, and that the three Armenian conscripts wounded in Nagorno Karabakh and interviewed by Helsinki Watch

in November 1992 were "lying" about where they served.

Armenia's criminal justice system was in desperate need of reform, a fact recognized by that country's interior ministry and procuracy officials. There was substantial to anecdotal evidence that criminal suspects were so routinely beaten after arrest that it was considered nothing out of the ordinary; Helsinki Watch did not conduct a formal investigation into this issue, however. Corruption in the criminal justice system was reportedly widespread.

On several occasions, arrests followed peaceful demonstrations, staged mostly by the Self-Determination Association (SDA), a small opposition movement. On February 18, Paruir Airikian, leader of the SDA, was arrested after a peaceful demonstration outside the presidential residence. After another similar demonstration in July, twelve people were arrested, ten were released later that evening.

The Right to Monitor
Helsinki Watch received no reports of threats to human rights monitors in Armenia.

U.S. Policy
The Clinton administration deserves credit for taking steps toward reaching a more balanced approach to the war in Nagorno Karabakh than that of the previous administration. (See sections on Nagorno Karabakh and Azerbaijan.)

A disturbing aspect of U.S. policy toward Armenia during 1993, however, was its consistent unwillingness publicly to acknowledge the fact that Armenia's economic and military support to Nagorno Karabakh had contributed to the egregious abuses by the Karabakh Armenians in their war for independence from Azerbaijan. No State Department observations on the conflict even suggested the critical role Armenia had played in financing Nagorno Karabakh's war effort and the concommitant violations of humanitarian law.

U.S. assistance to Armenia totaled some $200 million in 1993. The vast majority of these funds were used for humanitarian relief, which Helsinki Watch strongly welcomed to counter the disastrous effects of Armenia's economic blockade. Of the $30 million allocated for food for women and children throughout the former USSR, $12 million was earmarked for Armenia, according to Fred Hof, Deputy to Amb. Richard Hermitage. Helsinki Watch believes that all but humanitarian aid should be withheld from Armenia because of Armenia's financing of the war in Nagorno Karabakh.

The Work of Helsinki Watch

Helsinki Watch's June mission to Armenia investigated Azerbaijan's blockade of Armenia and the disastrous effects it has had on the lives of residents there. An op-ed article published in *The Los Angeles Times* following the mission described the blockade's effects and called on Azerbaijan to end it.

AZERBAIJAN

Human Rights Developments

Having suffered serious losses in the Nagorno Karabakh war, Azerbaijan's Popular Front (PFA) government, led by President Abulfaz Elchibey, was overthrown in June 1993 by a coalition of forces led by renegade Col. Surat Huseinov and Heidar Aliev. Aliev claimed that the change in government was legitimate and constitutional; he was elected President on October 3.

Neither regime distinguished itself with a good human rights record, choosing to harass its political opponents through arrests, censorship, police beatings, and other violations of basic civil rights.

Two people in 1992-1993 were charged with slander for insulting then-President Abulfaz Elchibey. In November 1992, prosecutors charged Social Democratic Party (SDP) leader Araz Alizade with allegedly calling President Elchibey a fascist; the charges were later dropped. Toward the end of 1992, Miralim Bakhronov, a discontented member of the PFA, was reportedly charged

with insulting the President and was imprisoned for organizing an unsanctioned demonstration. He was released from prison only after the Aliev government came to power.

Throughout the Popular Front period (June 1992 through June 1993), at least ten demonstrations were broken up by Azerbaijani police, who arrested and either imprisoned demonstrators or made them pay heavy fines. In late December 1992, demonstrators protesting language reform in Azerbaijan were reportedly beaten by police.

On March 27 the PFA government's Minister of Internal Affairs, Iskander Hamidov, attacked Zardusht Alizade, editor-in chief of *Istiglal* (Independence), at the office of the SDP. Alizade told Helsinki Watch that Hamidov, angered over several articles published about him in his paper, threw a heavy ashtray at the editor's head and punched another man in the face. Alizade was then thrown into the trunk of Hemidov's car and detained at Ministry of Interior Affairs, where he was beaten by law enforcement officials and held for several hours. Alizade reported that throughout the three months prior to this incident, he had received threatening phone calls—at times up to five or six per week—in response to politically controversial articles.

Due to this incident, and a March 27 incident in which Hamidov disrupted a live television debate between officials and the opposition National Independence Party of Azerbaijan (NDPA), Hamidov was chastised publicly by the President in April and dismissed in May.

The PFA government introduced a state of emergency on April 2 which, among other things, banned public demonstrations and sanctioned "military" censorship in view of the Karabakh war. Many believe, however, that it was aimed at suppressing political opposition in the face of the PFA government's weakness and waning popularity. *Istiglal*, the weekly newspaper of the Social-Democratic Party of Azerbaijan, was not published for more than two months, according to its editor, as a result of the censorship. The Russian-language *Zerkalo* reported that any article it attempted to publish on Heidar Aliev was routinely censored.

When Heidar Aliev came to power on June 24, he made a variety of public statements and pledges, including some to Helsinki Watch, that the new government would rule by democratic means only, based on human rights principles. Yet his government, instead of living up to these pledges, presided over waves of arrests, police beatings and censorship aimed at individuals and organizations in Azerbaijan's political opposition, mainly the PFA. From June through September 1993, police used violence to break up at least five reportedly peaceful demonstrations in support of the Popular Front of Azerbaijan, punching and clubbing more than one hundred peaceful demonstrators. Among the victims were at least eight journalists; their notebooks were snatched away and video cameras smashed; twelve journalists were arrested at two demonstrations and then released.

Each time Azerbaijan police broke up peaceful demonstrations, they detained large groups of opposition activists. One local human rights group estimated that at least 137 individuals were arrested for participating in unsanctioned demonstrations under Aliev's government in 1993. Some of the detained were released immediately, and others were kept in administrative detention. According to reliable reports, in some of the latter cases law enforcement officials refused to release political activists at the end of their brief terms of administrative detention while they gathered criminal evidence against them. In other cases, individuals were released after several hours, only to be re-arrested the next day.

Opposition activists were detained for other nonviolent political activity. On September 12 and 13, for example, Baku police arrested a group of Popular Front supporters for pasting up posters around the city announcing a demonstration to protest Azerbaijan's entry into the Commonwealth of Independent States. In mid-September, ten other Popular Front activists were arrested for printing and distributing leaflets, "agitation," "organizing provocations" and other activities that were either vaguely defined or qualified as civil and political rights. They were given fines and administrative penalties of up to fifteen or up to thirty days, but before the October elections, Aliev amnestied the ten.

High-ranking members of the PFA and Musavat, a party belonging to the Popular Front, also were arrested. In July, four Musavat party members were arrested while drinking tea at a Baky cafe. Ali Omarov, the general procurator of Azerbaijan, reportedly stated before the Milli Mejlis (parliament) that the men possessed texts that harshly criticized the Aliev government, and that this constituted a "state crime." All four were later released. On August 24, law enforcement officials arrested a group of political activists gathered in Tovuz at the coordinating council of the Popular Front, Musavat, and other political organizations.

Six high-ranking former government officials were arrested on July 16 in connection with events the previous month in the city of Gianja: in June the PFA government had attempted to put down a rebel army division (which eventually ousted President Elchibey). The six detained included the former chairman of the Milli Mejlis, the former deputy minister of security, the former deputy minister of justice, and the former deputy minister of interior, all of whom have been charged with using the army against the people and with misuse of public office. After much public outcry the former Chairman of the Milli Mejlis, Isa Gambar, was released on August 17, although charges against him were not dropped.

The Aliev government actively continued censorship, even after it suspended the state of emergency on September 20. Parts of Amnesty International's annual report on Azerbaijan, published in *Istiglal*, were cut by censors. The September 25 issue of *Milliet*, the National Independence Party newspaper, had contained a brief article on press censorship; the article was whited out by press censors. The wide-circulation daily

Azadlyg's entire print run—about 35,000 copies, according to some reports—was burned on September 11 because of a political cartoon depicting Aliev's visit to Moscow.

Because of the ongoing war in Nagorno Karabakh, Armenians remaining in Azerbaijan—mostly people in mixed marriages—faced the danger of being seized hostage, having their apartments confiscated and other forms of persecution. In February the Gray Wolves, a Turkish-oriented paramilitary group, repeatedly published lists of twenty-two Armenians who had changed their last names and national identity as indicated on Soviet-era passports, in order to escape persecution.

The Right to Monitor

On July 17 the Inter-party Commission on the Rule of Law and Human Rights, initiated by the Popular Front and representing a broad political spectrum, attempted to have its founding meeting. The gathering was disrupted by police troops, who reportedly broke into the Popular Front headquarters where the meeting was about to take place, shot into the air, ransacked the headquarters, and arrested a large group of people. Foreign human rights monitoring groups, including Helsinki Watch, were not harassed in Azerbaijan during 1993.

U.S. Policy

The Clinton administration firmly supported the Elchibey government, and publicly criticized the human rights policies that followed its overthrow. The U.S. Embassy in Baky issued a sharp protest after the arrest of Isa Gambar and other PFA government figures, and the U.S. ambassador was known to have raised human rights issues in his meetings with President Aliev.

This promotion of human right *in situ* was matched by statements from Washington. On August 30, for example, a State Department spokesperson unequivocally emphasized human rights in Azerbaijan, stating:

We have consistently urged the Azerbaijani government to take steps to restore Azerbaijan to a democratic path. We continue to watch events in Azerbaijan closely and remind the Azerbaijani government that we expect it to demonstrate its express commitment to democracy through free elections, freedom of speech and the press . . . We urge the Azerbaijani government to protect the rights of all citizens, and we will continue to stress the importance of human rights issues in our relations with Azerbaijan.

At the same time, the Clinton administration sought to reverse the restrictions on aid to Azerbaijan set out by the Freedom Support Act of 1992 in order to be an "honest broker" in the conflict in Nagorno Karabakh. (See section on Nagorno Karabakh.) Ambassador at Large for the New Independent States Strobe Talbott noted at a September 7 Senate Foreign Relations Committee hearing: "We have found by experience, including in [Azerbaijan,] that [assistance] is not a very good instrument of punishment or pressure." Helsinki Watch took the position that human rights would best be served by providing no aid, other than humanitarian assistance, to any party to the conflict, including Armenia. Helsinki Watch considered it unwise to reestablish aid to Azerbaijan after human rights abuses had worsened so dramatically in such a short period of time.

During 1993 the Clinton administration delivered humanitarian aid to Azerbaijan through the U.N. High Commissioner for Refugees (UNHCR) and the Red Cross. In June it distributed medical supplies through those organizations, and in September made grants of $1 million to each for relief.

The Work of Helsinki Watch

Early in the rule of Heidar Aliev, Helsinki Watch sought to have an immediate influence on human rights. To this end we sent a mission to Baky in June 1993, after the Popular Front government was overthrown, and met with Heidar Aliev. Mr. Aliev told Helsinki Watch that government in Azerbaijan "would be only by democratic means . . . [whose] main principles are human rights, political pluralism, and full rights for all people" and that although during this transition period "Azerbaijan faces many problems, one can be sure that we will not change our ways." Helsinki Watch gave a small press conference following the meeting. A Helsinki Watch letter to Aliev issued several weeks later, and published in *Azadlyg*, protested press censorship and the violent breakup of a peaceful demonstration in support of the PFA. Helsinki Watch sent Aliev another letter on October 1, on the eve of Azerbaijan's elections, pointing out the gap between the Aliev government's human rights pledges and its pattern of human rights violations from June through September. The letter was published in full in *Jumhurriat*.

In April, before Aliev took power, Helsinki Watch sent a letter to President Elchibey protesting Interior Minister Hamidov's beating of Zardusht Alizade, editor-in-chief of an opposition newspaper, and requesting that the Azerbaijan government take disciplinary action against Mr. Hamidov.

Nagorno Karabakh

Human Rights Developments

Now in its fifth year, the war between Armenian forces and Azerbaijan over the disputed, Armenian-populated enclave of Nagorno Karabakh in 1993 was marked by failed attempts to negotiate peace and by the capture by ethnic Armenians of at least five towns in Azerbaijan outside of the Nagorno Karabakh borders, including Kelbajar, Agdam, Fizuli, Goradiz, and Jebrail.

The towns' capture came at staggering human costs, creating 250,000 new Azerbaijani refugees. Civilians fled Kelbajar in April through high mountains still covered with snow. Refugees claimed that hundreds of people froze to death attempting to flee. Following the attacks on Fizuli, Goradiz and Jebrail, about 150,000 refugees flocked toward the Iranian border in August, where the U.N. High Commissioner for Refugees (UNHCR) and other relief organizations set up refugee camps. Hundreds of civilians were either killed or wounded in this offensive. The same Armenian offensive into towns in southern Azerbaijan, near its border with Iran raised fears that refugees would flood into Iran if attacks continued. The September 27 Armenian seizure of Gorodiz, near the Iranian border, would have cut off the population of that town from the rest of Azerbaijan had Iran not created a corridor to evacuate civilians. The U.N. announced a program of assistance to refugees and displaced persons who fled the war and the 1988 Armenian earthquake. The program provided $22.5 million to the displaced in Armenia and $12.5 million to Azerbaijan.

Ethnic Armenian forces developed a pattern of looting and burning villages after the withdrawal of Azerbaijani forces and the evacuation of civilians. (When they were on the offensive in 1992, Azerbaijani forces did the same to Armenian villages in Karabakh.) Some reports suggested that Azerbaijani forces also looted Azerbaijani villages as they retreated.

Azerbaijani forces continued their pattern of long-range shelling and aerial bombardments, which in the past had taken a heavy toll in civilian casualties. According to Armenian sources, long-range artillery rockets and aerial bombardments were used before the Azerbaijaini retreats from Agdam and Fizuli. On August 18, Azerbaijani forces bombed Kapan in southern Armenia, killing seven civilians.

On May 28, 1993, the mutilated remains of Armenian civilians killed during 1992 by Azerbaijani forces were found near Lachin. The civilians had attempted to flee Nagorno Karabakh to Armenia and were reportedly massacred by the Gray Wolves.

Both sides continued the widespread practice of seizing and maintaining hostages during 1993, although both the Karabakh authorities and the Azerbaijan government adopted decrees criminalizing the keeping of hostages in private homes. Ethnic Armenian forces seized about ninety-two hostages from Kelbajar, most of them children and the sick and elderly. Two months later they released four Kelbajar hostages, all infants. On August 24, Karabakh authorities released thirty-eight Azerbaijani detainees; several days later Azerbaijani authorities released twenty-eight Armenian detainees into the care of the International Committee of the Red Cross (ICRC). In late September, Karabakh Armenians released five more civilians. President Aliev of Azerbaijan claimed in August that Karabakh Armenian forces held 320 women, seventy-one children, and 173 elderly people as hostages; Karabakh authorities admit to holding 150. Azerbaijan also released to Russia five Russian mercenaries who had been sentenced to death in May.

The ICRC reported that, on August 2, Azerbaijani forces intentionally shelled its humanitarian convoy traveling along Armenia's border with Azerbaijan. One passenger was killed as a result.

During the year the United Nations gave some limited attention to the war in Nagorno Karabakh. U.N. Security Council resolution 822 condemned the Armenian attack on Kelbajar, called on Armenian forces to withdraw, and urged all sides to return to mediation efforts. A resolution adopted on July 29 condemned the seizure of Agdam and other occupied areas of Azerbaijan and demanded an end to hostilities and the withdrawal of troops from all occupied areas.

A June agreement, brokered by the Conference on Security and Cooperation in Europe (CSCE) and accepted by Armenia, Azerbaijan and Nagorno Karabakh authorities, based on Resolution 822, would have provided for a sixty-day cease-fire, an end to the Azerbaijani blockade of Nagorno Karabakh and Armenia, and the deployment of CSCE monitors with a mandate to observe troop withdrawal from all occupied areas, disarmament, provision of humanitarian assistance, and the creation of secure conditions for the return of refugees and displaced persons. It was disrupted when Azerbaijani President Elchibey was removed and ethnic

Armenian forces captured Azerbaijani territory, but a September cease-fire enjoyed some success.

A buildup of Turkish troops in early September along the Turkish border with Armenia raised fears that the conflict might widen. Prime Minister Tansu Ciller added to these fears when she announced in September that any Armenian advance on Nakhichevan would trigger a declaration of war against Armenia.

The Right to Monitor

Helsinki Watch received no reports of infringement on monitoring efforts during 1993. According to one Western journalist, however, Nagorno Karabakh authorities began in September to restrict journalists' access to the Nagorno Karabakh area and captured territories.

U.S. Policy

Responding to new offensives by Armenian forces, the Clinton administration appeared to be grappling for a more balanced approach to the war over Nagorno Karabakh, a departure from the previous administration's pro-Armenian inclinations. On April 6, Secretary of State Warren Christopher issued a statement in Washington that condemned the ethnic Armenian attack on Kelbajar, acknowledged the increased suffering it caused civilians, and called for the forces' withdrawal. Other statements expressed deep concern over continuing fighting and support for CSCE efforts to negotiate an end to the war.

The State Department also urged Congress to reconsider the Freedom Support Act's ban on U.S. aid to Azerbaijan. While human rights violations within Azerbaijan were serious indeed, it should be noted that the Freedom Support Act's ban on aid to Azerbaijan was based solely on the latter's blockade of Nagorno Karabakh and its military activities in the region. The Act made no mention of Armenia's responsibilities in the conflict. Ambassador at Large Strobe Talbott noted that a shift in policy had the goal of creating a role for the United States as "an honest broker in [the] conflict." Helsinki Watch considered that, rather than calling for a ban on Azerbaijan, the U.S. government could more effectively bring the war to an end by denying non-humanitarian assistance to both Azerbaijan and Armenia.

The Work of Helsinki Watch

Helsinki Watch monitored the conflict in Nagorno Karabakh during 1993, as it had since 1991. In 1993, in addition to monitoring violations of the laws of war, we worked to bring needed attention to this much-ignored and lengthy war. Helsinki Watch's newsletter on the appalling 1992 Azerbaijani air bombardment campaign was released in Yerevan and Baky in June, where it generated significant media attention and debate. During high-level meetings in the region, Helsinki Watch raised the issue of the air bombardment campaign, prospects for a negotiated end to the war, blockades and the Armenian advances.

BOSNIA-HERCEGOVINA

Human Rights Developments

The human rights situation in Bosnia continued to worsen throughout 1993. To varying degrees, all parties to the conflict were guilty of the practice of "ethnic cleansing"—the forcible deportation and displacement, execution, confinement in detention camps or ghettos, and the use of siege warfare, to force the flight of an "enemy" ethnic population. The forcible displacement of non-Serbs from Serbian-controlled areas of Bosnia continued, especially in Banja Luka and Bijeljina. In the Bosanski Samac region, non-Serbian women, children and elderly persons were held under house arrest and forced to do physical labor in a village controlled by Serbian paramilitaries. Serbian forces continued to detain hundreds, possibly thousands, of persons in detention camps. In March, as the humanitarian situation in east-

ern Bosnia deteriorated, Bosnian Serb forces repeatedly denied U.N. relief convoys access to tens of thousands of Bosnian civilians in besieged enclaves. In mid-1993, Serbian forces allowed the passage of humanitarian aid destined for Muslim populations through territory under their control.

The fighting between predominantly Muslim and Bosnian Croat forces (HVO) continued in 1993, beginning in January for a brief period and resuming in April, when Muslim forces in the Zenica area and Croatian forces in the Stolac area each forcibly displaced civilians from the opposing ethnic group. On April 16, HVO forces brutally executed over eighty-nine persons in the village of Ahmici.

On May 9, Bosnian Croat officials began evicting, arbitrarily arresting and detaining thousands of Muslim civilians in the Mostar area. In early June, Muslim forces launched an offensive against Bosnian Croat positions in central Bosnia, and thousands of Croats were forcibly displaced from their homes. After a mutiny of Muslim soldiers in the HVO in late June, Bosnian Croat forces arrested Muslim men in western Hercegovina. Those arrested in May and June were detained in camps at the Rodoc heliodrome outside Mostar and at the Dretelj and Gabela camps near Capljina, where they suffered from malnutrition and were beaten and forced to work along the front lines. Bosnian Croat forces obstructed delivery of humanitarian aid to the Muslim-controlled area of Mostar for over two months. Relief convoys were attacked by Bosnian Croat forces near Travnik.

Muslim forces summarily executed civilians and disarmed combatants in the villages of Trusina, Doljani, Mileteci and Uzdol and near the town of Konjic. Bosnian government troops beat prisoners in detention and forced them to work on the front lines. Muslim forces also obstructed humanitarian aid destined for wounded Croats in the village of Nova Bila.

The Right to Monitor

Human rights monitoring in Bosnia continued to be difficult and dangerous. Fighting between the warring factions and denial of access or restriction of movement by all parties to the conflict severely limited independent observers' ability to investigate reports of atrocities. Access to detention camps was denied by all parties to the conflict. Bosnian Croat forces denied the International Committee of the Red Cross (ICRC) and other relief workers access to the Gabela and Dretelj camps for over two months. The HVO-operated prison at the Rodoc heliodrome also was closed to outside observers for several weeks. The field staff of U.N. Special Rapporteur Tadeusz Mazowiecki were shot at while investigating the massacre of Muslims in the village of Ahmici. Muslim forces prevented access to Croatian villages in the Konjic and Jablanica municipalities, and as of mid-November, Serbian forces continued to hold prisoners in areas that had not been visited by outside observers. Although it was not their primary responsibility, the European Community Monitoring Mission, the United Nations High Commissioner for Refugees (UNHCR) and the United Nations Protection Force (UNPROFOR) monitored violations of human rights and humanitarian law to varying degrees. Occasionally, protests were issued to the authorities responsible for such abuses.

The Role of the International Community

The United Nations

U.N. efforts in 1993 focused on negotiating a peace, delivering humanitarian aid, enforcing a "no-fly" zone and establishing "safe areas" and a tribunal to try war criminals in the former Yugoslavia, including Bosnia. Despite much international activity, the UNPROFOR mission and the joint U.N.-E.C. Conference on the Former Yugoslavia became symbols of the world community's ineffectiveness in coping with the war crimes and crimes against humanity being perpetrated in Bosnia. The 9,000-troop UNPROFOR mission continued its operations in Bosnia in 1993 with a mandate that

did not reflect reality in the field. Initially a peacekeeping force, the UNPROFOR mandate was amended to empower U.N. troops to ensure the delivery of humanitarian aid. No efforts were made to revise the mandate to permit U.N. forces to prevent human rights abuses against civilians in Bosnia. U.N. personnel investigated human rights abuses in Bosnia, especially cases of summary execution by Bosnian Croat forces such as the Ahmici and stupni Do massacres. But U.N. personnel did not adequately investigate many other reports of egregious abuses, nor did they express much interest in such matters, claiming that the U.N. operation in Bosnia was understaffed and ill-equipped to deal with human rights issues.

Peace Negotiations

In early January 1993, then-U.N. Special Envoy Cyrus Vance and E.C. representative Lord David Owen began negotiating a peace proposal commonly referred to as the "Vance-Owen plan" with the leaders of Bosnia's warring factions. According to the plan, Bosnia was to be divided into ten semi-autonomous regions. However, on May 5, the self-proclaimed Bosnian Serb assembly rejected the Vance-Owen plan, and on June 18, Lord Owen declared that the U.N.-backed plan was "dead."

In late July, representatives of Bosnia's three warring factions entered into a new round of negotiations. On August 20, U.N. mediators unveiled a map that would partition Bosnia into three ethnic mini-states, in which Bosnian Serb forces would be given 52 percent of Bosnia's territory, Muslims would be allotted 30 percent and Bosnian Croats would receive 18 percent.

On April 1, Cyrus Vance announced his resignation as special envoy to the Secretary-General. He was replaced by Norwegian Foreign Minister Thorvald Stoltenberg on May 1.

Humanitarian Aid

To protest the failure of all sides to honor their agreements and provide safe passage for humanitarian aid, Sadako Ogata, the

United Nations High Commissioner for Refugees, suspended most relief operations in Bosnia on February 17. On February 19, U.N. Secretary-General Boutros Boutros-Ghali resumed relief efforts across Bosnia and implied that the blockade of supplies would be lifted as early as the next day, making clear that the UNHCR had acted without his approval. The UNHCR thus resumed its work with no new guarantees of protection by UNPROFOR troops or cooperation of the warring parties.

On March 4, the U.N. Security Council adopted a statement strongly condemning Bosnian Serb offensives in eastern Bosnia and demanding a cessation of killings and atrocities. On April 3, the Security Council issued another statement condemning Serbian offenses and calling for more peacekeepers in eastern Bosnia. Noticeably absent from both statements was a program of action should Serbian forces not comply with the Security Council's demands. In mid-March, following months of blockaded aid deliveries to Srebrenica, then-commander of U.N. forces in Bosnia, Lt. Gen. Phillipe Morillon, announced that he would remain in the town until a U.N. relief convoy was allowed to enter. On March 19, Serbian forces granted passage of the convoy into Srebrenica. U.N. Secretary-General Boutros-Ghali expressed anger at the general for "exceeding his mandate," despite the fact that the U.N. was empowered by the Security Council to use "all means necessary to deliver humanitarian aid." On April 14, French Defense Minister Francois Leotard confirmed that Morillon would be replaced as commander of U.N. forces in Bosnia.

After nearly two months of obstruction by Bosnian Croat forces, U.N. officials were able to deliver one truckload of medicine to the Muslim-controlled sector of Mostar on August 21. Five days later, a U.N. convoy of humanitarian aid finally reached the Muslim quarter of Mostar. Fearing that the departure of the U.N. convoy would result in resumed HVO shelling of the Muslim quarter, residents in the Muslim-controlled sector refused to allow U.N. personnel to leave the area. On August 28, the U.N. workers were allowed to leave the Muslim-controlled sector of Mostar but only after U.N. soldiers from the Spanish battalion agreed to remain in the Muslim-controlled sector of the city as a deterrent against further attacks by the Bosnian Croats.

The No-fly Zone

In October 1992, the U.N. Security Council declared a "no-fly" zone over Bosnia but, by March 1993, the flight ban had been violated nearly 500 times. The Security Council did not begin preparations to enforce the ban until March 18, after Serbian aircraft bombed two Muslim villages. However, action was delayed twice, apparently because of concern about weakening Russian President Boris Yeltsin's chances of political survival in his struggle with a Russian parliament sympathetic to the Serbs. Finally, on March 31, the Security Council authorized NATO to enforce the "no-fly zone," but the authorization proved to be a mostly symbolic gesture. While in the early stages of the Bosnian war, Yugoslav aircraft frequently attacked civilian targets, by April 1993, the destruction of civilian targets was being accomplished mainly by artillery, not aerial, bombardment.

NATO planes were instructed to use force only as a last resort, in order to lessen the possibility of a conflict with Serbian forces. Strict limitations were placed on pilots as to when they might fire. The Bosnian Serb military was unimpressed by the U.N. threat; on April 9, in blatant defiance of the flight ban, Bosnian Serb commander Gen. Ratko Mladic traveled to a meeting with U.N. General Morillon in a military helicopter.

Safe Areas

As part of a U.N.-brokered deal to prevent the fall of Srebrenica to Bosnian Serb forces, the Security Council declared Srebrenica a U.N.-protected "safe area" on April 17. Canadian troops entered the town the following day. The U.N. agreed to disarm the Muslim forces in Srebrenica and to protect the civilian population and disarmed combatants from Serbian attack. However, only 146 soldiers from the Royal Canadian Regiment and a dozen unarmed police officers were charged with protecting Srebrenica's approximately 30,000 residents from several thousand well-armed besieging Serbian troops.

In addition to Srebrenica, the Security Council issued a new resolution on May 6, declaring the cities and towns of Sarajevo, Tuzla, Zepa, Gorazde and Bihac as "safe areas." On June 5, the Security Council passed a resolution authorizing the deployment of as many as 10,000 new troops to defend the declared "safe areas." The resolution also authorized the U.S. and its allies to use air power to protect U.N. troops defending the six enclaves. However, the U.N. did nothing in response to continuing Serbian attacks against the "safe areas" throughout the year. On July 26, Serbian troops attacked a group of French U.N. troops in Sarajevo during a forty-five-minute barrage involving sixty-eight tank and mortar missiles. Despite a mandate clearly allowing for the self-defense of U.N. troops, the U.N. did nothing in response to the attack.

An International War Crimes Tribunal

On February 22, the U.N. Security Council passed Resolution 808 calling for the establishment of an international tribunal to investigate, prosecute, and punish those responsible for "grave breaches" of the 1949 Geneva Conventions and their 1977 First Additional Protocol in the former Yugoslavia, including Bosnia. The resolution required the Secretary-General to present a proposal for such a tribunal within sixty days. The Security Council finally approved a statute for the war crimes tribunal on May 25 and declared that the site of the tribunal would be in the Hague.

A list of twenty-three judges was compiled by the Security Council. The General Assembly elected eleven from the twenty-three in ten rounds of balloting between September 15 and 17. On October 21, Venezuela's State Prosecutor, Ramón Escovar Salom, was appointed chief prosecutor.

The European Community

The European Community's response to the crisis in Bosnia continued to be timid in 1993. While Germany favored tougher international involvement in Bosnia, Britain and France strongly opposed any such measures. French and British resistance was largely responsible for scuttling a U.S. effort in the spring of 1993 to arm the Bosnian Muslim forces and launch air strikes against Serbian military targets should the Bosnian Serbs reject the Vance-Owen peace plan. Following the demise of the Vance-Owen plan, the E.C. threw its support behind the establishment of U.N. "safe areas" in Bosnia. At a June summit, E.C. leaders pledged to donate more troops and money for the protection of these areas. Germany, constitutionally prevented from sending troops to Bosnia, has taken part in U.S.-initiated humanitarian airdrops over Bosnia while Greece, a traditional ally of Serbia, has avoided participating in the U.N. mission altogether.

U.S. Policy

Despite widespread expectations that President Clinton would adopt a more active stance than his predecessor toward the conflict in Bosnia, the new administration did little in reaction to the continued human rights violations occurring in the region. Indecision regarding Bosnia was arguably President Clinton's most glaring foreign policy failure in 1993. The Clinton administration vocally threatened to intervene militarily against Serbian forces three times only to renege on the threat each time. The appointment of a U.S. special envoy did nothing to facilitate the peace process. Internal disputes and lack of resolve further plagued the administration's policy toward Bosnia. Indeed, the Clinton administration's indecisiveness weakened the U.S.'s ability to influence its allies and to deal effectively with specific human rights problems in Bosnia.

The Clinton administration responded to the Vance-Owen plan when it was announced on January 30. Clinton officials considered that the Vance-Owen proposal was unjust toward Bosnia's Muslims. On February 10, however, Secretary of State Christopher said that the U.S. would engage in the Vance-Owen negotiations, that it had assigned Amb. Reginald Bartholemew to be the U.S. special envoy to those talks, and that it would seek to tighten the economic sanctions already imposed against Serbia and Montenegro. Promotion of wider delivery of humanitarian aid and the creation of a war crimes tribunal also were advocated. Christopher stopped short of endorsing imminent use of Western force or Bosnian government exemption from the U.N. arms embargo—steps that Clinton had previously endorsed.

On February 25, President Clinton ordered U.S. aircraft to begin airdropping food and medical supplies to civilians in besieged Bosnian towns. In early April, a team of experts sent to Bosnia by President Clinton to investigate the humanitarian situation produced a draft report recommending the use of international military force to protect Bosnia's civilians and urged the Clinton administration to consider a plan to establish internationally protected "safe havens" in Bosnia. At the instruction of senior administration officials, however, the committee omitted all recommendations of military force from closed-door briefings with Congress. The State Department, facing pressure after news of the incident was leaked to the press, made the report public on April 15.

On April 14, after a meeting with Serbian President Slobodan Milosevic, U.S. special envoy Reginald Bartholemew warned that if the Bosnian Serbs did not sign on to the Vance-Owen peace plan, the international community would make Serbia a "pariah state." He also stated that should the Serbs not comply, the U.S. would press for the exemption of the Bosnian government from the U.N.- imposed arms embargo. On April 19, in a move strongly supported by the U.S., the U.N. Security Council voted to impose tougher sanctions against Yugoslavia.

As the Bosnian Serb parliament continued to reject the Vance-Owen proposal, and as Bosnian Serb forces continued to attack Muslims in eastern Bosnia, President Clinton again began to contemplate military action against the Serbs. The administration was still deeply divided over what, if any, measures would be appropriate in Bosnia. Twelve State Department experts on the Balkans sent Secretary of State Christopher a letter in late April in which they urged military intervention on the side of the Bosnian government. In an April 23 news conference, President Clinton stated that the U.S. should take the lead on Bosnia but he qualified his statements by insisting that the U.S. would not act unilaterally and would not send ground troops to Bosnia.

In early May, President Clinton instructed Secretary Christopher to gain the agreement of European allies to arm Bosnian Muslim forces and to launch air strikes against strategic Serbian positions. After the secretary failed to persuade a number of European allies, most notably England and France, to endorse the U.S. proposal, President Clinton retreated from his threat of more forceful action and renounced a leadership role for the U.S. with regard to Bosnia.

On May 22, Secretary Christopher asserted that the U.S. would offer air cover to protect U.N. peacekeepers—but not Bosnian civilians—in the six U.N.-declared "safe areas." Only two weeks earlier, Christopher had criticized the "safe areas" plan, claiming that it condemned Muslims to ethnic "ghettos" and rewarded the Serbian policy of "ethnic cleansing." On June 17, President Clinton indicated that the United States was prepared to accept the partition of Bosnia into three separate states, acknowledging that such a partition would reward Serbian aggression.

On July 21, as Serbian forces continued to attack "safe areas" and appeared within reach of capturing Sarajevo, Christopher indicated that the U.S. would take no new initiatives. On July 22, President Clinton strongly endorsed the forthcoming peace talks in Geneva and stated that the U.S. would assist in the enforcement of any agreement that the Bosnian government would sign.

Following a Serbian attack on U.N. troops in Sarajevo, however, the U.S. began once again to contemplate military measures against Bosnian Serb forces. On July 26, a State Department spokesman insisted that the U.S. was prepared to protect peacekeepers in Bosnia with air power. On July 28, President Clinton met with senior military advisers to discuss possible U.S. air strikes in Bosnia. On July 30, the President sent a letter to the U.N. Secretary-General urging him to authorize the use of Western airpower. On July 31, administration officials announced that President Clinton had given his final approval to an air strike plan and was seeking allied support. On August 3, U.S. officials intensified the U.S. threat by announcing that the U.S. intended to start bombing Serbian positions within a week unless Serbian forces eased their siege of Sarajevo. In response, Bosnian Serb forces agreed to withdraw their troops from two strategic mountains near Sarajevo and to open two main roads into the city to all U.N. aid convoys.

Then, the U.S. came into conflict with the U.N. when it sought a consensus on giving NATO control of any possible air strikes. Secretary-General Boutros-Ghali asserted that only he had the authority to authorize air strikes, and Canada and France set up other obstacles. The final plan of August 9 represented a watered-down version of the U.S.'s original proposal: not only would the U.N. Secretary-General have to authorize any military action, but the NATO allies would also need to reconvene and unanimously approve the start of air strikes. The decision to start bombing would be contingent upon the judgment that the besieging Serbian forces were actually tightening their stranglehold on Sarajevo and other areas. In late August, the U.S. agreed to provide half of the proposed 50,000 NATO troops that would be deployed to enforce a future peace agreement in Bosnia. However, in September, President Clinton said that he would seek congressional approval before deploying U.S. troops.

Throughout 1993, the U.S. Department of State sent reports it had compiled on war crimes in Bosnia to the U.N. Security Council. However, the reports were not detailed and often did not indicate the specific source of the information. Three State Department officials resigned in August to protest U.S. policy and inaction in the Balkans.

In early November, Madeleine K. Albright, the U.S. Ambassador to the U.N., issued an important statement in support of the war crimes tribunal. According to Ambassador Albright, the Clinton administration would "not recognize—and we do not believe the international community will recognize—any deal or effort to grant immunity to those accused of war crimes." Should governments refuse to hand over persons indicted by the U.N. tribunal, she said, sanctions should be imposed upon them.

The Work of Helsinki Watch

In January, Helsinki Watch and the HRW Women's Rights Project sent a mission to Croatia and Yugoslavia to interview women who had been sexually abused in Bosnia. An article titled "Bosnia: Questions of Rape," appeared in *The New York Review of Books* on March 25. Helsinki Watch representatives traveled to Bosnia throughout 1993 to investigate violations of the rules of war by all three parties to the conflict.

Helsinki Watch released several reports and newsletters on Bosnia in 1993. In April, we issued Volume II of our series on *War Crimes in Bosnia-Hercegovina*. The 422-page report documented violations of the rules of war by the three parties to the conflict. Helsinki Watch published further information concerning abuses in Bosnia in a July 1993 newsletter titled "Abuses Continue in the Former Yugoslavia: Serbia, Montenegro and Bosnia-Hercegovina," and in September, released a newsletter on "Abuses by Bosnian Croat and Muslim Forces in Central and Southwestern Bosnia-Hercegovina." Also, on January 25, Helsinki Watch and Human Rights Watch sent a letter to Vladimir Lukic, the prime minister of the self-proclaimed Serbian state in Bosnia, protesting the murder of Bosnian Deputy Prime Minister Hakija Turajlic by a Bosnian Serb soldier as Turajlic was returning from the Sarajevo airport in a U.N. vehicle.

Throughout 1993, Helsinki Watch and Human Rights Watch wrote letters to U.N. officials asking that the U.N. address human rights concerns in Bosnia. On January 14, Helsinki Watch and Human Rights Watch sent a letter to U.N. Secretary-General Boutros-Ghali asking that the UNPROFOR mandate in Bosnia be expanded to allow for the use of force to ensure delivery of humanitarian aid. On February 3, a letter was sent to then U.N. Special Envoy Cyrus Vance, urging that U.N. peace negotiations not continue unless a neutral body such as the ICRC certified that grave breaches of the Geneva Conventions had been halted and that the parties to the conflict allowed and facilitated delivery of humanitarian aid to civilians in besieged communities. Also on February 3, Helsinki Watch and Human Rights Watch sent a letter to U.S. Secretary of State Warren Christopher calling on the U.S. government to support Helsinki Watch's stand regarding continuation of the peace negotiations. On April 22, a letter was sent to Secretary-General Boutros-Ghali expressing dismay at the delay in presenting a proposal for a war crimes tribunal and asking that the establishment of such a tribunal be expedited. Throughout 1993, Helsinki Watch continued to supply evidence of war crimes in Bosnia to the U.N. Commission of Experts, which was established by the Security Council in 1992 to collect such evidence.

Helsinki Watch kept up a constant pressure for the establishment of an international tribunal to try those accused of war crimes in Croatia and Bosnia. On August 1, Helsinki Watch released "Prosecute Now!," a newsletter that summarized eight cases that would be strong candidates for prosecution by an international war crimes tribunal. Also in August, Helsinki Watch published "Procedural and Evidentiary Issues for the Yugoslav War Crimes Tribunal: Resource Allocation, Evidentiary Questions and Protection of Witnesses." On September 7, Human Rights Watch sent a letter on the tribunal to Secretary-General Boutros-Ghali urging the se-

lection of a chief prosecutor with exceptional human rights and prosecutorial credentials and suggesting names of possible candidates. On August 25, Human Rights Watch submitted an *amicus curiae* brief in opposition to Bosnian Serb leader Radovan Karadzic's motion to dismiss charges of human rights abuse brought against him by two Bosnian women in a U.S. court.

BULGARIA

Human Rights Developments

Human rights abuses in Bulgaria were directed primarily at minority groups during 1993. In addition, the government sought to impose restrictions on thought and religion.

Helsinki Watch received numerous reports of police brutality. On June 3, 1993, Zaharie Aleksandrov Stefanov, a twenty-three-year-old ethnic Turk married to a Roma (Gypsy) woman, was arrested for allegedly having committed several thefts. Eyewitnesses to the arrest, and to his ensuing treatment at the police station, reported that Stefanov was severely beaten by the police. Stefanov was later taken to the regional police station where he died on June 5 under suspicious circumstances. Police claimed that Stefanov jumped from the window of a third floor interrogation room. Police reported that he was alone at the time.

On March 24, 1993, Khristo Nedialkov Khristov, a Roma man from Stara Zagora, was arrested and beaten with clubs and kicked repeatedly by the police. A police car then took him to his parents' home where, according to a report by the Bulgarian Helsinki Citizens Assembly, a policeman "pulled his belt tight around [Khristov's] neck and held him up like a dog." Khristov was released the next day and reported to his family that he had been tortured during the night, hit with truncheons and kicked all over his body. When he was released, Khristov was unable to stand on his feet. His physical condition deteriorated after his release, and he was hospitalized that same evening.

It remains difficult for members of the Roma minority to obtain redress when they are the victims of abuses. Local prosecutors frequently do not seriously investigate crimes against Romas and often close cases without filing charges. This is especially true when the alleged abuser is a police officer. There are few cases where abusive police officers are disciplined or charged, much less convicted, for crimes against the Roma minority.

Macedonians are not recognized as an ethnic minority in Bulgaria. Several Macedonian organizations, including United Macedonian Organization Ilinden (OMO Ilinden), have been denied permission to register because they are considered separatist organizations. In August, OMO Ilinden requested permission to organize a rally to celebrate the ninetieth anniversary of the Ilinden uprising of 1903. Their request was refused. Previously, on April 24, police intervened to stop efforts by Macedonians to hold a rally in honor of their revolutionary hero, Yane Sandanski. Police officers reportedly beat several of the demonstrators.

Bulgaria was struggling with the difficult transition from a repressive communist regime to a democracy. This decommunization process included the prosecution of abuses committed during the communist era, as well as legislative and administrative efforts to remove former Communist Party members from positions in a variety of governmental, economic and academic institutions. In December 1992, the National Assembly adopted the so-called Panev law, which provides that individuals who held, *inter alia*, certain positions within the Communist Party, who taught the History of the Communist Party of the Soviet Union, Marxist-Leninist Philosophy, or Scientific Communism, or had been on the teaching or research staff of the Academy of Social Sciences, can not be elected to positions in the executive bodies of scientific and academic organizations.

The Panev law was challenged by 102 members of the National Assembly, who submitted a petition to the Constitutional Court to review the law. This petition was joined by President Zhelyu Zhelev. On February 19, the Constitutional Court upheld the law, claiming that "professionalism" and "scientific commitment" were the only criteria applied. Despite the Constitutional Court's decision, Helsinki Watch concluded that:

> Although the Constitutional Court argued that the Panev law only deals with professional standards, in fact, the law establishes categories of people that are defined as unprofessional without any effort to evaluate their qualifications. Inherent in the law is the presumption that all who, for example, taught Marxism-Leninism were unprofessional.

The implementation of the Panev law, which began in early 1993, created severe tensions among colleagues within the university faculties in Bulgaria. In May, Radio Free Europe estimated that the law had already "led to the removal of several thousand formerly communist-affiliated academic staff from managerial positions."

There were also moves to restrict religious diversity. Growing public concern over an "invasion" of evangelical religious groups who were gaining in membership and influence led to calls for the banning or strict control of non-Orthodox religious sects. Legislation was introduced in parliament that would, among other things, establish government restrictions on non-Orthodox evangelical activities, including restrictions on church aid received from abroad.

In April, the Ministry of Foreign Affairs refused to grant a visa to Swedish Rev. Ulf Ekman, of the Word for Life religious sect. The government cited many complaints about the sect's activities in Bulgaria and claimed that the exclusion of Reverend Ekman would "protect the human rights" of Bulgarian citizens. Similarly, the Sofia daily *Duma* reported in April that a music teacher in the town of Plovdiv was fired for professing the teachings of the Krishna society.

The Right to Monitor

Helsinki Watch was not aware of any instance in 1993 in which human rights monitors had been hindered in their work by the government of Bulgaria.

U.S. Policy

Several high-level meetings between Bulgarian and U.S. government officials were held during the year to discuss such issues as cooperation on the environment and the war in the Balkans. However, the administration made no significant public comment on human rights developments in Bulgaria in 1993.

The Work of Helsinki Watch

Helsinki Watch's work in Bulgaria centered on two principal issues in 1993: the decommunization process and the rights of the Roma minority. Helsinki Watch sent a mission to Bulgaria to investigate police violence against the Roma minority. On the basis of that mission, Helsinki Watch issued a newsletter in April 1993 titled "Bulgaria: Police Violence Against Gypsies," which described the police raid in the town of Pazardzhik in mid-1992, noting the extraordinarily violent tactics used and the impunity enjoyed by the police responsible.

In June, Helsinki Watch sent a fact-finding mission to Bulgaria to investigate the decommunization process and the implementation of the Panev law. Having criticized the law when it was first considered by the parliament in 1992, Helsinki Watch wrote a letter in March 1993 urging the National Assembly to repeal the law. Helsinki Watch issued a newsletter in August titled "Decommunization in Bulgaria," which concluded that:

To the extent that the law deals with prior behavior of individuals, it imposes a penalty that is retroactive in nature. With the possible exception of some conduct that might be included within the extremely vague phrase "participation and involvement in the 'revival process,'" it is clear that none of the conduct

covered by the Panev law was prohibited by Bulgarian or international law.

CROATIA

Human Rights Development

Denial of citizenship on ethnic grounds, eviction from homes on the basis of past military affiliation, interference with freedom of the press, lack of due process for alleged "war criminals," and mistreatment of minorities and refugees blemished Croatia's human rights record in 1993.

Croatian ethnicity, parentage and place of birth—rather than established residency—were the criteria most frequently used to determine whether or not a person was granted Croatian citizenship. Without citizenship papers, a person was not entitled to welfare and medical benefits and was in danger of losing his or her job. Many non-Croats who were denied citizenship and could not keep their jobs or support their families chose to leave Croatia, thereby decreasing the number of minorities there. Some Croats also were denied citizenship. Those who appealed the denials sometimes were granted decisions in their favor.

In 1991, the Croatian Defense Ministry had assumed the right to ownership of all property belonging to the Yugoslav Army (JNA)—including apartments and homes owned by the JNA and in which its personnel lived. Throughout 1993, an administrative office of the Defense Ministry continued to forward eviction notices to the occupants of such homes—usually non-Croatian former JNA personnel. If the occupants did not move by the specified date, soldiers forcibly evicted them. The persons being evicted were not granted the opportunity to appeal to an independent entity, such as a civil court.

In 1993, the Croatian government completed its two-year-long effort to control the independent Split-based daily newspaper, *Slobodna Dalmacija*. Early in the year, a new editorial board was installed and most of the paper's journalists resigned to protest the government's *de facto* takeover. *Feral Tribune*, a bimonthly satirical and politically critical paper formerly part of *Slobodna Dalmacija*, was threatened with a 50 percent tax on all profits. Such a tax usually is imposed against pornography and would force the paper out of business. *Novi List*, a private daily based in the port city of Rijeka, continued to publish as of November without direct government interference.

Despite the promulgation of a law that would amnesty all those who fought on behalf of Serbian forces in Croatia, local and municipal courts continued to try persons accused of organizing the Serbian rebellion in Croatia. In addition to the inconsistency in enforcing the amnesty, there were several cases in which the defendant was not granted due process, such as the ability to call witnesses in his defense, or was mistreated while in police custody. Most of those indicted were tried *in absentia* in violation of due process norms.

Physical violence against Serbs declined in 1993, but abuses against Muslim refugees from Bosnia-Hercegovina escalated during the year. On several occasions, Muslims and some Croats and Serbs without proper refugee status—and some with proper papers—were forcibly repatriated to Bosnia. During the summer, the Croatian police arbitrarily arrested and detained Muslim and some Bosnian Croat refugees in a stadium and then bused them to Bosnia against their will. In general, the Croatian government stopped repatriating refugees after the U.N. High Commissioner for Refugees (UNHCR) and foreign governments publicly protested such actions.

The Croatian Interior Ministry improved its human rights record somewhat; abusive police chiefs were dismissed, and discipline within the police force was enforced. However, the military police continued to destroy property and physically abuse civilians throughout Croatia. The Croatian Defense Ministry did little, if anything, to ensure that military police officers observed a code of conduct.

Thirty percent of Croatia remained under the control of Serbian insurgents throughout 1993. Armed conflict between the Croatian army and troops belonging to the self-proclaimed Serbian Republic of Krajina escalated, beginning in January when the Croatian army launched an offensive to recapture a dam, an airport and a strategic bridge near the city of Zadar. Conflict in the areas of Sibenik and Zadar continued throughout the year. In September, Croatian Army troops launched a second offensive in the Lika region where they destroyed eleven Serbian villages and arbitrarily executed at least sixty-seven Serbs, including civilians. In October, the Croatian government reported that it had suspended two military commanders pending an investigation of their role in the massacre. Serbian forces responded to the Croatian offensive by attacking Croatian cities, including the suburbs of the country's capital, Zagreb. During the fighting in January and September, both sides attacked civilian targets.

Most non-Serbs were expelled from Serbian-controlled areas of Croatia by early 1993. After the Croatian offensive against Serbian-occupied areas on January 22, the few Croats that remained in the Krajina region were expelled by Serbian forces. Serbian authorities in the Knin area took steps to ensure the temporary safety of some Croats until arrangements could be made for their transfer to Croatian-controlled territory. Killings, beatings and intimidation continued against non-Serbs and liberal Serbs living in Serbian-controlled areas throughout the year.

The Right to Monitor

The Croatian government generally did not interfere with the ability of domestic and international groups monitoring human rights in their country. Peace groups in Zagreb, Rijeka and Osijek worked to prevent forcible evictions and other human rights abuses in their respective localities and brought their concerns to the attention of the local and national authorities. Similar human rights groups in Split, however, were harassed and intimidated by local extremists, and some of their members had their personal property vandalized or destroyed. A Croatian Helsinki Committee was formed in 1993, and on several occasions its members met with Croatian government officials to discuss human rights concerns. The Serbian Democratic Forum in Zagreb and its affiliate in Rijeka continued to document violations of human rights against Serbs throughout Croatia.

Several international and multilateral groups also monitored human rights abuses in Croatia, including Serbian-controlled areas of Croatia. Civilian affairs officers and police monitors for the U.N. peacekeeping mission regularly monitored human rights in Serbian-controlled areas of Croatia and in part of western Slavonia, which is controlled by the Croatian government. UNHCR officials also documented human rights violations against refugees, displaced persons and civilians throughout Croatia. When refugees were arbitrarily arrested and held for repatriation during the summer, U.N. officials initially were denied access to those arrested. The field staff of Tadeusz Mazowiecki, the Special Rapporteur for the U.N. Commission on Human Rights, also monitored human rights violations both in Serbian-controlled areas of Croatia and in areas under Croatian government control. However, in areas where active fighting or military operations were taking place, both Croatian and Serbian forces denied access to international observers.

The Role of the International Community

The United Nations

The United Nations Protection Force (UNPROFOR) faced considerable obstacles in Croatia in 1993. Originally deployed in May 1992 to oversee the terms of the January 1992 cease-fire agreement brokered by then U.N. Special Envoy Cyrus Vance, the 15,000-troop UNPROFOR mission was not able to fulfill its mandate of preventing the outbreak of armed conflict between Croats and Serbs

in January and September; it was not able to ensure the demilitarization of the U.N. Protected Areas (UNPAs); it could not prevent the continued displacement of non-Serbs from Serbian-controlled areas of Croatia; and it did not repatriate a single person who had been forcibly displaced from Serbian-controlled areas of the country. A U.N.-created civilian police unit (CIVPOL) was the most active in protecting the human rights of the local population in the UNPAs, and CIVPOL officers had the most success in implementing their part of the UNPROFOR mandate. However, U.N. peacekeeping forces generally failed to impose their authority in the UNPAs.

In January 1993, after months of tenuous peace in Croatia, the U.N. struggled to prevent the start of a new war there. After the January 22 Croatian army offensive, however, Serbian forces broke into a number of U.N.-monitored storage facilities and retook heavy weapons that had been turned over to joint U.N.-Serbian control. On January 25, the U.N. Security Council demanded an end to the fighting, ordering the retreat of Croatian troops to the pre-offensive front lines and the Serbs' return of the heavy weapons seized from the storage areas. Although the Croatian government and the local Serbian authorities signed an agreement to implement the terms of the U.N. resolution, neither side complied, and the U.N. did little to enforce its own demands.

On February 19, the Security Council extended UNPROFOR's original one-year mandate in Croatia to March 31, 1993. On March 30, the Council extended the mandate for another three months. In late September, the Croatian government and parliament threatened to cancel the acceptance of U.N. troops on its territory when UNPROFOR's present term expired on November 30, unless steps were taken to implement all U.N. resolutions and to seek enforcement of UNPROFOR's mandate. On October 4, the Security Council voted to extend for six months UNPROFOR's mandate, noting that sanctions against Yugoslavia would not be lifted until it used its influence with Serbs in

Croatia to make peace with the Croatian government in Zagreb.

The European Community

For the most part, the European Community's involvement in Croatia consisted of supporting the U.N. peacekeeping mission. France, Denmark and Belgium each contributed troops to the UNPROFOR operation. The E.C. maintained its own monitoring mission in Serbian-controlled areas of Croatia, usually assisting in the exchange of prisoners and remains of the deceased between the two warring factions. Representatives of the Croatian government and the Krajina Serb authorities were brought to the negotiating table under the auspices of the joint E.C.-U.N. Conference on the Former Yugoslavia.

Generally, the E.C. was silent on the issue of human rights abuses in Croatia. However, in the spring of 1993, it vocally condemned Croatia's support of Bosnian Croat forces. In June, the E.C. threatened to "initiate restrictive measures" against Croatia if it did not withdraw its military support from Bosnia. On July 19, the E.C. met again to debate ways in which it might apply diplomatic pressure to Croatia. Although German opposition prevented the community from considering the imposition of sanctions against Croatia, E.C. representatives agreed to warn Croatia that such sanctions were possible in the future.

U.S. Policy

U.S. policy toward the Republic of Croatia in 1993 was overshadowed by concern for the conflict in neighboring Bosnia, and the U.S. did not respond sufficiently to human rights abuses for which the Croatian government should be held accountable.

Since recognizing Croatia in April 1992, the U.S. government has maintained diplomatic relations with the newly formed republic. When Bosnian refugees were arbitrarily arrested and detained in a stadium in Zagreb, U.S. Ambassador Peter Galbraith visited the stadium and lodged a protest with the Croatian authorities. In September, Galbraith made clear to President Franjo

Tudjman that the U.S. would hold the Croatian government accountable for abuses perpetrated by the Bosnian Croat forces, which were politically, economically, and militarily dependent on the Croatian government in Zagreb.

The Work of Helsinki Watch

In order to monitor civil and political rights and laws of war violations in the country, Helsinki Watch maintained one or more staff members in Croatia throughout 1993. Staff representatives investigated human rights violations and sustained contacts with human rights activists, government officials, officials in Serbian-controlled areas and members of the press in Croatia. Helsinki Watch also conducted three missions to Croatia. In January, together with the HRW Women's Rights Project, Helsinki Watch investigated the treatment of Bosnian women who had sought refuge in Croatia. Staff members of Helsinki Watch and the Women's Rights Project spoke widely on the subject of rape and mistreatment of women in the conflicts in Croatia and Bosnia.

Between May and September, Helsinki Watch investigated civil and political rights in areas under Croatian government control for a report on the topic. In June, Helsinki Watch contributed a section on U.N. peacekeeping efforts in Croatia and Bosnia for the Human Rights Watch thematic report titled *The Lost Agenda: Human Rights and U.N. Field Operations*. Between May and September, Helsinki Watch continued its research of U.N. operations in the former Yugoslavia, including Croatia, for a detailed report on the UNPROFOR mission. Throughout the year, evidence was collected on war crimes perpetrated during the siege and after the fall of Vukovar in 1991. A report on the siege of Vukovar and current U.N. efforts to gather evidence of war crimes in the city will be released in 1994. Helsinki Watch and Human Rights Watch also lobbied for the establishment of an international tribunal to try those accused of war crimes in Croatia and Bosnia.

THE CZECH REPUBLIC

Human Rights Developments

On January 1, 1993, the Federal Republic of Czechoslovakia peacefully ceased to exist, after Czechs and Slovaks failed to agree on a workable federation during 1992. The Czech Republic, as one of the successor states, formally declared that it considers itself bound by the legal instruments ratified by the Federal Republic, including international human rights treaties and covenants.

The Czech Constitution, adopted in December 1992, incorporates Czechoslovakia's 1991 Charter of Fundamental Rights and Freedoms, which is similar in many respects to the U.S. Bill of Rights. In addition, Article 10 of the Czech Constitution states that "international treaties on human rights and fundamental freedoms ... are directly binding and take precedence over the [national] law."

In 1993, the Czech Republic continued to struggle to come to terms with its communist past. The controversial "lustration" law of October 1991 remained in effect, excluding for five years from a variety of appointive public positions anyone who may have collaborated with the Czechoslovak secret police agency (the StB) or who held high positions in the Communist Party or other specified institutions after 1948.

In November 1992, ninety-nine members of the Czechoslovak Parliament brought the lustration law before the Constitutional Court to determine its compliance with the Charter of Fundamental Rights and Freedoms. In November 1992, the Constitutional Court ruled that, primarily due to the questionable reliability of StB files, as well as difficulties of proof, those individuals identified in StB files as potential candidates for collaboration (otherwise know as Category C), could no longer be tried. The rest of the law, however, was upheld.

On July 9, the Czech parliament passed the Law on the Illegitimacy of and Resistance to the Communist Regime, which declares the Communist regime from 1948 to 1989 illegal and criminal. The new law invalidates any statute of limitations on and paves the way for possible prosecutions for past crimes committed in the name of communism. Helsinki Watch considered the law a retroactive criminalization of heretofore legal conduct, in violation of international law. Helsinki Watch had no information that charges had been brought under this law as of November.

By the end of 1993, over 96 percent of all those unjustly convicted under the communist regime had been rehabilitated by the Czech courts. In another attempt to deal with past abuses, in March 1993 the parliament established a commission to investigate repressive actions taken by the Czechoslovak security police against dissidents. The commission will work closely with the Prosecutor General's Office, as well as other government agencies.

On January 1, 1993, the Law of the Czech National Council on Acquisition and Loss of Citizenship, the republic's new citizenship law, went into effect. The law provides, *inter alia*, that Slovak citizens may apply for Czech citizenship until December 31, 1993 only if the applicant (a) has had official residency status in the territory of the Czech Republic continually for at least two years, (b) submits proof of having applied for exemption from Slovak citizenship, and (c) has not been sentenced in the past five years on charges of any intentional crime. After 1993, Slovak citizens will be treated the same as other foreigners when applying for Czech citizenship.

Helsinki Watch received reports that the citizenship law may have a negative impact on the Roma (Gypsy) minority. Many of the estimated 200,000 Romas living in the Czech Republic were forcibly resettled from Slovakia to the industrial areas of northern Bohemia after World War II, or resettled in the region by the communist regime in the 1960s. Many never applied for Czech residency, either because they did not believe it was necessary or because they lived in factory housing and thus were not eligible for permanent residency.

The Roma population may also be disproportionately affected by the requirement that the applicant have a clean criminal record. The Roma population is the poorest minority in the nation, with a high rate of unemployment that has been exacerbated by discriminatory hiring practices. As a consequence, the Roma population has a high rate of criminality. Moreover, many Romas are semi-literate, and some speak only a mixture of Slovak and the Romany language. Thus, they may not adequately understand the procedures required to obtain Czech citizenship or be able to prepare the necessary forms without assistance.

Several Czech towns initiated discriminatory policies against the Roma population during the past year. In late 1992, the town of Jirkov passed a controversial ordinance giving the town council wide discretion to evict or fine apartment occupants without a court order if certain hygiene or occupancy standards were violated. The town council of Jirkov acknowledged that these measures were aimed at controlling the migration of Romas to the town.

Similarly, at the end of December 1992, Jiri Setina, the Czech Prosecutor General, proposed a national anti-migration bill to deal with "the unrest caused by undisciplined groups of migrants" in certain areas. The migrants were clearly identified as Gypsies in the detailed report accompanying the bill.

The Jirkov ordinance and similar measures adopted by several other Bohemian villages, as well as the Prosecutor General's draft law, were severely criticized by human rights and minority rights organizations. These measures were voted down by the Czech parliament.

Some recent attempts have been made to improve conditions for the Roma minority, including a pre-school program launched in September by the Ministry of Education to provide higher-quality education and more individual attention for selected Roma children. Radio Free Europe reported that as many as 80 percent of the Roma children

living in Prague are classified as mentally backward and placed in special schools, often based on language and cultural differences, as well as racism.

Despite official efforts to improve the treatment of the Roma minority, prejudice remains widespread among the general populace. Reports of racially-motivated attacks on Romas by skinheads continued during 1993. Discrimination in housing, hiring, education and access to services also remained pervasive. What is more, reports persisted that the Czech police did not respond to crimes committed against Romas.

The Right to Monitor
Helsinki Watch was not aware of any attempt by the government of the Czech Republic to impede human rights observers in their monitoring activities.

U.S. Policy
The U.S. government officially recognized the Czech Republic on January 1, 1993. Several high-level meetings between Czech and U.S. government officials were held during the year to discuss such issues as cooperation in the environmental and military fields. The Czech Republic received over $171 million in investment insurance assistance from the Overseas Private Investment Corporation. However, the administration made no significant public comment on human rights developments in the Czech Republic in 1993.

The Work of Helsinki Watch
Helsinki Watch continued to monitor the treatment of minorities, and especially the Roma minority, during 1993. In May, Helsinki Watch sent a mission to the Czech Republic to meet with human rights and minority rights groups. Helsinki Watch representatives traveled to Usti nad Labem to meet with Roma leaders and discuss the implementation of the citizenship law. This delegation also met with Czech officials and expressed concern regarding the effect the law could have on the Roma minority.

On June 30, Helsinki Watch addressed

a letter to Prime Minister Vaclav Klaus regarding the provisions of the new citizenship law and its disproportionate impact on the Roma minority.

ESTONIA

Human Rights Developments

In its third year of independence from the former Soviet Union, Estonia slowly worked towards legalizing the status of its large non-citizen minority. In February 1992 the Estonian Parliament passed an *ius sanguinis* citizenship law that granted automatic citizenship only to citizens or their descendants of Estonia's inter-war republic (1918-1940). The law also provided for naturalization. This legislation effectively disenfranchised roughly 30 percent of the population that came to Estonia after Soviet annexation in 1940 or were born there in later years.

Language remains the most serious obstacle to naturalization. The Law on Estonian Language Requirements for Applicants for Citizenship" was not passed until February 10, 1993. The law presupposes a knowledge of about 1,500 words of Estonian. The Estonian parliament, the Riigikogu, passed amendments simplifying the language test for naturalization for the handicapped and for those born prior to 1930, but many non-citizens lived in areas where few Estonians reside and therefore had little opportunity to hear or speak Estonian. The cost of language instruction also hindered those seeking naturalization.

On June 21, 1993, the Riigikogu passed a Law on Aliens with the goal of regulating the residence of non-citizens in Estonia by granting them residency permits and aliens' passports. Non-citizens in Estonia had only their old internal Soviet passports and thus faced problems obtaining international travel documents. The law, however, did not contain any guarantee of residency and granted only five-year residency permits. Estonian President Lennart Meri refused to sign the law and sent it to the Council of Europe for expert legal advice. The council noted that, "The experts are of the opinion that the status of persons already resident on the territory of Estonia cannot be compared to that of non-citizens not presently residing [there]. . . ." The Riigikogu amended the law, granting a guarantee of residency to those who had lived in Estonia prior to independence. On July 8, President Meri signed the bill into law.

The law still, however, denied residency permits to career military retirees of the Soviet armed forces and convicted criminals. Legislation reportedly was planned to deal with each case individually, but to Helsinki Watch's knowledge no such law was passed as of November. While such exclusions may appear justified when applied to new immigrants, they are unwarranted and excessive with regard to Estonia's non-citizen population, most of whom have long residency in the country.

Estonia did, however, make progress in resolving tensions with its large non-citizen minority. On February 15, 1993, Estonia signed an agreement with the Conference on Security and Cooperation in Europe (CSCE) to set up a mission in Estonia to monitor human rights and the condition of the non-citizen population. The CSCE mission with offices in Tallinn, Kohtla-Jarve, and Narva, began to function in March 1993. On June 25, 1993, President Lennart Meri formed the "Round Table," a body composed of non-citizen organizations, parliamentarians, and representatives of national minority groups, to meet at least once a month to discuss legislation affecting the non-citizen population. Finally, the Estonian government granted citizenship to approximately one hundred non-citizens, allowing them to run in local elections held on October 17, 1993. According to the Local Government Council Election Law, non-citizens who have five-year residency may vote in local elections, but are forbidden to run for office. In some areas of heavy non-citizen settlement, the number of citizens able to run was quite small.

The Right to Monitor

Human rights fact finding missions have visited Estonia without interference since independence in August 1991. Some came on the invitation of the Estonian government.

U.S. Policy

The United States continued to support the growth of civil society and free market reform in Estonia and to call for the speedy withdrawal of Russian forces. The U.S. State Department viewed the condition of Estonia's non-citizen minority as a "practical problem," rather than a human rights concern.

A $2.5 billion aid package for the states of the former Soviet Union that President Clinton signed into law on September 30, 1993, conditioned aid to Russia on the withdrawal of Russian troops from the Baltic States. The U.S. also granted Estonia funds to finance the work of the "Round Table."

The Work of Helsinki Watch

Helsinki Watch's work in Estonia centered on two main issues: citizenship and non-citizen rights. In August and October 1993 Helsinki Watch sent missions to Estonia. A report issued in October 1993 concluded that the August 1993 mission "uncovered no systematic, serious abuses of human rights in the area of citizenship. . . . Problems exist, however, especially concerning the successful integration of Estonia's large non-citizen population, roughly 30 percent of the country's 1.6 million residents."

GEORGIA

Human Rights Developments

Political chaos, economic crisis, and armed conflicts in its territory gravely threatened Georgia's very existence as a state during 1993, with severe repercussions for its human rights situation. Georgia lost territory in its war against the secessionist republic of Abkhazia and lost important ground against armed bands supporting former President Zviad Gamsakhurdia, who was ousted in 1992. These crises paralyzed the parliament, courts and law enforcement agencies responsible for preventing and punishing human rights abuses.

Facing an extraordinarily high crime rate in a society where most civilians have guns, Georgian law enforcement agencies, infamous for beatings, torture and other cruel treatment of detainees, showed no sign of improvement in 1993. They also continued to allow semi-official paramilitary groups to take on the role of maintaining public order. In 1993 Helsinki Watch received several appalling reports of cruel beatings in pretrial detention. One concerned a man who was arrested for large-scale theft in a shoe factory and was beaten by police for several days in order to extract a confession, and then released. In another case, a supporter of former President Gamsakhurdia, who was awaiting trial on terrorism charges, was severely beaten by a convicted murderer who had mysteriously obtained the keys to the man's cell.

Tbilisi's chief of police estimated that mobs—sometimes numbering in the thousands—lynched about ten criminals in 1992 and 1993. Local journalists put the estimate higher (about one lynching per month) and added that the lynchings often took place in the presence of law enforcement officials, while suspects were being transferred from the scene of a crime or from one different prison to another. In August, a mob in Tbilisi attacked and killed two men who had killed a small girl that day in the course of an armed robbery. The lynching took place after police had arrived on the scene.

In a meeting with Helsinki Watch, the Tbilisi chief of police flatly denied that police brutality was a problem (although in an interview several months later with a Canadian journalist he was quoted as admitting it). The Georgian Procuracy—the nation's highest prosecutorial office—told Helsinki Watch it took disciplinary action against the convict in the above-mentioned case, but maintained that the beating took place for "personal" reasons. The procuracy in 1993 concluded that Zaza Tsiklauri, a man who reportedly was tortured and beaten in 1992, received his wounds during an attempt to escape from a police car.

Supporters of former President Gamsakhurdia continued to be subjected to various forms of harassment, which intensified as pro-Gamsakhurdia forces sought to take over parts of western Georgia. Police and paramilitary groups broke up several demonstrations, reportedly beating demonstrators in the process. At least five Gamsakhurdia supporters were fired from their university jobs, apparently for political reasons. Police broke up a meeting of Gamsakhurdia supporters in a private apartment on June 2, and brought all thirty-two participants to the police station; they were later released. The family members of Gamsakhurdia supporters also were rounded up by Mkhedrioni, one of the two main Georgian paramilitary groups, and there were allegations that Gamsakhurdia supporters who were imprisoned were beaten and possibly tortured.

The main pro-Gamsakhurdia weekly newspaper, *Iberia Spektr*, was unable to publish one of its issues in late April for reasons which, the editor believed, are connected with the controversial content of the previous issue. The paper was closed altogether in October. Its editor, Irakli Gotsiridze, was the target of several attacks in 1993, including one in February, when forty bullets were fired into his apartment. In October Mr. Gotsiridze was arrested for sedition and, according to his wife, was brutally beaten in detention, resulting in several broken ribs. Another pro-Gamsakhurdia newspaper, *The Georgia Sentinel*, was under pressure from government officials for its articles on the conduct of Georgian forces in Abkhazia and articles claiming that Gamsakhurdia had returned to power.

Pro-Gamsakhurdia newspapers were not the only ones to suffer harassment in 1993. In July the National Democratic Party (NDP) pressed a lawsuit against the independent weekly *Rezonans* for an article that included inaccurate information on a closed Council of Ministers meeting. The case was dropped. On September 17 another independent newspaper, *Shvidi Dre*, was attacked by eight armed men who said they were from the NDP. The men beat up staffers and fired pistols into the office's computers.

Thousands of civilians have been killed and wounded in the struggle for control of Abkhazia, an autonomous republic on the Black Sea, and over 100,000 driven from their homes since the outbreak of hostilities on August 14, 1992. All communities in this ethnically heterogeneous area suffered varying degrees of damage from shell and air attacks during 1992 and were heavily looted. The warring parties responsible were, on the Georgian side, disorganized forces from the Georgian National Guard, and paramilitary groups such as Mkhedrioni (Horsemen); and on the Abkhazian side, loosely coordinated volunteers from local villages and from the Confederation of Peoples of the North Caucasus, mercenaries from Russia, and probably some Russian Army personnel.

The Right to Monitor

Helsinki Watch received no reports of restrictions or attempted restrictions on the work of human rights monitors in 1993.

U.S. Policy

The U.S. government provided unwavering support for Head of State Eduard Shevardnadze both in the war with Abkhazia and in his struggle against supporters of former President Gamsakhurdia. Part of this unwavering support was the absence, in Washington, of public criticism of Georgia's dismal human rights record. This was particularly disappointing given the conscientious efforts of the U.S. Embassy in Tbilisi to gather information on human rights abuses, although the embassy's monitoring was far more assiduous in the capital than in the western conflict zone. Following Abkhazia's September offensive, President Clinton reportedly sent a message urging President Shevardnadze to resume peace negotiations with the Abkhazians.

U.S. aid to Georgia included Overseas Private Investment Corporation (OPIC) privileges and Most Favored Nation status (not yet ratified by the Georgian parliament as of November). A delay in granting coverage or a suspension of OPIC coverage for American investors on human rights grounds would have sent a strong signal to the Georgian government, but there was no evidence that the Clinton administration had invoked such leverage; nor, indeed, did it publicly criticize the poor human rights atmosphere in Georgia.

The murder of a U.S. Embassy official, Fred Woodruff, near Tblisi in August should have drawn administration attention to the extraordinarily high level of violence in Georgian society and to the ways in which law enforcement officials and paramilitary groups, which the government tolerates, contribute to this violence.

Of the $224 million allotted to Georgia in U.S. foreign assistance, $200 million was humanitarian assistance; monies were also allocated for C.I.A. training of President Shevardnadze's bodyguards. Helsinki Watch considered that, if police brutality and government tolerance of paramilitary groups acting as law enforcement authorities continued, this assistance should be cut.

The Work of Helsinki Watch

Helsinki Watch sent a mission to meet with Georgian government officials in June. The mission focused on police abuse, and was followed by a detailed letter to Head of State Shevardnadze in August calling attention to brutality on the part of police and paramilitary bands.

Helsinki Watch and the Human Rights Watch Arms Project also sent a joint mission to Georgia in July and August to investigate violations of the laws of war in connection with the secessionist conflict in Abkhazia. The mission helped identify Russia as a possible source of the weapons being used. Helsinki Watch and the Arms Project planned a report documenting violations by both sides, with recommendations to the Georgian government, Abkhazian authorities and

the government of the Russian Federation on how to prevent such violations in the future.

GERMANY

Human Rights Developments

Right-wing violence against foreigners escalated in Germany during 1993. Although the government initiated a series of measures in late 1992, these measures did not improve security for foreigners living in the country.

Following domestic and international outcry after violent events in Rostock in August 1992 and the death of three Turks in Mölln in November 1992, the German government adopted a series of measures to deal with the violence more effectively. These measures included the formation of a working group to develop ways in which the police would monitor and combat violent right-wing extremists in the various states. Police searched the offices and homes of members of neo-Nazi parties, confiscated propaganda materials and some weapons, and made numerous arrests. Police stepped up surveillance of the far-right groups generally, and banned several neo-Nazi political parties, including the National Front, the German Alternative and the National Offensive.

On May 26, the Bundestag (parliament) voted 521 to 132 to amend the country's constitutionally-guaranteed right to asylum. The new asylum law took effect on July 1. Under the new law, asylum-seekers arriving at airports can be held for nineteen days and then expelled if they do not qualify for asylum. Asylum-seekers from "safe countries of origin," countries where the German government has determined that there is no well-founded fear of persecution, can be immediately returned.

Asylum-seekers coming into the country by land can be expelled immediately if they have traveled to Germany through a "safe third" country where they could have applied for asylum. All countries sharing borders with German are considered "safe."

GERMANY | 219

The government had pushed for restrictions on the right to asylum, arguing that it was necessary to prevent further escalation of xenophobic violence. However, on May 29, only three days after the Bundestag voted to restrict the right of asylum, five Turkish residents died when four young skinheads set fire to their house in the town of Solingen. This was the worst single attack on foreigners since unification and set off yet another wave of attacks on foreigners.

Both the frequency and brutality of right-wing violence increased during the year. The government reported that there were 3,365 attacks against foreigners during the first six months of 1993, representing a 130 percent increase over the same period in 1992. Violent attacks against foreigners increased 72 percent in 1992 as compared to 1991.

Following the Solingen murders, angry Turks marched through the streets of the town demanding a stronger response from the German government and greater rights for the 1.8 million Turks living in Germany, including the right to dual citizenship.

Chancellor Helmut Kohl, faced with severe criticism of his handling of right-wing violence to date, vowed in June to crack down on German right-wing extremists, calling for tougher sentences, more police power and tighter restrictions on militant right-wing extremist groups. In response to demands from foreign residents, Kohl also agreed to seek reform of the eighty-year-old German citizenship law, which strictly emphasizes German ancestry. Kohl did not favor allowing dual citizenship, however.

Throughout 1993, Kohl continued to deny any connection between his party's vigorous pursuit of restrictions in the asylum law and the growing violence against foreigners. In a speech before the Bundestag on June 17, the chancellor denied any "connection between the asylum law and the arson attacks in Solingen and elsewhere." However, some representatives within Kohl's own government have been critical of the chancellor on these grounds. The Federal Ministry for Women and Youth issued a report in June concluding, among other things, that the public debate over asylum-seekers resulted in "anti-foreigner groups no longer feeling marginalized and stigmatized, but instead as the forefront of a larger movement."

The chancellor's failure to provide moral leadership on this crucial issue only exacerbated a situation in which—as Helsinki Watch noted in an article—asylum restrictions have "focused attention on the victims, implicitly shifting the blame for the violence onto them."

The Right To Monitor

Helsinki Watch received no information to indicate that human rights observers in Germany were prevented from conducting their investigations and reporting on their findings during 1993.

U.S. Policy

In response to a string of racist attacks against foreigners, then-U.S. Ambassador to Germany Robert M. Kimmitt stated, "Such violence is simply unacceptable in a modern democracy, where tolerance is an important element." Similarly, in a speech in Berlin, Ambassador Kimmitt urged that German officials "must make it understood that racist violence is not acceptable and will be punished very harshly."

The Work of Helsinki Watch

Helsinki Watch focused much of its efforts during 1993 on monitoring violent attacks against foreigners and the implementation of the asylum law. A Helsinki Watch staff person met with representatives of human rights and asylum organizations in Germany in June. On July 1, Helsinki Watch sent a letter to Chancellor Kohl criticizing the Bundestag's decision to tighten Germany's asylum law, stating:

> The action of the lower house of Parliament in curbing the influx of refugees to Germany is a serious human rights setback. . .The new law would make it far more difficult for

foreigners who have suffered persecution in their home countries to be granted political asylum in Germany, thus denying them protection guaranteed by international law.

During the latter half of 1993, Helsinki Watch representatives conducted an ongoing investigation of violence against foreigners, including the measures taken by the German government to deal with the violence, as well as the response of the police and judiciary. Helsinki Watch intends to conduct an additional fact-finding mission to Germany in early 1994. A report of the findings will be issued in 1994.

GREECE

Human Rights Developments

Human rights abuses in Greece involved freedom of speech, discrimination against minorities, physical abuse of detainees and prisoners, and violations of religious freedom.

A handful of free speech cases continued to be prosecuted and appealed during 1993. Minority issues were involved in six trials held in 1992 and 1993 against Greek citizens for the peaceful expression of their views. One case concerned two journalists who were found guilty of insult and sentenced to seven months in prison for a column about the "non-Greekness" of the Turkish minority in western Thrace. The other five cases, some dating from 1992, concerned speech about the Former Yugoslav Republic of Macedonia (FYRM), or members of the Macedonian minority in Greece. The subject of FYRM was extremely sensitive and emotional in Greece. The Greek government objected to the use of the world "Macedonia" to describe the former Yugoslav republic, since "Macedonia" is also the name of a region in northern Greece. A temporary compromise was reached in April 1993, when the republic was admitted to the U.N. under the temporary name "Former Yugoslav Republic of Macedonia."

The five prosecutions of dissenters involving "Macedonia" were based on publicly expressed opinions that conflicted with the views of the Greek government. None of the defendants was charged with violent acts or other criminal behavior. The five cases were:

· Five Trotskyites were charged with "spreading false information and rumors that might cause anxiety and fear to citizens and disturb international relations with Greece," and "inciting citizens to rivalry and division leading to disturbance of the peace." Their alleged crimes was to produce a pamphlet of nine short essays on "The Crisis in the Balkans: The Macedonian Question and the Working Class." On May 7 an Athens court acquitted all five after a week-long trial. On May 12 the public prosecutor's office appealed the verdict.

· In May, two Macedonian minority activists were sentenced to five months in prison and a fine of 100,000 drachmas (about $435) for telling *Ena* magazine that they "feel Macedonian," and for claiming that there are one million Macedonians in Greece. They were convicted of spreading false information about the non-Greekness of Macedonia, and with instigating conflict among Greek citizens by differentiating between speakers of a Slavic language and Greeks. The case was on appeal as of November.

· In May 1992, four members of an antinationalist group were convicted for distributing a leaflet calling for peace in the Balkans and opposing the Greek government's foreign policy and policy toward minorities. They were charged with spreading false information and attempting to incite citizens to violence or dissension, and for disturbing friendly relations with another country. The case was on appeal during 1993.

· A seventeen-year-old high school student was convicted in December 1992 for distributing a leaflet saying, "Alexander the Great: War Criminal; Macedonia belongs to its people." He was charged with attempting to incite division among citizens and disturbing the peace. His appeal was pending during 1993.

· Six members of an Organization for the Reconstruction of the Communist Party were convicted in January 1992 of defaming authorities, inciting citizens, dividing the community and illegally posting bills that read: "No to patriots. Recognize Slav-Macedonia." Sentenced to six-and-a-half months in prison, the men's cases were on appeal through 1993.

All of these prosecutions violated free expression rights guaranteed by international law.

The Greek government discriminated against ethnic minorities, including the ethnic Turks in western Thrace. Some significant improvements had been made since Helsinki Watch's first report in 1990 on the plight of the ethnic Turks: in 1993 ethnic Turks could buy, sell and repair houses and property; repair mosques; start small businesses; and obtain car, truck and tractor licenses. However, serious problems remained. Many ethnic Turks were deprived of their citizenship, and others were harassed by police. Associations and schools could not call themselves "Turkish." Turkish-language newspapers, books and magazines could not be imported from Turkey. Ethnic Turks faced discrimination in state employment and in the provision of municipal services. Problems in education included a lack of competent Turkish-language teachers and Turkish-language books, and insufficient secondary schools for ethnic Turkish students. Freedom of religion problems included the selection of muftis, the religious leaders of the Muslim community, and control of the *wakfs* (charitable foundations). The Turkish minority objected strongly to the state's appointment of its muftis, and elected its own; the dispute was unresolved. As to the wakfs, the ethnic Turks objected to the state's control of their charitable foundations.

Ethnic Turks were recognized as a minority by the Greek government, which referred to them, however, only as "Muslims." Associations were forbidden to use the word "Turkish" in their titles.

The Macedonian minority was not recognized as a minority. Authorities denied that a Macedonian minority existed or that a Macedonian language was spoken in northern Greece. Macedonian activists claimed that there were one million Macedonians in Greece; Greek authorities claimed that there was only a small group of "Slavophone" activists. Macedonian activists were followed, harassed by police, frequently refused state employment, and prosecuted for free speech offenses. They were not allowed to establish schools to teach the Macedonian language, and their children could not be educated in Macedonian in state schools.

Reliable reports, including those of Amnesty International, indicated that detainees and prisoners were physically abused. Reliable reports also indicated that religious freedom was under attack. Government permission was required (and often denied) to establish any sort of house of worship. Jehovah's Witnesses were reportedly harassed, and their ministers jailed for draft evasion in spite of laws stating that ministers (including Jehovah's Witnesses) were not subject to the draft. Helsinki Watch has not yet investigated these allegations.

The Right to Monitor

Greeks attempting to monitor human rights abuses are harassed. For example, in looking at the problems of the Macedonian minority, monitors are called "agents of Skopje," followed, and sometimes refused access to government officials. Outside organizations are allowed to monitor human rights, but their delegations in Greece are routinely followed. Helsinki Watch missions to both western Thrace and the Western Macedonian province have been openly and regularly followed.

U.S. Policy

Greece remained an important U.S. ally. In 1993, it received $315 million in military loans and $265,000 in military grants. In its 1992 country report, the State Department listed a series of human rights abuses in Greece: ill-treatment of detainees and prisoners; abuse of illegal aliens; restrictions on freedom of speech, association and religion; revocation of citizenship of Greek citizens who are not ethnic Greeks; discrimination against Gypsies; and violence against women. However, the Clinton administration has made no public efforts to persuade the Greek government to change its practices.

The Work of Helsinki Watch

Helsinki Watch's strategy for its work in Greece involved publicizing the government's human rights abuses; trying to persuade the Greek government to effect change (which was successful in regard to the Turkish minority); seeking to influence the international community and the U.S. government to persuade the Greek government to live up to international standards and agreements to which it is a state party.

Helsinki Watch's work in Greece during 1992 focused on three areas: free expression and the treatment of the Turkish and Macedonian minorities. In 1993, Helsinki Watch and the Fund for Free Expression sent a mission to Greece and issued a newsletter in July titled "Greece—Free Speech on Trial: Government Stifles Dissent on Macedonia." Also, in July, a mission was sent to northern Greece to examine the problems of the Macedonian minority; a report was planned for early 1994.

HUNGARY

Human Rights Developments

In recent years, Hungary has made significant progress toward implementing both legal and institutional protections for human rights. The amended constitution confers a broad array of rights and protections on all Hungarian citizens. On July 7, 1993, after two years of debate, the Hungarian parliament approved a Law on the Rights of National and Ethnic Minorities, which guarantees the use of names and education in the mother language. In June, the parliament also created an ombudsman's office to investigate allegations of constitutional violations of individual rights.

Despite these achievements, Hungary experienced a dramatic rise in xenophobia and right-wing violence. Although the Roma (Gypsy) minority, which is estimated at approximately 450,000, has organized politically, and Roma politicians entered the parliament, discrimination and racism remain prevalent. Romas were often the targets of discriminatory practices and faced severe discrimination in employment, housing, education and access to health care. Romas had little opportunity to obtain redress for their grievances. It remained unclear whether the newly established ombudsman's office would provide support to the Roma minority in seeking justice.

In the past two years, violence against Romas increased dramatically. In July, a young Roma man suffered brain damage after he was severely beaten by skinheads. This marked the twenty-fifth reported assault on the Roma community in Budapest since 1991. Moreover, experts believe that a very small percentage of attacks on Romas are ever reported. Helsinki Watch also received many reports that the police failed to intervene or to arrest those who attacked Romas.

Foreigners living in Hungary also became targets of skinhead violence. The Martin Luther King Association, a Hungarian organization documenting racist attacks, reported that in 1992 there were seventy-seven racist attacks on foreigners by nationalist youth groups. All involved foreign students from Africa, Asia and the Middle East. This trend continued in 1993. Helsinki Watch received reports that the police refused to disperse the attackers, were rude to those foreigners who complained, and were slow to investigate and resolve these cases. Police abuse against dark-skinned foreigners also appeared prevalent. In separate incidents in December 1992 and January 1993, the Fifth District Police Station in Budapest allegedly detained and beat about twelve people of Middle Eastern origin. Moreover, officials at the Kerepestarcs detention camp for illegal aliens were severely criticized by human rights groups because former detainees complained that guards used torture or very abusive treatment. The camp authorities and the government denied allegations of ill-treatment and torture.

Controversy surrounded the Hungarian media during 1993, as the government engaged in a dispute over the control of radio and television. Political parties and human rights organizations accused the government of monopolizing and manipulating the media. In December 1992, parliament had approved a bill that placed the budget of the radio and television under the prime minister's office. In the spring of 1993, the Constitutional Court upheld a moratorium on the privatization of radio and television until a media law could be passed. As of mid-November, no media law had been voted on by the parliament.

The Right to Monitor
Helsinki Watch was not aware of any attempt by the government to impede human rights observers in their investigations and reporting during 1993.

U.S. Policy
U.S. policy toward Hungary was responsive to human rights issues during 1993. The U.S. Embassy in Budapest used various opportunities to express concern about the growth of right-wing extremism and anti-

Semitism. For example, in an interview with the Hungarian daily *Magyar Hirlap* on July 3, Amb. Charles Thomas stated:

> There have been manifestations of anti-western, anti-democracy irredentism, pro-ethnic cleansing, and anti-Semitic concepts that appeared in writings last summer. Should these ideas prevail—and I am confident that they will not—it would be a disaster for U.S.-Hungarian relations. The U.S. could never be friends with a regime that attempted to summon up these demons from the past.

Similarly, when asked whether concern about extremist movements is "overemphasized in the western press" in an interview with *The Hungarian Observer*, Ambassador Thomas stated: "I think concern about the emergence of right-wing radicalism in Hungary is something that people should be very sensitive to and that's why I don't think reactions are exaggerated in the west and they should be deeply concerned about this." On October 21, Secretary of State Warren Christopher visited Budapest, reiterating U.S. support for democratization and economic reform in Hungary. It was Christopher's first visit to an East European country since becoming Secretary of State.

The Work of Helsinki Watch
Helsinki Watch's work in Hungary centered on two principal issues: the treatment of the Roma minority and freedom of the press. In January, Helsinki Watch sent a mission to Hungary to investigate the treatment of Romas. A report issued in July 1993 concluded that Romas were increasingly singled out as targets for violence by skinheads and other militant nationalists, and that public authorities had not responded adequately, either in apprehending or prosecuting the offenders. Moreover, Helsinki Watch concluded that excessive force and unlawful detention at the hands of the police appeared to be more prevalent against Romas than against ethnic Hungarians, as the authorities

apparently acted out the widely-held racist stereotype of Romas as dishonest and violent.

In September, Helsinki Watch sent a fact-finding mission to investigate allegations of Hungarian government interference with the print and broadcast media. A report on the mission's findings was planned for release in late November.

KAZAKHSTAN

Human Rights Developments

Kazakhstan remained relatively consistent during 1993 in its human rights practices, both those that protected human rights and those that restricted them. On January 28, it adopted a constitution enshrining many fundamental rights, and there were no substantial reports of ethnic discrimination during the year. However, the government maintained restrictions on freedom of association and continued to apply the law protecting the "honor and dignity" of the president and other government officials, in violation of the right to free speech.

Two cases of alleged violation of the "honor and dignity" law were prosecuted during 1993. The sixty-year-old scholar Karishal Asanov was charged with violating Article 170-3, parts 1 and 2, of the criminal code in August 1992, and his house was searched. He was subjected to a psychiatric examination, which found no signs of mental disturbance, and spent several months in pre-trial detention before being released for health reasons. Charges were brought in connection with his article "Don't Believe the President's Smile," a synthesis of arguments he made in a two-volume history of the Kazakh people that was critical of President Nursultan Nazarbaev. Numerous delays and reversals in court rulings prolonged the case into 1993, culminating in his conviction on May 25 and sentencing to three years of imprisonment, commuted to two years of probation. As of November, the case was on appeal.

Ruslanbek Chukurov, a doctor, also faced charges of violating the law on "honor and dignity" (Article 170-4, part 2, of the criminal code). Dr. Chukurov was first charged in 1992 when he publicly accused former Minister of Health Aliev of corruption. Conflicting decisions by two different courts have left the case unresolved.

More independent trade unions were registered during 1993, and *Birlescu*, the trade union movement's newspaper, reportedly was allowed to print again in August after being suspended by city authorities. Nonetheless, although Article 10 of the new Kazakhstan Constitution guaranteed the rights of public organizations, restrictive legislation continued to force parties, movements and independent trade unions to register in Kazakhstan.

The Right to Monitor

Helsinki Watch Watch received no reports of restrictions or attempted restrictions on the work of human rights monitors during 1993.

U.S. Policy

U.S. policy focused on providing humanitarian and technical assistance (the treaty granting Kazakhstan Most Favored Nation status went into effect in February) and supporting the Kazakhstan government's efforts to fulfill its promise to surrender all nuclear weapons by the year 2000.

The strong support of the Clinton administration stemmed from its assessment that Kazakhstan, according to a U.S. official in October, "is doing everything right."

The Work of Helsinki Watch

At the end of 1992, Helsinki Watch sent its first fact-finding mission to Kazakhstan since 1990, responding to allegations of violations of free speech and free association. Representatives met with human rights activists and with governmental and independent groups, and discussed their human rights concerns, such as the need to repeal the "honor and dignity" law.

In 1993 Helsinki Watch twice sent representatives to observe the ongoing trial of Karishal Asanov, and once to monitor the trial of Ruslanbek Chukurov. Both men were facing criminal charges for exercising their right to free speech.

LATVIA

Human Rights Developments

Citizenship and naturalization continued to be the most controversial rights issues in Latvia during 1993. Alone among the Baltic States, Latvia passed neither a naturalization nor a permanent residency law. Latvia took the idea of legal succession, the concept that the Baltic States were not new states but the legal successors to their inter-war predecessors, to its most literal end.

Consequently, the last Latvian Supreme Council, Latvia's legislative body from 1990 through mid-1993, refused to pass legislation concerning naturalization because a majority of deputies in the Supreme Council saw the council as a Soviet organ. Instead, on October 15, 1991, the Latvian Supreme Council passed legislation restoring citizenship to citizens and their descendants who resided in Latvia prior to the Soviet Union's 1940 annexation of the country. The October 1991 law left an estimated 34 percent of the population without citizenship. In parliamentary elections on June 5 and 6, 1993, in which only these "restored" citizens could participate, voters elected a new Saeima, or parliament. The Saeima was debating draft naturalization laws as of November.

In order to determine who was a citizen or the descendant of a citizen of Latvia prior to Soviet annexation in 1940 and therefore able to restore his citizenship under the October 1991 law, the Latvian Supreme Council passed a law on the registration of residents in December 1991. The Department of Citizenship and Immigration conducted registration, which lasted from spring 1992 to June 5, 1993.

Serious problems arose during the implementation of the registration guide-

lines. On its face, the law on registration was intended to register all of Latvia's residents, providing each with a personal code, similar to a Social Security number in the U.S. According to the law, only active-duty Russian military personnel and their families were not to be registered.

The Department of Citizenship and Immigration, however, intentionally and in violation of the law "On Registration," conducted a policy of denying certain non-citizen groups registration. Those denied registration included residents of temporary housing, retired Soviet military personnel, civilian employees—both past and present— of the Soviet military, and individuals who resided in housing built by the Soviet military but in many cases later transferred to civilian housing authorities. Estimates of those denied registration reached as high as 150,000. The unregistered had no right to receive social services and were considered temporary residents.

The Saeima's debate on a naturalization law also raised concern because the draft considered most likely to be passed into law included quotas severely limiting the number of non-citizens, estimated at 700,000, who could be naturalized in a given year. In the *The Baltic Observer*, Andrejs Pantelejevs, the ruling Latvia's Way party's parliamentary chairman, stated that only 300,000 of Latvia's non-citizens would be eligible for naturalization "in the next few years," while the plight of the remaining 400,000 would require an "international solution." Latvian politicians cited the precarious demographic situation of ethnic Latvians in Latvia, where they constituted a slim majority of 52 percent of the population, as the main reason behind a strict quota-based naturalization system. The Soviet government's policy of diluting the ethnic Latvian population through the forced immigration of non-Latvians, however heinous that policy may have been, does not justify a quota-based naturalization system that treats Latvia's non-citizen population en masse, and not as individuals.

The Right to Monitor

Helsinki Watch was not aware of any instance in which human rights monitors were hindered in their work by the Latvian Government.

U.S. Policy

The United States government noted no human rights violations in Latvia and called for the immediate withdrawal of all Russian troops. High-level official visits to Latvia toward the end of the year, however, including one by Secretary of State Warren Christopher on October 26 and 27, suggested heightened U.S. interest in ethnic relations in Latvia. Secretary Christopher called on the Latvian government "to act generously" regarding the adoption of a naturalization law, adding that it was "a matter of great concern to the United States. . .We want to pursue this vigorously." Other U.S initiatives included the nomination of Jerry Hamilton, Deputy Coordinator for East European Assistance for the State Department, as ambassador to the recently approved CSCE mission to Latvia, and funding for a "National Forum," a round table for negotiations among governmental, ethnic minority, and non-citizen groups.

The Work of Helsinki Watch

Helsinki Watch's work in Latvia during 1993 centered on two issues: the non-citizen community and naturalization legislation. Helsinki Watch sent two missions to Latvia, one in August and September and the other in October. A report issued in October 1993 commented that, "In its investigations, Helsinki Watch has uncovered sufficient evidence to substantiate serious, systematic abuses in Latvia's Department of Citizenship and Immigration. . . .the Department, in violation of the laws it was entrusted to implement, has targeted certain groups and denied them registration."

FORMER YUGOSLAV REPUBLIC OF MACEDONIA

Human Rights Developments

The Former Yugoslav Republic of Macedonia is the only one of the former Yugoslav republics to have become independent without bloodshed. It is bordered by Serbia (including the province of Kosovo), Bulgaria, Greece and Albania. Its population is about two million, composed of about 65 percent ethnic Macedonians, 22 percent ethnic Albanians, 5 percent ethnic Turks, 2 percent Macedonian Muslims, 3 percent Roma (Gypsies), 2 percent Serbs and .04 percent Vlachs. The human rights issues in Macedonia revolved around the rights of minorities.

A dispute with Greece over the country's name was resolved in April 1993 by admitting it to the United Nations with a temporary name, the "Former Yugoslav Republic of Macedonia." To simplify, we use the term "Macedonia" in this chapter.

Macedonia established itself as a parliamentary democracy. Following a public referendum, the country declared its independence and adopted a new constitution in November 1991. The present government is a coalition of the Social Democrats (formerly the Communist Party) the largest Albanian party, and others. During 1993 five of the twenty-four ministers in the government were ethnic Albanians; one was an ethnic Turk. Serbs, Turks, Vlachs and Albanians were represented among vice-ministers. An inter-ethnic council composed of two representatives of each minority was created by the parliament.

Macedonia was making the difficult transition from communism to democracy and a free market economy, while facing a grave threat of a spillover of the Bosnian war. A United Nations Protective Force

(UNPROFOR) of about 700 troops was deployed in Macedonia in December 1992; the U.S. added 300 troops in 1993.

The Macedonian constitution provides guarantees of equality, due process of law, free expression, freedom of religion, political freedom and other fundamental rights. But a stalemate in Parliament blocked passage of new laws needed to implement the constitution.

Free expression is guaranteed in the Macedonian constitution. There was no state censorship during 1993. In a legacy from communist times, the government owned the only newspaper printing facilities and controlled newsprint supplies (which were imported) and distribution. The government company, Nova Makedonija, printed daily newspapers in Macedonian as well as newspapers in Albanian and Turkish. Opposition views appeared in the government-controlled press. The largest opposition party, the Internal Macedonian Revolutionary Organization (VMRO, which was nationalist and anti-communist), published its own paper. Some in the opposition believed that the government limited free press by charging inordinately high fees for printing and distributing opposition journals. However, the only opposition journal issued during 1993, *Delo*, was printed at a government printing plant outside of Skopje, the capital. Three earlier independent journals shut down for economic reasons.

The government owned and operated several radio and television stations. Many hours of programs in Albanian, Turkish, Vlach and Romany (the Gypsy language), but none in Serbian, were broadcast daily. Many private TV and radio stations had sprung up since independence.

Demonstrations, including protests against government actions, were freely held.

The government reported that it was retraining the police, moving away from the political police practices of the old regime. Government opponents continued to complain of excessive use of force by police, however. The most serious incident took place in November 1992 following the police beating of a teenage Albanian cigarette seller. Hundreds of ethnic Albanians rioted; four people were killed. Police were also wounded by gunfire during the riot.

Equal treatment of minorities is guaranteed in the constitution. Minorities have the right to speak their own languages, issue newspapers or books in their own languages, and set up private schools. Government schools provide instruction in most minority languages where the number of minority children warrants it.

Nonetheless, many minority members have alleged discrimination in education. Most minorities argue that there were not enough elementary or secondary schools or universities for their children.

Job discrimination was another minority complaint. Ethnic Albanians asserted that they were discriminated against in government jobs and that, in areas where Albanians make up 80 percent of the population, the police force is 97 percent Macedonian. The prime minister confirmed this and told Helsinki Watch that the government had set a goal of 20 percent for minorities in the police academy, and that other affirmative action efforts were being undertaken in the army and the diplomatic service.

Ethnic Albanians contended that their representation in parliament was unequal; however, twenty-three of the 120 members of Parliament were Albanian. Ethnic Turks, whose members were not as concentrated, claim that voting districts were gerrymandered; Parliament contained no Turkish members.

A 1992 citizenship law established a fifteen-year residency requirement; Albanians argued for a five-year requirement. Thousands of ethnic Albanians have migrated to Macedonia from the Serbian province of Kosovo in recent years to escape abuse by the Serbian government. Because the 1991 census counted citizens, but not residents, ethnic Albanians boycotted it. A new census was planned for 1994.

The Serbian minority has some problems in addition to those shared with other minorities. Serbs are not mentioned by name in the preamble to the constitution, but are included only as an "other nationality"—a sore point with many Serbs.

During 1993, government television and radio stations provided no programs in Serbian, asserting that Serbs could receive programs from Serbia. Many Serbs, however, contended that Serbian programs provided news only about Serbia, and not about Macedonia.

Some Serbs alleged police brutality against young Serbs who wore Serbian hats or sang Serbian songs or in other ways asserted their Serbian identity.

Serbs could speak their own language and use their own names, although some alleged that Serbs with Serbian names were not given state jobs.

The Right to Monitor

No groups actively monitored general human rights abuses in Macedonia. The government cooperated fully with Helsinki Watch's monitoring mission in July.

U.S. Policy

The U.S. had not yet recognized the Former Yugoslav Republic of Macedonia as of November. State Department representatives had been stationed in Macedonia since before its independence; a liaison office was established in Skopje in November to provide support for the U.S. troops serving with UNPROFOR and to provide liaison with a mission of the Conference on Security and Cooperation in Europe (CSCE), which began monitoring conditions in Macedonia in 1992.

The U.S. allotted $10 million in SEED (Support for East European Democracy) funds for Macedonia for fiscal year 1993, and the administration requested $10 million for fiscal year 1994. As of November, $6 million had been obligated for specific projects.

The Work of Helsinki Watch

Helsinki Watch maintained a continuing presence in the former Yugoslavia, including Macedonia. Helsinki Watch sent a fact-finding mission to Macedonia in July and planned a report for early 1994. Its work in Macedonia involved monitoring human rights, particularly questions of free expression, minority rights, and the use of force by police.

MOLDOVA

Human Rights Developments

Compared with the gross violations committed in 1992, when armed conflict raged in Moldova's eastern territories, the country's human rights situation improved in 1993. Fear of large-scale ethnic discrimination—an ostensible cause of much of last year's conflict—proved largely unfounded. The situation remained worrisome, however.

The self-proclaimed "Dniester Moldovan Republic" (DMR), which took control of a strip of land between the Dniester River and the Ukrainian border in 1992, *de facto* seceded from the Republic of Moldova, and the government in the Moldovan capital of Chisinau ceased monitoring human rights practices or prosecuting violators in the secessionist area. Moreover, chaos reigned in the halls of government. The country debated whether to retain full independence or to join the Commonwealth of Independent States; several high-ranking government officials resigned; and Parliament was crippled by numerous walk-outs and the prospect of elections. As a result, human rights legislation fell from parliamentary agendas, and investigation and prosecution of civil and political violations were neglected by law enforcement bodies.

One of the most vivid cases of human rights abuse involved six men on trial on criminal charges in Tiraspol, the regional "capital" of the "DMR." They were arrested during the conflict of spring and summer 1992 on charges of terrorism; after several aborted beginnings of a trial, all six remained incarcerated as of November 1993. Violations of these defendants' right to due process included denial of their right to counsel and alleged gross mistreatment in detention. Since most were former members of the Popular Front of Moldova, which had vehemently opposed the "DMR" authorities, it was possible that the terrorism charges against these men were politically motivated.

Nina Maximovtsela, the defense attorney for one of those charged, reported that she had suffered from serious harassment in the "DMR" in connection with her work. She claimed she had been under surveillance, threatened by one of the investigators in the case and by several unidentified individuals, and attacked with a knife, and that her apartment had been broken into, all, she believed, for the purposes of intimidating her. The Moldovan government sent guards for her protection during the summer, but the "DMR" government rejected their authority, leaving her with no legal recourse.

The Right to Monitor

With the exception of minor harassment reported by members of the Romanian Helsinki Committee in the "DMR," such as apparent stalling on the part of local authorities in granting them a visit with a prisoner, Helsinki Watch received no reports of restrictions or attempted restrictions of the work of human rights monitors during 1993.

U.S. Policy

Four residents of Moldova participated in a program in the United States, sponsored by the U.S. Information Agency (USIA), to study protection of minority rights, an issue of particular concern in Moldova. Moldova was also the beneficiary of an Overseas Private Investment Corporation (OPIC) agreement and enjoyed Most Favored Nation status.

The Work of Helsinki Watch

Helsinki Watch tried during 1993 to focus international attention on the various violations committed in connection with the "terrorism" trial in Tiraspol. In August Helsinki Watch wrote to the International Commission of Jurists raising concerns about the

harassment of Nina Maximovtsela, the defense lawyer for one of the defendants, and requesting action for her protection. In September a letter was sent to the *de facto* authorities requesting clemency for Andrei Ivantoc, one of the six defendants facing terrorism charges in Tiraspol. Mr. Ivantoc was under medical observation for psychiatric and physiological disorders, yet, except for one month, was kept in prison pending the completion of the trial.

ROMANIA

Human Rights Developments

Respect for the rights of minorities remained an elusive goal during 1993. The Roma (Gypsy) minority continued to face severe discrimination and mistreatment in Romania, and was often unable to obtain effective remedy for abuses. In September 1991, Helsinki Watch issued a report documenting numerous incidents of mob violence against the homes and persons of Roma, and the failure of the Romanian authorities to provide protection against such violence. More than two years later, no person had been convicted for the vigilante attacks, and Helsinki Watch had no information that local officials or police officers had been prosecuted or disciplined for their role in these violent attacks.

There were additional reports of violence against Romas in 1993. On September 20, Romas in the town of Hadareni were attacked by a large mob. During the violence three Romas were killed. One Romanian, who was stabbed by a Roma man during the violence, also died. In addition, thirteen houses of Romas were set on fire and destroyed, and another twenty-five were partially or seriously damaged. Reports indicated that the police were slow to arrive on the scene of the violence and did little or nothing to intervene to protect the Romas who were being attacked. The Romanian government responded more aggressively in the Hadareni case by, among other things, dismissing the county police chief and taking disciplinary measures against two local police officers.

The Hungarian minority continued to face obstacles in equal treatment in education and culture, and were underrepresented in both local and national government administration. The most serious abuses against Hungarians occurred at the local level, where local officials placed restrictions on freedom of assembly, association and speech.

The Romanian government failed to take measures to adequately remedy these abuses. Government officials were rarely disciplined, much less prosecuted, for committing clear violations of Romanian law. The legal mechanisms for holding abusive officials accountable remained weak, and there were inadequate safeguards to ensure that minorities could obtain sufficient legal remedy when violations occur.

In the spring of 1993, the government announced that it was replacing the co-prefects of Covasna and Harghita counties (one Hungarian, one Romanian), with two Romanians; Hungarians make up 85 and 90 percent of the populations there respectively. Because of the government's decision, not a single ethnic Hungarian held this highest county government position. Moreover, as prefect of Covasna county, the government appointed a man who was closely associated with the highly nationalistic organization Vatra Romaneasca.

In the spring of 1993, the Romanian government announced the formation of the Council for National Minorities that had long been a demand of ethnic minorities in Romania and was viewed by many as a potentially significant step toward addressing minority concerns. However, little progress was made during the year to address the substantive concerns of minority groups.

Although the Romanian government made some recent attempts to distance itself from the extreme right-wing parties and their policies, it adopted at the same time several measures that were particularly insensitive to the concerns of minorities, as well as to all Romanians opposed to nationalistic and racist propaganda. In January 1993, President Ion Iliescu appointed Paul Everac to head the state-controlled Romanian Television. Everac had been widely criticized for being anti-Semitic and anti-minority.

In February 1993, the president of Romanian Television, Razvan Theodorescu, announced that the television program schedule would be reorganized, as a result of which the number of hours of minority programming would be reduced. Similarly, according to a directive by the Romanian Television leadership, news and current events were to be banned on minority-language broadcasts. The directive restricted such programming to cultural and "traditional" themes. While reports indicated that the directive might not be enforced in all cases, its existence left a strong impression that minority language programming was a target of the television leadership.

Helsinki Watch continued to receive reports of police brutality against detainees in 1993, including one case of a death in detention under suspicious circumstances. Costel Covalciuc, a thirty-five-year-old from the town of Dorohei, was arrested on June 29 for having allegedly threatened his wife and mother-in-law with a knife. He was tried and convicted the next day. On July 4, his family was informed that he had died that morning. Members of the family, who viewed Covalciuc's body at the morgue, reported visible signs of physical abuse. The autopsy report, however, concluded that Covalciuc had died of a heart attack, and the military prosecutor of Iasi concluded that there was no evidence of mistreatment in the case.

The Right to Monitor

Helsinki Watch was unaware of any instance in which human rights monitors had been hindered in their work by the Romanian government during the year.

U.S. Policy

In June, President Clinton issued the annual report to Congress on the implementation of the Helsinki Final Act and other Conference on Security and Cooperation in Europe

(CSCE) documents. The report concluded that respect for human rights had improved significantly in Romania, but also identified ongoing problems in the treatment of minorities such as the Hungarians and Romas.

On October 12, the U.S. House of Representatives approved by consensus a resolution restoring most favored nation (MFN) trading status to Romania. The Senate also approved restoration of MFN by unanimous consent on October 21. The Clinton administration had supported the resolution, stating that "to withhold MFN status would strengthen extremist groups and undermine the human rights progress made to date."

The Clinton administration made no significant public comment on human rights developments in Romania during 1993. An information sheet prepared by the State Department during Congress's consideration of MFN noted that Romania had "made vast progress on human rights." It also stated that "the government took steps to remedy scattered instances of racist violence in 1992/93."

The Clinton administration failed, however, to point out that the Romanian government had fueled ethnic tensions and hostilities by being slow to denounce firmly and clearly acts of vigilantism against Romas over the past four years. Moreover, the administration made no reference to the highly inflammatory role played by the state-controlled television by presenting highly biased reports on Romas.

The Work of Helsinki Watch

In addition to Helsinki Watch's ongoing effort to document the most serious human rights abuses in Romania, in 1993 Helsinki Watch focused extensive efforts on raising the profile of human rights issues in Romania in the Council of Europe, which was reviewing Romania's application for membership, and in the U.S. Congress, which was considering renewal of most favored nation trading status for Romania.

In January, Helsinki Watch issued a newsletter on conditions in police lockups in Romania. The newsletter concluded that:

Nearly every arrestee reported having been beaten by police investigators before arriving at the lockups. In some cases arrestees were beaten after they admitted to the crimes for which they were arrested but refused to confess to other, unsolved crimes.

In September, Helsinki Watch conducted an extensive investigation into the freedom of the press in Romania. A newsletter was planned for release in December 1993.

Helsinki Watch also concentrated, during 1993, on monitoring the treatment of ethnic minorities in Romania. On October 12, Helsinki Watch sent a letter to Prime Minister Nicolae Vacariou expressing concern about the death of three Romas and one Romanian during mob violence in the town of Hadareni, and about the police response to the violence. Helsinki Watch called on the Romanian government to take a clear position condemning violence against Gypsies and to guarantee the protection of all Romanian citizens from violence or bodily harm, regardless of their ethnic or national origin.

A report titled *Struggling for Ethnic Identity: Ethnic Hungarians in Post-Ceausescu Romania*, was issued in October documenting human rights abuses against the Hungarian minority since 1990, as well as the Romanian government's failure to take the measures necessary to remedy these violations. The report concluded that:

The government's willingness, on occasion, to manipulate ethnic tensions for political gain has done little to reassure Hungarians about the government's sincere commitment to the protection of minority rights. Inconsistent policies toward minorities, as well as positive statements accompanied by little or no specific action, have increased suspicion that the Romanian government is more concerned about its international reputation than addressing concerns of minorities.

In November, Helsinki Watch conducted an investigation into ongoing human rights abuses against the Roma minority. A newsletter was projected for early 1994.

RUSSIA

Human Rights Developments

The dramatic events of October 3 and 4 in Moscow, in which armed defenders of the parliament (or Supreme Soviet) attempted to seize power, threw into question the state of Russian democracy. Government sources estimated that 143 people died and more than 700 were wounded as a result of the armed uprising, which was crushed by the Russian army and troops under the Ministries of Interior. Unofficial sources, however, speculated that death figures might be as high as 400 or more.

The Supreme Soviet had throughout 1993 undermined President Boris Yeltsin's reform program and executive power in Russia. Although President Yeltsin's September 21 decree suspending parliament, which sparked the armed uprising, violated key articles of the Russian constitution, he was supported in his action by the heads of state of many democratic governments including the United States. But the consequences of Yeltsin's decision and his actions in the aftermath of the violence were very damaging to human rights in Russia.

In accordance with a state of emergency declared by President Yeltsin on October 3, about fifteen opposition newspapers were suspended, some of them well-known for racist and fascist tendencies. Two newspapers were restored a week later, and two others were offered the option of changing their titles, editors-in-chief, and general political line in exchange for regaining the right to operate. The right-wing news program "600 Seconds" was taken off the air, reducing further the meager access of opposition opinion to Russian state-owned television. During October 5 and 6, censors cut at least ten articles from major newspapers. When government censorship was lifted, the Ministry of Press and Information encouraged journalists and editors to practice self-censorship. Six political parties and organizations were suspended and banned from participating in the December 12 parliamentary elections. With Yeltsin's temporary suspension of the Constitutional Court, the opportunity to appeal these violations of civil rights on constitutional grounds was severely limited.

Police brutality, long a problem in Moscow, worsened during the two-week state of emergency. Dozens of supporters of the Supreme Soviet, including deputies themselves, were captured and beaten by riot police and Interior Ministry troops as they left the parliament building. Victims of police beatings included at least thirty-three journalists and hundreds of individuals detained for violating the 11 P.M. curfew.

Moscow Mayor Yuri Luzhkov used the state of emergency as a pretext to enforce the *propiska*, or residence requirement, system already established in the capital. Earlier, when the Russian Supreme Soviet finalized legislation abandoning the propiska system for Russia, the Moscow mayor's office had issued regulations that retained it for Moscow, but these regulations, on the whole, were not implemented. The regulations required non-Muscovites to register with the police and pay a fee for each day they remained in the city, and set out administrative penalties for violators. Although applicable to any non-Muscovite, the mayor's office told Helsinki Watch in May that they were intended mainly for people from the Caucasus, who, it said, were responsible for the lion's share of organized crime.

During the state of emergency, police strictly enforced these regulations, forbidding cars with license plates from the Caucasus to enter the city and forcing non-Russians in Moscow to leave. As of November the Ministry of Interior estimated that 9,000 individuals had been put on trains and sent out of Moscow, and that 10,000 others had left voluntarily. Detention centers sprang up in Moscow to hold individuals while they proved they were in the city legally. Most were from the Caucasus and Central Asia, which pointed out the discriminatory manner in which the regulations were conceived and enforced. Helsinki Watch and local human rights groups received many reports of individuals beaten by police in their homes, on the streets, and in police stations during passport checks.

Police brutality during the state of emergency brought to the surface the long-standing problem of police beatings during detention. Helsinki Watch received two reports of murder suspects who were so badly beaten as to require hospitalization; one of the victims also required exploratory surgery. Although police maintained that the two men incurred their bodily damage attempting to escape, a state medical examiner's report on one of the victims supported his claim that he had been beaten. The May 1 marches in Moscow demonstrated that police and riot police had poor crowd control techniques. Thousands of radical, anti-Yeltsin demonstrators, violating a city ordinance, marched from a major square in Moscow south, away from the city. When demonstrators approached a police barricade, they apparently attacked police and riot police, who responded violently. No tear gas was used, and water cannons did not function properly. One policeman died in the incident, and as many as 300 on each side are believed to have been wounded.

Several laws adopted by the Russian parliament in 1993 chipped away at civic freedoms. Amendments to the law on freedom of conscience adopted in August attempted to ban foreign missionary work, including proselytizing, publishing, and advertising, and would have required missionaries to be registered by Russian religious organizations. President Yeltsin's amendments proposed a softer variant, requiring foreign religious organizations to register (or re-register) with the Ministry of Foreign Affairs. July amendments to the Law on State Security Bodies granted the Ministry of Security the right to search private homes without warrants. During the summer the Supreme Soviet attempted unsuccessfully to disband the parliamentary human rights committee.

Hardships connected to economic reform disproportionately affected women, who in 1992-1993 accounted for 70 percent of layoffs. Gender discrimination in the workplace was reportedly rampant and ignored or even sanctioned by public officials. In a February press conference on privatization, the Minister of Labor remarked, "Why should we employ women when men are unemployed? It's better that men work and women take care of children and do the housework. I don't want women to be offended, but I seriously don't think women should work while men are doing nothing."

As a result of the 1992 armed conflict in the northern Caucasus between two indigenous ethnic groups, the Ossetians and the Ingush, 65,000 Ingush from the North Ossetian republic of Russia remained refugees in Ingushetia, and Ingush claimed that about 287 Ingush continued to be held hostage, although this figure may also have included disappeared persons. Ossetians claimed that Ingush continued to hold about forty Ossetians hostage. Ingush settlements in the mountains of North Ossetia remained basically in a state of blockade, relying heavily on accompaniment by Russian Interior Ministry troops or international relief organizations to travel to Ingushetia for supplies. The Russian Constitutional Court in September ruled unconstitutional a North Ossetian government decree stating that Ossetians and Ingush could not live peacefully together, thereby deflecting responsibility for resettling Ingush refugees.

Regions outside Moscow continued to enforce the propiska system, mainly to prevent the settlement of ethnic minorities. In the Mineralnye Vody region, for example, local government officials attempted to expel seventy-two families (most of them Armenian) dwelling in villages without propiskas, and between four and seven families were actually expelled, with the assistance of local Cossacks. Cossacks also attempted to expel nine Chechen families dwelling in the Don region. Cossacks reportedly forced six Armenian families to leave the village of Nizhny Podkumsk, located near the resort town of Piatigorsk; local authorities were either unwilling or unable to stop the action. Some reports indicated that Cossacks were targeting Jews as well in the Krasnodar area. Given the dangers that Cossacks pose to ethnic minorities the Russian government's decree, signed in March, granting Cossacks the right to set up their own military using special Interior Ministry and Defense Ministry forces was very troubling.

Far-right nationalist and neo-Nazi groups regularly published anti-Semitic newspaper articles and tracts, and anti-Semitism was palpable among the crowds supporting the parliament in September and October. Attackers twice during the summer broke windows of the Moscow synagogue and left graffiti saying "Kill the Kikes." After the second incident the Moscow city police set up a guard booth outside the synagogue, and although no further attacks occurred, "Kill the Kikes" graffiti reappeared around the synagogue during the September-October parliament uprising.

Russia's generous refugee law came into effect in March, but its implementation was disappointing. The newly created Federal Migration Service (FMS), overburdened and underfunded, processed 348,000 refugees and displaced persons in Russia from July 1992 through October 1993, while unofficial figures put the total number of refugees and displaced persons as high as two million. Many non-Russians complained of discriminatory treatment at FMS, whose staff often insisted that they had an overwhelming number of Russians to process and encouraged non-Russians (in cases that Helsinki Watch is familiar with, Tajiks and Uzbeks) who were facing no immediate problems simply not to apply.

Prison conditions in Russia remained a serious human rights concern, with overcrowding worsening in pre-trial detention centers. Five people died and forty were injured (about half of them law enforcers) during a prison uprising in Vladimir that was suppressed by police and mostly unarmed Interior Ministry troops using two armored personnel carriers. Local prisoners' rights groups noted no significant implementation of the much-acclaimed 1992 prison reform. Some reports indicated that, in institutions for the criminally insane, inmates were forceably drugged with Sulfazine, which had been forbidden in Russia.

Because Russia is the most powerful state to have emerged from the former Soviet Union, and because it sought to exercise considerable influence in the newly independent states, its foreign policy in the region (known in Russia as the "near abroad," a term deeply resented by many of its now-independent neighbors) merited close examination. In the area of human rights, a double standard prevailed. While the rights of ethnic Russians in the Baltics led the Russian government to maintain constant diplomatic and economic pressure on the Estonian and Latvian governments, the truly massive human rights violations committed by governments that Russia supported in Central Asia (in Tajikistan especially, with the country's economy and security heavily dependent on Russia) drew little or no public criticism. In February, President Yeltsin announced that Russia should be given special powers to conduct peacekeeping in the conflicts on the territory of the former Soviet Union, and in June he stated that Russia would seek to maintain its military bases in the former Soviet Union. This was a troubling development indeed, considering the Russian army's practice of taking sides in such conflicts, its reputation for providing the weapons that escalate conflict, and, as a result, its responsibility for worsening violations of humanitarian law in places like Moldova, Abkhazia, and Tajikistan.

The Right to Monitor

Human rights groups, local and international, operated basically freely in Russia. A Helsinki Watch representative was denied entry into the Supreme Soviet compound, as were all newspaper correspondents, on September 28, after it had been surrounded by police and Interior Ministry troops but several days before the outbreak of fighting.

U.S. Policy

The Clinton administration unswervingly supported President Yeltsin throughout 1993. This support was evident in the vigor with which the administration promoted a $2.5 billion aid package to the former Soviet Union, of which two-thirds was earmarked for Russia, and in the many public statements of support issued at critical moments during President Yeltsin's confrontations with the Supreme Soviet.

The unqualified nature of this support for Yeltsin was disturbing because it apparently crippled the administration's ability to offer criticism of Russia's human rights record. When Yeltsin suspended the Supreme Soviet on September 21, Secretary of State Warren Christopher remarked:

Just as we did at the time of the April referendum, the Clinton administration supports President Yeltsin and his program for democratic reform. We believe that the Russian people should have the right to determine the political future of their country at the ballot box. We urge Russian leaders at all levels to work together in a democratic process that maintains peace and stability while fully respecting civil liberties and individual human rights.

On September 29, five days before the Supreme Soviet building was stormed, Secretary Christopher expressed concern for the rights of those individuals holding out there.

Yet two weeks later, following the attempted coup by the Supreme Soviet, as the Russian government engaged in blatant violations of civil rights—including the closing of opposition newspapers and political organizations, routine and brutal police beatings, and the eviction from Moscow of ethnic minorities—the Clinton administration offered no substantial criticism. While Secretary Christopher rightly pointed out that Russians would determine their political future at the ballot box, distressing signs that the December elections would not be fully democratic drew no later remarks from the Clinton administration.

The administration's personalized Russia policy centered on President Yeltsin was reminiscent of the Bush administration's "Gorbymania." It became defined in late March, when Yeltsin first attempted to dissolve the ultra-conservative Supreme Soviet. On this occasion President Clinton announced:

The United States supports the historic movement towards democratic political reform in Russia. President Yeltsin is the leader of that process, he is a democratically elected national leader. He has United States support, as do his reform government and all reformists throughout Russia.

The Clinton administration apparently lobbied European governments to adopt such a personalized policy as well. According to the Associated Press, after German Chancellor Helmut Kohl's late September statement of support for democracy and democratic forces in Russia, President Clinton telephoned the German leader and convinced him to issue a statement backing Yeltsin personally. American embassies throughout Europe reportedly had instructions to likewise lobby their host governments.

On September 30, President Clinton signed into law the $2.5 billion aid package, perhaps the cornerstone to his administration's Russia policy. The aid breaks down into $750 million to assist privatization and private sector development, $500 million to encourage trade and investment, and $200 to $300 million for programs in each of the following areas: democracy development, humanitarian assistance, energy and environmental restructuring, and housing for demobilized Russian officers from the Baltic and other countries.

Conditions placed on aid included the timely withdrawal of Russian troops from Latvia and Estonia, respect for territorial integrity within the former Soviet Union, and ceasing aid to Cuba. No human rights conditions were attached to the aid, however, other than those set out elsewhere in U.S. foreign aid legislation. This was a serious shortcoming considering the fragile state of Russian democracy and civic freedoms. Indeed, the Clinton administration's failure to link human rights to U.S. aid was similar to that of the previous administration.

Ambassador at Large Strobe Talbott testified to the Senate Foreign Relations Committee on September 21 that "the Administration would rather not have these restrictions and conditionality, because we feel that it limits somewhat our ability to use these programs as a fully effective instrument of our foreign policy goals." This policy seemed to Helsinki Watch misguided: if it aimed to create and strengthen democracy and free markets, then surely the aid should have been connected to continued fulfillment of democratic freedoms and respect for human rights.

Russia's apparent involvement in the armed conflicts outside its borders, which seriously worsened human rights conditions in those areas, drew only mild criticism from the Clinton administration. In his September 7 testimony before the Senate Foreign Relations Committee, Ambassador Talbott stated that, for example, while there was evidence that elements of the Russian army may have been assisting the Abkhazian separatists in Georgia, the Russian role in Georgia was "overall a constructive and stabilizing one." During the summer of 1993, the Clinton administration unveiled a policy for peacekeeping in regions of armed conflicts in the former Soviet Union. Under the coordination of James Collins, former Chief of Mission to the U.S. Embassy in Moscow, American mediation would be available, within the framework of the CSCE and the United Nations, to those parties who requested it.

The Work of Helsinki Watch

Through published articles and reports and in consultation with officials, Helsinki Watch repeatedly cautioned the U.S. administration against employing a policy in Russia that gave unqualified support to one Russian leader, President Yeltsin, as the previous administration had done with Mikhail Gorbachev. Helsinki Watch carefully monitored any actions by President Yeltsin's government that were anti-democratic in nature and cautioned U.S. policymakers about Yeltsin's anti-democratic tendencies. During a May visit with Moscow Deputy Mayor Anatolii Braginskii, Helsinki Watch also objected to Moscow's unimplemented but discriminatory residence requirements.

In October Helsinki Watch wrote a letter to President Yeltsin protesting the crackdown on the media and police brutality following the October 4 uprising. The letter was published in full in *Nezavisimaia Gazeta* (The Independent Newspaper) and *Express Khronika*. After the October crackdown on residence requirement violators, Helsinki Watch wrote a letter of protest to Moscow Mayor Yuri Luzhkov and a press release protesting the regulations and their racist application, and gave many press interviews on the topic. A press release issued during Secretary Christopher's October visit to Moscow sharply criticized the Clinton administration's neglect of human rights in its Russia policy. During a November visit to Moscow, Helsinki Watch met with high-level government officials in Moscow in part to insist that the residence regulations be dropped.

A letter to President Yeltsin and Defense Minister Grachev sent in March expressed Helsinki Watch's deep concern over the proposal for the Russian army to play an expanded role in "peacekeeping" in the armed conflicts plaguing the former Soviet Union, and set out recommendations for preventing violations of humanitarian law in these conflicts.

In June, Helsinki Watch wrote a letter pressing the Russian Procurator General to release the opinion submitted by an independent medical expert in the case of a murder suspect reportedly beaten for ten hours during questioning and to investigate the beating itself. The medical information was later released to the man's attorney.

Committed to strengthening the human rights movement in the former Soviet Union, Helsinki Watch continued to maintain a staff and office in Moscow. During 1993, Helsinki Watch's Moscow representatives conducted a series of training seminars for local human rights groups and assisted in the formation of a Moscow-based human rights monitoring group for Central Asia.

Helsinki Watch selected Yuri Markovich Schmidt, a former dissident activist and well-known human rights lawyer, to be one of the international monitors honored by Human Rights Watch at its observance of Human Rights Day in December.

THE SLOVAK REPUBLIC

Human Rights Developments

The Slovak Republic ("Slovakia") became an independent state on January 1, 1993, with the peaceful breakup of the Federal Republic of Czechoslovakia. Slovakia declared that it considered itself bound by the legal instruments ratified by the Federal Republic, including international human rights covenants. The Slovak constitution went into effect in September 1992, providing, *inter alia*, that international instruments on human rights and freedoms ratified by the Slovak Republic shall take precedence over national laws.

In 1992, the government of Prime Minister Vladimir Meciar had announced that the Czechoslovak lustration law, which excludes former communist collaborators from certain appointive positions, would be abolished in Slovakia. However, a survey in early 1993 found that more than half of Slovak citizens supported retaining the law. Although it was not repealed, Helsinki Watch had no information that the law was being enforced.

Direct censorship did not occur, but the Slovak government used various means to prevent journalists from criticizing its policies and tried to force journalists to give only positive accounts of the government. During the 1992 election campaign, journalists who failed to present what the government called the "true picture of Slovakia" were not invited to government press conferences and not allowed to participate if they attended without an invitation. Helsinki Watch received reports that the government cut subsidies for various periodicals based on their political content, although the government claimed that its subsidy policy was based primarily on educational goals.

In January, the board of directors of the state-owned newspaper *Smena* fired Josep Weiss, the director, and Karol Jezik, the chief editor, who had printed articles critical of the Meciar government. This intensified fears that press freedom in Slovakia was being curtailed in the new state. Despite this effort to intimidate independent journalists, Weiss and Jezik were able to establish an independent daily called *Sme* shortly after they were fired from their previous job. *Sme* operated without government interference.

Helsinki Watch received numerous reports of discriminatory policies and statements by local and national government officials against the Roma (Gypsy) minority living in Slovakia. On July 1, 1993, the village of Spisske Podhradie instituted a curfew for "gypsies and other suspicious persons" between the hours of 11 P.M. and 4:30 A.M. After an outpouring of protest from human rights and minority rights groups, the curfew was declared unconstitutional by the Slovak National Council.

According to a report in the Slovakian *Pravda* on August 9, 1993, the management of a private hotel in Zilina decided not to allow Romas to enter the premises of its gambling halls in order "to protect private property and the good reputation of the hotel."

On September 3, in a clear reference to

Romas, Meciar stated that it was necessary to curtail family allowances that encourage "widespread reproduction" because Gypsies are having children who are "mentally and socially unadaptable." Meciar was criticized by human rights groups for fostering ethnic hostilities and prejudice.

There are approximately 600,000 ethnic Hungarians living in Slovakia. They are primarily concentrated along the border with Hungary, and constitute the country's largest ethnic minority. Although they have achieved greater rights and freedoms over the last four years, there are ongoing concerns regarding language rights and access to Hungarian-language education.

During 1993, the Slovak government initiated a series of measures criticized by the Hungarian minority as a policy of harassment. In many areas, even where Hungarians constitute the overwhelming majority, official road signs bearing Hungarian names of towns and streets were removed over the last year. Furthermore, a Slovak law on appropriate names for children also required that first names be chosen from an official list that excludes many Hungarian names. Ethnic Hungarian parents who attempted to give their children authentically Hungarian names were not allowed to register the children.

During the process of examining Slovakia's application for membership in the Council of Europe, a series of recommendations were made to the Slovak government, including amending its legislation to provide for bilingual signs and to allow Hungarian names. In response to the Council's recommendations, the Slovak Parliament passed a bill in July 1993 that would have allowed the use of Hungarian family names in official records without modification to comply with Slovak grammar and spelling rules. A week later, after Slovakia had been admitted to the Council of Europe, Meciar refused to sign the bill into law. Similarly, bilingual town and street signs, which had been installed as a concession to the Council of Europe prior to its vote on June 30, were ordered removed in early

August. The Minister of Transportation justified the action by saying that bilingual road signs confuse motorists and tourists.

On September 5, Chief Rabbi Baruch-Meyers, a U.S. citizen and Slovakia's first chief rabbi in over twenty-five years, was attacked and beaten by a group of skinheads. President Michal Kovac issued a statement condemning the attack and emphasizing that it did not represent the attitudes of most Czech citizens.

An alternative university in Trnava, which is viewed as a haven for academics critical of the Slovak government, experienced government harassment during 1993 as it had the previous year. The government delayed the appointment of Dr. Anton Hajduk as rector. After international criticism from academic and human rights groups, however, the Slovak government finally released bank account funds that had been frozen in 1992, and appointed Dr. Hajduk. Nevertheless, the government continued to discriminate against the university by apportioning a smaller budget than it was entitled to based on the size of its student body.

The Right to Monitor

Helsinki Watch was not aware of any interference in the work of human rights monitors by the government of the Slovak Republic.

U.S. Policy

On January 1, 1993, the United States officially recognized the Slovak Republic. In February 1993, the Committee on Foreign Affairs of the U.S. House of Representatives published the report of a November 1992 study mission, which included a visit to Slovakia. The report studied the implications for Slovakia of the dissolution of Czechoslovakia and recommended continued aid to support economic reform, democracy and human rights in Slovakia.

The report also noted some problems with the government's sensitivity to criticism and its desire to control the media and restrict academic freedom, as well as the concerns of the Hungarian minority. However, the committee recommended diplomacy and assistance to overcome these deficiencies, rather than condemnation.

Slovakia received over $80 billion of investment insurance assistance from the Overseas Private Investment Corporation.

The Clinton administration made no significant additional comment on human rights practices in Slovakia in 1993.

The Work of Helsinki Watch

During 1993 Helsinki Watch's work in Slovakia focused primarily on the rights of minorities and restrictions on press freedoms.

On January 15, 1993, Helsinki Watch sent a letter to Prime Minister Meciar expressing concern about reports that the Slovak government had interfered with the independence of the press by firing the editor-in-chief and director of the daily *Smena*, and had attempted to silence those critical of the government's policies.

Helsinki Watch conducted an extensive investigation into freedom of the press in Slovakia during 1993, and scheduled a report on freedom of the press for 1994.

On March 8, 1993, Helsinki Watch criticized a Slovak law that prevents ethnic Hungarians from freely choosing any name they want for their children. Helsinki Watch called the law "a violation of the fundamental right of an individual to express freely his or her ethnic identity and heritage." Helsinki Watch also criticized a decree from the director of the state-owned Slovak television banning Hungarian-language programs from using the Hungarian names for cities and towns. Helsinki Watch stated:

> Given that the Slovak state still exercises a virtual monopoly over television broadcasting, it is incumbent upon the government to encourage diversity in its programming. Helsinki Watch considers this recent decree an unnecessary restriction by the government on the Hungarian-language programs.

In May, Helsinki Watch sent a mission to Slovakia to investigate allegations of discrimination against the Hungarian minority.

TAJIKISTAN

Human Rights Developments

Following the government's victory in the civil war against an alliance consisting of the Democratic Party of Tajikistan (DPT) and the Islamic Revival Party (IRP), Tajikistan became a human rights disaster area. From early December 1992 through February 1993 the Tajikistan government, led by Emomali Rakhmonov, presided over an extraordinarily ruthless campaign of revenge against individuals believed to have supported or sympathized with the DPT-IRP coalition, which had governed Tajikistan for six months in 1992. In later months the government began arresting and convicting persons for their conduct during the DPT-IRP coalition period, continued a crackdown on the press, and banned the country's four main opposition political organizations.

The war brought disaster to Tajikistan, killing an estimated 20,000 to 50,000 people and wrecking the country's cotton-dependent economy. More than 500,000 residents of Tajikistan fled the civil war, seeking refuge either in other parts of Tajikistan or in Afghanistan. In the spring and summer, refugees and the displaced began to return to their homes and suffered harassment, beatings, and killings, partly due to inadequate protection measures on the part of local governments.

Pro-government paramilitary groups entered Dushanbe, the capital of Tajikistan, on December 10, 1992. Led by the Popular Front of Tajikistan, the main pro-government army in the civil war, they conducted a campaign of summary executions and "disappearances" of people of Pamiri and Garmi (regions of Tajikistan that had supported the DPT-IRP coalition) origins, killing more than 300 and disappearing hundreds of others. According to eyewitnesses interviewed by the Moscow-based human rights group

Memorial and Helsinki Watch, Popular Front soldiers and other pro-government forces stopped buses and trolley buses, stopped people on streets, and deployed forces at the Dushanbe airport in order to check individuals' documents. In many instances, those whose passports indicated that they were born in Pamir or Garm were killed or simply taken away and not heard from again. Graves containing as many as twenty or thirty corpses were exhumed in several places in and around Dushanbe.

The Popular Front committed summary executions in villages on the outskirts of Dushanbe after DPT-IRP rebels had already retreated, and, in at least one instance, the village of Subulak, in places that had never been a base for rebels. In another village called Kyrgyzon in January, the Popular Front, apportioning to itself law enforcement responsibilities, arrested and executed a thirty-one-year-old man (of Garmi origins) whom a neighbor had accused of murder. The summary execution was preceded by a two-minute "people's trial" in front of villagers.

The current government made no attempt to investigate the summary executions in Subulak and Kyrgyzon, and did not acknowledge that a campaign against Garmis and Pamiris took place from December 1992 through February 1992, attributing the large number of murders to the high rate of crime and banditry that characterized the government's first few months in power.

It is not known how many people disappeared in 1993. The disappeared were principally individuals who supported the DPT-IRP coalition or who were of Pamiri or Garmi origins. Their captors were paramilitary bands and warlords, mainly from Kuliab, one of the regions of Tajikistan that supports the current government. In some cases law enforcement officials may have been involved in the disappearances. A highly-placed Ministry of Internal Affairs (MVD) official, in an informal conversation with Memorial, alleged that MVD staff members sometimes collaborated in kidnapping. In addition, he stated that the MVD was most likely aware of the general pattern of disappearances and the reported existence of so-called informal prisons. In the second half of 1993, disappearances became more professional and, in at least two cases, took place in the full view of local government or law enforcement officials.

Some of the disappeared were believed to have been brought to informal prisons, or buildings appropriated by warlords and used as detention centers for their captives. Helsinki Watch had good reason to believe that the Tajikistan government was aware of the existence of at least two informal prisons.

Instead of leading an effort to punish all parties guilty of crimes during and after the civil war, the government imprisoned during the year at least nineteen people who supported the DPT-IRP coalition. These included four television journalists, some of whom were beaten in detention, accused of "agitation and spreading propaganda for the violent overthrow of the government"; at least three members of the Islamic Renaissance Party, two of whom were charged with publicly calling for the overthrow of the government; one of the most well-known poets in Tajikistan, who was charged with inciting ethnic hatred with his poetry and was accused of having made a speech at the spring 1992 mass demonstrations that criticized members of parliament, and which the current government considers was a signal for the crowd to seize as hostages a group of parliamentarians; and the former dean of the law faculty of Dushanbe, a co-chair of the DPT. In northern Tajikistan, which was left untouched by 1992's civil unrest and civil war, six members of the DPT, IRP, and the popular movement Rastokhez, were arrested in January. Five of these were charged with possession of bullets and pistols, but of the three who had been convicted as of November, including the chair of the Leninabad region DPT, fingerprint tests were never ordered on the weapons found.

On June 21, the Supreme Court of Tajikistan banned the DPT, IRP, the popular movement Rastokhez, and La'li Badakhshan (a Pamiri organization) for having organized the mass demonstrations in 1992 and for allegedly organizing fighters during the civil war. Freedom of expression suffered dramatically in Tajikistan after the current government came to power. In the first few weeks of December 1992, pressure on journalists stemmed from the apparent desire from armed groups associated with the Popular Front and the Kuliabi regional faction to take revenge on newspapers and journalists who had been their sharpest critics. In December, most of the latter fled Tajikistan under threat. The editorial offices of *Adolat* (Equality), the DPT newspaper, and *Charogi Ruz* (Light of Day), an independent newspaper, were ransacked; their writers and editors went into exile. Although Tajikistan government officials never officially closed the above newspapers, the harassment eliminated critical voices in the press, and during 1993 even newspapers loyal to the government were prevented from publishing material on such matters as government corruption.

The government attempted, but failed, to arrest two *Charogi Ruz* journalists. Officials of the Procuracy (the executive branch's investigative arm) searched the apartments of one opposition journalist who fled the country, confiscating all of his archives, journalistic material, and personal albums. As an extension of this harassment campaign, four Moscow-based journalists who write about Tajikistan were attacked in Moscow in the course of 1993.

Some 20,000 refugees and displaced persons returning to their homes in southern Tajikistan were beaten, harassed, and killed in 1993. Their homes had become areas where they were seen as the enemy, and where local government and police forces were led by former commanders of the Popular Front, the army that forced the refugees out in the summer and autumn of 1992.

Most of the internally displaced who returned to their homes did so on their own, with neither coercion nor aid. Toward the end of March, however, the government expelled many of the 30,000 to 40,000 refugees in Dushanbe. Government troops forced the displaced onto trains headed south for Kabodion, where local residents refused to allow them back to the villages. The displaced were then abandoned in an open area with no food, water, or electricity. Several were killed by local people. After they were reintegrated into their villages, the returnees suffered beatings for some time.

Killings and beatings of returnees decreased in June but became frequent again in several districts in southern Tajikistan after July 13, when Tajik rebels in Afghanistan attacked Russian border troops. Violence against returnees grew so severe that the U.N. High Commissioner for Refugees (UNHCR) temporarily suspended its repatriation program.

Returnees are frustrated by their inability to reclaim their property. In the Kabodion district, local officials allowed the displaced to return on condition that they sign a statement renouncing their claims to stolen property. Returnees are living in appalling conditions in mosques because their homes were either burned or are occupied.

The Right to Monitor

Helsinki Watch and Memorial attempted to visit four journalists who had reportedly been beaten in prison in Tajikistan. Despite their initial promises to help us gain access, high-level law enforcement officials deferred the decision to the case investigator, who at first refused, citing the need for secrecy during the investigation, and then "bargained" meters: Helsinki Watch and Memorial refused the investigator's final offer, which consisted of walking the journalists (shirts on) past us at a distance of five meters.

Local lawyers representing political prisoners in Dushanbe have reported receiving repeated telephone threats on their lives.

U.S. Policy

The State Department maintained almost complete silence on human rights abuses in Tajikistan during 1993. This degree of neglect was troubling in view of the grave human rights violations that continued there, and the key role played by Russia in the region. On those occasions when Tajikistan figured in the State Department's public agenda, the country's poor human rights record was not criticized.

The State Department has rarely raised concerns about human rights violations in Washington; fortunately, the U.S. Embassy in Tajikistan took seriously its human rights mandate. The ambassador has personally visited Mirbobo Mirakhimov in prison, and visited with the wife of Bozor Sobir, the imprisoned poet. The embassy staff has also attended his trial. He also regularly raises specific human rights cases in his meetings with Tajik government officials. Embassy officials have made themselves available to opposition members who suffer persecution.

Following intense rebel attacks along the Tajik-Afghan border, in July, a State Department spokesperson mentioned that the subject "was of great concern to the United States, something that we expressed our concern to Russia about." Following Ambassador Strobe Talbott's visit to Tajikistan, the State Department reported that the ambassador's delegation had had "serious discussions with President Rakhmonov on the need for political reconciliation within Tajikistan. President Rakhmonov indicated that he was willing to work with international organizations to bring peace to Tajikistan."

Tajikistan received close to $50 million in assistance in 1992 and 1993, most of it humanitarian relief. In September, Ambassador Talbott announced that the U.S. government would promise $45 million in humanitarian aid to Tajikistan, provided the latter observed international human rights norms. In July 1993, Congress signed a trade agreement with Tajikistan.

Despite Tajikistan's dismal human rights record, there was no evidence that the U.S. government had invoked the human rights provisions of the Overseas Private Investment Corporation (OPIC) mandate, which require that governments receiving this insurance for U.S. business operations respect basic human rights.

Russian Federation Policy

Tajikistan relies heavily on Russia for military, economic and other assistance. Russian officials—including President Yeltsin—consider Tajikistan's border with Afghanistan their own. During 1993 Russia provided 70 percent of Tajikistan's foreign aid and was believed to provide as much as 50 percent of Tajikistan's state budget. The Russian army assisted in the formation of the Tajik National Army, and its own 201st Motorized Division assisted in the defense of the Tajik-Afghan border and in internal security, and was implicated in humanitarian law violations, fighting on the side of the government in the civil war.

Russian policy in Tajikistan aimed to fight "Islamic fundamentalism" and to protect Russians living in Tajikistan. While the Russian-Tajik Friendship Treaty provides for an intergovernmental human rights commission, the latter had not yet been formed as of November 1993. Indeed, Russia appeared to have no publicly stated human rights agenda in Tajikistan, and Russian government officials spoke out only once against human rights violations in Tajikistan. To his credit, Foreign Minister Kozyrev, however, encouraged the Tajik government to negotiate with the Tajik rebels in Afghanistan. The Russian Supreme Soviet, in a joint effort with the Russian Ministry of Foreign Affairs, sent a delegation to Tajikistan in May to explore human rights conditions there, but had not issued a report as of November.

The Work of Helsinki Watch

Helsinki Watch devoted much time and resources to Tajikistan during 1993, seeking to have an effect both on the government of Tajikistan and on the Russian government. Beginning in December 1992, Helsinki Watch sent a series of five letters to Emomali Rakhmonov, chair of Tajikistan's Supreme Soviet, inquiring about or protesting human rights abuses. Four of the letters were released to the press.

The results of a June fact-finding mission, carried out jointly with Memorial, were released in a preliminary report at a press conference in July in Moscow. Thanks to Memorial's efforts the report was widely distributed in the Russian parliament and among the Russian Foreign Ministry's special working group on Tajikistan. A final report, *Human Rights in Tajikistan: In the Wake of the Civil War*, was scheduled for publication in December.

TURKEY

Human Rights Developments

Human rights abuses in Turkey continued at an appalling rate in 1993. Security forces continued to shoot and kill civilians in house raids and during peaceful demonstrations; brutal torture continued to be a routine and systematic interrogation technique (fifteen people died in suspicious circumstances while in police custody); hundreds of people were assassinated in southeast Turkey and the government failed to investigate their deaths; and members of the Kurdish minority in southeast Turkey were killed, tortured, detained and forced to abandon their villages and fields. Moreover, free expression continued to be sharply restricted, as were freedom of assembly and association.

The promises made by the coalition government that took office in November 1991 (made up of Suleyman Demirel's True Path Party and Erdal Inonu's Social Democratic Party) continued unfulfilled. Following the death of President Turgut Ozal in April, Parliament elected former Prime Minister Suleyman Demirel president. In June, Tansu Ciller, a member of the True Path Party, became prime minister—the first woman to hold that office. The coalition government endured; unfortunately, so did the pattern of gross violation of human rights.

In southeast Turkey, a guerrilla war started in 1984 by the Workers' Party of Kurdistan (PKK), a separatist group, escalated. Of more than 7,000 deaths that have taken place in the nine-year conflict, more than 2,000 took place in 1993. Support for the PKK in southeast Turkey appeared to grow rather than to decline.

In western Turkey, extremist groups that espouse political violence, chiefly Dev Sol (Revolutionary Path), continued to attack and kill current and former police and government officials; at least fifteen were killed in 1993.

Unfortunately, the government chose to deal with these problems by shooting and killing suspected members of extremist groups in violation of international agreements and standards. Rather than capture and try suspects, police and gendarmes (who perform police duties in rural areas) frequently raided houses or apartments believed to be used as homes or meeting places by suspects and shot and killed the occupants, announcing afterward that the suspects were killed in shoot-outs, although eyewitnesses often reported that no shots were fired by the victims. Tellingly, reports from the press and human rights groups indicate that, although many suspects died in such raids, security forces were rarely killed or injured in the same raids creating a strong presumption that the suspects were deliberately executed. Press reports show that forty-two people died in house raids during the first ten months of 1993: twenty in Istanbul, one each in Ankara and Izmir, and twenty in southeast Turkey. In these killings, police effectively acted as investigators, judges, juries and executioners.

Contrary to international agreements and standards, Turkish security forces continued to use deadly force against demonstrators in 1993. On August 15, police or gendarmes shot nineteen demonstrators dead during demonstrations in southeast Turkey celebrating the ninth anniversary of the start of the guerrilla war. Ten demonstrators were killed in Kars, six in Agri, and three in Malazgirt. One police special-team member was also killed.

Cruel torture of suspects of both ordinary and political crimes continued as a routine part of their interrogation by police and gendarmes, in violation of international standards and agreements. Eighteen people died in suspicious circumstances while in police custody through the end of October. Two deaths took place in Istanbul, one in Ankara, one in Gaziantep, and the rest in southeast Turkey. Officials explained the deaths variously as suicides or the results of heart attack or illness.

An appalling pattern persisted in southeast Turkey, in which civilians were killed in death squad fashion—frequently with one bullet to the back of the head. In almost no case did the government make serious efforts to investigate and to bring the killers to justice. Among those executed in this way were a Kurdish Member of Parliament; four journalists and two newspaper sellers, all connected to pro-Kurdish, left-wing journals; two human rights leaders; several members of the Democratic Party and its forerunner, the People's Labor Party; doctors, lawyers and other community leaders, as well as shepherds and villagers. The Turkish government was unresponsive to protests and pleas to investigate from Helsinki Watch and other human rights organizations. It was widely believed in Turkey that a counter-guerrilla organization tied to security forces had carried out the killings. Several of the murdered journalists had written articles describing a purported relationship between security forces and the alleged counter-guerrilla force.

As in previous years, Turkish authorities pressured villagers in the southeast to act as village guards prepared to fight against the PKK. When they refused, security forces often ordered their villages evacuated. More than 400 villages have reportedly been forcibly evacuated since January 1992. During 1993, many villages were bombed, houses deliberately incinerated, and livestock destroyed. Security forces' treatment of Kurdish villagers was often savage. In some instances, villagers were forced to gather in the village square, to lie on the ground and be beaten for hours by security forces. Many Kurds allegedly uninvolved with the PKK were detained, interrogated, tortured, and imprisoned.

For its part, the PKK violated the laws of war by increasingly targeting civilians.

Many were killed, others kidnapped, beaten and released. The PKK captured foreign tourists, detained them for days or weeks and then released them unharmed, in an attempt to focus international attention on southeast Turkey. In October, alleging false and incomplete reporting from the area, the PKK banned national and foreign journalists on threat of death.

Free expression continued to be sharply restricted by the government. While mainstream newspapers were largely untouched, left-wing and/or pro-Kurdish journals suffered harassment, raids, confiscations and trials. The newspaper *Ozgur Gundem* was particularly hard hit. Six of its journalists and five distributors were killed between June 1992 and July 1993. In addition, thirty-nine of its first 228 issues were confiscated by a state security court and proceedings begun to ban its publication. Charges against *Ozgur Gundem* included "separatist propaganda," "portraying Turkish citizens as Kurds," "using the words 'Kurd' and 'Kurdistan' in a way that breaches the Constitution in which Turkey is defined as a unitary state." Other journals suffered similar treatment.

At least seven journalists were tried, convicted, and sentenced to prison terms of from five to ten months. Moreover, in the course of the year, many newspaper offices were raided, journalists beaten, and dozens of journalists detained and interrogated.

Similar forms of intimidation restricted speech. Publishers and writers were charged and tried for their writings, speakers for their speeches, activists for hanging posters or distributing leaflets. One writer, Edip Polat, was sentenced in June to two years in prison. Frequent charges were: insulting Ataturk, or the president, or the armed forces, or holding symposiums on the Kurdish question. Many meetings and marches were banned, and demonstrators frequently beaten, interrogated and detained.

The Right to Monitor

The Human Rights Association (HRA), a large membership organization with forty branches throughout Turkey, continued to monitor human rights. The Human Rights Foundation, an independent group set up by the HRA, maintained a documentation center with detailed information on cases of abuse. Both operated legally.

Two HRA officials and one member were assassinated in 1993: Metin Can, the president of the Elazig HRA branch, was murdered with HRA member Dr. Hasan Kaya in February; a founding member of the Urfa branch, Kemal Kilic, a journalist, was also assassinated in February. No one had been charged with their deaths as of November.

HRA branches were harassed and raided, their documents seized and their members detained, tortured, and charged with various political offenses. The Istanbul branch was raided in January. In September, the Public Prosecutor took the Istanbul HRA to court and asked that it be closed down because of a panel discussion in December 1992 in which the Kurdish question was discussed. The trial began in October.

Several branches were closed: Elazig (one week), Mersin (first for fifteen days and then indefinitely), and Adana (re-opened in January after two months' closing). The Usak branch was investigated, its monthly bulletin said to contain writing based on racial and regional factors, provoking people to commit crimes. The monthly bulletin of the national HRA was seized because of an article on Kurds written by Ismail Besikci, a Turkish sociologist who has spent more than ten years in prison for his writings on Kurds.

Detained, tortured or threatened with death were HRA officers and members Husnu Undal, Mehmet Gokalp, Hafiz Uzun, Yavuz Binbay, Osman Ozcelik, Gulseren Baysungur, and Haci Oguz. Ercan Kanar, the Istanbul branch president, was tried for insulting the state when he said in a speech, "the state is not only a terrorist but also immoral." Four HRA members were among 126 people tried for making an application to the United Nations regarding human rights abuses.

In addition, meetings were banned, HRA members who wanted to meet with prisoners were themselves detained, and members were tried for distributing leaflets and for collecting signatures for a petition to end rape during war.

Human rights groups from outside Turkey have conducted fact-finding missions without difficulty.

U.S. Policy

Turkey continued to be an important U.S. ally; in 1993 it was the third-largest recipient of U.S. aid. In fiscal year 1993, Turkey received $450 million in military aid in the form of loans and $3.1 million in military grants, as well as "excess military equipment," including Cobra Helicopters and A-10 aircraft. It also received $125 million in economic grants.

The Clinton administration sent mixed signals on human rights abuses in Turkey. Speaking during Turkish Prime Minister Tansu Ciller's visit to Washington in October, President Clinton stated: "Like our own nation, Turkey is a shining example to the world of the virtues of cultural diversity," thus completely ignoring the Turkish abuses of the Kurdish minority.

On the other hand, meeting with Turkish leaders in Ankara in June, Secretary of State Warren Christopher reportedly asked them to cooperate with a detailed United States proposal to help end widespread human rights abuses in Turkey and indicated that the U.S. would reward "better behavior" by Turkey with economic cooperation and favors. Unfortunately, at the same time, the U.S. announced that it would provide Turkey with $336 million in aircraft and other military equipment.

The U.S. Department of State developed a new human rights strategy for Turkey, hoping to engage the Ciller government in a discussion of positive actions that would measurably improve the protection of human rights in Turkey. The three areas of concentration were torture, extrajudicial killings and freedom of expression.

Concerning torture, the U.S. has asked Turkey to work toward the elimination of torture, incommunicado detention, and arbitrary arrest by implementing the Criminal Trials Procedure Law (CMUK) and extending its jurisdiction throughout Turkey and to crimes in the jurisdiction of state security courts; establishing mechanisms for government oversight of police and gendarmes; human rights training for police; and prosecution of officials responsible for abuses. Helsinki Watch opposed implementation of the CMUK; although some useful provisions were included in the law, it provided for very long detention periods (eight days for non-political suspects; as much as thirty days for political suspects) in violation of international law and standards.

Regarding freedom of expression, the U.S. has recommended a dialogue with opinion makers representing many groups; the right to free speech, including the use of the Kurdish language; and protection of freedom of the press. No specifics were given in the plan released to the public. Helsinki Watch believed that Turkey should be pressed to investigate promptly, thoroughly and impartially the murders of the sixteen journalists assassinated since February 1992; and to release from detention or prison all those imprisoned for the peaceful expression of their views.

As to the U.S. objective of eliminating disappearances, extrajudicial killings, and excessive use of force by government forces, the State Department did not publicly release specific recommendations.

Turkey's dreadful abuse of its Kurdish minority—detention, torture, killings, forcible evacuations, bombing and shooting of civilians—was not addressed in the U.S. proposals.

The U.S. continued to provide anti-terrorism training to Turkish police. In 1992, Helsinki Watch representatives saw displayed on the wall of a police official's office a State Department certificate stating that he had been trained in the U.S. That official was in charge of a division of the police in which political suspects were routinely and systematically tortured. Helsinki Watch met with congressional staff members in an ef-

fort to persuade them to work toward ending such training; the policy was not altered, however. The State Department reported that it had established unspecified benchmarks to be used in future anti-terrorism assistance programs. Helsinki Watch strongly opposed U.S. training of Turkish police. In our experience, human rights training is useless unless the political will exists to order torture stopped. Moreover, when the U.S. provides training to police who continue to torture detainees, the U.S. is implicated in such torture.

U.S. efforts to increase the dialogue with Turkey on human rights abuses during 1993 were commendable; Helsinki Watch will monitor these efforts to see if they are fruitful.

The Work of Helsinki Watch

Helsinki Watch continued in 1993 to attempt to improve human rights in Turkey by focusing national and international attention on Turkey's dreadful human rights record and by urging the U.S. government to pressure the Turkish government to end human rights abuses. Helsinki Watch sent a mission to Turkey in June 1993 in cooperation with the HRW Women's Rights Project; the purpose was to investigate the government's use of "virginity controls" (examinations) to control and punish women. A report was planned for release in early 1994.

In March, Helsinki Watch issued a major report, *The Kurds of Turkey: Killings, Disappearances and Torture*, which described the government's abysmal abuse of the Kurdish minority. A comprehensive newsletter issued in August, "Free Expression in Turkey, 1993: Killings, Convictions, Confiscations," described in detail abuses of freedom of the press, publishing, speech and the arts. Four other newsletters were released denouncing deaths in detention and execution-style killings by unknowns.

TURKMENISTAN

Human Rights Developments

Patterns of abuse similar to those of the former communist regime and leveled at individuals critical of the government continued unabated in Turkmenistan during 1993. With its wealth of natural resources and small population, Turkmenistan was poised to become one of the wealthiest of the former Soviet republics. It boasted of stability to foreign investors when, in fact, such stability was maintained by a one-party system that restricted and punished critical voices in the media and alternative political circles with impunity.

The number of individuals openly critical of the government had dwindled from thousands in the late 1980s to several dozen in 1993, in large part due to persecution by law enforcement authorities. During the year government officials detained and interrogated dissenters, frequently without bringing charges; denied them the right to travel abroad; dismissed them, their relatives and associates from their places of work; stripped them of union membership; and maintained surveillance of them and their families.

Helsinki Watch was aware of one likely prisoner of conscience in Turkmenistan: Karadzha Karadzhaev, an accountant who had supported publication of an independent magazine, *Daianch*. He was arrested on August 12, reportedly on charges of embezzlement and slander. He remained incarcerated as of November although the charges against him did not warrant physical restraint, and he had not been afforded legal counsel of his choice, in violation of his rights under international law.

The ruling Democratic Party (formerly the Communist Party) was the only legal party in Turkmenistan. The government had consistently denied applications for registration submitted by the popular movement Agzybirlik (Unity), for example, a group that had been highly critical of President Saparmurad Niyazov, and had hounded its members. A provision in the 1992 constitution banned ethnically and religiously based political parties, a clause that was invoked arbitrarily in some cases.

The Turkmenistan government detained dissidents during 1993 to prevent them from meeting with visiting foreign dignitaries. On April 20, several individuals who were thought to be on their way to a meeting with representatives of the Conference on Security and Cooperation in Europe (CSCE) were rounded up by local law enforcement officials, interrogated and held without charges until the delegation left. The harassment was repeated on August 18 in connection with a scheduled meeting with U.S. Cong. Robert Torricelli (D-NJ): seven were detained for questioning before and after a meeting with the congressman at the home of a U.S. Embassy staff member.

Turkmenistan's four million residents were denied free access to information because of heavy censorship. Newspapers and television and radio stations tended to run virtually identical stories, consisting almost exclusively of government statements; the stories expressed a uniformly positive attitude toward the state. Local correspondents for Radio Liberty, the U.S.-sponsored radio station that frequently broadcast critical opinions, reported being harassed and prevented from leaving the country. President Niyazov publicly stated in September that censorship would not be lifted.

The Right to Monitor

Although several individuals were active in human rights monitoring and at least one was affiliated with the Central Asian Human Rights Society, which is based abroad, there continued to be no formal independent human rights groups in Turkmenistan.

There was a slight improvement in the ability of foreigners to monitor human rights in Turkmenistan as compared with conditions in October 1992 when the government deported two representatives of Amnesty International, using improperly processed visas as an excuse. By contrast, Helsinki Watch representatives who visited in April 1993 were hosted officially by the

Turkmenistan Ministry of Foreign Affairs, which largely kept its promise that no one with whom the delegation met would be harassed. However, during the Helsinki Watch visit, several of the individuals with whom we met were followed, and at least one reported having his telephone line cut during the period of our stay, preventing him from making contact with us. When a delegation from the CSCE, which is responsible for maintaining compliance with the human rights provisions of the CSCE documents, visited Turkmenistan in April, several local dissidents were detained by law enforcement officials and prevented from attending the scheduled meeting.

U.S. Policy

The State Department repeatedly protested human rights abuses in Turkmenistan. It issued numerous written protests, and reportedly raised human rights concerns at meetings with President Niyazov. Ambassador Joseph S. Hulings III reportedly advised top U.S. officials not to meet with President Niyazov, citing human rights grounds. In one particularly strong statement, Ambassador at Large Strobe Talbott declared in September that Washington would not provide economic aid if Turkmenistan did not enact democratic reforms. In at least one case (when the Turkmenistan government was proposing an educational exchange that discriminated on the basis of gender), protests from the U.S. side reversed the Turkmenistan government's practices.

The Clinton administration became particularly engaged in protesting violations when incidents affected U.S. diplomats. In the wake of Congressman Torricelli's ill-fated August visit to Turkmenistan, Ambassador Talbott refused to sign a bilateral assistance treaty, to signify U.S. protest of the treatment of those detained in connection with Congressman Torricelli's visit. The gesture was more ceremonial than real, however, because the treaty—which provided a certain amount of protection for American organizations operating in Turkmenistan— had no monetary value.

The force of verbal protests was undermined, moreover, by the administration's lack of will to condition economic development aid on an improved human rights record. There was no evidence, for example, that the U.S. government had invoked the human rights provisions of the Overseas Private Investment Corporation (OPIC) agreement, signed in 1992, despite Turkmenistan's failure to comply with those provisions. In addition, on March 23 the U.S. signed a trade agreement preliminary to ratification of Most Favored Nation (MFN) status, but State Department officials later expressed to Helsinki Watch serious ambivalence about MFN on human rights grounds.

The U.S. government's reprimands, although necessary, did not in themselves carry sufficient weight to prevent Turkmenistan law enforcement officials from harassing dissidents with impunity. The Turkmenistan government's blatant disregard for the U.S. government's censure of its human rights practices called for stronger action from the U.S.

The Work of Helsinki Watch

Helsinki Watch sent its first fact-finding mission to Turkmenistan in April 1993 to learn about the government's human rights policies and to make personal contact with government officials and victims of human rights abuses. Subsequently, Helsinki Watch launched a campaign to criticize publicly violations of civil and political rights, issuing an article and a comprehensive report on human rights abuses.

Helsinki Watch also wrote to President Niyazov protesting the detention of the individuals who were invited to meet with Congressman Torricelli in August, and inquiring about the progress of investigations into the suspicious deaths of two leading opposition figures in 1991. In October Helsinki Watch raised concerns in a letter to the procurator general about the probably illegal imprisonment of dissident Karaja Karajaev and the continuing denial of his access to legal counsel in detention.

UNITED KINGDOM

Human Rights Developments

The United Kingdom continued to receive little attention from the international human rights community in 1993. However, emergency legislation continued to suspend basic guarantees of due process in Northern Ireland; freedom of expression was still restricted throughout the U.K.; and conditions in many British prisons violated international standards.

As of November 1993, more than 3,000 people had been killed in political violence in Northern Ireland since 1969. A state of emergency significantly restricting human rights had been in effect in the province since 1922, more than seventy years. Emergency laws continued to give security forces—the Royal Ulster Constabulary (RUC, the Northern Ireland police force) and the British army—broad powers to stop people on the street, to question and search them, to search their homes, to detain them for as long as seven days without charges, and to exclude people from Northern Ireland or Great Britain.

The right to a fair trial was restricted in Northern Ireland. Jury trials were denied for offenses connected with political violence, the right to silence had been sharply curtailed, and evidentiary rules permitted the admission of confessions that might have been obtained by abusive treatment in detention. Moreover, lawyers representing political suspects continued to be harassed and intimidated in 1993.

In a positive development, three detectives and a retired senior officer were charged in 1993 with perjury and intending to pervert justice in the case of the UDR Four. The UDR Four were members of the Ulster Defense Regiment, a unit of the British army stationed in Northern Ireland; three were released in 1992, after six years in prison, when an appeals court held that police officers had lied at their trial in 1986.

In some troubled areas, the RUC abandoned normal policing. As a result, paramilitaries on both sides created alternative informal criminal justice systems in which suspects of ordinary crimes—both children and adults—could be informally tried and punished without due process. Punishments ranged in 1993 from warnings to brutal beatings, shootings and banishments.

Ill-treatment of detainees during interrogation continued. During 1993, adults and children under eighteen were psychologically abused, tricked and threatened. Following pressure from local and international human rights groups and criticism from the U.N. Subcommission on the Prevention of Discrimination, physical abuse in detention was markedly reduced.

In December 1992, an independent commissioner was appointed for the holding (detention) centers in Northern Ireland. Whether his appointment would significantly decrease abuses remained to be seen even late in 1993. The government had still not agreed to proposals by Helsinki Watch and other groups that interrogations be video- and audio-taped. Detainees could still be interrogated for up to forty-eight hours without the right to consult a solicitor. Moreover, political suspects could be detained for up to seven days. The U.K. had derogated from the provision of the European Convention on Human Rights that requires that a detainee be brought promptly before a judge. In May 1993, the UK's derogation was upheld by the European Court of Human Rights.

In a significant development, for the first time since 1969, no cases were reported in 1993 in which security forces killed people in disputed circumstances. Paramilitary groups, however, both Protestant and Catholic, continued to kill alleged opponents. Seventy-two people were killed through October 30 in connection with the troubles, thirty by the IRA (including twelve current or former members of the police or the army) and forty-two by the UFF (Ulster Freedom Fighters) or the UVF (Ulster Volunteer Force). In addition, two men were killed by paramilitaries as informers—one by loyalists, one by republicans. Killings by paramilitaries violated not only domestic criminal laws but also, in the case of civilians, the principles underlying international humanitarian law, or the laws of war. In addition to the killings, many were injured, police stations were attacked with rockets and mortars, and bombs were set off, causing both injuries and property damage estimated at millions of pounds.

In a positive development, one paratrooper was convicted of murder in the 1990 shooting of teenage joy-rider Karen Reilly and received a life sentence. A second paratrooper was sentenced to seven years in the same case.

Murder charges were also brought in three additional cases. Two Royal Marines were charged with murder for the December 1990 killing of twenty-year-old Fergal Caraher; a trial was set for November 1993. An RUC officer was charged with murder in the killing of nineteen-year-old student Kevin McGovern in Cookstown in September 1991. Finally, two soldiers were charged with murder in the shooting death of Peter McBride in September 1992.

Questions continued to be raised about the investigation of killings by security forces, and decisions as to whether to prosecute were still shrouded in secrecy. The Independent Commission for Police Complaints remained ineffective; in five years, not one of the hundreds of complaints filed with the ICPC had been substantiated by that organization.

Security forces continued to use plastic bullets for crowd control. A west Belfast man was wounded by a plastic bullet in June, and four others were hit by plastic bullets in July.

Street harassment of children and adults by security forces continued. Children under eighteen and adults were stopped on the street, hit, kicked, insulted, abused and threatened by security forces. In house searches, police continued to harass people and damage their homes; the Northern Ireland Office (the office delegated by the British government to run Northern Ireland) reported that 2.8 million pounds was paid out in 1992 and 1993 in compensation for damage caused by searches or patrols.

In the United Kingdom as a whole, serious curbs on free expression continued, made possible in part by the lack of written protection for individual liberties; the U.K. has no Bill of Rights. A wide range of government activities were screened from public view, primarily by operation of the Official Secrets Act, which criminalizes disclosure of broad categories of foreign policy, defense and military information. Suppression of information under this act was aggravated by the government's failure to adopt freedom of information legislation. During 1993, the British still did not enjoy an affirmative right of peaceful assembly, and the Public Order Act of 1986 afforded police extensive power to restrict or ban public demonstrations, marches and assemblies; in prior years, it had been used to prosecute anti-apartheid demonstrators and organizers of peaceful protests.

Regulatory bodies routinely interfered with the content of radio and television broadcasts, and the government ban on broadcast interviews with the Irish Republican Army (IRA), Sinn Fein and proscribed loyalist groups continued in Northern Ireland. The pro-plaintiff nature of British libel law—it requires the defendant to prove the truth of the allegedly defamatory statements—has a great chilling effect on journalists and writers, who, as in previous years, engaged in self-censorship out of the fear of a libel prosecution.

The United Kingdom had one of the highest prisoner-to-population ratios in Europe. Although the government made notable progress in improving prison conditions during 1992 and 1993, prisons remained overcrowded. The installation of in-cell plumbing continued during the year, with observers estimating that most prisoners would have access to in-cell sanitation by the end of 1994. The government also made significant progress in improving "problem" prisons, such as Wandsworth and Brixton.

The Right to Monitor

There was no evidence to indicate that human rights monitors were harassed by government officials in the U.K. Local and international groups monitored human rights openly and regularly.

U.S. Policy

There were no indications that the Clinton administration had tried publicly to persuade the U.K. to improve human rights conditions. U.S. policy toward Britain appeared unchanged from that of the Reagan and Bush administrations. The Clinton administration did not publicly criticize the U.K. for abuse of detainees during interrogations, for the suspension of due process in trials and other inadequacies in the criminal justice system, for in-house investigations of complaints against security personnel (all in Northern Ireland), or for restrictions on free expression and inhumane prison conditions throughout the U.K.

In April 1992, candidate Bill Clinton criticized human rights violations in Northern Ireland (citing the work of Helsinki Watch) and proposed that the U.S. send a "peace envoy" (mission unspecified) to Northern Ireland, but President Bill Clinton did not act on this proposal.

The administration's stated policy on Northern Ireland was support of peace and reconciliation between Ireland and Britain; opposition to terrorism from all quarters; careful review of accusations of human rights violations and urging all parties to respect human rights; and support for the International Fund for Ireland, which aimed to promote reconciliation in Ireland and Northern Ireland through economic and social development.

In 1993 the State Department again denied a visa to Gerry Adams, the president of Sinn Fein, a legal political party affiliated with the Irish Republican Army.

The U.S. contributed $20 million in fiscal year 1993 to the International Fund for Ireland.

The Work of Helsinki Watch

Helsinki Watch continued to monitor human rights developments in the U.K. during 1993. In February, Helsinki Watch and the HRW Prison Project sent a mission to the U.K. to follow-up the prison report issued in June 1992. In March, Helsinki Watch and the Fund for Free Expression issued an update on free expression in the U.K. In May, Helsinki Watch issued a newsletter reporting on human rights developments in Northern Ireland during 1992. Helsinki Watch's work in the U.K. involved the monitoring of human rights abuses, the publicizing of such abuses in the U.S., the U.K. and Europe, and at international fora, and work with other human rights groups toward effecting change.

UZBEKISTAN

Human Rights Developments

The Uzbekistan government's campaign to disband opposition groups and silence dissidents, launched intensively in the second half of 1992, continued in 1993, and was played out largely in the courtroom. Although the constitution adopted on December 8, 1992, enshrined many fundamental human rights and should have strengthened guarantees of protection in 1993, freedom of speech and religion and the right to form organizations continued to be violated. Uzbekistan's post-independence government continued to be run by largely unreformed Communist Party cadres who retained the previous era's *de facto* one-party rule and intolerance for dissent.

The government increasingly used legal mechanisms to silence dissent: by prosecuting leading members of the political opposition and religious groups and issuing ordinances closing organizations and political parties, it chilled free expression and association and put individuals who peacefully expressed criticism at risk of incarceration. At least eight prisoners of conscience remained in jail, and two more were believed to be in custody. Ten individuals, all of whom had publicly criticized the government of President Islam Karimov, were prosecuted and convicted in 1993 for criminal offenses, ranging from violating the "honor and dignity" of the president to illegal possession of narcotics. Approximately ten other criminal charges against dissidents were under investigation; others were suspended because the suspects were in hiding.

In all cases, the defendants were given prison sentences; all but one case ended in immediate release (in August, Pulatjon Okhunov, a teacher and local opposition movement leader, was sentenced to three years in a prison labor camp on narcotics and assault charges, which were likely to have been fabricated). In this way, the Uzbekistan government appeared to be showing "clemency" and avoided the stigma of holding many political prisoners. Such trials were merely another form of the repression of free speech practiced by the government under the guise of protecting law and order.

The opposition Democratic Party Erk (Will/Freedom) and Birlik (Unity) Popular Movement were the only political organizations legally registered to function in Uzbekistan except for the ruling Democratic Party (formerly the Communist Party). However, on January 19 the Supreme Court of Uzbekistan ordered Birlik closed for three months, and the headquarters of the Erk Democratic Party was sealed and party property confiscated in 1992.

In religious as in political activities, freedom of association was repressed. Although the right to freedom of conscience was enshrined in Uzbekistan's new constitution, and individual expression of religion was increasingly evident in daily life, the government continued to repress groups that attempted to organize on the basis of Islam, citing a 1992 ordinance. The government banned the Uzbekistan chapter of the Islamic Renaissance Party, and reportedly arrested its leader, Abdulla Utaev, in the last few days of 1992.

The government also banned Adolat (Justice), an Islamic group based in Namangan. In addition, it became known during 1993 that Adolat leader Khakim Satimov had been convicted the previous year of two criminal charges, which were believed to have been fabricated. Five individuals from Namangan reportedly were arrested near the Afghanistan border in what they claimed was an attempt to study in an institution of higher education in Afghanistan and make a pilgrimage to Mecca, Saudi Arabia; the government tried to prove a link between the defendants and Adolat, a connection the defendants and the head of Adolat reportedly denied. They were convicted on September 22 and sentenced to between ten and fifteen years of imprisonment on charges of betrayal of the motherland and illegally leaving the country; two were convicted on additional charges. The property of all defendants was reportedly confiscated. At least one of them, Khusnutdin Kubutdinov, reportedly claimed during his trial that he had been beaten in detention to extract a confession.

Article 54 of the new Uzbekistan criminal code, under which the men were sentenced, punishes both leaving the country "illegally" and failure to return, and carries a maximum sentence of death. Helsinki Watch denounced the arrests both for violating the right to freedom of movement and because charges were brought in a discriminatory manner.

There were no independent media for the twenty million residents of Uzbekistan. Newspapers published outside the country, including major papers from Russia containing articles criticizing Uzbekistan's repressive government, sometimes appeared in Uzbekistan with sections whited-out or with "offensive" articles replaced by advertisements.

Acts of violence against dissidents, already an established pattern, also persisted in 1993, including beatings and car bombs. On May 5, the co-chair of the Birlik Popular Movement, Shukhrat Ismatullaev, was beaten on the street by unidentified assailants and spent six weeks in the intensive care unit in Tashkent suffering from head injuries. That attack mirrored almost exactly the attack on his counterpart in Birlik, co-chair Abdurakhim Pulatov, in June of 1992. On October 4, Samad Murad was beaten in Karshi within days of his election as Erk's general secretary. No suspects had been apprehended in any of these cases as of early November 1993.

Tashkent police confirmed that on August 24 an explosive device destroyed the car used by Shukhrullo Mirsaidov, the former vice-president of Uzbekistan, who resigned in September 1992 after warning in an open letter that "democracy and a policy of openness are being replaced by an authoritarian regime." Mr. Mirsaidov and Shukhrat Ismatullaev were walking toward the car when it exploded, and narrowly escaped death. Several weeks later, on September 18, Mr. Mirsaidov and his son were beaten on the street; the elder Mirsaidov reportedly suffered multiple head injuries, a broken rib and several broken teeth. He claimed he was beaten by members of special security forces who had been following him for several days before his beating.

The Right To Monitor

Uzbekistan became the first of the Conference on Security and Cooperation in Europe (CSCE) signatory countries to refuse to issue visas to Helsinki Watch representatives since the Soviet Union lifted its ban on our observers in 1987. Despite verbal agreement by the Uzbekistan Ministry of Foreign Affairs, the ministry rescinded the promised visa support in April once Helsinki Watch representatives arrived in Moscow en route to Uzbekistan. Despite repeated requests, Helsinki Watch received no explanation for the denial.

Uzbekistan law enforcement authorities harassed, interrogated and expelled from the country numerous other foreign human rights observers, as well as several foreign defense attorneys and journalists. On February 22, security officials interrogated Helsinki Watch associate Alexander Petrov and Aleksei Tavrizov, a member of Memorial, the Moscow-based independent human rights organization, for ten hours following the two men's attempt to observe the trial of poet and Birlik activist Vasila Inoiatova, then forcibly escorted them to the airplane back to Moscow.

The fledgling independent human rights movement in Uzbekistan was severely restricted during 1992, and during 1993 functioned within very narrow limits. With few exceptions, all members of the Human Rights Society of Uzbekistan, formed in 1991, were also members of banned opposition movements or parties; thus it was not possible to determine whether they were persecuted—placed under surveillance, arrested, and prevented from leaving the country—because of their human rights activities or their political affiliations.

U.S. Policy

The Clinton administration was firm and consistent in public statements about human rights in Uzbekistan. But the U.S. government did not use its economic leverage by imposing the human rights conditions of the Overseas Private Investment Corporation (OPIC) agreement on Uzbekistan. Late in the year, the U.S. government was negotiating the trade agreement preliminary to granting Most Favored Nation status, which the State Department indicated it expected to grant to Uzbekistan.

The U.S. Embassy in Tashkent issued written protests on numerous occasions to express its displeasure with human rights abuses, such as several beatings and violations of free speech. The political officer at the embassy responsible for human rights concerns fulfilled her monitoring duties energetically, frequently attending trials in which due process was in jeopardy. When an Uzbek national working for the embassy was attacked on May 25, the State Department acted quickly and decisively, cutting short the visit of an Uzbekistan delegation on tour in the U.S. and threatening to consider freezing bilateral programs with Uzbekistan. The detention of at least one individual in connection with the visit of Ambassador Talbott on September 13 provoked both a formal protest from the embassy and a particularly strong statement by Ambassador Talbott that Washington would not provide economic aid if there were no democratic reforms in the country.

The U.S. Information Agency (USIA), however, sponsored a visit to the United States in March by the rector of Tashkent State University, who had been responsible for the dismissals of members of his faculty who had criticized the government. By sponsoring the visit, the USIA implicitly condoned abuses committed under his leadership.

As violations of human rights increased during the year, U.S. diplomatic and embassy staff increasingly became involved in incidents of harassment. Diplomats were removed from courtrooms; Uzbekistan nationals invited to meet with U.S. dignitaries were detained; and embassy workers were beaten before the eyes of U.S. diplomats. Despite this alarming increase in violations, there was no indication that the U.S. government used available economic leverage, such as the human rights language of the Overseas Private Investment Corporation (OPIC) agreement, which conditioned non-humanitarian aid on an improvement in Uzbekistan's human rights record. Late in the year, the U.S. government was negotiating the trade agreement preliminary to granting Most Favored Nation status, which the State Department indicated it expected to grant to Uzbekistan.

The Work of Helsinki Watch

Helsinki Watch responded to the escalation of human rights abuses in Uzbekistan by issuing frequent protests; by attempting to engage the Uzbekistan government in dialogue about its human rights record; by monitoring trials where due process rights appeared to be in jeopardy; and by increasing public awareness, especially within the business sector, of the nature and scope of these violations.

Helsinki Watch issued six letters and telegrams to President Karimov to protest trials in which defendants were denied their right to due process—most frequently, their right to consult legal counsel of their choice or their right to an open trial—or where criminal charges were brought to silence free speech. Helsinki Watch also spoke out against the beatings of dissidents Shukhrat Ismatullaev, Shukhrullo Mirsaidov and Samad Murad, and sent numerous appeals for the release of prisoners of conscience. Other letters by Helsinki Watch addressed the right to monitor: Helsinki Watch vehemently condemned the harassment and expulsion of its staff member from Uzbekistan, and in other letters attempted to clarify why requests to enter the country by Helsinki Watch representatives had been denied.

Despite obstacles, a Helsinki Watch representative attended two trials in the capital city of Tashkent: those of the poet and Birlik activist Vasila Inoiatova, and of members of the alternative political forum Milli Majlis (National Congregation).

In April, Helsinki Watch issued a newsletter documenting politically motivated dismissals from the workplace in Uzbekistan, primarily from institutions of higher learning. Numerous activist organizations responded to the newsletter by issuing their own protests. In May, Helsinki Watch published a comprehensive report on violations of civil and political rights in Uzbekistan. The documentation presented in the report, which was widely disseminated among international business and investment concerns, painted a disturbing picture of superficial stability masking profound domestic unrest. Helsinki Watch has urged the business and foreign aid communities to use the promise of increased economic investment to encourage an improvement in Uzbekistan's human rights record.

YUGOSLAVIA

Human Rights Development

Restrictions on freedom of the press, association and speech, abuses against minorities, increasing violence by police forces and paramilitary groups and continuing repression in Kosovo were causes for concern in Yugoslavia in 1993.

Police harassment and repression of organizations representing ethnic and political minorities intensified during the year. In February and March, police twice arrested the leader of Arkadia, a Belgrade-based gay and lesbian organization, demanding that he disclose the names of the groups' members. Muslims who tried to organize the Muslim community in Belgrade were arrested and beaten by the police in April. During a June 1 demonstration in Belgrade, police used excessive force against demonstrators. Members of the crowd were severely beaten with truncheons, and at least two police officers and five civilians suffered from gunshot wounds; one of the police officers later died. Opposition leaders Vuk and Danica Draskovic were arrested and severely beaten while in police custody; both were hospitalized in serious condition. In September, Dusan Reljic, the foreign affairs editor for the independent weekly *Vreme*, was abducted by two unknown persons and taken to an unknown location, where he was interrogated for two days about his contacts with foreigners. Reljic claims that the counter-intelligence service of the Yugoslav Army was responsible for his abduction, which appeared aimed at intimidating independent journalists.

Serbian paramilitary groups, with the apparent blessing of local, provincial and republican governments, continued to terrorize and forcibly to displace Croats, Hungarians, Slovaks and others in Vojvodina and Muslims in Sandzak. Although the government of former Yugoslav Prime Minister Milan Panic had arrested and indicted local government leaders responsible for inciting violence against non-Serbs in the village of Hrtkovci in mid-1992, such leaders were released almost immediately after Panic lost the December 1992 election for Serbian President to incumbent Slobodan Milosevic, and the terrorizing of non-Serbians resumed. Similarly, Muslims living in villages near the towns of Priboj in Montenegro and Plevlja in Serbia have been killed, shot at, harassed and terrorized by Serbian paramilitary groups and members of the Yugoslav Army. Muslims have been kidnapped or arrested in northern Montenegro and taken to Serbian-held areas of Bosnia, where they have been either disappeared or detained.

In early 1993, the Serbian parliament passed a law which called for the reorganization the Pristina-based Rilindja publishing house and its placement under Serbian government control. Workers at the publishing house were threatened with dismissal if they did not sign loyalty oaths to the new management. Police violence against Albanian civilians in Kosovo escalated in the summer and fall of 1993. Albanians who had formerly been members of the Yugoslav Army, Albanian political leaders and human rights activists and others who had met with foreign delegations were brutalized by the police and abused in detention. The police and paramilitary forces terrorized and raided Albanian villages, particularly along the border of Kosovo and Serbia proper.

The Right to Monitor

The Yugoslav government severely obstructed international observers from monitoring human rights developments in Kosovo, Sandzak and Vojvodina. The Conference on Security and Cooperation in Europe (CSCE) was forced to close its mission in Yugoslavia, and members of the mission were denied visas. The Special Rapporteur for the U.N. Human Rights Commission was refused permission to open an office in Yugoslavia. Amnesty International representatives were denied visas to visit the country. Helsinki Watch representatives were threatened with arrest by local government officials in the village of Hrtkovci in Vojvodina and were denied access to areas of Sandzak by the Serbian police.

Several domestic groups continued to monitor human rights in Yugoslavia throughout 1993. The Belgrade-based Humanitarian Law Fund investigated Serbian-perpetrated violations of humanitarian law in Bosnia and the rights of minorities in Vojvodina, Sandzak, Kosovo and

Montenegro. The Belgrade-based Center for Anti-War Action and leaders of some opposition political parties also lobbied on behalf of human rights. The Council for the Defense of Human Rights and Freedoms in Kosovo and Albanian political parties, Muslim groups in Sandzak and Croatian and Hungarian groups in Vojvodina also documented abuses committed against their ethnic groups.

The Role of the International Community

United Nations

Amplifying sanctions it had imposed in May 1992, the U.N. Security Council approved new sanctions against Yugoslavia on April 17 as punishment for its continued support of Bosnian Serb forces. Despite the imposition of further sanctions, Greece, Macedonia, Bulgaria and Romania continued to violate the U.N. sanctions, but the latter two quickly responded to international criticism and took steps to curb violations. In early February, there were reports in the London press that Russia had concluded a covert $360 million arms deal with Serbia, in direct violation of the U.N.-imposed arms embargo against the former Yugoslav republics. Apparently to avoid incriminating the Yugoslav government, the signatures on the final agreement were those of Serbian leaders from the Krajina region of Croatia.

Despite the U.N.-imposed flight ban over Bosnia, in mid-March light aircraft carried out bombing raids against Muslim villages in Bosnia and then flew back toward Serbia.

Several nonaligned countries voiced a demand that reparations be extracted from Serbia for the death and destruction caused during the war in the former Yugoslavia.

After the Bosnian Serbs rejected the Vance-Owen peace plan on May 6, Serbian President Milosevic promised to cut off all supplies to Bosnia and declared that Yugoslavia would accept international monitors along its borders to ensure that nothing but humanitarian aid passed between the Bosnian and Yugoslav border. However, on May 25, Milosevic told Russian Deputy Foreign Minister Vitaly Churkin that Yugoslavia was no longer prepared to accept international monitors on its borders.

U.S. Policy

In its last month in office, the Bush administration generally maintained its policy of limited involvement in the affairs of the former Yugoslavia. But in late December 1992, President Bush drafted a letter to Serbian President Milosevic and then-Yugoslav Army chief Zivota Panic threatening U.S. military action against Serbia should Serbian forces provoke an armed conflict in the majority-Albanian province of Kosovo. In January, U.S. intelligence reports indicated that Muslim and Croatian prisoners from Bosnia were being transferred to, and detained in, prison camps in Serbia. Bush administration officials held the information for months before releasing it to international humanitarian agencies in early 1993.

The Clinton administration took steps to punish Yugoslavia primarily for its support of Bosnian Serb forces but did not devote much attention to human rights within Serbia and Montenegro. However, U.S. Embassy personnel in Belgrade continued to monitor the human rights situation and to maintain contacts with human rights advocates, members of the political opposition and minority groups. After Vuk and Danica Draskovic were detained and beaten by police following the June 1 Belgrade demonstration, President Clinton sent a letter of support to the Draskovics in which he condemned the detention of, and denial of medical treatment to, the couple.

The Clinton administration took steps to tighten the U.N. embargo against Yugoslavia. In late February, the U.S. tracked a Greek ship carrying to Somalia weapons purchased from the Federal Directory of Supply and Procurement, an arms export agency for Yugoslavia. In March, the U.S. government publicly identified foreign companies that were helping Belgrade evade trade sanctions. The U.S. also offered to provide patrol boats to Romania and Bulgaria for use in enforcing the U.N.-imposed embargo on the Danube. Clinton offered to send teams of Treasury and State Department officials to work with European allies to crack down on Serbian financial transactions and imports. Such teams from the Treasury Department were sent to Cyprus, Germany and Austria.

On April 4, U.S. Secretary of State Warren Christopher discussed the possibility of new sanctions against Yugoslavia with Russian Foreign Minister Andrei Kozyrev. Two days later, the U.S. sought U.N. Security Council approval for additional sanctions against Yugoslavia. However, the U.S. agreed to delay a U.N. vote on new sanctions against Yugoslavia until after April 25; it was generally assumed to be a concession to the referendum in Russia, in which Russian President Boris Yeltsin sought to weaken the legitimacy of a conservative Russian Parliament that was sympathetic to the Serbs.

The Work of Helsinki Watch

In order to monitor human rights in Yugoslavia and Serbian-controlled areas in Bosnia and Croatia, Helsinki Watch maintained one or more staff members in Yugoslavia throughout 1993. Staff representatives investigated human rights violations and sustained contacts with human rights activists, government officials and members of the press in Yugoslavia.

On May 28, Helsinki Watch sent a letter to Serbian President Slobodan Milosevic condemning the closure of the publishing house Rilindja and calling for the re-opening of Rilindja and all other Albanian-language media in Kosovo that had been suppressed in the past. On June 4, Helsinki Watch sent a letter to Serbian President Slobodan Milosevic calling upon him to accept responsibility for Serbian police officers' excessive use of force against protestors and journalists on June 1 in Belgrade. In August, Helsinki Watch followed up its letter to President Milosevic and released a newsletter titled "Belgrade Demonstrations: Excessive Use of Force and Beatings in Deten-

tion."

Helsinki Watch published information concerning abuses in Serbia and Montenegro in a July 1993 newsletter titled "Abuses Continue in the Former Yugoslavia: Serbia, Montenegro and Bosnia-Hercegovina." A mission to Yugoslavia was conducted in September and October to investigate civil and political rights in Montenegro, Vojvodina, Kosovo and Serbia proper; a report will follow.

Helsinki Watch invited Nata a Kandi, the founder and executive director of The Humanitarian Law Fund, in Belgrade, to be honored by Human Rights Watch in its observance of Human Rights Day, December 10.

MIDDLE EAST
WATCH

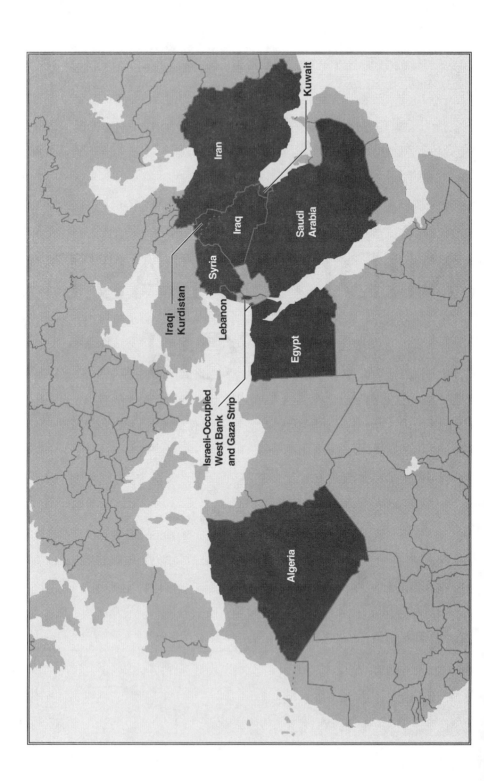

MIDDLE EAST WATCH OVERVIEW

Human Rights Developments

The political earthquake that shook the Middle East on September 13, when Israel and the Palestine Liberation Organization (PLO) signed an interim self-government accord, may have marked the beginning of the end of the forty-five-year-old Arab-Israeli conflict. In the medium term, it may also come to mark a parallel improvement in human rights conditions—not just in the Israeli-occupied territories, but in those front-line states that have long used the conflict as a pretext for violations of the fundamental rights of their own peoples.

Such aspirations could, equally, prove to be mere wishful thinking: human rights *per se* figured little in the interstate negotiations that took place during 1993, and few officials from any party to the talks, including the United States, publicly articulated concern for human rights. Under prodding, PLO Chairman Yassir Arafat was one of those who did, after the signing; but, misgivings persisted as to whether the PLO was truly committed to a future in which respect for human rights and a pluralistic democracy would be realized. In counterpoint, there were no early signs of an Israeli reassessment of long-established abusive policies and practices in the occupied territories.

Welcome though the Israel-PLO agreement was as an augury of peace, in the region as a whole—from the Maghreb states of North Africa to Iran—the accord was overshadowed by a broader conflict with pervasive implications for human rights: a contest for power, ideological domination, and control over social behavior between insurgent Islamists and established regimes, themselves often of little popular legitimacy and a secular, pro-Western cast. The contest became increasingly violent, and casualties mounted. In Egypt, over the eighteen months to October 1993, some 220 people lost their lives, sixty-six of them members of the security forces. In Algeria, in only the first nine months of the year the fatality toll reached over 700, of whom nearly 500 were Islam-

ists. Islamist gunmen were responsible for many acts of seemingly random violence, including murder and abductions, against secular figures and foreigners; but other unidentified forces also appeared to be taking advantage of the political unrest to carry out killings.

Not that this tragic struggle taking place in much of the Arab world can be accurately depicted only in secular versus religious terms. Even the rulers of Saudi Arabia and Iran, who drew their authority in part from religious wellsprings, faced challenges from hardline Islamists. In appeasing or fighting off these challengers, governments frequently made human rights the casualty.

After a period of several years in which acknowledgment of human rights as an issue with which local rulers had to contend, whatever their political system, appeared to be gaining greater acceptance, in 1993 this trend went into reverse. In the nine states actively monitored by Middle East Watch during the year, respect for fundamental human rights suffered a broad decline. (Middle East Watch was either unable to monitor other states such as Libya and Oman because of a lack of reliable information, or else, as in the case of Jordan, chose not to do so because of their relatively good human rights records.)

Perhaps out of concern for Western sensibilities and aid considerations, most regional governments continued to defend publicly their adherence to accepted human rights norms. Iraq jettisoned any such effort; while other states—the Islamic Republic of Iran and the Kingdom of Saudi Arabia, for instance—attempted to defend their records as being in conformity with Islamic, rather than universal, norms. Iraq and Syria, ruled by longstanding dictators who headed rival branches of the Arab Ba'th Socialist Party, were among those whose officials rejected external pressure over their human rights records as being a Western stick wielded for political purposes. Some of the regional dissatisfaction with attempts to enforce the Universal Declaration of Human Rights and other relevant treaties was aired at the U.N. World Conference on Human Rights, at Vienna in June, stirring debate about the universality of human rights and the claimed need to take cultural differences into account in their application.

Among the Arab nations of the Middle East and North Africa, only Jordan and Yemen, each of which held generally free and fair elections during the year, could plausibly claim to be in general compliance with the International Covenant on Civil and Political Rights—ratified by all regional nations except Saudi Arabia. The November elections in Jordan consolidated a democratic opening begun in 1989 by King Hussein. As a result of these two polls, and the 1992 election to a restored National Assembly in Kuwait, Saudi Arabia and other conservative Arab sheikhdoms on the Persian Gulf found themselves surrounded by lively examples of political life—in the process, exposing King Fahd of Saudi Arabia's arguments about the inappropriateness of democracy for the region's peoples. In 1993, the Saudi ruler instituted a long-promised Consultative Assembly; but, in Middle East Watch's view, the appointed advisory body did little to advance participatory democracy and may even have strengthened royal authority. Morocco, like Jordan a pro-Western monarchy with a developed civil society that operates with a qualified degree of freedom, also held parliamentary elections during the year; but the results were marred by allegations of fraud.

Presidential elections were held in two states with strong presidential systems: Egypt and Iran. In both countries the incumbents, Hosni Mubarak and Ali Akbar Hashemi-Rafsanjani, won easy victories, as had been predicted. Neither vote was a fair reflection of popular will, as the conditions under which the elections were held had been effectively predetermined by the government. Their respective regimes' deep political enmity notwithstanding, Mubarak and Rafsanjani shared several common problems. Both presided over states under great population and resources pressures; and attempted cautiously to open up the system to modernizing forces. Neither ruler, though, attempted to pursue the politics of inclusion, thus alienating important sectors of their populations.

Preconditions for genuine popular participation in elections are the interlinked freedoms of expression, association and assembly. In these key aspects of human rights, critical building blocks for the development of a healthy civil society, there was either no improvement during the year under review, or else there was backsliding. The only relatively bright spot in an otherwise bleak picture for the region covered by Middle East Watch was Israel's decision, following the September 13 accord, to relax its previously tight restrictions on peaceful demonstrations and forms of expression such as the display of Palestinian flags.

Otherwise, the regional record was an unending catalog of censorship; bans on meetings, demonstrations, publications and creative works; the closure of private associations; and the arrest of journalists, writers and government critics whose only offense was to espouse views unpopular with the political or religious establishment. Intolerance was driven by politically-backed religious zeal in countries as varied as Iran, Saudi Arabia and Egypt.

Fresh restrictions on freedom of expression were recorded by Middle East Watch in Iran and the seven Arab countries actively monitored in 1993. As described below, government actions increasingly hampered the ability of local and foreign organizations to monitor state abuses of basic human rights. Among certain offenders—Saudi Arabia, Iraq and Syria—freedom of expression was a virtual dead letter; while in countries such as Iran, Egypt, Lebanon and Kuwait the surface impression of lively public discourse and competing ideas was misleading as a guide to official tolerance of dissent or discordant voices.

In a footnote, the generally tolerant attitude toward expression displayed by the Kurdish regional authorities in northern Iraq should be noted. However, even in this Western-protected enclave, inhabited by approximately 3.5 million people the limits of political dissent were sometimes exposed during the year. Middle East Watch observed, with regret, the appearance of rights violations in the self-governing region, including the closure of a newspaper and a number of political detentions. These cases did not appear to represent any systematic policy or practice, however.

Ongoing conflicts within Iraq and Algeria, as well as the international conflict that took place in the Israel-Lebanon border region, in July, were marked by international humanitarian law violations. Middle East Watch argued that in the Israeli-occupied territories and Egypt, persistent and grave though actions by security forces and armed groups of opponents may have been at times, the localized violence did not reach the threshhold set by international humanitarian law. These two states were thus held to norms of behavior relevant to peacetime conditions. Israel is required to uphold the Fourth Geneva Convention covering occupied territory, an obligation that will not disappear as the Palestinian interim self-rule plan is implemented.

Israeli governments have consistently described security force actions in the West Bank and Gaza Strip as based on the upholding of law and order, rather than combat. However, during the year undercover army units continued to engage in shootings of suspects which amounted, in legal terms, to extrajudicial executions when arrests could have been effected without risk to the soldier.

While most violations derived from the repressive actions of the states concerned, Middle East Watch noted with much concern that grave human rights and humanitarian law violations were either being committed by nongovernmental groups or else were effectively condoned by them. Among the lengthening list of abusive militias and armed underground groups active in 1993 were Hizballa and the South Lebanon Army (Lebanon), Hamas (Israeli-occupied territories), the Islamic Group (Egypt), the Front Islamique du Salut (Algeria), and the Mujaheddin-e Khalq (Iran). Except for the SLA, a mainly Christian protegée of Israel, all were Islamist in their political ideology. The growing resort to violence by opposition groups in much of the Middle East and North Africa was a troubling feature of the year. In some cases, direct responsibility for assassinations and other acts of violence aimed at civilians, or in which noncombatants were placed at needless risk, could not be attributed to identifiable groups. But the fact that these groups usually did not denounce abusive acts committed by unidentified sympathizers was troublesome. While individuals identified with the regime were the main target of armed opposition groups, in several countries—for instance, Egypt and Lebanon—Middle East Watch noted that minorities or members of other groups were also victims.

The use of special courts that expedited legal procedures and afforded lower protection to defendants than standard criminal proceedings was a rash that spread throughout many parts of the region during the year. Even more disturbing were the large number of death sentences handed down by such courts, often on the basis of confessions that had been coercively extracted. In most cases, defendants did not have an opportunity to appeal their sentences to a higher court. Algeria, Egypt and Kuwait were the main offenders in this regard.

Undermining the fundamental concept of an independent judiciary, military courts answerable to government ministers were used to try civilians on charges unrelated to military matters in Lebanon, the Israeli-occupied territories, Egypt, Algeria and Tunisia. State security courts, usually empowered under emergency legislation, also dealt with human rights-related cases, in Syria and Kuwait.

In a sign of their residual vitality despite widespread official pressure, lawyers' associations and to a lesser extent civilian judges were sometimes able to fight back against the erosion of judicial independence and the rule of law. Among areas where this fight-back took place were Lebanon, Egypt,

Algeria, and the Israeli-occupied territories.

Iraq, where the rule of law had long been a charade in any case with political overtones, remained in a class of its own: hundreds of executions of suspected dissidents were believed to have been carried out in 1993 with little or no legal process. In November alone, dozens of prominent individuals apparently suspected of plotting against the regime were executed without charge or trial. Reports spoke of hundreds of Shi'a dissidents, arrested in southern Iraq after the March 1991 uprising or more recently, also being summarily executed, in August and September. While the precise scale of these bouts of extrajudicial executions was arguable, there could be no doubt that such killings had taken place in large numbers—in blatant defiance of many resolutions passed by the U.N. Security Council and Human Rights Commission.

In neighboring Iran, the problem with the judiciary was not so much subjugation to the executive branch as the arbitrary rulings of religious courts endowed with considerable decision-making autonomy. Continued recourse to Islamic revolutionary courts, which met behind closed doors in prisons and other undisclosed locations, augmented concerns over a judicial system that presided over one of the highest rates of execution in the world.

The Iranian authorities must also be held responsible for the continuation in 1993 of the *fatwa*, or religious ruling, issued in 1989 by the late Ayatollah Khomeini against the British writer Salman Rushdie over his book *The Satanic Verses*, and all those associated with its publication. Nor did the authorities disavow the $2 million "bounty" offered by a semi-independent Iranian foundation for the implementation of the fatwa. Since 1979, the Iranian government has been suspected of involvement in over sixty cases of assassination of exiled opponents; between December 1992 and November 1993, there were at least six successful or attempted killings in which evidence pointed to Tehran's official involvement. After lengthy delays, in late 1993 the trial of persons accused in connection with three celebrated assassinations of Iranians in Western Europe were either due to begin or had commenced. In each case, prosecutors claimed the Iranian authorities were directly involved.

While Iran, aware of the public relations damage caused, no longer released information about judicial executions on a regular basis, Saudi Arabia disclosed that capital punishment reached a record level in 1993. In the first seven months alone, executions—mostly public beheadings—exceeded the total for the preceding year. As in Iran, serious due process flaws often rendered nugatory the proceedings of Saudi courts based on uncodified *Shari'a*, or Islamic law. Drug offenses were said by officials to be the primary offense that drew the death sentence in both Saudi Arabia and Iran. Political opposition, suspected or actual, may also have added to the execution toll in Iran; but, given the paucity of reliable information, no firm conclusions could be drawn. Iranian opponents and human rights monitors have long claimed that political prisoners were being executed under the guise of being drug offenders.

Elsewhere, firmer assertions can be made about death sentences. In Kuwait, through November, seventeen death sentences were passed on persons charged with collaborating with the enemy during the 1991-92 Iraqi occupation. Another twelve defendants facing the death penalty were due to be sentenced after the publication of this report, and one execution was carried out. In Algeria, over 250 death sentences were passed by special courts. (Many were sentenced *in absentia*, and could be retried on surrender.) Even against the background of sharply higher levels of Islamist violence, this number was shockingly high. Barely two years earlier, Algeria had prided itself on its human rights record. Impelled by the same surge of Islamist-inspired violence as in Algeria, in Egypt too the government resorted to the death penalty in record numbers: between December 1992 and November 3, 1993, thirty-nine persons were sentenced to capital punishment, of whom seventeen were executed.

Contributing directly to the many travesties of justice that marred the region during 1993 was the endemic problem of torture in detention. Middle East Watch received credible testimony about the practice of torture— for the extraction of information, for punishment, to secure "confessions," or a combination of all three motives—in four countries: Iraq, Israel, Lebanon, and Saudi Arabia. All were long-standing abusers of human rights in this arena. Although first-hand testimony about torture was not taken during the year from the five other countries under review— Algeria, Egypt, Iran, Kuwait and Syria— Middle East Watch had no reason to believe that any of them had changed previously recorded interrogation practices. In a number of instances, mistreatment or medical neglect of detainees, itself an abuse, led to deaths in detention.

Administrative detention—detention without charge or trial of persons considered by the authorities to be security threats, but against whom sufficient evidence to warrant a trial was lacking—remained an obnoxious practice in Algeria, where it was used against militant Islamists, and the Israeli-occupied territories, where Palestinian activists were the target. However, the numbers in administrative detention in both countries were down significantly in 1993 compared with previous years. In part, this was due to a switch by the respective authorities to other means of dealing with the problem of peaceful opposition.

In Algeria, for example, much greater use was made of summary judicial proceedings before special courts apparently designed to process speedily as many defendants as possible. Meanwhile, in December 1992, in one fell stroke the Rabin government in Israel rounded up and deported 415 Palestinian activists suspected of involvement with Islamist groups. The use of some administrative punishments, such as house demolitions and sealings, lessened during 1993 in the Israeli-occupied territories. Nor was there any further resort to deportations. But collective punishments such as an in-

definite curfew on the entire Gaza Strip were continued, while other forms, notably a ban on travel by Palestinians across the 1967 "Green Line" border into Israel and East Jerusalem, were newly applied.

As often occurs amidst deteriorating human rights conditions, such as could be observed in 1993 in the Middle East and North Africa, minorities and dissident ethnic groups frequently bore the brunt of abusive government actions or else were not afforded the protection they should have enjoyed under the law. Outstanding examples were the Iraqi Kurds and Shi'a. As in the two previous years, among many other violations, they continued to endure mass arbitrary arrests and executions; the economic and military blockade of parts of regions where they formed a majority; discrimination in the allocation of scarce resources such as food and medicine, as well as in employment and education; and the absence of religious freedom. In the course of suppressing a Shi'a rebel insurgency in and around the southern marshes, the Iraqi government effectively destroyed the ancient way of life of the region's indigenous people, the Maadan. The region's lakes and marshes were drained; villages were shelled and burned; and their inhabitants were either forcibly relocated to areas under government control, or else forced to flee elsewhere. About 7,000 Shi'a refugees managed to cross into Iran between July and September, but most were trapped inside the country by intensive Iraqi military action.

Kurds were mistreated in the two other countries covered by Middle East Watch in which they form a significant minority, Iran and Syria (Turkey, where there is a major problem involving Kurds, is monitored by Helsinki Watch). Much of Iranian Kurdistan was turned into an armed camp during the year, as the authorities battled internal political unrest and guerrilla organizations based across the border in northern Iraq. While information about conditions affecting Iranian and Syrian Kurds was sketchy, arrests and executions were reported in Iran by opposition parties. In Syria, forty Kurds arrested the previous year during the course of demonstrations remained in custody accused of membership in a banned organization.

Apart from Iraq, discrimination against and persecution of religious minorities was reported from Iran and Egypt. In Iran, the 300,000-strong Baha'i sect was subjected to renewed official pressure during the year. In Egypt, the country's Coptic Christians were often the target of Islamist attacks. Thirty-six Copts died in Islamist violence in the eighteen months commencing March 1992. In Middle East Watch's view, government discrimination against the Copts, over freedoms of expression and church building and repair, contributed to a climate in which this vulnerable minority became fair game for extremists. The only positive note for minorities during the year was in Saudi Arabia, where Shi'a political prisoners were quietly released and exiled opponents permitted to return. The price, from a human rights monitoring perspective, was high: those self-exiled groups involved were required to cease publishing critical information about abuses inside the Kingdom.

The Right to Monitor

The ability of private individuals and groups, local or foreign, to gather information openly about government abuses without fear of punishment has rarely been tolerated in the Middle East, outside of Egypt, Israel and the occupied territories. The Maghreb region of North Africa has a better record. Established human rights organizations have long been at work in Morocco, Algeria and Tunisia, with a degree of freedom; and the governments' sensitivity to criticism on this score has led to the establishment of official human rights organizations in each of these countries. Nominally designed to be independent watchdogs, in practice these bodies became defenders of the official line.

In those parts of the Arab world where local groups have played a formal or informal monitoring role, they usually have done so cautiously. While the gathering of information about current abuses was tacitly permitted during 1993 in some relatively open societies, such as Lebanon, Morocco and Tunisia, advocacy work to promote change was much more problematic. Rarely did governments in the region respond substantively to complaints from local organizations, and only infrequently did they respond adequately to foreign human rights groups or U.N. human rights bodies. The *de facto* limits on local rights organizations put a greater burden on bodies such as Middle East Watch and Amnesty International, which had better access to the media and to governments in a position to exercise pressure on the abusive regional party.

Middle East Watch's ability to conduct missions and investigate alleged abuses in the region was highly qualified. Access to the country has never been a problem in Israel or Egypt, for instance, but to date has been consistently denied by Syria, Iraq and Saudi Arabia. In Iran, the government issued visas to permit the investigation of human rights abuses in neighboring Iraq; but was reluctant to discuss its own practices, much less to permit an above-board investigation. In Lebanon and Kuwait, the authorities were generally cooperative. But, until late 1993 the government in Morocco never responded to requests to send a mission to that country; following the receipt of an invitation, a mission to Morocco was planned for early 1994. While the Israeli government has put few obstacles in the way of fact-gathering, over the years it has shown itself reluctant to engage in a substantive dialogue with foreign human rights organizations about its practices.

This pervasive reluctance to deal with foreigners on sensitive issues such as political prisoners and the mistreatment of minorities was not unique to private groups. U.N. agencies and individual officials charged with investigating human rights conditions experienced similar difficulties. In 1993, both Iran and Iraq prevented the U.N. Secretary-General's representatives from conducting on-the-spot missions examining internal conditions, in defiance of U.N. resolutions. Iraq went further, preventing U.N. relief officials and guards from visiting troubled regions of the country. The Geneva-based International Committee of the Red Cross also faced many difficulties in gaining access to prisoners in most of the region, apart from the Israeli-occupied territories.

Consonant with the worsening human rights climate, fledgling local human rights organizations faced fresh restrictions in 1993. In Kuwait and Saudi Arabia, newly established groups were closed down on government order; in Saudi Arabia, members were arrested and dismissed from their jobs, but in more tolerant Kuwait it appeared as if the main human rights association, the Kuwaiti Association for the Defense of War Victims (KADWV), would in practice be permitted to continue operating. In Syria, fifteen members of the country's only monitoring body, the Committees for the Defense of Democratic Freedoms and Human Rights (CDF), remained in jail. Ten had previously been sentenced to prison terms of up to ten years, while another five faced trial before state security courts during the year.

Operating in the shadows, without official recognition, the KADWV found itself in late 1993 in a similar position to that long endured by the Egyptian Organization of Human Rights (EOHR). EOHR, an independent body with a strong record of investigating and publicizing abuses, had never been granted official recognition; nor did the authorities usually respond to its complaints. Elsewhere, the Tunisian Ligue des Droits de l'Homme reopened, after being effectively closed down under an amended law of association. But in Tunisia and Algeria, both of which were struggling with Islamist violence and government repression, local human rights groups engaged in little substantive work.

In the Israeli-occupied territories and in Jerusalem, several established human rights organizations were active during 1993. Movements of Palestinian workers and the gathering of field information were frequently difficult; otherwise, they suffered few restrictions in their activities. Israeli and Palestinian lawyers also acted as useful sources of information about current abuses, as did Egyptian and Algerian defense lawyers in their countries.

U.S. Policy

With regard to the Middle East and North Africa, the Clinton administration's approach to human rights differed little from that of the Bush administration. This was hardly surprising, given the primacy the administration continued to give to securing peace agreements between Israel and its Arab neighbors—a policy choice that went hand in hand with sublimating human rights concerns. Another constant was the unresolved dilemma of how to handle the Islamist movement challenging secular governments well disposed to the United States.

In international fora, such as the U.N. World Conference on Human Rights in Vienna, the vigorous espousal of human rights principles by the U.S. and the support given to letting the voices of nongovernmental organizations be heard at the conference was helpful. Middle East NGOs made good use of the occasion to embarrass their governments and lobby others to work for change.

The scheduled visit to Israel, the occupied territories and Egypt of John Shattuck, Assistant Secretary for Human Rights and Humanitarian Affairs, in late November was also a positive sign, on the heels of the Israel-PLO accord. But it remained to be seen whether the Clinton administration would pressure Israel to curb its longstanding abusive practices in the occupied territories, and work actively to promote a pluralistic society committed to the rule of law in the Palestinian-run regions.

The standard argument from Washington that public diplomacy on human rights-related matters would be counterproductive to the Middle East peace process could not be extended, however, to other key U.S. allies in the region, such as Saudi Arabia, Kuwait and Morocco. Concerning their record the administration remained equally silent. With respect to Saudi Arabia and Syria, the contrast between President Clinton's pre-election pledge to get tough on both of them on human rights grounds, and his administration's protective attitude toward them was striking.

Human rights concerns were said to have been raised privately at a high level with the governments of Egypt and Algeria, on one or more occasions during the year. This was welcome. But there was little evidence that the administration was prepared to follow up its verbal communications with public condemnation, or to use other forms of leverage. The resumption of U.S. military aid to Lebanon, in October, was a regrettable development, given the role of the Lebanese army in carrying out politically motivated arrests and holding military trials of civilians. Similarly, U.S. military cooperation with Kuwait, Bahrain and Saudi Arabia was not accompanied by any visible effort to help curb human rights violations.

The administration expressed a desire to promote the process of democratization in the region, particularly in emerging democracies such as Yemen and Jordan. It also aimed to push the embryonic Palestinian entity in this direction. High-level diplomatic support was given to the Iraqi National Congress, a coalition of opposition parties committed to a pluralistic future for Iraq. The administration also supported a proposal that the United Nations establish a commission of inquiry into Iraqi war crimes, crimes against humanity and genocide. But little diplomatic muscle was put into securing the implementation of this laudable proposal, or a parallel plan to deploy U.N. human rights monitors in Iraq. While there was no backtracking from the military protection given to the Kurdish enclave in northern Iraq, and substantial amounts of relief aid were appropriated by Congress for the Kurds, overall the administration's policy toward Iraq and President Saddam Hussein was largely one of maintaining established policy.

One unfortunate initiative was the June 26 missile attack on the Baghdad headquarters of the Mukhabarat, Iraq's external intelligence service. Launched in reprisal for an alleged plot by Iraqi agents to kill former President George Bush, during a visit to Kuwait, the missile attack killed eight civilians and caused property damage in the surrounding area. Middle East Watch considered the attack unwarranted, especially as the trial in Kuwait of those in custody over the alleged plot had not even commenced. During the year under review, senior administration officials frequently criticized Iraq's human rights behavior in strong terms. They also gave strong support to U.N. efforts to eliminate Iraq's weapons of mass destruction, while resisting efforts by Iraq and others to lift economic sanctions, in force for over three years.

The Clinton administration also adopted a strong position over human rights abuses committed by Iran and Libya, two other pariah states as far as the U.S. was concerned. Iran was criticized as the ringleader of global terrorism, and concerted efforts were made to restrict Western high-technology goods and financial aid going to Iran. Stringent sanctions were applied through the U.N. against Libya, on the basis of its alleged involvement in the bombing of American and French passenger aircraft.

But, in all of those Middle East states where the U.S. took a strong and principled position on human rights, there was no conflict with other U.S. policy considerations. Where the U.S. did have vital interests in play, particularly in Israel, Washington took a different approach. Human rights policy towards Israel was weaker than under the Bush administration, when occasional public criticism of Israeli practices in the West Bank and Gaza Strip was expressed. And, while the previous administration had shown its willingness to use U.S. financial leverage to bring about a desired political goal—a curb in the building of Jewish settlements in the occupied territories—President Clinton virtually gave away the candy store, promising Prime Minister Rabin that the $3 billion in annual U.S. aid to Israel would be preserved in future years, without demanding anything in exchange for this important concession.

When the administration faced its first major foreign policy test, in January 1993, over Israel's arbitrary deportation of 415 Palestinians to Lebanon, Secretary of State Christopher fought hard to secure a political deal with Israel that headed off U.N. sanctions and kept the peace talks on track, but abandoned principles long enunciated by the United States concerning the inadmissibility of deportations. In a gratuitous declaration that served to highlight for many states the selective approach taken by the U.S. to the enforcement of U.N. resolutions, the Secretary of State said that the compromise reached with Israel, to permit a phased return of the deportees, was consistent with the position taken on the deportations by the U.N. Security Council in December 1992. It was not.

The Work of Middle East Watch

In 1993 Middle East Watch prioritized its work and restricted active monitoring of human rights to nine of the eighteen countries in its regional bailiwick. In alphabetical order, these were Algeria, Egypt, Iran, Iraq, Israel, Kuwait, Lebanon, Saudi Arabia and Syria. Missions were conducted during the year to six of the nine—Egypt, Iran, Iraq, Israel, Kuwait, Lebanon—some of which were visited twice or even three times. Research was conducted by telephone to those countries where access was not possible. Particular effort was focused on Israel and Iraq.

After the extensive time spent the previous year in Kurdish-controlled northern Iraq, investigating the government's Anfal campaign against the Kurds, in 1993 comparatively less time was spent inside Iraq itself. Two missions were sent during the year, with the primary purpose of securing further consignments of captured Iraqi secret police documents. (In 1992, Middle East Watch brought out fourteen tons of such documents, for safekeeping and analysis into Iraqi abuses.) But research missions also went to Iran and London, to meet refugees and exiled activists and gather information on the comparatively neglected topic of abuses against the Iraqi Shi'a. These missions resulted in a report and extensive advocacy over the draining of the southern marshes

region of Iraq, and brutal treatment of its inhabitants.

In Israel, the second main focus of activity, a researcher was maintained in the field for eight months, through August, to work on selected issues in the occupied territories. Consistent with past emphases, these were the excessive use of force—in the form of extrajudicial killings of Palestinians by undercover army units—and the authorities' failure to investigate or prosecute possible violations by Israeli forces. Following work already published by regional human rights organizations, Middle East Watch also undertook a major research project into abusive interrogation practices amounting to torture. The persistence of reports of torture in detention under the Rabin government required a first-hand examination of a subject that could implicate U.S. financial aid to Israel.

Substantively, research work focused in the region on three themes of significance for Human Rights Watch. These were: freedom of expression, the treatment of minorities and other suppressed ethnic groups, and violations of international humanitarian law. Shorter interventions dealt regularly with the prisoners of conscience and with threatened local human rights groups and activists. Campaigns were mounted on behalf of groups or individuals in Algeria, Kuwait, Saudi Arabia, Syria and the Israeli-occupied territories.

A greater emphasis than in the past was placed in 1993 on advocacy work. Much of this was in the traditional arenas of the media, where Middle East Watch consolidated its reputation as a reliable source of timely information on regional human rights issues, other private associations, and government. Meetings were held with regional government officials in Israel, Iran and Lebanon and with diplomats posted to the United States or U.N. from much of the region. And book-length reports were released on, among other subjects, limits to freedom of expression in Iran, prison conditions in Egypt, and undercover killings in the Israeli-occupied territories. Refugee casework with immigration officials and asylum lawyers also formed a regular part of the staff's work.

But, the organization's biggest single advocacy and research effort was devoted to the huge task of bringing a case against Iraq at the International Court of Justice at The Hague. During the year, this task involved research into the captured Iraqi documents, development of the legal theory of the case to be brought by a state party to the Genocide Convention, and seeking a government or governments willing to act as the plaintiff. In addition, two books on the Anfal campaign were released during the year: a case study of the fate of one district, and an overview book on the whole of the 1988 campaign.

ALGERIA

Human Rights Developments

Mounting state repression and the increased targeting of civilians by well-armed opposition groups contributed to the abysmal state of human rights during 1993, the second year of emergency rule in Algeria.

The government took no concrete measures to revive the electoral process it had suspended in January 1992 after a first-round victory by the opposition Islamic Salvation Front (Front Islamique du Salut, or FIS). Nor did it act credibly to reverse the surge in abuses for which it had been responsible since the canceled elections.

The most disturbing development of 1993 was the spread of general political violence. According to a tally of official news reports, during the first nine months of 1993 over one hundred members of the security forces and over one hundred civilians were killed in assassinations attributed by the government to Islamist groups, while nearly 500 Islamists were killed. The civilian victims came from all walks of life, and included prominent writers, professors, and public figures.

In the absence of claims of responsibility, and given the difficulty of conducting independent research in Algeria, the author-

ship of specific acts was often difficult to attribute. But it was clear that armed Islamist groups were responsible for many, if not most, of the killings of both civilians and security force members that had been attributed to them by the authorities.

The principles of customary international humanitarian law which bind all parties to a conflict, include an absolute prohibition on killing or ill-treating persons once they are in custody or hors de combat, and a requirement to take all feasible precautions to avoid civilian casualties. These principles were repeatedly violated in Algeria.

During 1993, the government intensified its battle against the Islamic resistance, not only on the military but also on the judicial front. New "special courts," created by a 1992 decree, convicted many hundreds of defendants in what were officially described as "terrorism" cases. Their procedures fell short of international standards for a fair trial. The special courts pronounced nearly all of the more than 300 death penalties handed down between January and October, 1993. (Most of the death penalties were pronounced *in absentia*; persons convicted *in absentia* are entitled to new trials if they surrender or are captured.) Twenty-six death sentences, all in connection with "terrorist" offenses, were carried out during this period.

The current phase of turmoil in Algeria began with the cancelation of elections in January 1992 and the replacement of the president by a military-dominated executive council, the High State Council (Haut Conseil d'État, or HCE). In February 1992, the HCE declared a state of emergency and banned the FIS, the party that had won the first round of elections. The government then detained, by its own count, some 9,000 suspected FIS members and sympathizers and dismissed hundreds of party members from the local government posts to which they had been elected in 1990.

Meanwhile, an underground Islamist movement, whose structure and links to the overt political leadership of the FIS remained nebulous, took up arms against the regime.

Most of its operations consisted of hit-and-run ambushes targeting police and gendarmes, and acts of sabotage against state property. These attacks began to occur on an almost-daily basis in 1992 and intensified in 1993.

In December 1992, the HCE imposed an indefinite night-time curfew on the capital and six adjacent provinces, later extended to three more provinces. Elite troops were dispatched to begin flushing out suspected Islamist hideouts. Extended gun battles often resulted in casualties on both sides.

In February 1993, the state of emergency was renewed indefinitely and the new special courts began hearing cases. The HCE had established these courts of exception by Legislative Decree 92-03 of September 30, 1992, using the executive and legislative powers it had arrogated to itself. The special courts, which had potential jurisdiction over any case involving "subversion" and "terrorism," quickly replaced desert detention camps as the government's preferred means of dealing with the thousands of Islamists being arrested. The decree establishing the courts made clear that their purpose was to try a large volume of cases expeditiously and mete out harsh punishments to those they convicted. The decree doubled most punishments that Algeria's penal code provided for comparable offenses, and provided life sentences for what were previously ten- to-twenty year sentences, and the death penalty for what were life sentences.

Decree 92-03 prolonged from two to twelve days the permissible length of incommunicado detention in "subversion" and "terrorism" cases. It lowered the age of legal responsibility in such cases from eighteen to sixteen. It also defined "subversion" in an excessively broad fashion, and provided prison sentences for those who expressed sympathy, or distributed publications that express sympathy, for "subversive" acts.

Due process rights of defendants before special courts were restricted in a number of ways. Opportunities for appeal were more limited than in ordinary Algerian courts. The identity of judges was kept secret, under penalty of imprisonment; there was therefore no accountability or assurance that conflicts of interest would come to light. The courts were required to render a verdict within one month of receiving the case from the investigating magistrate. Such a deadline, while arguably guaranteeing a defendant's right to a prompt trial, ran counter to the higher duty of a court to determine the truth. Concern over the time limits was heightened by the fact that special courts often tried fifteen or more defendants at one time. In addition, Decree 92-03 violated the principle of non-retroactivity by subjecting defendants whose alleged offenses predated the creation of the special courts to the less protective procedures of those courts.

In April, the government issued an amendment to the decree that prompted a brief boycott of the special courts by most of the local bar associations around the country. The amendment stated that a lawyer could plead before a special court only after receiving the court's authorization to do so. It also threatened lawyers with suspension from practicing law for up to one year if a special court judge determined that they had been disruptive in court.

The most highly publicized trial of the year was that of fifty-five defendants accused of participating in an August 1992 bomb explosion at the Algiers airport that killed nine persons and wounded more than one hundred. The May trial, which was open to the press, brought to public attention some of the key human rights issues facing Algeria: several defendants testified that they had been held well beyond the twelve-day legal limit on incommunicado detention. They also asserted that they had been tortured into making false confessions. But the court did not probe these allegations, and sentenced thirty-eight of the defendants to death, twenty-six of them *in absentia*. Seven were executed in August.

The aura of unfairness in the "airport trial" dated back to October 1992, when confessions of two of the alleged ringleaders were broadcast by the government on the same day it announced having identified them. Viewers noticed bruises on the head of one of the suspects. When that suspect said at the trial that his confession had been extracted through torture, the prosecutor dismissed the bruises as the product of a suicide attempt the defendant allegedly made upon discovering that he was being filmed. Another defendant claimed the police had "destroyed his genital apparatus" during thirty-three days of torture. The two were among those put to death.

Middle East Watch was not granted permission by authorities to conduct a mission to Algeria during 1993. But it continued to receive reports from human rights lawyers, doctors, and others suggesting that the pattern of torture documented during its 1992 mission continued in 1993. There were reports of severe beatings and of interrogators choking defendants with wet rags placed tightly over their faces, as well as reports of the use of electric shock and other instruments of torture.

A government spokesman rejected a report published in March by Amnesty International alleging widespread torture, claiming the government was resolutely opposed to the practice. The government-created National Human Rights Monitoring Body (Observatoire national des droits de l'Homme, or ONDH) told Middle East Watch in September 1993 that there had been cases of police who had been charged or disciplined for abusing detainees, but could provide no details.

Prolonged administrative detention continued, although on a smaller scale than in 1992. The state of emergency gave authorities the power to detain indefinitely, without charge, any person whose "activity is shown to endanger the public order, public security, or the proper functioning of public services."

It was not possible to ascertain the precise number of detainees nor the conditions in the detention camps during 1993. The ONDH told Middle East Watch in early September that there were approximately 700 detainees being held in two military-run detention camps, Oued Namous in central Algeria and Ain Mguel in the south. The

ONDH also stated that there were no new cases of administrative detention during 1993 and that those being held had been detained since 1992. It was not possible to confirm this information. The government stopped releasing figures at frequent intervals about the detention camps; nor did it allow independent organizations or journalists to visit them.

As part of the battle against the Islamist opposition, the government bullied the once lively press into self-censorship, particularly where information and comments relating to the internal security situation were concerned. Both local media and foreign news agencies were pressured to rely almost exclusively on official dispatches for coverage of the rampant political violence. Meanwhile, the murder between May and October of seven journalists, in attacks attributed by the government to Islamists, undoubtedly deepened the chill on free expression. No one claimed responsibility for their murders.

El-Watan, a leading independent daily, was suspended for two weeks, and six of its staff were jailed for one week, after it ran an exclusive report in January on the slaying of five gendarmes. The authorities charged that *El-Watan* had jeopardized a criminal investigation, and announced that all reporting on security incidents would henceforth require official approval. Journalists who attempted to check unconfirmed reports risked getting into trouble for "disseminating false news." In December 1992, a reporter with Algiers Radio Three was dismissed for phoning the Reuter news agency to check a report on the assassination of a member of a government commission. In March 1993, the Reuter bureau chief was himself held for eighteen hours after filing a report that the government said was untrue about the assassination of an official.

Algiers-based foreign correspondents told Middle East Watch that their phone lines were tapped and that they exercised self-censorship in order to be permitted to continue working. The Algiers-based correspondent for Radio France Internationale was forced to leave the country in January because authorities refused to renew her work permit. Journalists applying to enter the country often faced delays in obtaining visas, or simply received no reply to their applications.

Although the Algerian dailies continued to criticize government policies and expose social ills, they were hauled into court on several occasions for violations of the repressive press code and other laws limiting expression. Although no journalist was sentenced to prison during 1993, a few were subjected to court-ordered temporary bans on writing or on traveling abroad. In July, the government used its emergency powers to suspend indefinitely the independent daily *El-Djezaïr el-Youm*. Although the government did not provide a reason, observers pointed to an advertisement the paper had run from a religious organization that warned against further executions of Islamists. As of late October, *El-Djezaïr el-Youm* remained suspended, as did the weekly *as-Sah Afa*, suspended in 1992.

The victims of the crackdown on the press were not limited to those who published news deemed favorable to the Islamists. Hachemi Cherif, leader of the leftist Ettahadi party—and the object of an unsuccessful assassination attempt in April—received a two-month suspended sentence for condemning in harsh terms the brief arrest of the editor of the leftist *Alger Républicain* for writing that the courts were being too lenient with "terrorist" defendants. The same sentence was imposed on a journalist and an editor at *El-Watan* for publishing Hachemi's remarks.

The *El-Watan* editor, Omar Belhouchet, exemplified the extent to which journalists were caught between government harassment on the one side and the terror of armed groups on the other. Three weeks before being sentenced, Belhouchet narrowly escaped an attempt on his life by unidentified assailants.

Many other prominent members of the intelligentsia were murdered in attacks attributed by the government to the Islamists. These included a professor of psychiatry, a sociologist, and two physicians. One of the physicians, Djilali Belkhenchir, was a leading member of the Algerian Committee Against Torture and of a national children's rights association. Former minister of higher education Djilali Liabes and former prime minister Kasdi Merbah (who served from 1988 to 1989) were also murdered. Many, but not all, of the victims had been outspoken advocates of a secular Algeria, or else critics of the country's Islamist movement.

Three of the fatalities were members of the National Consultative Council (NCC), an advisory body created by the regime in 1992 as a substitute for the parliament that had been prevented from taking office. Underground Islamist publications had denounced as illegitimate both the NCC and the government-appointed replacements for ousted local officials who were FIS-affiliated. According to Agence France-Presse (AFP), during 1992 and the first half of 1993 at least twenty of these appointees to local offices were assassinated.

There were many obstacles to assigning responsibility for the violence in Algeria. While no serious observers doubted that Islamist groups were responsible for some of the political violence, many Algerians, including those harboring no sympathy for the Islamist cause, suspected that there were other forces carrying out some of the killings, using the climate of violence and mayhem as a cover to settle political and personal scores, or to protect financial interests. For example, many Algerians believe that the persons behind the assassination of President Mohamed Boudiaf in June 1992 were foes of his reformist project rather than Islamists.

FIS leaders did, however, give their clear blessing to the armed struggle, even though the party did not claim responsibility for specific attacks. In an interview published on February 26, 1993 in the Paris-based daily *Libération*, exiled FIS leader Rabah Kebir said: "The violence stems from the dictatorship, which has left us no alternative to reciprocal violence." Asked about the first killings of foreigners in Algeria by armed groups in September and October, Kebir told Radio France Internationale, "The FIS has no policy of killing foreigners, but there is a popular movement that is difficult to control."

With the party banned, all of the FIS's leaders were either in jail, underground, or in exile. Its chief, Abbasi Madani, and deputy chief, Ali Belhadj, were serving long prison sentences on charges stemming from a strike and major disturbances in May and June 1991. The FIS leadership may have had few or no direct links to specific acts of violence committed by Islamist cells. Similarly, underground publications or statements that threatened or praised particular acts of violence may have emanated from activists who acted independently of the FIS leadership. But while the FIS denied responsibility for some assassinations and claimed responsibility for none, it never condemned and repudiated the killing of civilians in unequivocal terms. One prominent FIS representative in exile, Anouar Haddam, drew a distinction in an October 18 interview with Agence France-Presse between the FIS as "a political party that does not claim responsibility for any action," and the mujahidin. Haddam justified the targeting of certain civilians, saying "[T]he Algerian people have chosen as targets only those individuals upon whom the military-security system in Algeria relies. We know them one by one, and they are not innocent people." Haddam made similar statements to Middle East Watch in September. That month, Haddam was named to a newly created FIS steering committee in exile, headed by Rabah Kebir.

In June, Haddam was quoted by AFP as calling the fatal stabbing of psychiatry professor Mahfoud Boucebci "a sentence and not a crime. It is a sentence carried out by the mujahidin." In October, he said to the AFP, "Who are these so-called intellectuals? Among them are members of the National Consultative Council, which has usurped the place of the people's elected representatives, persons who wrote murderous editorials, and those who, through psychiatry, advised torturers on how to obtain confessions."

Middle East Watch unconditionally deplores the deliberate killing of civilians, whether by governments or armed opposition groups.

Having assumed power by annulling elections, the HCE put new voting off into the distant future. In June, the HCE pledged to turn over power at the end of 1993 to as yet unspecified institutions that would govern the country during a transitional period, lasting between two and three years; this would be followed by parliamentary and presidential elections. It later appointed a commission to set up a "national conference" to advise the HCE on the transitional period. But as of October—three months before the HCE was to cede power—the national conference had not begun, and the nature of the proposed transitional institutions had not been disclosed.

The HCE seized power on the grounds that it was rescuing Algeria's democratic future. While subsequent political violence vastly complicated the environment for the holding of fair elections, it did not excuse the failure of the HCE to take any meaningful steps toward restoring to Algerians their right to determine how they are governed.

The Right to Monitor

There were no formal obstacles to human rights monitoring in Algeria during 1993. However, human rights work was impeded by a fear of reprisals that kept many Islamists, their sympathizers, and ordinary citizens from providing testimony about government abuses. Those willing to speak often insisted on discreet meetings and on remaining anonymous. Many believed that their phones and mail were monitored by the government.

In 1993, the violence attributed to Islamist groups against civilians, several of whom had openly criticized Islamist intolerance, no doubt intimidated many Algerians from expressing such views. One of those felled in an attack attributed to Islamists was Djilali Belkhenchir, a pediatrician who was vice-president of the Algerian Committee against Torture. Belkhenchir, who had also been active in an organization that urged the government to cancel the parliamentary elections after the FIS had won the first round, was gunned down in the Algiers hospital where he worked on October 10. No one claimed responsibility for the killing.

Algeria had several independent women's and civil rights organizations that operated with minimal or no state interference. Among the human rights groups, the Algerian League for the Defense of Human Rights (Ligue Algérienne pour la Défense des Droits de l'Homme) was the only one inside Algeria that was outspokenly critical of government abuses. Its criticisms were covered by the local independent press, as are those of foreign human rights groups. However, as noted above, journalists were impeded by government pressures and restrictions from doing much critical reporting of their own on human rights abuses.

Near the start of the state of emergency in 1992, the government created a National Human Rights Monitoring Body (ONDH), with a mandate to "sensitiz[e] public opinion to the question of human rights and undertak[e] actions when abuses of these rights are reported or brought to its attention." In its first two years, the ONDH failed to emerge as a force for human rights that stood apart from the government. While it took principled positions against capital punishment and the administrative detention camps, it did not actively collect or publish data about the extent of abuses. For example, even though it was the only human rights body to be allowed into the detention camps during 1993, the information it had gathered remained private. Similarly, the ONDH could have enhanced its credibility by actively investigating and reporting on the extent of abuses of detainees under interrogation. But ONDH president Kemal Rezzag-Bara told Middle East Watch that his organization could act only if complainants approached it, and then only if they were willing to follow through on their complaints.

The Algerian government took a mixed approach to international human rights and humanitarian organizations. Amnesty International was permitted to visit, even after issuing a highly critical report in March. However, the International Committee of the Red Cross was unable to resume its program of visiting detention camps, suspended in early 1992 because of government conditions on the terms of visits. A request from the New York-based Lawyers Committee for Human Rights to observe trials of Islamists before the special courts, and repeated requests by Middle East Watch to conduct a mission, went unanswered. Meanwhile, the official press agency ran a story in May falsely accusing a Middle East Watch researcher of links to a network run by the Jewish charity B'nai B'rith, said to be arming and financing Islamists in Algeria.

The Role of the International Community

The U.S.
Algeria took a back seat to other U.S. concerns in the region during 1993. There were few public statements or initiatives by U.S. officials concerning human rights and democracy in Algeria, few high-level meetings between officials of the two countries, and little change in the modest aid program that the U.S. provides.

When a junta canceled elections and imposed a ruling council in January 1992, the Bush administration paused only momentarily before tilting toward the new regime, judging it preferable to a FIS-dominated parliament. Regrettably, its tilt was coupled with virtual silence toward the human rights abuses that the regime was perpetrating in the name of combatting Islamist terrorism.

If there was no major shift in policy toward Algeria between the Bush and Clinton administrations, there was at least a greater willingness on the part of the new administration to criticize the Algiers regime for failing to offer any response to its genuine security problem other than heightened repression. The Clinton administration's first major policy statement on Algeria contained blunt language on human rights. In testimony prepared for a May 12 hearing of the

House Foreign Affairs Committee, Assistant Secretary of State for Near East Affairs Edward P. Djerejian said:

Since the suspension of parliamentary elections, little progress has been made in restoring the democratic process and correcting the disturbing deterioration in the human rights situation. . . . Frankly, so far we have seen little in the way of action or specificity as to how the government plans to implement real political and economic reform. . . . [W]e do not believe that Algeria's problems can be resolved mainly through resort to security methods....In our contacts with the Algerian Government, we urge a measured approach to security, one which focuses on those guilty of violence but avoids wide-scale repression or renewed incommunicado detention.

Djerejian went on to express concern about press restrictions and allegations of torture.

U.S. officials made no further public comments about human rights in Algeria when Foreign Minister Redha Malek met with Secretary of State Christopher one week later. Nor were there any significant statements concerning Algeria in the months that followed.

Assistant Secretary Djerejian's laudable statement before Congress on May 12 needed to be followed by further steps to prod the regime in the direction of respect for human rights and democratic reform. As Algeria received little direct U.S. aid, Washington had little financial leverage. However, the U.S. maintained a number of programs whose continuation could have been reconsidered in light of Algeria's human rights record.

The U.S. was given Algeria $150,000 a year in the International Military Education and Training (IMET) program. The amount was tiny and restricted by the State Department to programs that, according to Djerejian's testimony, were "primarily designed to enhance democratization and respect for human rights in both the civilian and military sectors." The U.S. could have therefore sent a strong, albeit largely symbolic, message by suspending the program in protest at Algeria's deteriorating human rights record and its failure to move toward restoring democratic government. That is what the Senate's Foreign Relations Committee, in its official report accompanying the Foreign Assistance Act for the fiscal year 1994 budget, urged the administration to consider doing.

Far more important to Algeria were the U.S. government credits it received for the purchase of U.S. farm products, and the loans and loan guarantees given to U.S. corporations doing business in Algeria. For fiscal year 1994, Algeria was allocated $550 million in loan guarantees by the Department of Agriculture's Commodity Credit Corporation (CCC), making it the CCC's second-largest client. This program also helped make the U.S. the third-largest exporter to Algeria, after France and Italy. In addition, the Export-Import Bank (Eximbank) reported a total exposure in Algeria, as of September 30, 1993 of $2.2 billion in loan guarantees. The Eximbank's exposure was higher only in Mexico, Venezuela and Brazil.

While human rights restrictions on Eximbank activities are weak, the CCC is required to adhere to provisions of the Foreign Assistance Act that bar assistance to any government that engages in a consistent pattern of gross violations of internationally recognized human rights, "unless such assistance will directly benefit the needy people in such country." The Clinton administration should have considered ways to link the size of these programs to the government's progress in moving toward democracy and curbing human rights abuses.

The State Department could also have sharpened its reporting on Algeria in its Country Reports on Human Rights Practices. While the 1992 chapter acknowledged that the situation "deteriorated severely," and properly blamed the government for having "frustrated an electoral process that for the first time could have resulted in a democratic change of government," it failed to convey the systematic nature of the government's campaign to eradicate the main opposition force, the FIS.

The Report stated that torture declined in 1992 and occurred only in isolated cases. It provided no evidence for this assertion, which contradicted the findings of human rights organizations. The Report did not mention that detainees were commonly held incommunicado beyond the legal time limit, the phase of detention when most abuse occurs. The chapter also under-reported the extent of the crackdown on the FIS as a party. It ignored the removal of anti-government preachers, the effective dissolution in December 1992 of the pro-FIS union, the Syndicat Islamique du Travail, and the closure of Islamist charitable and cultural organizations following then-Prime Minister Belaïd Abdesslam's announcement of a crackdown on organizations that serve as "satellites" of the FIS.

France
With closer ties to Algeria than any other country in the West, France remained by far its largest creditor, with roughly $7 billion in outstanding loans. In 1993, France provided slightly more than $1 billion in new credit, most of it balance-of-payments assistance on favorable terms and commodity credits guaranteed by COFACE, the state export credit agency.

French policy toward Algeria during 1993 was driven in large part by concern that an Islamist takeover would swell the flow of immigrants to France and destabilize the rest of North Africa. French-Algerian relations are complicated by the legacy of France's colonial rule in Algeria and its eight-year war to prevent the country's independence; public evocation of human rights concerns by France prompts a backlash in Algerian official circles, complete with evocations of past atrocities.

The conservative government headed

by Prime Minister Edouard Balladur, installed in March, fortified French support for the Algiers regime. In June, Foreign Minister Alain Juppé offered "help in the struggle of the Algerian government against terrorism and religious fanaticism" without expressing any reservations about how the battle was being conducted. That month, Paris obliged Algerian authorities by banning a pro-FIS magazine published in France and forcing a number of Algerian Islamists to leave the country. Other than condemnations of political violence by opposition groups and cautious statements in favor of an expanded political dialogue in Algeria, the government was publicly silent during 1993 on Algeria's worsening human rights practices.

This policy followed the direction taken after some wavering by President François Mitterand and the ousted Socialist government in France. In early 1993 there were a series of high-level visits between Paris and Algiers, and agreements were signed for new French assistance. Then-Foreign Minister Roland Dumas termed as "courageous" Algiers's "policies of restoring the authority of the state and economic reform." President Mitterand, who had infuriated Algiers back in January 1992 by criticizing the interruption of the electoral process, changed tack and issued a statement condemning "extremism."

The Work of Middle East Watch
Middle East Watch monitored abuses by both the government and armed opposition groups, in keeping with the policy of Human Rights Watch of reporting on human rights violations by all sides to a conflict. Those efforts, however, were complicated by the failure of the government to authorize a Middle East Watch mission during 1993. Such authorization was deemed necessary by Middle East Watch in light of the extensive surveillance inside the country by the security forces.

As in other countries where access was effectively denied, Middle East Watch continued to gather information on human rights in Algeria by other means, including contacts by phone and correspondence, and through persons who had recently left Algeria. A report on governmental abuses and on Islamist-inspired political violence was scheduled for release in late 1993.

In May, Middle East Watch issued a newsletter urging the release of imprisoned lawyer Brahim Taouti, who had been active in defending Islamist clients. He was given a three-year sentence on the basis of a penal code article whose vague and overly broad prohibition on distributing material "harmful to the national interest" is inconsistent with the right to free expression.

Middle East Watch also wrote letters to the authorities condemning the killing of civilians by unknown assailants and urging thorough investigations. In June, Middle East Watch sent a letter of concern to the German minister of justice after Germany complied with an Algerian request via Interpol to arrest FIS activists Rabah Kebir and Ossama Madani. Middle East Watch opposed their extradition on the grounds that the two men had been sentenced to death *in absentia* by an Algerian court whose ability to insure a fair trial was very much in doubt. Reportedly unpersuaded by the evidence against the two men provided by the Algerian authorities, a German court released them in September.

EGYPT

Human Rights Developments

Egypt continued to be ruled under emergency law, imposed in October 1981 following the assassination of President Anwar el-Sadat. The law, which had previously been in continuous effect from June 1967 until May 1980, continued to provide the executive branch with exceptional legal powers that, in effect, voided the human rights guarantees set forth in Egypt's constitution. Those provisions included broad discretion to arrest and detain any individual and the option to try civilians in military courts. The inde-

pendent, Cairo-based Egyptian Organization for Human Rights (EOHR) stated in a July 1993 submission to the U.N. Human Rights Committee that the continuous application of the state of emergency had yielded "another constitution for the country" and "led to wide transgressions on the part of the security apparatus."

The political violence that marked 1992 continued in 1993, presenting the government of President Hosni Mubarak with a security crisis of serious proportions, as the death toll and human rights violations mounted. The government appeared increasingly sensitive to criticism of its human rights performance, and created human rights departments in key ministries, beginning with the Ministry of Foreign Affairs in February. Similar offices were organized in the Justice and Agriculture Ministries, and plans were announced for an office in the Ministry of Interior. It appeared that the primary task of the Foreign Ministry unit was to rebut the findings of international human rights organizations.

President Mubarak was elected to a third six-year term in a rubber-stamp national referendum on October 4, following his nomination on July 21 by the People's Assembly, the elected parliament overwhelmingly dominated by the ruling National Democratic Party. Mr. Mubarak ran unopposed. The Ministry of Interior said that almost sixteen million people (84 percent of those registered to vote) cast ballots, with 96.28 percent voting in favor of the president's re-election.

Armed Islamist extremists stepped up attacks in 1993 on Christian citizens, senior government officials, policemen and high-ranking security officers, causing casualties among intended victims and bystanders. There were also sporadic attacks during the year on tour buses and boats and at tourist attractions. From March 1992 to October 28, 1993, a total of 222 people lost their lives in the unrest: thirty-six Coptic Christians and thirty-eight other citizens; six foreigners; sixty-six members of security forces; and seventy-six known or suspected militants killed while allegedly resisting arrest. The latter died in raids by and shoot-outs with security forces, and at the scene of planned attacks. On March 9-10, a series of raids in Cairo, Giza, Qalyubiya province (north of the capital), and Aswan left dead a reported fifteen suspected militants and five members of security forces. In one of the raids in Giza, part of metropolitan Cairo, the fatalities included the wife and child of Khalifa Mahmoud Ramadan, a suspected militant who was himself killed. The government-owned Middle East News Agency (MENA) reported on March 10 that the raids were part of "a plan for an all-out confrontation to apprehend the fugitive leaders of the terrorist elements." The operations had been "prepared and planned at a high level," MENA reported, and had involved all of Egypt's internal security forces, including the powerful General Directorate of State Security Investigation (SSI).

The government's determination to crush the militants led to human rights violations on a large scale, including arbitrary arrests, incommunicado detention and torture. The government also resorted to military courts to try civilians accused of "terrorism" offenses. As of November 3, thirty-nine death sentences had been handed down against Islamist militants by these tribunals, and seventeen executions had been carried out.

Freedom of association, already significantly restricted in Egypt, was further circumscribed by measures designed to tighten state control of unlicensed political groups and private mosques, and to thwart Islamist electoral victories in the country's professional associations. Freedom of expression suffered a serious setback in October, when the government clamped down on the moderate Islamist opposition with the detention of two leaders of the Labor Party, a legal political party that is allied with the Muslim Brotherhood, and two journalists from the party's twice-weekly newspaper, al-Sha'ab. Coupled with the summoning of the newspaper's chief editor and board chairman for questioning, the move was prompted by articles in the newspaper critical of the Mubarak government.

The dismissal in April of Interior Minister Gen. Abdel Halim Musa did not bring an end to mass and arbitrary arrests, incommunicado detention, and torture. Ironically, the new interior minister, Gen. Hassan el-Alfi, said in a July interview with the Saudi weekly magazine al-Majalla that it was only Egyptian authorities' determination to "adhere to the law and human rights" that had hindered the elimination of extremist violence. In October, he claimed that reports about torture and other rights violations in Egypt were "mere purposeful rumors that seek to distort Egypt's image."

Despite public pledges by Gen. el-Alfi, the practice of "hostage-taking"—the arrest of family members of suspects wanted by authorities—continued. In one particularly shocking case, the parents and twelve other relatives of Ahmed Farouq, a thirty-year-old construction worker, were detained between August 20 and September 4, to put pressure on Farouq to give himself up. Farouq's father told EOHR that he was detained at SSI headquarters in Giza, where he was severely beaten while bound at the feet and wrists. His wife was beaten in his presence and suffered wounds to the head when thrown against a wall. Farouq himself surrendered to authorities on September 2. Police sources were reported as saying that he confessed to involvement in three bombing attacks in Cairo, including one in August that injured the interior minister and killed five people. Farouq died in custody the next day, after being held at Lazoughly, the Cairo headquarters of SSI, where torture of political and security detainees was routinely practiced. Farouq's death certificate noted that there were several bruises on his face, suggesting that he may have been tortured during interrogation. Farouq's father was not allowed to identify his son's body at the morgue, bring others to the burial, or hold a funeral. In a September 23 press release, EOHR noted that Farouq's death was the fourth since May believed to have been caused by torture.

Two other events were particularly egregious: a siege of Imbaba, a neglected neighborhood of one million residents in metropolitan Cairo that had become a stronghold of Islamist militants, and a raid on a mosque in Aswan, Egypt's southernmost city. On December 8, 1992, thousands of security force members began a weeks-long search-and-arrest operation in Imbaba. EOHR documented major abuses during the campaign. Security forces "entered the homes of suspects who belonged to Islamic militant groups in the late hours of the night and occasionally destroyed furniture and terrorized the inhabitants, assaulting and insulting them," EOHR reported. There were widespread arbitrary arrests. Persons were detained on mere suspicion or because they had beards; periods of detention typically ranged from fifteen to thirty days. Relatives of wanted suspects—including mothers, sisters and wives, and children as young as eight years old—were arrested "to force [suspects] to give themselves up or to obtain information from victims as to their whereabouts." EOHR found that some of the women were beaten with rods, forced to undress and sexually molested by officers at the Imbaba police station. Numerous male detainees were moved to security police camps on the Cairo-Alexandria desert road, where they were blindfolded and questioned by SSI officers. According to EOHR, torture methods during interrogation included beating with coiled wires, beating on the soles of the feet with the body held in awkward positions, electric shocks on sensitive body parts, and standing outdoors while naked, followed by dousing with cold water.

Among those from Imbaba held incommunicado at these camps was twenty-three-year-old Amhed Hamido al-Sawi, who was arrested on December 9, 1992. Ten days later, on December 19, al-Sawi's family was informed that he was dead. His brother was asked to sign a statement that al-Sawi had committed suicide. EOHR believed, however, that al-Sawi died under "severe torture" and submitted a written complaint to the prosecutor general. As of November 1993 EOHR had received no reply.

On March 9, 1993 in Aswan, eight militants and one policeman reportedly were killed when security forces raided the Rahman mosque, which was frequented by members and supporters of the Islamic Group, the clandestine organization that had claimed credit for numerous acts of political violence. Security sources cited by MENA claimed that the mosque was being used to store weapons and explosives and to harbor gunmen believed to have killed one local policeman and wounded another three days earlier. MENA reported that "terrorists opened fire on police, who retaliated in kind." But eyewitnesses interviewed by foreign journalists disputed the government's version of events, claiming that those inside the mosque were unarmed and that the assault, with tear gas and automatic weapons, began without warning.

Despite the aggressive pursuit of militants, anti-government violence only escalated during the year. There were attempted assassinations in Cairo of Information Minister Safwat el-Sherif in April and Interior Minister el-Alfi in August. Policemen and security officers, including high-ranking commanders, were frequently injured or killed in targeted attacks. On March 3, for example, Lt. Col. Mahran Abdel Rahim, an intelligence officer in Dayrut in Upper Egypt, and his eight-year-old son Muhammed were killed when assailants fired at their car. The Islamic Group claimed responsibility, stating: "Bullets against bullets, according to the law of retaliation."

Coptic Christians continued to live in fear and to fall victim to sectarian-inspired violence by suspected Islamist extremists, particularly in Upper Egypt. On April 19, author Shihatah Aziz Jirjis was shot and injured by two gunmen in his home in Dayrut, a a town north of Assyut. On July 22, Dr. Fawzi Mikhail, a gynecologist in his sixties, was shot dead in Manfalout, near Dayrut. Also in Dayrut, pharmacist Philip el-Komous was killed on August 5, Sami Shawfiq Mounis was shot and killed in his shop on September 3, and professor Edward Nakhou'a Iskandar was shot and killed on his way to work at a local college on September 21. Iskander was the thirty-fifth Christian killed since March 1992 by assailants believed to be Islamist extremists. Militants have also targeted the Christian community by attacking and killing security forces guarding churches. On March 6, gunmen shot two policemen stationed outside a church in Aswan, killing one of them; on May 9, in Qusiyah, a police officer guarding the Catholic church was killed, and a policeman was shot and wounded at the Coptic church thirty minutes later; and on September 28, gunmen shot at two police guards in front of the Anglican church in Dayrut, killing one of them.

During the twelve months under review, the government signaled its intention to clamp down on independent spheres of activity within civil society. It narrowed the limited political space available to opposition groups lacking legal status, notably the Muslim Brotherhood; announced a plan to phase out private mosques; and tightened controls over elections in nongovernmental professional associations. Also, moderate Islamist political leaders and journalists were interrogated and arrested for exercising their right to freedom of expression.

In December 1992, the People's Assembly passed an amendment to the political parties law. The amendment barred political activity by groups that lacked legal status and prohibited political alliances between such groups and legalized political parties. Although the government had previously tolerated its electoral alliance with legalized opposition political parties, the Muslim Brotherhood—by most accounts the largest and most vigorous opposition group in Egypt—was thus further excluded from formal participation in the political process.

In another development with serious implications for freedom of speech and association, the government announced in December 1992 that the state would gradually assume control over all of the country's mosques, in an apparent attempt to eliminate the influence of radical Islamists at private religious institutions. Only about 30,000 of Egypt's estimated 170,000 mosques were built and are administered by the Ministry of Religious Affairs. Sheik Ahmad Hindi, a ministry official responsible for Minya, Assyut and Sohag provinces in Upper Egypt, where militants have a strong base, said in February that the 2,835 private mosques in his area (of a total of 4,950) would be brought under government control over the following three years.

Al-Ahram Weekly newspaper reported in March that the ministry also planned to dictate topics for the sermons by imams at Friday noon prayers. According to the head of the ministry's Mosques Administration, Sheik Mansour al-Rifa'i Obeid: "Exercising control over all mosques is meant to guarantee that the sermons delivered therein are in strict compliance with true Islamic teachings." Dr. Muhammed Ali Mahjoub, the minister of religious affairs, said in an interview published in April in the semi-official *October* weekly that "the government respects freedom of speech" but added that "[i]f the word is poisonous and subversive, it must be stopped. . . .It is known that the ministry is earnestly working to annex all private mosques to control the Islamic call and secure the people ideologically."

The Mubarak government also set down controversial regulations governing elections in the country's professional associations, which have about 1.2 million members nationwide. Without consultation with the associations, a bill—which provided for what the state termed "guarantees for the democracy of professional associations"—had been rushed through the People's Assembly on February 16 and signed into law by President Mubarak the next day. Mubarak said that Law No. 100 of 1993 was intended to prevent "a minority from imposing its dictatorship over the majority." It mandated that 50 percent of the registered members of an association had to cast ballots; if this turnout fell short, a quorum of 33 percent had to be met in a second round of voting. In the continued absence of the required number of voters, the law provided for the appointment of a panel of judges and senior association members to administer the organization for a six-month period, until new elections could be organized. In the past, low voter turnout had facilitated victories by well-organized Islamists. Professionals across the political spectrum expressed vigorous opposition to the law.

In a move that belied the government's stated commitment to freedom of expression, state security prosecutors in October detained and questioned Salah Bedaiwy and Ali el-Qammash, journalists from *al-Sha'ab*, the twice-weekly newspaper of the opposition Labor Party; party vice-president Dr. Muhammed Helmi Murad, a seventy-three-year-old lawyer and former minister who writes for the paper; and party secretary-general Adil Hussein. Prosecutors also summoned for questioning the newspaper's chief editor, Magdi Hussein, and Ibrahim Shukri, the head of the Labor Party and chairman of the board of the newspaper. *Why We Say No to Mubarak*, a book of previously published articles by Dr. Murad and Adil Hussein, was ordered confiscated because, according to prosecutors quoted by Agence France-Presse, it constituted "propaganda for extremist ideas and a justification of terrorist operaitons."

In newspaper articles, Dr. Murad had advocated a boycott of the October 4 presidential referendum and called on President Mubarak to disclose details of government arms sales and purchases. According to EOHR, the charges against Dr. Murad included "contempt of the person of the President of the Republic." Among the charges against the two journalists—who had written articles critical of security forces and state agricultural policies—was publishing ideas harmful to national unity and social peace, a crime under the July 1992 "anti-terrorism" amendments to Egypt's penal code. In a newspaper interview on October 11, President Mubarak commented that Dr. Murad and the journalists were "supporting terrorism."

Egyptian courts figured prominently in human rights developments during the year. President Mubarak, using his powers under the emergency law, began to refer cases of civilians accused of "terrorism" offenses to three-judge military courts in October 1992; the hanging of those condemned to death by such courts commenced in June 1993. The president maintained that military court trials were necessary in cases where "quick measures" were required, and that the national interest permitted "no room for extended procedures." In December 1992, the Supreme Military Court in Alexandria handed down judgments in two trials. Eight militants were sentenced to death (seven of them *in absentia*), and the condemned man in custody was hanged on June 13. Other military court trials of civilians followed, including several mass trials each with over thirty defendants. Between December 1992 and November 3, 1993, military courts issued thirty-nine death sentences against Islamist militants; seventeen of the condemned men have been hanged.

Those trials violated human rights standards on three counts. First, the verdicts could not be appealed to a higher tribunal, as required by Egypt's obligations under the International Covenant on Civil and Political Rights, to which it is a state party. Civilians sentenced to death by military courts were denied the right provided to civilians condemned to death by regular criminal courts, who could appeal verdicts by applying for review by the Court of Cassation, Egypt's highest appeals court. Second, the military justice system—as part of the executive branch of government—lacks the fuller independence of Egypt's civilian judiciary. Last, the treatment of defendants and the court proceedings raised serious concerns about denials of due process and fair trial. Defense lawyers repeatedly complained that they were afforded insufficient time to review case files and prepare adequate defenses. They also said that some of their clients had been tortured and denied access to legal counsel during the initial days of custody and questioning.

In juxtaposition to the outcomes of military trials, on August 14 a civilian security court ruled as inadmissible confessions that had been extracted under torture, and acquitted the defendants of murder charges for lack of other evidence. The twenty-four Islamist militants (eight of them *in absentia*) accused of involvement in the assassination of People's Assembly speaker Dr. Rifaat al-Mahjoub in October 1990, were acquitted of murder charges by the Supreme State Security Court. Ten were sentenced to prison terms for other offenses. The president of the court, Judge Wahid Mahmoud Ibrahim, said that forensic medical reports indicated that some of the defendants had been subjected to the "ugliest forms of torture," including electric shocks. In a scathing rebuke to Egypt's security apparatus, Judge Ibrahim observed that the use of torture to obtain confessions constituted "proof of the failure and incapacity of the police to discover the truth."

Some scholars at al-Azhar—the prestigious institution of Islamic teaching and research supported with state funds and closely tied to the government—continued during the year to play a role in legitimizing intolerance in the name of religious orthodoxy. In an important development in June, one prominent sheik publicly condoned the killing of Muslims deemed apostates. Sheik Muhammed Ghazali appeared on June 22 as a defense witness at the security-court trial of thirteen defendants accused in the 1992 assassination in Cairo of the secular Muslim writer, Dr. Faraj Foda. Sheik Ghazali testified that a Muslim who opposed the implementation of Islamic law (as did Dr. Foda) was an apostate "liable to be killed." He further stated that in the absence of an apostasy law in Egypt, Islamic *sharia* law dictated that an individual who killed an apostate should not be punished, even though such an act constituted an encroachment on the state's authority. The testimony appeared to justify, and condone, murder; as EOHR noted, it constituted "an invitation to extrajudicial killing."

In another development, Sheik Mahmoud Abdel Mutagalli, another prominent scholar who sits on the *fatwa* (religious ruling) committee of al-Azhar, sought the banning of a low-priced series of forty contemporary and historical books on Islam, reprinted and published by the Ministry of Culture. According to Ahmed Selim, an official at the government's General Egyptian Book Organization as quoted by *al-Ahram Weekly*, the aim of the series was "to confront, from a liberal perspective, the misguided ideas embraced by the extremists." One of the books was *Islam and the Rules of Government*, written by *sharia* court judge Sheik Ali Abdel-Raziq. Originally published in 1925, the controversial book, which led to Abdel-Raziq's dismissal, postulated that an Islamic caliphate as a system of government was not prescribed in the Quran or the Sayings of the Prophet Muhammed, and that Islam and a civilian government therefore were not incompatible. Sheik Mutagalli was said to be particularly disturbed by the inclusion of this volume, and he petitioned al-Azhar Grand Sheik Ali Jad el-Haq to ban the series. The grand sheik referred the matter to Azhar's Islamic Research Center (IRC) for an opinion as to whether the contents of the books contradicted Islamic law. The IRC in previous years had taken unilateral action to ban and confiscate books on various political and religious subjects. Although its censorship authority under the law extended only to the Quran and the Sunna (The Traditions of the Prophet Muhammed), security forces and the General Egyptian Book Organization had taken action on the basis of al-Azhar's opinions.

The Right to Monitor

Locally based human rights groups are tolerated but not legalized, and continued to suffer from government restrictions on freedom of association. During 1993, the eight-year-old Egyptian Organization for Human Rights (EOHR) was able to carry out field work and advocacy, and issued numerous reports and press statements. But despite the group's growing prominence and international stature, it continued to be denied cooperative working relationships with, and information from, Egyptian authorities responsible for human rights oversight, most notably the prosecutor general's office. EOHR was forced to operate in a legal limbo because authorities had refused to grant it formal status as a private organization (Egypt's 1964 law governing private associations reserves broad power for the state to deny or rescind legalization of any group). The region-wide Arab Organization for Human Rights, founded in 1983 and also based in Cairo, was similarly denied legal status under the same law, as has the Egyptian section of Amnesty International.

The government was increasingly vocal in criticizing international human rights groups in 1993, declaring, for instance, that it no longer intended to respond to Middle East Watch. In an interview with *Rose al-Yousef* magazine published in June, the director of the newly created human rights department in the Foreign Ministry, Na'ela Gaber, stated that Middle East Watch had "held a press conference in Cairo [in July 1992 to release a major report on torture]. Their goal was to stir up trouble and to politicize the human rights issue, tying it to American aid. Now, there is no longer any dialogue with this organization since it does not respect the rules by which we operate." In a twenty-three-page statement to Middle East Watch dated June 9, the Foreign Ministry denied the existence of a pattern of human rights violations in Egypt. It stated: "We are astonished by the ever increasing and dutiful concern of MEW with regard to the conditions of the terrorists, and to the publication and repetition of their accusations. . . Our analysis of all the reports that the organization has prepared about Egypt. . .[indicates that it] has not proven the existence of a prevailing pattern of human rights violations." The Foreign Ministry also complained that MEW had "attacked Egypt and its ruling order" in press articles.

In a disturbing development, in February security forces in Upper Egypt interfered with the work of Middle East Watch and EOHR, and questioned two defense lawyers with whom the groups had made contact. Harassment included close surveillance by security forces in plainclothes. SSI questioned the executive director of EOHR about Middle East Watch's activities, with a re-

quest that additional information be provided as work proceeded. In a letter of protest to the Interior Minister, Middle East Watch said that these actions compromised the ability of rights monitors to gather information and created an atmosphere of intimidation. There was no reply to the letter. But the Ministry of Foreign Affairs, in its June statement, made note of this complaint and asserted that "security agencies reported that [Middle East Watch], during [its] visit, overstepped the internationally acknowledged functions regulating the activities of nongovernmental organizations concerned with human rights."

U.S. Policy

Public criticism of Egypt's human rights performance by U.S. officials continued to be taboo, despite mounting documentation of the Mubarak government's poor record. Middle East Watch understood, however, that behind-the-scenes U.S. government pressure was responsible for the creation of human rights departments in key ministries.

As in prior years, the only public comments about human rights were found in the State Department's *Country Reports on Human Rights Practices in 1992*, issued in February 1993. The country report accurately stated that many basic rights in Egypt "continue to be significantly restricted" and that "the pattern of human rights abuse...remained essentially unchanged in 1992." Among other violations, the State Department identified security forces' excessive use of lethal force; the widespread pattern of arbitrary arrest and detention; the systematic use of torture and the failure of authorities to investigate effectively allegations of abuse; substantial restrictions on freedom of peaceful assembly and association, including the right to form political parties; and important limitations on freedom of religion.

In an April 15 letter to Middle East Watch, the State Department's Bureau of Human Rights and Humanitarian Affairs asserted that its "interest in human rights conditions in Egypt will continue to be an important element in U.S.-Egyptian relations." It further stated that concerns and specific cases regarding torture, arbitrary arrest, prolonged detention without trial, and discrimination against Christians and women had been "raised...with Egyptian authorities at high levels."

Clinton administration officials made clear that bilateral relations with Egypt were guided by broad U.S. foreign policy concerns in the region. In testimony on April 28 before the House Foreign Affairs Committee's Subcommittee on Europe and the Middle East, Assistant Secretary of State for Near Eastern Affairs Edward P. Djerejian described the basis of bilateral relations. He cited Egypt's "important role in contributing to stability in the Middle East and furthering U.S. objectives in the region." He noted that Egypt "has provided essential support for the U.S. military presence in the Middle East," and said that U.S. security assistance to Egypt "has paid off handsomely."

The Clinton administration requested $2.15 billion in aid for Egypt for fiscal year 1994: $1.3 billion from the Foreign Military Financing Program; $1.8 million in International Military Education and Training program funds; $815 million in Economic Support Funds (ESF); and $35 million in food assistance. A small portion of the ESF is allocated for judicial exchanges and training, including human rights training, and the development of information systems in the People's Assembly, Egypt's elected Parliament. As in past years, the administration made no effort to link the continuation of assistance to the Mubarak government's undertaking of specific measures to improve human rights. In fact, Secretary Djerejian, pledged on April 28 that the administration would make its best effort to maintain aid levels in subsequent years. There was no evidence that President Clinton, in his meetings with President Mubarak in Washington, D.C., on April 6 and October 25, raised the subject of Egypt's poor human rights record.

In violation of U.S. law, security assistance to Egypt continued despite a pattern of gross human rights violations, including torture and long-term detention without charge or trial. Under Section 502B of the Foreign Assistance Act, these rights abuses should trigger either a cutoff of military aid or an explanation by the administration of the "extraordinary circumstances" that merit the continued assistance.

The Work of Middle East Watch

In 1993, Middle East Watch pursued a strategy of research, information dissemination and advocacy, in order to document and publicize rights violations, maintain pressure on the Egyptian government to acknowledge and remedy abuses, and urge the U.S. and the European Community to use their considerable leverage to press the Mubarak administration to correct abuses.

In January and February, Middle East Watch carried out fact-finding in Egypt, traveling to Cairo and six other cities and towns. One focus of the mission was to obtain information about the treatment of Christians, who constitute at least ten percent of Egypt's population of fifty-nine million. Middle East Watch examined how government policies and practices have undermined religious tolerance, and obtained testimony about abusive and violent actions by Muslim militants. The problems documented included specific anti-Christian activities by extremists and their followers; the state's discriminatory restrictions on church construction and repair; the mistreatment of Christians and Muslim converts to Christianity by SSI officers because of their suspected peaceful religious activities; and the failure of security forces to respond adequately to complaints by Christians about law-breaking and violence by extremists. The report based on this research was scheduled for an early 1994 release.

Middle East Watch also worked closely with the Fund for Free Expression, another division of Human Rights Watch, to provide support for its March-April mission to Egypt, undertaken jointly with the American Association of Publishers, to investigate freedom of expression and association. The mission was particularly concerned with the ways in which the tension between the government and Islamist opposition was manifested in freedom of the press, television and radio broadcasting, book publishing, and limitations on freedom of association—principally the restrictions on political parties and professional associations.

Following up on Middle East Watch's on-site inspections of six Egyptian prisons in 1992, a book-length report on prison conditions was released in February in Cairo. In July, Middle East Watch issued a newsletter about the trials of civilians before military courts, arguing that the trials violated international human rights norms.

Middle East Watch communicated human rights concerns directly to Egyptian government officials several times during the year. In February, a letter of protest was delivered to then-Interior Minister Musa about security forces' interference with the work of human rights monitors during a fact-finding mission to Upper Egypt that month. In May, a representative met in Washington with Egypt's ambassador to the U.S., Ahmed Maher el-Sayed, to discuss incommunicado detention and torture, and specific recommendations for addressing these abuses. The ambassador was presented with eight letters written by Middle East Watch to senior Egyptian officials between March 1992 and February 1993 that had gone unacknowledged.

In July, Middle East Watch and the Fund for Free Expression wrote to President Mubarak, expressing concern about the court testimony of Sheik Muhammed Ghazali, described above. The letter called on the president to denounce the sheik's legal opinion condoning the killing of apostates and to confirm publicly that the rule of law in Egypt wÿuld not be undermined by private religious versions of justice. In September, Middle East Watch wrote again to President Mubarak, urging that an independent investigation be conducted of the suspicious death in SSI custody of security suspect Ahmed Farouq on September 3. The only reply to these and earlier communications was the lengthy June 9 statement by the Foreign Ministry, which failed to address the specific cases raised.

In advance of President Mubarak's two visits to Washington, D.C., in April and October, Middle East Watch urged that human rights issues be discussed in Congressional and executive branch meetings with the Egyptian leader. An October newsletter, designed as a briefing document for policymakers, provided an overview of major human rights developments since December 1992. Middle East Watch selected Hisham Mubarah, a lawyer and executive director of the Egyptian Organization for Human Rights, as one of the thirteen international human rights monitors honored by Human Rights Watch in observance of Human Rights Day, December 10.

IRAN

Human Rights Developments

The negative attitude of the Iranian government to universal human rights did not change during 1993. The Islamic Republic was in the vanguard of the minority of states who argued strenuously at the U.N. World Conference, in June, that cultural and religious differences should permit the implementation of different standards of behavior. Officials continued to denounce the raising of human rights issues by foreign governments and nongovernmental organizations, and the United Nations, as attempts to undermine the 1979 revolution and impose "Western values" on Iran.

Iran is a signatory to most international treaties and conventions, including those in the field of human rights. In a significant step toward compliance with treaties governing banned weapons, in January, the Rafsanjani government added Iran's signature to the Chemical and Biological Weapons Convention.

On the other hand, Iran's compliance with U.N. resolutions dealing with human rights has usually been poor. Following a period of thaw, relations with the U.N. Human Rights Commission once again soured badly in late 1991, and remained hostile thereafter. Beginning in December 1991, the Special Representative of the Human Rights Commission, Reynaldo Galindo-Pohl, was barred from entering Iran, and cooperation by the Iranian authorities with U.N. human rights work almost ceased. The Special Representative reported in November 1992 that out of 500 Iranian cases submitted to the Working Group on Enforced or Involuntary Disappearances over the years only one had been cleared up—and a nongovernmental organization had resolved that case.

Strong resolutions condemning Iran's human rights record passed the U.N. General Assembly in November 1992 and the Human Rights Commission in February 1993, by wider margins than in previous years. In August 1993, the U.N. Commission on the Elimination of Racial Discrimination issued a scathing report on Iran's failure to provide adequate and timely information about its compliance with the relevant international convention. In particular, the U.N. body asked Iran about its treatment of Kurdish and Baha'i minorities.

In some arenas of national life, such as freedom of expression, women's rights and judicial reform, human rights had made some modest advances since President Ali Akbar Hashemi-Rafsanjani came to power in mid-1989. In other areas—freedoms of religion and association, for instance—there was little or no change in the government's repressive behavior. During 1993 political dissent continued to be dealt with severely, even within the ideological confines of the Islamic Republic's constitution. And prescription of every facet of public and private life—from clothing to schools curriculae—remained a principal tenet of governance.

Most serious of all, with respect to "the right to life, liberty and security of person," enshrined in Article 3 of the Universal Declaration of Human Rights, ÿ+1XIran's record remained one of the world's worst. An exceptionally high rate of judicial executions, following unfair trials; the hunting down, and murder, of exiled opponents; and the arbi-

trary detention of citizens on flimsy charges, added up to flagrant defiance of the letter and spirit of the Universal Declaration. Official explanations that Iran was engaged in a war against narcotic drugs and against armed opposition groups, accurate though these arguments might be, represented no justification for such gross violations.

A central dilemma—one shared by Iranian citizens concerned about the limits of appropriate behavior or expression and by human rights groups attempting to evaluate the Iranian government's record—was that of the arbitrary application of laws. Rapidly shifting norms set by competing factions in the clerical establishment added to the problem. Thus, the wide range of publicly expressed views, inconsistencies in judicial sentencing, and the unrest in border provinces could provide a misleading impression of tolerated diversity. Middle East Watch believed, however, that the absence of control in some areas of public life was not for lack of intent on the part of the central authorities; rather, it reflected the unique nature of the regime, with its dual spiritual and secular authority, and endemic factionalism, as well as latent Iranian individualism.

The June election of President Rafsanjani to a second, four-year term raised hopes that, with a fresh mandate, the President would feel strong enough to usher in a more tolerant era. In fact, the reverse occured. The most prolonged crackdown on "public vice" for years swept through the streets, shops and offices of the country within days of his re-election. The campaign, which resulted in over 4,000 arrests by September, was probably timed to the start of the holy Islamic month of Moharram. Whatever the rationale, Rafsanjani's inability or unwillingness to rein in the hard-liners was clear, despite his public pleas for restraint.

As in previous years, the streets were a good litmus test of the prevailing political climate. So, too, were the bookstores, newspaper stands and cinema theaters. Soon after the elections, a fresh drive against discordant voices in the press was launched. This time, the main targets were former allies, hardcore supporters of the revolution who, having lost an earlier battle for power in the Islamic Majlis, or parliament, had become champions of free expression and more relaxed state controls.

In August, the government acted to punish the daily newspaper *Salam*, aligned with the Militant Clerics Association, a breakaway group from the pro-government Tehran Militant Clergy Association. Since the radical faction's loss of its parliamentary majority in the 1992 national elections, *Salam* had become increasingly open in criticizing government policy. It had become a forum for dissident voices on a range of subjects. Abbas Abdi, its editor-in-chief, was arrested on the order of the Islamic Revolutionary Courts, on August 26. Two days later, the newspaper's publisher Mohammed Asqar Musavi-Kho'iniha, a prominent cleric, was summoned to appear before the Special Clerical Court on charges of slander. The same day, Mehdi Nassiri, editor-in-chief of the mass circulation daily, *Keyhan*, another radical newspaper, was summoned to the prosecutor's office over commentaries critical of the head of the judiciary, Ayatollah Mohammad Yazdi. He was released on bail and awaited trial on slander charges filed against him by Yazdi. Slander was the common criminal charge when government policy was criticized.

Keyhan's embroilment with the law was related to reports it had published concerning the activities of Ayatollah Hossein Ali Montazeri. The challenge to the regime's authority posed by Montazeri, a prominent government critic, touched one of its most sensitive subjects. Until 1989, when he fell out with Ayatollah Khomeini, Montazeri had been the late Iranian leader's designated successor; since then, he had been confined to the city of Qom, where he taught at a theological seminary. While the government attempted to silence Montazeri and his supporters as discreetly as possible, the problem was his religious eminence—especially when contrasted with the relatively low standing in the Shi'a hierarchy of Ali Khamenei, the

current Supreme Leader of Iran.

In a stern warning to other Montazeri supporters, in November, Mahmud Kheirollahi, a cleric, was sentenced to nine years in jail and seventy lashes. According to *Keyhan*, a religious court had found him guilty of "insulting the Islamic government" and distributing publications advocating Montazeri's elevation to the Supreme Leadership. Earlier in the year, the government had used both its formal and informal instruments of control in an unsuccessful attempt to silence Montazeri. After a critical speech to his theological class in February, several of the religious leader's aides, including his son-in-law, were arrested and their offices ransacked by paid thugs. Two months later, in April, a clerical court ordered the closure of the magazine *Rah-e Mojahed* because it dared to publish criticism of the February events.

Another prominent former supporter of the regime turned dissident, the philosopher Abdelkarim Soroush, increasingly found himself unable to express his opinions in public. Soroush had articulated a view held privately by many others, that the Shi'a leadership needed to choose between secular and spiritual power, arguing that, if they failed to choose, they ran the risk of losing both sources of authority.

During 1993, all the press remained vulnerable to unchecked vigilante attacks. Among those attacked were the daily *Ettela'at*, the magazine *Ettela'at-e Haftegi*, the magazine *Kiyan* (linked to Soroush) and the publishing house Nashr-e Nogreh. In June, a Ministry of Culture and Islamic Guidance spokesman acknowledged that the government was unable to stop these attacks. He exhorted publications to "behave in a way as not to offend the sentiments of the *hezbollahi* (hard-line revolutionaries)."

One of the worst abuses directly attributable to the authorities concerned Manouchehr Karimzadeh, a cartoonist accused in 1992 of insulting the memory of the late Ayatollah Khomeini. Despite standing orders from Ayatollah Yazdi, his first trial was conducted in secret before the Islamic

Revolutionary Courts. (Revolutionary Courts are used when the authorities deem the likely punishment levied by general courts to be insufficient.) Karimzadeh was first sentenced to one year in prison, fifty lashes and a fine. In 1993, the Supreme Court ratified the lower court's guilty finding, and sent the case back to the lower court for retrial. After the second hearing, Yazdi announced, in October, that Karimzadeh's prison sentence had been increased ten-fold.

In one small victory for press freedom, in December 1992 Abbas Maroufi, the editor-in-chief of *Gardoon* magazine, was tried by a criminal court before the press jury, and was acquitted. *Gardoon* was able to resume publication in April, after some delay. This case and another, earlier in 1992, marked the first applications of the 1985 Press Law, which required that press offenses be tried in general courts in the presence of a jury.

Women's rights—another key arena of ideological and social confrontation—fared indifferently in the twelve months under review. In some aspects, modest progress was made, in others there were reverses. Reinforced dress codes affected women more than men, descending even to such trivial offenses as wearing sun glasses. Violations frequently led to fines or flogging. Meanwhile, the separation of the sexes in public, a central precept of Islamic morality, was taken a step further in December 1992, when it became required that public transportation be segregated by gender.

Several developments improved women's conditions in the areas of employment and divorce. In July, Ayatollah Yazdi affirmed a right to work for women—an important, but controversial, issue in a country where conservative Muslim clergy argue that women must stay at home and bring up children. Yazdi qualified his endorsement of the principle, however, saying that in the absence of a private nuptial contract specifying a wife's right to work outside the house or continue her studies, her husband had the right to deny these prerogatives.

Amendments in divorce laws agreed upon in December 1992 were greeted by women as signs of progress. Legislation ratified by the Council of Expediency, a top-level arbitration body for the government, allowed women to claim "housework wages" from husbands who filed for divorce. Unfortunately, the practical consequences of this move were limited—in part, because of stringent preconditions applied to those seeking compensation and, in part, because of the high degree of illiteracy among rural women. Discriminatory policies against women in other legal areas, such as inheritance, child custody, education, travel and occupation remained unchanged.

The total number of political or security prisoners in Iran during 1993 was unknown. According to Ayatollah Yazdi, in April, there was "not even a single prisoner in Iran kept for his thoughts and beliefs." Hojatulislam Mir Abolfazl Musavi-Tabrizi, the Prosecutor-General, was equally categorical. The state radio quoted him as declaring at a press conference in January: "At present, there are no political prisoners in Iran." Yazdi conceded that the government was holding members of opposition parties, which he described as "counter-revolutionary grouplets;" but he claimed that the number of such detainees was "fewer than the number of fingers."

These official claims could not be accepted at face value. After anti-government disturbances in early 1992 in several parts of the country, many hundreds were arrested and accused of being "insurgents" or "corrupt on earth." Some were reported in the Iranian media to have been sentenced to long prison terms. In a submission to the Iranian government in September 1992, Galindo-Pohl listed the names and cases of eighty-nine persons believed being held at that time on political grounds.

Few cases of arrests of opposition activists become public. In one rare example, in November 1993, the left-wing organization Komala wrote to Middle East Watch about five of its activists who had been detained by Revolutionary Guards in the Kurdish city of Sanandaj, on October 21. Middle East Watch was also aware of the names of other long-term prisoners in Iranian jails who continued to be held because of their political beliefs or associations, and not because of any acts of violence.

Overcrowding and poor conditions were believed to be serious problems in Iranian detention facilities. In a rare admission, on January 3, Ayatollah Yazdi said on state television that, taking into account the number of incarcerated drug offenders, the state of the country's prisons presented "a big problem." Drug offenders and addicts, who were confined to compulsory treatment centers, made up between 50 and 70 percent of Iran's estimated 100,000 prisoners; the higher figure was given by Prosecutor-General Musavi-Tabrizi on January 24.

Supervisor of Prisons Asadollah Lajevardi disclosed in September that during the Iranian year to March 21, 1993, Iran's prison population had averaged 99,900. He broke down this figure by stating that 52,000 persons were held on drug-related charges, and 2,000 persons for vice crimes. Lajevardi also noted that 2,000 persons under the age of eighteen were among the prisoners. It was unclear whether detainees under interrogation or those awaiting trial or sentencing were included in these figures.

The number of executions carried out in 1993, while believed to remain high, could not be reliably estimated, largely because the Iranian media ceased its previous practice of publishing details of individual cases. In 1992, Amnesty International documented from press accounts at least 330 executions, including cases of juveniles. For his part, the U.N. Special Representative noted 224 cases where the death penalty had been applied in the first seven months of 1992 alone, at least sixty-six of which were on political grounds.

The government claimed that capital punishment was applied only to "major drug traffickers and those found guilty of premeditated murder." It also consistently denied allegations that political prisoners were being executed under the guise of drug traffickers. The scale of the drugs problem can be judged from a statement by a top Interior Ministry official, Brig.-Gen. Reza Seyfollahi,

that between March and August 1993—the first five months of the Iranian year—the authorities had seized a record twenty-two tons of narcotics.

In response to criticism about Iran's judicial shortcomings, during 1993, the country's top judicial officials were at pains to defend their practices. Musavi-Tabrizi emphasized that all judicial sentences were automatically reviewed, with the second stage being final and binding. Yazdi, responding to criticism over lengthy pre-trial detention of suspects claimed, in September, that Iran's practice was superior to international standards, "because charging a defendant with a crime before trial is tantamount to an official finding of guilt." His remarks underscored a disregard for the basic legal safeguards necessary for a fair trial. The judiciary's institutional weaknesses were its inconsistency and the dearth of qualified jurists.

Iran's disregard of the fundamental principle of the right to life was not, however, confined within its borders. In 1993, Middle East Watch noted four successful assassinations, one attempted assassination, and one case of abduction and disappearance of Iranians linked to exile opposition parties. In each of these cases there were strong grounds for the belief that the authorities in Tehran were behind the action. Since the Iranian revolution in 1979, the government has been suspected of involvement in the killing abroad of at least sixty opposition figures.

Incidents recorded during the twelve months to November 1993 consisted of the December 26, 1992 abduction in Istanbul of Abbas Gholizadeh, from the Organization for the Defense of Fundamental Freedoms in Iran (formerly Flag of Freedom); the January 18 attempted murder in Cologne of Mehdi Haeri, a dissident cleric; the March 16 killing in Rome of Mohammad Hossain Nagdi, an official of the National Resistance Council of Iran; the June 6 assassination in Karachi of Mohammed Hassan Arbab a People's Mojahedin of Iran member; the August 25 abduction in Ankara of Mohammad Ghaderi, member of the Kurdistan Democratic Party of Iran-Revolutionary Council; and the August 28 assassination in Ankara of Bahram Azadifar of the Kurdistan Democratic Party of Iran.

In none of the above cases were arrests made by the local authorities. Coincidentally, though, three important cases involving prominent Iranians assassinated in Western Europe either came to trial in late 1993, or were due to begin shortly. All of these cases carried political overtones for the states concerned—France, Germany and Switzerland—as local prosecutors in each case stated that evidence existed linking the Iranian authorities to the crimes. Iranian officials continued vehemently to deny the government's involvement in overseas assassinations—a denial expressed to Middle East Watch in February by Deputy Foreign Minister Jawad Zarif, in Tehran.

On October 28, a Berlin court began hearing a case against four Lebanese and an Iranian accused of participating in the 1992 murder of Sadiq Sharifkandeh and four of his colleagues on the orders of the Iranian intelligence service. A few days before the case began, Germany's top intelligence official held secret talks in Bonn with Hojatulislam Ali Fallahian, the Iranian Minister of Intelligence. The meeting drew protests from Britain and the United States; but the Kohl government insisted that it would continue the contacts, which it said dealt with unspecified "humanitarian matters." Four Germans were held in jail in Iran, one of whom had been sentenced to death, on charges of espionage, at the time. Several other foreigners, including an American travel agent, Milton Meier, who was informally accused of a number of offences, remained in jail in Tehran without trial.

The other Iranian cases due to come to trial in Europe at the end of 1993 or early in 1994 released were those involving the August 1991 murder in Paris of former Iranian Prime Minister Shahpour Bakhtiar, and the April 1990 murder near Geneva of Kazem Rajavi, brother of the leader of the opposition People's Mujaheddin of Iran.

Foreigners held against their will in Iran during the year included an estimated 20,000 Iraqi prisoners-of-war—still detained more than five years after the end of the war with Iraq. While many may not have wanted to return to Iraq, prior to 1993 the International Committee of the Red Cross (ICRC) had been unable to ascertain their wishes, in accordance with its standard procedures concerning the repatriation of POWs. After repeated official denials that Iran was holding so many Iraqis, in May Deputy Majlis Speaker Hassan Rouhani confirmed the 20,000 figure for the first time.

In what was described as a "good will" gesture, Iran released a total of 3,500 Iraqis, who returned to Iraq under ICRC supervision. At least 2,900 were not POWs, but military deserters who crossed the border into Iran during the 1991 Persian Gulf War. Iraq did not reciprocate these gestures and continued to claim that there were no Iranian POWs in its custody.

Based on testimonial evidence gathered by Middle East Watch in February, as well as information collected by other international organizations, Iranians being kept against their will in Iraq included an unknown, but large, number of ethnic Arabs and Kurds forcibly removed from their homes in the border areas to camps deep inside Iraq, in the early months of the eight-year war.

The two most significant issues during 1993 involving the rights of ethnic or religious minorities concerned the Kurds and the Baha'is. Little reliable information was available about security force actions inside Iranian Kurdistan involving human rights violations. But fighting with guerrillas of the Kurdistan Democratic Party of Iran and two smaller groups apparently grew in intensity, leaving casualties on both sides. In response to the deteriorating situation, the new Interior Minister, Ali Mohammed Besharati, was put in charge of a new security force in the border zone, in October. The Law and Order Forces, composed of *basij* volunteers— young Islamic zealots—was described as a rapid-reaction force to deal with unrest in Kurdistan; its establishment created a concern that further rights violations would occur in a region where grave abuses had been reported over the years since the 1979 revolution.

Along Iran's border with the Kurdish-held region of northern Iraq, Middle East Watch and other nongovernmental organizations observed the persistent shelling of border villages by Iranian forces, which caused much damage and forced an estimated 10,000 civilians to seek refuge elsewhere. Shelling and other military actions, ostensibly aimed at bases of Iranian Kurdish parties, began in March and continued on an almost daily basis throughout the rest of the year. In another breach of international humanitarian law, in July, Iranian forces seized thirteen Iraqi Kurdish civilians as hostages, to press for the return of five Iranian soldiers captured earlier by the Kurdish authorities. An exchange was arranged after some weeks of negotiation.

In a move with disturbing implications for the rights of thousands of Iranian refugees in Turkey, on October 18 Interior Minister Besharati and his Turkish counterpart, Mehmet Gazioglu, signed a protocol to counter "hostile acts along their common border." In return for Iran's cooperation in denying sanctuary to the mainly Turkish Kurdistan Workers Party (PKK) guerrillas, according to the Arabic daily *Asharq al-Awsat*, Besharati asked Gazioglu to expel or otherwise restrain 183 Iranian dissidents living in Turkey.

Members of the largest non-Muslim religious minority in Iran, Baha'is have long had to contend with discriminatory government policies. Persecution significantly abated over the years, but Baha'is were still not recognized by the state as a religious group and were not afforded any constitutional rights. In February, the U.N. Special Representative released a 1991 document apparently approved by Iran's highest-ranking officials which stated baldly that "the progress and development of the Baha'is shall be blocked." The document required that Baha'is be denied education and employment, if they identified themselves as Baha'i, and that they be prevented from assuming any position of influence.

Legislation that formalized the previously administrative discrimination applied against all persons deemed not to be good Muslims was passed by the Majlis on October 24. The wide-ranging bill made it illegal for public servants to engage in many actions with human rights implications. Among them were "unauthorized contact or communication with foreigners"; the "non-observance of Islamic dress code or Islamic principles and rights"; and "scaremongering, participation in illegal sit-ins, strikes and demonstrations, or encouraging others to [engage in] these acts."

Obnoxious for their group implications were those clauses of the bill that barred government employment to members of "deviant groups ... groups whose constitution is based on the denial of divine religions ... and Freemason organizations." As Baha'is are considered by mainstream Shi'a to be apostates, as a result of this bill they were automatically barred from work for any public employer. Although the legislation may have been aimed primarily at controlling corruption in government employment, as some Iranians claimed, its draconian nature gave officials a heavy stick to use at will against dissidents and minorities.

In response to criticism about Iran's treatment of Baha'is and peaceful dissidents, the Iranian Mission to the U.N. said on April 23 that: "neither Bahais nor any other groups including dissident groups have been prosecuted in Iran on grounds of their beliefs. Like other Iranian nationals, Bahais also enjoy equal protection of the law and like them Bahais have also been held accountable for their breaches of the law. For instance, in the last five years in Iran only one Bahai individual has been found guilty as charged in a court of law and sentenced to death." The individual concerned, Bahman Samandari, a prominent community leader, was executed on March 18, 1992, one day after being summoned on a pretext to Tehran's Evin Prison. His relatives were never informed of the charges, or whether he had been tried.

The Right to Monitor

No on-site monitoring of human rights conditions in Iran by international organizations was permitted during 1993. Reynaldo Galindo-Pohl, Special Representative of the U.N. Commission on Human Rights, had been denied access since December 1991. Similarly, Amnesty International, Middle East Watch and other nongovernmental organizations were consistently refused permission to enter Iran for the specific purpose of examining domestic human rights issues.

Middle East Watch was able to conduct a mission to Iran in 1991, aimed at gathering information about the uprising in neighboring Iraq; and it was permitted to return in early 1993 to investigate conditions in Iraq. On both these occasions, and during a September 1991 visit to Tehran, to take part in a government-sponsored conference on human rights, Middle East Watch representatives were able to meet with government officials, academics, nongovernmental organizations and private citizens.

In 1993, there was no genuinely independent domestic organization to monitor human rights conditions, although a dissident political party, the Freedom Movement, did issue occasional denunciations of governmental abuses of the rule of law, and other matters, through clandestinely printed and circulated statements. One ostensibly independent human rights organization, the Organization for the Defense of Victims of Violence, was backed by the government; its work was confined to combatting the propaganda of the opposition PMOI and to defending the official version of Iran's human rights record before international organizations.

In May, the Iranian parliament announced the formation of a "nongovernment" committee, consisting of seventeen members of parliament and lawyers, to "investigate the human rights situation in Iran and abroad and offer suggestions." No further details were available as to its role and functioning. Given parliament's independence from the Rafsanjani government, such a committee could potentially play a useful monitoring role, provided it was prepared to use its authority to call officials to account and demand changes in abusive practices.

The expulsion of the ICRC in March 1992, on the grounds that it had exceeded its mandate, closed a briefly opened window into prison conditions in Iran. For two months, the ICRC had been able to meet Iranian security prisoners on a regular basis, to register them and determine their wellbeing. However, it was not permitted to meet the estimated 20,000 Iraqi prisoners-of-war being held in Iran following the end of the war with Iraq, in August 1988.

International humanitarian organizations, such as the office of the United Nations High Commissioner for Refugees and private relief groups, were given relatively free access to the large refugee population in Iran. Iran housed over three million refugees from conflicts past and present among its neighbors—the heaviest refugee burden of any country in the world—and, during 1993, it appealed on several occasions for further outside assistance. The presence of foreign organizations in sensitive border regions was closely controlled by the authorities. Nevertheless, such bodies served informally as useful sources of information on human rights-related matters.

U.S. Policy

Impelled by Iran's outspoken opposition to the Arab-Israeli peace process, and by intelligence reports that the Islamic Republic was acquiring the means to develop nuclear weapons, the Clinton administration early on adopted a harsher stance against Iran than had the Bush administration. The shift to a more active policy of "containment" of Iran also reflected the urgings of two key U.S. allies in the Middle East, Israel and Egypt.

Secretary of State Warren Christopher, whose previous spell in government as Deputy Secretary of State had been marked by the U.S. Embassy hostage crisis of 1979 to 1981, set the tone at a March 30 Senate hearing. Branding Iran "an international outlaw," Secretary Christopher said the U.S. opposed World Bank lending to the Islamic

Republic, and would be urging U.S. friends and allies to follow suit. U.S. officials argued that low-cost World Bank loans enabled Iran to divert scarce financial resources to the acquisition of arms, including nuclear weapons. Against U.S. objections, the World Bank approved $458 million in loans to Iran, in March. However, persistent U.S. pressure led, in September, to a suspension of World Bank loans pending a broader review of lending to Iran, which has run into mounting credit problems.

Human rights formed one of the six areas of Iranian "objectionable behavior" cited by administration officials when asked about the preconditions for a changed attitude on the part of Washington. The others were: the acquisition of nuclear technology, support for terrorism abroad, pursuit of a military buildup in excess of its defensive needs, opposition to the Arab-Israeli peace talks, and the subversion of Arab governments friendly to the United States. The last point, referring to Egypt and Tunisia, was later dropped in public statements.

In a surprise move that highlighted the differences in approach to Iran between the Bush and Clinton administrations, on November 24 President Clinton met the British writer Salman Rushdie—in hiding for the previous four years under a death threat issued by the late Ayatollah Khomeini—at the White House. Despite the urgings of many freedom of expression organizations, the Bush administration had carefully distanced itself from the Rushdie affair. No high-level U.S. official had been willing to meet the writer in a show of solidarity with his plight. While security considerations were cited for this stance by the Bush administration, it appeared that Washington had previously been anxious not to give offense to Tehran with a gesture of this sort. This welcome shift by the administration to openly support a touchstone principle of universal human rights followed tougher stands on Rushdie by the British and German governments in 1993.

The most forthright exposition of the new U.S. policy toward Iran came in a May speech to the Washington Institute for Near East Policy by Martin Indyk, the senior Middle East aide on the National Security Council. In his speech, the NSC official said: "We do not seek a confrontation, but we will not normalize relations with Iran until and unless Iran's policies change—across the board." Indyk dubbed U.S. strategy toward Iran and Iraq as one of "dual containment." State Department officials later backed away from the "dual containment" line, emphasizing that Washington remained open to dialogue with Tehran, without preconditions on either side.

Although human rights were often cited in the lexicon of misbehavior, less emphasis was placed on domestic violations than on acts of overseas terrorism. Here, the U.S. took an expansive view of Iranian government responsibility. The State Department's annual report on terrorism featured Rafsanjani and Khamenei on its cover, and devoted more space to actions allegedly conducted by, or on behalf of, Iran than any other country. U.S. officials were particularly angered by Germany's secret talks with the Iranian Intelligence Minister, Ali Fallahian, in October. Regrettably, though, no statement emanated from Washington in response to the constant shelling of Iraqi Kurdish border villages—part of an area closely monitored, and ostensibly protected, by patrolling U.S. and allied aircraft.

The most practical aspect of U.S. policy was a concerted drive to deny Iran "dual-use" technology with civilian and military applications. Meeting with European Community Foreign Ministers in Luxembourg on June 9, Secretary Christopher urged European states to back the U.S. premise that Iran should not enjoy normal commercial relations. No blanket embargo exists on trade with Iran, although the U.S. forbids the import of most Iranian exports, including oil. Despite the prohibition, U.S. oil companies were reported to be among the largest purchasers of Iranian crude oil, shipping it to third destinations or to offshore refineries. A bid by the Boeing aircraft manufacturer to sell passenger aircraft to Iran, in an order potentially worth hundreds of millions of dollars, was held up by the White House.

Contrary to reports disseminated by the People's Mujaheddin, the principal opposition organization, the Clinton administration did not move closer than its predecessor to a rebel body that itself had a poor human rights record.

The Work of Middle East Watch

In 1993, Middle East Watch's work focused on freedom of expression in Iran. A 140-page report titled *Guardians of Thought: Limits on Freedom of Expression in Iran* was released in September and received widespread media coverage. Covering primarily the period from 1989 to 1993, the report examined the various mechanisms of state control of expression. It presented more than sixty cases of Iranian writers, filmmakers, journalists and intellectuals who had either been imprisoned or otherwise punished for the content of their work, or whose work had been banned or censored. The case studies illustrated tactics of direct, often violent, pressure by groups of ideological vigilantes, media vilification campaigns, and formal censorship; it also showed how the power play between different factions of the ruling élite had a deleterious effect on freedom of expression. Efforts to meet with Iranian government officials, to discuss the contents and recommendations contained in the report, were unsuccessful.

Publication of *Guardians of Thought* was followed up, in October, with a brief report on the detention of a dissident former army officer, Col. Nasrullah Tavakoli, and the imposition of a ten-year prison sentence on a cartoonist, Manouchehr Karimzadeh. The Tavakoli case, involving a lone individual who issued lengthy written attacks on the government, illustrated the limits of official tolerance. Middle East Watch organized an international campaign among cartoonists over the Karimzadeh case.

A delegation from Middle East Watch traveled to Iran in January and February, for a three-week mission. Team members interviewed Iraqi refugees and exiles in Tehran and Khuzestan province about human rights conditions inside Iraq. Informally, the delegation was also able to gather useful information on current conditions in Iran, to counter often distorted accounts received abroad from exile groups. Throughout the year, Middle East Watch met with activists living abroad or visiting from Iran. It participated in conferences on Iran, and addressed groups in the United States on human rights conditions in the country.

IRAQ AND IRAQI KURDISTAN

The regional Kurdish government and parliament based in Erbil, elected in May 1992, is treated in this chapter as a self-governing entity, with all due responsibilities for the maintenance of accepted norms of government behavior toward citizens and upholding of human rights standards. This approach by Middle East Watch does not imply recognition of the Kurds' right to self determination, a topic outside the mandate of Human Rights Watch, nor of the legitimacy of the local authorities.

Human Rights Developments

There were no indications during 1993 of improved respect on the part of the regime headed by President Saddam Hussein for the human rights of Iraq's eighteen million citizens. Iraq is a party to most international human rights instruments, but its compliance with their provisions has been only on paper. In the twenty-five years since the Ba'th Party seized power in a *coup d'état*, for the second time, in 1968, the party relied almost constantly on maintaining control through a system of "terror and reward"— the alliterative expression in Arabic is *tarhib wa targhib*.

After Iraq's defeat in the Persian Gulf War, in February 1991, the totalitarian nature of the regime became increasingly visible. A rubber-stamp National Assembly remained in existence. But President Saddam came to rely exclusively on a small circle of long-time aides from the ruling Revolutionary Command Council (RCC). All key government posts were held by close relatives of the President. In a new cabinet announced on September 5, 1993, Watban Ibrahim al-Hassan, Saddam's half brother, became Interior Minister; Hussein Kamel Hassan, his son-in-law, was made Minister of Minerals and Industry; and Ali Hassan al-Majid, the president's first cousin, retained the post of Defense Minister. An élite security agency, the *Amn al-Khas* (Special Security), responsible for the protection of the regime, was headed by Saddam's youngest son, Qusai Hussein.

In a little publicized move disturbing even by Iraq's standards of flagrant disregard for the rule of law, on December 12, 1992, the RCC issued a decree effectively absolving members of the Ba'th Party from criminal responsibility for their actions in defending security and order. As published by the state-run Iraqi News Agency, the decree stated that the RCC "bans the interrogation of members of the Party and popular patrols charged by the Arab Socialist Ba'th Party with the task of conducting security and observation missions under the slogan, 'the People's Guards never tire in establishing security and providing tranquillity for people.'" Members of the Ba'th were already a privileged caste in Iraq, provided with better employment and educational opportunities than non-members. Additionally, many Iraqis told Middle East Watch that, at a time of extreme food shortages and high prices in the country, as a consequence of U.N. sanctions, Ba'th members received favored access to the state-controlled food distribution system.

During 1993, the regime focused its energies at home on preserving its own survival and abroad on securing the lifting of economic sanctions imposed by the United Nations in August 1990, following Iraq's invasion of Kuwait, and periodically renewed. As sanctions are tied to compliance with U.N. Security Council Resolution 687

of March 1991, mandating the elimination of Iraq's weapons of mass destruction, the government avoided confrontation with UNSCOM, the U.N. agency charged with carrying out this task. It also issued a steady stream of propaganda about the effects of sanctions on vulnerable sectors of the Iraqi population.

While sanctions have undoubtedly had a highly negative impact on the health of the Iraqi population, Middle East Watch believes that an exclusive focus on the deleterious effect of U.N.-ordered actions ignores the government's own responsibility to ameliorate the situation, within its capabilities. Iraq continued to refuse to comply with U.N. Security Council resolutions 706 and 712 (of August and September 1992), which provided, *inter alia*, for a "food-for-oil" arrangement that could have alleviated hunger in the country. Negotiations between Deputy Prime Minister Tariq Aziz and U.N. Secretary-General Boutros Boutros-Ghali, at Geneva in August, broke down under Iraqi insistence that it had met the terms of Resolution 687, and should be permitted to resume oil exports without any constraint. Furthermore, the imposition of internal sanctions against northern Iraq and parts of the south exposed the government's bad faith in claiming to be concerned about the wellbeing of the people.

Economic and military blockades of the Kurdish enclave and of the marshes were maintained throughout the twelve months under review, preventing virtually all food, medicine and fuel from crossing army lines. Smuggling, made possible by rising levels of corruption in all corners of Iraqi society as the economy collapsed, was the principal means of survival for the embattled regions, in which the lives of an estimated four million persons were put at risk by the government actions. U.N. agencies, foreign nongovernmental organizations and—in the case of Kurdistan—the U.S. government took part in large-scale relief operations.

Following the expiration in March of a memorandum of understanding (MOU) between Iraq and the U.N. on relief arrangements, the activities of international bodies in Iraq became increasingly problematic. In early 1993, three foreign aid workers were killed by unknown gunmen, in attacks blamed on agents of the Baghdad government; visas for the workers of nongovernmental organizations (NGOs) to enter Iraq became hard to obtain; and U.N. guards charged with protecting relief operations could not be deployed outside Baghdad and the rebel-controlled north.

The blockades of regions of Iraq outside government control were accompanied, particularly in the south, by intensive military action. Scores of villages in the central Amara marshes were regularly shelled, causing thousands of civilian casualties. Marsh villages were burned and their inhabitants dispersed, denied medical care in government facilities or rationed food supplies. Mines placed in the waters of the marshes and on earth embankments protecting drainage schemes caused an untold number of casualties among noncombatants. All such actions were grave violations of international humanitarian law. While rebel groups based in Iran could be accused of similar violations, by using civilian settlements in the marshes as shields for military positions, or by targeting civilians for assassination as was claimed in frequent communiqués, the vast preponderance of abuses were on the government side of the conflict.

A vast hydrological scheme, to divert Euphrates and Tigris waters away from the Amara and Hammar marshes, advanced apace during 1993. U.S. government-released satellite photographs showed that, as of March, a significant part of the marshes had been drained, destroying the habitat and way of life of an ancient people, the Maadan or Marsh Arabs. Between July and September, as summer temperatures rose and water disappeared, an estimated 7,000 Iraqi Shi'a from the marshes region took refuge across the border in Iran. They reported that frequent army attacks on fleeing persons made the crossing highly precarious.

At least 105 Shi'a clerics, some of them very elderly, were rounded up in Najaf and Kerbala after the March 1991 uprising. They were not seen again by friends or relatives; nor did the government respond to enquiries from abroad as to their safety. However, contrary to some fears, Middle East Watch heard in September 1993 that the clerics were probably still all alive, and were being held in an undisclosed detention center. During the year, the regime moved to consolidate its control over Shi'a religious institutions in Iraq, particularly in Najaf and Kerbala. It also attempted to influence the succession to the late Grand Ayatollah Abdul Qasim Musawi al-Khoie, spiritual leader of Iraq's eleven million Shi'a and of many other Shi'a Muslims worldwide, who died in August 1992.

Iraq's maintenance of secret prisons and temporary detention centers, within the premises of security forces and in other locations, such as under public buildings, complicated the task of estimating the number of political prisoners in Iraq or determining their physical and mental condition. U.N. Special Rapporteur Max Van der Stoel estimated in February 1993 that there were over a hundred such detention facilities in different parts of the country. Access by the International Committee of the Red Cross and by other outsiders—except for one visit in 1991 by the Special Rapporteur—was barred.

Based on the rough estimates of Iraqi human rights organizations located abroad as well as information from opposition political parties, the total number of persons being detained without charge was estimated conservatively by Middle East Watch at 10,000 to 12,000. The majority were probably Shi'a men, detained on the grounds of their beliefs, and not because of any specific crimes. However, an estimated 70,000 to 100,000 Kurds—men, women and children—taken into government custody during the *Anfal* military operations, in 1988, and not seen again also remained to be accounted for. Most are believed to have been executed. But reports persisted during 1993 of Kurds being held in secret detention centers camouflaged to disguise their location. Following a July 1991 amnesty, hundreds—possibly thousands—of prisoners were released later that year. However, many other detainees remained incarcerated beyond their prison terms. The U.N. Special Rapporteur said in February 1993 that he had gathered the names of 153 persons who should have been released in the amnesty, but remained in detention as of that date. A small number of foreigners sentenced to excessively long prison terms for offences such as illegal entry into the country also remained in jail during 1993; among them were three British citizens. Three Swedes and an American were, however, quietly released.

The largest single detention facility in 1993 was believed to be the Radwaniya military camp, west of Baghdad, which was estimated to hold somewhere between 5,000 and 10,000 detainees. Most of the Radwaniyya inmates were arbitrarily detained after the 1991 uprisings. Former inmates described to Middle East Watch conditions of gross overcrowding at Radwaniyya, and of periodic public executions. Gross reports of torture, such as the rotation of prisoners strapped to metal drums over open fires, were also reported, but could not be confirmed.

The execution of many persons was reported periodically during the year under review by relatives who either managed to flee the country or were able to communicate to others abroad. In August, hundreds of young Shi'a men held at Radwaniyya were executed, most of them apparently after no legal process. Families in Amara and Nasiriyya said that bodies returned to them sometimes bore marks of torture.

In mid-November, dozens of prominent individuals detained in July and August, apparently on suspicion of participating in plots to overthrow the regime, were executed. Among them were serving and retired military officers. The total number could not be reliably estimated, because of an information blackout on this sensitive subject for the regime; but relatives claimed that the number ran into the hundreds. Many were members of major families from Mosul

and Tikrit, part of the Sunni heartland of the country. According to relatives, they were not informed of charges having been brought or of any trials having taken place. Several of the victims had been killed with a bullet to the head, gangster-style. Families were forbidden from burying the victims in family plots or holding mourning ceremonies. As of mid-November, there had been no reference to this wave of executions in the government-controlled Iraqi press.

Many thousands of Iraqis took advantage of the relative ease of travel abroad during 1992 and 1993 to move to Amman, the Jordanian capital, where they waited for visas to enter other countries. Even here, though, they were not safe from the attention of the Iraqi secret police. On December 7, an Iraqi nuclear scientist, Moayyad Hassan al-Janabi, was assassinated in front of his family in Amman by suspected Iraqi agents, as he was attempting to secure refuge abroad. In 1993, following reports of alleged plots to replace President Saddam, fresh travel restrictions on serving and former army officers were imposed.

The military-backed blockade of the Kurdish-held enclave, where approximately 3.5 million people were living, continued during 1993. As a consequence of the blockade, fuel prices in Iraqi Kurdistan were usually twenty times higher than in government-controlled parts of the country, imposing considerable hardship. In a further tightening of these internal sanctions, commencing in July, electricity supplies were cut off by the government to the Dohuk region of the enclave. Random bomb explosions occurred frequently during the year, causing many civilian casualties. The bombs were frequently left in crowded public places such as open-air markets, and appeared designed to destabilize the Kurdish authorities and increase the pressure on them to negotiate with Baghdad over the region's return to central control.

Outside the Kurdish enclave, foreign human rights groups gathered credible information about the renewal of pressure on Kurds living in the major city of Kirkuk to evacuate Kurdish-dominated districts. Periodic sweeps through Kurdish districts resulted in many arbitrary arrests, although detainees were often freed by paying bribes to their captors. The "Arabization" of Kirkuk and its surrounding oil fields region has been a longstanding goal of the Ba'th regime.

U.S. Policy

In January, shortly before taking office, President-elect Bill Clinton signaled that his administration would be taking a different approach to Iraq than had the Bush administration. In a newspaper interview, Clinton said he wanted to "depersonalize" the conflict with Saddam Hussein. Faced with uproar over the implication that the new administration was prepared to tolerate the continuation of Saddam's regime, U.S. officials scrambled to insist that there would be no change of policy. As evidence that nothing had changed, it was pointed out that "air exclusion" zones in northern and southern Iraq remained in force.

As if to prove the new administration's resolve, U.S. aircraft patrolling the "no-fly" zones acted preemptively on several occasions to strike at missile batteries they claimed had threatened allied aircraft monitoring Iraqi military behavior on the ground. In a signal to Baghdad that the new team would not be softer than its predecessor, in June President Clinton authorized the launch of a missile attack on the Baghdad headquarters of the Mukhabarat, Iraq's external intelligence service. Eight civilians were killed during the June 26 attack, justified by Washington as a legitimate defensive action, in reprisal for an alleged plot by Iraqi agents to kill former President George Bush during a visit to Kuwait. Middle East Watch considered both the rationale and the legal justification for the missile attack to be dubious.

Washington insisted that the U.S. still sought to promote a democratic form of government in Iraq. A clear manifestation of this commitment was meetings Secretary Christopher and Vice President Al Gore held in late April and early May with leaders of the Iraqi National Congress, a multiparty opposition coalition. At these meetings, the administration promised to continue protection for the Kurds, so long as the threat from Saddam Hussein remained potent. It also announced the U.S. intention to seek the establishment of a U.N. commission of inquiry into Iraqi "war crimes, crimes against humanity and acts of genocide." The commission could lead to the holding of a Nuremberg-style war crimes tribunal.

Together with its chief allies on Iraq policy, Britain and France, the U.S. remained admirably forthright in its condemnation of Iraqi human rights violations, politically convenient though this may have been. The administration gave solid support to a tough denunciatory resolution against Iraq, at the U.N. Human Rights Commission, in March, and was supportive of the work of the Special Rapporteur, including his proposal to establish a team of U.N. monitors for Iraq.

In late August, the State Department issued a statement of grave concern about Iraqi government actions in the marshes region. And, on September 8, this was followed by a written protest delivered to Iraq at the United Nations by four of the five Security Council permanent members: Britain, France, Russia and the United States. The four "noted an increasing pattern of repressive and unacceptable actions by the goverenment of Iraq, including the cut-off of electricity to civilians in the north, attacks against humanitarian workers, repression of civilians in the marshes, violations of the no-fly zones, and new military attacks in the south." The note also protested Iraq's lack of cooperation with international humanitarian organizations.

Faced with growing pressures from Arab and other developing countries to relax U.N. sanctions against Iraq, the U.S. led the group of U.N. members who insisted that there could be no let-up until Iraq complied fully with the terms of Security Council resolution 687, covering the elimination of Iraq's weapons of mass destruction.

The Right to Monitor

The freedom of private citizens, individually

or collectively, or of international organizations, to monitor government violations of human rights does not exist in Iraq. The dissemination of information about state abuses, even those affecting oneself or one's own relatives, is treated extremely severely. All Iraqi human rights organizations are thus either located abroad or, since October 1991, in the Kurdish-controlled enclave of northern Iraq.

The Iraqi government extended unprecedented cooperation to U.N. Special Rapporteur Van der Stoel during the first year of his mandate, to February 1992, permitting him to travel within the country, visit prisons and meet officials. The harshly critical report that Van der Stoel, a former Netherlands Foreign Minister, delivered to the U.N. Human Rights Commission that month terminated all cooperation. Since then, the Special Rapporteur has not been permitted to return to Iraq. (U.N. sensibilities over sovereignty have, unfortunately, prevented him even from taking advantage of the valuable information available in that part of Iraqi Kurdistan outside central government control.) Baghdad likewise made clear that it would not cooperate with U.N. resolutions calling for the deployment in Iraq of human rights monitors by the U.N., as proposed by Van der Stoel. Iraq's obdurate attitude and U.N. budget problems left this important initiative stillborn, as of November 1993.

When the MOU with the United Nations covering relief operations expired, in March 1993, the government refused to negotiate its renewal. An informal understanding permitted U.N. agencies to continue operating in Iraq on the same terms as before, but the practical consequence was to block the deployment of U.N. guards—a lightly armed security contingent—in any part of government-controlled Iraq outside the capital. The relief program, and guards designated to ensure the delivery of supplies and protect U.N. personnel, had been envisaged by some Western governments as a stratagem to ensure that international observers were present in all parts of the country, to guard against further human rights abuses.

In practice, this ploy was an utter failure.

In the year under review, no U.N. officials were based in southern Iraq, where the worst abuses took place. When the U.N. Department of Humanitarian Affairs was negotiating to send a mission to the southern region, Iraq conditioned its agreement on team members not attempting to monitor human rights-related matters or to speak about them on their return.

Middle East Watch requested permission in March 1993 to visit the marshes region of southern Iraq, to examine firsthand the claims and counter-claims of the government and rebel groups concerning the draining of marsh waters and forced depopulation of the region. No reply was received from the government. In common with most other nongovernmental human rights organizations, to date Middle East Watch has never been granted official permission to visit Iraq. It has, however, made frequent visits to the Kurdish enclave, entering through Turkey, in the process gathering valuable information about past and current abuses. In 1993, the focus of Iraqi government policy remained the lifting of U.N. trade sanctions; foreign groups interested in documenting the impact of sanctions on vulnerable sectors of the population were thus given ready access to the country and its institutions.

Monitoring by Iraqi exiles of human rights developments in their country was carried out primarily in Tehran, Damascus and London. The Iraqi National Congress, a London-based coalition of opposition parties; the Documental Centre on Human Rights in Iraq, affiliated with the Supreme Assembly of the Islamic Revolution in Iraq; the Organization for Human Rights in Iraq, a private London-based body; and Gulf War Victims, a private relief organization located in Tehran, were the principal sources of information. The last three named all focused on the rights of the Iraqi Shi'a.

The Work of Middle East Watch

After the intensive field activity of 1992 in Iraqi Kurdistan, which had examined the Anfal campaign against the Kurds, in the year under review Middle East Watch's efforts were concentrated on three areas: publication of two reports on the Anfal, examination of captured Iraqi secret police documents transported to the U.S. for safekeeping, and investigation of the lesser-known situation of the Iraqi Shi'a, particularly residents of the southern marshes.

While many foreign reporters and nongovernmental organizations were able to visit Iraqi Kurdistan, thanks to its Western military protection and shared border with Turkey, few were able to conduct independent studies of the Shi'a—the largest religious group in Iraq and one long suppressed by the Sunni-led Ba'th Party regime. Middle East Watch felt it necessary to redress this balance and make its own evaluation of grave reports from opposition parties about developments involving both human rights and humanitarian law in the southern marshes.

Denied permission from Baghdad to make an on-the-spot investigation in southern Iraq, in January and February, a Middle East Watch delegation spent three weeks in Iran meeting Iraqi exiles, activists and refugees; part of this time was spent at the marshes border, in southwest Iran. A report issued in March concluded that a "no-fly" zone imposed by the U.S., Britain and France in August 1992, as a means of protecting the population on the ground, had been of little or no practical consequence. It also alerted the international community to the speed with which the marshes were being deliberately drained by the government as a means of facilitating attacks on local inhabitants, including Shi'a rebels. Based on these findings, Middle East Watch engaged in extensive advocacy work with the U.N. and permanent members of the Security Council, to press for the deployment of U.N. monitors and a halt to the large-scale hydrological works being carried out.

Middle East Watch lobbied for the adoption of the U.S. plan to hold a U.N. commission of inquiry into Iraqi crimes, including genocide. However, as of mid-November, lack of enthusiam from Western allies on the Security Council, and strong opposition from China and other developing countries, had blocked the plan's progress. Of comparable, or even greater, importance to Middle East Watch, however, was the bringing of a Genocide Convention case against Iraq at the International Court of Justice (ICJ) at The Hague, based on the Anfal campaign against the Kurds. A team of researchers made steady progress in evaluating the documents brought from northern Iraq. And legal research was conducted into the theory of the case, to be brought by a putative state party to the convention.

In January, Middle East Watch published its first substantial report on the Anfal, *The Anfal Campaign in Iraqi Kurdistan: The Destruction of Koreme*. Based on forensic, testimonial and documentary research carried out in 1992, this report was a case study of the fate of one destroyed village in Dohuk governorate, where an on-site massacre occurred in August 1988. A second, overview report on the Anfal, *Genocide in Iraq: The Anfal Campaign Against the Kurds*, was released in July. A painstaking reconstruction of the seven-month-long Anfal campaign—during which an estimated 100,000 Kurds were taken away and killed at remote locations—the 350-page report marked the summation of eighteen months of research. Included in the media coverage on the subject generated by Middle East Watch's work, was a BBC television documentary on the Anfal based on this book and a cover article in *The New York Times Magazine* in early January that featured Middle East Watch's work on the Anfal.

Two missions were sent to Iraqi Kurdistan during the year, to recover further consignments of Iraqi documents. Advantage was taken of the presence of a researcher in the region, to investigate current issues such as the Iranian shelling of border villages and to meet with local human rights activists. Approximately four and a quarter tons of documents were shipped out of the region in August, to add to the fourteen tons already in the United States. Out of a total number of pages estimated at four million, about 40 percent had been examined as of mid-November.

Arrests without charge, and subsequent executions after summary trials or, in some cases, no legal procedures, involving Iraqi Shi'a detained after the March 1991 uprising and others accused of plotting against the regime, formed a significant part of Middle East Watch work on Iraq in the latter part of the year. In November, the organization reported the execution of dozens of prominent Sunni Iraqis detained in July and August. Hundreds of Shi'a young men were reportedly executed in August and early September at Prison Number One, at the al-Rashid military base outside the capital.

One focus of research attention, given Iraq's previous use of chemical weapons against Kurdish civilians in 1987 and 1988, was the government's maintenance, or use, of banned weapons of mass destruction in defiance of international treaties and U.N. Security Council Resolution 687. In its examination of the captured documents, Middle East Watch discovered, for the first time, explicit references to the use of chemical weapons against the Kurds in 1988. Documents referring to the maintenance of biological weapons stockpiles were also found. In November, Middle East Watch received unconfirmed reports about the use of chemical weapons by Iraqi troops against Shi'a rebels in the Hammar marshes, near Basra. This information was relayed to the U.N. Special Commission on Iraq, UNSCOM.

IRAQI KURDISTAN

Human Rights Developments

Human rights conditions in the rebel-controlled region of Iraqi Kurdistan were relatively good during 1993. The two major political parties, the Patriotic Union of Kurdistan (PUK) and Kurdistan Democratic Party (KDP), moved ahead with the integration of their rival *peshmergha* forces. Internal security was in the hands of a newly established body known as the *asaysh*, senior positions in which were also shared between the PUK and KDP. The PUK and KDP also control

the Kurdish regional parliament, elected by popular vote in May 1992, and the regional government. But minority Turkomans and Chaldean and Assyrian Christians were also allocated places in the legislature and executive.

This domination of the security forces by the big parties led to complaints from smaller parties and factions, particularly those on the far left and those associated with the mainly Turkish Kurdistan Workers Party (PKK), of the harassment and arbitrary detention of their members. In Erbil, a pro-PKK newspaper was closed down on the orders of the local authorities. In Dohuk, seven suspected extrajudicial executions were reported between August 1992 and August 1993. And in Koysinjaq one person, identified as Mohsen Mujammad Khan, died in detention under unexplained circumstances on September 5, 1993.

Scores of Iraqi Kurds disaffected with the regional leadership in their homeland took refuge in Turkey in 1992 and 1993; but their rights to refugee status were not recognized by the U.N. High Commissioner for Refugees or the Turkish authorities.

The Right to Monitor

The Kurdish regional authorities put few obstacles in the way of human rights monitoring by foreign organizations. During 1993, among others Middle East Watch, Amnesty International, the Federation International des Droits de l'Homme, and France Libertés (Danielle Mitterand Foundation) conducted missions to Iraqi Kurdistan. France Libertés and Medico International, a German relief organization with a rights monitoring mandate, maintained field offices in the enclave.

However, local Kurdish organizations at times encountered difficulties in gaining access to prisons run by the Asaysh, the Kurdish security service. Partly as a consequence of the politicization of all Kurdish life, with loyalties split between the two major parties, investigation of abuses for which one party was held responsible, in a region where it was dominant, was not easy.

U.S. Policy

When Secretary Christopher and Vice President Gore met the top Kurdish leaders, Masoud Barzani and Jalal Talabani, in Washington in May, they were careful to do so only in the context of a broader meeting with officeholders of the Iraqi National Congress. In 1993, the U.S. government remained opposed to recognition of the Western-protected northern Iraqi enclave as a jurisdictionally separate entity. Consonant with this policy, Washington declined to support appeals from the Kurds and from nongovernmental organizations for a selective lifting of U.N. trade sanctions to ease the economic plight of the self-governing enclave.

The maintenance in place of the Combined Task Force/Operation Provide Comfort, the two and a half-year-old military shield over regions of Iraq north of the 36th parallel, remained central to U.S. policy toward Iraqi Kurdistan. Aircraft patrolling northern Iraq and a small allied liaison force, at Zakho in the "security zone" region of Dohuk governorate, depend entirely on Turkey for base support and logistics.

In June, the Turkish parliament renewed its approval for the continuation of the allied operation for a further six months, to December 31. But U.S. officials told Middle East Watch that further renewals were looking increasingly difficult. Turkish Prime Minister Tansu Ciller has taken a less accommodating line than her predecessor, Suleiman Demirel, over U.S. policy toward Iraq, pushing hard for a lifting of U.N. sanctions. Turkish worries over the *de facto* establishment of an independent Kurdish state on Turkey's troubled southeast border were expressed in high-level meetings with Iran and Syria, to coordinate policies toward the northern Iraq enclave. As with the United States, U.N. room for maneuver over Iraq relief operations remained limited by Turkish considerations.

As the stalemate between the Western-backed Kurds and the central government in Baghdad persisted into a third year, the Clinton administration appeared to keep on a secondary plane its central dilemma of how to assure the continued protection of the Iraqi Kurds without promoting Kurdish self-determination. Privately, the administration made clear to Saddam Hussein that no major military assault on the Kurds would be tolerated. Public statements also condemned the continued Iraqi military siege of the region. However, the administration remained silent over Iranian shelling of Iraqi Kurdish border villages.

In the 1993 fiscal year, commencing October 1, 1992, Congress appropriated a total of $69 million for Kurdish relief aid, to be distributed through the Department of Defense; in addition, $15 million was carried over from fiscal year 1992. Of this total, about $40 million was disbursed during the year, and expenditure of a further $20 million was committed. In addition, the U.S. contributed $100 million to a U.N.-established escrow fund from Iraqi assets in the U.S. frozen under a U.N. Security Council resolution. The latter funds were used for relief programs and payment for U.N. operations in all parts of Iraq, including Kurdistan. In November, Congress approved a further $30 million in assistance to the Kurds during the 1993-94 winter, mostly for the purchase of fuel.

The Work of Middle East Watch

During 1993, Middle East Watch met with the principal Kurdish leaders, Jalal Talabani and Masoud Barzani, on several occasions. It also met frequently with lower-level Kurdish officials. A large part of the discussions concerned the documents captured by the Kurds. But current human rights concerns about developments in the self-governing region were also raised. On October 4, Middle East Watch wrote to the Kurdish authorities about alleged abuses, including arbitrary detention, torture and the closure of a newspaper that had occurred in the region under their control over the previous year. As of November 22, no reply had been received.

ISRAELI-OCCUPIED WEST BANK AND GAZA STRIP

Human Rights Developments

From a human rights perspective, 1993 ended far more optimistically than it had begun. Following the signing in Washington of a Declaration of Principles by Israel and the Palestine Liberation Organization (PLO) on September 13, there was a reduction in some human rights abuses by the Israeli authorities, notably killings by security forces. There were also hopes that, as Israeli forces began to withdraw from populated areas and turn over partial authority to the PLO, the human rights picture would improve.

Improvements would be welcome after a year that was one of the worst in human rights terms of the six-year-old Palestinian *intifada*. Since becoming prime minister in July 1992, Yitzhak Rabin's willingness to negotiate a political settlement with Palestinians had been accompanied by no trend toward greater respect for fundamental rights.

The winter of 1992-1993 provided many illustrations. On December 17, 1992, Rabin summarily expelled 415 suspected Islamist activists in response to a series of fatal attacks on Israeli soldiers, for which Hamas, the militant Islamist organization, had claimed responsibility. During December and January, security forces killed thirty-eight Palestinians in the West Bank and Gaza Strip. In March, Rabin imposed the most stringent closure in the occupied territories since their capture in 1967—indefinitely preventing Palestinians from entering both Israel and occupied East Jerusalem without difficult-to-obtain permits. And, throughout the year, the Israel Defense Forces (IDF) pursued a tactic adopted in late 1992 of using anti-tank missiles and other heavy weaponry against the suspected hideouts of armed fugitives, a tactic that usually destroyed or damaged dozens of neighboring dwellings and left innocent families homeless.

Established patterns of human rights abuses continued during 1993. These included the use of excessive force against demonstrators and "wanted" activists, the torture of detainees to extract information and confessions, and restrictions on movement affecting the entire population. Both before and after the signing of the accord with the PLO, Israel refused to recognize the *de jure* applicability to the occupied terrritories of the Fourth Geneva Convention, and violated many of its articles pertaining to the treatment of the protected population.

The number of Palestinians killed by Israeli security forces increased for the second straight year. Some of these killings were justified by life-threatening situations in which soldiers found themselves, such as when challenged by activists wielding firearms. (Palestinians killed sixteen soldiers in the occupied territories during the first ten months of 1993.) However, eyewitness testimony collected by human rights organizations and journalists indicated that many of these killings occurred when soldiers were dispersing stone-throwers or pursuing unarmed fleeing suspects, and were in no mortal danger.

The Israeli human rights organization B'Tselem reported that 126 Palestinians were killed between January 1 and September 30, compared to seventy-nine killed during the last nine months of Prime Minister Yitzhak Shamir's government. Forty-two of those killed during the first nine months of 1993 were younger than seventeen, compared to eleven during Shamir's last nine months.

Under the military orders applied by the Israeli authorities, demonstrations in the occupied territories were forbidden without a permit. Troops sent in to disperse demonstrators were often confronted by youths throwing stones, bottles, and sometimes Molotov cocktails. Although equipped with tear gas, shields and rubber bullets, the soldiers often resorted to live ammunition against the youths—whether or not their own lives were in danger. This disproportionate response was effectively condoned by the military command which, except in rare cases, allowed soldiers who used excessive force to go unpunished.

Demonstration-related deaths declined immediately after the signing of the Israeli-PLO accord in September. The principal cause of the drop appeared to be instructions issued to soldiers not to break up pro-accord demonstrations, and to avoid unnecessary friction with the Palestinian population. In the ensuing weeks, soldiers interfered little with the many rallies staged both for and against the accord, and the demonstrations ran their course with few clashes or casualties.

With regard to the killing of fleeing suspects, the IDF's open-fire orders violated internationally recognized police standards that forbid the use of lethal force, except in the presence of an imminent mortal danger. (See chapter titled "Applicable Legal Standards" in Middle East Watch's July 1993 report, *A License to Kill*.) Israeli soldiers were instructed to shoot at the legs of fleeing Palestinians suspected of grave offenses who refused to halt. Given the unreliability of aiming at the legs and the difficulty of enforcing such a command, the orders effectively gave soldiers a license to kill fleeing suspects, even when they posed no imminent danger.

Many fleeing suspects were killed during undercover hunts for "wanted" Palestinians—activists sought on suspicion of having attacked Israelis or Palestinians they suspected of collaborating with Israel. Middle East Watch, in common with other human rights groups, concluded that IDF and Border Police undercover units often killed activists in situations where they were not endangering the security forces and could have been arrested.

While the authorities depicted the undercover units as risking their lives against armed extremists, the units spent much of their time targeting lower-level activists who were not on any "wanted" list, but who donned masks and engaged in such actions

as stone-throwing, graffiti-writing, and enforcing political strikes. The masked youths often carried "cold" weapons such as axes or clubs but rarely carried firearms. When confronting these masked activists, undercover units frequently opened fire before the youths had an opportunity to surrender or as they attempted to flee. Several youths were killed in this fashion in 1993, and others were seriously wounded.

Undercover soldiers were rarely held accountable for their abuses. Despite clear evidence that their use of excessive force was systematic, Middle East Watch was aware of only two cases during the intifada in which an undercover soldier was criminally charged in connection with a killing. In one of the two cases, a lieutenant received a twelve-month prison term, half of it suspended, for the February 1993 shooting of a twelve-year old suspected stone-thrower; the child was attempting to flee at the time he was shot. The case exhibited the failure of the military justice system to hand out appropriately stern punishments in those rare cases when soldiers were court-martialed for using excessive force.

The main cause of killing, after security forces gunfire, was the slaying by Palestinians of other Palestinians suspected of collaborating with the authorities. Between January 1 and October 31 there were eighty-seven killings of suspected collaborators, according to the Associated Press news agency. Some collaborators carried Israeli-issued weapons and were themselves responsible for violent abuses against other Palestinians. They also assisted the security forces in operations that resulted in arrests and killings.

Many of the suspected collaborators were executed only after they had been abducted, and their bodies showed signs of torture. Middle East Watch condemns all killings of persons in formal or *de facto* custody as a violation of customary humanitarian law. The killing of suspected collaborators, often after a secret "trial" with little or no semblance of due process, cannot be excused by the absence of a formal Palestinian judicial system in the areas under Israeli occupation.

Even though many collaborator killings appeared to be the work of armed groups affiliated with the PLO and Hamas, the extent to which the latter groups were to be held responsible remained unclear. The perpetrators had ignored, and in some cases openly defied, public pleas from the political leadership of the PLO and local PLO-affiliated figures to halt the killings. It seemed clear, however, that even if the PLO could not rein in activists who captured and murdered suspected collaborators, at a minimum it could have unequivocally dissociated itself from those responsible. The PLO's failure during 1993 to do so seriously undermined its pleas that the killings be stopped.

As Palestinians prepared for the transition to limited self-rule, PLO chairman Yasser Arafat stated in early October that the PLO was committed to respect all internationally recognized standards and to incorporate them fully into Palestinian legislation. He also acknowledged the role of independent human rights organizations and pledged cooperation with those groups.

The PLO's commitment to these admirable goals will be tested in numerous ways during 1994, when it assumes authority over internal security in parts of the West Bank and Gaza Strip. Among the challenges will be the issue of violence against suspected collaborators. A Palestinian authority that does not strive to prevent acts of punishment delivered outside of a fair judicial process will be seen as complicit in these abusive acts.

Shortly after Prime Minister Rabin came to office, in mid-1992, the IDF began using a new tactic against wanted fugitives, in response to incidents in which undercover soldiers had been killed. When it suspected fugitives were hiding in a particular house, the IDF would seal off the surrounding neighborhood, evacuate its residents and call on the fugitives to surrender. If they did not respond, the troops would attack the suspected hideout using anti-tank missiles, grenades, machineguns, and dynamite. Invari-

ably, neighboring houses and their contents were damaged in the process.

There were more than thirty operations of this kind between September 1992 and October 1993, most of them in the Gaza Strip. Like the undercover hunts for "wanted" persons, the massive firepower assaults did not cease with the signing of the Israeli-PLO accord. On October 2, the IDF used heavy firepower in five separate locations in the Gaza Strip, destroying or damaging eighteen houses, according to the Gaza Center for Rights and Law, an independent monitoring group.

The Gaza Center charged that in some cases of the large-scale assaults carried out during 1993, authorities did not give the fugitives an opportunity to surrender before launching the attack. Other attacks were launched only to discover that the fugitives had escaped or had not been there in the first place.

While these raids achieved their stated goal of reducing the incidence of serious injuries and killings during confrontations with "wanted" activists, the tactic rendered homeless hundreds of Palestinians accused of no wrongdoing. According to the Ramallah-based human rights organization al-Haq, a total of eighty-four houses were destroyed during heavy assaults on suspected fugitives between January and mid-September. The IDF's stated policy of offering compensation to innocent residents produced few payments; those that were made were generally not commensurate with the losses suffered. The use of massive firepower against suspected hideouts involved in many instances a use of force that was highly disproportionate to the security advantage gained.

The Rabin administration chose during 1993 to avoid a more familiar, and much-criticized, form of house demolition—that of tearing down the home inhabited by the family of a person suspected of a grave violent offense. However, the government persisted in using a less drastic form of collective punishment against the families of suspects: sealing houses shut in twenty-four cases and sealing particular rooms in eighteen other cases, according to a tally compiled by the Israeli human rights organization B'Tselem from January 1 to September 1.

The torture of Palestinians by IDF and General Security Service (GSS) interrogators continued during 1993. An estimated 5,000 Palestinians have been arrested and interrogated each year during the intifada; most have been ill-treated or tortured during an initial period lasting up to several weeks during which time they were denied access to a lawyer.

A number of developments kept the issue of ill-treatment in custody in the public spotlight in Israel during 1993: the death of a Gazan under interrogation (an incident in which medical negligence played a role), a public scandal over the complicity of Israeli doctors in torture, and GSS admissions in court to using certain abusive methods.

Interviews by Middle East Watch of thirty-one Palestinians who underwent interrogations since mid-1992 found a continuation of the systematic mistreatment previously documented by other rights organizations. In both IDF and GSS interrogations, abuse occurred before and between questioning sessions, when virtually all detainees were confined or shackled in painfully cramped positions for prolonged periods with hoods placed over their heads, threatened, insulted, deprived of sleep for up to five days at a time, and denied access to toilets for prolonged periods.

While these methods of "position abuse" were more severe in GSS facilities than in IDF facilities, IDF interrogators tended to use more violence during the questioning sessions. While the IDF routinely beat detainees severely during interrogation sessions, GSS violence was less common.

Ayman Nasser died on April 2 from lung inflammation, thirteen days after he was arrested in Gaza. An independent pathologist, who was permitted by the Israeli authorities to attend the autopsy, concluded that proper medical care during the interrogation phase would probably have saved Nasser's life. There were also two deaths under interrogation in 1992 to which medical negligence apparently contributed.

The complicity of Israeli doctors in torture became a public scandal in the spring of 1993, when a human rights lawyer obtained, and made public, a form in use at a West Bank prison. The form asked the examining physician to state whether the person about to undergo interrogation was fit to withstand prolonged isolation, tying up, hooding, and prolonged standing. Publication of the "fitness form" prompted the chair of the Israel Medical Association, Dr. Miriam Tzangen, to instruct physicians publicly not to fill out such a form, which she characterized as "co-operation in torture." She was not dissuaded by a letter from Prime Minister Rabin claiming that the form had been "accidentally" put to use prior to interrogations, whereas it had been intended for use during interrogations when medical problems arose.

Further evidence that these methods were officially sanctioned, and were indeed routine, emerged from the 1993 trial in Hebron military court of accused Hamas activist Muhammad Adawi, who claimed that his confession had been coerced. His interrogator denied defense allegations that Adawi had been beaten, but readily told the court that Adawi had been hooded, confined to a small chair for prolonged periods, and deprived of sleep. The interrogator testified that Adawi was subjected to three lengthy periods without sleep, the longest of which was over 109 hours, interrupted only by two brief respites of several hours each, and by the moments when Adawi was able to doze off while confined to a painful position.

The number of Palestinians imprisoned for politically motivated offenses or charges remained one of the highest per capita rates found anywhere in the world. As of early November, approximately 11,000 Palestinians were being held in army or civilian-run prisons, following the first mass release of prisoners resulting from the Israeli-PLO accord. About 760 inmates were freed on October 25 and 26, most of them either under eighteen or over fifteen, or suffering from illness.

The prison population—according to an official tally in late September—included 277 administrative detainees who were being interned without charge or trial. The authorities have used administrative detention far less since 1991 than during the early years of the intifada. Roughly two-thirds of all prisoners and detainees were being held in facilities inside Israel, in violation of Article 76 of the Fourth Geneva Convention.

Mass expulsions in December 1992 were remarkable not only because they constituted the largest single act of deportation since 1967, but also because of the summary way they were carried out. Ignoring the appeals process accorded would-be deportees since 1980, Rabin ordered that several hundred Islamist activists be rounded up and transported immediately to the Lebanese border. Appeals were possible only from abroad.

The action came after Hamas claimed responsiblity for the killing of five Israeli soldiers and policemen in a one-week period, including the killing of a kidnapped border policeman. (Middle East Watch publicly condemned that in-custody slaying as an act of murder.) The Rabin government accused the deportees of being activists "who endanger human lives through their actions, or incite to actions of this sort." Rabin termed the deportations "temporary removals," explaining that, unlike previous deportees, the "removees" would be permitted to return within two years. Middle East Watch rejected this distinction, stating that the Fourth Geneva Convention's prohibition against deportations was absolute and was not negated by any time limit.

The deportees, who found themselves in Lebanon the morning after they were hastily rounded up from their homes and prison cells, remained camped on a hilltop near the Israeli border throughout much of 1993. Meanwhile, the governments of both Israel and Lebanon obstructed the delivery of humanitarian aid to them, each saying the deportees were the other's problem. Israel's Supreme Court upheld the legality of the deportations in January.

Under pressure from the United States and the United Nations, on February 1, Rabin announced that one hundred of the deportees would be permitted to return immediately and the others in stages before the end of 1993. However, he insisted that Israel reserved the right to "remove for a limited time hundreds of inciters, leaders, organizers" in the future.

The deportees collectively rejected Rabin's offer, saying that none would return until all could return. In August, they dropped their all-or-none position and the following month 181 returned. All were initially held in investigative detention, and some were subsequently released. As of the end of October, 216 remained in the mountainside camp. Thirty other Palestinians, out of over 1,200 deported between 1967 and 1991, were also permitted to return during 1993. Their return, granted in response to a demand made by the Palestinian delegation to the Arab-Israeli peace talks, was the largest such return of deportees since the beginning of the occupation.

The Israeli authorities' closure of the occupied territories, imposed in late March, was prompted by a wave of attacks by Palestinian assailants on Israelis. Many of the attacks occurred inside Israel. Like the deportations, in its execution the closure was an act of collective punishment, imposed arbitrarily on large numbers of persons not linked to specific offenses. The closure made it illegal for Palestinians to enter Israel or occupied East Jerusalem without a permit. Palestinians seeking permits were forced to wait for hours outside offices of the Civil Administration, the Israeli military-run local government. Many requests were turned down without explanation, while others were issued only after long waits, and then for only short periods of validity.

Those hardest hit by the new policy were Palestinians previously employed inside Israel, and their families. Before the closure, wages earned in Israel represented as much as one-third of the total income of West Bank Palestinians and one-half of the income of Gazans. Despite the fact that many Palestinians working in Israel had the same deductions taken from their paychecks as did Israeli workers, none were eligible for unemployment benefits. Also affected were Palestinians who needed medical care or had other pressing business inside Israel or East Jerusalem, and Palestinian farmers and businesses whose delivery routes were blocked by the new policy.

The closure compartmentalized the occupied territories, cutting off Palestinians from their main urban center, East Jerusalem, with its specialized hospitals, foreign consulates, and other institutions not found elsewhere in the occupied territories. In practice, the closure also made it illegal for Palestinians to travel between the northern West Bank and the southern half without a permit, since all connecting roads passed through Jerusalem.

By the summer, the number of Palestinians with permits to work inside Israel had crept up to 50,000, less than half the number previously employed. However, the closure continued to harm the Palestinian economy and inconvenience many Palestinians with compelling reasons to enter, or pass through, Israel or East Jerusalem.

On October 22, authorities eased restrictions on entering East Jerusalem. Physicians, lawyers, medical patients and Muslim worshippers were issued permits more readily than in previous months, and the permit requirement was dropped for men over forty and for women.

In Middle East Watch's view, Israel had no absolute obligation to allow residents of the occupied territories to enter its territory or provide them with jobs. However, it did have an obligation to attend to their welfare. After having transformed the West Bank and Gaza economies over the past twenty-six years into satellites of Israel's economy, the government of Israel had a duty to assist families suddenly deprived of their main source of income and for whom no employment was readily available. The small number of low-paying temporary public works jobs created by the Israeli government in the occupied territories after the closure were patently inadequate.

Curfews were another form of collective punishment imposed on security grounds. During 1993, the nightly curfew covering all 800,000 residents of the Gaza Strip entered its sixth year without interruption. In addition, the entire Gaza Strip was under round-the-clock curfews December 14-23 and 30-31, 1992. Shorter curfews were imposed on particular refugee camps, villages and towns on scores of occasions throughout 1993.

There were no long-term school or university closures during 1993, a form of collective punishment that was employed during 1988-1990 in response to demonstrations and disturbances that the authorities blamed on students. However, on about fifteen occasions between January and August, authorities closed particular schools and universities for up to two weeks at a time. Education was interrupted also by the closure of the occupied territories, which created obstacles for students who needed to obtain permits to travel between sectors of the territories.

The political breakthrough of 1993 raised hopes for general improvements in human rights. Under the Israeli-PLO declaration of principles, Israel committed itself to withdraw its troops from population centers and turn over responsibility for internal security in some areas to the PLO. However, as long as Israeli forces retain ultimate authority, the Fourth Geneva Convention continues to protect Palestinians resident in all territories captured in 1967—even areas from which Israeli troops withdraw. (For Israel's conduct in Lebanon, see section on Lebanon.)

The Right to Monitor

Human rights work was generally permitted in the occupied territories. However, there were constraints, which were far more onerous for Palestinians than for Israelis and foreigners.

Several Palestinian human rights organizations regularly denounced human rights conditions in the occupied territories, and their reports received international attention. New groups have been formed each year. The Jerusalem-based Palestinian press also reported critically on human rights issues, although the Israeli military censor often deleted or toned down the coverage.

Palestinian human rights workers and journalists risked harassment by soldiers at checkpoints and at the scene of disturbances or arrests. For example, Reuters photographer Ahmad Jadallah, a Gaza resident, was beaten by a group of soldiers on June 19 after he had filmed them assaulting a taxi driver in Gaza City. Several such incidents were reported during the year, involving both Palestinian and foreign journalists.

The indefinite closure of the occupied territories in March was a major obstacle to Palestinian rights workers, many of whom initially could not obtain permits to travel between different sections of the occupied territories. Prior to the closure, some human rights workers had already been barred from entering Israel and East Jerusalem.

At least in the case of the Ramallah-based rights organization al-Haq, all of its staff eventually obtained permits after the closure. Palestinian lawyers, except those residing in East Jerusalem, were prevented by the closure from traveling to consult with Palestinians imprisoned inside Israel, although most lawyers eventually obtained permits.

In contrast to previous years, no Palestinian human rights worker was jailed during the first ten months of 1993. However, Sha'wan Jabarin of al-Haq was barred from traveling to France to take part in a human rights course. Authorities stated, without furnishing evidence, that Jabarin was a "senior member" of the Popular Front for the Liberation of Palestine, and his travel would "endanger the security of the area."

Representatives of foreign human rights organizations were generally able to travel about freely, and to interview Palestinians without hindrance. The International Committee of the Red Cross (ICRC) maintained a large field staff in the West Bank and Gaza Strip, and was permitted by the Israeli authorities to visit all Palestinians arrested for security reasons within fourteen days of their arrest. The authorities permitted independent human rights organizations, including Middle East Watch, to inspect prisons and detention centers holding Palestinians. However, no group was permitted to visit interrogation wings, the part of the Israeli incarceration system in which the most serious human rights abuses were to be found.

U.S. Policy

The most dramatic moment in U.S. Middle East policy during 1993 was President Clinton's playing host to the signing of the Israeli-PLO accord at the White House. Middle East Watch hopes that the U.S. endorsement of the accord, and its efforts to promote international aid for West Bank and Gaza development, will lead also to a public role in promoting human rights during the difficult transitional phase due to begin by December 1993.

Such a role would represent a change of course for the administration. In his first year in office, President Bill Clinton showed no interest in openly challenging the poor human rights record of the Rabin government, and was quick to assure the Israeli prime minister that he favored maintaining U.S. aid to Israel at its annual level of over $3 billion. At no time did officials suggest that the aid, by far the largest annual amount that the U.S. gives to any country, should in some fashion be conditioned on curtailing abuses.

The only human rights issue that prompted public diplomacy by the Clinton administration was the deportation of 415 Islamists in December 1992, one month before inauguration day. It was in fact the new administration's first foreign policy crisis. The Bush administration had voted in favor of U.N. Security Council Resolution 799 on December 18, 1992 to condemn the deportations and urge Israel to rescind them. At that time, President-elect Clinton expressed concern that the deportations "may go too far and imperil the peace talks."

Upon taking office, the Clinton team lobbied against Security Council sanctions on Israel while Secretary of State Warren Christopher engaged in intensive consultations with Rabin. On February 1, Christopher and Rabin separately announced an Israeli compromise on the deportations. Christopher said Israel had agreed to allow about one hundred deportees to return immediately and to halve the period of exile for the remainder. He also announced that Israel would implement an appeals process that could further shorten the terms of exile, and that Israel would now assure the delivery of humanitarian assistance to the deportees. Notwithstanding the fact that Resolution 799 demanded the "immediate return" of all the deportees, Christopher pronounced the U.S.-brokered compromise as "consistent" with the U.N. resolution. Christopher argued that further steps by the Security Council were therefore "unnecessary and ... might undercut the [peace] process which is underway." The prospect of a U.S. veto effectively killed efforts at the Security Council to enact further resolutions on the issue.

It was ironic that Christopher should have announced the deal while at U.N. headquarters, since it represented a bilateral end-run of the U.N. machinery and fell short of the conditions set by Resolution 799. He also claimed that Israel had agreed to stop obstructing humanitarian aid to the deportees, a representation that went unfulfilled: Israel continued to bar the ICRC from conducting a mission to the deportees until September, a matter about which the U.S. remained publicly silent.

While Secretary Christopher worked hard to convince the rest of the world of the merits of the compromise, Prime Minister Rabin presented it to the Israeli public with the cynicism it deserved. On February 1, he described the compromise as a "package deal" that bound the U.S. to "prevent any decisions in international forums that would have operational significance against Israel." He even told Israel's parliament, "The principle of our ability to remove for a limited time hundreds of inciters, leaders, organizers, remains."

This claim begged for a U.S. clarifica-tion of its own position on deportations, be they indefinite or temporary. But U.S. officials ignored this comment, at least in public. Instead, when testifying on March 9 before the House Committee on Foreign Affairs, Assistant Secretary of State for Near East Affairs Edward P. Djerejian preferred to highlight another comment by Rabin—that the deportations were "unprecedented and an exception."

The Clinton administration handled the deportations with a focus primarily on renewing the peace talks. While this was logical, the U.S. at the same time weakened the cause of human rights by lending legitimacy to an inadequate Israeli appeals process, and by lobbying for a diplomatic compromise that left 300 arbitrarily deported persons in exile. In so doing, the U.S. undercut the credibility of a Security Council resolution and muffled its own objection to deportations in principle, a position that the Bush administration had repeatedly expressed.

On March 15, Rabin and Clinton met in Washington, for the first time as heads of government. According to senior aides cited in the press, Clinton assured the Israeli prime minister that he would oppose any attempt to reduce military and economic assistance to Israel not only in the coming fiscal year 1994 budget, but in subsequent years. At a news conference following their meeting, Clinton made no mention of Israel's human rights record. However, he stated that he and Rabin had not discussed the 400 deportees remaining in Lebanon.

During the rest of the year, the Clinton administration made no principled statements concerning Israeli abuses in the occupied territories. It said nothing publicly about the indefinite closure of the West Bank and Gaza Strip. When questioned about it on April 12, a State Department spokesman avoided raising concerns about its effects on Palestinians. He only noted that the U.S. viewed Israel as responsible for providing security for its people and for the territories under its control.

However, on the closure of the occupied territories and certain other human rights issues, the U.S. privately lobbied the Israeli government. Assistant Secretary Djerejian told reporters in May that the U.S. had asked Israel to ease the closure. A broader protest on human rights was described in the Israeli daily *Maariv* on June 28. According to that account, which State Department officials would neither confirm nor deny for the record, a senior official had warned the Israeli embassy that the U.S. would report a deterioration in human rights conditions if present patterns continued. The U.S. official expressed concern, according to *Maariv*, about the high number of children being killed by security forces gunfire and the demolition of houses caused by heavy weaponry used during the search for fugitives.

The Clinton administration did comment publicly when U.S. citizens became the victims of abuse. It lodged a formal protest with Israeli officials at the end of January, when consular officials were prevented for up to five days from visiting three Arab-Americans who had been arrested and interrogated on suspicion of helping Hamas. On February 9, the State Department sent a second letter, expressing concern about the men's allegations that they had been mistreated while in detention. The Israeli government responded that an investigation found no wrongdoing, according to a State Department official who asked not to be named. He called Israel's response "not satisfactory."

The Clinton administration never commented publicly on the routine abuse that Palestinian residents of the occupied territories undergo during interrogation. This, despite the death of a Gazan under interrogation in April and a scandal in Israel over a form that doctors in one detention center were using to verify a detainee's fitness for abuse during interrogation.

For years, successive U.S. administrations have argued that a policy of vocally criticizing Israel's human rights record was ill-suited to advancing the peace process in the region. Middle East Watch believes that Washington's generous annual aid to Israel bestows on it the authority, and the obliga-tion, to be a public advocate for human rights. Speaking out even-handedly on abuses throughout the region will not, in Middle East Watch's view, derail the peace process.

The Work of Middle East Watch

In its work on the Israeli-occupied territories, Middle East Watch devoted resources to one of the main issues it has focused on since the organization was created in 1989: the use of excessive force by Israeli troops.

In June Middle East Watch issued a book-length report titled *A License to Kill: Israeli Undercover Operations against "Wanted" and Masked Palestinians*. While other human rights organizations had already reported on the phenomenon, the Middle East Watch report made a timely contribution because it documented killings under the newly installed Rabin administration, and supplemented Palestinian accounts with testimony by Israeli soldiers.

Middle East Watch maintained a field researcher in the Israeli-occupied territories for eight months during 1993. Among other work, he conducted over thirty interviews with former detainees who had been interrogated either by the General Security Service or the IDF since the advent of the Rabin administration. The researcher also attended the trial of a Palestinian who said that his confession had been extracted under torture. A report on mistreatment during interrogations was scheduled for release in early 1994.

In December 1992, Middle East Watch issued three statements critical of the mass deportations of Palestinian Islamists to Lebanon. A researcher traveled to southern Lebanon to interview the deportees and inspect their living conditions. The data he collected were combined with information gathered in the occupied territories and released at a press conference in Jerusalem on January 12. Middle East Watch's executive director held a briefing in Jerusalem for the families of the deportees that day, and traveled to the Gaza Strip to make a similar presentation. He also met with Justice Minister David Libai and IDF officials.

Middle East Watch issued a statement

criticizing the decision by the Israeli Supreme Court to uphold the deportations, and wrote a letter on February 4 to Secretary Christopher questioning his enthusiastic endorsement of a compromise on the deportations that failed to secure the immediate return of all deportees. A Middle East Watch newsletter published in August updated the situation of the deportees.

In March, Human Rights Watch publicly urged President Clinton to raise human rights issued during his first official meeting with Prime Minister Yitzhak Rabin. In April, Middle East Watch issued a newsletter on the closure of the occupied territories and the isolation of occupied East Jerusalem. When the IDF issued a report defending its human rights record in July, Middle East Watch responded with a brief critique of that document. It also contributed a chapter on prison conditions in Israel and the occupied territories to Human Rights Watch's *Global Report on Prisons*.

During the year, Middle East Watch wrote to the Israeli authorities about restrictions imposed on a number of Palestinian human rights monitors. Letters were sent on behalf of members of the Khan Yunis-based Palestinian Lawyers for Human Rights who were not being given permits to enter or cross through Israel, and on behalf of Sha'wan Jabarin of al-Haq. Jabarin had been denied permission to attend a human rights course in Europe.

Middle East Watch took no position on the accord signed by the PLO and Israel on September 13, which was a political matter beyond the organization's mandate. However, three days before the signing ceremony, it issued a statement highlighting the absence of human rights provisions in the published declaration of principles, and arguing that a durable Israeli-Palestinian peace depended on respect for human rights by Israeli and Palestinian authorities. Identical letters on the subject were sent to Prime Minister Rabin and PLO Chairman Arafat.

Middle East Watch invited Mary Rock, a human rights lawyer and secretary of the Arab Lawyers Committee of the West Bank bar association, to be honored with other international monitors at the Human Rights Watch observance of Human Rights Day in December.

KUWAIT

Human Rights Developments

The year was marked by intensified persecution of those minority communities whose loyalty to the government was in doubt, especially Iraqis, Palestinians and Bedoons, the stateless longtime residents of Kuwait. After a year of relatively reduced tensions in 1992, the discovery in April of an alleged plot by Iraqi agents to assassinate former U.S. President George Bush during his visit to Kuwait that month sparked renewed pressure on those communities. The Kuwaiti government accelerated its long-term strategy of restructuring its population in a fashion that violated human rights, through arbitrary arrests and summary deportations. Those suspected of collaboration with the Iraqi government were either expelled or tried before the State Security Court, where defendants' rights are limited. Seven Iraqis and ten Palestinians were sentenced to death and, in May, another Iraqi, sentenced to death in 1992, was executed.

The government continued its effective ban on peaceful assembly and association. In August, the authorities closed down all unlicensed associations; the ban order included six human rights and humanitarian organizations.

Despite requests from human rights groups and families of those killed, disappeared or tortured in the post-liberation, martial-law period (February through June 1991), only a handful of such cases had been investigated. More than two years after a vicious attack on one Lebanese family resident in Kuwait city, a Kuwaiti official was charged in April 1993 with the crime of killing Ismael Farhat and his son Osama, and the rape and attempted murder of Naimat Farhat, his daughter. This was the first time a Kuwaiti government official had been tried for a human rights violation taking place during the martial-law period following the liberation of Kuwait in February 1991. With this notable exception, none of those implicated in the killing and torture of hundreds of prisoners were brought to justice. Kuwaiti officials told Middle East Watch that they had no plans to launch any further investigations of officials. In addition, mass unidentified graves of people buried after the war—apparent victims of Kuwaiti forces—remained to be exhumed.

During 1993, continuing a process begun immediately after liberation, the State Security Court tried scores of Iraqis, Palestinians and Bedoons charged with collaboration with the Iraqi occupying forces. Although the procedures followed in their trials were an improvement over those of the 1991 martial-law courts, serious shortcomings remained, including the use of confessions obtained through torture and the denial of legal counsel of the defendants' own choosing. The court often ignored the reasonable assertion of many defendants that they had been coerced into cooperating with the occupation authorities. Collaboration was defined by the prosecution to include many forms of minor association with the occupiers. All defendants before the court were charged under the broadly worded State Security Law of 1970, which imposed a mandatory death penalty on a wide range of crimes, including, for example, the peaceful expression of opinion, if it is deemed harmful to national morale.

In June, the State Security Court sentenced six Iraqis and ten Palestinians to death for collaboration. The six Iraqis were charged with belonging to the Ba'th Party, the ruling party in Iraq, and joining the Popular Army, a reserve militia which assisted the occupying forces. The ten Palestinians were charged with belonging to the Arab Liberation Front, a Baghdad-based faction of the Palestine Liberation Organization (PLO) financed and sponsored by Iraq, and with carrying arms in support of the occupation. The defendants had been detained since the first months

following liberation, when most detainees held on suspicion of collaboration were tortured. The court did not fully consider their claims that their early confessions had been secured through torture. None was allowed legal counsel before the trial, in violation of both Kuwaiti law and international standards.

On June 25, trial commenced before the State Security Court of eleven Iraqis and three Kuwaitis accused of plotting to assassinate former U.S. President Bush. The eleven Iraqis and one of the Kuwaitis faced the death penalty. During the proceedings, several defendants recanted their earlier confessions, which they said had been obtained through the use of torture. Ali Khudair, a sixty-eight-year old Iraqi defendant, told the court that he had been severely beaten by investigators to compel him to confess to the plot. Wali al-Ghazali and Ra'ad al-Asadi also maintained that they made their confessions after they had been subjected to torture, signs of which were clearly visible when they appeared in court. Although most of the accused faced the death penalty, all but one of the fourteen defendants were denied legal counsel until their first court appearance. Sentencing was scheduled for December 25.

Policies aimed at eventually expelling from Kuwait nearly all of its remaining Iraqi, Palestinian and Bedoon residents included arbitrary arrest and detention, torture and ill-treatment of prisoners, unlawful searches, heavy fines, threats, public humiliation and the denial of employment. During 1993, hundreds were arrested and placed in the Talha Deportation Prison and then given a choice between leaving voluntarily or remaining in that makeshift detention facility. This prison was the subject of a scathing parliamentary report about its deteriorating conditions and overcrowding. In June, Talha's inmates began a hunger strike to call attention to their plight. To dramatize the dismal conditions, six detainees—former Iraqi prisoners of war who were classified as refugees by the International Committee of the Red Cross (ICRC) and the U.N. High Commissioner for Refugees (UNHCR)—

sewed shut their mouths. Promises by Prime Minister Shaikh Sa'ad, who visited the facility in June, to improve conditions and relocate inmates from this facility to a more suitable building were not fulfilled. Faced with these conditions and no prospect of release, most of those detained chose to leave the country. They had to liquidate their assets quickly and use the proceeds to pay fines for residing in the country beyond August 1992, at a daily rate of two Kuwaiti dinars ($6.66). In the cases of former government employees, funds owed to them such as severance pay were used to satisfy those fines.

During the year, Kuwaiti authorities escalated pressure on the Bedoons to secure citizenship elsewhere in order for them to remain in Kuwait lawfully. Most Bedoons are long-term stateless residents of Kuwait who were born there and have lived there all their lives, but are not officially deemed to qualify for Kuwaiti citizenship. The pre-war community of 250,000 was estimated in 1993 at under 200,000 (according to official figures, only 120,000 Bedoons remained).

After Kuwait's liberation in 1991, long-standing anti-Bedoon policies took a violent turn. Accused *en masse* of aiding the Iraqi occupying forces, Bedoons were singled out for retribution, even though many had been killed by the Iraqi occupiers for acts of resistance. Bedoons suffered summary execution, disappearance and torture. All those employed by the government were dismissed from their jobs, prevented from sending their children to government schools and threatened with expulsion from the only country they had ever known. The military and the police, which before the invasion were largely composed of Bedoons, rehired only a small fraction of their pre-war employees—depriving the community of its chief source of income.

Most of the Palestinians who remained in Kuwait—fewer than 25,000, down from a pre-war high of over 350,000—were stateless refugees who came originally from the Gaza Strip but had not been allowed by Israel to return. They carried travel documents issued by Egypt, which refused to allow them to reside in its territory. Although these refugees had no place to go, Kuwaiti authorities denied them the right to remain in Kuwait until they found another country that would accept them. They were harassed, threatened with imprisonment, denied employment, and subjected to heavy fines for every day they stayed in Kuwait. Many exhausted their life savings to pay these fines.

In 1993, the Kuwaiti government ignored appeals by families and human rights organizations to retry or grant appeal to 118 persons sentenced by martial-law tribunals set up in May and June 1991. In those show trials, most defendants were convicted and sentenced on the basis of confessions extracted under torture.

Another vulnerable group of foreign residents subjected to violent mistreatment was Asian domestic employees, mainly from the Philippines, Sri Lanka, India and Bangladesh; their number was estimated at about 150,000 in 1993. Expressly excluded from the protection of labor legislation, these workers had been left at the mercy of their private employers. Their legal recourse severely limited, hundreds of abused Asian expatriates sought refuge in their respective embassies, charging their employers with rape, physical assault or withholding wages. Some 1,400 Filipina maids fled to their embassy in the year between April 1991 and April 1992. In 1993, several hundred runaway maids sought shelter in foreign embassies, notably that of the Philippines. In the spring, about four hundred maids, mostly from the Philippines, were repatriated, but by the end of October, hundreds more were sheltered in various Asian embassies. Only one case of an abusive employer was successfully tried: on July 24, a Kuwaiti and his Lebanese wife were sentenced to seven years each for causing the death of Sonia Panama, a twenty-three-year-old Filipina maid through ill-treatment.

The lifting of pre-publication censorship on newspapers in early 1992, although welcome, did not mark a trend toward greater freedom of expression. During 1993, the government continued to prosecute reporters who wrote critically of its policies. It also maintained other severe restrictions on peaceful expression, assembly and association. Since 1985, the Kuwaiti government had maintained a moratorium on the formation of new private groups, but in practice had allowed many to function without formal licenses. However, in 1993 this policy of benign neglect was abandoned. On August 6, the Council of Ministers issued a decree dissolving all unlicensed organizations, affecting all those groups engaged in human rights and humanitarian activities. Most had been formed since the liberation of Kuwait in 1991 but had not been formally legalized, despite their repeated requests.

Although the order was directed at all unlicensed organizations, in justifying the need for action government officials cited only human rights and humanitarian organizations, especially those working on the issue of those who disappeared during the Iraqi occupation of 1990 and 1991. The government singled out the Kuwaiti Association for the Defense of War Victims, the country's main human rights group, as being required to close down. All unlicensed groups were notified to cease operation and, on August 15, the Minister of Social Affairs threatened to use force against violators. On October 3, the Council of Ministers instructed the Minister of Social Affairs and Labor to implement the ban immediately.

While the parliament resumed functioning in 1992, the royal family continued its dominance of the executive branch. On October 5, 1992, elections for the National Assembly were held for the first time since it was dissolved by the Emir in July 1986. Only 81,400 first-class male citizens over the age of twenty-one were eligible to vote, accounting for less than 11 percent of the native population. Women and naturalized citizens did not have the right to vote, nor did the Bedoons.

However, the restoration of the National Assembly did not mean the beginning of parliamentary rule. Although the opposition and independent candidates gained a majority of the fifty contested seats, the majority's power was significantly curtailed when the Emir once again asked Crown Prince Shaikh Sa'ad to form a new government. The new cabinet, announced on October 14, 1992, was composed mostly of government loyalists, including five members of the royal family who retained the posts prime minister and first deputy prime minister, as well as the key portfolios of defense, foreign affairs, information and interior.

Although the success of independent candidates in gaining a majority in the National Assembly did not usher in parliamentary rule, deputies began in 1993 to assert their independence. They investigated reports of corruption and mismanagement of public funds during the six years (July 1986 through October 1992) when the parliament was dissolved—investigations that led to the indictment of several former officials, including members of the royal family. In addition, the assembly, for the first time in Kuwait's parliamentary history, formed two committees to deal exclusively with human rights. The Human Rights Committee conducted hearings on prison conditions and, in January 1993, conducted a surprise visit to the Talha Deportation prison. Following the hearing, the Prime Minister visited the prison and, in June, promised to relocate its inmates to a more appropriate facility. In July, the Human Rights Committee adopted a scathing (classified) report on the visit and urged the government to improve conditions there.

Until it resigned in August, the Assembly's Committee on POWs and the Hostages had become one of the most important parliamentary groups. It dealt almost exclusively with the issue of the 850 Kuwaitis (and others) who disappeared during Iraq's seven-month occupation of Kuwait (August 1990 to February 1991). The committee, headed by Deputy Mubarak al-Duwaila, supported private efforts to assist in securing information about their whereabouts. It introduced measures, later adopted by the full assembly, to urge the government to recognize and assist private groups in the country dealing with the issue of the disappeared. On August 17, this committee resigned *en masse* in protest of the government's decision to close down private groups dealing with the subject.

The second session of the 1992 National Assembly convened on October 26, 1993, amid growing competition between Islamist and secular deputies over the future direction of Kuwait, including the issue of how to treat human rights. In the first session, which had concluded in September, some Islamist opposition deputies appeared to side with the government's decision to close down human rights and humanitarian organizations, traditionally populated by secular and liberal activists.

The Right to Monitor

The right to monitor was dealt a severe blow with the closure in August of all human rights groups in Kuwait, including the Kuwaiti Association to Defend War Victims (KADWV). Established immediately after the Gulf War, the association had been the main independent local group devoted exclusively to monitoring human rights. The Kuwaiti government, which never formally recognized the organization's legal existence, announced in August that KADWV and the other human rights and humanitarian groups were illegal since they had not been licensed. On October 3, the government reiterated its decision to close down all unlicensed private associations.

KADWV and some of the other banned groups nevertheless continued to function and meet privately. As in previous years, a focal point for KADWV in 1993 was the fate of over 850 Kuwaitis and others who disappeared during Iraqi occupation. The organization also followed the fate of those who disappeared or went missing after liberation, mainly Palestinians and Bedoons; and it provided aid, including legal counsel, to prisoners and victims of official abuse.

Included in the government's ban were five other human rights and humanitarian groups. These were the Kuwaiti Association for Human Rights, League of Families of POWs and the Missing, Mutual Assistance Fund for the Families of the Martyrs and POWs, Popular Committee for Solidarity with POWs, Pro-Democracy Committee, Supporters of Single-Citizenship Committee, and Women Married to Non-Kuwaitis Support Association.

In 1993, the Kuwaiti government allowed visits by several international human rights organizations, but significant delays in granting approval were reported. Most non-Kuwaiti lawyers who volunteered to travel to Kuwait to represent those accused of state security offenses were not granted entry visas by Kuwaiti embassies without explanation. The few who were able to secure visas were not permitted to represent their clients in court.

U.S. Policy

Since the end of the 1991 Gulf War, the U.S. has been the main force protecting Kuwait from renewed Iraqi attack. A ten-year military agreement signed in September 1991 regulated the U.S.-Kuwaiti defense alliance. Under this agreement, the stationing of large numbers of land-based troops was eschewed in favor of maintaining a substantial naval presence nearby and holding frequent U.S.-Kuwaiti maneuvers. These exercises amounted to a semi-permanent presence in light of their frequency, their duration and the large number of troops involved. According to U.S. Defense Department officials, these exercises and the September 1991 agreement itself were intended as both a signal to Iraq and a demonstration of U.S. commitment to the security of Kuwait and stability of the Gulf. Similar agreements were concluded with France and the United Kingdom.

The U.S. continued to provide sophisticated weapons to Kuwait, during the year under review, with sales of tanks and fighter planes totalling over $1 billion. U.S. officials expressed their belief that the defense of Kuwait, as part of the defense of the Arabian Peninsula, was one of two key policy goals in the Middle East—the other being peace between Israel and her Arab neighbors. In April, David L. Mack, then-Deputy Assistant Secretary of State for Near Eastern Affairs, explained that Arab-Israeli peace was sought, in part, to "assure the security of this vital region." "Over the long term, peace between Israel and its Arab neighbors is essential to our continuing effort to encourage and help provide a credible defense of the Arabian Peninsula," Mack told the U.S.–GCC Business Conference in Washington. During visits by Secretary of State Warren Christopher to Kuwait and Saudi Arabia, Secretary Christopher reasserted longstanding U.S. policy. In February, he told Kuwaiti and Saudi leaders: "President Clinton's commitment to the security of friends in the Gulf, like that of every president since Franklin Roosevelt, is firm and constant," according to a statement by the State Department. There was no public reference to human rights during those visits.

The need to put an end to human rights violations committed by Iraq in Kuwait was one of the stated reasons that the U.S. administration went to war against Iraq. However, other than cataloguing human rights abuses in Kuwait, in the State Department's *Country Reports on Human Rights Practices*, U.S. officials shied away from publicly criticizing the serious human rights violations committed by Kuwaiti authorities against foreign and Bedoon residents. This reticence, which persisted during 1993, came despite what most Kuwaitis acknowledged to be their near-complete reliance on the U.S. to protect them from external threats.

In what may have been an effort to downplay human rights as a component of policy, the ranking Clinton administration official for the region described the U.S. relationship with Gulf countries as a purely commercial one. According to Mack, "I like to think of the ties between the U.S. and GCC as being based on a logic as ancient as that of the oriental bazaar, or souq. Simply put, the interests of the merchant in the bazaar and of his regular customers are complementary. If another party impeded or prevents the free and peaceful exchange of goods, or attempts to establish terms of trade through intimidation or extortion, both merchant and customer suffer."

By contrast to the State Department's assiduous efforts to help U.S. businesses who had problems or disputes in Kuwait, on human rights the U.S. refrained from taking the initiative: "We look instead to government and private sector leaders to devise, in consultation with their peoples, measures for democratic consensus building that flow naturally from their own established political traditions and cultural values," said Mack. The U.S. official reported, however, that, during his trip to Kuwait, Secretary Christopher had "applauded the reinstitution of the Kuwaiti parliament and encouraged the Kuwaiti government's consideration of expanding the electorate."

The Work of Middle East Watch

In 1993, Middle East Watch focused on advocacy to improve the observance of human rights in Kuwait, engaging in substantive discussions with Kuwaiti officials over human rights issues. It provided information to U.S. congressional staff, U.N. agencies and other groups investigating various aspects of the human rights situation in Kuwait. It also briefed immigration officials and refugee aid groups to help them deal with a flood of refugees from Kuwait pressured to leave or banned from returning.

To help especially vulnerable stateless refugees—Palestinians and Bedoons—stranded outside Kuwait, Middle East Watch filed a substantial number of affidavits and appeals to immigration officials and judges in Canada, Norway, Denmark, Switzerland and the United States.

When the State Security Court sentenced sixteen men to death in June, Middle East Watch protested the sentences and called for a full judicial review of the verdicts, in an open letter to the Emir of Kuwait. The June 24 letter was covered extensively in the Kuwaiti media. In August, when the Kuwaiti government banned all unlicensed organizations, targeting especially human rights and humanitarian groups, Middle East Watch sent an open letter to the Crown Prince protesting the action; the following month it issued a newsletter on the subject.

LEBANON

Human Rights Developments

The year was marked by frequent attacks on the peaceful exercise of civil and political rights, especially freedom of the press and assembly. In November 1992, President Elias el-Hrawi chose Rafiq al-Hariri to form a new government. The appointment improved the economic prospects of Lebanon by restoring a measure of confidence in the financial future of the country. But the government of al-Hariri, a Lebanese-Saudi billionaire and businessman, appeared to subordinate respect for civil and political rights to the strengthening of the armed forces and rebuilding the Lebanese economy, devastated by the fifteen-year civil war. The government often stated that Lebanon suffered from an "excessive freedom" that inflamed sectarian passions and made reconciliation difficult. Under the pretext of maintaining civil peace, the government jailed protesters, closed down news organizations and prosecuted reporters and publishers. Following an August ban of all demonstrations, on September 13 army troops used force to disperse demonstrations, with disastrous results: seven men and one woman were killed and about forty other peaceful demonstrators injured.

The year witnessed the government's growing reliance on special courts, such as military courts and the Publications Court, where procedures are abbreviated and the rights of defense are circumscribed. Critics of the government, including supporters of the Lebanese Forces, the largest Christian militia, and Gen. Michel Aoun, the ousted former prime minister, were frequently arrested, questioned and warned against further political activity. Others were tried before special courts and sentenced to lengthy prison terms.

During November and December 1992, scores were arrested after leaflets critical of President el-Hrawi were distributed on November 22, 1992, Lebanon's independence day. The leaflets criticized Syria and supported General Aoun, an outspoken critic who has lived in exile in France since August 1991. Many of those detained were known supporters of the general. As the government considered the offending leaflets defamatory of the commander-in-chief (President el-Hrawi), and weakening of the army morale, it deemed that the case fell under the competence of military courts, despite the fact that the defendants were civilian and the charges did not involve the use of violence. In late December 1992, twelve were formally charged by the military prosecutor. The following April, a military court sentenced most of the defendants to prison terms of up to seven years for the printing and distribution of those leaflets.

On July 6, Elie Mahfoud, head of the Movement for Change, a pro-Aoun opposition group, was arrested. He was charged with falsely accusing the government of arbitrarily holding hundreds of detainees, thus harming the reputation of the state. On July 13, after a summary trial before a military court, Mahfoud was convicted of "defaming official Lebanese institutions" by distributing the press statement. He was sentenced to two months in prison, later commuted to one week.

In July the Military Court of Cassation ratified in July judgments rendered by lower military courts in the case of suspects linked to an August 1992 deadly explosion in the headquarters of the Lebanese Army's First Brigade in Beirut. The two dead, Capt. Imad Abboud and Sgt. Philip Wanis, were suspected by the authorities of involvement in the explosion. Five officers and two civilians were sentenced to prison terms ranging from four months to five years. The defendants' confessions of guilt had been elicited through the use of force, according to defense lawyers.

Alarmed by the increase in detention of

government opponents and their ill-treatment, the Maronite Bishops Council criticized the security forces' excesses. In a statement issued on July 13, the council deplored "the arbitrary arrests of young men, including teenagers, which are accompanied by beatings, humiliation and insults. These actions are committed with disregard to the laws preventing arbitrary arrests, ignore the safeguards stipulated in these laws, and violate human rights."

Arbitrary arrests for peaceful expression resumed in October and continued in November. Between October 19 and November 4, dozens of Aoun supporters were arrested after some of them participated in a television program in which they voiced support for the General and criticized the Syrian presence in Lebanon. According to reports by Beirut-based lawyers and human rights monitors, the detainees included Abbad Zuwain, a writer and political activist, and his brother Najib Zuwain, Albert Shidyaq, Jean Eid, Paul Kallab, Tony Bitar and Patrick Khoury—all were arrested, without warrants, by plainclothes security forces. On October 29, Minister of Justice Bahij Tabbara confirmed the arrest of an unspecified number and described it as "precautionary detention." Other officials described the detainees as "suspected Aoun supporters," some of whom were also suspected of distributing pro-Aoun leaflets. When Abbad Zuwain, who is a prominent Aoun supporter, was released on October 29, it was learned that he had been beaten severely by Syrian intelligence officers during interrogation about his political activity.

Under Lebanese law, those arrested must be released or referred to the public prosecutor's office within twenty-four hours of their arrest. This rule was frequently violated, with detainees held incommunicado without charge for weeks or longer. Access to lawyers improved during 1993, thanks mainly to the efforts of a recently-formed Emergency Committee of the Lebanese Lawyers' Association. Nevertheless, many of those detained by the military were held for periods as long as several months

without access to family or lawyers. Lawyers complained about the lack of cooperation on the part of the chief military prosecutor's office in facilitating access. This was especially true in cases where politically motivated crimes were suspected. Between August 2 and 4, the army intelligence forces arrested several officials of the Lebanese Forces, an opposition group, including Jacques Zifikian, George al-'Alam, Tony Abou Younis and Jan 'Aqouri. Tens of other members and supporters of the Lebanese Forces were arrested and their houses and offices were raided. The authorities did not formally acknowledge the arrests until weeks later, when they responded to media reports by stating that those detained were suspected of involvement in acts of kidnapping and murder that had taken place during the civil war of 1975 to 1990, or in its immediate aftermath. This retrospective prosecution appeared to be politically selective. In August 1991, parliament had declared a sweeping amnesty for most civil-war crimes committed before March 28, 1991. Excluded were massacres and assassinations or attempted assassinations of political leaders, religious figures and diplomats. A number of senior officials, including members of the cabinet, had been leaders of militias implicated in such crimes, but had not been investigated.

Despite repeated demands by families of the missing, the government failed to search for those who were kidnapped and subsequently disappeared during the civil war. The number of missing, presumed dead, was estimated officially at about 14,000 persons. The government also failed to investigate vigorously more recent politically motivated abductions. After four months in captivity, Nasri al-Khouri Sader, a lawyer affiliated with an opposition faction, who had been kidnapped with two companions in August 1992, was released at the end of November. Sader's abduction, blamed on individuals affiliated with Hizballa, the pro-Iranian Shi'a party, prompted a lengthy strike by the members of the Lebanese Lawyers Union. Later in the year, one of his companions was found dead in southern Lebanon; the other was missing, as of November 5. Also missing since his abduction in September 1992 is Butrus Khawand, a member of the political bureau of the Lebanese Phalanges Party, a Christian opposition group.

During 1993, a number of judges resigned and others publicly complained about interference with the judiciary. At a press conference in February, Joseph Ghamroun, chief judge of the Criminal Court in the Beqa', announced his resignation, citing "deteriorating conditions under which judges must work". He referred specifically to executive interference with the judicial process. In March, 150 judges held a secret meeting at the Cassation Court at the Palace of Justice in Beirut, in which the independence of the judiciary was a main point of discussion, according to participants. After the meeting, the judges called for the adoption of a draft law—under consideration for some time—that would establish a clear separation between the executive branch and the judiciary. Despite a promise in March by Prime Minister Hariri to improve matters in the judicial branch so that "the basic rights of the Lebanese as stipulated in the Constitution will be guaranteed," there was no evident improvement.

Revealing a low tolerance threshold for criticism during 1993, the Hrawi government moved forcefully to carry out its previous threats against the media. In moves unprecedented since the civil war, in April and May the government shut down four news organizations and filed criminal charges against four journalists for violating press regulations. ICN, an outspoken television station, was closed down, as was the daily *Nida' al-Watan* (Call of the Nation)—both owned by Henry Sfair, an independent politician—for reporting an alleged plan by Prime Minister Hariri to "Islamize" Lebanon. Two other dailies, *al-Safir* (the Ambassador) and *al-Sharq* (the East), were also closed for publishing material considered offensive to the government. Court injunctions permitted the three newspapers to resume publica-

tion temporarily, pending the outcome of the criminal prosecution of their owners and reporters. But the closure of ICN was permanent. Throughout the year, criminal charges were filed against reporters, editors-in-chief, publishers and media owners, for violations of press regulations, including highly restrictive decrees issued without parliamentary approval during the civil war. The government's vigorous prosecution of violators of press laws was not matched by similar zeal in the investigation of attacks on the press, including assassinations and beatings of journalists.

In an attempt to enforce its monopoly over the ownership of television stations, the government threatened to close all forty-five private television stations. The Ministry of Information issued extremely restrictive media guidelines and put a legal and economic squeeze on these stations to drive them out of business, by directing advertising away from them and threatening them with closure and fines. On November 3, a court in Beirut fined *al-Mashriq*, a private station, $294,000 for infringing on the state's television monopoly. The only licensed station was the Lebanon Television Company (LTV), a company owned jointly by the Lebanese state and Prime Minister Hariri. LTV was granted a monopoly over television broadcasting until 2012.

During the year, the General Directorate of Public Security (GDPS), the national police force, revived its control over all non-periodical publications, including leaflets and press releases. All such publications were required to be submitted to the police for approval before being distributed. Violators were often prosecuted, and some received lengthy prison sentences. The GDPS also resumed prior censorship of books, plays and films. In a further imposition of censorship, in August Michel Samaha, Minister of Information, instructed LTV to submit its news bulletins to him before they were aired.

Freedom of assembly was dealt a severe blow when, on August 11, the Hariri government issued a categorical ban on all demonstrations. Prior to the ban, it had been the practice to grant permits, selectively, to hold demonstrations, albeit under very strict conditions. On September 13, as Israel and the Palestine Liberation Organization signed in Washington an interim self-rule accord for Gaza and Jericho, scores of protestors against the agreement were killed and injured in Beirut and Palestinian refugee camps in Lebanon. In one particularly bloody demonstration called that day in Beirut by Hizballa and other groups opposed to the peace accord, Lebanese army troops killed seven men and one women and injured around forty as they peacefully protested. Consistent reports pointed to the responsibility of senior officials of the government, including the President, the Minister of Defense and the army commander for giving the order to use force to disperse the demonstration.

Under the terms of Syria's September 1991 agreement with Lebanon, Lebanese officials consulted regularly with commanders of Syrian troops in Lebanon over most security matters, whether involving Syrian nationals or others. Officers of Syrian military intelligence were active in the Beirut international airport and other ports of entry into Lebanon, to prevent Syrian government opponents from entering or leaving the country without being interrogated or detained.

The 35,000 Syrian troops still deployed in most of Lebanon were an effective deterrent to the voicing of any criticism of Syria. There was little change in the deployment of troops despite earlier hints that Syrian forces would redeploy outside Greater Beirut, where half the Lebanese population lives, once the parliamentary elections were concluded. Although the elections brought, in October 1992, a largely pro-Syrian parliament, only minor redeployment took place; in the following January, troops were largely removed out of the Southern Suburb (of Beirut) and areas of West Beirut.

Israel and the Israeli-sponsored South Lebanon Army (SLA) were responsible for serious human rights violations in Lebanon during the year. Shelling and air raids by Israel and its allies on southern Lebanon, while ostensibly directed against guerilla bases, produced a heavy toll of civilian casualties. Between July 25 and 31, Israeli shelling of southern towns and villages resulted in several hundred civilian casualties and the flight of hundreds of thousands.

Israel continued to hold an undisclosed number of Lebanese detainees. As of October 31, Middle East Watch learned that at least twelve Lebanese detainees, most believed to belong to Hizballa, were being held in Beer Sheva prison in southern Israel. All were being held in custody beyond the expiration of their court-ordered sentences, in "administrative detention," without charge or trial, under British Mandate-era emergency regulations.

The SLA also engaged in the indiscriminate shelling of adjacent villages, the forced conscription of young men, and a policy of arbitrary arrest, lengthy incommunicado detention and torture of suspected opponents held in its notorious Khiam prison. In 1993, an estimated 200 detainees were being held in Khiam without charge or trial and without access to family or lawyers. The International Committee of the Red Cross continued to be denied access to these detainees.

Besides the SLA, the Iranian-supported Hizballa was the only other major militia that had not been disarmed by the Lebanese government. It, too, was implicated in a significant number of human rights violations, including abductions and beatings, in 1993. In light of the significant bloc of parliamentarians from Hizballa elected to the new Chamber of Deputies, the government appeared to be less inclined to curb human rights abuses by Hizballa loyalists. Ostensibly aiming to pressure Israel to abandon the Lebanese border area it controls, Hizballa also engaged in 1993 in indiscriminate shelling of northern Israel, causing civilian casualties, in violation of international humanitarian law. Hizballa's attacks on areas of southern Lebanon under SLA control caused extensive damage and casualties among noncombatants.

The Right to Monitor

There was no explicit prohibition against human rights work in Lebanon. However, local human rights groups and individual activists reported that various extralegal methods were used to restrict their freedom of activity in 1993. Security forces and militias employed violent tactics aimed at stifling human rights reporting, including arbitrary arrests and death threats.

While a number of independent groups operated openly, but cautiously, most functioned only clandestinely or abroad. Among the established groups inside Lebanon were, in Beirut, the Lebanese Association for Human Rights, the Foundation for Human and Humanitarian Rights, and the Lebanese Lawyers Association, especially its Emergency Committee. In Tripoli, the Center for Human Rights operated at al-Jinan University. Outside Lebanon, the Lebanese League for Human Rights was especially active in France and Belgium.

Humanitarian and academic organizations reported regularly on issues related to human rights in Lebanon. Among the Beirut-based groups were the Lebanese NGO Forum and the Movement of the Handicapped & Youth for Human Rights and Peace. *The Lebanon Report*, published monthly by the Lebanese Center for Policy Studies, a research institution in Beirut, provided information related to human rights.

Because of the dangers human rights monitors faced, most local groups avoided issuing public reports about specific abuses, restricting their activities to providing legal assistance to detainees and information to their families and other interested parties.

U.S. Policy

The United States significantly increased its support for the Lebanese government during 1993 in economic, military and political spheres. In the course of Middle East peace negotiations, Secretary of State Warren Christopher, twice visited Lebanon. In late September, bilateral relations were elevated further when President Bill Clinton met with Prime Minister Hariri in the U.S. American

officials appeared concerned primarily with bolstering the Lebanese government and armed forces, and ensuring Lebanon's active participation in the peace process. Regrettably, however, no concern over violations of human rights in Lebanon was voiced publicly by U.S. officials, when the Lebanese government waged a campaign against the press, jailed opponents and banned demonstrations, or when the Lebanese army attacked peaceful demonstrators. The gathering impression about the administration's attitude toward human rights was strengthened when the regional media gave prominence to comments attributed to President Clinton in a telephone conversation he had with President Hafez al-Asad of Syria on September 15; Clinton reportedly asked, in effect, that critics of the recently signed Israel-PLO accord be silenced.

During 1993, the U.S. increased its military assistance to Lebanon and ended an eight-year ban on the provision of lethal equipment. On October 6, Edward P. Djerejian, Assistant Secretary of State for Near Eastern and South Asian Affairs, cited military aid as the most important element of U.S. assistance to Lebanon. Less than a month after the Lebanese Army had opened fire, on September 13, on peaceful demonstrators in Beirut, killing eight and injuring dozens, Secretary Djerejian expressed unconditional praise for the army and its commander Gen. Emile Lahoud, and argued for additional military aid.

Economic assistance to Lebanon also increased during 1993. Although U.S. economic aid was relatively small, it had a specially high multiplier effect; Washington persuaded U.S. allies and multilateral institutions to provide record levels of economic aid. President Clinton personally communicated with a number of Arab and European heads of state to encourage their support and assistance to Lebanon. A study published in October by an investment guarantee group revealed that, on a per capita basis, Lebanon became the second-largest recipient of foreign aid in the Middle East, next only to Israel.

In March, partly due to Washington's efforts, the World Bank extended a $175 million loan to Lebanon, its first from the World Bank since 1978. The loan formed part of a $3 billion development plan the Lebanese government drew up for the period 1993 to 1996. New funding from elsewhere poured in. In July, Saudi Arabia announced a contribution of $130 million to co-finance eleven projects in Lebanon. Kuwait and Qatar made similar announcements following visits by Prime Minister Hariri during which he requested increased aid to Lebanon. In August, an Arab foreign ministers' meeting approved a $500 million aid package to Lebanon, in part at U.S. urging, according to State Department officials. Italy, France and Germany pledged substantial amounts of aid to Lebanon.

U.S. and allies' expressions of support for the Lebanese government were not accompanied by public concern over the serious human rights violations committed by the Hrawi/Hariri government, including the unprecedented attacks on freedom of the press and the death of peaceful demonstrators.

On September 15, two days after the bloody confrontation in Beirut and other protests in neighboring countries, President Clinton called President Asad of Syria to solicit his support for the Gaza-Jericho accord. Clinton asked Asad to silence Palestinians critics who were attacking the peace agreement. Absent public clarification of the President's remarks, which were widely reported in the front pages of Middle Eastern newspapers, an impression was strengthened in the region that the U.S. subordinated human rights, including the right of peaceful dissent, to other foreign policy considerations.

Critics of the Israel-PLO agreement voiced their conviction that President Clinton's September 15 phone call to President Asad was aimed at silencing those in Lebanon, and elsewhere, opposed to the Palestinian limited self-rule accord.

The Work of Middle East Watch

There were two points of special focus to Middle East Watch's work during 1993: Lebanese government attacks on the freedom of press and assembly, and the Israeli government's actions involving Lebanon.

In July, Middle East Watch issued a forty-eight-page report titled, "Lebanon's Lively Press Faces Worst Crackdown Since 1976," on the closure of news organizations and the restoration of strict censorship of the press, radio, television and all forms of political, cultural and artistic expression. The report concluded that the restrictive measures against the press were taken to safeguard the immediate interests of President Hrawi and Prime Minister Hariri and the policies of their government, and to shield the interests of Syria and Saudi Arabia, Lebanon's closest allies. Following the publication of the report, Middle East Watch coordinated a vigorous campaign involving several advocacy groups to draw attention to this unprecedented attack on the press and to call on the Lebanese government to end its crackdown. In September, it broadened this theme through a sixteen-page report on the government ban on demonstrations and the forcible dispersion of peaceful protests.

Following Israel's expulsion on December 17, 1992, of 413 Palestinians to Lebanon, Middle East Watch sent a mission to the region. After investigating the conditions under which the deportees were living in southern Lebanon, it held a press conference, on January 12, in Jerusalem to publicize its findings. While laying the primary responsibility for the deportees' plight on Israel, Middle East Watch criticized the Lebanese government for its failure to permit humanitarian assistance to reach them and for its denial of access by the ICRC. In a number of subsequent statements, Middle East Watch demanded that the U.S. take a leading role in urging Israel to repatriate the deportees, but its efforts to meet with U.S. officials to discuss their plight were unsuccessful. In August, Middle East Watch issued an updated report on the deportees' conditions.

The July fighting in Lebanon between Israel and Hizballa prompted Middle East Watch to issue press statements expressing concern over the apparent indiscriminate attacks by both sides on civilians. In October, Middle East Watch and the Arms Project, another division of Human Rights Watch, sent a mission to Lebanon to investigate possible violations of the rules of war. A report on the subject was scheduled for January 1994 release, after the completion of a November 1993 mission to Israel, to gather information from official and private sources.

SAUDI ARABIA

Human Rights Developments

During 1993, in some respects, the dismal human rights record of the Kingdom took a turn for the worse. Torture, ill-treatment and incommunicado detention without trial remained the norm during the year, especially for those accused of security and political offenses. Executions imposed after summary trials increased to more than double the rate of the previous year. The ban on free speech, assembly and association was strictly enforced; violators were jailed, deported, banned from travel or dismissed from their government positions. Fifteen university professors were jailed, and about sixty others banned from travel for the expression of views critical of the government. Formally sanctioned severe restrictions on the employment and movement of women remained in place. In a positive development, most political prisoners from the Shi'a minority were released in July. But discrimination against and harassment of Christians and non-Sunni Muslims continued unabated.

Senior government officials, meanwhile, continued to deny that human rights abuses occurred. Prince Nayef, Minister of Interior and the top security official in the country, said in May that Saudi Arabia "respects human rights much more than any other state or any other society in the world." The year was marked by a campaign in government-controlled media against human rights, which were dismissed as products of anti-Islamic Western bias and "Zionist intrigue."

The most significant development in 1993 was the Saudi government's swift crackdown on peaceful dissent by Islamist groups. The crackdown included formally banning the Committee to Defend Legitimate Rights (CDLR), established on May 3 by six prominent Islamist jurists and university professors. On May 12, the government-appointed Council of Senior Scholars, the highest religious body in the country, denounced the formation of the group as a violation of Islamic law. On May 13, King Fahd summarily dismissed the CDLR's founders from their government jobs. Two founders who were lawyers in private practice had their law offices closed down by royal order. The CDLR spokesman Dr. Muhammed al-Mas'ari, a physics professor at King Saud University, was arrested on May 15, after he defied an order not to talk to the foreign press about the committee. Fourteen other professors from King Saud and al-Imam universities were subsequently arrested and detained without trial. Lawyers supporting the new group had their offices closed and one, Sulaiman al-Rushudi, was also detained. Scores of the committee's other supporters, including about sixty university professors, were either dismissed from their official positions, banned from travel or both.

This crackdown on peaceful dissent was the first major test of the Basic Law of Government, issued by King Fahd in March 1992. Although this law was hailed by Saudi and United States officials as heralding a new era of respect for basic rights, the Saudi government's actions since its adoption proved such hopes to be premature. Ten days after the establishment of CDLR, the first nongovernmental organization of its kind to be formed in Saudi Arabia in decades, the government disbanded the group and jailed or dismissed its founders, most of whom were socially prominent and respected Islamist figures. The government-appointed clergy were induced to call for the banning of the group as un-Islamic, and to denounce its founders. Senior officials and the state-run media described the group as seditious or dismissed it as marginal.

According to its founders, the formation of the Islamist-inspired CDLR was in part prompted by widespread arrests and increased official harassment of Islamist activists. The Directorate of General Investigations (DGI), the secret police known as al-Mabahith, arrested and held without trial or formal charges hundreds of suspected followers of popular preachers and other sympathizers with Islamist groups during 1993. Scores arrested in Riyadh and al-Qasim were disciples of Salman al-'Awda and Safar al-Hawali, two popular Islamist speakers and university professors who advocated religion-based social and political reforms. The two scholars were banned in September from speaking in public and dismissed from their academic posts. Shaikh Ibrahim al-Dibayyan, another popular preacher, was arrested in February after he publicly criticized government policy in his sermons. In June, Shaikh Sa'id Ba Tarfi in Jidda, who advocated *jihad* (holy war) in Bosnia, and about twenty of his followers were also arrested. His followers, mostly from Egypt, Yemen and Afghanistan, were suspected of supporting Islamist groups in Egypt and Afghanistan. For similar reasons, over ten local and foreign supporters of Usama Bin Ladin, a prosperous businessmen who financed the *mujahideen* of Afghanistan, were arrested in Jidda. In most cases, no charges were filed against the detainees, but they were interrogated about their political activities. Most of the Saudis detained were later released after they signed statements expressing their regret and pledging not to engage in further political activity. Some of those who declined to sign such statements remained in prison while others were released but dismissed from their government jobs and banned from travel. Most of the foreigners were deported.

A violent protest in March at the Rafha refugee camp resulted in the death of at least eight Iraqi refugees and three Saudi government employees and the injury of over 140 refugees. The uprising at the camp, located near the Iraqi-Saudi border, was triggered by the refusal of Saudi authorities to permit family members fleeing Iraq to join their relatives in the camp. During the protest, fire was set to a camp administrative building and security forces subsequently opened fire to disperse the crowds. Following the incident, hundreds were detained. Many were known to have been tortured, in an apparent attempt by the authorities to find those who organized the protest.

Hostility between the refugees and the camp's guards predated this development. Since April 1991, a month after the Rafha camp was established for Iraqi refugees, there had been clashes between the camp's residents and guards in which scores of refugees were killed or injured. Refugees suspected of organizing protests were forcibly repatriated during 1991 and 1992. The government provided adequate levels of food, health care and education, and, until the March 1993, protest provided residents with additional monthly stipends. But the refugees' movement and their political expression and religious freedom were restricted. Less than 10,000 refugees were resettled in third countries between 1991 and the end of October, 1993, leaving about 25,000 refugees at the camp as of that date. The government denied press reports that it had forcibly repatriated some refugees after the March incident.

Middle East Watch received confirmed reports during 1993 of torture and ill-treatment of detainees during interrogation by the secret police and the religious police. To compel prisoners to provide information, they were frequently subjected to electric shock, falaqa (beating on the soles of the feet) and flogging with bamboo sticks on other sensitive parts of the body. Ill-treatment included prolonged incommunicado detention, sleep deprivation, threats, and insults. Visits by family members or lawyers were often denied for long periods.

There was one confirmed report of death in custody during the year. Hussein Ali al-

Shuwaikhat, a nineteen-year-old Shi'a from Saihat in the Eastern Province, died on January 18 after he was transferred, bleeding, to a hospital. Although officials at the 'Awwamiyya Western Prison, where he had been kept since March 1991, assured his family that he had died of natural causes, no autopsy was permitted. Authorities rejected the family's request to investigate the incident, and al-Shuwaikhat's father was coerced into signing a statement—five days after the death—declaring the cause of death to be natural.

The number of judicial executions in Saudi Arabia reached a record level in the first seven months of 1993. According to official figures, during that period, sixty-three persons were executed, nearly all beheaded. This figure surpassed the total for all of 1992, and was more than double the 1991 figure. In almost all of these executions, defendants were convicted after proceedings that fell far short of international standards for fair trials. Most were not represented by lawyers at the trials or assisted in preparing their defense. Out of the sixty-three, over forty were beheaded for drug offenses—more than during the preceding five years put together. Between 1987, the year the death penalty was introduced for drug smuggling, and October 1992, thirty-eight were executed, according to Gen. Mohammed al-Maleki, a drug enforcement official.

Arrest and detention procedures continued to be governed by Imprisonment and Detention Law No. 31 of 1978 and its 1982 bylaws issued by the Minister of Interior, Prince Nayef ibn Abdel Aziz. With few restrictions on the grounds or duration of pre-trial detention, these procedures allowed detainees to be held indefinitely without trial or judicial review. Although families were often able to find out informally if one of their members had been detained, rarely was there formal notification. This problem applied equally to foreigners arrested in Saudi Arabia, many of whom had no family in Saudi Arabia to notice that they were missing. Saudi authorities did not notify foreign missions of the arrest of their nationals and declined to sign international or bilateral consular agreements mandating such notification.

It was equally rare for a detainee to be informed of the charges against him or her. Saudi law permits interrogation of detainees without the benefit of counsel, and the use of force to elicit confessions was commonplace in the Saudi security system. This may be in part because of the Saudi legal system's over-reliance on confessions. Imprisonment and Detention Law No. 31 explicitly sanctioned flogging, indefinite solitary confinement, and deprivation of family visits, as methods for disciplining prisoners.

Detention without trial continued to be authorized for those involved in commercial disputes or business failures. Abdalla al-Rajhi, a forty-five-year-old Saudi banker detained without trial since 1979 when his firm collapsed, was released in February 1993. However, many others remained in debtors' prisons; some had been there for as long as ten years. Foreigners, estimated officially at about five million or 27 percent of the population, faced special hardships, including a ban on travel within the country or abroad without written permission from their employers. Hundreds of foreigners accused of violating the stringent visa regulations, by overstaying their residency permits or changing their employers, were being held in crowded, substandard deportation facilities throughout the Kingdom. Most were subsequently expelled without judicial review. Since regulations required that aliens secure clearance from their former employers before being permitted to leave the country, many were kept in deportation facilities awaiting these clearances.

Human rights abuses were facilitated by the absence of an independent judiciary and the lack of scrutiny by an elected representative body or a free press. Although the March 1992 Basic Law of Government formally recognized, for the first time, the principle of an independent judiciary, Middle East Watch continued to receive reports from within the judiciary that judges periodically came under pressure from senior members of the royal family and other government officials to influence their decisions. Not surprisingly, judges remained afraid to check official abuse of power. Moreover, under the Saudi government's interpretation of the Shari'a, the King is the spiritual as well as temporal head of the community (*waliyy al-amr*), and thus had broad discretion to override judicial decisions. Provincial governors in Saudi Arabia, as representatives of the King and usually close relatives, also exercised their authority to review court decisions.

A twenty-seven-page report sharply critical of the judicial system in the Kingdom was circulated during the U.N. World Conference on Human Rights, held in Vienna between June 14 and 25. Although written anonymously, Middle East Watch learned that the report was authored by a group of Saudi lawyers and judges. It was especially critical of the pervasive interference by members of the royal family in the judicial process.

The royal family's concentration of power—one that has few parallels in the world—was immunized from criticism by the absence of a free press or parliament. This left government officials and other prominent citizens, primarily members of the royal family and their associates, free to abuse their positions and act as if they were above the law. In early 1993, two men from the Qahtan tribe were killed after they had entered the estate of Prince Mish'al, King Fahd's brother, without his permission. Attempts by the families of the two men to bring the Prince, whom they accused of killing the two men, to trial were unsuccessful.

Expectations raised by the government when King Fahd decreed the Basic Law of Government in March 1992 were dashed by the experience of the subsequent eighteen months, in which there was no perceptible improvement in respect for human rights. Formally sanctioned discrimination based on gender or religious beliefs continued unabated. Glaring due process deficiencies

in the Saudi penal system were not rectified: based on Shari'a, as interpreted by government-appointed clergy, the unwritten criminal code for instance did not permit defendants to have legal representation in the courtroom. In May, the Council of Senior Scholars ratified the government's policy banning the formation of private human rights advocacy groups.

On August 20, King Fahd appointed the new Consultative Council, replacing a council by the same name that had been in existence since 1926 but had been almost completely ignored by the executive since 1953, when most of its powers were usurped by the King and his cabinet. Almost all of the sixty-one members of the new council were government loyalists, the majority of them longtime government employees. According to the Consultative Council Bylaws issued in August by King Fahd, the Council's members may retain their positions in the executive branch while serving their terms in the Consultative Council. By virtue of its mandate, composition and bylaws, the Council did not appear likely to provide a forum for significant political participation or act as a check on human rights abuses.

During 1993, the government initiated a dialogue with Shi'a political figures in exile. In exchange for ceasing their political activity abroad and discontinuing their publications, the government released political prisoners and promised to consider seriously Shi'a grievances. On July 25, the government released over thirty Shi'a men, representing nearly all Shi'a activists still in jail on political and security-related charges. Four exiled leaders returned to the Kingdom and some met with the King, a rare occurrence.

The *quid pro quo* also took place. In September, exiled groups suspended their publications. The Reform Movement, based in London, suspended its monthly *al-Jazeera al-Arabia* (The Arabian Peninsula), which reported regularly on human rights violations in the Kingdom and translated reports by Western human rights groups. The International Committee for Human Rights in the Arabian Peninsula and the Gulf, a group affiliated with the Reform Movement, suspended *Arabia Monitor*, its monthly English-language publication issued in Washington. However, as of the end of October, there was no evident change in institutionalized discrimination against the Shi'a.

In 1993, Islamists intensified their public criticism of the government. In mosque sermons and clandestinely distributed leaflets and audiocassettes, they criticized corruption and favoritism and called for more political participation. They also sought greater autonomy for Islamic preachers, including freedom of expression, as well as an end to torture and arbitrary arrests and searches. A number of Islamist leaders who publicly criticized the government were dismissed from their government jobs and banned from travel or from public speaking. On September 26, Salman Fahd al-'Awda and Safar Abdel Rahman al-Hawali, two popular Islamist speakers and university professors, were asked by senior Ministry of Interior officials to sign a statement apologizing for speaking out against the government and promising never again to discuss the "State's internal, foreign, financial, media or other policies," or "communicate with anyone outside the country, or any activist inside the country, by telephone or fax." When they refused to sign, they were informed of their dismissal from their university teaching positions. They were also banned from recording speeches, leading prayers or publishing books or articles. In May, the Ministry of Interior had once again warned pilgrims and other travelers to the Kingdom against importing any "political" publications.

The government owned and operated all radio and television stations in the Kingdom, and it kept the privately owned local press on a very short leash, preventing criticism of government policies. During the year, three editors-in-chief—Khaled al-Ma'eena and Luqman Younis, both of the *Arab News* English daily, and Yousef Damanhouri of the Arabic daily *al-Nadwa* (Symposium)—were either dismissed or suspended from their positions for publishing materials considered offensive. A large number of foreign publications, including daily newspapers and weekly magazines, were barred from the country in 1993 on the grounds of their supposedly offensive content. Most visa applications by journalists from major U.S. and British news organizations were turned down.

During 1993, the government continued its efforts to expand its considerable influence over major regional and international news organizations. On August 4, a cooperation agreement was signed between Ali al-Sha'ir, Minister of Information and Jacques Taquet, director general of Radio Monte Carlo's Middle East Division. Under this unusual agreement, Radio Monte Carlo, which has a large audience in the Kingdom for its Arabic broadcasts, undertook to publicize "the government's position on political, economic and oil issues, emphasizing the great achievements that have taken place during the reign of King Fahd, Custodian of the Holy Shrines," according to a Ministry of Information statement. In the two previous years, Saudi businessmen had acquired the U.S. news agency United Press International and *al-Hayat*, a major Arabic daily, and MBC, a London-based satellite TV network.

The Right to Monitor

Since monitoring human rights violations was considered by the government as political activity, Saudi Arabian law and practice strictly prohibited such an undertaking. Associations of any kind wishing to report on human rights violations in the Kingdom either had to work clandestinely inside the country, at the risk of arrest, or operate outside the Kingdom. In 1993, the ability to monitor human rights abuses in Saudi Arabia became even more restricted, with the shutdown of groups reporting on human rights and the arrests of activists attempting to monitor violations.

On May 3, seven distinguished Islamist jurists and professors publicly announced the formation of the Committee for the Defense of Legitimate Rights. The government reacted swiftly and harshly. The same month, the Saudi government banned the group and began to arrest its founders and core supporters. Others were dismissed from their government positions, had their law offices closed or were banned from travel.

A few months later, another important source of human rights information dried up under government pressure. Leaders of the Reform Movement, the main Shi'a opposition group, agreed in August to suspend their activities abroad, which had included the distribution of human rights information by groups affiliated with them and the translation of reports by international human rights organizations. In September, it suspended the publication of *Al-Jazeera al-Arabia* (The Arabian Peninsula), an Arabic monthly affiliated with the movement. Published in London, the magazine regularly published articles on human rights violations, especially those related to the Shi'a minority. That month, the London-based International Committee for Human Rights in the Gulf and Arabian Peninsula, which had close ties to the Reform Movement, suspended the publication of *Arabia Monitor*, an English-language monthly issued from Washington, D.C. After its representatives met with King Fahd in October, the International Committee suspended all public reporting on human rights in Saudi Arabia.

The government allowed humanitarian organizations to operate in the country; the United Nations High Commissioner for Refugees and the International Committee of the Red Cross maintained offices concerned mainly with the resettlement of Iraqi refugees and conditions at the Rafha refugee camp. However, no foreign human rights organizations were permitted to visit the country in 1993. As in the past, requests for information and inquiries that Middle East Watch made during the year on specific incidents of human rights violations went unanswered.

U.S. Policy

By virtue of a long and intimate relationship with Saudi Arabia spanning over fifty years, the United States is uniquely well-placed to help curb human rights abuses in Saudi Arabia. During the 1992 election campaign, Bill Clinton had cited Saudi Arabia, in a November 1992 magazine article, as a target for future human rights attention. Regrettably, his administration reverted to the practice of previous U.S. administrations, by emphasizing the special relationship and failing to criticize Saudi violations publicly. Human rights principles appeared to have been subordinated to strategic and economic interests, in the mistaken belief that promotion of human rights and participatory democracy in the Kingdom would have a deleterious effect on those other important interests.

The broad range of cooperation between the two countries was premised on a U.S. commitment to the defense of Saudi Arabia—a key goal of U.S. foreign policy. The Clinton administration reiterated this commitment. In his first visit to the region in February, Warren Christopher told Saudi leaders that President Clinton's commitment to the security of Saudi Arabia "like that of every president since Franklin Roosevelt, is firm and constant." There was no public reference to human rights during those visits.

U.S. officials expressed their belief that the defense of the Arabian Peninsula was one of two key policy goals in the Middle East—the other being peace between Israel and her Arab neighbors. In September and October 1992, Edward P. Djerejian, Assistant Secretary of State for Near Eastern Affairs, articulated this policy clearly in congressional testimony and other forums. David L. Mack, Deputy Assistant Secretary of State for Near Eastern Affairs, reiterated the same policy.

The administration's multi-tiered approach to ensuring Saudi Arabia's security included bilateral military arrangements and the provision of advanced U.S. weapons. A package of sophisticated weapons totaling $14 billion was signed in 1992, for delivery in 1992 and 1993. Although delivery of some of these system slowed down because of financial difficulties, arms sales to Saudi Arabia, at $4.2 billion, accounted for 31 percent of all U.S. arms sales in 1992, according to a study by the Congressional Research Service published in July. The U.S. military held periodic joint exercises with Saudi forces and maintained an enhanced naval presence in the Gulf with unrestricted access to Saudi facilities.

Considering this special relationship between the two countries, it was perhaps remarkable that the administration did not apparently consider utilizing its leverage to bring about a significant change in the Saudi human rights record. U.S. officials refrained in 1993 from voicing public criticism of Saudi human rights violations, some of which were catalogued, in some detail, in the State Department's most recent *Country Reports on Human Rights Practices*. In 1993, U.S. officials reported progress in resolving a number of long-standing commercial disputes between U.S. citizens and Saudi entities. But, even when the victims were U.S. citizens—there are nearly 40,000 U.S. citizens in the Kingdom—they shied away from publicly criticizing Saudi human rights practices. In 1993, Saudi Arabia failed to notify the U.S. Embassy of the arrest of American citizens and declined to approve a bilateral consular treaty providing for notification and immediate access to detainees.

When, in May, Saudi authorities banned the Committee for the Defense of Legitimate Rights and began to arrest its founders or dismiss them from their academic posts, the State Department refrained from criticizing the action. Despite the fact that embassy officials had met with the founders of the group before their arrest, a May 13 State Department written statement only promised that the U.S. Embassy would "look into the reports." Instead of addressing the Saudi action, the State Department went out of its way to defend the meeting as "routine, legitimate activity....The U.S. is in no way interfering in the internal affairs of Saudi Arabia. The meeting has been discussed between our two governments and it does not affect our excellent relations." On May 17, when a State Department spokesman was repeatedly questioned by reporters about the U.S.

reaction, he declined again to comment on the Saudi action, saying that the Department was still "looking into it."

Despite the fact the State Department's own *Country Reports*, published in early 1993, revealed detailed knowledge of human rights abuses in Saudi Arabia, a State Department spokesman declined to criticize the Saudi ban on public Christian worship, an issue researched extensively by U.S. diplomats. On September 14, asked whether he had any comment about reports of persecution of Shi'a and Christians, the spokesman declined to comment directly or to criticize the government. He added, "I will say that we, of course, support religious freedom. Our most recent human rights report contained substantial coverage of the situation in Saudi Arabia, and we have made our views and our concerns known about this at the highest levels within the Saudi government."

On March 23, the U.S. Supreme Court decided the case of *Saudi Arabia v. Nelson*, ruling that the Foreign Sovereign Immunities Act of 1976 (FSIA) denied U.S. courts jurisdiction to hear suits by U.S. citizens against foreign governments unless the dispute related to commercial activity. The court decided that this did not apply to Nelson's suit against Saudi Arabian government agencies, on the grounds that police action, no matter how monstrous, was by definition a sovereign matter. Scott Nelson, a former safety engineer, had filed legal action against Saudi authorities for torture and unlawful detention. The Bush administration filed an *amicus* brief with the U.S. Supreme Court in support of the Saudi position that U.S. courts had no jurisdiction in this case (Human Rights Watch filed a brief with the court in support of Nelson's claim).

On September 23, 1992, despite objections by the Bush administration, the House Judiciary Committee adopted an amendment to the FSIA enabling Americans subjected to torture abroad, and the families of American victims to extrajudicial execution abroad, to obtain remedy in U.S. courts. The bill did not reach the House floor before the end of the term. A similar amendment was introduced in the new Congress. In September 1993 the House Judiciary Committee adopted this new measure, adding the crime of genocide to the list of human rights abuses included in the previous amendment. The Clinton administration did not express a view on this amendment. A State Department official told Middle East Watch in October that the administration was "still formulating a position" on the proposed legislation.

The Work of Middle East Watch

In 1993, Middle East Watch's Saudi Arabia work focused on advocacy. In one notable case, on January 29, Canadian authorities granted asylum to a Saudi woman known as Nada (her family name was withheld). Nada fled Saudi Arabia in 1991, claiming fear of persecution for her feminist beliefs. Middle East Watch had supported Nada's claim and urged Canadian authorities, in 1992, to grant her asylum. After the Canadian landmark decision was announced, Middle East Watch issued a statement applauding the decision, and called for wider application of the principle of granting asylum to women who were persecuted on grounds either of their gender or feminist beliefs. In March, Canada's Immigration and Refugee Board issued guidelines widening the scope of the definition of women refugees, giving support to the concept that women should be treated as a social group under the terms of the 1951 Refugee Convention. In May, Middle East Watch called on the U.S. to introduce similar measures in its immigration policy.

In April, Middle East Watch called on the Congress to adopt legislation allowing for legal action in the U.S. to remedy human rights violations committed abroad. The recommendation was in response to the Supreme Court decision in *Saudi Arabia v. Nelson*. Middle East Watch had acted as *amicus curiae* in support of Scott Nelson, an American worker who was suing the government of Saudi Arabia for torture and arbitrary arrest during his employment with a Saudi government agency.

When Saudi university professors were arrested in connection with the founding of CDLR, Middle East Watch participated in a campaign to free them. Human Rights Watch's International Committee on Academic Freedom sent similar protests.

SYRIA

Human Rights Developments

In 1993, Syria's fifteen million residents lived their thirtieth year under emergency law, imposed in March 1963 when the Arab Ba'th Socialist Party seized power. The reference by President Hafez al-Asad in a June 1991 speech to the need to "increase popular participation in political decision-making" had generated hope that an opening of Syria's political system might be in the offing. But, towards the end of the year, anticipated reforms had not been realized. As in past years, opposition political activity was not tolerated, independent institutions of civil society were not permitted to exist, and the media remained under total state control. The regime of President Hafez al-Asad, which has ruled in authoritarian fashion since 1970, has earned the ignominious distinction of holding some of the world's longest-serving political prisoners, detained without charge or trial for over twenty years. One of them, Gen. Salah Jadid, by many accounts the most powerful figure in Syria from 1966 to his arrest in 1970, died in detention in August. Jadid's death —and the release earlier in the year of five former government and Ba'th Party officials arrested in 1970 or 1971—left eight long-term political prisoners, all arrested between 1969 and 1972, incarcerated without trial.

Despite the welcome mass releases over the last two years of thousands of Syria's security and political prisoners—including 4,018 in three successive amnesties between December 1991 and December 1992— Middle East Watch estimated that some 4,000 remained incarcerated. Among them were individuals held for association with political groups not engaged in violence, and writers and other professionals held merely for peaceful expression and association. Fifteen human rights activists from the Committees for the Defense of Democratic Freedoms and Human Rights in Syria (CDF), an independent human rights organization formed in Damascus in 1989 that is barred from working openly inside the country, were part of this group of prisoners of conscience. The CDF members were arrested between December 1991 and March 1992.

There were reports in 1993 of arrests under the emergency law, incommunicado detention, and deaths believed to have been caused by torture. Additionally, during the year, the Supreme State Security Court began to hand down verdicts in trials begun the previous June of some 500 detainees accused of membership in outlawed political groups. Most had been held without charge since the 1980s. The legal proceedings fell short of international fair-trial standards and the court's decisions could not be appealed to a higher tribunal. Five detained CDF members were among those tried by the court; in a disgraceful move in 1992, the security court had sentenced fourteen other CDF members to prison terms of up to ten years (four were released in a subsequent amnesty).

Kurds, Palestinians and Jews all continued to be at risk as minorities. The large Kurdish population of over one million suffered from blatant state-sponsored discrimination. Most of Syria's 300,000 Palestinians remained as refugees under the law, pending final resolution of their status through the Arab-Israeli peace process. Thus, while Palestinian residents were issued identity cards, they were not granted Syrian citizenship and passports, even if born in Syria to refugee parents. In the second half of 1993, some thirty Palestinian families of Gazan origin were expelled after authorities confiscated their identity papers. Syria's tiny remaining Jewish community faced fresh obstacles in securing exit permits, in a reversal of the regime's April 1992 liberalization of departure rules that led 2,650 Syrian Jews to emigrate to the U.S.

Freedom of expression continued to be a casualty of the longstanding state of emergency. Syria's media served as state organs, and no independent publications were permitted to exist. In a clear articulation of the government's philosophy, Information Minister Muhammed Salman unabashedly stated, in an interview published in the Jordanian daily *al-Dustur* on May 10, that the role of Syria's media since 1970 has been to "express and explain the state's domestic development policy and Arab and foreign policy." He added: "We express in our media the policy drawn up by our political leadership, away from sensationalism or competition, or any other heading that could be used as a cover to propagate policies or ideas that are like harmful weeds that have a deceptive appearance." The minister cited Syria's state of war with Israel, and the occupation of the Golan Heights, as reasons for tight control of the media: "This requires immunizing citizens politically and culturally all the time through the official media, as well as through the parties of the National Progressive Front, and the popular, professional and cultural organizations."

In a June 1 report from Damascus, CDF noted that the Ministry of Information and the security apparatus both played a prominent role in monitoring and suppressing independent thought. Manuscripts, articles and other works—as well as Friday sermons in mosques—had to be authorized by state agents. Syrian writers and intellectuals had been interrogated for what they had said in public fora; many were blacklisted from traveling abroad. Special intelligence-service units at each university conducted surveillance of all activities and compiled periodic reports about the content of academic lectures.

Despite the regime's poor rights record, Syrian officials in 1993 celebrated the country's political system, glossing over the lack of pluralism, the absence of an independent civil society, and the thousands of victims of human rights abuse. Vice-President Abdel Halim Khaddam, quoted on April 27 in the Kuwaiti newspaper *al-Watan*, proclaimed that Syria was "the most stable country in the Third World." He said that the political system had "proved its efficacy because of this stability over the past twenty-three years." During an official visit to France in February, Foreign Minister Farouq al-Shar`a was asked by the London-based Arabic daily *al-Hayat* about human rights. "As regards human rights," he stated, "we believe that no state in the world, not even a superpower interested in a new world order, has a right to dictate the political regimes of other states." But when the foreign minister addressed the U.N. World Conference on Human Rights in Vienna on June 17, he declared that Syria was "committed to the Universal Declaration of Human Rights" and "reflected in its different legislation and laws the humanitarian yardsticks which are encapsulated in [international human rights] charters and covenants." He neglected to mention that exceptional powers under the longstanding emergency law have essentially voided any human rights guarantees enshrined in Syrian law.

The regime demonstrated sensitivity to its human rights image abroad, however, when it dispatched three representatives to an October 18 conference in Paris organized by CDF, the International Federation of Human Rights and Amnesty International. The three were: Ghassan Rifa'i, former editor-in-chief of the government daily *Tishrin*; Gen. Asad Muqaed, president of the official association of the Syrian community in France; and Dr. Adel Zaaboub, head of the state-run Syrian Arab News Agency (SANA) in France and a former government censor. In their remarks, Mr. Rifa'i and Gen. Muqaed noted that the government was involved in a struggle against terrorism, and acknowledged that some abuses had occurred from the state's efforts to protect society from terrorist actions. (According to CDF, there had not been a terrorist incident in Syria since 1983.) They also misleadingly characterized the efforts of CDF and international human rights organizations on Syria as political rather than human rights work.

There was no space for opposition political parties independent of the ruling Ba'th Party and the National Progressive Front (NPF), which the Ba'th dominates. Law No. 49 of July 1980, which banned the Muslim Brotherhood and made membership in the organization a capital offense, remained in effect. President Asad offered a defense of Syria's one-dimensional political landscape in an interview with his English-language biographer Patrick Seale. As published in the May 10 to 16 issue of the London-based Arabic weekly *al-Wasat*, Asad maintained that the seven political parties in the NPF were "deep-rooted movements" with "differences among them." Seale responded that these parties had extremely limited power, and asked the Syrian leader if he intended to give them more room to maneuver. Asad's reply provided no indication that any form of political pluralism was in the offing, despite some signs to that effect at the end of 1991.

The Syrian leader provided his own view of the system: "I believe that these parties have real power. They participate...in the decisions that affect the fate of every citizen. They monitor the government's work....There is nothing that prevents them from voicing their opinion on any issue....Not one member of these parties has been arrested for his activities within the Front." He did not mention that political activity outside the narrow band of the state-controlled NPF was not permitted.

Despite the dramatic and encouraging reduction in the number of security and political prisoners in Syria during 1992 and 1993, developments in 1993 demonstrated that independent political activity not only would not be tolerated, but also would be punished severely, as would human rights work inside Syria by Syrians. Trials of over 500 detainees, which started in June 1992, continued before the Supreme State Security Court, a tribunal created in 1968 to try violations of emergency-law regulations. The defendants, almost all of whom had been arrested between 1980 and 1992, included suspected members or supporters of communist, rival Ba'thist, Nasserite, and Kurdish nationalist organizations. The trials of five CDF members arrested in February and March 1992—Kurdish writer Ahmad Hasso, Palestinian writer Salama George Kila, freelance journalist Ibrahim Habib, athletics teacher Najib Ata Layqa and merchant Jihad Khazem—also began.

All of the defendants faced charges of membership in organizations attempting to change the structures of the state or the foundations of the society through the use of violence; the dissemination of false information in order to undermine public confidence in the goals of the revolution; and opposition to Arab unity, socialism and other objectives of the revolution—offenses itemized in a 1965 military decree. Amnesty International reported in June 1993 that, while a small number of the 500 defendants stood accused of participation in violent incidents, the majority had neither advocated nor participated in political violence but were prisoners of conscience "detained simply because they are suspected of membership of links with illegal political parties, distribution of leaflets and attending their meetings."

On June 24 and June 29, the security court handed down a first set of verdicts and sentences against thirty-four defendants, all accused of supporting the illegal Party for Communist Action (PCA). Harsh prison terms were imposed on twenty-two defendants. Twelve men were sentenced to fifteen years with hard labor: two were political prisoners who had already been detained for over ten years, Malik al-Asad and Rustum Ahmad Rustum; a third was Dr. Ayman Daghistani, detained since 1987 and sentenced for reading the banned PCA newsletter *Red Flag*. Ten other defendants received sentences of ten to thirteen years with hard labor, and seven received lesser terms. All of those sentenced were stripped of civil rights, including the right to vote, travel abroad and hold government jobs. Amnesty International observers who attended some of the trial proceedings found gross violations of internationally accepted fair-trial norms, including a failure to investigate complaints of torture, lack of full access by defense law-

yers to the files of their clients, and the denial of private meetings between lawyers and their clients.

The continuing practice of incommunicado detention in Syria—coupled with the lack of independent mechanisms for investigating suspicious deaths in detention—rendered conclusive documentation of torture extremely difficult. CDF reported in 1993 that six political prisoners were believed to have died under torture at two prisons between October 1992 and January 1993. Ahmad Mattar, Abdel Karim Dhouehi, and Muhammed Barakat died at al-Riqqa prison, east of Aleppo, some time between December 20, 1992, and January 15, 1993. Three others died at Sednaya prison, north of Damascus. The body of one of them—Shakour Ta'ban, a lawyer in his fifties who had been arrested in connection with a communique issued in January 1991 in opposition to the Gulf War—was returned to the family in November 1992. (Two other lawyers arrested in the same case, Mrs. Naif al-Hamaoui and Walid Mouteiran, remained in detention as of the end of October 1993.) The other deaths at Sednaya prison were those of sixty-year-old Muhsen Abdallah, who died in November 1992, and sixty-three-year-old Qasem Hesso, who died sixteen days after his arrest in October 1992.

Suspected Kurdish political activists remained detained for freedom of expression. On October 5, 1992, four illegal Kurdish organizations had published materials to mark the thirtieth anniversary of Decree Law No. 93 of 1962, which effectively stripped about 120,000 Kurds of their Syrian citizenship and passports (the number of stateless Kurds has since risen by natural increase to 180,000). The groups had called upon Syrian citizens to support equal civil and cultural rights for the Kurds. The authorities responded with the arrest of about 260 Kurds in al-Hassakah, Ras al-'Ain and al-Qamishli in the northeast, and in Aleppo and Afrin in the northwest. Forty of the Kurds remained in detention in 1993, most of them suspected of membership in the banned Kurdish Popular Union Party. CDF reported that authorities prevented some Kurdish intellectuals from traveling abroad throughout 1993, and prohibited the formation of Kurdish cultural centers, bookshops, publishing houses and other associations. In a further mark of discrimination against Kurdish culture, a September 1992 decree (No. 122) prohibited Syrian civil servants from registering children with Kurdish first names.

Syrian prisons, known for their abysmal conditions in violation of minimum international standards, remained off-limits to independent domestic or foreign scrutiny. There continued to be grave concerns about inadequate medical care for prisoners suffering from serious illnesses. In August, CDF submitted to the U.N. Human Rights Commission the names of fourteen prisoners believed to be in poor health, including lawyer Riad al-Turk, arrested in 1980, and former government minister Muhammed 'Id Ashshawi, arrested in 1970.

Some of the longest-serving political prisoners in the world remained incarcerated in Syrian jails. Their advanced age, coupled with conditions of confinement and medical care, raised humanitarian and human rights concerns. In 1993, the government released five prisoners, former high-ranking officials, who had been held for over twenty-two years; these releases reportedly left thirteen men in detention who had been arrested between 1969 and 1972: eight of them were never tried, and four (all arrested in 1970) had been held beyond the expiry of their sentences in 1985. One of the prisoners never charged or tried was sixty-nine-year-old Gen. Salah Jadid, a key figure in the 1963 coup and *de facto* head of the Ba'th Party at the time of his arrest in November 1970 following a bloodless coup led by his former colleague, then-Defense Minister Hafez al-Asad. Gen. Jadid had been held in al-Mezze military prison in Damascus and died on August 19. Rights groups and Jadid loyalists called for an independent investigation of the circumstances of his death. CDF received information that ten members of Jadid's family were arrested after his death, including his grandsons Nidal Jadid and

Salah Jadid.

On March 24, fifty-seven prisoners perished in a fire in al-Hassakah prison in northeastern Syria. Most of them reportedly were Kurds, and at least four were political prisoners. Following the fire, one political prisoner at al-Hassakah wrote in a letter to his brother that sleeping quarters designed for fifty or sixty had been packed with up to 115 inmates, and that political detainees were not separated from criminal prisoners, as required by international standards. The Ministry of Interior appointed a four-member committee of high-ranking military and security figures to investigate the fire. The committee found eight prisoners culpable, and condemned five to death, two to life imprisonment, and a seventeen-year-old to twelve years in prison. SANA reported on May 20 that the five condemned men—described as "criminals"—were hanged that morning in a public square in the city of Hassakah. According to CDF, the condemned men were not afforded the right to legal counsel or the right to appeal the committee's decision.

Syria's remaining Jewish community of 1,100 to 1,200 persons faced renewed obstacles to emigration, following the liberalization of exit-visa procedures in April 1992. According to the New York-based Council for the Rescue of Syrian Jews (CRSJ), beginning in October 1992 the issuance of exit permits slowed down again to a trickle. CRSJ reported in October 1993 that exit permits were not being issued to entire families (a pre-liberalization practice); Jewish prisoners released in 1992 had not been permitted to travel abroad; harassment by security forces had noticeably increased; and the sale of personal and business property continued to be barred, government promises notwithstanding.

The Right to Monitor

The Syrian government did not recognize the right of local human rights monitors to carry out work inside the country. But in a welcome change of policy, beginning in 1992 several international human rights organizations received permission to undertake missions to Syria.

The regime sent an unmistakably strong signal in 1992 that human rights work by Syrians inside Syria would not be tolerated when the Supreme State Security Court tried seventeen members of the independent, four-year-old Committees for the Defense of Democratic Freedoms and Human Rights in Syria (CDF). In March 1992, the court sentenced fourteen CDF members to prison terms ranging from three to ten years. Four given three-year sentences were released in March and April, as part of the March 1992 amnesty, but ten remained in prison as of November 1993. In 1993, the security court began to try another five CDF members, all arrested in February and March 1992.

On August 10, the fifteen imprisoned CDF members—held in Sednaya and Adra prisons near Damascus—began a hunger strike to protest their continued detention. In remarks to the U.N. Human Rights Commission in Geneva on August 18, the Syrian government representative, Clovis Khouri, denied that the rights activists were on hunger strike. He accused CDF, whose representative had addressed the Commission two days earlier and publicized the hunger strike, of making false claims. He denounced CDF, stating that the organization's name was "a cover-up of their crimes against the internal and external security of Syria." He noted that CDF was an illegal organization and claimed that the "political" goal behind CDF's reports was "to distort Syria's reputation abroad."

To date, two international human rights organizations have been granted permission to undertake work in Syria. Amnesty International conducted its first fact-finding mission in December 1992, followed by a second mission in May 1993. Syrian authorities also granted permission for a representative of the International Commission of Jurists to observe a portion of the March 1992 security trial of the CDF members. In November 1993, Middle East Watch transmitted a letter to President Asad through the Syrian Embassy in Washington, D.C., requesting permission to conduct a fact-finding mission in Syria in 1994. Previous requests made by Middle East Watch to visit Syria went unanswered.

The Role of the International Community

U.S. Policy

There were numerous high-level meetings during the year between the Clinton administration and Syrian government officials concerning the Arab-Israeli peace process and U.S.-Syria relations, but no evidence that Syria's thirty-year state of emergency and poor human rights record occupied a prominent place on the bilateral agenda. Early in the year, U.S. Secretary of State Warren Christopher summarized the relationship with Syria. "In recent years, the U.S. and Syria worked together to advance the peace process and regional security, and we expect that this cooperation will continue and we look forward to it," he was quoted by the Syrian government news agency SANA as saying upon his arrival in Damascus on February 20.

Middle East Watch was aware of only one specific human-rights problem in Syria on which the Clinton administration spoke out publicly in 1993—freedom of travel for the remaining Syrian Jews. If other rights abuses were raised and discussed in the numerous bilateral meetings during the year, the issues were not publicly disclosed by either side. For example, after Secretary Christopher met President Asad on February 21 in Damascus, he declined to offer specifics about discussions on improving bilateral relations between Syria and the U.S.: "My talks with President Hafez al-Asad covered a wide range of issues. The discussions lasted for more than three and a half hours. I do not want to get into the details of the issues we discussed together. However, I can say that there was common ground between myself and President al-Asad." Asked to comment about a possible political opening in Syria and the removal of Syria from the U.S. terrorism list, the Secretary of State was equally opaque. "We discussed both issues and I do not wish to go into more details about the nature of these discussions," Syria Television Network quoted him as saying.

In October, Syrian Foreign Minister Farouq Shar'a visited Washington, the first visit to the U.S. capital by a senior Syrian official in almost two decades. The State Department said that human rights were among the topics discussed but would not disclose details of the talks. On October 5, Foreign Minister Shar'a met with Secretary Christopher in a ninety-minute private meeting. The State Department's spokesman said that the talks focused "on all aspects of our bilateral relations," including the Arab-Israeli peace process. Asked to describe the types of issues discussed, said: "We've discussed terrorism, we've discussed human rights, we've discussed the situation involving Syrian Jews, there have been other aspects as well." He provided no additional details.

On October 7, the Syrian foreign minister met briefly with President Clinton. According to the White House press secretary, the "constructive" discussion focused on developments and next steps in the peace process.

The European Community

European Community (E.C.) aid to Syria was delayed, and also blocked, due to concerns about the human rights record of the Asad regime by members of the European Parliament. In 1992, the European Parliament twice blocked implementation of the ECU 158 million, ($178.4 million) five-year Protocol on financial and technical cooperation, the fourth such protocol between the E.C. and Syria. On January 15 and again on October 28, the parliament did not give its assent to the aid package because of concern about the human rights situation in the country. (An earlier protocol with Syria—ECU 146 million in loans and grants, or $164.834 million—did not receive final approval until November 1992.)

In 1993, the E.C.-Syria fourth protocol again ran into difficulty because of human rights concerns. Prior to the European Parliament's first 1993 vote on the protocol, Foreign Minister al-Shar'a visited the E.C. headquarters in Brussels and met on February 26 with E.C. Commissioner for Foreign and Security Affairs Hans van den Broek, the former Dutch foreign minister. During the visit, the Syrian foreign minister "rejected any link between the domestic situation in Syria and cooperation with the [European] Community," the *Bulletin of the European Communities* reported. The vice-chair of the Green Group in the European Parliament, Brigit Cramon Daiber, called on Commissioner van den Broek to ask the Syrian foreign minister for details about the human rights situation in Syria and information about Alois Brunner, the alleged Nazi fugitive who reportedly has lived in Syria since the 1950s. Mrs. Cramon Daiber demanded clear answers from the Syrian government as a condition for assent to the fourth financial protocol by the parliament.

Commissioner Van den Broek told the European Parliament that he wanted an end to the E.C.'s "isolation" of Syria. "Syria is an important player in the Middle East peace process," the March 5 issue of *Middle East International* quoted him as saying. "Our relations with Syria must be relaunched." But, on March 10, the fourth protocol was turned down by the European Parliament. The vote was 249 in favor and 75 opposed, with 29 abstentions; the proposal fell just eleven votes short of the 260 required for assent. Another vote on the protocol, scheduled for October, was postponed.

The Work of Middle East Watch

Middle East Watch pursued a strategy of monitoring and advocacy with respect to Syria during the year under review, focusing in particular on long-term detainees and the jailed human rights activists.

Throughout the year, Middle East Watch participated in the efforts of the U.S. Congressional Friends of Human Rights Monitors to free the fifteen CDF activists imprisoned since 1992. It selected imprisoned Palestinian writer and CDF member Salama

George Kila as one of the thirteen international human rights monitors that Human Rights Watch would honor in December 1993.

Middle East Watch also provided information to the U.S. Congressional Human Rights Caucus, which in January sent a letter to President Asad expressing concern over the fate of long-term detainees and criticizing the state security trials then in progress. In August, it provided information to members of the U.S. Senate working on behalf of those detained in Syria for union activities.

In November, Middle East Watch distributed a report on human rights developments in Syria to members of the European Parliament, in advance of an anticipated vote by the parliament on the European Community aid package to Syria. It recommended that aid, with the sole exception of assistance of a humanitarian nature that directly benefits the needy, be conditioned upon specific human rights improvements.

At the initiative of Middle East Watch, the American Association for the Advancement of Sciences (AAAS) launched in December 1992 a campaign on behalf of detained Syrian professionals. Based on research conducted by Middle East Watch the previous year, the effort involved, in addition to AAAS, four engineering societies, five health professional associations and three general scientific societies. These organizations sent a stream of letters in support of jailed professionals to Syrian officials and to their counterpart professional associations in Syria. With backing from Middle East Watch, a similar effort was undertaken by the Washington-based National Academy of Sciences (NAS).

Middle East Watch selected Salama George Kila, a member of CDF imprisoned since March 1992 for his human rights work, as one of the international monitors to be honored by Human Rights Watch in its observance of Human Rights Day, December 10.

HUMAN
RIGHTS
WATCH

UNITED STATES

In 1993, Human Rights Watch reported on several types of human rights abuse in the United States. Together with the American Civil Liberties Union, Human Rights Watch published a major report detailing U.S. compliance and noncompliance with the International Covenant on Civil and Political Rights, whose ratification by the U.S. in 1992 significantly expanded the protection of human rights in this country. Americas Watch released "Frontier Injustice," a follow-up to its 1992 report on human rights abuses by U.S. Border Patrol agents. Human Rights Watch collaborated with three other non-governmental organizations to produce a study of physician participation in the death penalty, and the Prison Project continued to monitor U.S. prison conditions. Finally, Human Rights Watch participated in the U.S.-based litigation against Bosnian Serb military commander Radovan Karadzic, who stands accused of a multitude of crimes, including genocide, torture, and crimes against humanity.

U.S. Compliance with the International Covenant on Civil and Political Rights

On September 8, 1992, the United States formally adopted the International Covenant on Civil and Political Rights (ICCPR). In doing so, the United States undertook "to respect and to ensure to all individuals within its territory and subject to its jurisdiction the rights recognized in the ... Covenant, without distinction of any kind ..." This duty is modified only by the explicit reservations entered by the United States.

Under the terms of the ICCPR, the United States had one year from the date of ratification in which to file a report on its compliance with ICCPR provisions. In anticipation of this report, Human Rights Watch and the American Civil Liberties Union collaborated to produce their own report on U.S. compliance with the ICCPR. Scheduled for release in December 1993, this report examined several areas of concern and found the U.S. to be in violation of numerous Covenant provisions. For example:

· *Immigration and Refugee Law.* The U.S. policy of interdicting and summarily repatriating Haitian boat people violated Article 12 of the ICCPR, which states that "[e]veryone shall be free to leave any country, including his own." The indefinite detention of HIV-positive Haitian asylum-seekers at Guantánamo Bay Naval Base, a practice discontinued in the summer of 1993 by court order, violated Article 9, which requires a statutory basis for detention. It also violated Article 10, which forbids inhumane conditions of confinement, and Article 26, which forbids discrimination on the basis of national origin (only Haitians were subject to medical screening and detention based on HIV status; intercepted Cubans, for example, were not medically screened and were transported directly to the United States). Misconduct by agents of the Immigration and Naturalization Service (INS), detailed below with regard to border violence, violated Article 7 (the right to be free from torture or cruel, inhuman or degrading treatment), Article 9(1) (the right to liberty and security of the person), and Article 16 (the right to recognition everywhere as a person before the law).

· *Prison Conditions.* United States treatment of prisoners and conditions of confinement violated each of the three paragraphs of Article 10 of the ICCPR. Article 10(1) requires that all persons deprived of their liberty "be treated with humanity and with respect for the inherent dignity of the human person." Conditions of confinement in the U.S. increasingly violated this mandate, with extreme overcrowding stripping prisoners of dignity and privacy and endangering their health and safety. The brutal treatment of the new "maxi-maxi" high-security prisons also contravened this provision. Confinement of pretrial detainees in facilities that were often older, more crowded and more dangerous than prisons violated Article 10(2), which requires that pre-trial detainees be separated from convicted persons and accorded treatment "appropriate to their status as unconvicted persons." Finally, Article 10(3) states that prisoners must be given treatment that aims for "reformation and social rehabilitation." This stands in marked contrast to current U.S. law and practice, which had rejected an affirmative right to rehabilitation.

Language Rights. Article 2 of the ICCPR requires that the rights of the covenant be recognized "without distinction of any kind, such as race, colour, sex, language, religion, political or other opinion, national or social origin, property, birth or other status." Similarly, Article 26 forbids discrimination on the basis of any of these grounds. In contrast, domestic U.S. law provides no explicit protection against language discrimination. Those small pockets of protection that do exist reflect piecemeal legislation rather than a comprehensive policy, and have done little to stanch the ongoing attacks against minority language use in the schools, workplace and electoral arena. Federal courts have refused to equate language discrimination with national origin discrimination, which, like race and religion, warrants the highest level of judicial scrutiny; instead, language-based claims have been slotted into the lowest level of the three-tier system of evaluating discrimination claims, which requires only that the government show a "rational basis" for discriminatory government action. By attaching to its ratification an understanding that distinctions based on race, color, sex, language, religion, etc. are permissible when they are, "at minimum, rationally

related to a legitimate governmental objective," the U.S. diluted the protection of the ICCPR to match that of the U.S. courts. Nonetheless, the ICCPR's specific prohibition on language discrimination adds a greater scope of protection than was previously available. The Human Rights Watch/ACLU report also examined U.S. compliance with the ICCPR in regard to free expression, race discrimination, women's rights, language rights, and religious freedom.

Border Violence

In May 1993, Americas Watch released "Frontier Injustice: Human Rights Abuses Along the U.S. Border with Mexico Persist Amid Climate of Impunity." The forty-six-page newsletter followed the 1992 publication of *Brutality Unchecked: Human Rights Abuses Along the U.S. Border with Mexico*, a major report detailing severe human rights abuses committed by the U.S. Border Patrol of the INS. One year later, Americas Watch found the situation unchanged; serious abuses continued and mechanisms to ensure accountability were thoroughly inadequate. Documented abuses included numerous beatings, sexual assault, arbitrary detention, unjustified shootings, and murder. Border Patrol agents often covered up abuses of fellow agents by observing a "code of silence," complaints were discouraged, procedures for investigating alleged violations were ineffective, and abusive agents often went undisciplined.

Those vulnerable to mistreatment included undocumented immigrants, refugees, U.S. citizens and legal residents. They might be abused during apprehension or while in detention; although the majority of such abuses occurred in the border region, abuses were documented in interior regions as well, including Nevada and Nebraska. High school students had been harassed and assaulted while on or near their school campuses. Instances of abuse were not limited to agents of the border patrol; "Frontier Injustice" included allegations of abuse by customs agents at points of entry, which, although less widespread than border patrol violations, shares the same disregard for the rights of the person and the same freedom from accountability. Racially motivated verbal abuse by immigration law enforcement agents was also extremely common.

The case of border patrol agent Michael Andrew Elmer was a stark example of the impunity surrounding even the most violent border patrol agents. On June 12, 1992, Elmer was patrolling the border region near Nogales, Arizona when he and his partner spotted three men they suspected to be lookouts for drug smugglers. As the men fled, Elmer shot at one of them a dozen times, hitting him twice in the back. He then hid the wounded man, Darío Miranda Valenzuela, behind a tree trunk in a gully, where the victim subsequently died. Elmer's partner, agent Thomas Watson, broke the traditional code of silence and reported the shooting fifteen hours later.

Although he was acquitted of murder on the grounds of self-defense, Elmer's trial revealed his alleged perpetration of other human rights abuses: on March 18, 1992, he reportedly assaulted a motorist, leaving him wounded and in need of stitches; later that night Elmer was alleged to have shot at a group of thirty undocumented immigrants, wounding one in the stomach and leg. In keeping with the code of silence, none of the agents present during these incidents reported them; were it not for the publicity surrounding the investigation into the Miranda murder, they would have remained hidden and unaccounted for. (Two of the victims of the March shooting reported the incident at a border patrol station, but it was not investigated.) Significantly, agent Watson, who reported the killing of Miranda Valenzuela, was fired by the border patrol. Although the ostensible reason was his fifteen-hour delay in reporting the shooting, he believed the real cause to be his breach of the code of silence.

Other documented abuses included:

· Border Patrol agent Luis Santiago Esteves was reported to have sexually harassed or assaulted three different women whom he first encountered while on duty. The first incident was reported to his supervisor on October 9, 1989; no disciplinary action was taken against him. The second incident led to his arrest in December 1989 for rape. Although Esteves was temporarily suspended, the border patrol reinstated him when the victim failed to appear in court, forcing the prosecutor to drop charges. He was arrested a third time in 1991, again for rape. That arrest led to a conviction and, in July 1992, he was sentenced to twenty-four years in prison.

· On December 23, 1992, a border patrol agent allegedly beat an unarmed man who had been apprehended near the border. The agent then warned the man not to report the beating. Agents took him and his female companion, who was detained by a second agent and witnessed the beating, to the San Ysidro, California detention center, where they were held for several hours. Despite the man's obviously severe pain and his repeated requests for medical attention, no assistance was provided for several hours. He was eventually taken to a hospital, where he remained under observation for ten days, at which time his condition worsened and he underwent surgery to repair damage that had been done to his pancreas. Two weeks later the border patrol issued a statement claiming the man had injured himself by falling into a drainage ditch. Although both the Federal Bureau of Investigation (FBI) and the Office of the Inspector General of the Justice Department subsequently began investigations, the agent was reportedly still on active duty as of November 1993. In keeping with INS policy, the agent's name was withheld from the victim and his attorney.

· In February 1992, a customs agent

injured a U.S. citizen whose car was being inspected at an El Paso/Juarez checkpoint. According to the victim and witnesses, the agent twisted the woman's arm behind her back and held it there for a long period of time, despite her protests that he was hurting her. She was taken by ambulance to a nearby hospital, where a cast was placed on her severely sprained arm. An investigator with the Office of Internal Affairs of the Customs Service took statements from customs agents at the scene, yet never contacted the victim, even though her name and phone number were available from police officers who had been called to the scene. When the victim returned to the checkpoint days later to ask whether the agent had been disciplined, she was told that he had been suspended; Customs Service officials later admitted that she had been misinformed and that the agent remained on duty.

· In December 1992, a federal court ruled that border patrol agents committed a number of abuses over a period of years against students and faculty at Bowie High School in El Paso, Texas, including the use of excessive force (beatings, rough physical treatment, and the unnecessary brandishing of a weapon), verbal abuse, and harassment. *Murillo v. Musegades*, EP-CA-319-B, (W.D. Tex. Dec 1, 1992). "Frontier Injustice" also reported numerous instances of border patrol agents' harassment on high school campuses in Phoenix, Arizona.

Americas Watch concluded that these and similar incidents of misconduct were fostered by a protective climate of impunity sustained by a variety of factors. First, incidents of abuse often went unreported, due both to victims' fears of deportation or further harassment and to the absence of information regarding complaint procedures. Second, attempts to lodge complaints were often obstructed by immigration officials.

"Frontier Injustice" reported that complainants were ridiculed, given incomplete or wrong information, directly discouraged from filing complaints, and threatened with counter-charges. Reports by fellow agents were also rare, in adherence with the strict code of silence.

In addition to these informal obstacles, existing complaint procedures within the INS were found to be inadequate. Most abuse cases were investigated by INS and Border Patrol managers themselves, calling into question the independence of the investigators. And, although the Office of the Inspector General of the Justice Department maintained a hotline to receive complaints, its existence was almost wholly unknown, its operation hours limited, and it staff not equipped to respond to Spanish speakers.

Those investigations that did take place were shrouded in secrecy, with the Justice Department refusing to divulge the names of agents involved or the status or results of investigations. Agents under investigation might remain on active duty at the discretion of their supervisors, even when the alleged abuse was a serious criminal offense. Finally, Americas Watch found a consistent failure to discipline agents involved in human rights abuses. Where disciplinary action was taken it was carried out in an arbitrary fashion, turning more on the agent's relationship with his supervisor than on the seriousness of the abuse committed.

There were some encouraging developments following the release of "Frontier Injustice" in May 1993. Citing the Americas Watch report, Acting INS Commissioner Chris Sale sent a letter to all district directors and chief patrol agents in July 1993. Saying she was "seriously concerned about these allegations," Ms. Sale declared her intention "to ensure strict adherence to policies and procedures for investigating allegations of abuse and disciplining ... [violators of] principal human rights." She also promised "imminent approval" of an INS policy for the use of non-deadly force. In October 1993, Doris Meissner was confirmed as commissioner of the INS. In a written statement submitted at her confirmation hearing, Ms. Meissner stated that the work of the INS "must always be done with care, compassion and respect for human and civil rights."

In the meantime, Americas Watch followed up on the recommendations first made in our 1992 report, *Brutality Unchecked*. In addition to detailed recommendations regarding the use of force, Americas Watch advocated the creation of an independent federal commission to receive complaints of abuse, investigate those complaints, hold public hearings when warranted, and relay its findings to the INS or Customs Service for disciplinary action. During 1993, Human Rights Watch worked closely with members of Congress who supported the creation of such a commission. In May, Rep. Xavier Becerra (D-CA) introduced the "Immigration Enforcement Review Commission Act," which would provide for independent review of the INS and the Customs Service. Hearings on the proposal were held in September, and the bill continued to gain cosponsors.

Prisoners' Rights
The Prison Project of Human Rights Watch continued to monitor the treatment of U.S. prisoners. In April 1993, Human Rights Watch wrote to Attorney General Janet Reno, drawing her attention to three U.S. prison matters: (1) the case of federal inmate Brett Kimberlin, who was denied access to the press and placed in administrative detention after alleging during the 1988 presidential campaign that he had sold marijuana to then vice-presidential candidate Dan Quayle; (2) the administrative transfer of twenty inmates from the Lewisburg, Pa. penitentiary to the super-maximum security facility at Marion, Ill.; and (3) new regulations imposing a variety of restrictions on the use of telephones by federal inmates.

In September 1993, a Justice Department report of its investigation into the Kimberlin case was made public. This report admitted that Kimberlin had been subject to "disparate treatment," that his placement in detention had been due to his attempts to

contact members of the press, and that the personal involvement of Bureau of Prisons director J. Michael Quinlan, who canceled a scheduled Kimberlin press conference and ordered Kimberlin's special detention, was "quite unusual." Nonetheless, the report denied that political considerations played any role in Kimberlin's extraordinary treatment.

In October, Human Rights Watch again wrote to Attorney General Reno, renewing its request that she address the Marion transfers and restrictive new telephone regulations.

Death Penalty
In September 1993, Human Rights Watch wrote to Governor Tucker of Arkansas, urging him to grant a stay of execution to Barry Lee Fairchild, a mentally retarded man who was found guilty of murder on an accomplice-liability theory. In addition to Fairchild's low mental capacity, reports indicated that his confession may have been coerced through physical abuse by sheriffs investigating the murder. On the day he was to be executed, September 22, a federal district court judge vacated Fairchild's death sentence.

Human Rights Watch collaborated with the American College of Physicians, the National Coalition to Abolish the Death Penalty, and Physicians for Human Rights in producing a report on physician participation in capital punishment in the United States. This report provided a brief history of physician involvement in U.S. executions and surveyed current state laws and practices and the responses of medical associations. Most significantly, the report explored the ethical implications of physician involvement in capital punishment, and recommended bringing laws into compliance with prevailing medical ethics, which forbid physician participation in executions. The report was scheduled for a December 1993 release.

Asylum Reform Proposals
During the year, the rights of individuals

with legitimate asylum claims were threatened by proposals made by the Clinton administration and by legislation introduced in Congress. Those proposals sought to "streamline" and "expedite" the asylum process by turning back individuals without proper documentation at points of entry if they could not prove their claims at immediate airport interviews; they would also have reduced opportunities for asylum-seekers already within the U.S. to present their case. Human Rights Watch warned lawmakers that many provisions of these proposals ignored internationally recognized standards and treaty obligations protecting asylum-seekers.

In response to the public outcry over criminal acts carried out by individuals in the United States illegally—some of whom may have abused the asylum process—dozens of bills were introduced in Congress, and reforms were proposed by the Clinton administration. In letters criticizing these initiatives, Human Rights Watch argued that the asylum system itself was basically sound but not functioning properly due to mismanagement and inadequate funding. As a result, individuals were able to abuse the system—and might continue to do so even if improvements were made.

Any modifications to the asylum system must comply with customary international law and international treaties which prohibit *refoulement*, the forcible repatriation of any refugee whose life or freedom would be threatened. The 1951 Convention on the Status of Refugees and its 1967 Protocol, which the United States has ratified, provide:

> No Contracting State shall expel or return ("*refouler*") a refugee in any manner whatsoever to the frontiers of territories where his life or freedom would be threatened on account of his race, religion, nationality, membership of a particular social group or political opinion.

This prohibition of *refoulement* must be the central principle in any asylum reform plan. Human Rights Watch believes that the only way to ensure compliance with the *refoulement* prohibition is by granting individualized hearings in which asylum applicants have a fair opportunity to prove possible persecution and a right of appeal.

Among the objectionable provisions of pending legislation were: overly rigorous or ambiguous standards of persecution; arbitrary time limits restricting an asylum-seeker's right to file a claim; restrictions on independent or judicial review of denied claims; and return of asylum-seekers stopped at points of entry to countries through which they traveled on their way to the United States, even though these countries might or might not protect refugees.

High Seas Interdiction

In 1993, the Clinton administration continued the Bush policy of interdicting and summarily repatriating all Haitians encountered on the high seas. As discussed below, Human Rights Watch participated in litigation challenging this practice, on the grounds that it violates the international legal principle of *nonrefoulement*.

A disturbing new development in U.S. interdiction policy occurred in July 1993, when the Coast Guard intercepted three boats carrying a total of 659 Chinese immigrants in international waters off the coast of Mexico. Allowing the Chinese into U.S. territory would have made it possible for them to apply for political asylum. To avoid this, the United States asked the Mexican government to accept the immigrants just long enough to deport them back to China. The U.S. offered to pay the cost of the deportations, which Mexico refused.

In letters to Presidents Clinton and Salinas, Human Rights Watch urged that the prohibition against *refoulement* be observed and that the detainees be screened to ensure that those facing possible persecution on political and other grounds not be forcibly repatriated to China. Reports that previous deportees had been subjected to months of "reeducation" and other forms of persecution increased the concern. Human Rights

Watch argued that the *refoulement* prohibition is binding on both Mexico and the United States as a matter of customary international law; furthermore, the U.S. has ratified the Protocol Relating to the Status of Refugees, which codifies the prohibition. In its letter to President Clinton, Human Rights Watch explained the implication of this.

> What the U.S. by its own interpretation of international law cannot do directly, it should not be able to do indirectly by enlisting the Mexican government as an intermediary. Otherwise, the U.S. government sends the signal that international refugee standards can be avoided simply by getting another government to do the dirty work. Refugee law would be crippled by such subterfuge.

Approximately one-third of the detainees were given a cursory screening for refugee status (in the form of a questionnaire) by the United States while still in international waters. Mexico then allowed the boats to enter its territory. Thirty crew members were arrested for trafficking in human beings. All but two of the other occupants of the boats were deported to China. Both were allowed to enter the United States, where they applied for political asylum.

Litigation in the U.S. Courts

In 1993, Human Rights Watch continued its active involvement in U.S. civil litigation involving the application of international human rights law.

· *Doe v. Karadzic.* This class action suit was brought against Bosnian Serb military commander Radovan Karadzic in February 1993. The suit charged Karadzic with genocide, war crimes and crimes against humanity, summary execution, torture, cruel, inhuman or degrading treatment, wrongful death, assault and battery, and intentional infliction of emotional harm. The two named plaintiffs, Jane Doe I and Jane Doe II, are teenage Muslim women from Bosnia and Hercegovina currently living as refugees in Zagreb, Croatia. Jane Doe I was allegedly raped by at least eight Bosnian Serb soldiers, beaten and slashed with a knife; Jane Doe II and her younger brother were allegedly forced to witness the rape of their mother by Bosnian Serb soldiers, who then allegedly murdered her. Their claims were representative of the entire class, estimated to number in the thousands and consisting of all women and men who had suffered these and similar abuses at the hands of the Bosnian Serb military forces acting under the command and control of defendant Karadzic. The plaintiffs argued that Karadzic knew or should have known that his forces were committing these abuses, that he failed to prevent or punish these abuses, and that he was liable to the class members under international law, as well as two U.S. laws—the Torture Victim Protection Act and the Alien Tort Claims Act.

Filing an *amicus curiae* brief in response to Karadzic's motion to dismiss for lack of jurisdiction, Human Rights Watch argued that the United States had a vital interest in redressing the atrocities alleged. The international conventions on which the plaintiffs base their claim, including the Genocide Convention, the Geneva Conventions and the Torture Convention, provide States parties with not only a compelling interest but an affirmative obligation to hold violators legally accountable for their human rights abuses. Federal law, including the Torture Victim Protection Act, underscores this interest and obligation. In addition, customary international law provides universal jurisdiction for allegations of genocide and war crimes. Under the doctrine of universal jurisdiction, neither the nationality of the perpetrator or the victims nor the location of the crime constrains jurisdiction, since the perpetrators of such atrocities are enemies of all humankind.

· *Haitian Centers Council v. McNary.*
United States treatment of Haitian refugees was litigated in two related cases beginning in 1992. One case challenged the discrimination against HIV-positive Haitian asylum-seekers, who were being held indefinitely at Guantánamo Bay Naval Base under adverse conditions and without access to attorneys, visitors, telephone calls, or letters. The second case challenged the "Kennebunkport Order" issued by President Bush and continued under President Clinton despite earlier vows to the contrary. This policy called for the immediate and summary repatriation of all Haitians interdicted on the high seas, without screening to exclude refugees. Human Rights Watch submitted *amicus curiae* briefs in both cases. In June 1993, the Supreme Court overturned a Second Circuit decision and approved the Kennebunkport Order. In their brief to the court, Human Rights Watch had argued that this blanket policy of forcible repatriation violated the international law of *non-refoulement*, which prohibits the forcible return of refugees to countries where they face persecution. Human Rights Watch issued a press release in response to the Supreme Court's decision, describing it as "a devastating setback for the international protection of refugees." Meanwhile, the Guantánamo detention camp was ordered closed by Federal District Court Judge Sterling M. Johnson, Jr. "The Haitian camp at Guantánamo is the only known refugee camp in the world composed entirely of HIV-positive refugees," he said in his opinion. "The Haitians' plight is a tragedy of immense proportion and their continued detainment is totally unacceptable to this Court."

· *Saudi Arabia v. Nelson.* Scott Nelson was a safety engineer in a government-run hospital in Saudi Arabia in 1984. He sued the Saudi government in 1988, alleging that he had been arrested, tortured and unlawfully detained for thirty-nine days after he reported an unsafe condition to his supervisors and a government commission. Invoking the Foreign Sovereign Immunities Act (FSIA), the Saudi government moved for dismissal based on lack of jurisdiction; as it currently stands, FSIA denies U.S. courts jurisdiction to hear suits by U.S. citizens against foreign governments, unless the dispute relates to "commercial activity." Nelson prevailed before the circuit court, but at the urging of the Saudi and U.S. governments, the United States Supreme Court agreed to review the case. Human Rights Watch submitted an *amicus curiae* brief to the Supreme Court on behalf of Nelson, emphasizing the obligation imposed by international law on all states to provide a remedy to torture victims. In light of this obligation, and because Nelson was almost certain not to receive redress in Saudi courts, Human Rights Watch argued for an expansive interpretation of the commercial activity exception to the FSIA. On March 23, 1993, the Supreme Court allowed the Saudi government's motion to dismiss. Middle East Watch responded by publicly urging passage of a proposed bill (H.R. 934) that would amend the FSIA and extend U.S. court jurisdiction to include claims against foreign states that allege injury or death to U.S. citizens caused by foreign security forces. The House Judiciary Committee approved the bill in September 1993.

THE ARMS PROJECT

The Arms Project was organized in September 1992 with a grant from the Rockefeller Foundation. Its purpose is to monitor and seek to prevent transfers of weapons, military assistance, and training to regimes or groups that commit gross violations of internationally recognized human rights or of the laws of war. In addition, the Arms Project seeks to promote freedom of expression and freedom of information about arms and arms transfers worldwide.

The Arms Project is therefore a human rights undertaking that seeks to prevent the physical means of human rights abuse from reaching the hands of known abusers. It seeks accountability from both suppliers and recipients of weapons for the human rights consequences of their transfer. It is a human rights rather than disarmament organization; the touchstone of its activities is human rights, rather than broader agendas of peace, stability, security, proliferation, or arms control.

Two distinguishing features of the Arms Project in 1993 were its commitment to field research and its emphasis on the trade in small arms and other less than major weapons. With respect to the trade in less than major weapons, the Arms Project was particularly (although not exclusively) interested in those weapons most prevalent in human rights abuse—small arms, light weapons, and land mines. Although the Arms Project took into account any transfer of security material or training to a violator of human rights or the laws of war, including major weapons systems, dual-use technology, and training, much of its research program focused on transfers and abuse of less than major weapons.

The project's field research attempted to connect the documented abuse of weapons in the field to their supply. Thus, field research undertaken by the Arms Project began with the demand side of weapons transfers—their use and abuse—and worked from there to the supply side. By focusing on abuse, the Arms Project was able to bring to bear the traditional tools of the human rights movement, international denunciation and stigmatization for the violation of international standards. This emphasis on field research made the Arms Project nearly unique among groups researching arms transfers, which generally emphasized research among government and other public documents. Because transfers of less than major weapons have not been tracked in the way that major weapons are, however, field research was the best way of investigating this trade.

Regarding weapons of mass destruction, the Arms Project had an active program on the use of chemical and biological weapons that violated the current laws of war. The Arms Project committed itself to examining the question of whether to undertake the issue of nuclear weapons, but believed that its limited resources were best put toward weapons systems that had not received adequate attention in the international security field, but that most gravely threatened the developing world and produced the most severe violations of international human rights.

An area of special consideration were weapons which as a class were, or in the view of the Arms Project should be, prohibited by the laws of war. The Arms Project identified in this area chemical or biological weapons and anti-personnel land mines. The Arms Project sought to eliminate these weapons under the laws of war, without consideration of the human rights record of the country or group possessing them.

Field Research

Taking advantage of Human Rights Watch's extensive field operations, the Arms Project in its 1992-93 year sent researchers to Angola, Argentina, Brazil, Chile, Georgia, India, Iraqi Kurdistan, Israel, Lebanon, Mozambique, Pakistan, Russia, Rwanda, and Uganda. The field missions typically focused on a particular question, such as where the parties to a conflict, who have been shown to be abusive of human rights or the laws of war, were obtaining their weapons. These field missions produced completely new information on arms transfers and the abuse of weapons that was not available in public documents in Washington or Western capitals.

In Angola, working with Africa Watch, the Arms Project began initial work on a study of weapons and violations of the laws of war in the renewed fighting that had left tens of thousands dead. The size of the conflict meant that this work would be completed and published in 1994.

In Brazil, Argentina and Chile, a mission was undertaken in April and May 1993 to research conventional arms transfers by countries of the Southern Cone. The purpose of this research was to inaugurate a series of reports on transfers of weapons to the developing world by countries of the developing world, in addition to the more usual investigation of transfers by "first-world" countries to the developing world.

In cooperation with Helsinki Watch, the project conducted a mission to Georgia and Abkhazia to investigate violations of the laws of war and abuses of weaponry in the Abkhazian separatist war in August 1993. The investigation focused on the role of Russian military forces and weapons in the conflict.

An Arms Project consultant visited India and Pakistan in March and April 1993 to conduct research on how weapons were reaching the hands of abusive armed groups in both countries. This research focused on small arms.

The Arms Project, following up on research conducted for Middle East Watch and Physicians for Human Rights (PHR), released with PHR the findings of tests conducted by the British Ministry of Defence on soil samples obtained by a HRW/PHR field research team from the site of a 1988 Iraqi army chemical weapons attack against a civilian village; the tests showed remnants of mustard gas and nerve gas in the soil. This marked the first time ever that the use of chemical weapons was proven by traces of the chemicals or their degradation products. The implications for arms control verification regimes were of considerable importance, as were the implications of being able to prove such massive violations of the laws of war as took place in Iraqi Kurdistan.

Arms project staff visited Israel in November 1993 as part of an Arms Project/Middle East Watch investigation into violations of the laws of war and abuses of weapons in the summer 1993 Israeli army and Hizbollah attacks in southern Lebanon. A Middle East Watch expert visited southern Lebanon in October 1993 and conducted extensive interviews among Lebanese refugees and documented physical destruction. The research from the two missions was directed toward publication of a single report, scheduled for January 1994.

Field work on land mines in Mozambique was scheduled for publication in a December 1993 report.

An Arms Project consultant visited Pakistan in March 1993 in the course of researching a report, to be released in December 1993, on weapons transfers to abusive armed groups in India and Pakistan.

In July 1993 research was carried out in Russia on the role of the Russian military and Russian-supplied weapons in the Georgian-Abkhazian conflict. A report was planned for release in January or February 1994.

A consultant conducted field work in Rwanda for the purpose of determining the sources of weapons to each of the extremely abusive sides of the Rwandan civil war. His work also took him to Belgium, and resulted in the discovery of previously unpublicized South African and Egyptian arms connections. The resulting report was scheduled for release in French and English in December 1993. The same consultant also undertook research in Uganda in the course of investigating arms transfers to insurgent forces in the Rwandan civil war.

The purpose of these field missions was to develop new information not published elsewhere, to target specific instances of abuse, and to demand accountability from the suppliers of weapons by confronting them with the evidence of abuses.

Data Base Research

An ultimate aim of the Arms Project is to develop a systematic data base on transfers of weapons to and from regimes that violate human rights or the laws of war. To this end the Arms Project established a central data base, concentrating on less than major weapons systems. The Arms Project was the only organization in the United States attempting to monitor the trade in less than major weapons on a systematic basis.

The project undertook the collection of arms transfer information on an initially short list of countries of particular interest, for human rights reasons, to the regional divisions of Human Rights Watch. It was anticipated that over several years this data base would grow. Experts universally agree that no data base on transfers of less than major weapons can be exhaustive, given the lack of official information, the number of unofficial and black market transfers, resistance to sharing information, and general lack of monitoring of small arms transfers. Therefore, while the Arms Project is systematic in its collection of information, it makes no claim to be exhaustive with respect to transfers.

Advocacy

The Arms Project's advocacy program aims to provide policy makers, in the U.S. and internationally, with information about arms being transferred to human rights abusers. In addition to information about arms transfers and abuse in particular countries, by particular regimes and groups, the Arms Project also seeks to give information about how law and policy in the United States and elsewhere, including the United Nations, should be reformed to ensure that human rights are taken into account as an explicit consideration in the approval of arms transfers. The Arms Project also seeks to increase transparency concerning arms transfers worldwide, and to reform laws and regulations to that end.

Thus, for example, the Arms Project in 1993, in conjunction with other components of HRW, helped to develop proposals with respect how both U.S. human rights law and arms control law should be reformed. The Arms Project conducted a study in 1993 on how the United Nations Register of Conventional Arms should be expanded to cover less than major weapons systems. The Arms Project also undertook advocacy outside the United States; its Rwanda report, for example, was released in Europe in French. The project has also served as co-counsel to a Russian scientist, Vil Mirzayanov, who was under indictment in Russia for speaking out on alleged Russian government violations of U.S.-Russian chemical weapons treaties.

Antipersonnel Land Mines

During 1993, the Arms Project undertook a special research and advocacy program on land mines. The research program involved the writing and publication, with Physicians for Human Rights, of a 528-page book on all aspects of land mines, including extensive, original research into the production and trade of land mines worldwide. This book, *Landmines: A Deadly Legacy*, is unique in its multidisciplinary approach to the issue of land mines and was a major source of new information in debates over land mines in the U.S. Congress and the U.N. General Assembly.

The Arms Project's advocacy program on land mines involved extensive work in 1993 on a worldwide nongovernmental organization campaign to ban the production, stockpiling, transfer, and use of land mines. The project participated in meetings sponsored by the International Committee of the Red Cross on land mines in Geneva in April 1993; it also co-sponsored a major meeting of nongovernmental organizations in London in May 1993 to formulate strategies for the ban campaign. It has taken an active role in educating U.S. lawmakers and administration officials, as well as U.N. officials and delegations, to the risks posed by land mines.

The staff of the Arms Project consists of director Kenneth Anderson, Washington director Stephen D. Goose, counsel Monica Schurtman, New York staff associates Barbara Baker and Cesar Bolaños, and Washington staff associate Kathleen Bleakley.

Members of the international advisory committee of the Arms Project are: Morton Abramowitz, Nicole Ball, Frank Blackaby, Frederick C. Cuny, Ahmed H. Esa, Jo Husbands, Frederick J. Knecht, Andrew J. Pierre, Gustavo Gorriti, Di Hua, Edward J. Laurance, Vincent McGee, Aryeh Neier, Janne E. Nolan, David Rieff, Kumar Rupesinghe, John Ryle, Mohamed Sahnoun, Gary Sick, and Tom Winship.

THE FUND
FOR FREE
EXPRESSION

The Fund for Free Expression works with the regional divisions of Human Rights Watch to investigate and analyze freedom of expression problems in particular countries; publishes thematic studies about global freedom of expression problems (in the past, these have included reports on the link between governmental corruption and censorship and the persecution of environmental advocates); and brings an international perspective to U.S. freedom of expression problems. In addition, the fund administers the Hellman/Hammett grants to persecuted writers and journalists, and manages the work of two casework committees, the Committee for International Academic Freedom and Filmwatch.

In April, the fund joined the International Freedom to Publish Committee of the Association of American Publishers (AAP) on a mission to Egypt to investigate government restrictions on freedom of expression and association, particularly as they relate to the growing power of Islamists who advocate implementation of Islamic law. A report based on their findings was planned for publication early in 1994. With Middle East

Watch, the fund wrote to Egyptian President Hosni Mubarak calling on him to denounce a government-connected sheik's testimony, in the trial of the accused killers of Farag Fouda, a prominent secular writer and intellectual, that Dr. Fouda's murder was justified because he was an "apostate."

The fund joined Middle East Watch to analyze the laws and decrees used to regulate the media in Lebanon and to report on repressive measures designed to stifle dissent. The forty-eight-page report, released in July, detailed actions that forced the closure of three daily papers and a television network and caused the arrest of four journalists. The government claimed that the closings and prosecutions were necessary to avoid the kind of religious and ethnic strife that fueled its disastrous civil war. But the report argued that by closing outlets for nonviolent opposition, the government heightened such tensions and encouraged dissidents to resort to lawless actions.

Helsinki Watch and the Fund for Free Expression published reports on free expression issues in Poland, Greece and Great Britain. The Poland report, released in August, warned that freedom of expression was threatened by government use of a repressive Communist-era law to prosecute its critics and by a new law which required all broadcast programming to respect "Christian values."

The report on Greece covered six cases in which criminal prosecutions were used to stifle the views of citizens who questioned government policy on Macedonia, relying on statutes that targeted peaceful political expression and violate international human rights guarantees.

In an update of their 1991 report on "Freedom of Expression in the United Kingdom," the fund and Helsinki Watch reviewed recent developments in Great Britain. The report, released in May, noted some movement toward more open government, including the first official recognition of MI6, the Secret Intelligence Service. But the government also opposed adoption of a Bill of Rights and a Freedom of Information Act and stepped up moves toward tighter regulation of the media; Scotland Yard impounded record albums under the Obscene Publications Act; and the government sued under the Prevention of Terrorism Act to force disclosure of the names of confidential news sources.

In September, the fund joined with Helsinki Watch to conduct an investigation of media freedom in Hungary, with particular attention to the battle for control of state radio and television. A newsletter was scheduled for release in December.

The fund joined other free expression groups to found the Rushdie Defense Committee, USA. With the Arthur Garfield Hays Civil Liberties Program at New York University Law School, the fund sponsored a symposium in October titled "Speech and Equality: Do We Have to Choose?"

Committee for International Academic Freedom

The Committee for International Academic Freedom acts on behalf of professors, teachers and students around the world when they are harassed or imprisoned for attempting to exercise their rights of free expression and inquiry and when their work is censored or universities are closed for political reasons. The committee sends cables and letters to appropriate government authorities and publicizes the cases of abuse in the U.S. academic community.

In 1993, the committee wrote protest letters to thirteen countries in all parts of the world. Among the issues addressed were: the confiscation of a scientific journal for criticizing the lack of political reform in China; also in China, the arrest and torture of a retired professor and a middle-school teacher for having peacefully supported students in the 1989 pro-democracy movement; in Ethiopia, the violent suppression of a student demonstration, closing Addis Ababa University and firing the president and forty-one senior faculty members; in Indonesia, banning a student newspaper and politically selective prosecution of students; in Peru, holding a professor in prison after the gov-

ernment acknowledged that it found no evidence to support the charges of terrorism for which he had been arrested; in Saudi Arabia, the dismissal and/or arrest of three professors for forming an association intended to protect the political rights of the opposition; Serbian government-imposed curriculum changes and new language regulations so that the Serbian minority was favored over the Albanian majority in Kosovo; the arrest and dismissal in Uzbekistan of seven teachers and professors who appeared to have been targeted merely for their connections with political groups that peacefully criticized government officials or public policy.

The committee is composed of twenty-three university presidents and scholars. Jonathan Fanton of the New School for Social Research, Hanna Holborn Gray of the University of Chicago, Vartan Gregorian of Brown University and Charles Young of the University of California at Los Angeles are co-chairs.

Hellman-Hammett Funds

In 1989, the estates of American writers Lillian Hellman and Dashiell Hammett asked the Fund for Free Expression to set up and administer a special fund to assist writers from around the world who are in financial need as a result of political persecution. Grants from the Hellman-Hammett funds are awarded every spring after nominations have been reviewed by a five-person selection committee composed of Fund for Free Expression board members. Throughout the year, the selection committee makes smaller emergency grants, usually to writers who have an urgent need to leave their country or who are otherwise in dire material circumstances.

In addition to offering financial assistance, by highlighting individual cases, the grants help publicize repression and censorship around the world. While some recipients have asked to remain anonymous for safety reasons, many others have used the grant to call attention to human rights conditions in their own countries.

In 1993, the grants ranged from $3,000

to $10,000 and were awarded to twenty-two writers in fifteen countries. The recipients included Mariella Sala Eguran, a Peruvian novelist who had been targeted for assassination by Sendero Luminoso; Liu Qing, a Chinese journalist who was imprisoned and tortured for his repudiation of the Cultural Revolution; Nader Naderpour, an Iranian poet who voluntarily left Iran in vocal opposition to the cultural policies of the government and who signed a declaration condemning the death sentence, or *fatwa*, against Salman Rushdie; five writers from three Central Asian republics which were formerly part of the Soviet Union.

The committee also selected two groups of writers to receive Hellman-Hammett grants: twelve journalists in Peru at the newsmagazine *Caretas* and twenty-four writers in Bosnia. Six writers received emergency funds.

THE PRISON PROJECT

The Human Rights Watch Prison Project was formed in 1987 to focus international attention on prison conditions worldwide. Drawing on the expertise of the regional divisions of Human Rights Watch, the Prison Project investigates conditions for sentenced prisoners, pre-trial detainees, and those held in police lockups. The project is distinctive in the international human rights field in that it examines conditions for all prisoners, not simply those held for political reasons.

In addition to pressing for improvement in prison conditions in particular countries, the project seeks to place the problem of prison conditions on the international human rights agenda. We believe that a government's claim to respect human rights should be assessed not only by the political freedoms it allows but also by how it treats its prisoners, including those not held for political reasons. Our experience has repeatedly

shown that a number of democratic countries that are rarely or never a focus of human rights scrutiny are in fact guilty of serious human rights violations within their prisons.

The project has a self-imposed set of rules for prison visits: investigators undertake visits only when they, not the authorities, can choose the institutions to be visited; when the investigators can be confident that they will be allowed to talk privately with inmates of their choice; and when the investigators can gain access to the entire facility to be examined. These rules are adopted to avoid being shown model prisons or the most presentable parts of institutions. When access on such terms is not possible, reporting is based on interviews with former prisoners, prisoners on furlough, relatives of inmates, lawyers, prison experts and prison staff, and on documentary evidence. The project uses the U.N. Standard Minimum Rules for the Treatment of Prisoners as the chief document with which to assess prison conditions in each country. Prison investigations are usually conducted by teams composed of a member of the Human Rights Watch staff with expertise on the country in question and a member of the Prison Project's advisory committee. Occasionally, the project invites an outside expert to participate in an investigation.

The project publishes its findings in book-length reports and in newsletters. These are released to the public and the press, both in the United States and in the country in question, and whenever possible, also in translation.

In previous years, the project conducted studies and published reports on prison conditions in Brazil, Czechoslovakia, India, Indonesia, Israel and the Occupied Territories, Jamaica, Mexico, Poland, Romania, the former Soviet Union, Spain, Turkey, United Kingdom, and the United States (including Puerto Rico, with a separate newsletter published).

The Global Report

The main focus of the project's work in 1993 was the *Global Report on Prisons*, produced for and released at the United Nations World Conference on Human Rights, held in Vienna in June. The 340-page report, which reflected six years of investigations of prison conditions on five continents, included findings on pre-trial detention, physical conditions, classification of prisoners, women inmates, life on death row, activities, prison labor, availability of prison rules, disciplinary measures, beatings and physical abuse, aftermath of prison riots, contacts with the outside world and other issues. It also featured separate chapters on the prison systems of nineteen countries. The report concluded that the great majority of the millions of persons who are imprisoned worldwide at any given moment, and of the tens of millions who spend at least part of the year behind bars, are confined in conditions of filth and corruption, without adequate food or medical care, with little or nothing to do, and in circumstances in which violence—from other inmates, their keepers, or both—is a constant threat. Despite international declarations, treaties and standards forbidding such conditions, this state of affairs is tolerated even in countries that are more or less respectful of human rights, because prisons, by their nature, are out of sight, and because prisoners, by definition, are outcasts.

We also concluded that by and large, it is not possible for prisoners themselves to call attention to the abuses they suffer. Except for political prisoners, the great majority are not skilled in organizing or communicating; while in prison, they are cut off from the rest of the world, and once out of prison, they are eager to avoid continuing identification with prisons. Accordingly, it is up to others, acting out of a willingness to redress the suffering of their fellow human beings and a desire to uphold the rule of law, to concern themselves with prisons. In the report, we urged our fellow human rights organizations to expand their mandates to include prison conditions.

The Enforcement of Standards

The U.N. Standard Minimum Rules for the Treatment of Prisoners is the most widely known and accepted document regulating prison conditions. Unfortunately, these standards, although known to prison administrators virtually all over the world, are seldom fully enforced. To strengthen the enforcement of standards, in the *Global Report* the project recommended creating a U.N. human rights mechanism to inspect prisons and disseminate information about prison conditions and abuses. Throughout 1993, the project maintained contacts with U.N. bodies that concern themselves with prison matters. The project also urged U.S. representatives to these bodies to strengthen the human rights component of the U.N.'s work related to prisons. In November, a representative of the project traveled to the Netherlands to give a presentation at an international gathering of non-governmental and inter-governmental organizations working on devising methods to make existing standards on prison conditions work more effectively.

Fact-Finding

The project continued its fact-finding work and the publication of country-specific prison conditions reports throughout 1993.

In January and February, a representative of the project traveled to South Africa to continue the investigation started in 1992. Five prison complexes were visited in the course of this trip, including prisons in the "homeland" of Transkei. In addition, numerous ex-prisoners, prison guards and prison rights advocates were interviewed. A report based on this and the earlier research was planned for January 1994.

A book-length report on prison conditions in Egypt was published in February, based on investigations carried out in 1992. That investigation was the first time that any human rights organization had inspected Egyptian prisons.

In March and April, the project undertook an investigation of prison and police lockup conditions in Zaire. Our representative visited several prisons and detention camps, as well as police jails. The report that resulted from this mission was published in

November.

The project's request to the Chinese authorities for permission to inspect the country's prisons was ignored. A representative traveled to China and Hong Kong in February and March and interviewed former prisoners. Further interviews were conducted in New York. A report is planned for 1994.

Follow-up on Earlier Work

In response to the British government's critique of the project's 1992 report on prison conditions in the U.K., in February a project representative traveled to London and conducted visits to two prisons that had been most harshly criticized by the report and where, according to the government, significant improvements took place subsequently. An extensive memorandum resulting from the follow-up visit was sent to the British government in May. We had found some improvements but informed the government that overall conditions were still inadequate.

Two developments related to the project's earlier work took place in Brazil. In February, state prosecutors in Sao Paulo recommended the indictment of 120 policemen for their role in the October 1992 massacre in which at least 111 prisoners lost their lives (those indicted, however, had not been arrested as of early November, and no trials had taken place). In addition, the overall number of extrajudicial executions by the police in São Paulo decreased in the course of the year, a decline that was attributed to the outcry following the 1992 massacre. In September, a ground-breaking decision found a civil policeman guilty of the 1989 killing of eighteen prisoners in a Sao Paulo jail and sentenced him to 516 years in prison for the killings. This was the first time that a policeman was found guilty of killing prisoners. In both cases, the project had sent representatives in the immediate aftermath of the massacres and contributed to publicizing the cases both in Brazil and internationally.

Domestic Prison Issues

For several years, the project had been involved in domestic prison-related issues.

The project continued monitoring conditions for U.S. prisoners in 1993, with particular focus on the proliferation of super-maximum security institutions (or "maxi-maxis"), a problem to which the project first called attention in its 1991 report on prison conditions in the U.S. On two occasions, the project sent letters to the Attorney General, raising issues that included administrative transfers of prisoners and new restrictions on access to the telephone for federal prisoners.

Human Rights Watch and the American Civil Liberties Union planned to publish in December 1993 a report on U.S. compliance with the International Covenant on Civil and Political Rights, which includes important safeguards of relevance to prison conditions. The covenant, ratified by the United States in June 1992, provides an additional, and extremely valuable, tool for establishing accountability for prison abuse. Because in important respects the United States falls short of international standards relevant to prisons, we believe that scrutiny under these standards, and in light of international practices, can be particularly effective.

The project collaborated with the American College of Physicians, the National Coalition to Abolish the Death Penalty and Physicians for Human Rights in producing a report on physician participation in capital punishment in the U.S. For this report also, a December 1993 release was planned.

The HRW Prison Project invited Peter Loggenberg, of the South African Police and Prison Officers Civil Rights Union, an illegal organization of mostly black professionals, to be honored for his organization's work at Human Rights Watch's observance of Human Rights Day in December.

THE WOMEN'S RIGHTS PROJECT

The Women's Rights Project of Human Rights Watch was established in 1990 to work in conjunction with Human Rights Watch's regional divisions to monitor violence against women and discrimination on the basis of sex that is either committed or tolerated by governments. The project grew out of Human Rights Watch's recognition of the epidemic proportions of violence and gender discrimination around the world and of the past failure of human rights organizations, and the international community, to hold governments accountable for abuses of women's basic human rights. The project monitors the performance of specific countries in securing and protecting women's human rights, highlights individual cases of international significance, and serves as a link between women's rights and human rights communities at both national and international level.

Women's Human Rights Developments

This chapter does not evaluate progress in women's human rights throughout the world, but describes developments in countries most closely monitored by the Women's Rights Project in 1993: Peru, the former Yugoslavia, Thailand, Turkey, Kenya, Kuwait, Pakistan and Brazil.

Peru

In January 1993, the HRW Women's Rights Project and Americas Watch released *Untold Terror: Violence Against Women in Peru's Armed Conflict*. The report found that both the government security forces and the Shining Path insurgency used violence, including rape and murder, against noncombatant women as a tactic of warfare. Soldiers and police routinely raped women, while the Shining Path often murdered them, either to punish, intimidate, or coerce particular female victims or as part of their efforts to achieve broader political ends. These violations of women's basic rights as well as other human rights abuses routinely went unpunished. Accused rapists are rarely prosecuted and punished. The problem was compounded for rape victims as questions of a woman's "honor," age, and sexual past were considered relevant in judicial proceedings and often discriminated against women victims and unfairly diverted scrutiny away from the accused rapist.

In response to letters of concern from the U.S. Congress which followed the report, President Alberto Fujimori vowed to "drastically punish" soldiers and police officers who committed rape. However, despite his assertions, the pattern of impunity for rapists continued in Peru: Human Rights Watch knew of no case where an active member of the military had been punished for rape. In one incident, known as the Santa Bárbara massacre and detailed in *Untold Terror*, an army patrol entered several villages in the department of Huancavelica in July 1991 and proceeded to rape women, destroy houses and steal livestock. Fifteen villagers were then taken away and killed. In February 1993, an army lieutenant was sentenced to ten years in prison for abuse of authority and falsehood for his role in the massacre. No military men were prosecuted or punished for the more egregious offenses of rape and murder. Second Sgt. Dennis Pacheco Zambrano was charged with rape and cattle theft but was acquitted.

New allegations of rape by the police and military emerged in 1993. In January 1993, forty members of the anti-terrorist police were accused of gang-raping and impregnating a twenty-year-old women detained for alleged ties the Shining Path. The woman, María de la Cruz, was detained after appearing with her mother in Lima to testify on behalf of a relative accused of being a member of the Shining Path. Shortly after her detention, she was reportedly taken to a beach outside Lima where she and five other women were raped by police officers over a period of four days. Doctors who examined Ms. de la Cruz found that she conceived while in police custody. Ms. de la Cruz was acquitted of all charges connecting her to the Shining Path by the military courts, but remained in a maximum security prison in Lima while a military prosecutor appealed the decision. In August, Peru's congress, under the auspices of the congressional human rights commission, agreed to conduct an investigation into the case. In another incident, the *New York Times* reported that soldiers broke into the home of a sixteen-year-old girl on March 22, 1993 in the town of Acayacu and raped her. Another soldier reportedly raped her fourteen-year-old neighbor.

Former Yugoslavia

In January 1993, representatives of the HRW Women's Rights Project and Helsinki Watch traveled to the former Yugoslavia to investigate allegations of widescale rape in Bosnia-Hercegovina. The mission found that rape was being used by Serbian forces as a weapon of terror against non-Serb, civilian women as part of the policy of "ethnic cleansing." To a lesser extent, Croatian and Bosnian Muslim forces also had committed rape against Serbian women. These findings were incorporated into the Helsinki Watch report, *War Crimes in Bosnia-Hercegovina: Volume II*, released in April 1993.

Women refugees from Bosnia-Hercegovina described being raped in their homes or in the streets as soldiers swept through their villages, destroying property and attacking civilians. Other women were arrested and raped during the course of interrogation or as part of the torture they were subjected to in military-directed detention camps. In some areas, women and girls were detained in abandoned houses or municipal buildings, where they were raped and abused repeatedly for days or even weeks on end. The effect of rape was often to ensure that women and their families would flee and never return.

Women victims of rape reported being threatened with forcible impregnation. A number of women recounted that, as they were being assaulted, rapists taunted them with ethnic slurs or stated their intention to impregnate their victims. J., a thirty-nine-year-old Croatian woman who was raped by a reserve captain of the self-proclaimed "Serbian Republic" in the Omarska detention camp, told us, "They said I was an Ustasa and that I needed to give birth to a Serb—that I would then be different."

The failure to punish rapists was as consistent and widespread as rape itself. Despite the many reports of rape, Human Rights Watch found no evidence that any soldier or member of a paramilitary group had been punished or held to account for raping women and girls. Not only did military commanders fail to punish soldiers who rape, in many instances they themselves committed rape or organized "rape camps." Human Rights Watch released "Prosecute Now!" on August 1, 1993, detailing cases of human rights abuses, including rape, for which there has evidence implicating officers who committed abuses, including rape, or turned a blind eye to the abuses committed by their subordinates.

Thailand

In February 1993, the Women's Rights Project and Asia Watch traveled to Thailand to document the trafficking of Burmese women and girls into Thailand for the purposes of forced prostitution. An estimated 20,000 to 30,000 Burmese women and girls were believed to be held in Thai brothels, primarily in the northern provinces, Bangkok, and Ranong Province in the south. Expecting to work in restaurants and factories, most of them became trapped in brothels instead, under deplorable conditions that amounted to a modern form of slavery. The Burmese were being held in debt bondage and compelled to have sex with as many as ten to fifteen customers a day in order to pay off their recruitment, transportation and living expenses. Not only did the local police fail to enforce Thai laws against trafficking and prostitution, but they were often directly involved in trafficking as drivers and clients and were known to take protection money from brothel owners.

In the 1992 State Department *Country Reports on Human Rights Practices*, the State Department acknowledged that "senior [Thai] government officials themselves have cited corruption as a major factor in police willingness to turn a blind eye to the problem. Reliable sources report that police can earn $120 to $200 per month in protection fees." The department's analysis failed, however, to identify more invidious forms of participation by local police and border patrols in sex trafficking.

During 1993, the government of Prime Minister Chuan Leekpai began to crack down on forced and child prostitution, with very mixed results. While the highly-publicized brothel raids heightened public awareness of the problem, the crackdown in fact discriminated against the Burmese women and girls. Whereas the women were arrested during raids on brothels, detained and often deported as illegal immigrants, the brothel owners, pimps and traffickers were rarely arrested and prosecuted. At most, some police implicated in sex trafficking were transferred. With the exception of one 1992 case involving the murder of a Thai prostitute in the province of Songkla, no Thai official had been prosecuted or imprisoned for involvement in prostitution or trafficking as of November 1993.

The ordeal of the Burmese women and girls did not end with their "rescue" from the brothels, as the detention and deportation process was rife with additional abuses. Conditions at some of the immigration detention centers fell drastically short of the United Nations Standard Minimum Rules for the Treatment of Prisoners. The Bangkok detention center, where adults and minors were held together, was so overcrowded that detainees had to take turns just to lie down head to toe. At the Kanchanaburi detention center, there were consistent allegations of rape and physical abuse during 1992 and 1993. Furthermore, many of the women we interviewed at the detention centers did not know what, if any, charges were pending

against them. Most did not understand the Thai language and they were rarely provided with translators during their hearings and sentencing. The length of detention, in many cases, was dependent on the women's ability to cajole or in some instances bribe their way out.

With the alarming spread of AIDS in Thailand, Burmese women and girls in closed brothels were at extreme risk of HIV infection, since very few had the power to negotiate either condom use or the number of customers. During 1993, an otherwise commendable national AIDS prevention campaign largely failed to reach the Burmese women in the brothels. NGOs and health care workers estimated that 50 to 70 percent of the Burmese women and girls in the brothels in northern Thailand were HIV-positive. Notwithstanding widely-circulated reports of Burmese government persecution of people who were HIV-positive, Burmese women and girls infected with the AIDS virus were summarily repatriated. In September 1922, the Thai government completed a high-profile official deportation of ninety-five Burmese women and girls, half of whom were subsequently reported by the Burmese authorities to be HIV-positive and detained for treatment. As of November, there had been no official Thai mission to verify the status of those returnees.

Turkey

In July 1993, the Women's Rights Project and Helsinki Watch conducted a mission to Turkey to investigate reports that police and other state actors were forcing women and girls to undergo gynecological exams to determine whether they were virgins. The social stigma associated with the exams and the lack of appropriate complaint procedures made the exact incidence of such exams difficult to determine. However, numerous Turkish women, doctors, and lawyers told us that the threat—and in some cases the actual imposition—of forced virginity control exams followed Turkish women throughout their lives.

We found that police and other state

authorities had abused broadly-worded statutes regulating the treatment of detainees and pertaining to the duties and responsibilities of the police to monitor public behavior—none of which specifically required anything resembling virginity exams—by compelling women and girls, often against their will, to undergo exams to assess the status of their hymens. A report planned to follow-up on the trip would document several incidents in which women in detention were forcibly examined before and after interrogation, police stopped women on the street for engaging in "immoral" behavior and threatened them with virginity "control," and local public health authorities forced hospital patients to submit to compulsory vaginal exams. The virginity of men was never investigated, even by superficial questioning.

In one case, two young, female journalists traveling in southeastern Turkey were detained by the police. Prior to being interrogated about whether they were carriers for the Kurdish Workers' Party (PKK), the women were taken to the local state hospital for virginity examinations. At first the women refused to be examined. According to the women's testimony, the police responded "[w]e do this to all of the women we detain, even if they are detained only for two hours. We do it two times—when we detain women and again before we release them. We do this to protect ourselves, so that you won't say we raped you." The doctor then cautioned them, "You'd better do this or they will force your legs apart for you." Both women were forcibly examined twice.

In May 1992, two female high school students in western Anatolia reportedly killed themselves after being forced by school authorities and family members to submit to virginity exams. The girls, along with several of their female classmates, were taken by school authorities to have their hymens examined after being seen picnicking in the woods with boys. When the suicides became public, Turkish activists protested against the imposition of virginity exams and decried such exams as an extreme manifestation of state-tolerated violence against women and discrimination. According to local activists, government officials dismissed the cases as isolated incidents.

In interviews with the Women's Rights Project, Turkish police officials denied that woman in custody were forced to undergo virginity exams. However, we obtained several forms signed by local police authorities directing that individual women in detention have their virginity determined by a doctor.

Kenya

In July 1993, the Women's Rights Project and Africa Watch conducted a mission to Kenya, to investigate allegations of sexual abuse of Somali refugee women in camps in Kenyan territory. We found that from January through August 1993, 192 rapes were reported to the United Nations High Commissioner for Refugees (UNHCR), which administers the Kenyan camps.

In a majority of reported cases, refugee women and girls were violently attacked by unknown armed bandits at night or when they went to the outskirts of the camp to herd goats or collect firewood. These bandits increasingly joined forces with former Somali military men or fighters from the various warring factions who launched raids across the Kenya-Somali border. To a lesser extent, refugee women reported attacks by Kenyan police officers posted in the area, who were responsible for seven of the reported rape cases. UNHCR estimated that reported cases amount to only one-tenth the number of actual rapes occurring in the camps, at the hands of either bandits, warring parties or local police.

Somali women as old as fifty and girls as young as four were subjected to violence and sexual assault. Most of the cases involved gang-rape at gunpoint, some by as many as seven men at a time. Some women were raped twice or three times in the camps. In the vast majority of cases, female rape victims were also robbed, brutally beaten, knifed or shot. Those women refugees who had been circumcised often had their vaginal openings torn or cut by their attackers. Many suffered ongoing medical and psychological problems.

For nearly half of the women who reported being raped, rape was a factor in causing them to become refugees. Eighty-five of the 192 reported rape cases involved women who were raped in Somalia before fleeing to Kenya. Once in Kenya, women were again targeted with rape as a particularly effective form of intimidation, further destabilizing the refugee population and rendering women refugees in particular vulnerable to exploitation for money, goods and perverse sexual gratification.

The Kenyan government's response to rising sexual assault in its camps was wholly inadequate. The authorities did not provide sufficient protection or security to the refugee camps, nor did they prosecute a single individual responsible for rape. Moreover, the office of the President callously accused the Somali refugee women of fabricating the rape claims to "attract sympathy and give the government negative publicity" and asserted, despite ample evidence to the contrary, that the police had received no rape reports. Relief officials, including UNHCR, belatedly began to establish programs designed to respond to the sexual assault of women refugees, but services were still severely limited, and relief organizations had made insufficient efforts to protect the women refugees against rape in the first instance.

Like Human Rights Watch as a whole, the HRW Women's Rights Project is committed to conducting sustained monitoring efforts in the countries on which it reports. In addition to the new country studies discussed above, we also conducted follow-up efforts in three countries we visited in 1991 and 1992: Kuwait, Pakistan and Brazil.

Kuwait

As documented in *Punishing the Victim: Rape and Mistreatment of Asian Maids in Kuwait*, a report released by the Women's Rights Project and Middle East Watch in August 1992, over 2,000 Asian guestworkers employed as maids in Kuwait fled from abusive employers following that country's liberation. Most of these women were from Sri Lanka, Bangladesh, India and the Philippines and were drawn to Kuwait by the hope of higher wages. Instead, they experienced physical and sexual assault, debt bondage, passport deprivation, illegal confinement, and contract violations.

The Kuwaiti government did little to address the Asian maids' plight despite its full knowledge of their deplorable situation. A decree to regulate Kuwaiti recruitment agencies was not consistently enforced. A draft bill to include maids in labor laws was left pending for months.

Following the report's release, the HRW Women's Rights Project learned that many women continued to seek refuge in their embassies and to complain of abuse and mistreatment at the hands of their employers. The Kuwaiti government's efforts to repatriate women who had fled abusive employers did not address the underlying problem or provide legal restitution. In July 1993, approximately 400 Filipina and one hundred Indian and Sri Lankan maids who had sought refuge in their respective embassies were repatriated at Kuwaiti government expense. In August 1993, the Philippines Embassy reported that over 120 women were staying in the embassy. More women arrived daily.

In September, another 100 Indian and Sri Lankan maids were sent home. Although the repatriation of maids may have solved the women's immediate need to return home, the Kuwaitis conducted the returns without gathering in advance adequate evidence of the alleged abuses. Thus, once the women left Kuwait their allegations of abuse and mistreatment were effectively dropped.

To our knowledge, only one case of abuse was successfully prosecuted as of November 1993. Sonia Panama, a twenty-three-year-old Filipina working as a maid, died on March 8, 1993 after being admitted to the hospital with severe injuries. Press reports indicated that hospital staff found signs that she had been beaten and raped. One ear was virtually severed, cigarette burns covered her body, and there were bite marks on her stomach. In July 1993, Panama's employers, a Kuwaiti husband and Lebanese wife, were sentenced to seven years' imprisonment for causing her death through ill-treatment.

Pakistan and Brazil

The Women's Rights Project also conducted follow-up missions on its previous work on trafficking in women in Pakistan and violence against women in Brazil.

From June to August 1993, the project and Asia Watch conducted preliminary research in Pakistan which indicated that, although brothel raids and arrests of Bangladeshi women trafficked into Pakistan for prostitution appeared to have diminished, Bangladeshi women continued to be trafficked across the Pakistani border and to be arrested, either as prostitutes or as illegal immigrants, once in Pakistan. In one case we investigated, twenty-year-old Saira Bano was abducted from Bangladesh and taken with a group of twenty to thirty other Bengali women on a bus to India and ultimately across the border into Pakistan. Saira was arrested in Karachi on March 24, 1992, prior to being sold into prostitution, and spent the next twelve months in detention. On February 4, 1993 she was released to Darul Aman, a quasi-penal institution, where she remained as of November 1993. She had no papers to prove that she was Bengali and no financial means to return home.

Both Bangladesh and Pakistan are signatories to the Convention for the Suppression of Traffic in Persons and of the Exploitation of the Prostitution of Others which, among other things, obligates states parties to repatriate victims of trafficking and to provide temporary care and maintenance until repatriation takes place. While the convention requires a state party to pay for repatriation at least to the frontier of the victim's country of origin, unfortunately it only requires repatriation "after agreement is reached with the state of destination." In general, the Bangladesh High Commissioner in Pakistan consistently refused applications like Saira's on the grounds that, without documentation, the women could not prove they are Bengali.

In November the Women's Rights Project and Americas Watch launched a mission to follow up on violence against women in Brazil, with particular emphasis on the forced prostitution of Brazilian girls in the Amazon region.

The International Response

International work and, in particular, work at the United Nations continued to be a crucial element in efforts to advance the protection and promotion of women's human rights worldwide. At the 1993 session of the United Nations Commission on the Status of Women, in Vienna, which the Women's Rights Project attended, the commission called for the full integration of women's rights into the work of the World Conference on Human Rights in June and adopted a draft declaration on violence against women to be considered by the United Nations General Assembly in November. At its 1993 session in Geneva, the U.N. Commission on Human Rights adopted a resolution calling for the "full integration of women's rights into the human rights mechanisms of the United Nations," and agreed to consider the appointment of a Special Rapporteur on Violence Against Women at its 1994 session.

Following the U.N. Women's Commission and Human Rights Commission meetings, the Women's Rights Project circulated to government delegates a series of talking points in support of the appointment of a Special Rapporteur on Violence Against Women to be used in advance of the 1993 World Conference on Human Rights. We called for the rapporteur's mandate to encompass sex discrimination as well as violence on the grounds that gender-based violence cannot be effectively understood or remedied if it is examined separately from gender discrimination. In May, we wrote a letter to Assistant Secretary of State John Shattuck assessing the draft U.S. human rights action plan for Vienna. We called in particular for the U.S. more thoroughly to integrate women's human rights throughout its action plan, rather than artificially segregating "women's issues" from the plan's substantive sections and to more vigorously support the appointment of a special rapporteur.

At the World Conference itself, the Women's Rights Project participated in several NGO working groups and panels addressing women's human rights and worked closely with women's rights activists worldwide to integrate women's rights into the conference's final declaration. In a victory for women's human rights activists, the Vienna Declaration affirmed that "the human rights of women and of the girl-child are an inalienable, integral and indivisible part of universal human rights. The full and equal participation of women in the political, civil, economic, social and cultural life, at the national, regional and international levels, and the eradication of all forms of discrimination on grounds of sex are priority objectives of the international community."

In October 1993, the U.N.'s Division for the Advancement of Women invited the Women's Rights Project to participate in an expert group meeting on measures to eradicate violence against women. Women's rights activists from Asia, Africa, Latin America, the Caribbean and North America analyzed various forms of gender-based violence worldwide and crafted recommendations for national, regional and international bodies to combat such violence more effectively as part of efforts to combat human rights abuse more generally.

U.S. Policy

Women's human rights assumed a higher profile in U.S. foreign policy during 1993, largely due to increased attention from the Clinton administration, revelations about atrocities in the former Yugoslavia, and the World Conference on Human Rights. Heightened visibility, however, did not translate into consistent and effective demands for accountability. The U.S. government's response to violations of women's human rights in particular countries continued to suffer from a lack of coordination among the many federal agencies and bureaus with responsibility for foreign policy.

At the international level, the United States supported the U.N. Human Rights Commission resolution calling for the full integration of women's rights into the U.N.'s human rights mechanisms and co-sponsored the draft declaration on violence against women. The U.S. also played a significant role in advancing women's human rights at the official U.N. Human Rights Conference in Vienna. Secretary of State Warren Christopher set the tone for the U.S. at Vienna by calling it "a moral imperative" to guarantee to women their human rights. Firm advocacy by the U.S. delegation helped assure that key components of the U.S. human rights action plan concerning women's human rights were incorporated into the Vienna Declaration.

However, for these commitments to have more than symbolic significance, the U.S. must develop concrete monitoring and enforcement mechanisms. Assistant Secretary of State for Human Rights John Shattuck, in testimony before the House Subcommittee on International Security, International Organizations and Human Rights in October, committed the administration to taking the following steps in this regard: appoint a staff person within the Human Rights Bureau to work full-time on women's human rights issues; assess U.S. aid and trade relations, and votes at the multilateral lending institutions with regard to human rights; direct U.S.-funded democracy and administration of justice programs to support women's rights in new and emerging democracies; and incorporate abuses targeted at women into all relevant sections of the State Department *Country Reports on Human Rights Practices*.

Assistant Secretary Shattuck also made specific pledges with respect to U.S. relations with the U.N. The Human Rights Bureau committed itself to advocate U.S. ratification of U.N. Convention on the Elimination of All Forms of Discrimination Against Women (CEDAW); to support the appointment of a U.N. Special Rapporteur on Violence Against Women and a U.N. High Commissioner for Human Rights; and to press for the assembly of evidence for prosecuting systematic rape as a war crime and a tool of ethnic cleansing in the former Yugoslavia.

Assistant Secretary Shattuck's commitment to the appointment of a senior advisor on women's human rights to the State Department Bureau for Human Rights and Humanitarian Affairs came in response to recommendations introduced by Reps. Olympia Snowe and Howard Berman and Sen. Paul Simon as amendments to the 1994 State Department authorization bill, which was awaiting passage by Congress as of November. Among other things, the proposed senior advisor would be tasked "to assure that the issue of abuses against women, along with human rights issues generally, are a factor in determining bilateral assistance as well as United States votes at the multilateral development banks."

Even before the Clinton administration announced its intent to ratify CEDAW, members of Congress were urging ratification. In April, sixty-eight senators wrote to President Clinton asking him to take the necessary steps to ratify CEDAW. The letter noted that "[d]elayed action on the Convention only signals to the international community that the U.S. doesn't recognize discrimination of women as a violation of human rights." In the House, Representatives Woolsey and Hamilton introduced a Resolution calling on President Clinton to move expeditiously on CEDAW.

Notwithstanding these welcome developments, the record of the U.S. executive branch's responses to country-specific cases of violations of women's human rights clearly indicated that the U.S. could and should engage in more vigorous and systematic international and bilateral initiatives to promote and protect women's human rights.

The Clinton administration at times missed important opportunities to exercise U.S. leverage to ensure the protection of women's human rights. For example, the State Department in September approved the release of $3.73 million in security assistance to Kenya to enhance security on its border with Somalia. In his September 24, 1993 press statement accompanying the release, the State Department's spokesperson said that "the United States has welcomed the Kenyan government's efforts to improve conditions along the border, and believes that those efforts merit support." This decision to disburse security assistance should have been, but was not, accompanied by pressure on the Kenyan government to adopt specific measures to protect Somali refugees from widespread abuses, including rape of Somali women refugees. Such abuses had been documented by UNHCR, Human Rights Watch and other human rights organizations over a period of months. On the positive side, the Refugee Bureau responded in November to a funding appeal from UNHCR for a special project to assist Somali women refugees by allocating $250,000 in humanitarian aid directly to UNHCR.

Thailand was another case where the U.S. has failed to integrate women's human rights into its bilateral relations. Even as the U.S. spent some $4 million in fiscal year 1993 to combat drug trafficking in Thailand, the State Department never publicly raised the problem of sex trafficking with the Thai government. Again, Congress was more active in advocating the human rights of women trafficking victims. In its report accompanying the 1994 foreign appropriations bill, the Senate Foreign Relations Committee for the first time raised concerns about the illegal trafficking of Burmese women and children into Thailand for the purposes of forced prostitution. While acknowledging the Thai government's periodic efforts to rescue women held captive in brothels, the committee also noted that "these efforts have unfortunately led to the arrest and detention of Burmese women as illegal immigrants rather than to the arrest of brothel owners and officials, often local police, involved in the trafficking." The committee called upon the Thai government "to prosecute those responsible for the trafficking, forced labor, and physical and sexual abuse of these [Burmese] women."

By contrast, U.S. advocacy to establish

an international tribunal to prosecute war crimes in the former Yugoslavia has consistently taken into account crimes against women. In February, in her statement supporting U.N. Security Council Resolution 808 to establish an ad hoc tribunal, Ambassador Madeleine Albright specifically condemned rape as one aspect of "ethnic cleansing." The U.S. also successfully nominated a woman, Judge Gabrielle Kirk McDonald, to one of the eleven judgeships on the tribunal. In addition, the State Department drafted rules of evidence and procedures for the tribunal that included a ban on inquiry into survivors' past sexual histories. These rules were under consideration by the panel of judges.

Various members of Congress circulated resolutions to condemn rape and forced pregnancy as war crimes and crimes against humanity, and to urge the U.N. to investigate expeditiously all forms of abuse. Despite such efforts, U.N. progress toward establishing a war crimes tribunal was shamefully slow; as of November, the staff had not even been selected. Meanwhile, evidence disappeared and witnesses dispersed.

In some cases, Congress played an important role in placing the U.S. on record and pressuring foreign governments on significant abuses of women's human rights. In March, for example, following the release of the Women's Rights Project/Americas Watch report on Peru, twenty-three senators and forty-two representatives wrote to President Alberto Fujimori to deplore the widespread rape and killing with impunity of civilian women during that country's protracted internal conflict. Beyond condemning both the Peruvian government and the Shining Path for consistently failing to discipline their combatants, the signatories criticized the Peruvian government's maneuvers to retaliate against Raquel Martín Castillo de Mejía, whose case was detailed in our report, for speaking out against the military for raping her.

Congress also assumed the lead in pressing for Japanese accountability for past abuses against women. While welcoming the Japa-nese government's recent admission of official involvement in the establishment of a vast network of military brothels during World War II, members of the House of Representatives called upon Prime Minister Morihiro Hosokawa to take additional steps. To ensure justice for women who were forced to work as prostitutes to the Japanese military during World War II, they urged the Japanese government "to cooperate fully [with the U.N. Special Rapporteur on Sexual Slavery] in order to provide a complete account of the 'comfort women' policy." The letter also supported the demands of numerous former "comfort women" for official apologies and compensation from the Japanese government as part of the overall process of accountability.

In the case of Kuwait, the U.S. engaged in high-level discussions regarding abuses against Asian domestic workers by their Kuwaiti employers. However, little changed in Kuwait during the fourteen months since we first reported on this problem. Additional pressure from the U.S. government was needed to ensure that Kuwait extended the protection of labor laws to domestic workers and prosecuted employers for criminal behavior.

As in previous years, Human Rights Watch testified before the House Foreign Affairs Subcommittee in March 1993 on the State Department's *Country Reports on Human Rights Practices*. While commending the 1992 Country Reports for generally improved coverage of women's human rights, we reiterated that more data was needed on violence against women to underscore the enormity of this problem, and that abuses against women should be more consistently integrated into all appropriate sections on substantive rights, rather than concentrated under "discrimination."

The accurate categorization of abuses against women was directly pertinent to the application of U.S. human rights law to women's human rights. U.S. human rights law mandates sanctions only against those countries that consistently commit "gross violations," including torture, degrading treatment and flagrant violations of the right to life, but not "discrimination."

To generate urgent support for individual women who were at imminent risk of abuse, or who were seeking legal redress for past abuse, Sen. Patty Murray and Reps. Jan Meyers and Joe Moakley initiated the Congressional Working Group on International Women's Human Rights. The cases, to be identified and researched by Human Rights Watch and other human rights organizations, are also to highlight patterns of state-sponsored or state-tolerated violence or severe discrimination against women that merit Congressional attention beyond action on the individual cases.

The Work of the
Women's Rights Project

The Women's Rights Project and Americas Watch continued advocacy to end violence against women in Peru by government forces and Shining Path insurgents, which we first reported in our report, *Untold Terror*. In February, we sent letters to Peruvian President Alberto Fujimori and the Shining Path leadership to condemn ongoing attacks on civilian women as a tactic of war. We called upon both parties to investigate and discipline their combatants. In May, the Women's Rights Project and Americas Watch wrote to President Fujimori to protest the alleged rape of twenty-three-year-old María de la Cruz by Peru's anti-terrorist police, DINCOTE. Ms. de la Cruz, who became pregnant, was still being held in maximum security prison as of November, even though the military court acquitted her of all connections to the Shining Path.

In July, responding to new threats of extradition and trial-*in-absentia* by the Peruvian government against Raquel Martín de Mejía, the Women's Rights Project and Americas Watch appealed to Peruvian Ambassador to Sweden Jaime Stiglich Berninzon to write to his government stating that there was no information that showed any links whatsoever between Ms. Martín de Mejía and Sendero Luminoso. Ms. Martín had been living in exile in Sweden after being raped by Peruvian soldiers in 1989. The false charges against Ms. Martín were still pending in November.

Human Rights Watch called on the United Nations to prosecute rape and forced pregnancy as war crimes in the Bosnian war. In a February 1993 letter to the U.S. delegation to the U.N. Human Rights Commission, the Women's Rights Project urged the U.S. to press the commission for a resolution recognizing explicitly that rape is a war crime and calling for the establishment of an international war crimes tribunal to ensure the prosecution of war crimes, including rape, in the former Yugoslavia. The commission subsequently adopted such a resolution. The project also assisted congressional efforts to draft similar resolutions and to call on the administration and its U.N. delegation to support the tribunal and to ensure that prosecuting rape remained a priority. When, in March 1993, the U.S. released its proposed charter for the war crimes tribunal, the Women's Rights Project highlighted issues pertaining to the prosecution of sexual abuses in its contributions to Human Rights Watch's commentary on the charter's provisions.

Once the U.N. began the process of appointing judges and the chief prosecutor of the tribunal, the project worked to submit the names of qualified female candidates for these crucial positions. The U.N. General Assembly ultimately selected two women— Elizabeth Odio Benito of Costa Rica and Gabrielle Kirk McDonald of the United States—to sit on the tribunal's eleven-judge panel. The project continued its efforts to ensure women's participation in the U.N. Commission of Experts reviewing evidence of war crimes in the former Yugoslavia, and in the tribunal's prosecutorial team.

The project participated actively in two non-governmental *ad hoc* coalitions against war crimes in the former Yugoslavia. The coalitions called attention to the situation of women refugees and victims of human rights abuse in Bosnia, worked with the U.S. government and the U.N. to condemn and seek eventual prosecution of war crimes against women, and urged that international relief efforts respond to the needs of victims of sexual violence and torture. Human Rights Watch also filed an *amicus* brief supporting a civil suit brought by the Center for Constitutional Rights on behalf of Bosnian victims of human rights abuses and charging the leader of the Bosnian Serbs, Radovan Karadzic, with responsibility for rape and other gross violations of humanitarian law.

Just prior to the State Department's announcement in September that the U.S. would release $3.73 million in security assistance to Kenya, the Women's Rights Project urged the department to appropriate a portion of the funds to protection of women refugees against rape. Following the aid's release, we met with State Department officials to express concern that no portion of the approved funds—for the purchase of spare parts for military helicopters, parts for heavy equipment transporters, equipment for drilling water wells in the border region and related training and services—was allocated to address the specific protection needs of Somali refugees, particularly women refugees, in Kenya. The Women's Rights Project strongly urged the State Department to press the Kenyan government to meet its international refugee protection obligations, and to prosecute all wrongdoers.

In a follow-up letter to the State Department's Kenya desk officer, the project urged the administration to press the Kenyan government to fulfill its obligations under the 1951 Refugee Convention by committing to specific refugee safety measures. At a minimum, such measures should include additional physical barriers around the refugee camps, protection for women who report sexual violence from reprisal, prosecution and punishment of all wrongdoers to the full extent of the law, and collaboration with UNHCR to enhance camp security and to provide legal and medical assistance to rape survivors.

In a May 1993 letter to Kuwait's Minister of Justice, the Women's Rights Project and Middle East Watch called on the government to take steps to respond to the problem, including (1) revising labor laws to afford maids the same level of protection as other private sector employees; (2) ceasing the wrongful arrest and detention of Asian maids; (3) establishing adequate shelter for women who allege abuse and mistreatment until their cases are resolved; (4) explicitly denouncing and punishing passport deprivation; and (5) investigating and prosecuting all those accused of rape and assault.

In September, the Women's Rights Project offered testimony at a hearing held by the House Foreign Affairs Subcommittee on Human Rights, on women's human rights and U.S. foreign policy. The Women's Rights Project emphasized the need to advance beyond the enumeration of violations and dependence on *ad hoc* responses, toward the systematic integration of women's human rights into U.S. foreign policy.

In October, the Women's Rights Project submitted to Secretary of State Warren Christopher a memorandum with extensive recommendations to fully integrate women's human rights into all aspects of U.S. foreign policy. The memorandum suggested ways to increase the State Department's capacity to promote and protect women's human rights, and to improve coordination across federal agencies involved in U.S. foreign policy. We also recommended ways to enhance the effectiveness of U.N. mechanisms in safeguarding women's human rights. To implement these suggestions, we fully endorsed Secretary Shattuck's plan to designate a full-time staff person within the Human Rights Bureau to work on women's human rights, with the proviso that this individual must be appointed at a senior level with sufficient authority and staff.

In addition to our country-specific work, and our work on national and international policy regarding women's human rights generally, we continued to take up specific women's human rights cases which had broad ramifications for women's human rights. In March, the project wrote to President Daniel arap Moi protesting harassment and threats against Prof. Wangari Maathai, an outspoken advocate for democratic reform in Kenya and co-founder of the Tribal Clashes

Resettlement Volunteer Service, for her criticism of the government's handling of the ethnic violence in the Rift Valley.

In April, the project and Middle East Watch issued an urgent press release strenuously protesting the Moroccan government's decision to ban a demonstration against sexual harassment. Scheduled to occur in the wake of the sensational trial of Moustapha Tabet, a senior police official sentenced to death for abducting and raping over 500 women, the march was to make the point that Tabet could have abused so many only because the government generally condoned police abuse of authority.

In October 1992, the Women's Rights Project and Middle East Watch joined other advocates in petitioning the Canadian government to grant political asylum to Nada, a Saudi woman fleeing gender-based persecution in her country. Nada fled Saudi Arabia because she feared persecution as a woman who had refused to heed the travel, dress and employment restrictions imposed on women by the government and strictly enforced by the religious police, who are empowered to flog transgressors on the street. On January 29, 1993, Canada's Minister of Employment and Immigration, Bernard Valcourt, finally granted Nada asylum.

Our work on Nada's case led us to engage in work on women refugees issues more generally. Like Nada, many women become refugees in order to escape gender-based persecution. Often these women are subject to further persecution as female refugees. Yet current refugee law does not explicitly recognize gender-based persecution. Thus, women seeking asylum in the United States due to their well-founded fear of such persecution may be presumptively excluded because the basis of their claims is not acknowledged by law.

Even as UNHCR and human rights organizations were beginning to document and analyze the particular problems that confronted refugee and displaced women, the administration was proposing to reform the U.S. asylum system in ways that were likely to have a negative impact on women's ability to seek refuge in the U.S. Measures under review included a higher, more difficult standard for establishing persecution claims in summary proceedings, and drastic limits on access to judicial review of asylum claims. Commenting on the administration's proposals, which were introduced in the Senate by Sen. Edward Kennedy and in the House by Rep. Jack Brooks, Rep. Nancy Pelosi argued that "refugee women fleeing gender-related persecution, often victimized by rape, will be unable, under the proposed legislation, to present evidence in a summary hearing sufficient to meet the 'credible fear' test."

Echoing Rep. Pelosi's main criticisms, the Women's Rights Project wrote to Vice-President Al Gore on August 10, 1993 to express concern that "the [legislation's] proposed expedited exclusion proceedings could effectively deny women the time and resources necessary to demonstrate the legitimacy of their [asylum] claims." The Women's Rights Project further urged that any amendment to U.S. asylum law include an explicit recognition of gender-based persecution as a grounds for asylum.

In March 1993, the Canadian Immigration and Refugee Board promulgated guidelines for considering the petitions of women refugee claimants fearing gender-related persecution. The guidelines explicitly state that the definition of refugee may be interpreted to include women who demonstrate a well-founded fear of gender-related persecution. The Women's Rights Project contributed during the year to efforts underway in the United States to draft guidelines similar to those adopted in Canada. The draft U.S. guidelines were designed to assist immigration officers in analyzing and interpreting gender-based persecution claims. The project's participation in drafting the guidelines was rooted in the work of Human Rights Watch documenting both gender-specific human rights abuses and the plight of women refugees in, for example, the former Yugoslavia, Kenya, and Bangladesh.

HUMAN RIGHTS WATCH —CALIFORNIA

Human Rights Watch-California was formed in April 1987 by a group of concerned Californians who sought to mobilize their state's unique resources to help people whose human rights were being violated. The Los Angeles office, which opened in 1989, is responsible for Americas Watch's research and advocacy on Mexico and the U.S.-Mexico border area; investigation and campaign tasks for all aspects of Human Rights Watch; and litigation and other legal work to support cases in U.S. courts that raise international human rights questions.

Human Rights Watch-California places a high priority on human rights education and community outreach. During 1993, public education program events addressed, among other topics, the incipient U.N. crimes tribunal for the former Yugoslavia, United Nations operations in Somalia and Haiti, the North American Free Trade Agreement (NAFTA), and womens' rights. In October, the Human Rights Watch Film Festival was screened in Los Angeles.

Development also was a priority in 1993. In addition to expanding our advisory board, members of Human Rights Watch-California hosted private informational meetings to introduce potential new supporters to our work. In August, with foundation support, a regional development director joined the Los Angeles office staff.

At the same time, the Los Angeles office continued its research and advocacy on human rights conditions in Mexico and along the U.S.-Mexico border. A chapter on prison conditions in Mexico was included in the *Human Rights Watch Global Report on Prisons*, and reports were written or edited on the intimidation of activists in Mexico, police abuse in Mexico City, and human rights abuses along the border by the U.S. Border Patrol and the Customs Service. Work

continued on a forthcoming Human Rights Watch-Yale University Press book on human rights in Mexico and on a joint Human Rights Watch-Natural Resources Defense Council report on intimidation of environmentalists and interference with environmental due process rights in Mexico.

In addition, the Los Angeles office staff gave frequent speeches and press interviews concerning human rights on both sides of the border. They helped prepare testimony on human rights in Mexico for the U.S. House of Representatives Small Business Committee, and the Subcommittee on International Security, Human Rights, and International Organizations of the House Committee on Foreign Affairs. They also met with key senior government officials in both countries including Mexican Attorney General Jorge Carpizo and U.S. Attorney General Janet Reno.

The Los Angeles office continued to provide legal and campaign support to other divisions of Human Rights Watch. For example, the California director participated in a working group organized by the United Nations Sub-Commission on Prevention of Discrimination and Protection of Minorities special rapporteur that drafted proposed basic principles and guidelines concerning reparation to victims of gross violations of human rights; assisted in the preparation of a Human Rights Watch *amicus* brief to the U.S. District Court for the Southern District of New York in *Doe v. Karadzik*; drafted a letter to Secretary of State Christopher urging U.S. ratification of the major human rights treaties; participated in the Stanley Foundation conference on Global Changes and Domestic Transformations: Southern California's Emerging Role; spoke at the American Public Health Association conference on the legal aspects of prevention and treatment of torture; and consulted with attorneys representing inmates at California's Pelican Bay State Prison regarding international human rights norms relevant to litigation on prisoner mistreatment.

The group's co-chairs took part in missions for Human Rights Watch (to the former

Yugoslavia and Cuba) and in work against the death penalty in the United States, including addressing state legislatures and speaking at vigils for death row inmates.

In December 1992 we brought to Los Angeles the international human rights monitors invited to the United States by Human Rights Watch. As part of that visit, the human rights monitors toured those Los Angeles neighborhoods most heavily impacted by the disturbances that followed the acquittal in the state trial of the police defendants accused of beating Rodney King, where they had an opportunity to exchange personal experiences with community activists. They also met with the mayor's office, the senior staff of the *Los Angeles Times*, and other senior community leaders. A similar program was planned for December 1993.

HUMAN RIGHTS WATCH FILM FESTIVAL

With the rapid advances in technology and global communications, the visual media are playing an increasingly important role in the evolving international dialogue on human rights. Human Rights Watch has developed the capacity through our film festival and related activities to promote and distribute the enormous wealth of important human rights-related films and videos from around the world. The Human Rights Watch Film Festival, established in 1988, advances public education on rights issues and concerns by exhibiting the finest works each year in commercial and archival theaters in the U.S. and on television and in film festivals internationally.

Since its inception, the Human Rights Watch Film Festival has presented 150 fiction, documentary, and animated films and videos from more than fifty countries. The sum of the festival's first four years of programming constitutes a unique, cumulative visual record of the contemporary global struggle for human rights.

The film festival opened its 1993 season in New York in May. Films presented over a two-week schedule, on two screens in a Manhattan theater, included sixty films and videos (of which thirty-eight were premieres) from more than thirty countries. The works ranged in type from fiction and documentary to experimental and animated, and formats ranged from feature-length to shorts to works-in-progress.

In 1992 the festival had presented the first-ever retrospective of the works of acclaimed documentarian Marcel Ophuls ("The Sorrow and the Pity," "Hotel Terminus"). The 1993 festival featured a retrospective of the films of Argentina's internationally-known director Fernando Solanas.

In its brief history, the festival has premiered works from familiar directors like Agnieska Holland ("Europa, Europa"), Jonathan Demme ("My Cousin Bobby"), Bertrand Tavernier ("The Undeclared War"), and Andrzej Wajda ("The Katyn Forest"); and has introduced the artistry and potent moral voices of emerging directors like Pawel Pawlikowski ("Serbian Epics"), Iris F. Kung ("Escape from China"), and Harriet Eder ("Mein Krieg").

Additional films appearing for the first time in the U.S. have included Suzanne Osten's "Speak Up! It's So Dark," a Scandinavian meditation on the renewed fervor of neo-Nazism among European youth, and Sahin Gok's "Siyabend and Xece," the first film made in the Kurdish language.

The 1993 festival schedule included customized daytime programming for high school audiences, accompanied by panel discussions on related human rights themes. Students participating in the project to date have come from seventeen, mainly inner-city schools throughout the New York area.

In selecting films for the festival, Human Rights Watch concentrates equally on artistic merit and human rights content. The festival's full-time programmer travels extensively and maintains close contacts with film appraisers around the world who scout for deserving works. The festival's programming committee has screened more than 400 films and videos each year; once a film is nominated for a place on the program, staff of the relevant division of Human Rights Watch also view it, primarily to confirm accuracy in the portrayal of human rights issues.

In conjunction with the opening night festivities each year in New York, the festival awards a prize in the name of the legendary cinematographer and director Nestor Almendros, who was a cherished friend of the festival. The award, which includes a cash prize of $5,000, goes to a deserving filmmaker in recognition of his or her contribution to human rights. The 1993 recipient was German director Helke Sander for "Liberators Take Liberties," her inquiry into the prevalence of rape during World War II.

The traveling sections of the festival expanded significantly in 1993, a reflection of both the national scope of the festival and the increasingly global appeal that the project has generated. The festival has itself become a worldwide distribution vehicle for the human rights films in our program.

In June 1993, the festival sent a special film showcase to Vienna in conjunction with the World Conference on Human Rights. A European television station, SuperChannel, whose broadcast market covers East and Western Europe and former Soviet republics, also aired a collection of films from the festival showcase following the conference.

In early September, selections from the Human Rights Watch Film Festival appeared in the Venice Film Festival and the Boston Film Festival; festival selections were also programmed in September at the Pacific Film Archive in Berkeley, California. In October, the festival as a whole appeared at the UCLA Film and Television Archive in Los Angeles, and selections from the festival were featured in the Sarajevo Festival, held in Bosnia.

The schedule for the remainder of 1993 included showings in Portland, Seattle and Olympia, Washington; and Hong Kong, where the Festival was presented under joint sponsorship with Amnesty International.

HUMAN RIGHTS WATCH AND CONGRESSIONAL CASEWORK

Human Rights Watch continued to work closely with two casework groups composed of members of Congress—the Congressional Friends of Human Rights Monitors and the Congressional Committee to Support Writers and Journalists. Both groups are bipartisan and bicameral. Human Rights Watch initiated the formation of these groups to enable concerned members of Congress to write letters and urgent cables to governments that violate the basic rights of human rights monitors, writers and journalists. Human Rights Watch supplies the groups with information about appropriate cases of concern; the groups, in turn, determine which cases they would like to pursue.

The goals of the congressional casework groups are three-fold. Most important, their letters and cables help to pressure governments to end their persecution of human rights monitors, writers and journalists who criticize repressive acts by their governments. Second, members of the congressional groups are informed about these important incidents of violence and intimidation against human rights activists and writers. Finally, copies of letters and cables are sent to U.S. ambassadors in the relevant countries to inform them about cases of concern.

The Congressional Friends of Human Rights Monitors, which was formed in 1983, is composed of thirty-four senators and 119 members of the House of Representatives. The five members of the steering committee for the group are Sen. Dave Durenberger, Sen. James Jeffords, Sen. Daniel Patrick

Moynihan, Rep. Tony Hall and Rep. Constance A. Morella.

In 1993, the committee took up the cases of dozens of human rights monitors who had been killed, arrested arbitrarily, assaulted or harassed. For example:

· The Congressional Friends expressed its concern over the Kuwaiti government's August order to dissolve all unlicensed associations, including all independent human rights organizations. The Congressional Friends noted that the government had repeatedly denied licenses for human rights organizations, whose work has at times been critical of the government. The Congressional Friends urged the Kuwaiti government to reverse its decision banning unlicensed private organizations.

· The Congressional Friends wrote to the Uzbekistan government to express its concern over the consistent harassment and interrogation of human rights activists. The Congressional Friends noted that this harassment had led to the virtual eradication of the human rights community within the country. As part of the apparent intimidation campaign, human rights activists have been arrested and interrogated. The Congressional Friends urged the government to guarantee human rights activists the right to carry out their work.

· In Guatemala, the Congressional Friends again expressed its deep concern over serious attacks against human rights activists. The letter noted that one human rights activist, Tomas Lares Sipriano, was killed, another "disappeared," and others received death threats. In addition, several human rights activists were fired upon during a peaceful protest in August, and a bomb exploded at the offices of the Guatemalan Association of Jurists. The Congressional Friends urged the government to carry out a thorough investiga-

tion into the murder of Lares Sipriano and to bring those responsible to justice. The group also requested that the government make every effort to determine the whereabouts of the disappeared activist, and to ascertain who was responsible for threats, unjustified shootings and bombings directed at several other human rights monitors.

· In Syria, the Congressional Friends wrote about the continuing detention and criminal charges faced by fifteen members of the Committee for the Defence of Democratic Freedoms and Human Rights in Syria (CDF). Ten of the CDF members had already been convicted and sentenced, apparently in response to their human rights work. Sentencing was pending against five of the CDF members, who had been detained for nearly two years and who faced up to fifteen years of hard labor in prison. The Congressional Friends urged the government to overturn the convictions of the fifteen human rights activists if they had been charged and convicted because of their human rights work.

· In Colombia, the Congressional Friends expressed its continuing concern over the April disappearance of Colombian human rights monitor Delio Vargas and the frequent death threats received by human rights activists throughout Colombia. The Congressional Friends noted that the death threats appeared to be part of an intimidation campaign to prevent monitors from reporting on human rights violations. The Congressional Friends urged the government to make every effort to determine the whereabouts of the disappeared monitor, to investigate death threats against human rights activists and to bring to justice those found responsible.

· The Congressional Friends again expressed its concern over continuing arrests of Nigerian human rights activists. Three human rights leaders continued to be detained and faced sedition and conspiracy charges, apparently as a result of their human rights work; two of the human rights leaders suffered from ill health and there was serious concern for their well-being in detention, where they were denied medical attention. Three more human rights activists with the Civil Liberties Organization were arrested in July, held for a month and then hospitalized upon their release. The Congressional Friends urged the government to release all human rights activists and to drop all charges against them if they had been charged and detained as a result of their human rights activities.

· In Turkey, the Congressional Friends expressed its deep concern over the murders of three human rights activists: Kemal Kilic, Metin Can and Dr. Hasan Kaya. The Congressional Friends also expressed its continuing concern over the alleged torture suffered by human rights activists detained and charged by Turkish authorities. The Congressional Friends urged the government to investigate the murders of the three human rights monitors and to punish appropriately those found responsible. The Congressional Friends also urged the government to end the alleged torture of detainees and to release all those detained who had been arrested as a result of their human rights work.

· In Korea, the Congressional Friends expressed its concern over the July arrest of human rights activist Noh Taehun. The Congressional Friends noted that his arrest took place without a proper arrest warrant and that Noh was subjected to long hours of interrogation and sleep deprivation during his detention. After being detained for two months, Noh was freed on a suspended eighteen-month sentence. The Con-

gressional Friends urged the government to drop all pending charges against Noh if they stemmed from his involvement in legitimate human rights work.

Other cases raised by the group included: the unwarranted arrests and continuing harassment of Cuban human rights monitors; the death threat received by Indonesian human rights lawyer Ahmad Jauhari and the warrant for the arrest of human rights activist Dedi Ekadibratal; the escalating number of arrests of human rights activists in Tibet and the serious sentences they faced if convicted; the continuing detention and mistreatment of human rights advocate Mohamed Houmed Soulleh in Djibouti; the violent attacks and threats against human rights activists in Rwanda, including those working with the government-approved human rights commission; the harassment by police of Tunisian human rights lawyer Radhia Nasraoui and the Tunisian League for Human Rights; the continued imprisonment of Moroccan human rights activist Ahmed Belaichi; the attack and death threat against Peruvian human rights lawyer Rosa Elena Mandujano Serrano; the death threats received by two human rights lawyers defending clients facing execution in Trinidad and Tobago; and the February murder of Philippine human rights activist Chris Batan, killed while in transit to an interview with victims of human rights abuses during the Marcos regime.

The Congressional Committee to Support Writers and Journalists was formed in 1988 and is composed of sixteen senators and seventy-six members of the House of Representatives. During 1993, the members of the steering committee for the group were Sen. William Cohen, Sen. Bob Graham, Rep. Jim Leach and Rep. John Lewis.

During the year, the committee denounced attacks against individual writers and journalists, as well as acts of censorship. For instance:

· In October, the Committee expressed its concern over several violent attacks against journalists in Argentina. One reporter, Hernán Lopez Echagüe with *Página 12*, was seriously beaten twice during a two-week period. During the attacks, the assailants threatened Lopez with death and warned him that he should stop "publishing those things." Lopez, as well as other journalists who had been threatened or assaulted, had reported critically about the Menem administration. The Committee urged the government to investigate these attacks and to bring to justice those found responsible.

· The committee wrote to the Cameroonian government to protest actions taken against several independent weeklies and their reporters. After the weeklies published articles critical of President Biya, reporters and publishers were criminally charged and some also received anonymous death threats. In addition, copies of one of the weeklies, *La Nouvelle Expression,* were confiscated. The committee urged the government to cease its harassment of the independent press and to drop all pending charges against journalists and publishers engaged in legitimate journalistic activities.

· After three Chinese journalists received harsh sentences, the committee wrote a letter to officials in October protesting the sentences and the continuing crackdown against the press. The committee, which had written letters of protest to the Chinese government several times during past years, expressed its deep concern over the life sentence received by Xinhua editor Wu Shishen. Wu was charged with selling "state secrets" after allegedly providing a copy of a speech by Communist Party chief Jiang Zemin to a reporter in Hong Kong. Another journalist received a six-year sentence for allegedly delivering the copy of the speech to the Hong Kong reporter. The third journalist, Fu Shenqi, received a three-year sentence at a labor re-education camp for allegedly speaking to the Australian prime minister. The committee urged the Chinese government to release these journalists immediately and unconditionally if they were being detained for carrying out legitimate journalistic duties.

· The Committee wrote to the *de facto* rulers in Haiti after several reporters were detained and seriously beaten by members of the armed forces or armed "attachés" working with the police and army. Some of the targeted reporters were abducted and then beaten after covering demonstrations, while others were attacked at their homes. In each case, the assailants questioned the victims about their critical reporting about the army or about their support for exiled president Jean-Bertrand Aristide. The committee urged the *de facto* leaders to cease these attacks and to punish those found responsible.

· In India, the committee wrote to protest the beating of three journalists in Srinagar by members of the Border Security Force (BSF). The journalists reported that a commander of the BSF threatened to kill the journalists and then commanded troops to beat the reporters. The reporters, from *Agence France-Presse, DPA* and *Srinagar News*, were subsequently hospitalized as a result of the injuries they sustained during the beatings. The committee urged the government to investigate the beatings and to punish members of the BSF found responsible.

· In October, the committee wrote to the Israeli government to protest attacks against journalists reporting in Gaza. Soldiers shot one reporter who was filming a clash between soldiers and demonstrators at a refugee camp. The apartment of another reporter was raided, and the reporter was arrested and mistreated while detained. Soldiers assaulted another reporter and confiscated his film of soldiers beating a taxi driver in Gaza City. The committee urged the government to investigate the attacks and to punish appropriately those found responsible.

· The Congressional Committee wrote to the Nigerian government to protest the banning of most of the independent press following the aborted June 12 elections. Two daily newspapers were banned, and five publishing houses were raided by the government and closed. Many reporters and editors working for the banned publications were detained and faced sedition charges. The government also issued decrees to curtail press freedoms further. The committee urged the government to end its suppression of the independent press and to annul the new decrees which ban many publications and severely curtail the right to freedom of expression.

· In Rwanda, the committee protested the murder of a veteran journalist, a shooting incident involving two Swedish journalists, and charges pending against a newspaper editor. Callixte Kalissa, a television producer and former photographer with the state-run press, was shot in April by assailants presumed to be members of the army. Two Swedish journalists were fired upon by Rwandan soldiers even though they had obtained permission to travel to a rebel zone and carried a white flag. The editor of *Umurava* was detained and charged with insulting the head of state after reporting on alleged connections between the President and death squads. The committee urged the Rwandan government to investigate the attacks against the journalists and to bring to justice those found responsible. The committee also asked the government to drop charges against the *Umurava* editor if they stemmed from his involvement in legitimate journalistic activities.

Other cases taken up by the Congressional Committee included: the murders and beatings of several journalists reporting on Tajikistan; the murder and disappearance of several journalists in Turkey; the harassment of journalists in Zaire, including arrests of reporters and suspensions of newspapers; the continuing death threat against Salman Rushdie, as well as violent attacks against those working with him; the murder of television reporter Rabah Zenati in Algeria; repressive measures taken by the Lebanese government against the independent press, including the shutting down of one television network and three daily newspapers; acts of intimidation carried out by the Kenyan government against the printing houses that publish independent magazines; criminal charges against journalists in Greece who have written about sensitive political or historical issues; threats allegedly made by the Brazilian military police against journalist Reinaldo Cabral for his reports on police violence; and statements by a prominent Egyptian sheik appearing to condone the murder of secular journalist Faraq Fuda.

UNITED NATIONS

The Vienna Conference

For the worldwide human rights movement, 1993 was notable in being the year of the second United Nations World Conference on Human Rights—the first having taken place twenty-five years earlier, when world conditions were markedly different and the human rights movements of many countries were in their infancy or not yet born. After preparatory conferences in the various regions, some 1,500 nongovernmental human rights organizations gathered in June in Vienna to review the state of human rights and to look ahead. The official conference of governments met separately from the nongovernmental groups, but both considered the same issues and both produced documents at the close of the conference.

Human Rights Watch sent several senior staff to Vienna and distributed two reports there. The *Human Rights Watch Global Report on Prisons* was a compilation of our work in twenty countries over a period of six years, and was issued as a call on the worldwide human rights movement and on U.N. bodies to stop averting their eyes from the horrifying conditions in which prisoners—a forgotten and profoundly vulnerable group in any society—must survive. The second report was titled *The Lost Agenda: Human Rights and U.N. Field Operations.* Focusing on the U.N. peace-making, humanitarian and peacekeeping operations in El Salvador, Cambodia, the former Yugoslavia, Somalia and Iraq, the report analyzed why incorporating human rights concerns was critical to the success of the El Salvador process; why unwillingness to seek accountability for ongoing abuses weakened the mission in Cambodia; and how the U.N. had failed to give human rights the necessary priority in the remaining three cases. The report was the first such cross-regional critique of the U.N.'s field performance from a human rights organization.

The meaning and impact of the Vienna conference appeared mixed. Although the conference was a welcome opportunity to gather monitors and governments together—and as such should take place more often than every twenty-five years—it also pointed up the areas of division that exist among governmental approaches to human rights. The argument of some authoritarian Asian governments that differing cultural norms should exempt their countries from the universal application of international human rights instruments was one flashpoint of discussion. There was also a perception, among countries of the South, that the U.N. had not adequately addressed their human rights priorities where those priorities involved economic, social and cultural rights, but had rather responded to an agenda of the developed, westernized North which emphasized predominantly civil and political rights.

Among the nongovernmental groups, such divisions were far less pronounced, although the issue of economic and social rights as priorities was widely discussed. In clear contrast to their governments, Asian and other Southern human rights organizations embraced the universality of human rights law. Particularly notable was the strength of women's groups from around the world and virtually unanimous criticism of the U.N.'s existing human rights machinery. The NGO Forum comprising all the human rights groups participating in the conference produced a strong position paper in which three elements stood out: first, that human rights, for the U.N., must mean all five categories of human rights; second, that women's basic rights must be fully integrated into the U.N.'s human rights agenda, beginning with the appointment of a Special Rapporteur on Violence Against Women; and third, that the U.N. General Assembly must create a High Commissioner for Human Rights, to ensure that a human rights component is included in all the U.N.'s developmental, humanitarian and peacekeeping work and that the U.N. can become capable of early warning and flexible action on human rights crises.

The Work of Human Rights Watch

In July, Human Rights Watch succeeded in obtaining consultative status at the United Nations. Resistance from abusive governments had previously blocked our application, and on this occasion China and Cuba spoke against the petition. On July 30, however, in a departure from established procedure, the Economic and Social Council (ECOSOC) decided on the status issue for Human Rights Watch with a vote rather than by consensus; the vote was 30 in favor and 3 against, with 13 abstentions. Consultative status enables a nongovernmental organization to attend working sessions of U.N. bodies and to lobby national delegations more effectively.

We used our consultative status during the General Assembly, which began in New York in late September, to focus in particular on the creation of a High Commissioner for Human Rights. Human Rights Watch representatives met with U.N. Secretary-General Boutros Boutros-Ghali to discuss the commissioner post. We developed a joint proposal for the commissioner's role, function and authority with five other international human rights organizations and distributed it widely within the U.N. And through the regional divisions of Human Rights Watch we kept in contact with our colleague organizations in the various regions to urge them to follow up on this issue with their governments, where possible. As of mid-November, it was unclear whether the General Assembly would agree on the post before year's end.

Human Rights Watch also followed closely the progress of the U.N.'s war crimes tribunal on the former Yugoslavia. During the long search for a chief prosecutor, when the Security Council was repeatedly deadlocked on the appointment, Human Rights Watch successfully opposed one unqualified candidate and suggested a number of distinguished advocates of human rights as possible alternatives. We considered it essential that the tribunal be headed by a prosecutor of exceptional moral stature and proven commitment to accountability. The Security Council selected Ramón Escovar Salom, the incumbent Prosecutor General of Venezuela, whose record in that post had been strong on rhetoric but less so on substance. That mixed record placed a burden on Mr. Escovar to show his commitment to the tribunal's urgent and historic mission. It was therefore with concern that Human Rights Watch learned that the new prosecutor would not even be developing his staff for the tribunal until after the New Year.

The Women's Rights Project, which in February called on the U.N. to prosecute rape and forced pregnancy as war crimes in the former Yugoslavia, also participated in the Vienna conference and there engaged in developing such proposals as the one for the Special Rapporteur on Violence Against Women, which was due to be taken up by the U.N. Human Rights Commission

in early 1994. In October, representatives of the Women's Rights Project were invited, by the U.N.'s Deparatment for the Advancement of Women, to participate in an expert group meeting on measures to eradicate violence against women.

HUMAN RIGHTS WATCH MISSIONS

Africa Watch

January/Somalia: To gather information about the human rights situation since the U.S.-led intervention.

January-February/South Africa: To investigate human rights in KwaZulu as part of a series of reports focusing on the homelands, and, in conjunction with the Prison Project, to investigate prison conditions.

January/Rwanda: As part of an international commission, to investigate human rights abuses in Rwanda and to excavate two mass graves where victims had been buried.

March/Liberia and the Ivory Coast: To evaluate the ECOMOG intervention in Liberia from a human rights perspective, with emphasis on the period of renewed warfare since October 1992.

March/Sudan: To investigate human rights conditions in southern Sudan.

March-April/Zaire: To investigate prison conditions in Zaire for a joint report with the Prison Project, as well as to document the government manipulation of the ethnic conflict in Shaba province.

April-May/Nigeria: To investigate the role of the government in religious and ethnic conflict in northern Nigeria.

June-July/Kenya: To investigate the ethnic clashes in western Kenya and, in conjunction with the Women's Rights Project, to document the rape of Somali women refugees in northeastern Kenya.

June-July/Mozambique: To investigate the types of land mines employed and their use during the civil war for a joint report with the Arms' Project.

July-August/Sudan and Kenya: To document violations of the laws of war by all sides to the war in southern Sudan.

October/Somalia and Kenya: To investigate problems of returning refugees and displaced people in southern Somalia.

October-November/Senegal: To interview Mauritanian refugees about abuses against the black ethnic groups in Mauritania since the "democratization" of 1992.

Americas Watch

January/Nicaragua: To research the problem of violence against former *contras* and former Sandinista soldiers.

January/Honduras: To conduct research on clandestine detainees.

February-March/Colombia: To conduct research on violations of laws of war by Mobile Brigades and by guerrillas.

May/Bolivia: To research a report on García Meza trial.

February/Costa Rica, Inter-American Court on Human Rights: To argue at a hearing on Advisory Opinion OC-13 (regarding powers of the Inter-American Commission).

February/Peru: To conduct research for a report on one year after Fujimori's "self-coup."

April/Peru: To conduct interviews on disappearance of students from La Cantuta University and revelations about a military death squad.

April/United States, Southwestern states: To research problem of violations by Border Patrol against intending immigrants.

May/Guatemala: To establish presence during attempted coup.

May-June/Venezuela: To conduct final research for first comprehensive report.

May-June/Brazil: To conduct research on violence against street children in four major urban areas.

June/Argentina: To interview senior Peruvian military chief in exile about the military death squad and La Cantuta case.

July/Brazil: To research problem of forced labor.

June/Nicaragua: To attend General Assembly of the Organization of American States, and hold press conference.

June/Haiti: To research U.S. program of in-country processing of applicants for asylum.

June-July/El Salvador: To conduct follow-up on Truth Commission report.

July/Costa Rica, Inter-American Court: To try the case on the merits against Peru for El Frontón prison massacre.

July/Costa Rica, Inter-American Court: To argue on preliminary objections, *Caballero v. Colombia*.

July/Peru: To research La Cantuta-Cieneguilla case, talk to press, government officials.

August-September/Guatemala: To follow up on July mission.

September/Brazil: To talk with government and press, and research massacre in Rio de Janeiro slum.

September/Guatemala: To conduct further research on new situation after fall of Serrano and appointment of new President.

October/Mexico and Guatemala: To conduct research on repatriation of Guatemalan refugees.

October/Nicaragua: To conduct further research on mechanisms to protect rights of *contras* who had returned to private life.

October/Honduras: To research human rights situation on the eve of elections.

October/El Salvador: To update human rights cases.

November/Paraguay: To talk with press, government and local monitors about attacks on press.

November/Brazil: (with Women's Rights Project) To conduct follow up investigation on violence against women and investigate forced prostitution of Brazilian girls in the Amazon region.

November/Argentina: To talk with government about press attacks, compensation of victims.

Arms Project

March/India, Pakistan: To investigate transfers of weapons to abusive forces in both India and Pakistan.

May/Argentina, Brazil, Chile: To investigate commercial transfers of weapons and licensing requirements of Southern Cone countries to human rights abusers elsewhere in the world.

June/Rwanda, Uganda, Belgium: To investigate where both sides in the abusive Rwandan civil war obtain weapons.

June/Mozambique: To investigate land mines abuse in Mozambique.

July-August/Georgia: To investigate violations of the laws of war and abuses of weapons in the Abkhazia civil war.

October-November/Israel-Lebanon: To investigate violations of the laws of war and abuses of weapons in the fighting in July between Israeli forces and Hizbollah in southern Lebanon.

Asia Watch

January-February/Thailand: Researched and interviewed Burmese girls and women being trafficked into brothels in Thailand and the consequences faced by those "rescued" by Thai police which entailed arrest, detention and deportation as illegal immigrants.

February-March/Cambodia: To evaluate UN mission and extent of human rights abuses throughout Cambodia's northwest and eastern regions prior to elections.

March/Vietnam: Introduced Asia Watch to a wide variety of Vietnamese officials and opened dialogue on human rights and law reform.

March/East Timor and Indonesia: Observation of Xanana Gusmao trial.

March/Thailand: Attended the Bangkok NGO forum and regional conference on human rights and discussed issues of concern with Asian NGOs.

March/Hong Kong and China: Updated the religious situation, particularly among Catholics and Protestants, in China. Collected data on prison conditions.

April/Sri Lanka and southern India: Investigated reports of involuntary repatriation and human rights violations against Tamil refugee returnees from India.

April/Japan: Held discussions with government officials, NGOs and others on the role of Japan in promoting human rights in Asia.

May/Kashmir: Investigated human rights abuses in Kashmir.

May/Bangladesh: Investigated reports of abuse by Bangladeshi security forces against Burmese refugees.

August/Thailand (with the Jesuit Refugee Service, USA): Observed situation of Burmese in Thailand and investigated their reasons for leaving Burma.

August/Indonesia: Collected information on human rights in Irian Jaya, Java and Sumatra.

September/Philippines: Investigated relationship between human rights violations and logging.

October/Pakistan: Investigated human rights abuses associated with bonded labor.

Fund for Free Expression

March/Egypt: To investigate restrictions of freedom of expression and association (with the Association of American Publishers).

September/Hungary: To assess the independence of broadcasting and investigate other press freedom issues (with Helsinki Watch).

Helsinki Watch

January/Croatia and Bosnia: To investigate human rights and humanitarian problems in Bosnia-Hercegovina.

January/Croatia and Serbia: To investigate sexual abuse of women in Bosnia-Hercegovina.

January/Hungary: To investigate the treatment of Romas.

April-May/Russia and Turkmenistan: To conduct a preliminary investigation into human rights conditions there. To release the report on *Human Rights in Uzbekistan* at a press conference in Moscow on May 5. Attempted to visit Uzbekistan (thwarted by Uzbekistan authorities).

May/Kazakhstan: To monitor a trial of a human rights activist.

May/Czech Republic and Slovakia: To investigate press restrictions and treatment of ethnic Hungarians and Romas.

June/Bulgaria: To investigate the decommunization process and the treatment of Romas.

June/Germany: To investigate the treatment of refugees in Germany.

May-September/Croatia and Bosnia: To conduct fact-finding missions in the republics of former Yugoslavia; to investigate civil and political rights in Croatia; to further investigate and update UN performance in the former Yugoslavia; to document rules of war violations in central and western Bosnia.

May-June/Tajikistan: To investigate violations of civil and political rights and meet with government officials about human rights conditions.

May/Czech Republic and Slovakia: To meet with activists and government officials to discuss Helsinki Watch's concerns.

June/Armenia, Georgia, Azerbaijan: To meet with government officials, present our mission findings and discuss our concerns about human rights in the region, and release newsletter on Azerbaijani air raids in Nagorno Karabakh.

July/Turkey: To investigate virginity controls through gynecological exams by state agents.

July/Greece: To investigate the situation of the Macedonian minority.

July/Macedonia: To investigate minority questions and the state of human rights in general.

July-August/Russia and Georgia: To investigate violations of the rules of war, and reinforce contact with regional human rights groups.

August-September/Estonia and Latvia: To investigate treatment of the non-citizen minority, to investigate restrictions on citizenship and establish initial contacts in the region.

September-October/Serbia and Montenegro: To investigate civil and political rights in Kosovo and Montenegro.

October-November/Estonia, Latvia: To meet with government officials about Helsinki Watch findings and release two reports.

October-November/Russia: To meet with government officials about the recent upheaval in Moscow and address Helsinki Watch's concern about human rights.

November/Romania: To investigate recent mob violence against the Roma minority as well as the government's failure to investigate and prosecute past violence against Romas.

Middle East Watch

December-January/Lebanon and Israel: To investigate deportation of Palestinians and take up our findings with Israeli authorities.

January-February/Iran: To interview Iraqi refugees about abuses against the Shi'a of southern Iraq, particularly in the marshes.

February/Egypt: To investigate abuses against Christian Copts and release prisons report.

April/Iraqi Kurdistan: To secure the retrieval of additional captured Iraqi documents and investigate continued human rights abuses against the Kurds.

June/Israel: To release *A License to Kill* report at a press conference.

August/Iraqi Kurdistan: To supervise the collection and escort to the U.S. a second consignment of captured Iraqi documents.

September/London: To interview Iraqi exiles and human rights activists.

October/Lebanon: To collect evidence in the field of possible violations of the rules of war during July 1993 fighting with Israel (conducted jointly with Arms Project).

November/Israel: To collect evidence in the field of possible violations of the rules of war during July 1993 fighting with Israel (conducted jointly with Arms Project).

N.B.: Middle East Watch maintained a field researcher in the Israeli-occupied territories to August 1993, to monitor current conditions and research reports on undercover killings and torture.

Prison Project

January-February/South Africa: (with Africa Watch) To investigate prison conditions.

February/United Kingdom: To visit two London-area prisons.

March/Hong Kong and China: Collected data on prison conditions.

March-April/Zaire: (with Africa Watch) To investigate prison conditions in Zaire.

Women's Rights Project

January/Former Yugoslavia: (with Helsinki Watch) To investigate reports of widespread rape of women by all parties to the conflict and to work with local groups to develop methods for accurate documentation of rape.

February/Thailand: (with Asia Watch) To document the trafficking of Burmese women and girls into Thailand for the purposes of forced prostitution and state complicity or toleration of such abuse.

July/Turkey: (with Helsinki Watch) To investigate reports of forced gynecological exams by police and other state actors to control women's and girls' virginity.

July/Kenya: (with Africa Watch) To investigate reports of rape of Somali refugee women in camps in Kenyan territory.

June-August/Pakistan: (with Asia Watch) To conduct research on the trafficking of Bangladeshi women into Pakistan.

November/Brazil: (with Americas Watch) To conduct follow-up investigation on violence against women and investigate forced prostitution of Brazilian girls in the Amazon region.

1993 PUBLICATIONS

To order any of the following, please call our Publications Department at 212-972-8400 and ask for the most recent publications catalog.

Africa Watch

Angola
Land Mines in Angola, 1/93, 80 pp.

Eritrea
Freedom of Expression and Ethnic Discrimination in the Educational System, Past and Future, 1/93, 9 pp.

Kenya
Seeking Refugee, Finding Terror: The Widespread Rape of Somali Women Refugees in North Eastern Kenya, 10/93, 25 pp.

Divide and Rule: State-sponsored Ethnic Violence in Kenya, 11/93, 66 pp.

Liberia
Waging War to Keep the Peace: The Ecomog Intervention and Human Rights, 6/93, 34 pp.

Nigeria
Military Injustice: Major General Zamani Lekwot and Others Face Government-Sanctioned Lynching, 3/93, 11 pp.

Threats to a New Democracy: Human Rights Concerns at Election Time, 6/93, 23 pp.

Democracy Derailed: Hundreds Arrested and Press Muzzled in Aftermath of Election Annulment, 8/93, 20 pp.

Rwanda
Beyond the Rhetoric: Continuing Human Rights Abuses in Rwanda, 6/93, 29 pp.

South Africa
Half-Hearted Reform: The Official Response to the Rising Tide of Violence, 5/93, 82 pp., 100-2

"Traditional" Dictatorship: One Party State in KwaZulu Homeland Threatens Transition to Democracy, 9/93, 45 pp.

Somalia
Beyond the Warlords: The Need for a Verdict on Human Rights Abuses, 3/93, 29 pp.

Sudan

The Copts: Passive Survivors under Threat, 2/93, 9 pp.

Africa Watch Letters Protest Abuses of Human Rights by all Parties to the Conflict in Southern Sudan, 4/93, 10 pp.

War in South Sudan: The Civilian Toll, 10/93, 9 pp.

Zaire

Inciting Hatred: Violence Against Kasaiesn in Shaba, 6/93, 25 pp.

Zambia

Model for Democracy Declares State of Emergency, 6/93, 7 pp.

Americas Watch

Bolivia

The Trial of Responsibilities: The Garcia Meza Tejada Trial, 9/93, 12 pp.

Brazil

Urban Police Violence in Brazil: Torture and Police Killings in São Paulo and Rio de Janeiro after Five Years, 5/93, 26 pp.

Cuba

"Perfecting" the System of Control: Human Rights Violations in Castro's 34th Year, 2/93, 26 pp.

El Salvador

Accountability and Human Rights: The Report of the U.N. Commission on the Truth for El Salvador, 8/93, 38 pp.

Guatemala

Clandestine Detention in Guatemala, 3/93, 18 pp.

Haiti

Silencing a People: The Destruction of Civil Society in Haiti, 3/93, 152 pp.

No Port in a Storm: The Misguided Use of In-country Refugee Processing, 9/93, 37 pp.

Jamaica

Human Rights in Jamaica: Death Penalty, Prison Conditions and Police Violence, 4/93, 13 pp.

Mexico

Human Rights Watch/Americas Watch Writes to President Clinton Urging NAFTA Summit on Human Rights, 10/93, 23 pp.

Peru

Human Rights in Peru: One Year After Fujimori's Coup, 4/93, 56 pp.

Anatomy of a Cover-up: The Disappearances at La Cantuta, 12/93, 20 pp.

United States

Frontier Injustice: Human Rights Abuses Along the U.S. Border with Mexico Persist Amid Climate of Impunity, 5/93, 46 pp.

Venezuela

Human Rights in Venezuela, 10/93, 118 pp.

Asia Watch

Bangladesh

Abuse of Burmese Refugees from Arakan, 10/93, 15 pp.

Cambodia

Human Rights Before and After the Elections, 5/93, 41 pp.

An Exchange on Human Rights and Peace-keeping in Cambodia, 9/93, 28 pp.

China

Democracy Wall Prisoners: Xu Wenli, Wei Jingsheng & other Jailed Pioneers of the Chinese Pro-Democracy Movement, 3/93, 51 pp.

Economic Reform, Political Repression: Arrests of Dissidents in China since mid-1992, 3/93, 28 pp.

Continuing Religious Repression in China, 6/93, 60 pp.

China in 1993: One More Year of Political Repression, 11/93, 36 pp.

General
Human Rights in the APEC Region, 11/93, 60 pp.

Indonesia & East Timor
Charges and Rebuttals over Labor Rights Practices: Analysis of Submissions to the U.S. Trade Representative, 1/93, 25 pp.
Military Repression against the Batak Church, 1/93, 9 pp.
Students Jailed for Puns, 3/93, 4 pp.
Remembering History in East Timor: The Trial of Xanana Gusamao and a Follow-up to the Dili Massacre, 4/93
More Restrictions on Workers, 9/93, 9 pp.
Government Efforts to Silence Students, 10/93, 13 pp.
Human Rights Abuses in North Sumatra, 11/93, 18 pp.

India
The Crackdown in Kashmir: Torture of Detainees and Assaults on the Medical Community, 2/93, 62 pp.
No End in sight: Human Rights Violations in Assam, 4/93, 22 pp.
Rape in Kashmir: A Crime of War, 5/93, 20 pp.
The Human Rights Crisis in Kashmir: A Pattern of Impunity, 7/93, 240 pp.
Halt Repatriation of Sri Lankan Tamils, 8/93 18 pp.

Pakistan
Persecuted Minorities and Writers in Pakistan, 9/93, 22 pp.

Vietnam
The Case of Doan Viet Hout and Freedom Forum: Detention for Dissent in Vietnam, 1/93, 10 pp.
Human Rights in U.S.-Vietnam Relations, 8/93, 12 pp.

Helsinki Watch

Azerbaijan
Bloodshed in the Caucasus: Indiscriminate Bombing and Shelling by Azerbaijani Forces in Nagorno Karabakh, 7/93, 24 pp.

Bulgaria
Police Violence against Gypsies, 4/93, 14 pp.
Decommunization of Bulgaria, 8/93, 42 pp.

Estonia
Integrating Estonia's Non-citizen Minority, 10/93, 41 pp.

General
Threats to Press Freedoms: A Report Prepared for the Free Media Seminar Commission on Security and Cooperation in Europe, 11/93, 41 pp.

Greece
Free Speech on Trial: Government Stifles Dissent on Macedonia, 7/93, 7 pp.

Hungary
The Gypsies of Hungary, 8/93, 80 pp.

Lativa
Violations by the Latvian Department of Citizenship and Immigration, 10/93, 27 pp.

Moldova
Human Rights in Moldova: The Turbulent Dneister, 3/93, 80 pp.

Poland
Freedom of Expression Threatened by Curbs on Criticism of Government and Religion, 8/93, 9 pp.

Romania
Lockups in Romania, 1/93, 19 pp.

Turkmenistan
Human Rights in Turkmenistan, 7/93, 56 pp.

Turkey

Sixteen Deaths in Detention in 1992, 2/93, 5 pp.

The Kurds of Turkey: Killings, Disappearances and Torture, 3/93, 64 pp.

Killings Mount: Human Rights Activist and Doctor Latest Murder Victims, 4/93, 3 pp.

Four Deaths in Detention, 6/93, 3 pp.

Free Expression in Turkey, 1993: Killings, Convictions, Confiscations, 8/93, 40 pp.

United Kingdom

Freedom of Expression in the U.K.: Recent Developments, 3/93, 33 pp.

Northern Ireland: Human Rights Abuses by All Sides, 5/93, 9 pp.

Uzbekistan

"Straightening Out the Brains of 100": Discriminatory Political Dismissals in Uzbekistan, 4/93, 13 pp.

Human Rights in Uzbekistan, 5/93, 70 pp.

Former Yugoslavia

War Crimes in Bosnia-Hercegovina: Volume II, 4/93, 460 pp.

Abuses Continue in the Former Yugoslavia: Serbia, Montenegro and Bosnia-Hercegovina, 7/93, 40 pp.

Procedural and Evidentiary Issues for the Yugoslav War Crimes Tribunal: Resource Allocation, Evidentiary Questions and Protection of Witnesses, 8/93, 15 pp.

Belgrade Demonstrations: Excessive Use of Force and Beatings in Detention, 8/93, 22 pp.

Prosecute Now!: Helsinki Watch Releases 8 Cases for War Crimes Tribunal on Former Yugoslavia, 8/93, 25 pp.

Middle East Watch

Egypt

Prison Conditions in Egypt, 2/93, 160 pp.

Trials of Civilians in Military Courts Violate International Law, 7/93, 18 pp.

Iran

Guardians of Thought: Limits on Freedom of Expression in Iran, 8/93, 152 pp.

Iraq

The Anfal Campaign in Iraqi Kurdistan: The Destruction of Koreme, 1/93, 126 pp.

Background on Human Rights Conditions, 1948-1992, 8/93, 18 pp.

Genocide in Iraq: The Anfal Campaign Against the Kurds, 7/93, 400 pp.

Israel & occupied territories

Isolation of Jerusalem: Restrictions on Movement Causing Severe Hardship in Occupied Territories, 4/93, 9 pp.

A License to Kill: Israeli Undercover Operations Against Wanted & Masked Palestinians, 8/93, 288 pp.

Kuwait

Kuwait Closes All Human Rights Organizations, 9/93, 12 pp.

Lebanon

Lebanon's Lively Press Faces Worst Crackdown since 1976: Government Shuts Down 3 Dailies, 1 Network, 7/93, 48 pp.

Palestinian Deportees Continue to Suffer from Poor Conditions in Lebanon Camp, 8/93, 26 pp.

All Demonstrations Banned Israel/PLO Peace Accord Opponents Killed, 9/93, 16 pp.

Syria

European Parliament Should Condition E.C. Aid on Human Rights Improvements, 11/93, 14 pp.

Human Rights Watch

The Human Rights Watch World Report 1993, 1/93, 424 pp.

Persecuted Writers Receive Grants: 36 Writers from 15 Countries Recognized with Funds from the Lillian Hellman/Dashiell Hammett Estates, 6/93, 4 pp.

The Lost Agenda: Human Rights and U.N. Field Operations, 6/93, 184 pp.

The Human Rights Watch Global Report on Prisons, 6/93, 344 pp.

Landmines: A Deadly Legacy, 10/93, 528 pp.

COMMITTEES AND STAFF

Human Rights Watch

Executive Committee

Robert L. Bernstein, Chair; Adrian W. DeWind, Vice Chair; Roland Algrant, Lisa Anderson, Peter D. Bell, Alice L. Brown, William Carmichael, Dorothy Cullman, Irene Diamond, Jonathan Fanton, Alan Finberg, Jack Greenberg, Alice H. Henkin, Stephen L. Kass, Marina Pinto Kaufman, Alexander MacGregor, Peter Osnos, Kathleen Peratis, Bruce Rabb, Orville Schell, Gary G. Sick, Malcolm Smith.

Staff

Kenneth Roth, Executive Director; Holly J. Burkhalter, Washington Director; Gara LaMarche, Associate Director; Susan Osnos, Press Director; Ellen Lutz, California Director; Jemera Rone, Counsel; Richard Dicker, Associate Counsel; Cynthia Brown, Consultant; Allyson Collins, Dinah PoKempner, Research Associates; Robert Kimzey, Editor; Virginia Muller, Librarian; Anastasia Clubb, Anthony Levintow, Linda D. Long, Loren K. Miller, Urmi Shah, Scott Turner, Associates. **Development:** Michal Longfelder, Director; Rachel Weintraub, Special Events Director; Desireé A. Colly, Regional Development Director; Giuliana Capone, Jennifer Lavenhar, Associates. **Operations:** Stephanie C. Steele, Director; Barbara Guglielmo, CPA, Accounting Man-

ager; Anderson Allen, Laura McCormick, Office Managers; Suzanne Guthrie, Publications Manager; Lemual Thomas, Production Manager; Fredrick Evans, Production Assistant; Natalie Clarke, Dominique Dieudonne, Stacey Wolfson, Receptionists. **Film Festival:** Hamilton Fish, Director; Bruni Burres, Programmer; Heather Harding, Coordinator. **Fellowship Recipients:** Susan Forrester, Deborah Krisher, Henry R. Luce Fellows; Deborah Blatt, NYU Public Service Fellow; Farhad Karim, Fatemeh Ziai, Orville Schell Fellows; Uche Ewelukwa, Leonard Sandler Fellow; LaShawn Jefferson, Sophie Silberberg Fellow; Lee Tucker, Bradford Wiley Fellow.

Africa Watch

William Carmichael, Chair; Alice L. Brown, Vice Chair; Roland Algrant, Robert L. Bernstein, Julius L. Chambers, Michael Clough, Roberta Cohen, Carol Corillon, Alison L. DesForges, Adrian W. DeWind, Thomas M. Franck, Gail M. Gerhart, Jack Greenberg, Alice H. Henkin, Robert Joffe, Richard A. Joseph, Thomas Karis, Russell Karp, Stephen L. Kass, John A. Marcum, Gay McDougall, Vincent McGee, Toni Morrison, Barrington Parker, III, James C. N. Paul, Robert Preiskel, Norman Redlich, Randall Robinson, Sidney S. Rosdeitcher, Aristide R. Zolberg, David S. Tatel, Howard P. Venable, Claude E. Welch, Jr.

Staff

Abdullahi An-Na'im, Executive Director; Janet Fleischman, Washington Representative; Karen Sorensen, Research Associate; Abdelsalam Hasan, Bronwen Manby, Alex Vines, Consultants; Kimberly Mazyck, Associate.

Americas Watch

Peter D. Bell, Chair; Stephen L. Kass, Marina Pinto Kaufman, Vice Chairs; Roland Algrant, Robert L. Bernstein, Albert Bildner, Paul Chevigny, Dorothy Cullman, Peter W. Davidson, Patricia Derian, Adrian W. DeWind, Stanley Engelstein, Tom J. Farer, Jamie Fellner, Alejandro Garro, Wendy

Gimbel, John S. Gitlitz, Robert K. Goldman, James Goldston, Jack Greenberg, Wade J. Henderson, Alice H. Henkin, Russell Karp, Margaret A. Lang, Robert S. Lawrence, MD, Jocelyn McCalla, Theodor Meron, Marshall Meyer, David E. Nachman, John B. Oakes, Victor Penchaszadeh, Clara A. "Zazi" Pope, Michael Posner, Bruce Rabb, Jeanne Richman, Tina Rosenberg, Jean-Marie Simon, Sanford Solender, George Soros, Alfred Stepan, Rose Styron, Arturo Valenzuela, Jorge Valls.

Staff

Juan E. Méndez, Executive Director; Cynthia Arnson, Anne Manuel, Associate Directors; Mary Jane Camejo, Gretta Tovar Siebentritt, Research Associates; Robin Kirk, Consultant; Vanessa Jiménez, Ben Penglase, Associates.

Asia Watch

Jack Greenberg, Chair; Orville Schell, Vice Chair; Floyd Abrams, Maureen Aung-Thwin, Edward J. Baker, Robert L. Bernstein, Julie Brill, Jerome A. Cohen, Adrian W. DeWind, Clarence Dias, Delores A. Donovan, Timothy A. Gelatt, Adrienne Germaine, Merle Goldman, Deborah M. Greenberg, Charles Halpern, David Hawk, Paul Hoffman, Sharon Hom, Rounaq Jahan, Virginia Leary, Daniel Lev, Perry Link, The Rt. Rev. Paul Moore, Jr., Sheila Rothman, Barnett Rubin, James Scott, Ivan Shapiro, Judith Shapiro, Nadine Strossen, Maya Wiley.

Staff

Sidney Jones, Executive Director; Mike Jendrzejczyk, Washington Director; Robin Munro, Hong Kong Director; Therese Caouette, Patricia Gossman, Jeannine Guthrie, Research Associates; Marianne Spiegel, Consultant; Grace Oboma-Layat, Associate.

Helsinki Watch

Jonathan Fanton, Chair; Alice H. Henkin, Vice Chair; Roland Algrant, Robert L. Bernstein, Charles Biblowit, Martin Blumenthal, Roberta Cohen, Lori Damrosch,

Istvan Deak, Adrian W. DeWind, Fr. Robert Drinan, Stanley Engelstein, Alan R. Finberg, Ellen Futter, Willard Gaylin, MD, Michael Gellert, John Glusman, Paul Goble, Robert K. Goldman, Jack Greenberg, Rita E. Hauser, Robert James, Rhoda Karpatkin, Stephen L. Kass, Bentley Kassal, Marina Pinto Kaufman, Joanne Landy, Margaret A. Lang, Leon Levy, Wendy Luers, Theodor Meron, Deborah Milenkovitch, Toni Morrison, John B. Oakes, Herbert Okun, Jane Olson, Yuri Orlov, Srdja Popovic, Bruce Rabb, Peter Reddaway, Stuart Robinowitz, John G. Ryden, Herman Schwartz, Stanley K. Sheinbaum, George Soros, Susan Weber Soros, Michael Sovern, Fritz Stern, Svetlana Stone, Rose Styron, Liv Ullman, Gregory Wallance, Rosalind Whitehead, Jerome Wiesner.

Staff

Jeri Laber, Executive Director; Lois Whitman, Deputy Director; Holly Cartner, Julie Mertus, Counsels; Erika Dailey, Rachel Denber, Ivana Nizich, Christopher Panico, Research Associates; Christina Derry, Ivan Lupis, Alexander Petrov, Lydda Ragasa, Isabelle Tin-Aung, Associates.

Middle East Watch

Gary G. Sick, Chair; Lisa Anderson, Bruce Rabb, Vice Chairs; Shaul Bakhash, M. Cherif Bassiouni, Hyman Bookbinder, Paul Chevigny, Helena Cobban, Patricia Derian, Stanley Engelstein, Edith Everett, Mansour Farhang, Robert K. Goldman, Rita E. Hauser, Reverend J. Bryan Hehir, Edy Kaufman, Marina Pinto Kaufman, Samir Khalaf, Judith Kipper, Pnina Lahav, Ann M. Lesch, Richard Maass, Stephen P. Marks, David K. Shipler, Sanford Solender, Shibley Telhami, Sir Brian Urquhart, Napoleon B. Williams, Jr., James J. Zogby

Staff

Andrew Whitley, Executive Director; Eric Goldstein, Research Director; Aziz Abu-Hamad, Virginia N. Sherry, Associate Directors; Suzanne E. Howard, Associate.

Arms Project

Morton Abramowitz, Nicole Ball, Frank Blackaby, Frederick C. Cuny, Dr. Ahmed H. Esa, Gustavo Gorriti, William Green, Di Hua, Jo Husbands, Frederick J. Knecht, Edward J. Laurance, Vincent McGee, Aryeh Neier, Janne E. Nolan, Andrew J. Pierre, David Rieff, Kumar Rupesinghe, John Ryle, Mohamed Sahnoun, Gary Sick, Tom Winship.

Staff

Kenneth Anderson, Director; Stephen D. Goose, Washington Director; Monica Schurtman, Counsel; Barbara Baker, Kathleen Bleakley, Cesar Bolaños, Associates.

Fund for Free Expression

Roland Algrant, Chair; Aryeh Neier, Peter Osnos, Vice Chairs; Alice Arlen, Tom A. Bernstein, Hortense Calisher, Geoffrey Cowan, Dorothy Cullman, Patricia Derian, Adrian W. DeWind, Irene Diamond, E. L. Doctorow, Norman Dorsen, Alan R. Finberg, Frances FitzGerald, Jack Greenberg, Vartan Gregorian, S. Miller Harris, Alice H. Henkin, Pam Hill, Joseph Hofheimer, Lawrence Hughes, Ellen Hume, Mark Kaplan, Stephen L. Kass, William Koshland, Judith F. Krug, Jeri Laber, Anthony Lewis, William Loverd, Wendy Luers, John Macrae, III, Michael Massing, Nancy Meiselas, Arthur Miller, The Rt. Rev. Paul Moore, Jr., Toni Morrison, Peter Osnos, Bruce Rabb, Geoffrey Cobb Ryan, John G. Ryden, Steven R. Shapiro, Jerome Shestack, Nadine Strossen, Rose Styron, John Updike, Luisa Valenzuela, Nicholas A. Veliotes, Kurt Vonnegut, Jr., Roger Wilkins.

Staff

Gara LaMarche, Executive Director; Marcia Allina, Program Associate; Lydda Ragasa, Associate.

Prison Project

Herman Schwartz, Chair; Nan Aron, Vivian Berger, Haywood Burns, Alejandro Garro, William Hellerstein, Edward Koren, Sheldon Krantz, Honorable Morris Lasker, Benjamin Malcolm, Diane Orentlicher, Norman Rosenberg, David Rothman, Clarence Sundram.

Staff

Joanna Weschler, Director; Anthony Levintow, Associate.

Women's Rights Project

Kathleen Peratis, Chair; Mahnaz Afkhami, Alice Brown, Cynthia Brown, Charlotte Bunch, Rhonda Copelon, Patricia Derian, Joan Dunlop, Mallika Dutt, Martha Finemen, Claire Flom, Adrienne Germain, Zhu Hong, Stephen Isaacs, Helene Kaplan, Marina Pinto Kaufman, Wangari Maathai, Joyce Mends-Cole, Marysa Navarro-Aranguren, Susan Peterson, Celina Romany, Margaret Schuler, Jeane Sindab, Nahid Toubia.

Staff

Dorothy Q. Thomas, Director; Regan Ralph, Staff Attorney; Sarah Lai, Research Associate; Evelyn Miah, Associate.

Human Rights Watch—California

Stanley K. Sheinbaum, Honorary Chair; Mike Farrell, Jane Olson, Co-chairs; Raquel Ackerman, Rabbi Leonard Beerman, Alan Gleitsman, Danny Glover, Paul Hoffman, Barry Kemp, Maggie Kemp, Donna LaBonte, Daniel Levy, Lynda Palevsky, Lucille Polachek, Clara A. "Zazi" Pope, Tracy Rice, Vicki Riskin Rintels, Cheri Rosche, Pippa Scott, Honorable Phillip R. Trimble, Joan Willens, Dianne Wittenberg.